THE BLACKWELL READER IN

Developmental
PSYCHOLOGY

EDITED BY

ALAN SLATER AND **DARWIN MUIR**

BLACKWELL
Publishers

Copyright © Blackwell Publishers Ltd 1999

First published 1999

2 4 6 8 10 9 7 5 3 1

Blackwell Publishers Ltd
108 Cowley Road
Oxford OX4 1JF
UK

Blackwell Publishers Inc.
350 Main Street
Malden, Massachusetts 02148
USA

British Library Cataloguing in Publication Data

A CIP catalogue record for this book is available from the British Library.

Library of Congress Cataloging-in-Publication Data

The Blackwell reader in developmental psychology / edited by Alan Slater and Darwin Muir.
p.   cm.
Includes bibliographical references and index.
ISBN 0–631–20718–X (alk. paper).—ISBN 0–631–20719–8 (pbk.: alk. paper)
1. Developmental psychology.   I. Slater, Alan.   II. Muir, Darwin.
BF713.B57   1998   155—dc21   98–29201   CIP

Typeset in Palatino on 10/12.5pt
by Pure Tech India Ltd, Pondicherry
http://www.puretech.com
Printed in Great Britain by
T.J. International, Padstow, Cornwall

This book is printed on acid-free paper

THE BLACKWELL READER IN DEVELOPMENTAL PSYCHOLOGY

CONTENTS

LIST OF FIGURES

LIST OF TABLES

LIST OF PLATES

PREFACE

The aim of this collection of papers is to provide an introduction to developmental psychology using original articles which span a broad range of the subject. It is often the case that students cannot find original articles in their libraries, perhaps because the library does not take the relevant journals, or because there are too many people searching for the same papers. This collection will provide the student with immediate access to 39 papers which cover the whole range of developmental psychology.

Any choice of a set of articles in an area as extensive and dynamic as developmental psychology is bound to be somewhat idiosyncratic. We acknowledge that different editors could have made a quite different selection, but in making our choice we have been guided by a number of considerations. One major concern is that the articles should reflect the dynamic and changing nature of the subject, and the current 'state of the art'. Thus, 24 of the 39 articles have been published or written in the 1990s (some of these have been specially commissioned and written for this book). Many of these articles are already highly cited and in the editors' opinion the most recent ones (those published in 1995 and later) are 'classics in the making'. A few articles were published in the 1980s, and are still important. There are only four papers published prior to 1980. Three of these (not surprisingly) are in Part I – 'Methods, History and Developmental Theory' – and for the other (article 12) the authors (who are still rather young!) have kindly contributed an update on the topic, which is printed after their original article. We were also concerned to cover the range of developmental psychology, and in this we were greatly assisted by Blackwell, who sought the advice of a great number of reviewers – our first selection of articles has been considerably modified (and improved) as a result of their suggestions!

Another important consideration is that the articles selected should be accessible, and make sense, to students at all levels of their studies in developmental psychology. We have therefore not included articles, however important, that would only be understood by specialists in the area. There are Editors' Introductions for many of the articles where we feel that it will be helpful to the reader. These introductions sometimes put the article into context, sometimes add information not to be found in the article, or provide an abstract where there isn't one with the article. This means that each of the articles has at least one sort of introduction and sometimes two! – the Editors' Introduction and the authors' abstract.

Developmental psychology is one of the most exciting and dynamic areas of enquiry to be found. This book of readings is representative of some of the best research in the different areas of the subject, and it can be used either in conjunction with, or as a replacement for, a textbook that offers an introduction to the area. Developmental psychology is taught at all levels, both as a "whole", where the aim is to give the student an introduction to the major areas it covers, and also at a more specialized level where the student is offered courses into its various subdisciplines. In order to do justice to this diversification Blackwell are publishing smaller *Readers* which will offer original articles in the major areas of developmental psychology.

We would like to thank Nathalie Manners at Blackwell, who helped to get this project started. We thank a large number of anonymous reviewers who guided our selection of articles. In particular we thank Martin Davies of Blackwell, whose enthusiasm is infectious and who will be pleased to see the finished product!

Alan Slater
Darwin Muir

ACKNOWLEDGEMENTS

Nameera Akhtar, Malinda Carpenter and Michael Tomasello, "The Role of Discourse Novelty in Early Word Learning", *Child Development*, **67** (1996), pp. 635–45. © The Society for Research in Child Development, Ann Arbor, 1996.

L. Bradley and P. E. Bryant, "Categorizing Sounds and Learning to Read – A Causal Connection", *Nature*, **301**, 5899 (1983), pp. 419–21. © 1983 Macmillan Journals Ltd.

Stephen J. Ceci and Mary Lyn Crotteau Huffman, "How Suggestible are Preschool Children? Cognitive and Social Factors", *Journal of the American Academy of Child and Adolescent Psychiatry*, **36** (1997), pp. 948–58. Reprinted by permission of Dr S J Ceci.

Charles Darwin, "A Biographical Sketch of an Infant", originally published in 1877; reprinted from *Mind: A Quarterly Review of Psychology and Philosophy*, **7** (July 1877), pp. 285–94.

Anthony J. DeCasper and William P. Fifer, "Of Human Bonding: Newborns Prefer their Mothers' Voices", *Science*, **208** (1980), pp. 1174–6. Reprinted with permission; copyright © 1980 American Association for the Advancement of Science.

Judy S. DeLoache, "Rapid Change in the Symbolic Functioning of Very Young Children", *Science*, **238** (1987), pp. 1556–7. Reprinted with permission; copyright © 1987 American Association for the Advancement of Science.

John H. Flavell, "Development of Children's Knowledge about the Appearance–Reality Distinction", *American Psychologist*, **41** (1986), pp. 418–25. Copyright © 1986 The American Psychological Association; reprinted with permission.

Uta Frith, "Cognitive Development and Cognitive Deficit", *The Psychologist*, **5** (1992), pp. 13–19. Copyright © 1992 The British Psychological Society, Leicester.

Susan Goldberg, "Recent Developments in Attachment Theory and Research", *Canadian Journal of Psychiatry*, **36** (1991), pp. 393–400.

Willard W. Hartup, "The Company They Keep: Friendships and their Developmental Significance", *Child Development*, **67** (1996), pp. 1–13. © The Society for Research in Child Development, Inc., Ann Arbor, 1996.

Jerome Kagan, J. Steven Reznick and Nancy Snidman, "Biological Bases of Childhood Shyness", *Science*, **240** (1988), pp. 167–71. Reprinted with permission; copyright © 1988 American Association for the Advancement of Science.

Mary Kister Kaiser, Michael McCloskey and Dennis R. Proffitt, "Development of Intuitive Theories of Motion: Curvilinear Motion in the Absence of External Forces", *Developmental Psychology*, **22** (1986), pp. 67–71. Copyright © 1986 The American Psychological Association; reprinted with permission.

Annette Karmiloff-Smith, "The Connectionist Infant: Would Piaget Turn in his Grave?", *SRCD Newsletter*, Fall (1996), pp. 1–3; reprinted by permission of the author.

Kang Lee, Catherine Ann Cameron, Fen Xu, Genyao Fu and Julie Board, "Chinese and Canadian Children's Evaluations of Lying and Truth Telling: Similarities and Differences in the Context of Pro- and Antisocial Behaviours", *Child Development*, **68** (1997), pp. 924–34. © The Society for Research in Child Development, Inc., Ann Arbor, 1997.

Kang Lee and Bruce Homer, "Children as Folk Psychologists: the Developing Understanding of the Mind", original article.

Michael Lewis, Catherine Stanger and Margaret W. Sullivan, "Deception in 3-Year-Olds", *Developmental Psychology*, **25** (1989), pp. 439–43. Copyright © 1989 The American Psychological Association; reprinted with permission.

Michael Lewis, Margaret Wolan Sullivan, Catherine Stanger and Maya Weiss, "Self Development and Self-Conscious Emotions", *Child Development*, **60** (1989), pp. 146–56. © The Society for Research in Child Development, Inc., Ann Arbor, 1989.

Andrew N. Meltzoff and M. Keith Moore, "Imitation of Facial and Manual Gestures by Human Neonates", *Science*, **198** (1977), pp. 75–8. Reprinted with permission; copyright 1977 American Association for the Advancement of Science.

Andrew N. Meltzoff and M. Keith Moore, "Resolving the Debate about Early Imitation", original paper.

Darwin Muir, "Theories and Methods in Developmental Psychology", original paper.

Darwin W. Muir, Diane E. Humphrey and G. Keith Humphrey, "Pattern and Space Perception in Young Infants", *Spatial Vision*, **8** (1994), pp. 141–65. Reprinted courtesy of VSP, Zeist.

Debra Pepler, Wendy M. Craig and Paul O'Connell, "Understanding Bullying from a Dynamic Systems Perspective", original theoretical article.

Laura Ann Petitto and Paula F. Marentette, "Babbling in the Manual Mode: Evidence for the Ontogeny of Language", *Science*, **251** (1991), pp. 1493–6. Reprinted with permission; copyright 1991 American Association for the Advancement of Science.

Jean Piaget, "The Stages of the Intellectual Development of the Child", *Bulletin of the Menninger Clinic*, **26** (New York: Guilford Publications, 1962), pp. 120–8.

Steven Pinker, "Rules of Language", *Science*, **253** (1991), pp. 530–5. Reprinted with permission; copyright 1991 American Association for the Advancement of Science.

Robert Plomin, Michael J. Owen and Peter McGuffin, "The Genetic Basis of Complex Human Behaviors", *Science*, **264** (1994), pp. 1733–9. Reprinted with permission; copyright 1994 American Association for the Advancement of Science.

Carolyn K. Rovee-Collier, Margaret W. Sullivan, Mary Enright, Debora Lucas and Jeffrey W. Fagen, "Reactivation of Infant Memory", *Science*, **208** (1980), pp. 1159–61. Reprinted with permission; copyright 1980 American Association for the Advancement of Science.

Sandra Scarr, "American Child Care Today", *American Psychologist*, **53** (1998), pp. 95–108. Copyright © 1998 The American Psychological Association; reprinted with permission.

Helen I. Shwe and Ellen M. Markman, "Young Children's Appreciation of the Mental Impact of their Communicative Signals", *Developmental Psychology*, **33**

(1997), pp. 630–6. Copyright © 1997 The American Psychological Association; reprinted with permission.

B. F. Skinner, "Baby in a Box", in B. F. Skinner, *Cumulative Record* (New York: Appleton Century Crofts, 1959), pp. 419–26.

Alan Slater, "Helen Keller: An Extraordinary Life", original article.

Alan Slater, Rachael Carrick, Clare Bell and Elizabeth Roberts, "Can Measures of Infant Information Processing Predict Later Intellectual Ability?", original paper.

L. Alan Sroufe and Michael Rutter, "The Domain of Developmental Psychopathology", *Child Development*, **55** (1984), pp. 17–29. © Society for Research in Child Development, Inc., Ann Arbor, 1984.

Liliana Tolchinsky Landsmann and Annette Karmiloff-Smith, "Children's Understanding of Notations as Domains of Knowledge versus Referential-Communicative Tools", *Cognitive Development*, **7** (1992), pp. 287–300. Courtesy of Ablex Publishing Corporation, Stamford.

Laura H. Weiss and J. Conrad Schwarz, "The Relationship between Parenting Types and Older Adolescents' Personality, Academic Achievement, Adjustment and Substance Use", *Child Development*, **67** (1996), pp. 2101–14. © The Society for Research in Child Development, Inc., Ann Arbor, 1996.

Janet F. Werker and Renée N. Desjardins, "Listening to Speech in the First Year of Life: Experiential Influences on Phoneme Perception", *Current Directions in Psychological Science*, **4** (June 1995), pp. 76–81. © 1995 American Psychological Association, published by Cambridge University Press, reproduced with permission.

Emmy E. Werner, "Children of the Garden Island", *Scientific American*, **260** (1989), pp. 106–11. Reprinted with permission; copyright © 1989 by Scientific American, Inc. All rights reserved.

Jennifer G. Wishart, "Learning and Development in Children with Down's Syndrome", original article.

Karen Wynn, "Infants Possess a System of Numerical Knowledge", *Current Directions in Psychological Science*, **4** (1995), pp. 172–7. © 1995 American Psychological Association, published by Cambridge University Press, reproduced with permission.

Edward Zigler and Sally J. Styfco, "Head Start: Criticisms in a Constructive Context", *American Psychologist*, **49**(2) (1994), pp. 127–32. Copyright © 1994 The American Psychological Association; reprinted with permission.

Part I

METHODS, HISTORY AND DEVELOPMENTAL THEORY

1

THEORIES AND METHODS IN DEVELOPMENTAL PSYCHOLOGY

Darwin Muir

In this paper, the framework used by developmental psychologists to study the development of human behaviour will be discussed. Craig (1996), author of a developmental textbook, defines developmental psychology as the discipline which attempts to describe and explain 'the changes over time in the structure, thought, or behaviour of a person due to both biological and environmental influences' (p. 5). While all developmental psychologists may study behaviour change over time, not all would agree with Craig's definition. In fact, the manner in which development is defined can lead researchers to adopt different methods of studying development. We will begin by discussing different definitions of development which have been offered by psychologists holding different world views. According to Lerner (1986), a world view (also called a 'paradigm', 'model', or 'world hypothesis') is 'a philosophical system of ideas that serves to organize a set or family of scientific theories and associated scientific methods' (p. 42). They are beliefs we assume, which are not open to empirical test. Lerner and others note that many developmental theories appear to fall under one of two basic world views: Organismic and Mechanistic. Only a superficial description of these two world views will be presented, given space limitations (see Lerner, 1986, ch. 2, for a detailed discussion and Hultsch and Deutsch, 1981, for a concise summary). This will be followed by examples of different developmental functions which are used as evidence to support various theories, and a discussion of the strengths and weaknesses of the various methods used to collect developmental data.

DEFINING DEVELOPMENT ACCORDING TO WORLD VIEWS

Organismic World View

According to the Organismic World View a person is represented as a biological organism which is inherently active and continually interacting with the environment. This world view emphasizes the interaction between maturation and experience which leads to the development of new internal, psychological structures for processing environmental input. As Lerner states: 'The Organismic model stresses the integrated structural features of the organism. If the parts making up the whole become reorganized as a consequence of the organism's active construction of its own functioning, the structure of the organism may take on a new meaning; thus qualitatively distinct principles may be involved in human functioning at different points in life. These distinct, or new, levels of organization are termed stages . . .' (p. 57). An analogy is the qualitative change that occurs when molecules of two gases, hydrogen and oxygen, combine to form a liquid, water.

The point is that the new stage is not simply reducible to components of the previous stage; it represents new characteristics not present in the previous stage. For example, the organism appears to pass through structural stages during foetal development. In the first stage (Period of the Ovum – first few weeks after conception) cells multiply and form clusters; in the second stage (Period of the Embryo – 2 to about 8 weeks) the major body parts are formed by cell multiplication, specialization, and migration as well as cell death; in the last stage (Period of the Foetus) the body parts mature and begin to operate as an integrated system (e.g., head orientation towards and away from stimulation, arm extensions and grasping, thumb sucking, starting at loud noises, and so on). Similar stages of psychological development are postulated to occur as well. Piaget is perhaps the best example of an Organismic theorist (Lerner, 1986). Piaget (1962, this reader) postulates the existence of qualitatively different levels of behavioural organization in cognitive development, such as the shift from activity-based sensori-motor processing in infancy to the use of symbolic representations (e.g., language) between 1 and 2 years of age. It should be noted that the shift from one stage to another occurs in a relatively rapid, step-like fashion which leads to higher levels of functioning – in Piaget's case, abstract reasoning. Thus, the job of the developmental psychologist subscribing to an Organismic viewpoint is to determine when different psychological stages operate and what variables, processes, and/or laws represent the differences between stages.

Mechanistic World View

According to the Mechanistic World View a person can be represented as a machine (e.g., computer), which is inherently passive until stimulated by the environment. Ultimately, human behaviour is reducible to the operation of fundamental behavioural units (e.g., habits) which are acquired in a gradual, cumulative manner, reflected by a more continuous growth function. Behaviourists represent this world view. While they recognize the existence of maturational norms, some (e.g., Baer, 1970) have argued that psychologists need not study the onset of various motor skills (walking and talking – which are determined to a large extent by maturation of muscles), the adolescent growth spurt (which is caused by hormone changes), and even major divisions in the life span such as infancy, childhood, adolescence, adulthood, and old age. Baer defines development as behaviour change *over time* which involves 'learning procedures: patterns of reinforcement, punishment, extinction, differentiation and discrimination, in general...development is behavior change which requires programming; and programming requires time, but not enough of it to call it age' (p. 245). Given this definition, behaviour change may be multidirectional. The frequency of behaviour can increase with age (time) as a result of various learning processes (e.g., classical and operant conditioning and observational learning) and it can decrease with age when it no longer has any functional consequence (extinction) or leads to a negative consequence (punishment).

Baer rejects the methods used by developmental psychologists such as Piaget, who catalogue age differences in behaviour and explain them by the operation of qualitatively different mental structures. To illustrate his position, Baer describes an experiment by Jeffrey (1958) in which children were given the task of learning to name a stick figure pointing to the left 'Jack' and the same figure pointing to the right 'Jill'. Seven-year-olds learned this task rapidly while 4-year-olds failed to learn it at all after many trials. However, Jeffrey eliminated this age difference by training 4-year-olds to push a button on the left for the left-pointing figure and on the right for the right-pointing one. They learned this motor association task quickly and when they returned to the first, verbal-association task they solved it easily as well. Baer's point is that the process of development can be revealed by providing the proper sequence of learning experiences which, under poorly constructed natural conditions, might take several years to occur. He argued that 'Age' per se is not a useful concept. He suggested that the developmentalist's job is to study the environmental factors, or principles of learning, which determine the way organisms respond to stimulation. Indeed, it appears that we are born to learn, as illustrated by the demonstration of DeCasper and Fifer (1980, this reader) that newborns learn to change their sucking pattern in order to hear their mother's voice. However, as shown by Flavell (1986, this reader), some abilities which appear to develop in a stage-like manner, such as understanding the appearance–reality distinction (one object can have two incompatible properties – e.g., a sponge remains a sponge even if it looks like a rock), are difficult to advance.

Two additional perspectives

Two other perspectives not covered above need to be considered in our discussion of developmental functions: the Nativist and the Life Span perspectives. Karmiloff-Smith (1996, this reader) notes that the Nativist sees the infant as being pre-programmed to process faces, language, space, number, social interaction, and so on at birth. These abilities may be revealed at birth, or they may arise later when the structures needed to display the ability mature. The developmentalist's job is to invent clever experimental procedures to reveal these hidden skills, as exemplified by the elegant demonstration by Wynn (1995, this reader) that very young infants may be capable of simple addition and subtraction.

The Life Span tradition is reflected in Vander Zanden's (1993) definition of development as 'the orderly and sequential changes that occur with the passage of time as an organism moves from conception to death...[and] includes those processes that are biologically programmed within the organism and those processes by which the organism is changed or transformed through interaction with the environment' (p. 4). This definition clearly emphasizes the need to determine the interaction between biological and environmental factors as we study both behavioural and biological change *across the life span*. Why should we be interested in the life span? There are several reasons. First, growth and development do not stop at adolescence. Secondly, developmental declines are part of the story too; indeed, while they may predominate in old age, they also occur even in infancy. For example, Werker and Desjardins (1995, this reader) show that very young infants distinguish phonetic contrasts (e.g., 'b' from 'd') in their parents' native language as well as phonetic contrasts which are not part of the parents' native language. Some of these phonetic contrasts can be discriminated by the infants but not by their parents! This amazing infant ability disappears by 12 months of age. In other instances, during adulthood, one ability may decline while another increases; these developmental functions may be causally related as noted below. Finally, infant behaviour may be influenced by parental behaviour which was instilled by grandparents, as suggested by studies in the cross-generational transmission of patterns of attachment, discussed by Goldberg (1991; this reader, article 28).

EXAMPLES OF DEVELOPMENTAL FUNCTIONS

Given that all developmental psychologists study some aspect of psychological and biological change in an organism as a function of age (time), we will consider several examples of developmental functions – the actual data developmental psychologists collect, analyse and interpret. Developmental functions are presented in graphs similar to those in figure 1.1. Usually, the measure of behavioural or structural change is represented on the vertical, Y-axis, and age or time is on the horizontal, X-axis. The picture we obtain has both practical and theoretical value because it provides an index of how humans typically grow and change with age. The practical value is that it allows us to detect unusual developmental functions (e.g., developmental delays) and to intervene with treatment when appropriate. The theoretical value is that the data can be used to evaluate hypotheses derived from various theoretical perspectives by comparing theoretical schematic plots such as those in figure 1.1 with empirically-derived functions. Several examples of phenomena which match one of the different functions in figure 1.1 are drawn from this reader while others can be found in general developmental textbooks.

Continuous function

Perhaps the most common developmental function found in textbooks is the one described above for the Mechanistic World View, which simply increases

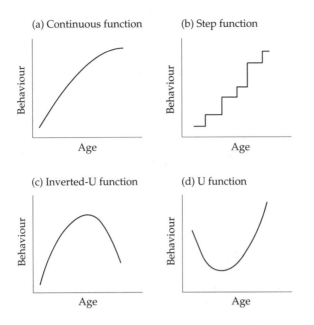

FIGURE 1.1   Four schematic developmental functions illustrating a change with age in the form of: (a) continuous, (b) step- or stage-like, (c) inverted U-shaped, and (d) upright U-shaped functions

with age (figure 1.1a). Examples include the negatively accelerating change in the height and weight of children, which increase rapidly during the first few years of life, more gradually during childhood, and level off after adolescence. Another example with a shorter time scale is the precision in reaching for and grasping an object, which gradually increases during the first year of life as infants practise and receive feedback from their errors.

Discontinuous (step) function

A second, common developmental function found in textbooks looks like a series of stages, reflecting the Organismic World View. This developmental function might be theoretical. Authors of developmental textbooks describe different 'stages' in the human life span such as infancy, preschool childhood, middle childhood, adolescence, adulthood, and later adulthood. As noted above, this function matches Piaget's description of stages of cognitive development. Stage-like progressions of specific skills or processes also exist, such as in the development of mobility. Here the Y-axis could be distance travelled by an infant, which suddenly accelerates at different points in time matching the onset of various mobility accomplishments. Infants are relatively immobile during the first few months of life, begin to crawl at around 6–8 months of age, stand up and toddle around furniture a few months later, and begin to walk on their own between 12 and 18 months of age. The onset of these mobility milestones seems to occur rather abruptly and each one represents a qualitatively different type of locomotion, suggesting a stage-like progression.

Another example is the development of speech – an initial period of no word production, followed by a period of babbling beginning around 9 months of age when infants make speech-like sounds in a flowing conversation which contains no words. Infants begin to use single words around 12 months of age, produce 2-to-3-word phrases at about $1\frac{1}{2}$ years of age, and finally, produce complex grammatical sentences. These major milestones, which appear to be qualitatively different, also have been conceptualized as stages.

U-shaped functions

Two other types of developmental functions are inverted and upright U-shaped functions. When we consider development across the life span, an inverted U-shaped developmental function, illustrated in figure 1.1c, is commonly observed. One example is the development of visual acuity, which is poor at birth, increases rapidly during the first few years of life, and diminishes during the latter part of the life span. Inverted U-shaped functions can also be found during shorter time periods. For example, babbling (Petitto and Marentette, 1991, this reader) emerges around 6 months of age, and disappears without a trace a few months later! Of course, some might argue that it does emerge again during adulthood – perhaps during university lectures.

The other U-shaped function, shown in figure 1.1d, involves abilities which may be present early in life and disappear to re-emerge at a later age. One example is the common observation that infants will display coordinated alternating step-like movements at birth, if they are supported, of course. This amazing ability seems to disappear when infants are a few months old and re-appears when they begin to stand and walk, around 12 months of age. Another example is the ability of newborns to turn towards off-centred sound sources at birth. This dramatic auditory localization response diminishes or disappears at around 6 weeks of age and re-appears around 4 months of age (see Muir, Humphrey and Humphrey, 1994, this reader).

Comparing developmental functions

It can be useful to plot more than one developmental function on the same graph. Possible causal relationships may be suggested by doing so. In the case of the U-shaped response for stepping, Thelen (see Thelen and Ulrick, 1991) discovered that the form of the alternating stepping in newborns looked like their kicking response when they were supine. Thelen looked for other developmental functions which might contribute to the suppression of the stepping response. One candidate was the increase in body weight, which progressed ahead of development of muscle strength in the legs. To demonstrate a causal relationship, Thelen reduced the need for muscle strength to lift the legs of infants who were not stepping, by, for example, placing them in water, and alternating stepping was recovered. In the case of the U-shaped auditory localization function, Humphrey, Dodwell, Muir and Humphrey (1988) compared the developmental functions for auditory localization responses and orientation to schematic faces from birth to 5 months of age, shown in

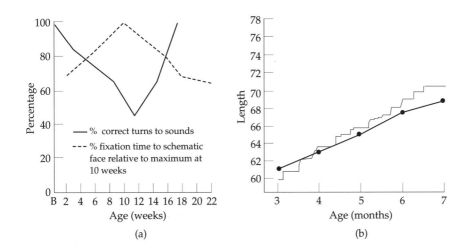

FIGURE 1.2 Illustrations of comparisons between different developmental functions. (a) compares the developmental course of the U-shaped auditory localization response function with that of the inverted U-shaped function, for interest in a schematic face (reported in Humphrey et al., 1988). (b) compares the continuous-growth function for height derived from averaged data with that derived from daily measures of a single infant

figure 1.2A. When there is a minimum in the performance of headturning to off-centred sounds there is a maximum in looking time for schematic faces. Although no causal relationship was determined by Humphrey et al., they speculated that competition between the two stimulus-response systems occurred, with the most rapidly changing system, visual attention, predominating. Alternative causal explanations for the U-shaped developmental function for auditory localization, related to other developmental functions, are discussed by Muir et al. (1994).

Uttal and Perlmutter (1989) provide a number of comparisons between developmental functions for older children and adults which illustrate possible causal relationships. One example has to do with the maintenance of typing speed by professional typists as they age. The developmental function tends to be flat over much of the life span. This is a puzzle because it is well known that as people age they have a slower reaction time, which slows down the typist's keystroke speed. It turns out that as keystroke speed declines, older typists increase their letter span (the number of words they code as a unit, which are then run-off automatically by the fingers). This cognitive skill, which increases with practice, may compensate for the loss of keystroke speed.

Conclusions

Developmental functions are a fundamental aspect of any course in developmental psychology. They allow us to evaluate our theories about how different processes develop over time. For example, we might ask: Is the child's visual face perception essentially adult-like at birth, following the Nativist perspective? Or, does it develop slowly over time, in a cumulative fashion, as a consequence of certain experiences, following the Mechanistic perspective? Or, does it emerge suddenly, in a step-like fashion, when the internal perceptual structure matures, following the Organismic perspective?

DEVELOPMENTAL METHODS

Now that some of the developmental functions developmental psychologists study have been reviewed, it is necessary to discuss how the data presented in these graphs are actually collected; what are the experimental designs employed by developmental psychologists?

Developmental psychologists employ a variety of methods. Perhaps the simplest in form is the case study, which involves repeated observations of the same person over time. Piaget began his work by observing his own children. Another famous example is Darwin's (1877) biographical sketch of his own child's development of different skills and aptitudes, which is included in this reader. While such case studies provide a rich source of ideas and insights, they have many obvious weaknesses. For example, there are problems of generalization – one or two children hardly constitute a representative sample of the population. Also, the observations tend to be unsystematic, and in many cases are retrospective – i.e., events are described long after their occurrence. Baby biographers may have strong theoretical biases which lead them to note anecdotes supporting their own theories. This is illustrated by Darwin's observations on gender differences in the develop-ment of anger. Of course, case studies can be done using more systematic methods by more objective observers than parents, but the reliability of the observations and generalization of the results may still be a problem. A brief review of different techniques for obtaining objective data will be followed by a discussion of the methods developmentalists employ to provide a greater degree of generalization of the results to the population at large.

From the collection of papers in this reader, you will find that researchers use many different types of instruments designed to obtain objective informa-tion about age differences. The instruments have been carefully constructed to fit the questions being asked, within the constraints of the age group being assessed. For example, cognitive development might be evaluated in infants by using visual habituation procedures, given that infants cannot talk, and in older children by administering IQ tests. Slater, Carrick, Bell and Roberts (1998, this reader) discuss difficulties in relating the results derived from different measures of children's intelligence. The development of infant–parent relationships may be studied by recording the frequency of various activities that the parties engage in during home observations, or by videotap-ing face-to-face interactions in a laboratory (e.g. Muir, et al., 1994, this reader). Tests of older infants include recording infant responses when parents leave them alone in a laboratory room (Ainsworth's Strange Situation Test, dis-cussed by Goldberg, 1991) or by interviewing children and having them sort picture cards depicting various family activities. The development of antisocial behaviour has been assessed using questionnaires filled out by parents and teachers, and by field observations of children's activity in class rooms and in the playground. In some cases, observers use check-lists to record the occurrence of various behaviours every few minutes (a time-sampling technique) from the live or videotaped observations, as in the studies of bullying made by Pepler, Craig and O'Connell (1998, this reader). These are only a few examples of the wide variety of measurement techniques used by the authors of papers in this reader. In all cases, the emphasis is on obtaining reliable, accurate, objective and valid measures of the operation of some psychological process.

Research designs

In all studies which describe behavioural changes with age, one of two general developmental designs, either the cross-sectional or the longitudinal, are used. The strengths and weaknesses of these designs are discussed and the sequential design is offered as a partial solution for the limitations imposed by the use of only one method.

Cross-sectional method   People of different ages are tested once; thus, each point on the X-axis is represented by a different age group. This is the most common method employed by developmental researchers because it is least expensive and provides a quick estimate of the shape of the developmental age function. However, it only describes age differences. There is no way to derive an estimate of the continuity or discontinuity of various processes over age (e.g., stability of personality; sudden shifts in language comprehension or production) because performance is averaged over different individuals at each age. Thus, the developmental function we plot could be due to either age or non-age differences between groups.

Longitudinal method   People of the same age are tested repeatedly as they grow older. This method is powerful because each individual's development is measured over time, allowing one to assess within-person changes with age, and between-person differences in age changes. In many cases the data are summarized by plotting the group average as a function of age; but, by looking at each individual's data, we can determine if there is a gradual change with age, similar to figure 1.1a, or a sudden shift in performance more characteristic of stage-like development, similar to figure 1.1b. Unfortunately, there are several problems with the longitudinal method as well. The cost is very high in several respects. It is time-consuming and difficult to schedule repeated visits, and the drop-out rate can be very high. If those who find the task difficult withdraw from the study, this selective survivorship can produce a population bias which distorts the developmental function and limits the generality of the results. Perhaps the biggest problem is the time it takes to complete a study – it equals the age span being tested. If, for example, the task is to map changes in performance on IQ tests between age 20 and 80, it would take about 60 years to complete the study. And, after all that work, the results may only be true for the particular age cohort studied (those born at about the same time), producing yet another population bias.

Design problems: when longitudinal and cross-sectional results tell a different story

Usually we try to obtain both longitudinal and cross-sectional data on any topic. Hartup (1996, this reader) compares the results of longitudinal and cross-sectional studies of aggression and comments on the limitations in generalizations we can derive from each method. In general, we expect to obtain similar developmental functions from cross-sectional and longitudinal data, and generally this is the case. For example, the U-shaped function for auditory localization is the same using either procedure (Muir, Clifton and Clarkson, 1989). However, this does not always happen. Two instances of conflicting results will be discussed; the first concerns the length of time between measures (the age scale) and the second concerns cohort effects.

Time between tests   In designing a developmental study one must decide what intervals to use on the X-axis, i.e., how many age groups are to be tested or how often repeated tests will be administered. When studying infants, it is common to test them monthly or bi-weekly in longitudinal studies, depending on when we expect to see an age difference in performance appear. The transition point for changes in performance with age can be estimated using cross-sectional data. While this may be appropriate in most cases, sometimes different distances between test ages can result in very different developmental functions.

An interesting example involves physical growth, which usually is represented as a continuous, increasing growth curve. This is shown in figure 1.2b, where the filled circles connected by a solid line have been estimated from a normative study by Babson and Benda (1976) which is based on a combination of cross-sectional and longitudinal data. The function looks continuous and the shape matches the monthly longitudinal data they reported for a few 'normally' growing individual infants. By contrast, a step-like function was found by Lampl, Veldhuis and Johnson (1992) when they made daily or weekly measures of the growth in length of a small number of infants during their first 21 months of life. Lampl et al. analysed individual growth functions and discovered that the main change in length occurred in sudden bursts followed by longer periods of no change. Indeed, in daily measures, children were found to grow substantially, as much as 1 centimetre, in a sudden burst, in many cases overnight, and then not change for an average of 12 days. This is shown in figure 1.2b where a summary of the growth pattern of one infant in Lampl et al.'s study is pictured by the thin line overlaying Babson and Benda's normative curve.

This may come as no great surprise to some parents, who report that their babies seemed suddenly to outgrow their sleepers overnight. The main point is that according to Lampl et al. changes in size occur in a stage-like progression with the most common state being 'no change' at all. This developmental function is not revealed unless frequent measures are taken on individuals. It should be noted that if all of Lampl et al.'s data were collapsed across individuals and plotted as a function of monthly age groups, the curve probably would look like Babson and Benda's normative age function.

Cohort effects and sequential designs　A serious design problem, which is particularly relevant for studies covering a large age range, involves cohort effects alluded to above. This is illustrated by the classic work on changes in performance on IQ tests as a function of age by Schaie and co-workers (e.g., Schaie and Strother, 1965). An idealized drawing of typical results derived from their work is shown in figure 1.3a (see Woodruff and Birren, 1975, for a detailed discussion of Schaie's work). This figure illustrates a common finding that the developmental functions of intellectual performance derived from cross-sectional studies decrease with age, while those derived from longitudinal studies may show little change with age. One explanation for these contradictory results is the existence of cohort differences in cultural experiences such as education (which is correlated with performance on intelligence tests). Possible years of education for the different cross-sectional age groups are also shown in figure 1.3a as filled circles (for these points, the Y-axis should read years of education from 7 to 12 years), which illustrates this confounding variable. Longitudinal studies are also flawed – as discussed above, practice and selective survivor effects could artificially inflate the longitudinal developmental function.

　　How then does one estimate the true developmental function for human performance over the life span? Schaie simply combined cross-sectional and short-term longitudinal designs, which is called a sequential (Hultsch and Deutsch, 1981) or sequential/age cohort (Craig, 1996) design. A schematic drawing of performance on one intellectual test (visualization performance – adapted from Nesselroade, Schaie and Baltes, 1972) is shown in figure 1.3b. In this figure, adults in five different age groups (7 years apart) were tested twice (7 years apart) giving us overlapping age groups. The results show both the

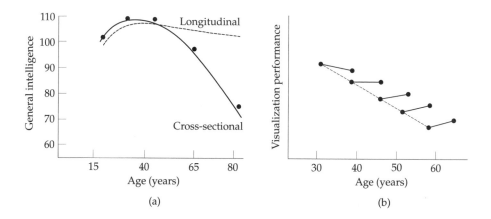

FIGURE 1.3　(a) and (b) Schematic illustrations of different developmental functions which may be produced by longitudinal versus cross-sectional studies of intellectual performance across a wide age span. See text for details

cohort effect – a drop in performance by older age groups, illustrated by the dotted line connecting cross-sectional data, and the contrasting, longitudinal effect, where groups show a slight improvement in performance over age, illustrated by the solid lines connecting each pair of longitudinal points for the five age groups.

Although sequential designs are not used often in studies with younger age groups, when they are used they provide a measure of individual differences and reveal whether or not longitudinal and cross-sectional results agree. Two examples of studies using this design with younger age groups are Kisilevsky, Muir and Low's (1992) study on the maturation of human foetal responses to vibroacoustic stimulation (in this case the developmental functions matched), and Miller, Ryan, Sinnott and Wilson's (1976) study of serial visual habituation in 2- to 4-month-olds (in this case, the developmental functions did not match). Failure to show matching developmental functions needs to be known and explained.

Summary

The Organismic and Mechanistic World Views have been summarized in order to provide a general framework within which the reader can place various types of research included in this reader, and elsewhere. The Organismic World View leads investigators to identify different stages of development humans pass through as they progress to the final adult level. In cognitive development, for example, the mental structures for processing environmental input are qualitatively different, and studies are constructed to reveal the differences in the operations of these structures at each stage, and to identify the age at which a lower structure is reorganized into a more advanced form. Investigators who subscribe more to the Mechanistic World View use behavioural technology to measure the development of processes such as memory, face processing, social behaviour, and so on, to discover how various abilities can be advanced (e.g., prosocial behaviour) and how to eliminate unwanted behaviours (e.g., antisocial behaviours). In fact, both world views emphasize the importance of the interaction between the organism and its environment, and both world views acknowledge the existence of differences in the abilities of children and adults. However, by including the Nativist position it is possible, at least as an exercise, to identify the orientation of most of the research included in this reader. The task is not easy, and in some cases it may be inappropriate to label a particular study as a derivative of only one world view. For example, DeCasper and Fifer's (1980) demonstration of infant preferences for the maternal voice might be considered to be support for a Nativist's position because it is present at birth; but, this preference may have developed as a result of the association between positive intrauterine events and maternal vocalizations experienced by the foetus during the prenatal period (Turkewitz, 1993), supporting a learning perspective.

A major job of developmental psychologists is to describe the developmental functions for various processes. Theories are generated to explain their shape, and in many cases they reflect one of the world views – some being relatively continuous patterns of growth or decline, and others appearing to be stage-like. U-shaped functions are particularly interesting. Some might reflect a learning perspective; for example, reinforcement and extinction/punishment may operate to increase and decrease auditory localization responses in young infants. However, the same phenomenon could reflect a stage process; the drop and recovery in auditory localization may reflect shifts from subcortical to cortical structures for processing the position of sound in space. When developmental functions are plotted on the same figure, depending on the timing of the shifts in behaviour, we may be able to establish causal relationships between different processes. It is to be hoped that a more comprehensive picture of development will arise as more developmental functions are described and compared.

References

Babson, T., and Benda, G. (1976). Growth graphs for the clinical assessment of infants of varying gestational age. *Journal of Pediatrics*, **89**, 814–20.

Baer, D. (1970). An age-irrelevant concept of development. *Merrill-Palmer Quarterly*, **16**, 238–45.

Craig, G. (1996). *Human Development* (7th edn). New Jersey: Prentice-Hall.

Darwin, C. (1877). A biographical sketch of an infant. *Mind: A Quarterly Review of Psychology and Philosophy*, **7**, 285–94.

DeCasper, T., and Fifer, W. (1980). Of human bonding: newborns prefer their mothers' voices. *Science*, **208**, 1174–6.

Flavell, J. (1986). Development of children's knowledge about the appearance–reality distinction. *American Psychologist*, **41**, 418–25.

Goldberg, S. (1991). Recent developments in attachment theory and research. *Canadian Journal of Psychiatry*, **36**, 393–400.

Hartup, W. (1996). The company they keep: friendships and their developmental significance. *Child Development*, **67**, 1–13.

Hultsch, D., and Deutsch, F. (1981). *Adult Development and Aging: A Life-Span Perspective*. New York: McGraw-Hill.

Humphrey, G., Dodwell, P., Muir, D., and Humphrey, D. (1988). Can blind infants and children use sonar sensory aids? *Canadian Journal of Psychology*, **42**, 94–119.

Jeffrey, W. (1958). Variables in early discrimination learning: I. Motor responses in the training of left–right discrimination. *Child Development*, **29**, 269–75.

Karmiloff-Smith, A. (1996). The Connectionist infant: Would Piaget turn in his grave? *SRCD Newsletter*, Fall 1996, 1–3 and 10.

Kisilevsky, B., Muir, D., and Low, J. (1992). Maturation of human fetal responses to vibroacoustic stimulation. *Child Development*, **63**, 1497–1508.

Lampl, M., Veldhuis, J., and Johnson, M. (1992). Saltation and stasis: A model of human growth. *Science*, **258**, 801–3.

Lerner, R. (1986). *Concepts and Theories of Human Development* (2nd edn). New York: Random House.

Miller, D., Ryan, E., Sinnott, J., and Wilson, M. (1976). Serial habituation in two-, three-, and four-month-old infants. *Child Development*, **47**, 341–9.

Muir, D., Clifton, R., and Clarkson, M. (1989). The development of a human auditory localization response: A U-shaped function. *Canadian Journal of Psychology*, **43**, 199–216.

Muir, D., Humphrey, D., and Humphrey, K. (1994). Pattern and space perception in young infants. *Spatial Vision*, **8**, 141–65.

Nesselroade, J., Schaie, K., and Baltes, P. (1972). Ontogenetic and generational components of structural and quantitative change in adult behavior. *Journal of Gerontology*, **27**, 222–8.

Pepler, D., Craig, W., and O'Connell, P. (1998). Understanding bullying from a dynamic systems perspective. In A. Slater and D. Muir (eds), *The Blackwell Reader in Developmental Psychology*, Oxford: Blackwell.

Petitto, L., and Marentette, P. (1991). Babbling in the manual mode: Evidence for the ontogeny of language. *Science*, **251**, 1493–6.

Piaget, J. (1962). The stages of the intellectual development of the child. *Bulletin of the Menninger Clinic*, **26**, 120–28.

Schaie, K., and Strother, C. (1965). A cross-sequential study of age changes in cognitive behavior. *Psychological Bulletin*, **70**, 671–80.

Slater, A., Carrick, R., Bell, C., and Roberts, E. (1998). Can measures of infant information processing predict later intellectual ability? In A. Slater and D. Muir (eds), *The Blackwell Reader in Developmental Psychology*, Oxford: Blackwell.

Thelen, E., and Ulrick, B. (1991). Hidden skills: A dynamic systems analysis of treadmill stepping during the first year. *Monographs of the Society for Research in Child Development*, **56** (1).

Turkewitz, G. (1993). The influence of timing on the nature of cognition. In G. Turkewitz and D. Devenny (eds), *Developmental Time and Timing*, New Jersey: Erlbaum.

Uttal, D., and Perlmutter, M. (1989). Toward a broader conceptualization of development: The role of gains and losses across the life span. *Developmental Review*, **9**, 101–32.

Vander Zanden, J. (1993). *Human Development* (5th edn). New York: McGraw-Hill.

Werker, J., and Desjardins, R. (1995). Listening to speech in the first year of life: Experiential influences on phoneme perception. *Current Directions in Psychological Science*, **4**, 76–81.

Woodruff, D., and Birren, J. (1975). *Aging: Scientific Perspectives and Social Issues*. New York: Van Nostrand.

Wynn, K. (1995). Infants possess a system of numerical knowledge. *Current Directions in Psychological Science*, **4**, 172–7.

2

A Biographical Sketch of an Infant*

Charles Darwin

Charles Darwin (1809–1882) was one of the finest observers of natural behaviour the world has ever seen. His observations of subtle variations in behaviour and form culminated in his account *On the Origin of Species* (1859): 'I have called this principle, by which each slight variation, if useful, is preserved, by the term of Natural Selection.' Charles and Emma Darwin had their first child, William Erasmus (nicknamed 'Doddy'), on 27 December 1839, and soon afterwards Charles began a diary record – a 'baby biography' – to detail his son's early development. Such biographies constitute some of the earliest systematic studies of children's development, and this account was published 37 years later.

It is of interest to note that, despite his considerable powers of observation, Darwin often got it wrong. With respect to vision he suggested that early capabilities were severely limited: 'his eyes were fixed on a candle as early as the 9th day, and up to the 45th day nothing else seemed thus to fix them'. However, we now know that even the newborn baby sees well enough to be able to imitate the facial gestures of adults (see Meltzoff and Moore's account in this collection of readings, article 12). With respect to hearing, Darwin wrote that 'Although so sensitive to sound in a general way, he was not able even when 124 days old easily to recognise whence a sound proceeded, so as to direct his eyes to the source.' We now know that in the appropriate setting even the newborn infant will readily localize, and turn his/her head in the direction of a sound (see Muir, Humphrey and Humphrey's account, article 11).

EDITORS'
INTRODUCTION

* Previously published in *Mind: A Quarterly Review of Psychology and Philosophy*, **7** (July 1877), pp. 285–94.

Darwin addresses a broad range of topics in his account of his son's development: innate and learned behaviour, instinct, memory, the development of pleasure, fear, affection, shyness and communication, among others. This account is a clear indication of how careful observation can provide substantive information about child development, and can lead to careful experiments which act to develop and complement diary studies.

REFERENCE

An excellent account and evaluation of baby diaries is to be found in: Wallace, D. B., Franklin, M. B., and Keegan, R. T. (1994). The observing eye: A century of baby diaries. *Human Development*, **34**, 1–29.

M. Taine's very interesting account of the mental development of an infant, translated in the last number of *Mind* (p. 252), has led me to look over a diary which I kept thirty-seven years ago with respect to one of my own infants. I had excellent opportunities for close observation, and wrote down at once whatever was observed. My chief object was expression, and my notes were used in my book on this subject; but as I attended to some other points, my observations may possibly possess some little interest in comparison with those by M. Taine, and with others which hereafter no doubt will be made. I feel sure, from what I have seen with my own infants, that the period of development of the several faculties will be found to differ considerably in different infants.

During the first seven days various reflex actions, namely sneezing, hickuping, yawning, stretching, and of course sucking and screaming, were well performed by my infant. On the seventh day, I touched the naked sole of his foot with a bit of paper, and he jerked it away, curling at the same time his toes, like a much older child when tickled. The perfection of these reflex movements shows that the extreme imperfection of the voluntary ones is not due to the state of the muscles or of the co-ordinating centres, but to that of the seat of the will. At this time, though so early, it seemed clear to me that a warm soft hand applied to his face excited a wish to suck. This must be considered as a reflex or an instinctive action, for it is impossible to believe that experience and association with the touch of his mother's breast could so soon have come into play. During the first fortnight he often started on hearing any sudden sound, and blinked his eyes. The same fact was observed with some of my other infants within the first fortnight. Once, when he was 66 days old, I happened to sneeze, and he started violently, frowned, looked frightened, and cried rather badly: for an hour afterwards he was in a state which would be called nervous in an older person, for every slight noise made him start. A few days before this same date, he first started at an object suddenly seen; but for a long time afterwards sounds made him start and wink his eyes much more frequently than did sight; thus when 114 days old, I shook a paste-board box with comfits in it near his face and he started, whilst the same box when empty or any other object shaken as near or much nearer to his face produced no effect. We may infer from these several facts that the winking of the eyes, which manifestly serves to protect them, had not been acquired through experience. Although so sensitive to sound in a general way, he was not able even when 124 days old easily to recognise whence a sound proceeded, so as to direct his eyes to the source.

With respect to vision, – his eyes were fixed on a candle as early as the 9th day, and up to the 45th day nothing else seemed thus to fix them; but on the 49th day his attention was attracted by a bright-coloured tassel, as was shown by his eyes becoming fixed and the movements of his arms ceasing. It was surprising how slowly he acquired the power of following with his eyes an object if swinging at all rapidly; for he could not do this well when seven and a half months old. At the age of 32 days he perceived his mother's bosom when three or four inches from it, as was shown by the protrusion of his lips and his eyes becoming fixed; but I much doubt whether this had any connection with vision; he certainly had not touched the bosom. Whether he was guided through smell or the sensation of warmth or through association with the position in which he was held, I do not at all know.

The movements of his limbs and body were for a long time vague and purposeless, and usually performed in a jerking manner; but there was one exception to this rule, namely, that from a very early period, certainly long before he was 40 days old, he could move his hands to his own mouth. When 77 days old, he took the sucking bottle (with which he was partly fed) in his right hand, whether he was held on the left or right arm of his nurse, and he would not take it in his left hand until a week later although I tried to make him do so; so that the right hand was a week in advance of the left. Yet this infant afterwards proved to be left-handed, the tendency being no doubt inherited – his grandfather, mother, and a brother having been or being left-handed. When between 80 and 90 days old, he drew all sorts of objects into his mouth, and in two or three weeks' time could do this with some skill; but he often first touched his nose with the object and then dragged it down into his mouth. After grasping my finger and drawing it to his mouth, his own hand prevented him from sucking it; but on the 114th day, after acting in this manner, he slipped his own hand down so that he could get the end of my finger into his mouth. This action was repeated several times, and evidently was not a chance but a rational one. The intentional movements of the hands and arms were thus much in advance of those of the body and legs; though the purposeless movements of the latter were from a very early period usually alternate as in the act of walking. When four months old, he often looked intently at his own hands and other objects close to him, and in doing so the eyes were turned much inwards, so that he often squinted frightfully. In a fortnight after this time (i.e. 132 days old) I observed that if an object was brought as near to his face as his own hands were, he tried to seize it, but often failed; and he did not try to do so in regard to more distant objects. I think there can be little doubt that the convergence of his eyes gave him the clue and excited him to move his arms. Although this infant thus began to use his hands at an early period, he showed no special aptitude in this respect, for when he was 2 years and 4 months old, he held pencils, pens, and other objects far less neatly and efficiently than did his sister who was then only 14 months old, and who showed great inherent aptitude in handling anything.

ANGER

It was difficult to decide at how early an age anger was felt; on his eighth day he frowned and wrinkled the skin round his eyes before a crying fit, but this may have been due to pain or distress, and not to anger. When about ten weeks old, he was given some rather cold milk and he kept a slight frown on his forehead all the time that he was sucking, so that he looked like a grown-up person made cross from being compelled to do something which he did not like. When nearly four months old, and perhaps much earlier, there could be no doubt, from the manner in which the blood gushed into his whole face and scalp, that he easily got into a violent passion. A small cause sufficed; thus, when a little over seven months old, he screamed with rage because a lemon slipped away and he could not seize it with his hands. When eleven months old, if a wrong plaything was given him, he would push it away and beat it; I presume that the beating was an instinctive sign of anger, like the snapping of the jaws by a young crocodile just out of the egg, and not, that he imagined he could hurt the plaything. When two years and three months old, he became a great adept at throwing books or sticks, &c., at anyone who offended him; and so it was with some of my other sons. On the other hand, I could never see a trace of such aptitude in my infant daughters; and this makes me think that a tendency to throw objects is inherited by boys.

FEAR

This feeling probably is one of the earliest which is experienced by infants, as shown by their starting at any sudden sound when only a few weeks old; followed by crying. Before the present one was $4\frac{1}{2}$ months old I had been accustomed to make close to him many strange and loud noises, which were all taken as excellent jokes, but at this period I one day made a loud snoring noise which I had never done before; he instantly looked grave and then burst out crying. Two or three days afterwards, I made through forgetfulness the same noise with the same result. About the same time (*viz.* on the 137th day) I approached with my back towards him and then stood motionless: he looked very grave and much surprised, and would soon have cried, had I not turned round; then his face instantly relaxed into a smile. It is well known how intensely older children suffer from vague and undefined fears, as from the dark, or in passing an obscure corner in a large hall, &c. I may give as an instance that I took the child in question, when $2\frac{1}{4}$ years old, to the Zoological Gardens, and he enjoyed looking at all the animals which were like those that he knew, such as deer, antelopes &c., and all the birds, even the ostriches, but was much alarmed at the various larger animals in cages. He often said afterwards that he wished to go again, but not to see "beasts in houses"; and we could in no manner account for this fear. May we not suspect that the vague but very real fears of children, which are quite independent of experience, are the inherited effects of real dangers and abject superstitions during ancient savage times? It is quite conformable with what we know of the transmission of formerly well-developed characters, that they should appear at an early period of life, and afterwards disappear.

PLEASURABLE SENSATIONS

It may be presumed that infants feel pleasure whilst sucking, and the expression of their swimming eyes seems to show that this is the case. This infant smiled when 45 days, a second infant when 46 days old; and these were true smiles, indicative of pleasure, for their eyes brightened and eyelids slightly closed. The smiles arose chiefly when looking at their mother, and were therefore probably of mental origin; but this infant often smiled then, and for some time afterwards, from some inward pleasurable feeling, for nothing was happening which could have in any way excited or amused him. When 110 days old he was exceedingly amused by a pinafore being thrown over his face and then suddenly withdrawn; and so he was when I suddenly uncovered my own face and approached his. He then uttered a little noise when was an incipient laugh. Here surprise was the chief cause of the amusement, as is the case to a large extent with the wit of grown-up persons. I believe that for three or four weeks before the time when he was amused by a face being suddenly uncovered, he received a little pinch on his nose and cheeks as a good joke. I was at first surprised at humour being appreciated by an infant only a little above three months old, but we should remember how very early puppies and kittens begin to play. When four months old, he showed in an unmistakable manner that he liked to hear the pianoforte played; so that here apparently was the earliest sign of an æsthetic feeling, unless the attraction of bright colours, which was exhibited much earlier, may be so considered.

AFFECTION

This probably arose very early in life, if we may judge by his smiling at those who had charge of him when under two months old; though I had no distinct evidence of his distinguishing and recognising anyone, until he was nearly four months old. When nearly five months old, he plainly showed his wish to go to his nurse. But he did not spontaneously exhibit affection by overt acts until a little above a year old, namely, by kissing several times his nurse who had been absent for a short time. With respect to the allied feeling of sympathy, this was clearly shown at 6 months and 11 days by his melancholy face, with the corners of his mouth well depressed, when his nurse pretended to cry. Jealousy was plainly exhibited when I fondled a large doll, and when I weighed his infant sister, he being then $15\frac{1}{2}$ months old. Seeing how strong a feeling jealousy is in dogs, it would probably be exhibited by infants at an earlier age than that just specified, if they were tried in a fitting manner.

ASSOCIATION OF IDEAS, REASON, &C.

The first action which exhibited, as far as I observed, a kind of practical reasoning, has already been noticed, namely, the slipping his hand down my finger so as to get the end of it into his mouth; and this happened on the 114th day. When four and a half months old, he repeatedly smiled at my image and his own in a mirror, and no doubt mistook them for real objects; but he showed sense in being evidently surprised at my voice coming from behind him. Like all infants he much enjoyed thus looking at himself, and in less than two months perfectly understood that it was an image; for if I made quite silently any odd grimace, he would suddenly turn round to look at me. He was, however, puzzled at the age of seven months, when being out of doors he saw me on the inside of a large plate-glass window, and seemed in doubt whether or not it was an image. Another of my infants, a little girl, when exactly a year old, was not nearly so acute, and seemed quite perplexed at the image of a person in a mirror approaching her from behind. The higher apes which I tried with a small looking-glass behaved differently; they placed their hands behind the glass, and in doing so showed their sense, but far from taking pleasure in looking at themselves they got angry and would look no more.

When five months old, associated ideas arising independently of any instruction became fixed in his mind; thus as soon as his hat and cloak were put on, he was very cross if he was not immediately taken out of doors. When exactly seven months old, he made the great step of associating his nurse with her name, so that if I called it out he would look round for her. Another infant used to amuse himself by shaking his head laterally: we praised and imitated him, saying 'Shake your head'; and when he was seven months old, he would sometimes do so on being told without any other guide. During the next four months the former infant associated many things and actions with words; thus when asked for a kiss he would protrude his lips and keep still, – would shake his head and say in a scolding voice 'Ah' to the coal-box or a little spilt water, &c., which he had been taught to consider as dirty. I may add that when a few days under nine months old he associated his own name with his image in the looking-glass, and when called by name would turn towards the glass even when at some distance from it. When a few days over nine months, he learnt spontaneously that a hand or other object causing a shadow to fall on the wall in front of him was to be looked for behind. Whilst under a year old, it was sufficient to repeat two or three times at intervals any short sentence to fix firmly in his mind some associated idea. In the infant described by M. Taine (pp. 254–6) the age at which ideas readily became associated seems to have been considerably later, unless indeed the earlier cases were overlooked. The facility with which associated ideas due to instruction and others spontaneously arising were acquired, seemed to me by far the most strongly marked of all the distinctions between the mind of an infant and that of the cleverest full-grown dog that I have ever known. What a contrast does the mind of an infant present to that of the pike, described by Professor Möbius,[1] who during three whole months dashed and stunned himself against a glass partition which separated him from some minnows; and when, after at last learning that he could not attack them with impunity, he was placed in the aquarium with these same minnows, then in a persistent and senseless manner he would not attack them!

Curiosity, as M. Taine remarks, is displayed at an early age by infants, and is highly important in the development of their minds; but I made no special observation on this head. Imitation likewise comes into play. When our infant was only four months old I thought that he tried to imitate sounds; but I may have deceived myself, for I was not thoroughly convinced that he did so until he was ten months old. At the age of $11\frac{1}{2}$ months he could readily imitate all sorts of actions, such as shaking his head and saying 'Ah' to any dirty object, or by carefully and slowly putting his forefinger in the middle of the palm of his other hand to the childish rhyme of 'Pat it and pat it and mark it with T'. It was amusing to behold his pleased expression after successfully performing any such accomplishment.

I do not know whether it is worth mentioning, as showing something about the strength of memory in a young child, that this one when 3 years and 23 days old on being shown an engraving of his grandfather, whom he had not seen for exactly six months, instantly recognised him and mentioned a whole string of events which had occurred whilst visiting him, and which certainly had never been mentioned in the interval.

Moral Sense

The first sign of moral sense was noticed at the age of nearly 13 months: I said 'Doddy (his nickname) won't give poor papa a kiss, – naughty Doddy.' These words, without doubt, made him feel slightly uncomfortable; and at last when I had returned to my chair, he protruded his lips as a sign that he was ready to kiss me; and he then shook his hand in an angry manner until I came and received his kiss. Nearly the same little scene recurred in a few days, and the reconciliation seemed to give him so much satisfaction, that several times afterwards he pretended to be angry and slapped me, and then insisted on giving me a kiss. So that here we have a touch of the dramatic art, which is so strongly pronounced in most young children. About this time it became easy to work on his feelings and make him do whatever was wanted. When 2 years and 3 months old, he gave his last bit of gingerbread to his little sister, and then cried out with high self-approbation 'Oh kind Doddy, kind Doddy.' Two months later, he became extremely sensitive to ridicule, and was so suspicious that he often thought people who were laughing and talking together were laughing at him. A little later (2 years and $7\frac{1}{2}$ months old) I met him coming out of the dining room with his eyes unnaturally bright, and an odd unnatural or affected manner, so that I went into the room to see who was there, and found that he had been taking pounded sugar, which he had been told not to do. As he had never been in any way punished, his odd manner certainly was not due to fear and I suppose it was pleasurable excitement struggling with conscience. A fortnight afterwards, I met him coming out of the same room, and he was eyeing his pinafore which he had carefully rolled up; and again his manner was so odd that I determined to see what was within his pinafore, notwithstanding that he said there was nothing and repeatedly commanded me to 'go away', and I found it stained with pickle-juice; so that here was carefully planned deceit. As this child was educated solely by working on his good feelings, he soon became as truthful, open, and tender, as anyone could desire.

Unconsciousness, Shyness

No one can have attended to very young children without being struck at the unabashed manner in which they fixedly stare without blinking their eyes at a new face; an old person can look in this manner only at an animal or inanimate object. This, I believe, is the result of young children not thinking in the least about themselves, and therefore not being in the least shy, though they are sometimes afraid of strangers. I saw the first symptom of shyness in my child when nearly two years and three months old: this was shown towards myself, after an absence of ten days from home, chiefly by his eyes being kept slightly averted from mine; but he soon came and sat on my knee and kissed me, and all trace of shyness disappeared.

Means of Communication

The noise of crying or rather of squalling, as no tears are shed for a long time, is of course uttered in an instinctive manner, but serves to show that there is suffering. After a time the sound differs according to the cause, such as hunger or pain. This was noticed when this infant was eleven weeks old, and I believe at an earlier age in another infant. Moreover, he appeared soon to learn to begin crying voluntarily, or to wrinkle his face in the manner proper to the occasion, so as to show that he wanted something. When 46 days old, he first made little noises without any meaning to please himself, and these soon became varied. An incipient laugh was observed on the 113th day, but much earlier in another infant. At this date I thought, as already remarked, that he began to try to imitate sounds, as he certainly did at a considerably later period. When five and a half months old, he uttered an articulate sound 'da' but without any meaning attached to it. When a little over a year old, he used gestures to explain his wishes; to give a simple instance, he picked up a bit of paper and giving it to me pointed to the fire, as he had often seen and liked to see paper burnt. At exactly the age of a year, he made the great step of inventing a word for food, namely, *mum*, but what led him to it I did not discover. And now instead of beginning to cry when he was hungry, he used this word in a demonstrative manner or as a verb, implying 'Give me food.' This word therefore corresponds with *ham* as used by M. Taine's infant at the later age of 14 months. But he also used *mum* as a substantive of wide signification; thus he called sugar *shu-mum*, and a little later after he had learned the word 'black', he called liquorice *black-shu-mum*, – black-sugar-food.

I was particularly struck with the fact that when asking for food by the word *mum* he gave to it (I will copy the words written down at the time) 'a most strongly marked interrogatory sound at the end'. He also gave to 'Ah,' which he chiefly used at first when recognising any person or his own image in a mirror, an exclamatory sound, such as we employ when surprised. I remark in my notes that the use of these intonations seemed to have arisen instinctively, and I regret that more observations were not made on this subject. I record, however, in my notes that at a rather later period, when between 18 and 21 months old, he modulated his voice in refusing peremptorily to do anything by a defiant whine, so as to express 'That I won't,'; and again his humph of assent expressed 'Yes, to be sure.' M. Taine also insists strongly on the highly expressive tones of the sounds made by his infant before she had learnt to speak. The interrogatory sound which my child gave to the word *mum* when asking for food is especially curious; for if anyone will use a single word or a short sentence in this manner, he will find that the musical pitch of his voice rises considerably at the close. I did not then see that this fact bears on the view which I have elsewhere maintained that before man used articulate language, he uttered notes in a true musical scale as does the anthropoid ape Hylobates.

Finally, the wants of an infant are at first made intelligible by instinctive cries, which after a time are modified in part unconsciously, and in part, as I believe, voluntarily as a means of communication, – by the unconscious expression of the features, – by gestures and in a marked manner by different intonations, – lastly by words of a general nature invented by himself, then of a more precise nature imitated from those which he hears; and these latter are acquired at a wonderfully quick rate. An infant understands to a certain extent, and as I believe at a very early period, the meaning or feelings of those who tend him, by the expression of their features. There can hardly be a doubt about this with respect to smiling; and it seemed to me that the infant whose biography I have here given understood a compassionate expression at a little over five months old. When 6 months and 11 days old he certainly showed sympathy with his nurse on her pretending to cry. When pleased after performing some new accomplishment, being then almost a year old, he evidently studied the expression of those around him. It was probably due to differences of expression and not merely of the form of the features that certain faces clearly pleased him much more than others, even at so early an age as a little over six months. Before he was a year old, he understood intonations and gestures, as well as several words and short sentences. He understood one word, namely, his nurse's name, exactly five months before he invented his first word *mum*; and this is what might have been expected, as we know that the lower animals easily learn to understand spoken words.

NOTE

1. *Die Bewegungen der Thiere, &c.,* 1873, p. 11.

REFERENCES

Taine, H. A. (1877). Taine on the acquisition of language by children. *Mind: Quarterly Review of Psychology and Philosophy*, **2**, pp. 252–9.

3

BABY IN A BOX*

B. F. Skinner

EDITORS'
INTRODUCTION

Burrhus Frederick Skinner (1904–90) became America's most famous psychologist. He used conditioning procedures and reinforcement to shape animals' behaviour and develop laws of learning, and under his influence Behaviourism became one of the most powerful theoretical views in psychology. He gave an account of how it was easily possible to use the same principles of learning with infants and children:

> The human baby is an excellent subject in experiments of the sort described here [Skinner was describing how conditioning and reinforcement could be used to train animals]. You will not need to interfere with feeding schedules or create any other state of deprivation, because the human infant can be reinforced by very trivial environmental events; it does not need such a reward as food. Almost any 'feedback' from the environment is reinforcing if it is not too intense. A crumpled newspaper, a pan and a spoon, or any convenient noisemaker quickly generates appropriate behavior, often amusing in its violence. The baby's rattle is based upon this principle.
> One reinforcer to which babies often respond is the flashing on and off of a table lamp. Whenever the baby lifts its hand, flash the light. In a short time a well-defined response will be generated. (Human babies are just as 'smart' as dogs or pigeons in this respect.) Incidentally, the baby will enjoy the experiment.
> (*Cumulative Record*, p. 418)

He also described how the mother might unintentionally reinforce behaviour that she does not want in her child:

* From B. F. Skinner, *Cumulative Record* (New York: Appleton-Century-Crofts, Inc., 1959), pp. 419–26.

A familiar problem is that of the child who seems to take an almost pathological delight in annoying its parents. In many cases this is the result of conditioning.... The mother may unwittingly promote the very behavior she does not want. For example, she may answer the child only when it raises its voice. The average intensity of the child's vocal behavior therefore moves up to another level. Eventually the mother gets used to this level and again reinforces (with her attention) only louder instances. This vicious circle brings about louder and louder behavior. The child's voice may also vary in intonation, and any change in the direction of unpleasantness is more likely to get the attention of the mother and is therefore strengthened. The mother behaves, in fact, as if she had been given the assignment of teaching the child to be annoying! The remedy in such a case is simply for the mother to make sure that she responds with attention and affection to most if not all the responses of the child which are of acceptable intensity and tone of voice and that she never reinforces the annoying forms of behavior. (Ibid., p. 419)

Skinner's experiments with animals were almost invariably carried out with the animal in some sort of cage, usually with a lever for the animal (e.g., a pigeon) to peck or (a rat) to press. It wasn't long before such cages were called boxes, and the expression 'Skinner box' caught on. Skinner also turned his hand to inventing, and one device was the 'Air-Crib' in which one of his daughters was reared. When the following article was first published in the *Ladies' Home Journal* in October 1945 it was entitled 'Baby in a Box'. Skinner commented that 'The title "Baby in a Box" was not mine; it was invented by the editors of the Journal.' The title was perhaps unfortunate, because the impression was quickly gained, from those who had not read the article, that his daughter was reared in a Skinner box, and subjected to a variety of different reinforcement schedules. In fact, the 'Air-Crib' seems a rather pleasant and hygienic environment for an infant.

Reference

Skinner, B. F. (1961). *Cumulative Record*. London: Methuen.

OVERVIEW Since publication of this article in the *Ladies' Home Journal* in October 1945, several hundred babies have been reared in what is now known as an "Air-Crib." The advantages reported here have been generously confirmed. Although cultural inertia is perhaps nowhere more powerful than in child-raising practices, and in spite of the fact that the device is not easy to build, its use has steadily spread. The advantages to the child and parent alike seem to be too great to be resisted. One early user, John M. Gray, sent a questionnaire to 73 couples who had used Air-Cribs for 130 babies. All but three described the device as "wonderful." The physical and psychological benefits reported by these users seem to warrant extensive research.

In that brave new world which science is preparing for the housewife of the future, the young mother has apparently been forgotten. Almost nothing has been done to ease her lot by simplifying and improving the care of babies.

When we decided to have another child, my wife and I felt that it was time to apply a little labor-saving invention and design to the problems of the nursery. We began by going over the disheartening schedule of the young mother, step by step. We asked only one question: Is this practice important for the physical and psychological health of the baby? When it was not, we marked it for elimination. Then the "gadgeteering" began.

The result was an inexpensive apparatus in which our baby daughter has now been living for eleven months. Her remarkable good health and happiness and my wife's welcome leisure have exceeded our most optimistic predictions, and we are convinced that a new deal for both mother and baby is at hand.

We tackled first the problem of warmth. The usual solution is to wrap the baby in half-a-dozen layers of cloth – shirt, nightdress, sheet, blankets. This is never completely successful. The baby is likely to be found steaming in its own fluids or lying cold and uncovered. Schemes to prevent uncovering may be dangerous, and in fact they have sometimes even proved fatal. Clothing and bedding also interfere with normal exercise and growth and keep the baby from taking comfortable postures or changing posture during sleep. They also encourage rashes and sores. Nothing can be said for the system on the score of convenience, because frequent changes and launderings are necessary.

Why not, we thought, dispense with clothing altogether – except for the diaper, which serves another purpose – and warm the space in which the baby lives? This should be a simple technical problem in the modern home. Our solution is a closed compartment about as spacious as a standard crib (plate 3.1). The walls are well insulated, and one side, which can be raised like a window, is a large pane of safety glass. The heating is electrical, and special precautions have been taken to ensure accurate control.

After a little experimentation we found that our baby, when first home from the hospital, was completely comfortable and relaxed without benefit of clothing at about 86° F. As she grew older, it was possible to lower the temperature by easy stages. Now, at eleven months, we are operating at about 78°, with a relative humidity of 50 per cent.

Raising or lowering the temperature by more than a degree or two produces a surprising change in the baby's condition and behavior. This response is so sensitive that we wonder how a comfortable temperature is ever reached with clothing and blankets.

The discovery which pleased us most was that crying and fussing could always be stopped by slightly lowering the temperature. During the first three months, it is true, the baby would also cry when wet or hungry, but in that case she would stop when changed or fed. During the past six months she has not cried at all except for a moment or two when injured or sharply distressed – for example, when inoculated. The "lung exercise" which so often is appealed to to reassure the mother of a baby who cries a good deal takes the much pleasanter form of shouts and gurgles.

PLATE 3.1   The Skinner box

How much of this sustained cheerfulness is due to the temperature is hard to say, because the baby enjoys many other kinds of comfort. She sleeps in curious postures, not half of which would be possible under securely fastened blankets.

When awake, she exercises almost constantly and often with surprising violence. Her leg, stomach, and back muscles are especially active and have become strong and hard. It is necessary to watch this performance for only a few minutes to realize how severely restrained the average baby is, and how much energy must be diverted into the only remaining channel – crying.

A wider range and variety of behavior are also encouraged by the freedom from clothing. For example, our baby acquired an amusing, almost apelike skill in the use of her feet. We have devised a number of toys which are occasionally suspended from the ceiling of the compartment. She often plays with these with her feet alone and with her hands and feet in close co-operation.

One toy is a ring suspended from a modified music box. A note can be played by pulling the ring downward, and a series of rapid jerks will produce Three Blind Mice. At seven months our baby would grasp the ring in her toes, stretch out her leg and play the tune with a rhythmic movement of her foot.

We are not especially interested in developing skills of this sort, but they are valuable for the baby because they arouse and hold her interest. Many babies seem to cry from sheer boredom – their behavior is restrained and they have nothing else to do. In our compartment, the waking hours are invariably active and happy ones.

Freedom from clothes and bedding is especially important for the older baby who plays and falls asleep off and on during the day. Unless the mother is constantly on the alert, it is hard to cover the baby promptly when it falls asleep and to remove and arrange sheets and blankets as soon as it is ready to play. All this is now unnecessary.

Remember that these advantages for the baby do not mean additional labor or attention on the part of the mother. On the contrary, there is an almost unbelievable saving in time and effort. For one thing, there is no bed to be made or changed. The "mattress" is a tightly stretched canvas, which is kept dry by warm air. A single bottom sheet operates like a roller towel.[1] It is stored on a spool outside the compartment at one end and passes into a wire hamper at the other. It is ten yards long and lasts a week. A clean section can be locked into place in a few seconds. The time which is usually spent in changing clothes is also saved. This is especially important in the early months. When we take the baby up for feeding or play, she is wrapped in a small blanket or a simple nightdress. Occasionally she is dressed up "for fun" or for her play period. But that is all. The wrapping blanket, roller sheet, and the usual diapers are the only laundry actually required.

Time and labor are also saved because the air which passes through the compartment is thoroughly filtered. The baby's eyes, ears, and nostrils remain fresh and clean. A weekly bath is enough, provided the face and diaper region are frequently washed. These little attentions are easy because the compartment is at waist level.

It takes about one and one-half hours each day to feed, change, and otherwise care for the baby. This includes everything except washing diapers and preparing formula. We are not interested in reducing the time any further. As a baby grows older, it needs a certain amount of social stimulation. And after all, when unnecessary chores have been eliminated, taking care of a baby is fun.

An unforeseen dividend has been the contribution to the baby's good health. Our pediatrician readily approved the plan before the baby was born, and he has followed the results enthusiastically from month to month. Here are some points on the health score: When the baby was only ten days old, we could place her in the preferred face-down position without danger of smothering, and she has slept that way ever since, with the usual advantages. She has always enjoyed deep and extended sleep, and her feeding and eliminative habits have been extraordinarily regular. She has never had a stomach upset, and she has never missed a daily bowel movement.

The compartment is relatively free of spray and air-borne infection, as well as dust and allergic substances. Although there have been colds in the family, it has been easy to avoid contagion, and the baby has completely escaped. The neighborhood children troop in to see her, but they see her through glass and keep their school-age diseases to themselves. She has never had a diaper rash.

We have also enjoyed the advantages of a fixed daily routine. Child specialists are still not agreed as to whether the mother should watch the baby or the clock, but no one denies that a strict schedule saves time, for the mother can plan her day in advance and find time for relaxation or freedom for other activities. The trouble is that a routine acceptable to the baby often conflicts with the schedule of the household. Our compartment helps out here in two ways. Even in crowded living quarters it can be kept free of unwanted lights and sounds. The insulated walls muffle all ordinary noises, and a curtain can be drawn down over the window. The result is that, in the space taken by a standard crib, the baby has in effect a separate room. We are never concerned lest the doorbell, telephone, piano, or children at play wake the baby, and we can therefore let her set up any routine she likes.

But a more interesting possibility is that her routine may be changed to suit our convenience. A good example of this occurred when we dropped her schedule from four to three meals per day. The baby began to wake up in the morning about an hour before we wanted to feed her. This annoying habit, once established, may persist for months. However, by slightly raising the temperature during the night we were able to postpone her demand for breakfast. The explanation is simple. The evening meal is used by the baby mainly to keep herself warm during the night. How long it lasts will depend in part upon how fast heat is absorbed by the surrounding air.

One advantage not to be overlooked is that the soundproofing also protects the family from the baby! Our intentions in this direction were misunderstood by some of our friends. We were never put to the test, because there was no crying to contend with, but it was never our policy to use the compartment in order to let the baby "cry it out."

Every effort should be made to discover just why a baby cries. But if the condition cannot be remedied, there is no reason why the family, and perhaps the neighborhood as well, must suffer. (Such a compartment, by the way, might persuade many a landlord to drop a "no babies" rule, since other tenants can be completely protected.)

Before the baby was born, when we were still building the apparatus, some of the friends and acquaintances who had heard about what we proposed to do were rather shocked. Mechanical dish-washers, garbage disposers, air cleaners, and other laborsaving devices were all very fine, but a mechanical baby tender – that was carrying science too far! However, all the specific objections which were raised against the plan have faded away in the bright light of our results. A very brief acquaintance with the scheme in operation is enough to resolve all doubts. Some of the toughest skeptics have become our most enthusiastic supporters.

One of the commonest objections was that we were going to raise a "softie" who would be unprepared for the real world. But instead of becoming hypersensitive, our baby has acquired a surprisingly serene tolerance for annoyances. She is not bothered by the clothes she wears at playtime, she is not frightened by loud or sudden noises, she is not frustrated by toys out of reach, and she takes a lot of pommeling from her older sister like a good sport. It is possible that she will have to learn to sleep in a noisy room, but adjustments of that sort are always necessary. A tolerance for any annoyance can be built up by administering it in controlled dosages, rather than in the usual accidental way. Certainly there is no reason to annoy the child throughout the whole of its infancy, merely to prepare it for later childhood.

It is not, of course, the favorable conditions to which people object, but the fact that in our compartment they are "artificial." All of them occur naturally in one favorable environment or another, where the same objection should apply but is never raised. It is quite in the spirit of the "world of the future" to make favorable conditions available everywhere through simple mechanical means.

A few critics have objected that they would not like to live in such a compartment themselves – they feel that it would stifle them or give them claustrophobia. The baby obviously does not share in this opinion. The compartment is well ventilated and much more spacious than a Pullman berth, considering the size of the occupant. The baby cannot get out, of course, but that is true of a crib as well. There is less actual restraint in the compartment because the baby is freer to move about. The plain fact is that she is perfectly happy. She has never tried to get out nor resisted being put back in, and that seems to be the final test.

Another early objection was that the baby would be socially starved and robbed of the affection and mother love which she needs. This has simply not been true. The compartment does not ostracize the baby. The large window is no more of a social barrier than the bars of a crib. The baby follows what is going on in the room, smiles at passers-by, plays "peek-a-boo" games, and obviously delights in company. And she is handled, talked to, and played with whenever she is changed or fed, and each afternoon during a play period which is becoming longer as she grows older.

The fact is that a baby will probably get more love and affection when it is easily cared for, because the mother is not so likely to feel overworked and resentful of the demands made upon her. She will express her love in a practical way and give the baby genuinely affectionate care.

It is common practice to advise the troubled mother to be patient and tender and to enjoy her baby. And, of course, that is what any baby needs. But it is the exceptional mother who can fill this prescription upon demand, especially if there are other children in the family and she has no help. We need to go one step further and treat the mother with affection also. Simplified child care will give mother love a chance.

A similar complaint was that such an apparatus would encourage neglect. But easier care is sure to be better care. The mother will resist the temptation to put the baby back into a damp bed if she can conjure up a dry one in five seconds. She may very well spend less time with her baby, but babies do not suffer from being left alone but only from the discomforts which arise from being left alone in the ordinary crib.

How long do we intend to keep the baby in the compartment? The baby will answer that in time, but almost certainly until she is two years old, or perhaps three. After the first year, of course, she will spend a fair part of each day in a play-pen or out-of-doors. The compartment takes the place of a crib and will get about the same use. Eventually it will serve as sleeping quarters only.

We cannot, of course, guarantee that every baby raised in this way will thrive so successfully. But there is a plausible connection between health and happiness and the surroundings we have provided, and I am quite sure that our success is not an accident. The experiment should, of course, be repeated again and again with different babies and different parents. One case is enough, however, to disprove the flat assertion that it can't be done. At least we have shown that a moderate and inexpensive mechanization of baby care will yield a tremendous saving in time and trouble, without harm to the child and probably to its lasting advantage.

NOTE

1. The canvas and "endless" sheet arrangement was soon replaced with a single layer of woven plastic, which could be cleaned and instantly wiped dry.

4

THE STAGES OF THE INTELLECTUAL DEVELOPMENT OF THE CHILD*

Jean Piaget

The impact of Jean Piaget (1896–1980) on our understanding of child development has been extraordinary. He developed a theory of child development that was both original and comprehensive. While he wrote on many aspects of child development he is best known for his stage theory of intellectual development, and in this article he gives a brief account of these stages.

EDITORS'
INTRODUCTION

A consideration of the stages of the development of intelligence should be preceded by asking the question, What is intelligence? Unfortunately, we find ourselves confronted by a great number of definitions. For Claparède, intelligence is an adaptation to new situations. When a situation is new, when there are no reflexes, when there are no habits to rely on, then the subject is obliged to search for something new. That is to say, Claparède defines intelligence as groping, as feeling one's way, trial-and-error behavior. We find this trial-and-error behavior in all levels of intelligence, even at the superior level, in the form of hypothesis testing. As far as I am concerned, this definition is too vague, because trial and error occurs in the formation of habits, and also in the earliest established reflexes: when a newborn baby learns to suck.

Karl Bühler defines intelligence as an act of immediate comprehension; that is to say, an insight. Bühler's definition is also very precise, but it seems to me too narrow. I know that when a mathematician solves a problem, he ends by having an insight, but up to that moment he feels, or gropes for, his way; and to

* From *Bulletin of the Menninger Clinic*, **26** (1962), pp. 120–8. The three lectures by Doctor Piaget contained in this issue of the *Bulletin* were presented as a series to the Menninger School of Psychiatry, March 6, 13 and 22, 1961.

say that the trial-and-error behavior is not intelligent and that intelligence starts only when he finds the solution to the problem, seems a very narrow definition. I would, therefore, propose to define intelligence not by a static criterion, as in previous definitions, but by the direction that intelligence follows in its evolution, and then I would define intelligence as a form of equilibration, or forms of equilibration, toward which all cognitive functions lead.

But I must first define equilibration. Equilibration in my vocabulary is not an exact and automatic balance, as it would be in Gestalt theory; I define equilibration principally as a compensation for an external disturbance.

When there is an external disturbance, the subject succeeds in compensating for this by an activity. The maximum equilibration is thus the maximum of the activity, and not a state of rest. It is a mobile equilibration, and not an immobile one. So equilibration is defined as compensation; compensation is the annulling of a transformation by an inverse transformation. The compensation which intervenes in equilibration implies the fundamental idea of reversibility, and this reversibility is precisely what characterizes the operations of the intelligence. An operation is an internalized action, but it is also a reversible action. But an operation is never isolated; it is always subordinated to other operations; it is part of a more inclusive structure. Consequently, we define intelligence in terms of operations, coordination of operations.

Take, for example, an operation like addition: Addition is a material action, the action of reuniting. On the other hand, it is a reversible action, because addition may be compensated by subtraction. Yet addition leads to a structure of a whole. In the case of numbers, it will be the structure that the mathematicians call a "group." In the case of addition of classes which intervene in the logical structure it will be a more simple structure that we will call a grouping, and so on.

Consequently, the study of the stages of intelligence is first a study of the formation of operational structures. I shall define every stage by a structure of a whole, with the possibility of its integration into succeeding stages, just as it was prepared by preceding stages. Thus, I shall distinguish four great stages, or four great periods, in the development of intelligence: first, the sensorimotor period before the appearance of language; second, the period from about two to seven years of age, the pre-operational period which precedes real operations; third, the period from 7 to 12 years of age, a period of concrete operations (which refers to concrete objects); and finally after 12 years of age, the period of formal operations, or positional operations.

SENSORI-MOTOR STAGE

Before language develops, there is behavior that we can call intelligent. For example, when a baby of 12 months or more wants an object which is too far from him, but which rests on a carpet or blanket, and he pulls it to get to the object, this behavior is an act of intelligence. The child uses an intermediary, a means to get to his goal. Also, getting to an object by means of pulling a string when the object is tied to the string, or when the child uses a stick to get the object, are acts of intelligence. They demonstrate in the sensori-motor period a certain number of stages, which go from simple reflexes, from the formation of the first habits, up to the coordination of means and goals.

Remarkable in this sensori-motor stage of intelligence is that there are already structures. Sensori-motor intelligence rests mainly on actions, on movements and perceptions without language, but these actions are coordinated in a relatively stable way. They are coordinated under what we may call schemata of action. These schemata can be generalized in actions and are applicable to new situations. For example, pulling a carpet to bring an object within reach constitutes a schema which can be generalized to other situations when another object rests on a support. In other words, a schema supposes an incorporation of new situations into the previous schemata, a sort of continuous assimilation of new objects or new situations to the actions already schematized. For example, I presented to one of my children an object completely new to him – a box of cigarettes, which is not a usual toy for a baby. The child took the object, looked at it, put it in his mouth, shook it, then took it with one hand and hit it with the other hand, then rubbed it on the edge of the crib, then shook it again, and gave the impression of trying to see if there were noise. This behavior is a way of exploring the object, of trying to understand it by assimilating it to schemata already known. The child behaves in this situation as he will later in Binet's famous vocabulary test, when he defines by usage, saying, for instance, that a spoon is for eating, and so on.

But in the presence of a new object, even without knowing how to talk, the child knows how to assimilate, to incorporate this new object into each of his already developed schemata which function as practical concepts. Here is a structuring of intelligence. Most important in this structuring is the base, the point of departure of all subsequent operational constructions. At the sensori-motor level, the child constructs the schema of the permanent object.

The knowledge of the permanent object starts at this point. The child is not convinced at the beginning that when an object disappears from view, he can find it again. One can verify by tests that object permanence is not yet developed at this stage. But there is there the beginning of a subsequent fundamental idea which starts being constructed at the sensori-motor level. This is also true of the construction of the ideas of space, of time, of causality. What is being done at the sensori-motor level concerning all the foregoing ideas will constitute the substructure of the subsequent, fully achieved ideas of permanent objects, of space, of time, of causality.

In the formation of these substructures at the sensori-motor level, it is very interesting to note the beginning of a *reversibility*, not in thought, since there is not yet representation in thought, but in action itself. For example, the formation of the conception of space at the sensori-motor stage leads to an amazing decentration if one compares the conception of space at the first weeks of the development with that at one and one-half to two years of age. In the beginning there is not one space which contains all the objects, including the child's body itself; there is a multitude of spaces which are not coordinated: there are the buccal space, the tactilokinesthetic space, the visual and auditory spaces;

each is separate and each is centered essentially on the body of the subject and on actions. After a few months, however, after a kind of Copernican evolution, there is a total reversal, a decentration such that space becomes homogenous, a one-and-only space that envelops the others. Then space becomes a container that envelops all objects, including the body itself; and after that, space is mainly coordinated in a structure, a coordination of positions and displacements, and these constitute what the geometricians call a "group"; that is to say, precisely a reversible system. One may move from A to B, and may come back from B to A; there is the possibility of returning, of reversibility. There is also the possibility of making detours and combinations which give a clue to what the subsequent operations will be when thought will supersede the action itself.

Pre-Operational Stage

From one and one-half to two years of age, a fundamental transformation in the evolution of intelligence takes place in the appearance of symbolic functions. Every action of intelligence consists in manipulating significations (or meanings) and whenever (or wherever) there are significations, there are on the one hand the "significants" and on the other the "significates." This is true in the sensori-motor level, but the only significants that intervene there are perceptual signs or signals (as in conditioning) which are undifferentiated in regard to the significate; for example, a perceptual cue, like distance, which will be a cue for the size of the distant object, or the apparent size of an object, which will be the cue for the distance of the object. There, perhaps, both indices are different aspects of the same reality, but they are not yet differentiated significants. At the age of one and one-half to two years a new class of significants arises, and these significants are differentiated in regard to their significates. These differentiations can be called symbolic function. The appearance of symbols in a children's game is an example of the appearance of new significants. At the sensori-motor level the games are nothing but exercises; now they become symbolic play, a play of fiction; these games consist in representing something by means of something else. Another example is the beginning of delayed imitation, an imitation that takes place not in the presence of the original object but in its absence, and which consequently constitutes a kind of symbolization or mental image.

At the same time that symbols appear, the child acquires language; that is to say, there is the acquisition of another phase of differentiated significants, verbal signals, or collective signals. This symbolic function then brings great flexibility into the field of intelligence. Intelligence up to this point refers to the immediate space which surrounds the child and to the present perceptual situation; thanks to language, and to the symbolic functions, it becomes possible to invoke objects which are not present perceptually, to reconstruct the past, or to make projects, plans for the future, to think of objects not present but very distant in space – in short, to span spatio-temporal distances much greater than before.

But this new stage, the stage of representation of thought which is super-imposed on the sensori-motor stage, is not a simple extension of what was referred to at the previous level. Before being able to prolong, one must in fact reconstruct, because behavior in words is a different thing from representing something in thought. When a child knows how to move around in his house or garden by following the different successive cues around him, it does not mean that he is capable of representing or reproducing the total configuration of his house or his garden. To be able to represent, to reproduce something, one must be capable of reconstructing this group of displacements, but at a new level, that of the representation of the thought.

I recently made an amusing test with Nel Szeminska. We took children of four to five years of age who went to school by themselves and came back home by themselves, and asked them if they could trace the way to school and back for us, not in design, which would be too difficult, but like a construction game, with concrete objects. We found that they were not capable of representation; there was a kind of motor-memory, but it was not yet a representation of a whole – the group of displacements had not yet been reconstructed on the plan of the representation of thought. In other words, the operations were not yet formed. There are representations which are internalized actions, but actions still centered on the body itself, on the activity itself. These representations do not allow the objective combinations, the decentrated combinations that the operations would. The actions are centered on the body. I used to call this egocentrism; but it is better thought of as lack of reversibility of action.

At this level, the most certain sign of the absence of operations which appear at the next stage is the absence of the knowledge of conservation. In fact, an operation refers to the transformation of reality. The transformation is not of the whole, however; something constant is always untransformed. If you pour a liquid from one glass to another there is transformation; the liquid changes form, but its liquid property stays constant. So at the pre-operational level, it is significant from the point of view of the operations of intelligence that the child has not yet a knowledge of conservation. For example, in the case of liquid, when the child pours it from one bottle to the other, he thinks that the quantity of the liquid has changed. When the level of the liquid changes, the child thinks the quantity has changed – there is more or less in the second glass than in the first. And if you ask the child where the larger quantity came from, he does not answer this question. What is important for the child is that perceptually it is not the same thing any more. We find this absence of conservation in all object properties, in the length, surface, quantity, and weight of things.

This absence of conservation indicates essentially that at this stage the child reasons from the configuration. Confronted with a transformation, he does not reason from the transformation itself; he starts from the initial configuration, then sees the final configuration, compares the two but forgets the transforma-tion, because he does not know how to reason about it. At this stage the child is still reasoning on the basis of what he sees, because there is no conservation. He is able to master this problem only when the operations are formed and these operations, which we have already sensed at the sensori-motor level, are not formed until around seven to eight years of age. At that age the elementary problems of conservation are solved, because the child reasons on the basis of the transformation per se, and this requires a manipulation of the operation. The ability to pass from one stage to the other and be able to come back to the point of departure, to manipulate the reversible operations, which appears around seven to eight years of age, is limited when compared with the operations of the superior level only in the sense that they are concrete. That is to say, the child can manipulate the operations only when he manipulates the object concretely.

Stage of Concrete Operations

The first operations of the manipulation of objects, the concrete operations, deal with logical classes and with logical relations, or the number. But these operations do not deal yet with propositions, or hypotheses, which do not appear until the last stage.

Let me exemplify these concrete operations: the simplest operation is concerned with classifying objects according to their similarity and their difference. This is accomplished by including the subclasses within larger and more general classes, a process that implies inclusion. This classification, which seems very simple at first, is not acquired until around seven to eight years of age. Before that, at the pre-operational level, we do not find logical inclusion. For example, if you show a child at the pre-operational level a bouquet of flowers of which one half is daisies and the other half other flowers and you ask him if in this bouquet there are more flowers or more daisies, you are confronted with this answer, which seems extraordinary until it is analyzed: The child cannot tell you whether there are more flowers than daisies; he reasons on the basis either of the whole or of the part. He cannot understand that the part is complementary to the rest, and he says there are more daisies than flowers, or as many daisies as flowers, without understanding this inclusion of the subclass, the daisies, in the class of flowers. It is only around seven to eight years of age that a child is capable of solving a problem of inclusion.

Another system of operation that appears around seven to eight years of age is the operation of serializing; that is, to arrange objects according to their size, or their progressive weight. It is also a structure of the whole, like the classification which rests on concrete operations, since it consists of manipulating concrete objects. At this level there is also the construction of numbers, which is, too, a synthesis of classification and seriation. In numbers, as in classes, we have inclusion, and also a serial order, as in serializing. These elementary operations constitute structures of wholes. There is no class without classification; there is no symmetric relation without serialization; there is not a number independent of the series of numbers. But the structures of these wholes are simple structures, groupings in the case of classes and relations, which are already groups in the case of numbers, but very elementary structures compared with subsequent structures.

STAGE OF FORMAL OPERATIONS

The last stage of development of intelligence is the stage of formal operations or propositional operations. At about eleven to twelve years of age we see great progress; the child becomes capable of reasoning not only on the basis of objects, but also on the basis of hypotheses, or of propositions.

An example which neatly shows the difference between reasoning on the basis of propositions and reasoning on the basis of concrete objects comes from Burt's tests. Burt asked children of different ages to compare the colors of the hair of three girls: Edith is fairer than Susan, Edith is darker than Lilly; who is the darkest of the three? In this question there is seriation, not of concrete objects, but of verbal statements, which supposes a more complicated mental manipulation. This problem is rarely solved before the age of 12.

Here a new class of operations appears which is superimposed on the operations of logical class and number, and these operations are the propositional operations. Here, compared with the previous stage, are fundamental changes. It is not simply that these operations refer to language, and then to operations with concrete objects, but that these operations have much richer structures.

The first novelty is a combinative structure; like mathematical structures, it is a structure of a system which is superimposed on the structure of simple classifications or seriations which are not themselves systems, because they do not involve a combinative system. A combinative system permits the grouping in flexible combinations of each element of the system with any other element of that system. The logic of propositions supposes such a combinative system. If children of different ages are shown a number of colored disks and asked to combine each color with each other two by two, or three by three, we find these combinative operations are not accessible to the child at the stage of concrete operations. The child is capable of some combination, but not of all the possible combinations. After the age of 12, the child can find a method to make all the possible combinations. At the same time he acquires both the logic of mathematics and the logic of propositions, which also supposes a method of combining.

A second novelty in the operation of propositions is the appearance of a structure which constitutes a group of four transformations. Hitherto there were two reversibilities: reversibility by inversion, which consists of annulling, or canceling; and reversibility which we call reciprocity, leading not to cancellation, but to another combination. Reciprocity is what we find in the field of a relation. If A equals B, by reciprocity B equals A. If A is smaller than B, by reciprocity B is larger than A. At the level of propositional operations a new system envelops these two forms of reversibility. Here the structure combines inversion and reversibility in one single but larger and more complicated structure. It allows the acquisition of a series of fundamental operational schemata for the development of intelligence, which schemata are not possible before the constitution of this structure.

It is around the age of 12 that the child, for example, starts to understand in mathematics the knowledge of proportions, and becomes capable of reasoning by using two systems of reference at the same time. For example, if you advance the position of a board and a car moving in opposite directions, in order to understand the movement of the board in relation to the movement of the car and to other movement, you need a system of four transformations. The same is true in regard to proportions, to problems in mathematics or physics, or to other logical problems.

The four principal stages of the development of intelligence of the child progress from one stage to the other by the construction of new operational structures, and these structures constitute the fundamental instrument of the intelligence of the adult.

5

THE CONNECTIONIST INFANT: WOULD PIAGET TURN IN HIS GRAVE?*

Annette Karmiloff-Smith (1996)

A HISTORY OF PSYCHOLOGY IN 1000 WORDS...

Let us begin with a very brief history of psychology as it pertains to theorizing about the starting state of the human neonate. It will necessarily be rather superficial given the space limits, but it will set the stage for the rest of the discussion. I will compare and contrast four theories. Behaviourism, Piagetianism, Nativism, and Connectionism. While there are fundamental differences between the theories, I shall point to some interesting similarities and invite the reader to rethink the whole issue of innateness. I will argue that there is a trade-off in nature between prespecification, on the one hand, and plasticity, on the other, leading ultimately to the kind of flexibility one finds in the human mind. Much of my earlier work centred on cognitive flexibility in later development (Karmiloff-Smith, 1979, 1992a, 1992b), but in the present discussion I shall focus on infancy.

THE BEHAVIOURIST INFANT

Figure 5.1 gives a caricature of the mind/brain of the Behaviourist infant: a tabula rasa, faced with the blooming, buzzing confusion of inputs from the environment. There is no built-in content, and domain-general laws of learning obtain. The infant gradually accumulates information about language, number, face processing, etc. The Behaviourist infant is a passive accumulator of

---

* Previously published by the Society for Research in Child Development, in *SRCD Newsletter*, Fall 1996, pp. 1–3 and 10, adapted from a talk given at ISIS in April 1996.

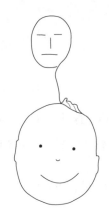

FIGURE 5.1   The Behaviourist infant

knowledge via the *same* mechanisms throughout its life. No underlying structural changes take place as learning proceeds

THE PIAGETIAN INFANT

In contrast, the Piagetian infant (see caricature in figure 5.2) will pass through major stages of development involving fundamentally different underlying structural organization. However, like the Behaviourist infant, Piaget's baby is initially assailed by chaotically competing inputs. Of course, in Piaget's case the infant is an active seeker of knowledge, rather than a passive storer of knowledge. However, at one level of description Behaviourism and Piagetianism have a common approach to the newborn: domain-general mechanisms of learning suffice to explain how children learn about language, number, space, faces, etc. Of course, the domain-general mechanisms invoked are radically

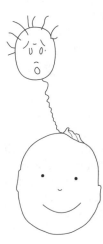

FIGURE 5.2   The Piagetian infant

different. Piaget's theory calls on the biologically-inspired mechanisms of assimilation, accommodation, and equilibration, but like the Behaviourist, he argues that such domain-general mechanisms are applied across all linguistic and cognitive domains. Let it be clear that I am not of course suggesting that Piagetian theory is Behaviourist. There are fundamental differences between the two theories. But there are two general-level commonalities between the theories as they pertain to the young infant: domain-general learning mechanisms and initially chaotic inputs.

THE NATIVIST INFANT

Let us now turn to the Nativist infant (see caricature in figure 5.3) which flourished in the past 20 years, deeply influenced by Chomskyan linguistics and by Fodorian modularity theory. Here we have a very different kind of infant. It comes into the world well prepared for processing different domains of knowledge. In fact, many Nativist theorists would do away with the notions of learning and development altogether (e.g., Piatelli-Palmerini, 1989; Fodor, 1983). The Nativist infant is not assailed by chaotic inputs. Each input is neatly cordoned off from the others by virtue of the dedicated representations that serve it. The Nativist infant comes pre-prepared for processing faces, language, space, number, social interaction, and so forth, each in very different ways. Nativist theorists invoke pre-adapted modules which are specialized *from the outset* in processing proprietary inputs. A surprisingly large number of so-called 'developmentalists' have been deeply influenced by what is in essence a non-developmental form of theorizing.

Part of the popularity of the Nativist position stemmed from convincing demonstrations that very young babies display capacities hitherto

FIGURE 5.3   The Nativist infant

unsuspected by Piagetians. This led to a challenge of Piaget's theory and to the argument that such capacities must be innately specified. Yet, as I have repeatedly argued, specialization and domain-specificity can actually be the product of a developmental process, rather than its starting point (Karmiloff-Smith, 1992a). Not only have precocious infant abilities been used to back the Nativist position, but research on normal adult brain-damaged patients has also been invoked. It is true that particular brain circuits seem to be specialized in processing particular kinds of inputs and that these can display double dissociations in brain-damaged adults. This has led researchers to jump to the conclusion that such abilities must be innately specified. Dissociations are grist for the Nativist mill. But do we necessarily need to jump to a Nativist conclusion in the face of such facts?

THE CONNECTIONIST INFANT

It is in turning now to the Connectionist infant that I shall argue against such strong forms of Nativism. But first it is necessary to divide the Connectionist infant in two: first, I shall deal with what I call 'Stone Age' Connectionist infant (or the 'Perception Kid'!), followed by the Modern-Day Connectionist infant, which I believe to be a very close cousin of the Piagetian infant, albeit with some interesting differences. The Stone Age Connectionist infant (see figure 5.4) started life with a strong anti-Nativist, anti-Piagetian bent. In 1986, two 'bibles' on Connectionism were published (Rumelhart and McClelland, 1986; McClelland and Rumelhart, 1986). Researchers who embraced the new approach initially had a somewhat 'Billy Graham' attitude towards Connectionism, proclaiming that the human mind can do without propositions, rules, and representations. Learning, it was argued, takes place simply via input/output relations. At first blush Connectionism came across as a new form

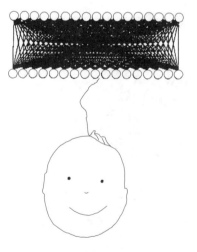

FIGURE 5.4   The Stone Age Connectionist infant

of Behaviourism–Associationism in high-tech clothing! In my view, the initial proclamations did much disservice to the potential interest of Connectionist ideas. Connectionist theorists focused on dethroning Chomsky, Fodor, and the Piagetian concept of stage-like development (e.g, McClelland and Jenkins, 1990). As we shall see below, some of the potential merits of Connectionist thinking got temporarily buried during the early years of research.

Although fascinated with the potential of Connectionist principles, in my earlier writings I focused on criticizing their anti-Nativist claims by demonstrating that more was actually built into a Connectionist network than was immediately obvious (Karmiloff-Smith, 1992a, b, c). For example, although the starting state of a network – its weights and connections – may be random, it is only random with respect to a highly constrained architecture and learning algorithm. In other words, while there is no built-in representational content, which is derived in interaction with the structure of the input, there are built-in architectural, computational, and temporal constraints. Here are some examples:

1. The choice of architecture is made in advance, as a function of the type of input to be learnt. Feed forward, recurrent, autoassociative and other types of networks are differently suited to different types of input, e.g., a recurrent network is used for sequentially structured input, whereas an auto-associative network is not. This choice is a crucial starting state of learning, say, linguistic strings (e.g., Elman, 1991).
2. The number of layers in the architecture of a network is decided upon in advance.
3. The number of units within each layer is again preset (except in cascade-correlations networks which recruit new units as learning proceeds, e.g., Schultz, 1991).
4. The spatial connections between units are fixed in advance.
5. The speed with which weights change is part of the built-in constraints.

RETHINKING INNATENESS

These were some of the criticisms which I initially levelled at the anti-Nativist claims of Connectionism. However, what I had focused on as criticisms could in fact be turned on their head and seen in a positive light, as ways of exploring the kinds of architectural, computational, temporal, and representational constraints that might be innately specified (Karmiloff-Smith, 1992a, b, c). It was then that I joined forces with a group of colleagues in a concerted effort to spell out these ideas in much greater detail, not only at the level of constraints within networks but also at the level of the developing brain (Elman, Bates, Johnson, Karmiloff-Smith, Parisi and Plunkett, 1996).

Enter here the Modern-Day Connectionist infant (see figure 5.5). This is an infant with several biases specified prior to processing the input: a recurrent network, an autoassociative network, and so forth, each of which is suited to a different type of input, but with weights and connections left random. This illustrates how the infant brain might start out with a number of architectural,

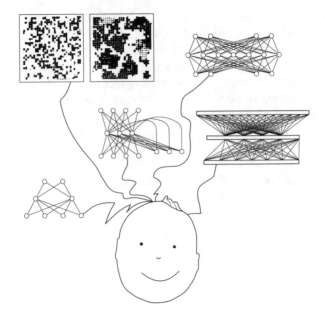

FIGURE 5.5   The Modern-Day Connectionist infant

computational, temporal, and other biases or constraints, without building in representational content. Representations *emerge* from the interaction between such constraints and the structure of particular types of input. Such a view retains much of Piaget's sensori-motor infant: the representation/processing distinction is blurred, representations are implicit in the network's processing of the input and are distributed throughout the network rather than being propositions located in a specific location. Networks learn by slowly assimilating the input via tiny changes each time an input is processed, as well as by accommodating to the progressively changing representations of the network to the particularities of the structure of the input. This retains Piaget's deep intuition that systems have to learn, and that when they learn, this affects the way in which they subsequently process the input. Representational content does not have to be built in; it *emerges* from the network's activities.

One aspect of Piagetian theory has, in my view, been successfully challenged by Connectionist simulations. Connectionist models, and dynamical systems in general, are based on non-linear learning curves. Tiny changes accrue and for a long time they give rise to no overt behavioural change. Then at some point, another similar tiny change will give rise to a sudden change in overt behaviour. Piaget and others have interpreted these overt changes as particularly meaningful: they are thought to be the point at which important developmental change takes place (e.g., a new stage). A good example of this is the so-called vocabulary spurt. However, it has since been shown (Bates and Carnavara, 1993) that abrupt change in dynamical systems is not a clue to fundamental internal structural change, but simply the outcome of a single process. Thus, stage-like change in *external* behaviour is not necessarily the point at which stage-like change occurs in *internal* organization (Elman, Bates,

Johnson, Karmiloff-Smith, Parisi and Plunkett, 1996; McClelland and Jenkins, 1990; Thelen and Smith, 1994).

Rather than simply reject the Nativist stance and the compelling infancy data brought to light in recent years, let us now explore the implications that the Modern-Day Connectionist infant might have for rethinking the issue of innateness. First, we can avoid invoking pre-specified blueprints for language, for theory-of-mind, for number, for faces, and so forth. But secondly, we can also avoid the opposite extreme of a single, general-purpose learning mechanism. Rather, connections modelling makes it possible to explore in detail the interactions between architectural, computational, temporal, and representation biases which infants bring to bear on the learning situation. What kind of constraints might obtain?

ARCHITECTURAL–COMPUTATIONAL CONSTRAINTS

Let us take the example of the so-called "where" and "what" pathways in the human brain which serve to process where things are in the environment, on the one hand, and what they are, on the other. It is known that in brain-damaged adults one of these circuits may be damaged while the other is intact. It is also true that infants process differentially where and what things are in the environment. Do we conclude from this that the "where" pathway and the "what" pathway must be innately specified? A Connectionist simulation suggests that this need not be the case. O'Reilly and McClelland (1992) designed a simple network with no initial representational content, but in which identical inputs are fed to two types of unit which differ only in the speed with which their activation levels are specified (something like "fast units" and "slow units"). With time, the network progressively develops such that one set of units represents where things are in the network's environment and the other set represents what objects are present. In other words, two very specialized, differential pathways *emerge* from slightly different parameters in the initial processing. In my view, this is perfectly consistent with Piagetian thinking. Such architectural–computational biases interact with environmental inputs to produce emergent representations (see numerous other examples in Elman, Bates, Johnson, Karmiloff-Smith, Parisi and Plunkett, 1996). The point is that some relatively minimal built-in biases can give rise to crucial representational differences as a product of learning.

TEMPORAL CONSTRAINTS

Architectural–computational biases can be accompanied by temporal biases. First, it is known that certain areas of the infant brain come on line at different times ontogenetically (Turkewitz and Kenny, 1982). Furthermore, there are periods of neuronal over-production and subsequent pruning that take place at certain moments in the development process. These constitute natural temporal constraints on what is processed, and when. Furthermore, recent work on foetal development points to the importance of timing during embryogenesis (see Karmiloff-Smith, 1995, for discussion). Take, for example, two pregnant women chatting in their seventh month of pregnancy. There are four, not two, eavesdroppers on the conversation. During the final three months of intrauterine life, foetuses actively process the auditory input that they receive filtered through the amniotic fluid. As one example amongst many, at birth neonates show a preference for their mother's voice over other similar female voices despite the fact that their mother's voice ex-utero sounds very different from her voice heard in-utero (see Karmiloff-Smith, 1995, for discussion). This suggests that during foetal life infants extract abstract components of their mother's voice, not simply surface auditory form. Timing and modality biases are such that the foetus naturally starts to process language prior to birth, as opposed to visual input that they can only start processing after birth. These timing differences serve to make the environment far less chaotic than Piaget originally assumed.

REPRESENTATIONAL CONSTRAINTS

At birth visual processing starts with a vengeance. How can we guarantee that infants will pay particular attention to the faces of their conspecifics? Do we need to build in a detailed blueprint of the human face? Again, we shall avoid such strong Nativism in favour of minimal representational biases. Work by my colleagues in London, Johnson and Morton (1991), focused on the neonate's tracking of various stimuli to ascertain whether, like in the case of the chick Johnson previously studied (Johnson, Bolhuis and Horn, 1985), certain stimuli are more attractive to the newborn than others. Figure 5.6 gives four examples from the array of stimuli presented to subjects (see Johnson and Morton, 1991, for full details). Now, if infants were just attending to interesting patterns, then (a), (b) and (d) would be equivalent. If it were just symmetry that neonates attend to, then items (a), (c) and (d), as well as (c) and (d) turned upside down, should be equivalently interesting. By contrast, if the neonate came to the task with a pre-specified blueprint of the human face, then (d) should be the most interesting and be tracked the furthest. In fact, (c) and (d) are tracked further than the others and equivalently for the first couple of months of life. In other

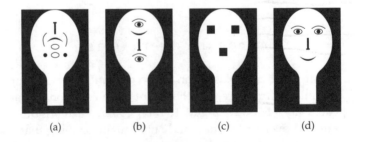

(a)   (b)   (c)   (d)

FIGURE 5.6   Examples of stimuli presented to neonates

words, there does seem to be *some* representational bias (three blobs in the location of eyes and mouth) that the neonate brings to the learning situation for faces. But this is not at the level of cortical connectivity. It is simply a minimal sub-cortical bias that ensures that at birth babies attend to an important input in the environment. The bias is not even species specific but something very general (Sargeant and Nelson, 1992). By 3–4 months, infants start to prefer (d) over all the other stimuli, suggesting that by then they have learnt much more about the human face of their own species from massive postnatal exposure to environmental input. This learning takes place at the cortical level and is quite different from the bias that ensured that they attended to face-like stimuli in the first place.

PIAGET AND THE CONNECTIONIST INFANT

We have briefly touched on four types of bias or constraint that may interact, as networks or infants process different kinds of input. The ideas have been developed in great detail in a book I have just finished with Jeff Elman, Liz Bates, Mark Johnson, Domenico Parisi, and Kim Plunkett (1996). Connectionist modelling can be used as a tool for manipulating each of these biases separately or in conjunction with one another to explore the issue of what might be innately specified and what can be derived from processing patterns in the input. In other words, it directly addresses the Nature/Nurture issue. It is important to note how little representational content or "knowledge" has been invoked. In the main, the interaction of architectural, computational and temporal biases, together with the structure of different kinds of inputs, suffice to generate representations that simply emerge from the processing.

In my view, Piaget would not turn in his grave at the thought of the Connectionist infant. He would have approved of its dynamic learning capacities, its constant assimilation and accommodation as learning proceeds. Piaget would probably have embraced the notion that certain architectural, computational, temporal and, rarely, representational biases can kick-start infant learning, thereby obviating the need to build in more than a minimum of representational content. Piaget's theory is fundamentally *developmental*. Paradoxically quite a lot of infancy studies are not developmental at all. Researchers focus on babies, to be sure, but concentrating on infancy does not imply a developmental approach per se. In such studies, the focus is on steady-state systems. The research does not explore *how* systems change over time, but tends to measure whether a particular type of representation is present or not at one age compared with another. It does not address the question of how increasingly abstract representations *gradually emerge* over time. This was Piaget's agenda. Piaget's notion of epigenesis at the biological level – gene expression instead of genetic pre-specification – and his notion of constructivism at the psychological level, are in my view entirely compatible with connectionist thinking.

REFERENCES

Bates, E., and Carnavara, G. F. (1993). New directions in research on language development. *Developmental Review*, **13**, 436–70.

Elman, J. L. (1991). Distributed representations, simple recurrent networks, and grammatical structure. *Machine Learning*, **7**, 195–225.

Elman, J. L., Bates, E., Johnson, M. H., Karmiloff-Smith, A., Parisi, D., and Plunkett, K. (1996). *Rethinking Innateness: A Connectionist Perspective on Development*. Cambridge, MA: MIT Press.

Fodor, J. A. (1983). *The Modularity of Mind*. Cambridge, MA: MIT Press.

Johnson, M. H., Bolhuis, J. J., and Horn, G. (1985). Interaction between acquired preferences and developing predispositions during imprinting. *Animal Behaviour*, **33**, 1000–6.

Johnson, M. H., and Morton, J. (1991). *Biology and Cognitive Development*. Oxford: Blackwell.

Karmiloff-Smith, A. (1979). Micro- and macro-developmental changes in language acquisition and other representational systems. *Cognitive Science*, **3** (2), 91–118.

Karmiloff-Smith, A. (1992a). *Beyond Modularity: A Developmental Perspective on Cognitive Science*. Cambridge, MA: MIT Press/Bradford Books.

Karmiloff-Smith, A. (1992b). Abnormal phenotypes and the challenges they pose to connectionist models of development. *Technical Reports in Parallel Distributed Processing and Cognitive Neuroscience, TR. PDP.CNS.92.7, Carnegie-Mellon University*.

Karmiloff-Smith (1992c). Nature, Nurture and PDP: Preposterous Developmental Postulates? *Connection Science*, **4** (3/4), 253–69.

Karmiloff-Smith, A. (1995). Annotation: The extraordinary cognitive journey from foetus through infancy. *Journal of Child Psychology and Child Psychiatry*, **36**, 1293–1313.

McClelland, J. L., and Jenkins, E. (1990). Nature, nurture and connectionism: Implications for connectionist models for cognitive development. In K. van Lehn (ed.), *Architectures for Intelligence*, Hillsdale, NJ: Erlbaum.

McClelland, J. L., Rumelhart, D. E., and the PDP Research Group (1986). *Parallel Distributed Processing: Explorations in the Microstructure of Cognition*. Cambridge, MA: MIT Press.

O'Reilly, R. C., and McClelland, J. L. (1992). The self-organization of spatially invariant representations. *Technical Reports in Parallel Distributed Processing and Cognitive Neuroscience PDP.CNS.92.5, Carnegie-Mellon University*.

Piatelli-Palmerini, M. (1989). Evolution, selection, and cognition: From 'learning' to parameter setting in biology and the study of language. *Cognition*, **31**, 1–44.

Rumelhart, D. E., McClelland, J. L., and the PDP Research Group (1986). *Parallel Distributed Processing: Explorations in the Microstructure of Cognition*. Cambridge, MA: MIT Press.

Sargeant, P. L., and Nelson, C. A. (1992). Cross-species recognition in infant and adult humans: ERP and behavioral measures. Poster presentation. *International Conference of Infant Studies, Miami Beach, May 1992*.

Schultz, T. R. (1991). Simulating stages of human cognitive development with connectionist models. In L. Birnbaum and G. Collins (eds), *Machine Learning: Proceedings of the Eighth International Workshop*, Morgan Kaufman.

Thelen, E., and Smith, L. B. (1994). *A Dynamic Systems Approach to the Development of Cognition and Action*. Cambridge, MA: MIT Press.

Turkewitz, G., and Kenny, P. A. (1982). Limitations on input as a basis for neural organization and perceptual development: A preliminary theoretical statement. *Developmental Psychobiology*, **15**, 357–68.

Part II

BASIC ISSUES: CONTINUITY, DISCONTINUITY, NATURE AND NURTURE

6

CAN MEASURES OF INFANT INFORMATION PROCESSING PREDICT LATER INTELLECTUAL ABILITY?

Alan Slater, Rachael Carrick, Clare Bell and Elizabeth Roberts

Some things are sacred.
For developmental psychology, predicting later behavior from early behavior is sacred.... And so the search for early predictors of later IQ continues.
McCall (1981, p. 141)

EDITORS' INTRODUCTION

McCall was commenting on 50 years of research that had shown that there was no relationship between infant behaviour or test scores and mental performance in early (or later) childhood. This finding gave support to theoretical views that emphasized the instability or discontinuity of development from infancy to childhood, with the accompanying suggestion that infant intelligence is different in kind from intelligence in the post-infancy years. In the last 20 years, however, it has become clear that a moderate degree of predictability of development may be possible, leading McCall to the view that 'the current promise of greater predictive accuracy...represents one of the most exciting contemporary fields of enquiry' (1989, p. 177).

In this article Slater and his colleagues survey the current state of this research, but conclude that we need a greater number of reliable measures of infant cognitive performance before a useful test of infant mental or cognitive development will emerge.

REFERENCES

McCall, R. B. (1981). Early predictors of later IQ: the search continues. *Intelligence*, **5**, 141–7.

McCall, R. B. (1989). Commentary. *Human Development*, **32**, 177–86.

By the end of the 1970s some 50 years of research had shown fairly clearly that prediction coefficients from measures of infant behaviour to later measures of intelligence in childhood were so low as to indicate that, except in extreme cases such as severe subnormality, the early measures had no predictive validity (Bayley, 1970; Clarke, 1978; Lewis and Brooks-Gunn, 1981). These findings led to theoretical views that emphasized the discontinuity of development from infancy to childhood, with the accompanying suggestion that infant intelligence is different in kind from intelligence in the post-infancy years. Clarke (1978, p. 256) expressed this view succinctly when he commented that 'The rather poor long-term predictions of individual development which characterise our science *do not primarily rest on inadequacies in the methods of measurement. . . . They lie in development itself'* (italics added).

From about this time, however, researchers began to question the nature and validity of the infant tests on which these findings were based. It was argued that the 'mental scales' on these tests primarily measure perceptual and motor development, rather than mental or cognitive growth, and there is little reason to expect measures of such abilities to predict later IQ (Bornstein and Sigman, 1986; Slater, Cooper, Rose and Morison, 1989). Accordingly, the search began for cognitive or information-processing measures of infant performance which might more reasonably be considered to tap abilities that are similar to, and may be predictive of, the abilities measured by the childhood intelligence tests. A major focus of this research has been on measures of visual information processing and attentiveness, and it has become clear that a moderate degree of predictability may be possible, leading some to the view that the 'promise of greater predictive accuracy using recognition memory and habituation rate represents one of the most exciting contemporary fields of inquiry' (McCall, 1989).

In the next section the failings of the existing developmental scales are discussed, followed by an account of the use of visual information processing as a possible predictor of later intellectual development.

Problems with Standardized Infant Tests

One of the best known and most widely used tests of infant development is the *Bayley Scales of Infant Development* (BSID). In the Second Edition of these scales (1993) many items on the Mental Development Index (MDI) appear to measure perceptual-motor, rather than mental or cognitive development. At 4 months, items include: no. 36 'eyes follow rod'; no. 44 'uses eye–hand coordination in reaching'; no. 45 'picks up cube'. At 12 months items include: no. 73 'turns pages of book'; no. 79 'fingers holes in pegboard'; no. 97 'builds tower of three cubes'. By 2 years of age, such seemingly perceptual-motor items are fewer in number, and they have been replaced with a preponderance of items that would generally be considered more mental or 'cognitive' – many to do with verbal comprehension, recall of geometric forms, and comparison of masses. From about 2 years of age predictive validity of the BSID increases (Bayley, 1949; Lewis and Brooks-Gunn, 1981). Similar comments apply to other well-known tests of infant development, such as the Griffiths Scales (1954).

Several studies have introduced programmes in which infants at risk of intellectual retardation have been given educational intervention designed to enhance their cognitive development, and at the end of the first year the groups do not seem to differ from non-intervention control groups (Brooks-Gunn, Klebanov, Liaw and Spiker, 1993; Ramey, Yeates and Short, 1984). A likely interpretation of these findings is that the Mental Scales that have been used to evaluate the effectiveness of these programmes are simply not measuring mental or cognitive growth, and there is, therefore, a great need for a valid test of infant cognitive development.

Visual Information Processing

Control of attention, memory formation, and the ability to process information quickly and efficiently have traditionally been conceived of as being central to mature cognitive functioning (Bornstein, 1985; Bornstein, Slater, Brown, Roberts and Barrett, 1997), and in the search for predictors of later intelligence a major focus has been on measures of visual information processing and attentiveness since these appear to be measuring these abilities: 'attentiveness reflects not only the detection of information but also the ongoing processing of that information and the status of the relation between the new information and the child's existing knowledge' (Reznick, Corley and Robinson, 1997, p. 29). Measures of habituation to visual stimuli in particular have been seen as potential predictors of later intelligence.

Habituation is an aspect of learning in which repeated presentations of a stimulus result in decreased responsiveness: when an infant is placed in an otherwise homogeneous environment and shown a visual stimulus the stimulus will initially attract the infant's attention, but as time passes the baby's attention will wane (as measured by reduced looking). Habituation refers to this decrement in visual attention, and measures of this decrement reflect memory formation (of the now familiar stimulus), and therefore processing of information from the stimulus, and may also be an indication of infant's ability to inhibit attention to the familiar stimulus (McCall, 1994).

For several other reasons measures of habituation have been seen as potential predictors of later intellectual functioning: (1) there are inter-age differences in speed of habituation, with older infants taking less time to reach a criterion of habituation than younger ones (Slater and Morison, 1985), and there are also intra-age differences; (2) infants who habituate in shorter times have been found to process information more rapidly and more efficiently than 'long lookers' (Colombo, Mitchell, Coldren and Freesman, 1991); (3) simpler stimuli provoke more rapid habituation than do more complex stimuli in infants of a given age (e.g., Bornstein, 1981; Caron and Caron, 1969); (4) infants 'at risk' for cognitive delay or handicap habituate less effectively than non-risk age-matched infants (Cohen, 1981; Friedman, 1975; Lester, 1975).

Psychometric Considerations

There are many different habituation procedures, and many different dependent measures that can be drawn from them (Slater, 1995). An important enterprise is to establish the psychometric adequacy of these measures, particularly by examining their test–retest reliabilities. Those measures that give the best reliabilities are likely to be the best potential predictors, since if a measure does not correlate with itself it is unlikely to correlate well with other concurrent or future measures.

Several groups of researchers have assessed the short- and long-term reliability of various measures of habituation in the first year from birth (Colombo, Mitchell, O'Brien and Horowitz, 1987; Pêcheux & Lécuyer, 1989; Rose, Slater and Perry, 1986) and the results are both encouraging and discouraging. What is encouraging is that measurements at points close in time (separated by a few days or weeks) tend to give reliability estimates in the range $r = 0.40$ to 0.60, but what is discouraging is that measurements separated by a month or more tend to yield lower estimates, with rs in the range from zero to 0.20. Thus, these infant measures tend to have low test–retest reliabilities, and this will inevitably limit the maximum predictive correlations that might be found.

Predictive Validity of Visual Information Processing

Three measures can be distinguished which have some predictive power: (a) visual recognition memory (preferences for a novel stimulus following a brief look at a 'familiarized' stimulus); (b) time taken to reach a criterion of habituation, and associated measures (such as the duration of the longest single [peak] look); (c) the duration of individual fixations to visual stimuli, independent of habituation. There are many studies that have reported predictive correlations, and several reviews of these studies are available (Bornstein and Sigman, 1986; McCall and Carriger, 1993; Slater, 1995). The measures predicted are usually scores of the subjects on childhood intelligence tests, and the delay between testing as infants and testing as children can vary between months and several years. The predictive correlations that have been reported occasionally approach 0.6, but are usually in the range 0.3 to 0.5, with a median correlation of around 0.45 (McCall and Carriger, 1993).

Failures to Replicate and the 0.05 Syndrome

Lécuyer (1989) refers to what he calls 'the 0.05 syndrome' and points out that 'It is difficult to publish an experimental paper if no statistical tests reach this magical level of significance. So, how many studies exist that show no correlation between infancy and childhood measures?' One failure to replicate was reported by Lewis and Brooks-Gunn (1981) who found rate of habituation in

3-month-olds to be predictive of 2-year Bayley MDI for one group of infants ($N = 22$, $r = 0.61$), but for a second group the identical measure gave a non-significant negative correlation of -0.18. In a more recent study with 226 3-month 'at risk' infants eleven measures of looking were extracted and very few of these correlated either with the Bayley MDI at 2 years or with several cognitive tests at 4.5 years (Laucht, Esser and Schmidt, 1994).

One finding that is relevant is that the size of the predictive correlations to be found in the literature is correlated with sample size ($r = -0.6$) (Bornstein and Sigman, 1986). The most reasonable interpretation of this is that very high and very low correlations are likely to be found with smaller samples, and the studies finding low, non-significant correlations are not likely to be published. Recently, data have been collected from some 420 infants who, as 4-month-olds, completed an habituation task as part of the Avon Longitudinal Study on Pregnancy and Childhood (ALSPAC), Bristol, UK, and they have subsequently been tested on later measures of language acquisition and abilities, and at 4 years on the Wechsler Preschool and Primary Scales of Intelligence (WPPSI). This is the largest sample that, to date, has been tested on an habituation task. At the time of writing the data have not been analysed in detail, but a preliminary analysis suggests that although several of the across-age correlations from infant habituation to the later measures are significant none of them is likely to reach the median correlation of 0.45 suggested by McCall and Carriger (1993), and many will be considerably lower. These findings are in line with those of Laucht et al. (1994), and indirectly seem to offer support for Lécuyer's (1989) suspicion that there may be unpublished studies that have not found statistical support for the claim that measures of infant information processing predict later cognitive abilities.

What these findings and considerations suggest, unfortunately, is that the predictive correlations to be found in the published literature are almost certainly an overstimate of the 'real' predictive correlations, biased by the difficulty of publishing non-significant findings. Thus, the usefulness of habituation as a predictor of later outcome is in doubt.

PREDICTORS OTHER THAN VISUAL INFORMATION PROCESSING

Many studies have used measures other than those derived from visual information processing. These measures include differential vocal responsiveness to mother and stranger, visual anticipation, mother's encouraging attention, cross-modal transfer, symbolic play, means–ends problem solving, perception of causal relations, and various measures of language development (Bornstein et al. 1997; Canfield, Smith, Brezsnyak and Snow, 1997; Dougherty and Haith, 1997; Slater, 1995). These studies are not reviewed here, but at present it seems reasonable to conclude that (with the exception of the language measures, which are inevitably taken in late infancy) at present none of them has been shown to have greater predictive validity than measures of visual information processing.

PRACTICAL IMPLICATIONS: CAN WE PREDICT LATER DEVELOPMENT?

The predictive correlations from measures of infant information processing with later IQ rarely exceed 0.5 and are usually 0.4 or lower. Figures 6.1 to 6.4 show scattergrams to illustrate correlation coefficients of 0.2, 0.4, 0.6 and 0.8. Let us suppose that values along the horizontal axis represent the scores for individual infants, and those along the vertical axis the scores a year or so later for the same subjects on childhood IQ tests. It is apparent that with correlations of 0.2 and 0.4 there is so much variability in the data that it would be quite misleading to attempt to make predictions about later IQ from the infancy measures. Even with a correlation of 0.6 individual predictions would be very risky, and it is only when the correlations approach 0.8 that meaningful prediction becomes possible. It is clear that with the low predictive correlations that are currently available attempts at predictions of individual infants' development would result in a substantial number of children being misclassified. The predictive correlations therefore have more theoretical than practical implications.

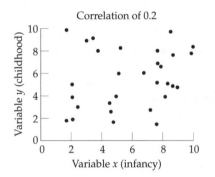

FIGURE 6.1   Scatterplot of the (hypothetical) relationship between infant IQ scores and those on later childhood tests, to illustrate the predictive value of a correlation of 0.2

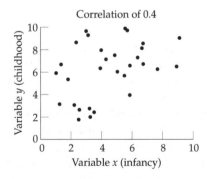

FIGURE 6.2   Scatterplot to illustrate the predictive IQ value of a correlation of 0.4

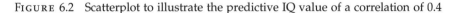

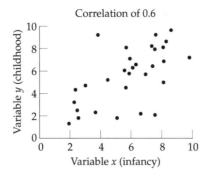

FIGURE 6.3   Scatterplot to illustrate the predictive IQ value of a correlation of 0.6

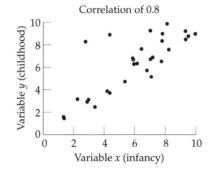

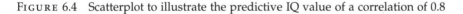

FIGURE 6.4   Scatterplot to illustrate the predictive IQ value of a correlation of 0.8

THEORETICAL IMPLICATIONS

Some twenty years ago the poor long-term predictive validity of infant tests led to theoretical views that emphasized discontinuity of intellectual functioning from infancy to childhood: 'No science can predict accurately qualities which have not yet made any appearance in the development of the pre-school child' (Clarke, 1978, p. 256). Thus, it was reasonable to argue that the types of intelligence one wanted to predict, and which would be important in the school years – language, numeracy, thinking, problem solving, and reasoning – developed in the post-infancy years, and that measures of intelligence in infancy (if it existed) would not predict these later-appearing abilities (McCall, 1979).

The demonstrations of developmental continuity (however modest the predictive correlations) mean that we can probably reject such extreme models, and suggest that it is reasonable to look for genuine precursors of childhood intellectual abilities in infancy. However, predictive correlations of the magnitude reported give ample scope for theorists who wish to emphasize discontinuity, change, and open-endedness, rather than continuity of development.

Continuity and Change

Development, by its very nature, is characterized by change as well as continuity and any approach that puts continuity and discontinuity into opposition is meaningless. The reasonable view is that we should 'be thinking in terms of ways in which development is simultaneously continuous and discontinuous with respect to different dimensions of analysis' (Sternberg and Okagaki, 1989, p. 158). An excellent illustration of the way in which continuity and discontinuity go hand-in-hand was given by Lipsitt (1981):

> The preservation of sameness is not what development and developmental continuity are about. The essence of continuity is *predictable* and *explicable* change. That the tadpole and the frog, or the pupa and the butterfly do not look like one another or behave like one another does *not* mean that the later stages are discontinuous with the earlier. Nor does it mean that the later stages could not, and cannot, and may not be well predicted and understood in terms of the organism's earlier history. It is the nature of life processes that change will occur, that some later stages of the same organism may only bear superficial resemblances to earlier, and that progressive, orderly, lawful, and understandable rules for these changes will be discovered.

Social and Cultural Influences on IQ

However good our measures of infant function, they can only give an indication of mental growth, or cognitive ability, *at the time of testing*. Clearly, later IQ will be considerably modified by social factors (Slater, 1995), and a valid test of infant cognitive abilities will be of inestimable value in allowing the quantification of the role of such factors in the early months from birth.

Conclusions

Measures of visual information processing taken in infancy have been shown to predict measures of intelligence in childhood. However, the predictive correlations are modest (usually in the range 0.3 to 0.5), and correlations for identical or similar measures have a habit of fluctuating from one study to another. This is to be expected, given variations in sample characteristics, and in the social and cultural factors that influence development, but it is a little more worrying when the correlations disappear altogether! What is certainly the case is that prediction of an individual infant's current cognitive ability, or future intellectual development, is not possible as yet (Bornstein et al. 1997; Cohen and Parmelee, 1983).

While it may be possible to use measures of visual information processing to make predictions for groups of infants, the search must continue for a greater number of reliable measures of infant cognitive performance before a useful test of infant mental or cognitive development will emerge. Nevertheless, it is reasonable to claim that the research has considerable potential for practical application since it is leading in the direction of developing valid tests of cognitive abilities, with the accompanying possibilities of detecting infants 'at risk' for cognitive delay, suggesting courses of remedial treatment, and evaluating the effects of such treatment.

ACKNOWLEDGEMENTS

This article is an updated version of two articles: A. Slater, Individual differences in infancy and later IQ. *Journal of Child Psychology and Psychiatry*, **36**, (1995) 69–112; and A. Slater, Can measures of infant habituation predict later intellectual functioning? *Archives of Disease in Childhood*, **77**, (1997) 474–6. The author's research was supported by research grant R000232967 from the Economic and Social Research Council, UK.

REFERENCES

Bayley, N. (1949). Consistency and variability in the growth of intelligence from birth to eighteen years. *Journal of Genetic Psychology*, **75**, 165–96.

Bayley, N. (1970). *The Bayley Scales of Infant Development*. New York: Psychological Corporation.

Bornstein, M. H. (1981). Psychological studies of color perception in human infants: Habituation, discrimination and categorization, recognition and conceptualization. In L. P. Lipsitt (ed.), *Advances in Infancy Research*, vol. 1, Norwood, NJ: Ablex, pp. 1–40.

Bornstein, M. H. (1985). Habituation of attention as a measure of visual information processing in human infants: Summary, systematization, and synthesis. In G. Gottlieb and N. A. Krasnegor (eds), *Measurement of Audition and Vision in the First Year of Postnatal Life: A Methodological Overview*, Norwood NJ: Ablex, pp. 253–300.

Bornstein, M. H., and Sigman, M. D. (1986). Continuity in mental development from infancy. *Child Development*, **57**, 251–74.

Bornstein, M. H., Slater, A., Brown, E., Roberts, E., and Barrett, J. (1997). Stability of mental development from infancy to early childhood: Three 'waves' of research. In J. G. Bremner, A. Slater and G. Butterworth (eds), *Infant Development: Recent Advances*, Hove: Psychology Press, pp. 191–215.

Brooks-Gunn, J., Klebanov, P. K., Liaw, F-R., and Spiker, D. (1993). Enhancing the development of low-birthweight premature infants: Changes in cognition and behavior over the first three years. *Child Development*, **64**, 736–53.

Canfield, R. L., Smith, E. G., Brezsnyak, M. P., and Snow, K. L. (1997). Information processing through the first year of life. *Monographs of the Society for Research in Child Development*, **62** (Serial no. 250).

Caron, A. J., and Caron, R. F. (1969). Degree of stimulus complexity and habituation of visual fixation in infants. *Psychonomic Science*, **14**, 78–9.

Clarke, A. (1978). Predicting human development: Problems, evidence, implications. *Bulletin of the British Psychological Society*, **31**, 249–58.

Cohen, L. B. (1981). Examination of habituation as a measure of aberrant infant development. In S. L. Friedman and M. Sigman (eds), *Preterm birth and Psychological Development*, New York: Academic Press, pp. 241–53.

Cohen, S. E., and Parmelee, A. H. (1983). Prediction of five-year Stanford–Binet scores in preterm infants. *Child Development*, **54**, 1242–53.

Colombo, J., Mitchell, D. W., Coldren, J. T., and Freesman, L. J. (1991). Individual differences in infant visual attention: Are short lookers faster processors or feature processors? *Child Development*, **62**, 1247–57.

Colombo, J., Mitchell, D. W., O'Brien, M., and Horowitz, F. D. (1987). The stability of visual habituation during the first year of life. *Child Development*, **58**, 474–87.

Dougherty, T. M., and Haith, M. M. (1997). Infant expectations and reaction time as predictors of childhood speed of processing and IQ. *Developmental Psychology*, **33**, 146–55.

Friedman, S. (1975). Infant habituation: Process, problems, and possibilities. In N. Ellis (ed.), *Aberrant Development in Infancy: Human and Animal Studies*, New York: Halstead Press, pp. 217–39.

Griffiths, R. (1954). *The Abilities of Babies: A Study in Mental Measurement*. New York: McGraw-Hill.

Laucht, M., Esser, G., and Schmidt, M. (1994). Contrasting infant predictors of later cognitive functioning. *Journal of Child Psychology and Psychiatry*, **35**, 649–62.

Lécuyer, R. (1989). Habituation and attention, novelty and cognition: Where is the continuity? *Human Development*, **32**, 148–57.

Lester, B. M. (1975). Cardiac habituation of the orienting response to an auditory signal in infants of varying nutritional status. *Developmental Psychology*, **11**, 432–42.

Lewis, M., and Brooks-Gunn, J. (1981). Visual attention at three months as a predictor of cognitive function at two years of age. *Intelligence*, **5**, 131–40.

Lipsitt, L. (1981). Presidential address to Division 7 of the American Psychological Association, reported in M. Shatz, On transition, continuity and coupling. In M. Golinkoff (ed.) (1983), *The Transition from Prelinguistic to Linguistic Communication*, Hillsdale, NJ: Lawrence Erlbaum Associates.

McCall, R. B. (1979). Qualitative transitions in behavioral development in the first two years of life. In M. Bornstein and W. Kessen (eds), *Psychological Development from Infancy: Image to Intention*, Hillsdale, NJ: Erlbaum Associates, pp. 183–224.

McCall, R. B. (1989). Commentary. *Human Development*, **32**, 177–86.

McCall, R. B. (1994). What process mediates predictions of childhood IQ from infant habituation and recognition memory? Speculations on the roles of inhibition and rate of information processing. *Intelligence*, **18**, 107–25.

McCall, R. B., and Carriger, M. S. (1993). A meta-analysis of infant habituation and recognition memory performance as predictors of later IQ. *Child Development*, **64**, 57–79.

Pêcheux, M. G., and Lécuyer, R. (1989). A longitudinal study of visual habituation between 3, 5 and 8 months of age. *British Journal of Developmental Psychology*, **7**, 159–69.

Ramey, C. T., Yeates, K. O., and Short, E. J. (1984). The plasticity of intellectual development: Insights from preventive intervention. *Child Development*, **55**, 1913–25.

Reznick, J. S., Corley, R., and Robinson, J. (1997). A longitudinal twin study of intelligence in the second year. *Monographs of the Society for Research in Child Development*, **62**, (Serial no. 249).

Rose, D. H., Slater, A. M., and Perry, H. (1986). Prediction of childhood intelligence from habituation in early infancy. *Intelligence*, **10**, 251–63.

Slater, A. (1995). Individual differences in infancy and later IQ. *Journal of Child Psychology and Psychiatry*, **36**, 69–112.

Slater, A., Cooper, R., Rose, D., and Morison, V. (1989). Prediction of cognitive performance from infancy to early childhood. *Human Development*, **32**, 137–47.

Slater, A., and Morison, V. (1985). Selective adaptation cannot account for early infant habituation: A response to Dannemiller and Banks. *Merrill-Palmer Quarterly*, **31**, 99–103.

Sternberg, R. J., and Okagaki, L. (1989). Continuity and discontinuity in intellectual development are not a matter of 'either-or.' *Human Development*, **32**, 158–66.

7

Biological Bases of Childhood Shyness*

Jerome Kagan, J. Steven Reznick and Nancy Snidman

EDITORS' INTRODUCTION

Two temperamental categories that display stability across age are shyness (behavioural restraint, perhaps introversion) and boldness (spontaneity in unfamiliar contexts, perhaps extroversion). Kagan, Reznick and Sidman demonstrate that 2-year-olds who were at one of these two behavioural extremes displayed similar behaviour when 7-year-olds. In a recent paper Kagan (1997) extends the age range downwards and presents evidence that 'Four-month-old infants who show a low threshold to become distressed and motorically aroused to unfamiliar stimuli are more likely than others to become fearful and subdued during early childhood, whereas infants who show a high arousal threshold are more likely to become bold and sociable' (p. 139). In the present paper Kagan, Reznick and Sidman speculate on possible biological determinants and correlates of these extreme temperamental types, and on the role of environmental experiences in actualizing, or promoting the different temperaments.

Reference

Kagan, J. (1997). Temperament and the reactions to unfamiliarity. *Child Development*, **68**, 139–43.

OVERVIEW

The initial behavioral reaction to unfamiliar events is a distinctive source of intraspecific variation in humans and other animals. Two longitudinal

---

* Previously published in *Science*, **240** (8 April 1988), pp. 167–71.

studies of 2-year-old children who were extreme in the display of either behavioral restraint or spontaneity in unfamiliar contexts revealed that by 7 years of age a majority of the restrained group were quiet and socially avoidant with unfamiliar children and adults whereas a majority of the more spontaneous children were talkative and interactive. The group differences in peripheral physiological reactions suggest that inherited variation in the threshold of arousal in selected limbic sites may contribute to shyness in childhood and even extreme degrees of social avoidance in adults.

A child's initial reaction to unfamiliar events, especially other people, is one of the few behavioral qualities that is moderately stable over time and independent of social class and intelligence test scores. About 10 to 15 percent of healthy, 2- and 3-year-old children consistently become quiet, vigilant, and affectively subdued in such contexts for periods lasting from 5 to 30 minutes. An equal proportion is typically spontaneous, as if the distinction between familiar and unfamiliar were of minimal psychological consequence.[1] Empirical indexes of a pair of related, but not identical, constructs in adults, often called introversion and extroversion, are among the most stable and heritable in contemporary psychology.[2]

Comparative psychologists and behavioral biologists may be studying an analogous form of variation among members of a species or closely related strains. Mice, rats, cats, dogs, wolves, pigs, cows, monkeys, and even paradise fish differ intraspecifically in their initial tendency to approach or to avoid novelty.[3] Some investigators have explored the physiological correlates of these behavioral differences. For example, about 15 percent of kittens (*Felis catus*) show prolonged restraint before approaching novel objects and people and, as adults, do not attack rats. These avoidant cats, compared with a larger complementary group that does not retreat from novelty, show greater neural activity in the basomedial amygdala following exposure to a rat, as well as larger evoked potentials in the ventromedial hypothalamus following direct stimulation of the basomedial amygdala.[4] Laboratory born and reared rhesus monkeys also vary in their response to novelty. Those who are slow to explore show higher heart rates in unfamiliar settings and larger increases in plasma cortisol following separation from the mother or peers than do animals who are much less avoidant.[5] The total corpus of evidence suggests that both animals and children who consistently show an initial avoidance of or behavioral restraint to novelty display distinctive behavioral and physiological profiles early in development, implying the influence of genetic factors.

INHIBITED AND UNINHIBITED CHILDREN

Our laboratory has used a longitudinal design in the study of three cohorts of Caucasian children from working- and middle-class Boston homes. The first two cohorts were selected at either 21 or 31 months of age to include approximately equal numbers of children who were either consistently shy, quiet, and timid (inhibited) or consistently sociable, talkative, and affectively spontaneous (uninhibited) when exposed to unfamiliar people, procedures, and objects in unfamiliar laboratory settings. About 15 percent of a total sample of 400 children evaluated was classified as belonging to one of the two extreme groups with similar proportions of boys and girls in each group.[6]

Descriptions of procedures

The children in cohort 1, selected at 21 months, were observed on two occasions with unfamiliar women and objects in several unfamiliar laboratory rooms. The major behavioral signs of inhibition coded from videotape were prolonged clinging to or remaining proximal to the mother, cessation of vocalization, and reluctance to approach or actual retreat from the unfamiliar events. The children who displayed these behaviors consistently across most incentives, as well as those who did not, were selected to form one group of 28 inhibited and another group of 30 uninhibited children.

The initial selection of children for cohort 2 at 31 months was based on behavior with an unfamiliar child of the same sex and age in the same laboratory playroom, with both mothers present, and a subsequent episode in which the child encountered an unfamiliar woman dressed in an unusual costume. The indexes of inhibition, similar to those used with cohort 1, were long latencies to play, speak, and interact with the unfamiliar child and woman, as well as long periods of time proximal to the mother. This selection process yielded 26 consistently inhibited and 23 consistently uninhibited children.

Each of these two cohorts was observed on three additional occasions. Cohort 1 was observed subsequently at 4, 5.5, and 7.5 years of age; cohort 2 at 3.5, 5.5, and 7.5 years, with about 20 percent attrition by the time of the last assessment at 7.5 years when there were 41 children in each cohort. The phenotypic display of the two temperamental tendencies changes with age because of learning and maturation. A 2-year-old will become uncertain in an unfamiliar room with unfamiliar objects, but older children require more potent incentives, especially unfamiliar children and adults. Thus, the specific laboratory procedures we used changed for the four evaluations.

The index of inhibition on the second assessment (3.5 or 4 years) was based on behavior in two, separate 40-minute laboratory play sessions with an unfamiliar child of the same sex and age with both mothers present. At 5.5 years the children in both cohorts were observed in four different unfamiliar situations. The indexes of inhibition, for each situation, were based on (i) long latencies to initiate play or interact with an unfamiliar child as well as time proximal to the mother in a laboratory playroom, (ii) spatial isolation and infrequent interaction with classmates in the child's school setting, (iii) long latencies to talk and infrequent spontaneous comments with a female examiner who administered a 90-minute cognitive battery (including recall and recognition memory, match to sample, and discrimination of pictures), and (iv) reluctance to play with novel toys suggestive of risk in an unfamiliar laboratory room (a large black box with a hole or a beam set at an angle to the floor). The theoretically relevant variables from each situation were aggregated to form a composite index of behavioral inhibition.[7]

The index of behavioral inhibition at 7.5 years was based on two situations separated by several months. The first was a laboratory play situation involving seven to ten unfamiliar children of the same age and sex; a single unfamiliar child does not generate sufficient uncertainty in a child this old. Approximately 50 minutes was devoted to structured, competitive games and a total of 30 minutes to unstructured free-play intervals interposed between each of the games. The two variables indexing behavioral inhibition were infrequent spontaneous comments to the other children and long periods of playing or standing apart from any other child in the room. The second assessment context was an individual testing session with an unfamiliar female examiner. The two variables were latency to the sixth spontaneous comment to the examiner and the total number of spontaneous comments over the testing session. The results are similar if latency to any of the first six comments is used as the component of the index. The reliabilities between coders (correlation coefficients) for the variables quantified from video tapes were generally above 0.90 at each age.

Preservation of behavioral differences

The initial behavioral differences between inhibited and uninhibited children predicted theoretically reasonable derivatives at the older ages (the adjectives inhibited and uninhibited refer to the original classification at 21 or 31 months, unless stated otherwise). The slopes of the regression lines relating an index of inhibited behavior at one age to an index at a later age, which reflect the stability of behavior, ranged from 0.40 to 1.12 ($P < 0.01$). The standard error of the slopes ranged from 0.09 to 0.22 and the standard deviation of the values around the slope ranged from 0.45 to 0.83.[8] Each mother's rating of her child's shyness with unfamiliar people was only moderately related to the child's behavior in the laboratory (correlations between the two variables ranged from 0.3 to 0.6). Additionally, the mothers of inhibited children in both cohorts more often reported a history of excessive irritability, colic, and sleeplessness during the infant's first year.

Figure 7.1 illustrates values for children in each cohort on the two indexes of behavioral inhibition with the group of unfamiliar peers at age 7.5 – that is, the percentage of time distant from any other child during the free-play intervals and total number of spontaneous comments. More inhibited, than uninhibited, children were above the median on the first variable and below on the second ($\chi^2 = 7.9$, $P < 0.05$ for cohort 1; $\chi^2 = 5.2$, $P < 0.05$ for cohort 2; and $\chi^2 = 15.2$, $P < 0.001$ for the pooled cohorts). A frequent scene during the play sessions was a cluster of three or four children playing close to each other, often talking, and one or two children standing or playing alone one to several meters from the center of social activity. These isolated, quiet children were typically those who had been classified as inhibited 5 or 6 years earlier.[9]

After 4 years of age remaining quiet with an unfamiliar adult in an evaluative setting is an extremely sensitive sign of behavioral inhibition. The inhibited children were much less talkative with the examiner than uninhibited children during the testing session at 4 and 5.5 years. During the testing

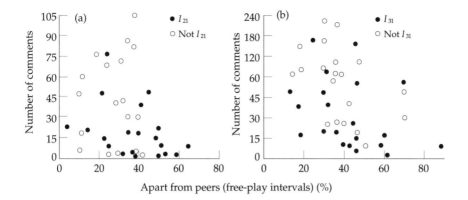

FIGURE 7.1   Relationship between total number of spontaneous comments and the percentage of time each child was distant from a peer in a free-play situation at 7.5 years for (a) cohort 1 children selected at 21 months, and (b) cohort 2 children selected at 31 months. The free-play intervals were longer for cohort 2; hence, the larger number of spontaneous comments. I = inhibited; Not I = uninhibited

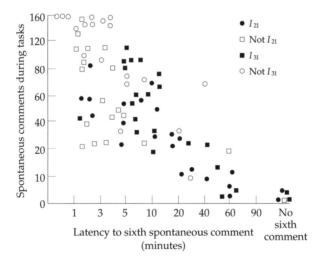

FIGURE 7.2   Relationship between latency to the sixth spontaneous comment and total number of spontaneous comments at 7.5 years for cohort 1 children selected at 21 months and cohort 2 children selected at 31 months. I = inhibited; Not I = uninhibited

session with an unfamiliar female examiner at 7.5 years, 60 percent of the inhibited and 15 percent of the uninhibited children uttered their sixth spontaneous comment later in the session and, in addition, spoke less often than uninhibited children (based on median values for the two variables, $\chi^2 = 20.9$, $P < 0.0001$) (figure 7.2).

The mean of the two standardized indexes of inhibited behavior from the peer play procedure (proportional amount of time distant from peers and total number of spontaneous comments) was combined with the mean of the two

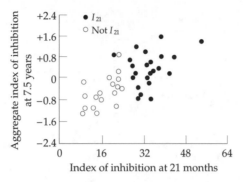

FIGURE 7.3   Relationship between the original index of inhibition at 21 months and the aggregate index of inhibition (z score) at 7.5 years for cohort 1 children. I = inhibited; Not I = uninhibited

standardized indexes from the testing situation (latency to the sixth spontaneous comment and total number of spontaneous comments; $r = 0.40$ between the two indexes) to yield an aggregate index of inhibition for the 41 children in cohort 1 at 7.5 years. Figure 7.3 illustrates the relation between this aggregate score and the original behavioral index. The predictive relation between the indexes at 21 months and 7.5 years had a slope of 0.50 ($P < 0.001$), with a standard error of 0.09 and a standard deviation of the values around the regression line of 0.56. A comparable analysis of cohort 2 data revealed a slope of 0.59 ($P < 0.001$) between the indexes at 3.5 and 7.5 years with a standard error of 0.12 and a standard deviation of the points around the line of 0.45. Furthermore, the children in both cohorts who had the most extreme scores on the original index were most likely to have remained behaviorally consistent through 7.5 years.

An unselected cohort

In a third longitudinal study, Caucasian middle-class children of both sexes were selected who were extreme on the two behavioral profiles. The children in cohort 3 were observed initially at 14 months ($n = 100$), and again at 20 ($n = 91$), 32 ($n = 76$), and 48 months ($n = 77$). The indexes of inhibition at 14 and 20 months were based on behavior with an unfamiliar examiner and with unfamiliar toys in laboratory rooms. The index of inhibition at 32 months was based on behavior in a 30-minute free-play situation with two other unfamiliar children of the same sex and age with all three mothers present. The index of inhibition at 48 months was based on behavior with an unfamiliar child of the same sex and age, with an unfamiliar examiner in a testing situation and in an unfamiliar room containing objects suggestive of risk. The original variation in inhibited behavior for the entire group at 14 months was correlated with the variation at 20 and 32 months ($r = 0.52$ and 0.44; $P < 0.01$), but the indexes at 14 and 20 months did not predict differences in behavioral inhibition at 4 years of age. However, when we restricted the analysis to those children who fell at the top and bottom 20 percent of the distribution of behavioral inhibition at both 14 and 20 months (13 children in each group), the two groups showed statistically significant differences at 4 years of age ($t = 2.69, P < 0.01$). Almost half the inhibited but 8 percent of the uninhibited group had a positive standard score on the index of inhibition at 4 years of age. This finding, together with the data from cohorts 1 and 2, implies that the constructs inhibited and uninhibited refer to qualitative categories of children. These terms do not refer to a behavioral continuum ranging from timidity to sociability in a volunteer sample of children, even though such a continuum can be observed phenotypically.

Physiology and Inhibition

As noted, intraspecific variation in behavioral withdrawal to novelty in rats, cats, and monkeys is often related to physiological reactions that imply greater arousal in selected hypothalamic and limbic sites, especially the amygdala.[3] If this relation were present in humans, inhibited children should show more activity in biological systems that originate in these sites. Three such systems are the sympathetic chain, reticular formation with its projections to skeletal muscles, and the hypothalamic–pituitary–adrenal axis.[10]

Sympathetic reactivity

Five potential indexes of sympathetic reactivity include a high and minimally variable heart rate, as well as heart rate acceleration, pupillary dilation, and norepinephrine level to psychological stress and challenge. We measured each child's heart period and heart period variability both under minimally stressful baseline conditions as well as during moderately stressful cognitive tasks on every one of the four assessments. Heart period variability was the average standard deviation of the interbeat intervals during the trials of the test episodes. Mean heart period and heart period variability for a multitrial episode were based on the values for the separate trials of that episode. Although we use the terms heart rate and heart rate variability in the text, all statistical analyses were performed on the heart period values.

Mean heart rate and variability were always inversely correlated – a higher heart rate associated with lower variability – both under relaxed conditions as well as during cognitive activity (product moment correlations were between -0.6 and -0.7). Individual differences in heart rate and variability were preserved from 21 months to 7.5 years in cohort 1 ($r = 0.62, P < 0.001$ for heart rate; $r = 0.54, P < 0.001$ for variability); from 31 months to 5.5 years for cohort 2 ($r = 0.59, P < 0.001$ for heart rate and $r = 0.61$ for $P < 0.001$ variability). Correlations are reported because the children were not selected to be extreme on the cardiac variables and both heart rate and variability were normally distributed at all ages. Further, the index of inhibited behavior was typically associated with a higher and more stable heart rate on the early evaluations (average $r = 0.4$), but on the last assessment at 7.5 years this relation was less

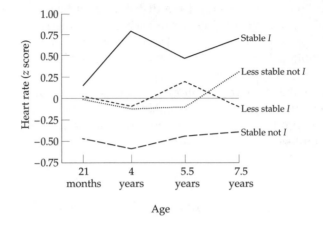

FIGURE 7.4 Mean heart rate (z score) for cohort 1 children at each of the four assessments. Stable I refers to 12 children who were inhibited at every age; Less stable I, to 10 children who were inhibited originally but were uninhibited on one or more of the later assessments; Stable not I, to 12 children who were consistently uninhibited; and Less stable not I, to 7 children who were classified as uninhibited originally but were inhibited on one or more of the later assessments. The standard errors of the mean for each of the four groups at the four ages averaged 0.29, 0.26 for the consistently inhibited children, and 0.34 for the consistently uninhibited children

robust ($r = 0.3$). However, the inhibited children with the highest heart rates on the first two assessments were more likely to have remained inhibited through 7.5 years than the inhibited children who had lower heart rates earlier. We computed for each child in cohort 1 a standard score representing his or her index of inhibition and heart rate on each of the four assessments. At every age the consistently inhibited children (those with positive standard scores on the index of inhibition on each assessment) and the consistently uninhibited children had the highest and lowest heart rates, respectively (figure 7.4).

Unusual fears at 5.5 and 7.5 years (violence on television or in movies, kidnappers, or going to the bedroom alone in the evening) were most frequent in inhibited children with the highest heart rates (60 percent of the group) and least frequent in uninhibited children with the lowest heart rates (no child in this group had any unusual or intense fears).

In addition, at every age inhibited children were more likely than uninhibited ones to show an increase in heart rate, about ten beats per minute, across the trials of a test or across the entire battery of cognitive tests.[7,11] This fact was also true for the cohort 3 children who had extreme scores on the index of inhibition at 4 years of age. The inhibited children were more likely to attain their maximal heart rate early in the testing session, usually during the first cognitive procedure following the initial baseline. We also evaluated, for the first time at 7.5 years in cohort 2, and 4 years in cohort 3, the change in heart rate when the child's posture changed from sitting to standing. Inhibited children showed a larger increase in mean heart rate (ten beats per minute) during a 60-second period than did uninhibited children, despite a slightly higher heart rate during the preceding sitting baseline. This result suggests that the inhibited children maintained a brisker sympathetic response to the drop in blood pressure that accompanies the rise to a standing position. In addition, the inhibited children in cohort 2 showed higher diastolic, but not a higher systolic, blood pressure during the testing session at 7.5 years, implying greater sympathetic tone in the vessels of the arterial tree.

Several months after the laboratory session with cohort 1 at 7.5 years we recorded the child's heart rate during one night of sleep. We eliminated the first and last hours of sleep on the assumption that sleep would be lighter during these times, and a continuous respiration record permitted elimination of epochs of active sleep. The mean quiet heart rate during sleep was 76 beats per minute, with a range of 59 to 92 beats, and there was no statistically significant relation between heart and respiration rate. The mean sleeping heart rate was correlated with heart rate obtained in the laboratory at each of the four ages ($r = 0.37, 0.40, 0.61$, and $0.49, P < 0.05$). Although the sleep heart rate had only a low positive association with the aggregate index of inhibition at 7.5 years, two of the four components of the composite index of inhibition at 5.5 years (reluctance to play with novel toys suggestive of risk in an unfamiliar room and shy, restrained behavior with an unfamiliar peer) were associated with higher sleeping heart rates 2 years later ($r = 0.48$, $P < 0.01$; $r = 0.35$, $P < 0.05$).

Pupillary dilation, which is another potential index of sympathetic activity,[12] was assessed only at 5.5 years. Although both cohorts showed a reliable increase in pupil size of about 0.3 millimeter to cognitive test items (an increase of about 5 percent), the inhibited children in both cohorts had larger pupil diameters during test questions as well as during the intervals between test items [$F(1, 269) = 20.9$, $P < 0.1$ for test trials; $F(1, 154) = 17.3$, $P < 0.001$ for periods before trials; F values based on repeated measures analysis of variance].

Muscle tension

Projections from limbic structures to the skeletal muscles of the larynx and vocal cords also appear to be at higher levels of excitability in inhibited children. Increased tension in these muscles is usually accompanied by a decrease in the variability of the pitch periods of vocal utterances, which is called perturbation.[13] The increased muscle tension can be caused by discharge of the nucleus ambiguus as well as sympathetic activity that constricts arterioles serving the muscles of the larynx and vocal folds. Because the vocal cords do not maintain a steady rate as they open and close, the perturbations in the rate at which they open and close is a consequence of many factors, one of which is the degree of tension in the laryngeal muscles.[14] We measured the vocal perturbation of single-word utterances at 5.5 years in cohort 1 and 3.5 years in cohort 2. The inhibited, compared with the uninhibited, children showed a significantly greater decrease in vocal perturbation when the single words were spoken under moderate as opposed to low stress. The inhibited children also showed less variability in the fundamental frequency of all the single-word utterances spoken during the episode.[15]

Urinary norepinephrine

Norepinephrine is the primary neurotransmitter in the postganglionic synapses of the peripheral sympathetic nervous system. A urine sample collected from each child in cohort 1 as the end of the test battery at 5.5 years was tested for norepinephrine and its derivatives (normetanephrine, MHPG, and VMA) by mass fragmentography.[16] Concentrations of each compound were transformed to micrograms per gram of creatinine, and a composite index of total norepinephrine activity was computed. There was a modest correlation between this index and inhibited behavior at both 4 and 5.5 years ($r = 0.34$, $P < 0.05$ with the index at age 4; $r = 0.31$, $P < 0.05$ with the index at age 5.5 years).

Salivary cortisol

In order to assess activity in the hypothalamic–pituitary–adrenal axis, samples of saliva were gathered on cohort 1 at 5.5 years when the child came to the laboratory, as well as at home on three mornings before breakfast and before the stress of the day had begun. Analysis of unbound cortisol in these saliva samples by a modification of the standard radioimmunoassay method revealed that the average cortisol level for the three morning home samples was correlated with the original index of inhibition ($r = 0.39$, $P < 0.05$).[17]

Aggregate of physiological variables

With the exception of heart rate and heart rate variability, correlations among the remaining physiological variables were low, ranging from -0.22 to $+0.33$ with a median coefficient of $+0.10$. This phenomenon has been noted by others.[18] However, it is likely that an aggregate index of physiological activity might be more highly correlated with inhibited behavior because any single variable could be the result of a factor unrelated to the hypothetical processes mediating inhibited and uninhibited behavior. Pooling several indexes would dilute the contribution of any of these factors. For example, a child who did not belong to the inhibited category but who was highly motivated to solve the cognitive problems might show a high and minimally variable heart rate and a large pupil, but this child should show average cortisol levels and variability in the vocal perturbation index. Consider the following analogy. Body temperature, fatigue, thoracic discomfort, and pneumococci in the sputum are not highly correlated in a random sample of the population. But persons with high values on all four variables meet the criterion for a special disease category. We averaged the standard scores for eight peripheral psychophysiological variables gathered at 5.5 years on cohort 1 to create a composite index of physiological arousal (mean heart period, heart period variablity, pupillary dilation during cognitive tests, total norepinephrine activity, mean cortisol level at home and in the laboratory, variablity of the pitch periods of vocal utterances under cognitive stress, and the standard deviation of the fundamental frequency values of the vocal utterances). There was a substantial positive relation between this composite physiological index and the index of inhibition at every age ($r = 0.70$ with the index at 21 months and $r = 0.64$ with the index at 7.5 years of age).

DISCUSSION

A majority of children who had been selected from a much larger sample at 1.5 or 2.5 years because they were extremely shy, quiet, and restrained in a variety of unfamiliar contexts became 7-year-olds who were quiet, cautious, and socially avoidant with peers and adults, whereas a majority of children who had been selected to be extremely sociable and affectively spontaneous were talkative and socially interactive at 7 years of age. However, the preservation of these two behavioral styles, albeit modest and different in form at the two ages, holds only for children selected originally to be extreme in their behavior. The data from cohort 3 indicate that there is no predictive relation in an unselected sample between indexes of inhibited behavior assessed during the second and fourth years. Only when we restricted the analysis to the behavioral extremes did we find preservation of the two behavioral categories as well as an association between inhibition and both heart rate acceleration to mild stress and high early morning levels of salivary cortisol.

The behavioral differences between the two groups were most consistently associated with peripheral physiological variables implying greater sympathetic reactivity among the inhibited children, especially larger cardiac accelerations to cognitive activity and to a postural change from sitting to standing. We suggest, albeit speculatively, that most of the children we call inhibited belong to a qualitatively distinct category of infants who were born with a lower threshold for limbic–hypothalamic arousal to unexpected changes in the environment or novel events that cannot be assimilated easily. This hypothesis is consonant with comparable data gathered on rhesus monkeys,[5] the views of a number of physiologists,[19] and especially animal data implying that the amygdala is an important mediator of states which would be regarded as resembling anxiety or fear in humans.[20] Although the reasons for the lower thresholds in limbic–hypothalamic sites are unclear, and likely to be complex, tonically higher levels of central norepinephrine, greater density of receptors for norepinephrine in these areas, or both, are possible contributing factors.[21] This suggestion is supported by evidence indicating a close covariation in free-moving cats between activity of the locus coeruleus, the main source of central norepinephrine, and acceleration of heart rate to the stresses of white noise and restraint.[22]

However, we suggest that the actualization of shy, quiet, timid behavior at 2 years of age requires some form of chronic environmental stress acting upon the original temperamental disposition present at birth. Some possible stressors include prolonged hospitalization, death of a parent, marital quarreling, or mental illness in a family member. These stressors were not frequent in our samples. However, in both longitudinal cohorts, two-thirds of the inhibited children were later born while two-thirds of the uninhibited children were first born. An older sibling who unexpectedly seizes a toy, teases, or yells at an infant who has a low threshold for limbic arousal might provide the chronic stress necessary to transform the temperamental quality into the profile we call behavioral inhibition. Thus, it is important to differentiate between those children and adolescents who are quiet and restrained in unfamiliar social situations because of the influence of temperamental factors and those who behave this way because of environmental experiences alone. Physiological measures might be helpful in distinguishing between these two groups. We suspect that the contemporary construct of introversion, usually applied to adults, contains both types.[23] Finally, we note that these data support Jung's claim, which Freud rejected, that temperamental factors contribute to the development of social anxiety and avoidance and to the symptoms of panic and agoraphobia that had been classified earlier in the century as components of hysteria.[24]

ACKNOWLEDGEMENTS

Supported by grants from the John D. and Catherine T. MacArthur Foundation and NIMH grant MH-40691. We thank J. Gibbons, M. Johnson, P. Ellison, H. O'Rourke, C. Kagan, R. J. Wyatt, F. Karoum, K. Baak, T. Shea, C. Raver, Xiao Ping, and J. Miller for their contributions.

NOTES

1. J. Kagan, J. S. Reznick, C. Clarke, N. Snidman, C. Garcia-Coll, *Child Dev.* **55**, 2212 (1984); A. Thomas and S. Chess, *Temperament and Development* (Brunner Mazel, New York, 1977).
2. J. J. Conley, *J. Pers. Soc. Psychol.* **49**, 1266 (1985); R. Plomin, *Development, Genetics and Psychology* (Erlbaum, Hillsdale, NJ, 1986); J. Kagan and H. A. Moss, *Birth to Maturity* (Wiley, New York, 1962); I. M. Marks, *Fears, Phobias and Rituals* (Oxford, New York, 1987).
3. D. A. Blizard, *Behav. Genet.* **11**, 469 (1981); R. T. Blanchard, K. J. Flannelly, D. C. Blanchard, *J. Comp. Psychol.* **100**, 101 (1986); R. M. Murphey, F. A. M. Duarte, M. C. T. Penendo, *Behav. Genet.* **10**, 170 (1980); K. McDonald, *J. Comp., Psychol.* **97**, 99 (1988); V. Csanyi and J. Gervai, *Behav. Genet,* **16**, 553 (1986); R. Dantzer and P. Mormode, *Animal Stress,* G. P. Moberg, ed. (American Physiological Society, Bethesda, MD, 1985), pp. 81–95; D. O. Cooper, D. E. Schmode, R. J. Barrett, *Pharmacol, Biochem. Behav.* 19, 457 (1983); J. Stevenson-Hinde, R. Stillwell-Barns, M. Zunz, *Primates 21*, 66 (1980); T. C. Schneiria, *Advances in the Study of Behavior,* D. S. Lehrman, R. A. Hinde, E. Shaw, eds (Academic Press, New York, 1965), pp. 1–74; J. P. Scott and J. L. Fuller, *Dog Behavior: The Genetic Basis* (Univ. of Chicago Press, Chicago, IL, 1965); M. E. Goddard and R. G. Beilharz, *Behav. Genet.* **15**, 69 (1985).
4. R. E. Adamec and C. Stark-Adamec, *The Limbic System,* B. K. Doane and K. E. Livingston, eds (Raven, New York, 1986), pp. 129–45.
5. S. J. Suomi, *Perinatal Development: A Psychobiological Perspective,* N. A. Krasnegor, E. M. Blass, M. A. Hofer, W. P. Smotherman, eds (Academic Press, New York, 1987), pp. 397–420.

6. C. Garcia-Coll, J. Kagan, J. S. Reznick, *Child Dev.* **55**, 1005 (1984); N. Snidman, thesis, University of California, Los Angeles (1984). During the initial selection at 21 or 31 months, it was most difficult to find extremely inhibited boys.

7. J. S. Reznick et al., *Child Dev.* **51**, 660 (1986).

8. Because the two groups of children in cohorts 1 and 2 were selected originally to represent behavioral extremes, the slope of the regression line, rather than the product moment correlation, is the more appropriate statistic to summarize the degree to which the children retained their relative position on the behavioral indexes of inhibition across the assessments at the different ages.

9. K. Miyake (personal communication) of the University of Hokkaido in Sapporo, Japan, who has been studying 13 children from the first week through 6 years of age, implemented this same procedure with one group of boys and one of girls. The two 6-year-olds who were the most distant from the other children in their play group had been extremely shy and fearful during the first 2 years of life while the two children who were most often proximal to a peer had been the least fearful.

10. A. S. Kling, R. L'. Lloyd, K. M. Perryman, *Behav. Neural Biol.* **47**, 54 (1987); D. H. Cohen, *Limbic and Autonomic Nervous System Research*, L. V. DiCara, ed. (Plenum, New York, 1974), pp. 223–75; G. J. Mogenson, *Progress in Psychobiology and Physiological Psychology*, A. N. Epstein and A. R. Morrison, eds (Academic Press, New York, 1987), pp. 117–70.

11. See B. Giordani, S. B. Manuck, and J. C. Farmer [*Child Dev.* **52**, 533 (1981)] and J. W. Hinton and B. Craske [*Biol. Psychol.* **5**, 23 (1977)] for comparable findings with adult introverts; and J. Kagan, J. S. Reznick, and N. Snidman [*Child Dev.* **58**, 1459 (1987)] for details of the heart rate analyses.

12. J. Beatty, *Psychol. Bull.* **91**, 276 (1982); F. Richer and J. Beatty, *Psychophysiology* **24** 258 (1987); R. F. Stanners, M. Coulter, A. W. Sweet, P. Murphy, *Motiv. Emotion* **3**, 319 (1979).

13. K. N. Stevens and M. Hirano, *Vocal Fold Physiology* (Univ. of Tokyo Press, Tokyo, 1981).

14. P. Lieberman, *J. Acoust. Soc. Am.* **33**, 597 (1961).

15. W. Coster, thesis, Harvard University, Cambridge (1986); N. Snidman, P. Lieberman, J. S. Reznick, J. Kagan, unpublished manuscript; see J. Kagan, D. R. Lapidus, and M. Moore [*Child Dev.* **49**, 1005 (1978)] for evidence of a significant positive relation between frequency of crying to discrepant events in a laboratory setting at 4 and 8 months of age – a characteristic of inhibited infants – and resting electromyogram levels at 10 years of age.

16. F. Karoum, *Methods in Biogenic Amine Research*, S. Parvez, T. Nagatsu, I. Nagatsu, H. Parvez, eds (Elsevier, Amsterdam, 1983), pp. 237–55.

17. R. F. Walker, *Steroid Hormones in Saliva*, D. B. Ferguson, ed. (Karger, Basel, 1984), pp. 33–50; the inhibited children in cohort 2 also generated higher morning cortisol levels than uninhibited children at 5.5 and 7.5 years of age.

18. D. Kelley, C. C. Brown, J. W. Shaffer, *Psychophysiology* **6**, 429 (1970); J. Fahrenberg, F. Foerster, H. J. Schneider, W. Muller, M. Myrtek, ibid. **23**, 323 (1986); R. M. Nesse et al., *Psychosom. Med.* **47**, 320 (1985).

19. J. P. Aggleton and R. E. Passingham, *J. Comp. Physiol. Psychol.* **95**, 961 (1981); P. Gloor, *Limbic Mechanisms*, K. E. Livingston and O. Hoznykiewicz, eds (Plenum, New York, 1978), pp. 189–209; M. Sarter and H. J. Markowitsch, *Behav. Neurosci.* **99**, 342, (1985); A. Tsuda and M. Tanaka, ibid., p. 802.

20. J. Hitchcock and M. Davis, *Behav. Neurosci.* **100**, 11 (1986); D. H. Cohen, *Memory Systems of the Brain*, N. M. Weinberger, J. L. McGaugh, G. Lynch, eds (Guilford,

New York, 1985), pp. 27–48; L. T. Dunn and B. J. Everitt, *Behav. Neurosci.* **102**, 3 (1988).

21. G. Aston-Jones and F. E. Bloom, *J. Neurosci.* **1**, 887 (1981); A. Bandura et al., *J. Consult. Clin. Psychol.* **53**, 406 (1985); M. F. Reiser, *Mind, Brain, Body* (Basic Books, New York, 1984); D. S. Charney and D. E. Redmond, *Neuropharmacology* **22**, 1531 (1983); D. B. Cubicciotti, S. P. Mendoza, W. A. Mason, E. N. Sassenrath, *J. Comp. Psychol.* **100**, 385 (1986).

22. E. D. Abercrombie and B. L. Jacobs, *J. Neurosci.* **7**, 2837 (1987).

23. H. J. Eysenck, *Personality, Genetics and Behavior* (Praeger, New York, 1982).

24. C. J. Jung, *Psychological Types* (Harcourt Brace, New York, 1924).

8

THE GENETIC BASIS OF COMPLEX HUMAN BEHAVIORS*

Robert Plomin, Michael J. Owen and Peter McGuffin

EDITORS'
INTRODUCTION

Robert Plomin and his colleagues give an account of behavioural and quantitative genetic research which is building a strong case for 'the importance of genetic factors in many complex dimensions and disorders of human behavior'. Much of the evidence they present comes from twin and adoption studies: monozygotic (MZ) twins are genetically identical and their phenotypic resemblance gives some indication of genetic influence; adopted children share a similar environment to their foster parents and siblings but are genetically unrelated, and their resemblance indicates environmental influence. These studies suggest that schizophrenia is under genetic influence – twin studies show a much higher concordance rate (about 45%) for MZ twins than for dizygotic (DZ or fraternal) twins (about 15%).

The evidence suggests that genetic influence is substantial for such behavioural disorders as Alzheimer's disease, autism, affective disorders, and reading disability, and is high for such medical conditions as rheumatoid arthritis, peptic ulcers and types of epilepsy; but it is low for alcoholism, Parkinson's disease and breast cancer. With respect to the controversial topic of the heritability of intelligence they suggest that genetic research shows that genetic influence increasingly affects cognitive abilities throughout the life span.

Plomin and his colleagues suggest that quantitative genetic research, allied with behavioural studies, will increasingly identify those areas of behaviour and behavioural disorders that are influenced by genetic factors.

* Previously published in *Science*, **264** (17 June 1994), pp. 1733–9.

OVERVIEW   Quantitative genetic research has built a strong case for the importance of genetic factors in many complex behavioral disorders and dimensions in the domains of psychopathology, personality, and cognitive abilities. Quantitative genetics can also provide an empirical guide and a conceptual framework for the application of molecular genetics. The success of molecular genetics in elucidating the genetic basis of behavioral disorders has largely relied on a reductionistic one gene, one disorder (OGOD) approach in which a single gene is necessary and sufficient to develop a disorder. In contrast, a quantitative trait loci (QTL) approach involves the search for multiple genes, each of which is neither necessary nor sufficient for the development of a trait. The OGOD and QTL approaches have both advantages and disadvantages for identifying genes that affect complex human behaviors.

The received wisdom of the behavioral sciences concerning the importance of "nature" (genetics) and "nurture" (environment) in the origins of behavioral differences among people has changed dramatically during the past few decades. Environmentalism, which attributes all that we are to nurture, peaked in the 1950s. A more balanced view that considers both nature and nurture swept into psychiatry in the 1960s and 1970s. Although this balanced view has been slower to reach some realms of psychology, there are signs that it has arrived. For example, at its centennial meeting in 1992, the American Psychological Association identified genetics as one of the themes that best represent the present and especially the future of psychology.[1]

Behavioral genetic research began in the 1920s with inbred strain and selection studies of animal behavior and family, twin, and adoption studies of human behavior.[2] These quantitative genetic designs assess the "bottom line" of transmissible genetic effects on behavior, regardless of the number of genes involved, the complexity of their interactions, or the influence of nongenetic factors. As discussed in the first part of this article, quantitative genetic research has built a strong case for the importance of genetic factors in many complex dimensions and disorders of human behavior.

Although more quantitative genetic research is needed, the future of behavioral genetics lies in harnessing the power of molecular genetics to identify specific genes for complex behaviors. In the second part of this paper, initial successes are described and research strategies are discussed. Although more powerful methods and results are available for the investigation of animal than human behavior, animal work is discussed in accompanying articles in this issue.

QUANTITATIVE GENETICS

The change from antipathy to acceptance of genetic factors in the behavioral sciences has occurred so rapidly and thoroughly, especially in psychiatry, that a reminder is warranted about how environmentalistic the behavioral sciences were, even in the 1960s. For example, the major explanation for schizophrenia was abnormal parenting.

Adoption studies were pivotal in leading psychiatrists to consider nature as well as nurture. Schizophrenia was known to run in families, with a risk of 13% for offspring of schizophrenic parents, 13 times the population rate of about 1%.[3] Adoption experiments allow a determination of whether schizophrenia runs in families for reasons of nature or of nurture. In a classic study, Heston[4] examined the offspring of schizophrenic mothers who had been adopted at birth and compared their rate of schizophrenia to a control group of adopted offspring. Of the 47 adopted-away offspring of schizophrenic mothers, 5 were diagnosed as schizophrenic, as compared with none of the 50 control adoptees. Indeed, the risk of schizophrenia for the adopted-away offspring of schizophrenic mothers is the same as the risk for individuals reared by a schizophrenic parent.

These findings implicating substantial genetic influence in schizophrenia have been replicated and extended in other adoption studies, and they confirm the results of twin studies that show greater concordance for identical twins (about 45%) than fraternal twins (about 15%).[3] This twin method is a natural experiment in which the phenotypic resemblance for pairs of genetically identical individuals [identical, monozygotic (MZ) twins] is compared with the resemblance for pairs of individuals whose coefficient of genetic relationship is only 0.50 [fraternal, dizygotic (DZ) twins].

The convergence of evidence from family, twin, and adoption designs – each with distinct assumptions – provides the most convincing argument for the importance of genetic factors in behavioral traits.

Behavioral disorders

Evidence for genetic influence has been found for nearly all behavioral disorders that have been investigated.[5] Figure 8.1 summarizes the results of twin studies for some of the best studied disorders. Genetic influence is substantial for schizophrenia, Alzheimer's disease, autism, major affective disorder, and reading disability.[6] Not all behavioral disorders are influenced to the same degree by genetic factors. For example, diagnosed alcoholism has been assumed to be highly heritable, but new twin studies show only modest genetic influence for males and negligible genetic influence for females. Interestingly, the amount of alcohol consumed shows greater genetic influence than diagnosed alcoholism.[7] In contrast to diagnosed alcoholism, autism, which until the 1970s was assumed to be environmental in origin, appears to be among the most heritable psychiatric disorders.

In addition to the examples in figure 8.1, the following disorders have also shown some evidence of genetic influence: specific language disorder, panic disorder, eating disorders, antisocial personality disorder, and Tourette's syndrome. Some behavioral disorders such as mild mental retardation have not yet been analyzed by genetic research.

Figure 8.2 summarizes results from twin studies for some of the best studied common medical disorders. Like behavioral disorders, some medical disorders show substantial genetic influence – rheumatoid arthritis, peptic ulcers, and idiopathic epilepsy. Others show more modest genetic influence, such as

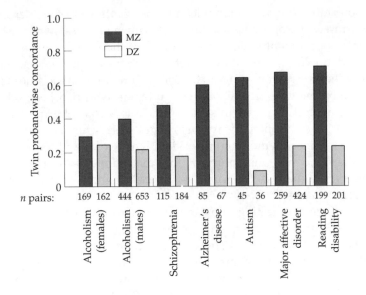

FIGURE 8.1   Identical twin (MZ – monozygotic) and fraternal twin (DZ – dizygotic) probandwise concordances for behavioral disorders. For source of average weighted concordances, see note 60

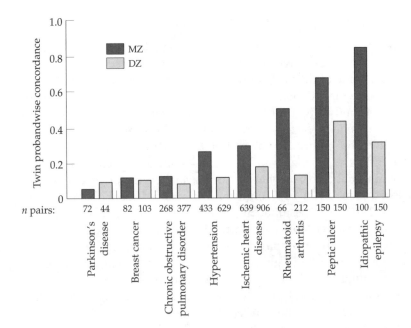

FIGURE 8.2   Identical (MZ) and fraternal (DZ) twin probandwise concordances for common medical disorders. For source of average weighted concordances, see note 61

hypertension and ischemic heart disease. Several common medical disorders show negligible genetic influence. For example, twin studies suggest negligible heritability for breast cancer as a whole in the general population, even though a rare early onset familial type is linked to markers on chromosome 17.[8] By comparing figures 8.1 and 8.2, it appears that behavioral disorders on average show greater genetic influence than common medical disorders.

Behavioral dimensions

Data on behavioral variability within the normal range also indicate widespread genetic influence. Figure 8.3 summarizes results of twin studies for personality (neuroticism and extraversion), vocational interests, scholastic achievement, cognitive abilities (memory, spatial reasoning, processing speed, verbal reasoning), and general intelligence. For quantitative dimensions, the size of the genetic effect can be estimated roughly by doubling the difference between MZ and DZ correlations. This estimate is called heritability, which is a statistic that describes the proportion of phenotypic variance in a population that can be attributed to genetic influences. Heritabilities range from about 40 to 50% for personality, vocational interests, scholastic

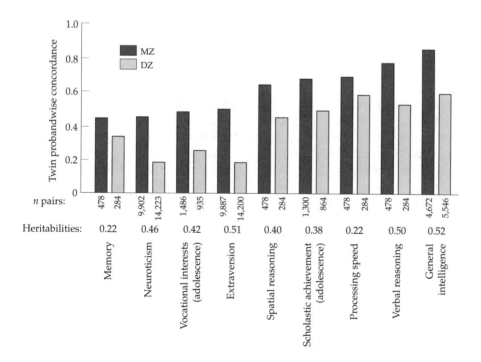

FIGURE 8.3 Identical (MZ) and fraternal (DZ) twin intraclass correlations for personality (neuroticism and extraversion), vocational interests in adolescence, scholastic achievement in adolescence (combined across similar results for English usage, mathematics, social studies, and natural science), specific cognitive abilities in adolescence (memory, spatial reasoning, processing speed, verbal reasoning), and general intelligence. For source of average weighted correlations, see note 62

achievement, and general intelligence. For specific cognitive abilities, heritabilities are also in this range for spatial reasoning and verbal reasoning but lower for memory and processing speed. Recent research also suggests genetic influence for other cognitive measures such as information processing, electroencephalographic evoked potentials, and cerebral glucose metabolism.[9] Examples of recently studied noncognitive behaviors that show genetic influence are self-esteem,[10] social attitudes,[11] and sexual orientation.[12] Little is known about genetic effects for perception and learning and for many health-related behaviors (for example, responses to stress, exercise, and diet).

Beyond heritability

Quantitative genetic research has gone beyond merely demonstrating the importance of genetics for complex human behaviors. Three new techniques are especially useful for this advancement, as can be seen most clearly in research on cognitive abilities, the most studied domain of behavior. First, developmental genetic analysis monitors change in genetic effects during development. For cognitive ability, genetic factors become increasingly important for general intelligence throughout the life span, reaching heritabilities as high as 80% later in life.[13] This is the highest heritability reported for any behavioral dimension. In addition, with longitudinal genetic designs, it is possible to investigate the etiology of age-to-age change – that is, to what extent do genetic effects at one age overlap with genetic effects at another age? For general cognitive ability, longitudinal genetic analyses during childhood suggest that genetic effects do not completely overlap from age to age, indicating changes in genetic effects, especially at the early school years.[14]

A second advance is multivariate genetic analysis, which assesses genetic contributions to covariance among traits rather than to the variance of each trait considered separately. Multivariate analyses of specific cognitive abilities suggest that genetic influences on all specific cognitive abilities overlap to a surprising degree, although some genetic effects are unique to each ability.[15] This finding implies that genes associated with one cognitive ability are likely to be associated with other cognitive abilities as well. Multivariate analyses also indicate that genetic effects on scholastic achievement overlap completely with genetic effects on general cognitive ability.[16] Such techniques can also be used to address the fundamental issues of heterogeneity and comorbidity for psychiatric disorders, contributing to a nosology at the level of genetic effects rather than at the level of symptoms. Longitudinal and multivariate approaches have been facilitated by advances in analysis that test the fit between a model and observed data.[17]

The third example, called extremes analysis, addresses genetic links between normal and abnormal behavior. If, as seems likely, multiple genes are responsible for genetic influences on behavioral dimensions and disorders, a continuum of genetic risk is likely to extend from normal to abnormal behavior. For example, is major depressive disorder merely the extreme of a continuous dimension of genetic and environmental variability? A quantitative genetic technique developed during the past decade investigates the extent to which a disorder is the etiological extreme of a continuous dimension.[18] Preliminary research with this approach suggests that some common behavioral disorders such as depressive symptoms,[19] phobias,[20] and reading disability[21] represent the genetic extremes of continuous dimensions.

Nurture as well as nature

Another way in which genetic research has gone beyond merely documenting genetic influence is to focus on the implications of genetics research for understanding environmental influences. Genetics research provides the best available evidence for the importance of nonheritable factors. Usually genetic factors do not account for more than about half of the variance for behavioral disorders and dimensions. Most of the disorders and dimensions summarized in figures 8.1 and 8.3 show as much nonheritable as heritable influence. The current enthusiasm for genetics should not obscure the important contribution of nonheritable factors, even though these are more difficult to investigate. For environmental transmission, there is nothing comparable to the laws of hereditary transmission or to the gene as a basic unit of transmission. It should be noted that the "environmental" in quantitative genetics denotes all nonheritable factors, including nontransmissible stochastic DNA events such as somatic mutation, imprinting, and unstable DNA sequences.[22]

Two specific discoveries from genetic research are important for understanding environmental influences. First, the way in which the environment influences behavioral development contradicts socialization theories from Freud onward. For example, the fact that psychopathology runs in families has reasonably, but wrongly, been interpreted to indicate that psychopathology is under environmental control. Research shows that genetics generally accounts for this familial resemblance. Environmental influences on most behavioral disorders and dimensions serve to make children growing up in the same family different, not similar.[23] This effect, called nonshared environment, leads to the question of how children in the same family experience such different environments. For example, what are the nonshared experiences that make identical twins growing up in the same family so often discordant for schizophrenia?

The second genetic discovery about the environment concerns what has been called the nature of nurture.[24] Many widely used measures of the environment show genetic influence in dozens of twin and adoption studies. Research with diverse twin and adoption experimental designs has found genetic influence on parenting, childhood accidents, television viewing, classroom environments, peer groups, social support, work environments, life events, divorce, exposure to drugs, education, and socioeconomic status.[25] Although these results might seem paradoxical, what they mean is that ostensible measures of the environment appear to assess genetically influenced characteristics of individuals. To some extent, individuals create their own experiences for genetic reasons.[26] In addition, genetic factors contribute to the prediction of developmental outcomes from environmental measures.[25] For example, genetics is part of the reason why parenting behavior predicts children's cognitive development and why negative life events predict depression.

Quantitative genetics and molecular genetics

Quantitative genetic research is needed to inform molecular genetic research. Most fundamentally, quantitative genetic research can steer molecular genetic research toward the most heritable syndromes and combinations of symptoms. Genes are less likely to be identified for complex behaviors that show little genetic influence in the population unless some aspect of the trait can be found that is more highly heritable, as in the case of breast cancer. Although genetic influence has been detected for many behavioral disorders and dimensions (figures 8.1 and 8.3), little is known about the most heritable aspects within these domains.

Even more useful is quantitative genetic research that goes beyond heritability to take advantage of new techniques mentioned above. For example, developmental genetic research shows that genetic influence increasingly affects cognitive abilities throughout the life span. This suggests that molecular genetic research on cognitive abilities is most likely to be successful later in life when phenotype better represents genotype. Multivariate genetic research indicates that genes associated with one cognitive ability are likely to be associated with other cognitive abilities. The clue here is that molecular genetic research will profit from focusing on what cognitive abilities have in common. Quantitative genetic research suggests that common disorders represent the quantitative extremes of continuous dimensions. This suggests that genes associated with disorders can be found by investigating continuous dimensions and vice versa. Finally, quantitative genetic research suggests that non-genetic factors generally account for as much variance as genetic factors, that behavior-relevant environmental factors generally operate in a nonshared manner to make children growing up in the same family different, not similar, and that genetic factors play a role in individuals actively creating their own experience. Molecular genetic research will benefit from incorporating environmental measures, especially measures of nonshared environment.

MOLECULAR GENETICS

Quantitative genetic research leaves little room for doubt about the importance of genetic influence in behavior. The next step is to begin to identify some of these genes. This is obviously a more difficult step, especially in the case of complex traits, and some of the initial steps in this direction have faltered. However, the difficulty of identifying specific genes underlying complex traits should not obscure the evidence for the importance of genetic influence.

Many rare disorders such as Huntington's disease show simple Mendelian patterns of inheritance for which defects in a single gene are the necessary and sufficient cause of the disorder. Linkage analysis and the rapidly expanding map of the human genome guarantee that the underlying genes will be mapped and eventually cloned, as has already happened for scores of single-gene disorders. The new frontier for molecular genetics lies with common and complex dimensions, disorders, and diseases. The challenge is to use molecular genetic techniques to identify genes involved in such complex systems influenced by multiple genes as well as multiple nongenetic factors, especially when any single gene is neither necessary nor sufficient. Because this challenge is the same for complex behaviors as for common medical disorders, their futures will be intertwined.

One gene, one disorder?

Complex traits that show no simple Mendelian pattern of inheritance are unlikely to yield simple genetic answers. For this reason, it has often been assumed that complex disorders consist of a concatenation of several disorders, each caused by a single gene, or at least a gene of major effect that largely accounts for genetic influence. Indeed, one definition of the word "complex" is a composite of distinguishable constituents. This could be called the one gene, one disorder (OGOD) hypothesis. The OGOD hypothesis is more than a simple single-gene hypothesis. It does not look for a single gene for complex traits, but rather assumes that complex traits comprise several subtraits each influenced by a single gene. Even if single genes corresponding to subtypes of a disorder cannot be found throughout the population, the hope is that by analyzing linkage in large pedigrees, it may be possible to find a single gene responsible for a family's particular version of the disorder.

The OGOD strategy has already been successful for some complex behavioral disorders, especially severe mental retardation. A classic example is the distinct type of mental retardation, phenylketonuria (PKU), caused by recessive mutations in the phenylalanine hydroxylase (PAH) gene on chromosome 12.[27] Although its incidence is low (fewer than 1 in 10,000 births), PKU accounted for about 1% of institutionalized mentally retarded individuals before diets low in phenylalanine were implemented.

Recently, another distinct type of mental retardation was discovered, fragile X, which is caused by an unstable expansion of a CGG repeat in the *FMR-1* gene on the X chromosome.[28] Its incidence is 1 in 1250 males and 1 in 2500 females, making it the single most important cause of mental retardation after Down's syndrome. Another fragile site on the X chromosome has been linked to a less common form of mental retardation.[29] In addition to these defects in single genes necessary and sufficient to develop distinct forms of mental retardation, more than 100 other rare single-gene disorders include mental retardation among their symptoms.[30]

Another example of the success of the OGOD approach for behavior involves a common syndrome, dementia, which is marked by progressive memory loss and confusion. Dementia of the Alzheimer's disease (AD) type includes a rare, familial dementia that appears in middle age, shows a dominant Mendelian pattern of inheritance, but which accounts for fewer than 1% of AD cases. Mutations in the amyloid precursor protein gene on chromosome 21 segregate with the disease in some families with autosomal dominant AD.[31]

The majority of such cases are linked to chromosome 14,[32] although the gene is not yet identified.

An example of a successful OGOD approach outside the cognitive realm of retardation and dementia involves a particular type of violence. A point mutation in the monoamine oxidase A (MAOA) gene, which disrupts MAOA activity, has been linked to impulsive violence in one Dutch family.[33]

The well-known false positive linkage results for bipolar affective disorder and schizophrenia[34] and the more recent failure to replicate reported X-linkage for bipolar affective disorder[35] were caused by procedural and interpretative problems rather than by faults with the analytic technology itself. If a single gene is responsible for genetic influence on a trait, linkage can detect it. Although the entire genome has not yet been screened for linkage with these disorders, it is possible that there are no genes of major effect to be found despite clear twin and adoption evidence for genetic influence. Conventional linkage analysis of extended pedigrees is unlikely to have sufficient power to detect a gene unless the gene accounts for most of the genetic variance. Newer linkage methods such as "affected-relative-pair" linkage designs are more robust than traditional pedigree studies because they do not depend on assumptions about mode of inheritance.[36] These newer methods may be able to detect genes of somewhat smaller effect size if large samples (for example, several hundred sibling pairs) are used. They can also incorporate quantitative measures.[37] Nonetheless, linkages found with these methods imply that a single gene explains most of the genetic effects on the trait, especially if sample sizes are not large.

Two behavioral examples involve linkages reported for sexual orientation and for reading disability. For sexual orientation, linkage has been reported with markers on the X chromosome in a study of 40 homosexual brothers selected for pedigrees consistent with maternal transmission.[38] Reading disability has been linked to markers on chromosome 15 and possibly to chromosome 6 in a family pedigree linkage analysis[39] as well as sib-pair linkage analyses of sibling pairs in these same families,[40] although later reports show less evidence for chromosome 15 linkage.

Quantitative trait loci

Quantitative geneticists assume that genetic influences on complex, common behavioral disorders are the result of multiple genes of varying effect size. These multiple-gene effects can contribute additively and interchangeably, like risk factors, to vulnerability to a disorder. In this case, the word "complex" means "complicated" in the sense of multigenic and multifactorial rather than a composite of OGOD constituents. Any single gene in a multigene system is neither necessary nor sufficient to cause a disorder. In other words, genetic effects involve probabilistic propensities rather than predetermined programming.

Genes that contribute to genetic variance in quantitative traits are called quantitative trait loci (QTL).[41] One implication of a multigene system is that genotypes are distributed quantitatively (dimensionally) even when traits are assessed phenotypically by dichotomous diagnoses. For this reason, the term QTL is apropos for the liability to diagnosed disorders, not just quantitative traits. The term QTL replaces the word "polygenic," which literally means "multiple genes" but has come to connote many genes of such infinitesimal effect size that they are unidentifiable. QTL denote multiple genes of varying effect size. The hope is to be able to detect QTL of modest effect size. "Oligogenic" is another word that has been used as a substitute for polygenic, but it presupposes that only a few ("oligo") genes are involved.

QTL examples have been detected by allelic association, often called linkage disequilibrium. Allelic association refers to a correlation in the population between a phenotype and a particular allele, usually assessed as an allelic or genotypic frequency difference between cases and controls. Allelic association has often been used to pin down a single-gene effect, but it also provides the statistical power to detect small QTL effects, as discussed below. Allelic associations involving small genetic effects in multiple-gene systems could be called QTL associations. The best QTL example for a common medical disorder is provided by the associations between apolipoprotein genes and risk for cardiovascular disease, accounting for as much as a quarter of the genetic variance.[42]

Two recent QTL associations from medical research are especially noteworthy in relation to complex behaviors. A deletion polymorphism in the angiotensin-converting enzyme (ACE) gene is associated with cardiovascular disease independent of effects on lipid metabolism.[43] The frequency of individuals homozygous for the ACE deletion was 32% for patients with myocardial infarction and 27% for controls. This slightly increased relative risk of 1.3, which accounts for less than 1% of the liability for the disorder, is significant statistically because the sample was extremely large (610 cases and 733 controls). The second example involves longevity, which is only modestly heritable. Significant associations with longevity have recently been reported for both the ACE deletion and allele 4 of the apolipoprotein E (Apo-E) gene.[44] Allelic frequencies for 325 centenarians differed from 20- to 70-year-old controls for the ACE deletion (62% as compared with 53%) and for Apo-E4 (5% as compared with 11%). Again, these modest allelic frequency differences are statistically significant because the sample size was so large. In addition, Apo-E2 was associated with increased longevity.

The best QTL example for a behavioral disorder is the recently discovered association between late onset AD and Apo-E4.[45] Unlike the rare, early onset, autosomal dominant form of dementia discussed above, the prevalence of AD increases steeply with age from less than 1% at age 65 years to 15% in the ninth decade.[46] The frequency of the Apo-E4 allele is about 0.40 in individuals with AD as compared with 0.15 in control populations. The odds ratio, or approximate relative risk, is 6.4 for individuals with one or two Apo-E4 alleles.[47] The Apo-E4 allele is neither necessary nor sufficient to develop the disorder: many individuals with AD do not possess an Apo-E4 allele, and many individuals with an Apo-E4 allele do not develop AD. It has been estimated that Apo-E4 contributes approximately 17% to the population variance in liability to develop the disorder.[47] Although this is a large effect for a QTL, it is much too small to qualify as a single-gene effect. A linkage study of 32 pedigrees found only relatively modest evidence of linkage for the *Apo-E4* region of chromosome 19.[48] A QTL of this magnitude may be near the lower limit of detection by linkage analysis with realistic sample sizes, as discussed below.

We predict that QTL associations will soon be found for other complex human behaviors. For example, a weak association has been suggested for paranoid schizophrenia in seven of nine studies with the *A9* allele of human leukocyte antigen (HLA), yielding a combined relative risk of 1.6, which accounts for about 1% of the liability to the disorder.[49] Severe alcoholism[50] and other forms of drug abuse[51] have been reported in several studies to be associated with the *A1* allele of dopamine receptor D_2, but the association remains controversial.[52] A QTL association study of general cognitive ability has found two suggestive but as yet unreplicated associations for DNA markers in or near neurally relevant genes.[53] Thyroid receptor – β gene has been associated with symptoms of attention deficit – hyperactivity disorder.[54] However, because this allelic association was found in individuals hospitalized for resistance to thyroid hormone, it is possible that symptoms of hyperactivity were due to the disease itself.

As illustrated in figure 8.4 for mental retardation, both the OGOD and QTL approaches are likely to contribute to the elucidation of the genetic basis of complex behaviors. Although we have emphasized the distinction between the OGOD and QTL approaches, we recognize that in fact there is a continuum of varying effect sizes. The relative contributions of single-gene effects at one end of the continuum and undetectably small effects at the other end are unknown. If genetic effects on complex behaviors are single-gene effects, traditional linkage approaches will detect them. If effects are infinitesimal (for example, accounting for less than 0.1% of the variance), they will never be detected. In the middle of the continuum, QTL of large effect size (for example, genes accounting for 10% of the variance) might be detected by the newer linkage

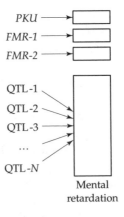

FIGURE 8.4   Complex behaviors such as mental retardation are likely to involve single genes, each responsible for a distinct subtype of the disorder, as well as QTL that contribute probabilistically and interchangeably to genetic risk

TABLE 8.1   Reported linkages and associations with complex behaviors*

Behavior	Gene, chromosome	Note containing reference
Mental retardation		
Phenylketonuria	PAH, 12	(27)
Fragile X-1	FMR-1, X	(28)
Fragile X-E	FRAX-E, X	(29)
Alzheimer's disease		
Early onset, dominant	APP, 21	(31)
	?, 14	(32)
Late onset	Apo-E, 19	(43)
Violence	MAOA, X	(33)
Hyperactivity	Thyroid receptor–β, 3	(54)
Paranoid schizophrenia	HLA-A, 6	(49)
Alcoholism, drug abuse	Dopamine receptor–D_2, 11	(50, 51)
Sexual orientation	?, X	(38)
Reading disability	?, 15	(39, 40)

* Previously published in *Science*, **264** (17 June 1994), pp. 1733–9.

strategies. In the example of *Apo-E* and AD, linkage analysis suggested the possibility of a gene in this region of chromosome 19, and association analysis identified the gene. QTL of small effect size (for example, genes accounting for 1% of the variance) cannot be detected by linkage. Allelic association can detect such QTL, as in the example of *ACE* and myocardial infarction.

Of the few loci that have been implicated to date for complex behaviors (table 7.1), most are genes of major effect rather than QTL, especially the indisputable linkages for PKU, fragile X, and early onset, dominant dementia. This may be the result of reliance on linkage approaches that are only able to detect genes of major effect. The replicated association between *Apo-E4* and AD makes it likely that more systematic association studies will be undertaken to identify QTL with modest effects on complex behaviors.

Allelic association

The advantage of linkage approaches is that they can identify genes without a priori knowledge of pathological processes in a systematic search of the genome by using a few hundred highly polymorphic DNA markers. Such systematic screens of the genome can also exclude the presence of genes of major effect. However, they cannot exclude small QTL effects, at least when realistic sample sizes are used. We predict that failure to find major gene effects by exclusion mapping for complex behaviors will by default provide the best evidence for QTL. The disadvantage of traditional linkage designs is that they are only able to detect single genes or genes largely responsible for the trait.

Although linkage remains the strategy of choice for detecting single-gene effects and for identifying the largest QTL effects, other strategies are needed to detect QTL of smaller effect size. Most likely, new techniques will soon be developed to reach this goal. For the present, allelic association represents an increasingly used strategy that is complementary to linkage.[55] Allelic association can provide the statistical power needed to detect QTL of small effect size. As in the examples of allelic associations between myocardial infarction and the *ACE* deletion polymorphism and between longevity and *ACE* and *Apo-E*, statistical power can be increased to detect small QTL associations by increasing sample sizes of relatively easy-to-obtain unrelated subjects. Such small QTL effects could not be detected by linkage analysis with realistic sample sizes.

As noted above, allelic association refers to a correlation between a phenotype and a particular allele in the population. Loose linkage between two loci does not result in allelic associations in the population because alleles on the same chromosome at all but the tightest linked loci are separated by recombination with sufficient frequency that both sets of alleles quickly return to linkage equilibrium in the population. When allelic association depends on linkage disequilibrium between a DNA marker and the trait locus, the marker must be very close to the trait locus and both must have low rates of mutation. For example, when the marker and trait locus are separated by about one million base pairs (that is, a recombination fraction of 0.01), an allelic association would return halfway to equilibrium in about 70 generations or about 2000 years.[56] For this reason, allelic association research on complex traits can use markers in or near relevant genes, because the markers are likely to be in linkage disequilibrium with any functional polymorphism in the gene.

Linkage disequilibrium is not the only cause of allelic association between a marker and a trait. Allelic association can also occur because the marker itself codes for a functional polymorphism that directly affects the phenotype (pleiotropy). Use of such functional polymorphisms greatly enhances the power of the allelic association approach to detect QTL.[57] It is noteworthy that both the *Apo-E4* and *ACE* deletion markers show direct physiological effects. The new generation of complementary DNA markers and techniques to detect point mutations in coding sequences are rapidly producing markers of this type.

Another distinction between linkage and allelic association involves the issue of dimensions and disorders. As mentioned earlier, complex behaviors in multigene systems are likely to be distributed as continuous quantitative dimensions rather than as qualitative dichotomies. Quantitative dimensions cannot be easily analyzed by linkage, which is based on cosegregation between a DNA marker and a disorder, although a newly developed sib-pair linkage technique for use with quantitative measures employing interval mapping is promising.[37] In contrast, allelic association is as easily applied to quantitative dimensions as to qualitative disorders.

Limitations of allelic association analysis include ethnic stratification and chance positive results when many markers are examined. The possibility that an allelic association might be the result of ethnic differences can be investigated by using within-family controls.[58] False positives can best be addressed by replication.[59] The major limitation to the use of allelic association analysis is that a systematic search of the genome would require thousands of DNA markers separated by about 500 kb or less and would detect only QTL with low mutation rates.

Until such massive genotyping is feasible, allelic association will be limited to screening functional polymorphisms or DNA markers in or near possible candidate genes. For complex behaviors, the problem is that few candidate genes are known that are as specific as the apolipoprotein genes associated with cardiovascular disease. Nonetheless, many genes expressed in the brain are likely to make very small contributions to the genetic variance for complex behaviors, which can be detected with large samples. A single very large representative sample could be used to screen functional polymorphisms for a multitude of common behavioral as well as medical dimensions and disorders. Inclusion of sib pairs would permit sib-pair linkage analyses as well as provide within-family control groups for allelic association analyses. Such a sample could serve as a cumulative and integrative resource for QTL allelic association research.

The goal of the genome project is to sequence the entire human genome. However, there is no single human genome. We need to determine the variability of genes between individuals and then to determine how this variation contributes to phenotypic differences between individuals. For complex traits (including behavior), this will be facilitated by a merger between quantitative genetics and molecular genetics.

CONCLUSIONS

Most of what is currently known about the genetics of complex human behavior comes from quantitative genetic research. Twin and adoption studies have documented ubiquitous genetic influence for most reliably measured behavioral dimensions and disorders. More quantitative genetic research is now needed that goes beyond merely documenting the presence of genetic influence. This will guide molecular genetic research by identifying the most heritable domains of behavior and the most heritable dimensions and disorders within domains. New quantitative genetic techniques can also track the developmental course of genetic contributions to behavior, identify genetic heterogeneity, and explore genetic links between the normal and abnormal. The same quantitative genetic data that document significant and substantial genetic influence for complex behavior also provide the best available evidence for the importance of nongenetic factors. Possible environmental factors need to be investigated in the context of genetically sensitive designs to follow up on the far-reaching findings of nonshared environment and genetic influences on experience and to explore the developmental processes of genotype–environment correlation and interaction by which genotypes become phenotypes. This research will in turn facilitate molecular genetic attempts to identify specific genes that contribute to genetic variance in complex behaviors. The confluence of quantitative genetics and molecular genetics will be synergistic for the elucidation of complex human behaviors.

ACKNOWLEDGEMENTS

Supported by grant HD-27694 from the National Institutes of Child Health and Human Development. The article benefited from suggestions by J. C. Crabbe, J. C. DeFries, L. Rodriguez, and K. J. Saudino.

NOTES

1. R. Plomin and G. E. McClearn (eds), *Nature, Nurture, and Psychology* (American Psychological Association, Washington, DC, 1993).
2. R. Plomin, J. C. DeFries, G. E. McClearn, *Behavioral Genetics: A Primer* (Freeman, New York, edn 2, 1990).
3. I. I. Gottesman, *Schizophrenia Genetics: The Origins of Madness* (Freeman, New York, 1991). Resemblance for fraternal twins is often greater than for nontwin siblings. This suggests greater shared environment for twins, which may be a result of shared prenatal environment or growing up in the same family at exactly the same age. This does not affect the twin design's test of genetic influence, which compares the resemblance of fraternal twins with the resemblance of identical twins.
4. L. L. Heston, *Br. J. Psychiatry* **112**, 819 (1966).
5. P. McGuffin, M. J. Owen, M. C. O'Donovan, A. Thapar, I. I. Gottesman, *Seminars in Psychiatric Genetics* (Gaskell, London, 1994).
6. Although the size of the difference between MZ and DZ twin concordances suggests the magnitude of the genetic effect, dichotomous concordance data present statistical problems in providing estimates of heritability, the statistic representing the effect size of genetic influence in a population. For this reason, concordances are usually converted to liability (tetrachoric) correlations, which assume that a continuous distribution of liability underlies the dichotomous data (see note 5). Heritability estimates based on liability correlations estimate genetic influence on a hypothetical construct of continuous liability that is derived from a dichotomous diagnosis; it is not the heritability of the disorder as diagnosed. Such estimates of the heritability of liability are often higher than the twin concordance data would suggest. For example, for schizophrenia, some estimates of the heritability of liability exceed 0.80, even though the MZ concordance is less than 0.50. Such high liability heritabilities might be misleading to molecular geneticists searching for specific genes when their research is based on the disorder as diagnosed. As discussed later, there is good reason to believe that multiple-gene influences on complex disorders result in continous dimensions rather than dichotomous disorders. An important research direction that will increase the power of genetics research is to attempt to assess dimensions directly rather than to assume them from dichotomous diagnoses.
7. J. K. Kaprio et al., *Alcohol. Clin. Exp. Res.* **11**, 249 (1987).
8. J. M. Hall et al., *Science* **250**, 1684 (1990).
9. P. A. Vernon (ed.), *Biological Approaches to the Study of Human Intelligence* (Ablex, Norwood, NJ, 1993).
10. R. Plomin, *Social Dev.* **3**, 37 (1994).
11. L. J. Eaves, H. J. Eysenck, N. G. Martin, *Genes, Culture, and Personality: An Empirical Approach* (Academic Press, New York, 1989).

12. J. M. Bailey and R. C. Pillard, *Arch. Gen. Psychiatry* **48**, 1089 (1991); ——, M. C. Neale, Y. Agyei, ibid. **50**, 217 (1993).

13. M. McGue, T. J. Bouchard Jr., W. G. Iacono, D. T. Lykken, in Plomin and McClearn, pp. 59–76.

14. D. W. Fulker, S. S. Cherny, L. R. Cardon, in Plomin and McClearn, pp. 77–97.

15. N. L. Pedersen, R. Plomin, G. E. McClearn, *Intelligence* (in press).

16. L. A. Thompson, D. K. Detterman, R. Plomin, *Psychol. Sci.* **2**, 158 (1991); S. J. Wadsworth, in *Nature and Nurture during Middle Childhood*, J. C. DeFries, R. Plomin, D. W. Fulker, eds (Blackwell, Cambridge, MA, 1994), pp. 86–101.

17. M. C. Neale and L. R. Cardon, *Methodology for Genetic Studies of Twins and Families* (Kluwer Academic, Norwell, MA, 1992).

18. J. C. DeFries and D. W. Fulker, *Behav. Gen*, **15**, 467 (1985).

19. R. Plomin, in *Biological Risk Factors for Psychosocial Disorders*, M. Rutter and P. Casaer, eds (Cambridge Univ. Press, Cambridge, 1991), pp. 101–38.

20. J. Stevenson, N. Batten, M. Cherner, *J. Child Psychol, Psychiatry* **33**, 977 (1992).

21. J. C. DeFries and J. J. Gillis, in Plomin and McClearn pp. 121–45.

22. P. McGuffin, P. Asherson, M. J. Owen, A. Farmer, *Br. J. Psychiatry* **164**, 593 (1994).

23. R. Plomin and D. Daniels, *Behav. Brain Sci.* **10**, 1 (1987).

24. R. Plomin and C. S. Bergeman, ibid. **14**, 373 (1991).

25. R. Plomin, *Genetics and Experience: The Interplay between Nature and Nurture* (Sage, Newbury Park, CA, 1994).

26. D. C. Rowe, *The Limits of Family Influence* (Guilford, New York, 1994); S. Scarr, *Child Dev.* **63**, 1 (1992).

27. S. L. C. Woo, in *Genes, Brain, and Behavior*, P. R. McHugh and V. A. McKusick, eds (Raven, New York, 1991), pp. 193–203.

28. A. J. Verkerk et al., *Cell* **65**, 905 (1991).

29. S. J. L. Knight et al., ibid. **74**, 127 (1993).

30. J. Walhsten, *J. Ment. Defic. Res.* **34**, 11 (1990).

31. A. Goate et al., *Nature* **349**, 704 (1991).

32. G. D. Schellenberg et al., *Science* **258**, 668 (1992).

33. H. G. Brunner, M. Nelen, X. O. Breakefield, H. H. Ropers, B. A. van Oost, ibid, **262**, 578 (1993).

34. M. J. Owen and M. J. Mullan, *Trends Neurosci.* **13**, 29 (1990).

35. M. Baron et al., *Nature Genet.* **3**, 49 (1993).

36. N. Risch, *Am. J. Hum. Genet.* **46**, 229 (1990).

37. D. W. Fulker and L. R. Carbon, ibid, (in press).

38. D. H. Hamer, S. Hu, V. L. Magnuson, N. Hu, A. M. L. Pattatucci, *Science* **261**, 321 (1993).

39. S. D. Smith, W. J. Kimberling, B. F. Pennington, H. A. Lubs, ibid, **219**, 1345 (1993); S. D. Smith, B. F. Pennington, W. J. Kimberling, P. S. Ing, *J. Am. Acad. Child Adolesc. Psychiatry* **29**, 204 (1990).

40. S. D. Smith, W. J. Kimberling, B. F. Pennington, *Read. Writ. Interdiscipl. J.* **3**, 285 (1991); D. W. Fulker et al., ibid, **4**, 107 (1991).

41. H. Gelderman, *Theor. Appl. Genet.* **46**, 319 (1975); E. S. Lander and D. Botstein, *Genetics* **121**, 185 (1989).

42. S. E. Humphries, *Atherosclerosis* **72**, 89 (1988); C. F. Sing and E. A. Boerwinkle, in *Molecular Approaches to Human Polygenic Disease*, G. Bock and G. M. Collins, eds (Wiley, Chichester, UK, 1987), pp. 99–122.

43. F. Cambien et al., *Nature* **359**, 641 (1992).

44. F. Schächter et al., *Nature Genet*, **6**, 29 (1994).

45. E. H. Corder et al., *Science* **261**, 921 (1993).

46. I. Skoog, L. Nilsson, B. Palmertz, L. A. Andreasson, A. Svanborg, *N. Engl. J. Med.* **328**, 153 (1993).

47. M. J. Owen, M. Liddle, P. McGuffin, *Br. Med. J.* **308**, 672 (1994).

48. M. A. Pericak-Vance et al., *Am. J. Hum. Genet*, **48**, 1034 (1991).

49. P. McGuffin and E. Sturt, *Hum, Hered.* **36**, 65 (1986).

50. E. P. Noble, *Behav. Genet.* **23**, 119 (1993).

51. G. Uhl, K. Blum, E. P. Noble, S. Smith, *Trends Neurosci*, **16**, 83 (1993).

52. J. Gelernter, D. Goldman, N. Risch, *J. Am. Med. Assoc.* **269**, 1673 (1993).

53. R. Plomin et al., *Behav. Genet.* **24**, 107 (1994).

54. P. Hauser et al., *N. Engl. J. Med.* **328**, 997 (1993).

55. M. J. Owen and P. McGuffin, *J. Med. Genet.* **30**, 638 (1993).

56. N. E. Morton, *Outline of Genetic Epidemiology* (Karger, Basel, Switzerland, 1982).

57. J. L. Sobell, L. L. Heston, S. S. Sommer, *Genomics* **12**, 1 (1992).

58. C. T. Falk and P. Rubinstein, *Ann. Hum. Genet.* **51**, 227 (1987); J. D. Terwilliger and J. Ott, *Hum. Hered.* **42**, 337 (1992).

59. J. L. Sobell, L. L. Heston, S. S. Sommer, *Am. J. Med. Genet. (Neuropsychiatr. Genet.)* **48**, 28 (1993).

60. Alcoholism: M. McGue, in Plomin and McClearn, pp. 245–68; schizophrenia: I. I. Gottesman, *Schizophrenia Genetics: The Origins of Madness* (Freeman, New York, 1991); Alzheimer's disease: A. L. M. Bergem and E. Kringlen, *Psychiatr. Genet.* **2**, 9 (1991); A. F. Wright, in *The New Genetics of Mental Illness*, P. McGuffin and R. Murray, eds (Butterworth-Heinemann, London, 1991), pp. 259–73; autism: S. L. Smalley, R. F. Asarnow, M. A. Spence, *Arch. Gen. Psychiatry* **45**, 953 (1988); major affective disorder: P. McGuffin and M. P. Sargeant, in *The New Genetics of Mental Illness*, P. McGuffin and R. Murray, eds (Butterworth-Heinemann, London, 1991), pp. 165–81; reading disability: J. C. DeFries and J. J. Gillis, in Plomin and McClearn, pp. 121–45.

61. Parkinson's disease: R. Eldridge and W. A. Rocca, in *The Genetic Basis of Common Diseases*, R. A. King, J. I. Rotter, A. G. Motulsky, eds (Oxford Univ. Press, New York, 1992), pp. 775–91; breast cancer: N. V. Holm, M. Hauge, O. M. Jensen, *Cancer Surv.* **1**, 17 (1982); chronic obstructive pulmonary disease, hypertension, and ischemic heart disease: K. S. Kendler and C. D. Robinette, *Am. J. Psychiatry* **140**, 1551 (1983); rheumatoid arthritis: R. A. King, in *The Genetic Basis of Common Diseases*, R. A. King, J. I. Rotter, A. G. Motulsky, eds. (Oxford Univ. Press, New York, 1992), pp. 596–624; peptic ulcer (diagnosed by X-ray): J. I. Rotter, T. Shohat, G. M. Petersen, in ibid., pp. 240–78; epilepsy; T. D. Bird, in ibid., pp. 732–52.

62. Neuroticism and extraversion: J. C. Loehlin, *Genes and Environment in Personality Development* (Sage, Newbury Park, CA, 1992); vocational interests: J. C. Loehlin and R. C. Nichols, *Heredity, Environment, and Personality* (Univ. of Texas Press, Austin, 1976); C. A. Roberts and C. B. Johansson, *J. Vocational Behav.* **4**, 237 (1974); scholastic achievement: J. C. Loehlin and R. C. Nichols, *Heredity, Environment, and Personality* (Univ. of Texas Press, Austin, 1976); specific cognitive abilities: L. F. Schoenfeldt, *Meas. Eval. Guid.* **1**, 130 (1968); M. Wictorin, *Bidrag til Raknefardighetens Psykologi, en Tvillingundersokning* (Elanders, Göteborg, Sweden, 1952); general intelligence: T. J. Bouchard Jr. and M. McGue, *Science* **212**, 1055 (1981).

Part III

PERCEPTION AND COGNITION IN INFANCY

9

OF HUMAN BONDING: NEWBORNS PREFER THEIR MOTHERS' VOICES*

Anthony J. DeCasper and William P. Fifer

Although this paper was published 20 years ago it remains influential as one of the first demonstrations that newborn infants (within the first three days from birth) prefer to listen to their mother's voice. This has implications for auditory perception in the young infant, and we now know that infants are responsive to speech sounds in the last trimester of foetal life: near-term foetuses can discriminate between male and female voices, and soon after birth they will show a preference for sounds they have heard in the womb (Hepper, 1988, 1997; Lecanuet et al., 1993). Recent findings suggest remarkable auditory and speech perception abilities in the young infant: two-day-old infants can even discriminate between their native and a foreign language – they prefer to listen to their native tongue! (Moon et al., 1993). An up-to-date account of auditory and visual perception in the foetus and infant is to be found in Slater, 1998.

EDITORS' INTRODUCTION

REFERENCES

Hepper, P. G. (1988). Fetal 'soap' addiction. *Lancet*, **1**, 1147–8.
Hepper, P. G. (1997). Memory in utero. *Developmental Medicine and Child Neurology*, **39**, 343–5.
Lecanuet, J-P., Granier-Deferre, C., Jacquet, A-Y., Capponi, I., and Ledru, L. (1993). Prenatal discrimination of a male and female voice uttering the same sentence. *Early Development and Parenting*, **2**, 217–28.
Moon, C., Cooper, R. P., and Fifer, W. P. (1993). Two-day-olds prefer their native language. *Infant Behavior and Development*, **16**, 495–500.
Slater, A. (ed.) (1998). *Perceptual Development: Visual, Auditory and Speech Perception*, Psychology Press.

* Previously published in *Science*, **208** (6 June 1980), pp. 1174–6.

OVERVIEW   By sucking on a nonnutritive nipple in different ways, a newborn human could produce either its mother's voice or the voice of another female. Infants learned how to produce the mother's voice and produced it more often than the other voice. The neonate's preference for the maternal voice suggests that the period shortly after birth may be important for initiating infant bonding to the mother.

Human responsiveness to sound begins in the third trimester of life and by birth reaches sophisticated levels,[1] especially with respect to speech.[2] Early auditory competency probably subserves a variety of developmental functions such as language acquisition[1,3] and mother–infant bonding.[4,5] Mother–infant bonding would best be served by (and may even require) the ability of a newborn to discriminate its mother's voice from that of other females. However, evidence for differential sensitivity to or discrimination of the maternal voice is available only for older infants for whom the bonding process is well advanced.[6] Therefore, the role of maternal voice discrimination in formation of the mother–infant bond is unclear. If the newborn's sensitivities to speech subserves bonding, discrimination of and preference for the maternal voice should be evident near birth. We now report that a newborn infant younger than 3 days of age can not only discriminate its mother's voice but also will work to produce her voice in preference to the voice of another female.

The subjects were ten Caucasian neonates (five male and five female).[7] Shortly after delivery we tape-recorded the voices of mothers of infants selected for testing as they read Dr Seuss's *To Think That I Saw It On Mulberry Street*. Recordings were edited to provide 25 minutes of uninterrupted prose, and testing of whether infants would differentially produce their mothers' voices began within 24 hours of recording. Sessions began by coaxing the infant to a state of quiet alertness.[8] The infant was then placed supine in its basinette, earphones were secured over its ears, and a nonnutritive nipple was placed in its mouth. An assistant held the nipple loosely in place; she was unaware of the experimental condition of the individual infant and could neither hear the tapes nor be seen by the infant. The nipple was connected, by way of a pressure transducer, to the solid-state programming and recording equipment. The infants were then allowed 2 minutes to adjust to the situation. Sucking activity was recorded during the next 5 minutes, but voices were never presented. This baseline period was used to determine the median interburst interval (IBI) or time elapsing between the end of one burst of sucking and the beginning of the next.[9] A burst was defined as a series of individual sucks separated from one another by less than 2 seconds. Testing with the voices began after the baseline had been established.

For five randomly selected infants, sucking bursts terminating IBIs equal to or greater than the baseline median (t) produced only his or her mother's voice (IBI $\geq t$), and bursts terminating intervals less than the median produced only the voice of another infant's mother.[10] Thus, only one of the voices was presented, stereophonically, with the first suck of a burst and remained on until the burst ended, that is, until 2 seconds elapsed without a suck. For the other five infants, the conditions were reversed. Testing lasted 20 minutes.

A preference for the maternal voice was indicated if the infant produced it more often than the nonmaternal voice. However, unequal frequencies not indicative of preference for the maternal voice per se could result either because short (or long) IBIs were easier to produce or because the acoustic qualities of a particular voice, such as pitch or intensity, rendered it a more effective form of feedback. The effects of response requirements and voice characteristics were controlled (i) by requiring half the infants to respond after short IBIs to produce the mother's voice and half to respond after long ones, and (ii) by having each maternal voice also serve as the nonmaternal voice for another infant.

Preference for the mother's voice was shown by the increase in the proportion of IBIs capable of producing her voice; the median IBIs shifted from their baseline values in a direction that produced the maternal voice more than half the time. Eight of the ten medians were shifted in a direction of the maternal voice (mean = 1.90 seconds, a 34 percent increase) (sign test, $P = .02$), one shifted in the direction that produced the nonmaternal voice more often, and one median did not change from its baseline value (figure 9.1).

If these infants were working to gain access to their mother's voice, reversing the response requirements should result in a reversal of their IBIs. Four infants,

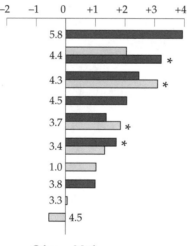

FIGURE 9.1 For each subject, signed difference scores between the median IBIs without vocal feedback (baseline) and with differential vocal feedback (session 1). Differences of the four reversal sessions (*) are based on medians with differential feedback in sessions 1 and 2. Positive values indicate a preference for the maternal voice, and negative values a preference for the nonmaternal voice. Filled bars indicate that the mother's voice followed IBIs of less than the baseline median, open bars indicate that her voice followed intervals equal to or greater than the median. Median IBIs of the baseline (in seconds) are shown opposite the bars

two from each condition, who produced their mother's voice more often in session 1 were able to complete a second session 24 hours later, in which the response requirements were reversed.[11] Differential feedback in session 2 began immediately after the 2-minute adjustment period. The criterion time remained equal to the baseline median of the first session. For all four infants, the median IBIs shifted toward the new criterion values and away from those which previously produced the maternal voice. The average magnitude of the difference between the medians of the first and reversal sessions was 1.95 seconds.

Apparently the infant learned to gain access to the mother's voice. Since specific temporal properties of sucking were required to produce the maternal voice, we sought evidence for the acquisition of temporally differentiated responding. Temporal discrimination within each condition was ascertained by constructing the function for IBI per opportunity: IBIs were collected into classes equal to one-fifth the baseline median, and the frequency of each class was divided by the total frequency of classes having equal and larger values.[12] When IBIs less than the baseline median were required, the likelihood of terminating interburst intervals was highest for classes less than the median (figure 9.2), whereas when longer intervals were required, the probability of terminating an IBI was maximal for intervals slightly longer than the median. Feedback from the maternal voice effectively differentiated the temporal character of responding that produced it: the probability of terminating IBIs was highest when termination resulted in the maternal voice.

Repeating the experiment with 16 female neonates and a different discrimination procedure confirmed their preference for the maternal voice.[13] The discriminative stimuli were a 400-Hz tone of 4 seconds duration (tone) and a 4-second period of silence (no tone). Each IBI contained an alternating sequence of tone–no-tone periods, and each stimulus was equally likely to begin a sequence. For eight infants, a sucking burst initiated during a tone period turned off the tone and produced the Dr Seuss story read by the infant's

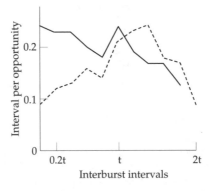

FIGURE 9.2 Interburst interval per opportunity when the maternal voice followed intervals less than the baseline median (solid line) and intervals equal to or greater than the median (dashed line). The IBIs are represented on the abscissa by the lower bound of interval classes equal to one-fifth the baseline median (t)

mother, whereas sucking bursts during a no-tone period produced the non-maternal voice. The elicited voice remained until the sucking burst ended, at which time the tone–no-tone alternation began anew. The discriminative stimuli were reversed for the other eight neonates. Testing with the voices began immediately after the 2-minute adjustment period and lasted 20 minutes. Each maternal voice also served as a nonmaternal voice.

During the first third of the testing session, the infants were as likely to suck during a stimulus period correlated with the maternal voice as during one correlated with the nonmaternal voice (table 9.1). However, in the last third of the session the infants sucked during stimulus periods associated with their mother's voice approximately 24 percent more often than during those associated with the nonmaternal voice, a significant increase $[F(1, 14) = 8.97, P < .01]$. Thus, at the beginning of testing there was no indication of stimulus discrimination or voice preference. By the end of the 20-minute session, feedback from the maternal voice produced clear evidence of an auditory discrimination; the probability of sucking during tone and no-tone periods was greater when sucking produced the maternal voice.

The infants in these studies lived in a group nursery; their general care and night feedings were handled by a number of female nursery personnel. They were fed in their mothers' rooms by their mothers at 9:30 a.m. and at 1:30, 5:00, and 8:30 p.m. At most, they had 12 hours of postnatal contact with their mothers before testing. Similarly reared infants prefer the human voice to other acoustically complex stimuli.[14] But, as our data show, newborns reared in group nurseries that allow minimal maternal contact can also discriminate between their mothers and other speakers and, moreover, will work to produce their mothers' voices in preference to those of other females. Thus, within the first 3 days of postnatal development, newborns prefer the human voice, discriminate between speakers, and demonstrate a preference for their mothers' voices with only limited maternal exposure.

The neonate's capacity to rapidly acquire a stimulus discrimination that controls behavior[15] could provide the means by which limited postnatal experience with the mother results in preference for her voice. The early preference demonstrated here is possible because newborns have auditory competencies adequate for discriminating individual speakers: they are sensitive to rhythmicity,[16] intonation,[17] frequency variation,[1,13] and phonetic

TABLE 9.1 Mean ($\bar{X}$) and standard deviation (S.D.) of the relative frequency of sucking during a stimulus associated with the maternal voice divided by the relative frequency of sucking during a stimulus associated with the nonmaternal voice. A ratio of 1.0 indicates no preference

Stimulus associated with maternal voice	First third		Last third	
	$\bar{X}$	S.D.	$\bar{X}$	S.D.
Tone	0.97	0.33	1.26	0.33
No tone	1.04	0.31	1.22	0.19
Combined	1.00	0.32	1.24	0.27

components of speech.[18] Their general sensory competency may enable other maternal cues, such as her odor[19] and the manner in which she handles her infant,[20] to serve as supporting bases for discrimination and vocal preference. Prenatal (intrauterine) auditory experience may also be a factor. Although the significance and nature of intrauterine auditory experience in humans is not known, perceptual preferences and proximity-seeking responses of some infrahuman infants are profoundly affected by auditory experience before birth.[21]

ACKNOWLEDGEMENTS

Supported by Research Council grant 920. We thank the infants, their mothers, and the staff of Moses Cane Hospital, where this work was performed, and A. Carstens for helping conduct the research.

NOTES

1. R. B. Eisenberg, *Auditory Competence in Early Life: The Roots of Communicative Behavior* (University Park Press, Baltimore, 1976).
2. P. D. Eimas, in *Infant Perception: From Sensation to Cognition*, L. B. Cohen and P. Salapatek, eds (Academic Press, New York, 1975), vol. 2, p. 193.
3. B. Friedlander, *Merrill-Palmer Q.* **16**, 7 (1970).
4. R. Bell, in *The Effect of the Infant on Its Care-giver*, M. Lewis and L. A. Rosenblum, eds (Wiley, New York, 1974), p. 1; T. B. Brazelton, E. Tronick, L. Abramson, H. Als, S. Wise, *Ciba Found. Symp.* **33**, 137 (1975).
5. M. H. Klaus and J. H. Kennel, *Maternal Infant Bonding* (Mosby, St. Louis, 1976); P. DeChateau, *Birth Family J.* **41**, 10 (1977).
6. M. Miles and E. Melvish, *Nature (London)* **252**, 123 (1974); J. Mehler, J. Bertoncini, M. Baurière, D. Jassik-Gershenfeld, *Perception* **7**, 491 (1978).
7. The infants were randomly selected from those meeting the following criteria: (i) gestation, full term; (ii) delivery, uncomplicated; (iii) birth weight, between 2500 and 3850 grams; and (iv) APGAR score, at least eight at 1 and 5 minutes after birth. If circumcised, males were not observed until at least 12 hours afterward. Informed written consent was obtained from the mother, and she was invited to observe the testing procedure. Testing sessions began between 2.5 and 3.5 hours after the 6 a.m. or 12 p.m. feeding. All infants were bottle-fed.
8. P. H. Wolff, *Psychol. Issues* **5**, 1 (1966). The infants were held in front of the experimenter's face, spoken to, and then presented with the nonnutritive nipple. Infants failing to fixate visually on the experimenter's face or to suck on the nipple were returned to the nursery. Once begun, a session was terminated only if the infant cried or stopped sucking for two consecutive minutes. The initial sessions of two infants were terminated because they cried for 2 minutes. Their data are not reported. Thus, the results are based on 10 of 12 infants meeting the behavioral criteria for entering and remaining in the study.
9. With quiet and alert newborns, nonnutritive sucking typically occurs as bursts of individual sucks, each separated by a second or so, while the bursts themselves are separated by several seconds or more. Interburst intervals tend to be unimodally

distributed with modal values differing among infants. [K. Kaye, in *Studies in Mother–Infant Interaction*, H. R. Schaffer, ed. (Academic Press, New York, 1977)]. A suck was said to occur when the negative pressure exerted on the nipple reached 20 mm-Hg. This value is almost always exceeded during nonnutritive sucking by healthy infants, but is virtually never produced by nonsucking mouth movement.

10. The tape reels revolved continuously, and one or the other of the voices was electronically switched to the earphones when the response threshold was met. Because the thresholds were detected electronically, voice onset occurred at the moment the negative pressure reached 20 mm-Hg.

11. Two infants were not tested a second time, because we could not gain access to the testing room, which served as an auxilliary nursery and as an isolation room. The sessions of two infants who cried were terminated. Two other infants were tested a second time, but in their first session one had shown no preference and the other had shown only a slight preference for the nonmaternal voice. Their performance may have been affected by inconsistent feedback. Because their peak sucking pressures were near the threshold of the apparatus, very similar sucks would sometimes produce feedback and sometimes not, and sometimes feedback would be terminated in the midst of a sucking burst. Consequently, second session performances of these two infants, which were much like their initial performances, were uninterpretable.

12. D. Anger, *J. Exp. Psychol.* **52**, 145 (1956).
13. Three other infants began testing with the voices, but their sessions were terminated because they cried. Their data are not included. This study is part of a doctoral thesis submitted by W.P.F.
14. E. Butterfield and G. Siperstein, in *Oral Sensation and Perception: The Mouth of the Infant*, J. Bosma, ed. (Thomas, Springfield, Ill., 1972).
15. E. R. Siqueland and L. P. Lipsitt, *J. Exp. Child. Psychol.* **3**, 356 (1966); R. E. Kron, in *Recent Advances in Biological Psychiatry*, J. Wortis, ed. (Plenum, New York, 1967), p. 295.
16. W. S. Condon and L. W. Sander, *Science* **183**, 99 (1974).
17. R. B. Eisenberg, D. B. Cousins, N. Rupp, *J. Aud. Res.* **7**, 245 (1966); P. A. Morse, *J. Exp. Child. Psychol.* **14**, 477 (1972).
18. E. C. Butterfield and G. F. Cairns, in *Language Perspectives: Acquisition, Retardation and Intervention*, R. L. Schiefelbusch and L. L. Lloyd, eds (University Park Press, Baltimore, 1974), p. 75; A. J. DeCasper, E. C. Butterfield, G. F. Cairns, paper presented at the fourth biennial conference on Human Development, Nashville, April 1976.
19. A. MacFarlane, *Ciba Found. Symp.* **33**, 103 (1975).
20. P. Burns, L. W. Sander, G. Stechler, H. Julia, *J. Am. Acad. Child Psychiatry* **11**, 427 (1972); E. B. Thoman, A. F. Korner, L. Bearon-Williams, *Child Dev.* **48**, 563 (1977).
21. G. Gottlieb, *Development of Species Identification in Birds: An Inquiry into the Prenatal Determinants of Perception* (Univ. of Chicago Press, Chicago, 1971); E. H. Hess, *Imprinting* (Van Nostrand–Reinhold, New York, 1973).

10

LISTENING TO SPEECH IN THE FIRST YEAR OF LIFE: EXPERIENTIAL INFLUENCES ON PHONEME PERCEPTION*

Janet F. Werker and Renée N. Desjardins

EDITORS' INTRODUCTION

We have known for some 30 years that young infants are extremely sensitive to small differences in phonemes – the basic units of sound that distinguish one word from another. Subsequent research has revealed that young infants can discriminate phonemes from all of the world's languages, even phonemes that are not used in their own native language. In this paper Janet Werker and Renée Desjardins describe their own, and others' research which has shown clearly that as they get older infants *lose* the ability to make many phonemic discriminations that are not used to differentiate words in their native language! As they put it: 'The biases and proclivities that allow the neonate to detect regularities in the speech stream are, by 1 year of age, exquisitely tuned to the properties of the native language.' By the time infants start to produce their first words they have become 'native listeners'.

REFERENCES

Werker, J. F. (1989). Becoming a native listener. *American Scientist*, **77**, 54–9.
For a detailed account of speech perception in infancy, see A. Slater (ed.) (1998), *Perceptual Development: Visual, Auditory, and Speech Perception*. Psychology Press.

The use of language to share thoughts, ideas, and feelings is a uniquely human characteristic. And to learn a language is one of the biggest challenges of

* Previously published in *Current Directions in Psychological Science*, **4** (3) (June 1995), pp. 76–81.

infancy and early childhood. In order to be successful at this momentous task, the child must break down the speech stream, which consists of highly encoded and overlapping information, into smaller units such as clauses, phrases, and words. A yet smaller unit is the phoneme. Two words may differ by only one phoneme (e.g., *bat* vs. *pat*), yet this difference is enough to convey different meanings. Thus, a critical part of the language acquisition process is the ability to distinguish individual syllables on the basis of minimal differences in phonemes. In this review, we discuss the kinds of initial abilities infants bring to the task of phoneme perception, how these sensitivities are influenced by experience in a particular linguistic community, and whether events that occur during the prelinguistic period help prepare the child for the important task of language acquisition.

MAPPING THE CHANGES IN PHONEME PERCEPTION

Sensitive experimental techniques that were developed in the early 1970s allowed testing of very young infants' speech perception abilities. These techniques revealed that infants can not only discriminate minimally distinctive phonemes, but can also distinguish phonemes from all the world's languages – including phonemes not used in their language-learning environment. In contrast, research with adults, using different techniques, had led scientists to believe that adults cannot readily discriminate all phonemic distinctions that are not used in their native language. Because adults typically perform better than infants at virtually any task given to them, this counterintuitive pattern of results was most intriguing. Our work was designed to explore the age at which experience first begins to influence phonemic perception and the mechanisms that might be responsible for this change.[1]

To explore the counterintuitive suggestion that infants discriminate nonnative phonemes better than adults, we first compared the two groups directly. In order to do this, we needed a procedure that would be adaptable to both infants and adults. The procedure we chose is a category change procedure. In this task, the subject monitors a continuous background of syllables from one phonemic category (e.g., /ba/) and presses a button to signal when the stimuli change to a contrasting phonemic category (e.g., /da/). Correct button-presses are reinforced with the presentation of a flashing light (as feedback for older children and adults) or an electronically activated animal (as a reward for younger children). Incorrect button-presses are not reinforced, and misses are not signaled.

In the infant version of this procedure, called the conditioned head turn task, the infant sits on the parent's lap facing an experimental assistant who maintains the infant's interest by showing toys. The infant is conditioned to turn his or her head toward the sound source when he or she detects a change in the phonemic category (see plate 10.1). Correct head turns are reinforced with the illumination and activation of clapping and drumming toy animals inside a Plexiglas box. In addition, the experimental assistant claps and gives praise and encouragement. As is the case with children and adults, incorrect

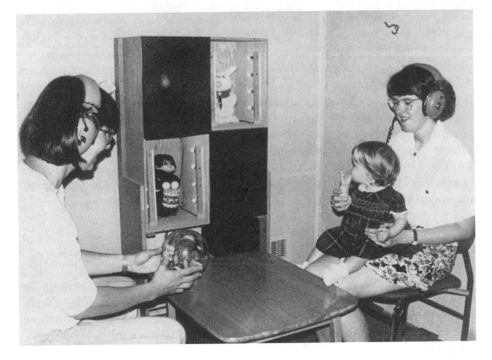

PLATE 10.1   Madeleine performing in the conditioned head turn procedure (photograph courtesy of Steven Heine)

responses are not reinforced. In our laboratory, the criterion for successful discrimination is set at 9 out of 10 correct consecutive responses within a series of 25 trials, approximately half of which are control trials in which no change occurs.

In the first series of experiments, we compared infants and adults on their ability to discriminate two distinctions that are phonemic (i.e., can differentiate words) in Hindi but not in English and one that is phonemic in both Hindi and English. The Hindi-only contrasts were chosen to vary in their potential difficulty. The first contrast, /Ta/–/ta/, involves two phonemes that both sound like *t* to a native English speaker. The difference between them involves where the tongue is placed. For /Ta/, the tongue is curled back and the tip of the underside hits the roof of the mouth. This is called a retroflex consonant. For /ta/, the tip of the tongue is placed against the front teeth. This is called a dental consonant. An English speaker makes a /t/ by placing the tongue against the alveolar ridge directly behind the front teeth. This alveolar consonant is articulated at a place in between the dental and retroflex consonants.

The second contrast was a Hindi voicing contrast that also involves two phonemes that sound like *t* to an English speaker. In this case, the difference involves the timing and shape of the opening of the vocal cords. Hindi /t^h/ and /d^h/ involve a slightly different combination of timing and shape than is used in production of English phonemes. For linguistic and acoustic reasons, this voicing contrast is potentially easier to discriminate than the retroflex–dental contrast.

Subjects were also tested on the contrast between /ba/ and /da/, which is used in both Hindi and English. This contrast served as a control to ensure that the subjects understood (and, in the case of the infants, were willing to perform) the task.

In the first study, done collaboratively with Richard Tees, John Gilbert, and Keith Humphrey, English-learning infants aged 6 to 8 months were compared with both English-speaking adults and Hindi-speaking adults. Virtually all subjects in all groups could discriminate the /ba/–/da/ contrast, and the English-learning infants and the Hindi-speaking adults could easily discriminate both Hindi contrasts. However, the English-speaking adults had difficulty discriminating the Hindi contrasts, and showed particular trouble with the difficult retroflex–dental distinction. A short training procedure (25 trials) was effective in raising the proportion of English-speaking adults who could discriminate the Hindi voicing contrast, but this amount of training did not improve adult performance on the retroflex–dental distinction.

This experiment confirmed what many researchers had expected. Testing using comparable procedures verified that infants discriminate nonnative phoneme contrasts better than adults. But we had no idea as to the age in development when the performance decrement occurs. An influential view at the time was Lenneberg's hypothesis that there is a "critical period" for language acquisition up to the onset of puberty. Extrapolating from this hypothesis led us to test children on the verge of adolescence, as well as two younger age groups. To our surprise, the results indicated that English-speaking children 12, 8, and even 4 years old perform as poorly as English-speaking adults on the Hindi contrasts not used in English. This effect was evident even though the 4-year-old children could easily discriminate the English contrast, and even though Hindi-learning children of age 4 discriminated both Hindi contrasts successfully when tested with the same procedure.

These results showing that language experience affects phoneme perception by age 4 led to additional tests of children between 6 months and 4 years old. A series of pilot tests led to a focus on the first year of life.

Infants between 6 and 12 months of age were tested on the difficult retroflex–dental contrast taken from Hindi, as well as on a new contrast taken from a Native Canadian language, Nthlakampx (one of the Interior Salish languages). The new contrast, glottalized velar /k'/ versus glottalized uvular /q'/, involves a difference in the position of the tongue in the back part of the vocal tract. English listeners hear these two sounds as "funny" ks. We found that although English-learning infants aged 6 to 8 months can discriminate both of these contrasts with ease, infants of 10 to 12 months, like English-speaking adults, fail to discriminate the difference in either non-English contrast. The same pattern of results was replicated in a study in which the same infants were tested at 6 to 8, 8 to 10, and 10 to 12 months of age. Thus, it appeared that the change occurs between 6 and 12 months of age.

In a final manipulation, we tested a small number of 11- to 12-month-old infants who were being exposed to either Hindi or Nthlakampx in the home. Infants in each language group discriminated the contrast from their native language with ease, confirming that the change between 6 and 12 months reflects language-specific experience and is not just an age-related decrement in performance on difficult contrasts.

In a subsequent study, we tested English-learning infants using synthetically produced stimuli that varied in equal steps along a continuum from bilabial / ba/ to dental /da/ to retroflex /Da/. We found that English-learning infants aged 6 to 8 months can group stimuli according to the English boundary between labial and dental stimuli, and according to the Hindi boundary between retroflex and dental, but not according to an arbitrary boundary location that does not correspond to any known phonemic category. English-learning infants aged 10 to 12 months can group only according to the bilabial–dental boundary. These results confirm that the sensitivities shown by young infants prior to language-specific tuning are not arbitrary, but rather conform to potential phonemic categories. Also, with these synthetic stimuli, we replicated our finding that language-general perception shifts to language-specific perception between 6 and 12 months of age.

More recently, Best and colleagues replicated this finding with both the Nthlakampx /k'/–/q'/ contrast and three contrasts from the Zulu language that are not used in English.[2] Best found that infants 6 to 8 months old could discriminate nonnative contrasts, whereas infants 10 to 12 months old could not. These findings are of particular interest as Best used a habituation–dishabituation looking procedure,[3] rather than the conditioned head turn procedure. Taken together, these replications with new phonemic contrasts and different testing procedures provide strong confirmation that listening experience brings about a change in nonnative consonant perception within the first year of life.

How to Explain this Pattern of Results?

One possible explanation to account for these results is that phoneme sensitivities that exist in the young infant will be maintained only if those phonemes are present in the language input (a maintenance/loss view). Without such experience, the infant will lose the ability to discriminate those phonemes permanently. Originally, we thought the loss was tied to events at the level of neuronal functioning. However, a series of experiments with adults convinced us that this explanation was not adequate. Specifically, we found that adult performance varied as a function of the testing conditions. Under conditions that match the demands required in natural language use, adults fail to discriminate the nonnative contrasts. However, when memory demands are minimized (via a shortened interstimulus interval), or uncertainty is diminished (via practice or training), adults show a continued sensitivity even to the most difficult nonnative phoneme distinctions. For this reason, we began to refer to the age-related change in cross-language perception as a reorganization rather than a loss. We assumed the reorganization resulted in a restructuring of initial sensitivities to map on to those required to contrast meaning in the native language.

Recently, Best has developed a model that predicts how listeners will perceive nonnative phoneme contrasts on the basis of how those contrasts map on to the sound system of the native language. According to her perceptual assimilation model (PAM), English-learning infants 10 to 12 months old fail to discriminate the retroflex–dental distinction because retroflex and dental *t* are assimilated to a single phonemic category in English. Nonnative phonemes that fall into two different English phonemic categories may be easier to discriminate. Finally, if the two nonnative phonemes are completely unlike any sounds used in the native language, there should be no pressure for reorganization, and high levels of discrimination should be maintained.[4]

To test this model, Best, McRoberts, and Sithole used a series of clicks from the Zulu language.[4] These clicks are not recognizable as speech to native English speakers. In one such contrast, [||]–[|||], the first click sounds to an English speaker like a "tsk-tsk" of disapproval, and the second sounds something like the click used to make a horse move faster. Consistent with their predictions, Best and her colleagues found that English-learning infants of all ages and English-speaking adults discriminate this contrast easily. However, Best has shown that other Zulu contrasts that can be assimilated into English phonemic categories pattern like the consonants in our previous work: they are easily discriminated by young infants, but not by English-learning infants of 10 to 12 months or by English-speaking adults.

Recently completed research in our laboratory has shown that similarity to native language sounds is not the only factor influencing reorganization. Pegg tested infants on their ability to discriminate two variants of a single phonemic category (allophones) that occur systematically in the English language but are not used to distinguish meaning.[5] The allophones she tested can be illustrated by the phonetic difference between "the stalls" and "these dolls." Both the [t] in *stall* and the [d] in *doll* sound like the English phoneme /d/; however, there are subtle differences that are discriminable to adults and that may help listeners find word boundaries. Pegg found that many English-learning infants 6 to 8 months old are sensitive to these subtle differences and can distinguish the two allophones. Infants 10 to 12 months old, however, cannot. The performance of the older infants suggests that exposure to a systematic difference in speech sounds is not enough to maintain discriminability. Apparently, it is necessary that the distinction be used to contrast meaning in the native language.

New Directions

The work we have discussed so far focused exclusively on consonant perception. An area of current interest is whether experience affects vowel perception similarly. There are several reasons why vowel perception might pattern differently. Vowels carry paralinguistic information concerning the speaker's identity, emotional tone, and pragmatic context in addition to carrying specifically phonemic information. Thus, very young infants may listen to vowels for their prosodic as well as for their phonemic information. Also, the boundaries between vowel categories are less rigid than the boundaries between consonant categories: both adults and infants can discriminate "within-category" differences better for vowels than for consonants. Finally, discrimination of nonnative vowel contrasts is typically easier than is discrimination of nonnative consonant contrasts.

In an early study of cross-language vowel perception in infancy, Trehub reported that English-learning infants aged 5 to 17 weeks discriminated a French vowel contrast that is not used in English, thus showing the same pattern of language-general sensitivity in vowel perception as has been shown for consonant perception.[6] In recent work, Kuhl and colleagues showed there are language-specific influences on the internal structure of vowel categories by 6 months of age in both Swedish- and English-learning infants.[7] This finding suggests that language-specific experience might affect vowel perception at a younger age than it affects consonant perception. However, because Kuhl's research involved testing infants' ability to generalize to other exemplars within a single vowel category rather than to discriminate across two phonemic vowel categories, it is not analogous to the studies of consonant perception.

To compare vowel and consonant perception directly, Polka and Werker tested English-learning infants and English-speaking adults on their ability to discriminate two German vowel contrasts.[8] Each pair contrasted a "high, front, rounded" with a "high, back, rounded" German vowel in a "d-VOWEL-t" context. For example, in one pair, the vowel in "boot" (high, back, rounded) was contrasted with a German vowel produced like the vowel in "beet" but with the lips rounded (high, front, rounded). Pretesting with adults showed that although these distinctions are not phonemic in English, they are relatively easy for English-speaking adults to discriminate. All subjects were also tested on an English contrast (/dit/ vs. /dat/) to make sure they could perform the task.

Using two different procedures to test English-learning infants from 4 to 12 months of age, we found that the effects of experience begin earlier for vowels than for consonants, but that experiential influences continue to be seen up to 10 to 12 months of age. Infants aged 4 months performed better than infants aged 6 months on the German contrast when tested in a habituation–dishabituation looking procedure (a procedural change necessary for testing younger infants). When tested in the conditioned head turn procedure, infants aged 6 to 8 months performed significantly better than the 10- to 12-month-old infants, but not as well as 6- to 8-month-old infants typically perform on nonnative consonant contrasts (see figure 10.1).

This study suggests that vowel perception is like consonant perception, but that experience begins to influence initial language-general capabilities at an earlier age for vowels than for consonants. However, as this is the first cross-language study of this type that has been reported using vowels, additional research is required before we can be confident about the results. Indeed, there are some reports that vowel perception may initially be organized quite differently than consonant perception, and that the effects of experience may not always be as pronounced for vowel perception as they are for consonant perception.[9]

It is important to note that researchers have begun to investigate whether experience affects other aspects of language processing in addition to phoneme

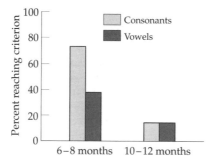

FIGURE 10.1   Percentage of infants reaching criterion in the conditioned head turn procedure. Results are shown separately for 6- to 8-month-old infants and for 10- to 12-month-old infants. The consonant data (see note 1) represent the average of two consonant contrasts, one Hindi and one Nthlakampx. The vowel data (see note 8) represent the average of two German vowel contrasts.

perception. Although it is beyond the scope of this article to review this burgeoning literature, it seems that infants become increasingly sensitive to many aspects of the native language, including stress pattern, rules for sequencing sounds, and cues to word boundaries.[10] Indeed, infants may show sensitivity to the global prosody of the native language within the first few days after birth.[11] Finally, there is evidence that babbling changes across the first year of life to reflect the characteristics and distribution of sounds used in the native language.[12] An exciting question is how all these capabilities come together to prepare the child to move on to the task of word learning.

SUMMARY

During the first year of life, long before uttering his or her first words, an infant makes remarkable progress toward mastering the sound structure of the native language. The biases and proclivities that allow the neonate to detect regularities in the speech stream are, by 1 year of age, exquisitely tuned to the properties of the native language. Our work documents the infant's movement from universal to language-specific phoneme perception. What we have described, however, represents only a part of the infant's remarkable journey toward becoming a native listener. The challenge for future work is to determine what makes the movement from language-general to language-specific perception possible, and how sensitivity to the various properties of the native language is linked to the functional task of language acquisition.

ACKNOWLEDGMENTS

This work was supported by Natural Sciences and Engineering Research Council of Canada Grant OGP0001103 to J. F. Werker.

Notes

1. For a review of the studies discussed in this introduction, see J. F. Werker, Becoming a native listener, *American Scientist*, **77**, 54–9 (1989).
2. C. T. Best, Learning to perceive the sound pattern of English, in *Advances in Infancy Research*, C. Rovee-Collier and L. Lipsitt, eds (LEA, Hillsdale, NJ, in press).
3. In this procedure, infants' looking time to a visual display is used as an index of their attention to the speech stimuli. During the habituation phase, the infants are familiarized to instances of a single phoneme. Across trials, looking time decreases. A novel phoneme is then presented. If infants are able to discriminate the difference between the novel and familiar phonemes, they show an increase in looking time.
4. C. T. Best, G. W. McRoberts, and N. N. Sithole, The phonological basis of perceptual loss for non-native contrasts: Maintenance of discrimination among Zulu clicks by English-speaking adults and infants, *Journal of Experimental Psychology: Human Perception and Performance*, **14**, 345–60 (1988).
5. J. E. Pegg and J. F. Werker, Infant perception of an English allophone [Abstract], *Infant Behavior and Development*, **17**, 862 (1994).
6. S. E. Trehub, The discrimination of foreign speech contrasts by infants and adults, *Child Development*, **47**, 466–72 (1976).
7. P. A. Kuhl, K. A. Williams, F. Lacerda, K. N. Stevens, and B. Lindblom, Linguistic experience alters phonetic perception in infants by 6 months of age, *Science*, **255**, 606–8 (1992).
8. L. Polka and J. F. Werker, Developmental changes in perception of nonnative vowel contrasts, *Journal of Experimental Psychology: Human Perception and Performance*, **20**, 421–35 (1994).
9. L. Polka and O. Bohn, *A cross-language comparison of vowel perception in English-learning and German-learning infants*, poster presented at the International Conference on Infant Studies, Paris (June 1994).
10. See, e.g., P. W. Jusczyk, A. Cutler, and N. J. Redanz, Infants' preference for the predominant stress patterns of English words, *Child Development*, **64**, 675–87 (1993); P. W. Jusczyk, A. D. Friederici, J. I. Wessels, V. Y. Svenkerud, and A. M. Jusczyk, Infants sensitivity to the sound patterns of native language words, *Journal of Memory and Language*, **32**, 402–20 (1993).
11. J. Mehler, P. W. Jusczyk, G. Lambertz, N. Halstead, J. Bertoncini, and C. Amiel-Tison, A precursor of language acquisition in young infants, *Cognition*, **29**, 143–78 (1988).
12. See, e.g., B. De Boysson-Bardies and M. Vihman, Adaptation to language: Evidence from babbling and early words in four languages, *Language*, **61**, 297–319 (1991); D. H. Whalen, A. G. Levitt, and Q. Wang, Intonational differences between the reduplicative babbling of French- and English-learning infants, *Journal of Child Language*, **18**, 501–16 (1991).

Further Reading

Jusczyk, P. W. (1994). Infant speech perception and the development of the mental lexicon. In *The Transition from Speech Sounds to Spoken Words: The Development of Speech Perception*, J. C. Goodman and H. C. Nusbaum, eds (MIT Press, Cambridge, MA).

Werker, J. F., Lloyd, V. L., Pegg, J. E., and Polka, L. B. (in press). Putting the baby in the bootstraps: Toward a more complete understanding of the role of the input in infant speech processing. In *Signal to Syntax: The Role of Bootstrapping in Language Acquisition*, J. Morgan and K. Demuth, eds (LEA, Hillsdale, NJ).

Werker, J. F., and Tees, R. C. (1992). The organization and reorganization of human speech perception. *Annual Review of Neuroscience*, **15**, 377–402.

11

Pattern and Space Perception in Young Infants*

Darwin W. Muir, Diane E. Humphrey and G. Keith Humphrey

OVERVIEW Research is reviewed which reveals the surprisingly advanced perceptual skills of very young infants and some changes in these capacities which occur early in life; possible mechanisms which may underlie these changes are discussed. Newborns readily turn toward visual, auditory, and tactual stimulation, indicating that primitive localization systems operate at birth. However, their pattern perception appears to be more limited, with the notable exception of certain facial configurations, which may have a privileged status. During the period from 1 to 3 months of life, auditory localization responses decrease substantially from neonatal levels while interest in visual patterns increases; indeed, during this period infants seem to become "captured" by visual stimuli. By 4 months of age, infants turn rapidly and accurately towards off-centered sounds again, as they begin to reach for visible and invisible sounding objects. Between 3 and 4 months of age, they become sensitive to various types of static pattern regularities such as symmetry and other global configurational properties, and to dynamic aspects of faces (e.g. changes in facial expressions). Major structural maturation of the visual cortex at this age may underlie these new levels of auditory–visual spatial integration and pattern analysis abilities.

INTRODUCTION

This review of the development of spatial perception during infancy will update and extend earlier reviews by Dodwell (1983a) and Dodwell et al.

* Previously published in *Spatial Vision*, **8**, 1 (1994), pp. 141–65.

(1987). This early work was conceptualized on the basis of an old division of spatial senses into localizing ("where") and pattern recognition ("what") functions (Held, 1968). This dichotomy is exemplified by the conceptualizations of two functionally independent visual systems developed by Held (1968) and others (e.g. Trevarthen, 1968; Schneider, 1969). The "where" system, based on collicular structures, is specialized for the localizing of stimuli in egocentric space, that is, in relation to one's body. The "what" system, mediated by cortical structures, is concerned with the detailed analysis and identification of patterns and objects.[1] Building on this research, Bronson (1974) proposed a model of visual development during infancy in which he argued that the cortical visual areas were not functional at birth, and for the first month or two of life visual abilities depended on the superior colliculus.[2] Because the superior colliculus contains neurons responsive to visual, auditory, and somatosensory information (e.g. Cynader, 1979), we generalized from Bronson's model of visual development and expected to see reliable orientation responses in newborns to visual, auditory, and tactile stimuli. Sensitivity to the internal structure, or the pattern properties of stimuli, should emerge later, with experience and cortical maturation.

Newborn Perceptual Abilities

Early research by the authors was devoted to understanding sensory orientation in newborn humans in auditory, visual, and tactile modalities. In these experiments, the direction and degree of head and/or eye turning toward the source of stimulation were measured. The procedure consisted of holding the infant in a semi-supine position, centering the infant's head with a visual target, and then removing the fixation target and presenting an off-midline stimulus. Visual and auditory stimuli were presented at a distance of approximately 20 cm from an infant's head; stimulus position on the horizontal plane differed depending on stimulus modality (see below). Reliable head or eye turning toward the target was taken to be evidence of perceptual–motor coordination.

Neonatal spatial responses to auditory, visual, and tactile stimuli

First, it was demonstrated that reliable orienting to a sound source can be elicited in newborns, even within minutes after birth. The auditory stimulus was usually a rhythmic, rattle sound (see Muir and Field, 1979, for procedural details) presented 90 degrees from midline, opposite one ear, for 15–20 seconds or until the infant turned to face toward or away from the sound source. It was found that newborns turned 88% of the time toward the sound source, averaged across a series of studies (summarized in Muir et al., 1989, and shown in figure 11.1). It should be noted that the highest number of correct responses was consistently obtained when visual conflict was eliminated by testing infants in the dark (Muir et al., 1989).

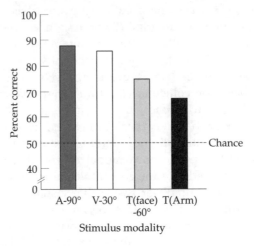

FIGURE 11.1   Percentage of trials in which newborns oriented their heads in the correct direction, toward various laterally presented auditory stimuli (A-90° – a rattle sounded 90 degrees from midline – averaged data from Muir et al., 1989, top section of table 2), visual stimuli (V-30° – a circular red light presented approximately 30 degrees away from the center of the infant's visual field – averaged data from Muir and Clifton, 1985, table 2), and tactile stimuli (T(Face)- 60° – an air puff delivered to the infant's face approximately 60 degrees from midline; T(Arm) – an air puff or a gentle stroking of the infant's forearm – averaged data from Dodwell, 1983a, figure 11.3). In all modalities, directional responding was above chance, but it was lower for tactile stimulation

Next, the auditory localization procedure described above was used to compare neonatal responses to off-centered auditory, visual, and tactile stimulation (see Muir and Clifton, 1985, for procedural details). All testing was conducted in the dark. In three studies, the auditory stimuli were recorded or live rattle sounds presented 90 degrees from midline. The visual stimuli were static, circular patterns of red light (4–6 degree visual angle in diameter) presented approximately 30–45 degrees off midline. Although the within-subject experimental designs and stimuli were not identical in the three studies, the neonates' performance was similar: they turned 86% of the time (averaged across the three studies) toward the visual target (see figure 11.1), comparable to 82% on rattle trials. In one study, infants were also tested with a regular, pulsing, air puff presented to one side of their faces. The experimenter simultaneously squeezed two nasal aspirators, one with its nozzle pointed toward the cheek, approximately 1.5 cm from the corner of the infant's mouth, and the other on the opposite side, pointed away from the infant's head, to balance the non-tactile stimulation on each side. As shown in figure 11.1, neonatal head turning was directed toward the tactile stimulus above chance levels (75% correct). However, when responses to the different stimuli were compared in that study, the air puff elicited significantly fewer head turns in its direction than did the auditory and visual stimuli.

   To explore further newborn sensitivity to lateral tactile stimulation, a gentle stroking or a puff of air was delivered to the forearm's outer surface of 32 neonates (Dodwell, 1983a; D. E. Humphrey, D. Muir, P. C. Dodwell, and G. K. Humphrey, unpublished ms). Tactile stimulation to the forearm is more distal on the body than stimulation of the cheek and perioral region, which normally elicits a rooting reflex in the newborn. Thus, orienting to touch on the arm would demonstrate that the tactile orientation response is more than a simple reflex, as it generalizes to stimulation of parts of the body other than the head. Again, infants turned their heads reliably toward (67%) the side of tactile stimulation, but their responses were not as strong as those to tactile stimulation of the face.

A detailed analysis of infants' responses to touch on the arm revealed a more complex sequence of responses. Typically, when eye, head, and ispilateral arm movement latencies were recorded, an infant first moved the touched arm, followed by a head turn and then an eye movement toward the limb being touched, a proximal–distal action sequence. Also, most babies showed, at least once during the testing session, a response consisting of bringing the hand of the touched arm up to the face in what Trevarthen (1986) described as "self-regulating" gestures, and Brazelton (1980) labeled "self-quieting." Such gestures were only executed by the stimulated arm. The consistency of such a complex, functional response directed toward the site of tactile stimulation may reflect the operation of an early localization ability.

Another spatial response which can be elicited from newborns is an oriented arm movement which Trevarthen (1986) called "prereaching." Two-week-olds exhibit arm movements directed toward small, graspable objects when they are presented at a location within the infants' reach (Bower, 1972; Trevarthen, 1975; DiFranco et al., 1978). While this pre-reaching is spatially coordinated, it does not appear to be sensitive to the 3D quality of objects. In our studies, these responses were very infrequent, and neonates did not display differential responses toward a photograph of a ball vs the real ball, at least according to their reaching behavior (Dodwell et al., 1976; Ruff and Halton, 1978). Neither the frequency nor the components of visually elicited reaching (e.g. hand shaping, extent of the reach, coordination of reaching, and direction of gaze) differentiated between reaching for a ball vs its picture (DiFranco et al., 1978 – see plate 11.1). Of course, the possibility that neonates are responding to 3D cues contained in any 2D picture cannot be ruled out. Although visually elicited arm movements are present in newborns, much development is required before infants actually reach for and grasp 3D objects reliably and accurately at 4–5 months of age, as described later.

Pattern and face perception in neonates

Almost 20 years ago, Goren et al. (1975) reported that 9-minute-old infants visually tracked a schematic facial configuration, as it slowly moved from directly in front of the baby to one side, further than patterns containing the same elements in non-facial configurations – i.e. schematic "scrambled faces." This theoretically challenging result suggests that, despite their poor acuity (Banks and Ginsburg, 1985), infants may possess a "primal" structure for recognizing conspecifics at birth (see Johnson and Morton, 1991). Muir et al.

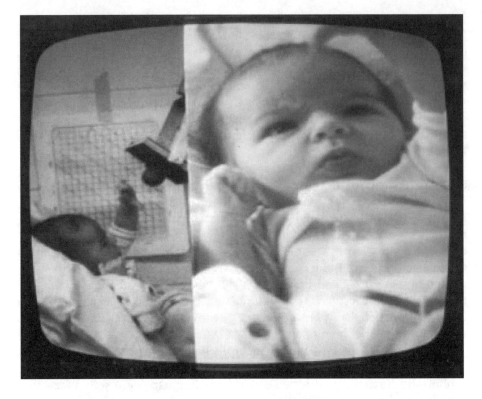

PLATE 11.1   Photographs of video-records from DiFranco et al.'s (1978) study illustrating an instance of a neonate's mature-looking, but infrequent reaching response which involved raising the arm with extended fingers, formed in a well-shaped grasp, toward both the object (on the left) and the object's picture (on the right). This response constituted 48% of the responses displayed by "frequent reachers" in DiFranco et al.

(1977) attempted to obtain a similar preference for facial patterns from 3-day-olds, using a modified procedure and a different set of patterns (shown in figure 11.2). They tested four groups; the performances of matched control groups were compared with those of two high-risk (asphyxiated and growth-retarded) groups of neonates (control ($n = 31$) vs asphyxiated ($n = 19$) groups – see details in Low et al., 1978a, and control ($n = 43$) vs growth-retarded ($n = 31$) groups – see Low et al., 1978b). Muir et al.'s (1977) face, checkerboard, and striped patterns were matched for space-average luminance and presented in random order. Each stimulus was moved from the infant's midline slowly around a perimeter at a distance of approximately 20 cm from the infant's forehead in a 60 degree arc and back again, once to the left and once to the right, or vice versa. The presenter, unaware of the pattern type, scored the degree of visual pursuit on each trial as: 0 for none, 1 for intermittent, and 2 for continuous. Average visual pursuit scores of each group, for each pattern, are shown in figure 11.2. Clearly, infants tracked pattern stimuli farther than the blank field, but none of the groups displayed differential tracking as a function of pattern type. The fact that growth-retarded neonates turned reliably less far than the asphyxiated and control infants gave us confidence that

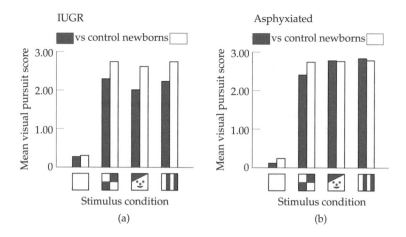

FIGURE 11.2   The average visual pursuit score for neonates presented with the various patterns displayed below each pair of bars, representing (a) performance of intrauterine growth-retarded (IUGR) infants vs non-IUGR neonates, and (b) performance of infants who experienced asphyxia (clinically significant metabolic acidosis, determined by umbilical cord artery blood samples) at birth (asphyxiated) vs non-asphyxiated controls. While group differences were significant for IUGR vs controls, no pattern differences were found except for the patterns vs the blank field

our measure was sensitive enough to differentiate between infants with and without certain major perinatal insults.

Given the lack of pattern preference for facial over other configurations by the infants, and the collective wisdom of the time which suggested that infants would not prefer facial configurations until about 2 months of age (see Maurer's 1985 review), further work on differential responses to visual patterns was abandoned. However, this conclusion was premature. Maurer and Young (1983), attempting to replicate the results of Goren et al. (1975), found that neonates tracked with their eyes a schematic face further than a "severely" scrambled face, but not farther than a "moderately" scrambled face. Although differential head turning was not found, Maurer and Young's results partially confirm Goren et al.'s (1975) findings.

More recently, Johnson et al. (1991 – see also Morton and Johnson's, 1991, review) replicated and extended Goren et al.'s work. After a successful replication they varied the stimuli along several dimensions, attempting to specify which aspects of the facial configuration were driving neonatal attention. For example, they compared the original face and scrambled face patterns with one having only three dark squares in place of the eyes and mouth, and with the same 3-squared patterns rotated 180 degrees. Like Maurer and Young (1983), they found that the degree of head turning did not differentiate between the four stimuli, but eye-turns did. Neonates visually tracked the face pattern further than the scrambled face and inverted squares patterns. However, the difference in visual tracking of the more complete schematic face and the "three-square" face was not reliable. Thus, neonates appear to respond to "faces" at a very "gross" level. Interestingly, Morton and Johnson (1991, pp. 118–19) also reported that infants tracked some non-facial patterns, similar to those we used (Muir et al., 1977), farther than their highly schematic facial pattern, making the current story both complex and incomplete[3] (also see Slater and Morison's, 1993, comments).

DEVELOPMENT OF AUDITORY LOCALIZATION: A U-SHAPED FUNCTION

Given the impressive directional response to off-centered sounds displayed by newborns, the results of classic normative studies which placed the onset of reliable auditory localization responses at 4–5 months of age were perplexing (Muir et al., 1989). To resolve this apparent discrepancy, several longitudinal studies were conducted in which the same infants were assessed bi-weekly (Muir et al., 1979) or monthly (Field et al., 1980) using the neonatal procedure described above. During the newborn period, infants turned their heads toward the sound source reliably (75–100% correct), but slowly (taking about 5–7 seconds to complete a turn), on almost every trial. Their responding remained slow and decreased in frequency and magnitude between 1 and 3 months of age. Then, rather suddenly, they began to respond accurately

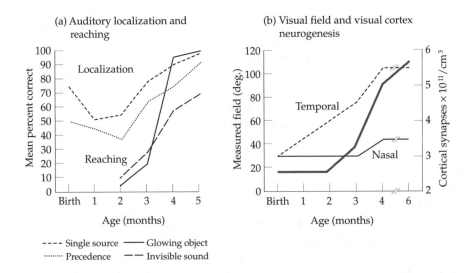

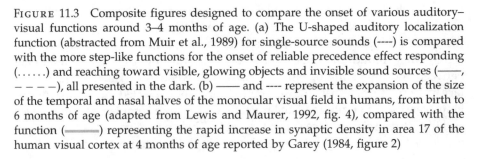

FIGURE 11.3 Composite figures designed to compare the onset of various auditory–visual functions around 3–4 months of age. (a) The U-shaped auditory localization function (abstracted from Muir et al., 1989) for single-source sounds (----) is compared with the more step-like functions for the onset of reliable precedence effect responding (......) and reaching toward visible, glowing objects and invisible sound sources (——, – – – –), all presented in the dark. (b) —— and ---- represent the expansion of the size of the temporal and nasal halves of the monocular visual field in humans, from birth to 6 months of age (adapted from Lewis and Maurer, 1992, fig. 4), compared with the function (▬▬) representing the rapid increase in synaptic density in area 17 of the human visual cortex at 4 months of age reported by Garey (1984, figure 2)

(90–100% correct) and rapidly (1–2 seconds latency) around 4–5 months of age. This U-shaped auditory localization function has been replicated in subsequent studies, including a recent cross-sectional study (Muir et al., 1989) of 84 infants ranging in age from 3 days to 5 months (see figure 11.3a).

Visual interference hypothesis

A number of explanations for this surprising developmental function were considered. For example, perhaps as visual acuity improved over the first few months of life (Banks and Ginsburg, 1985) visual events in the infant's central visual field might absorb the infant's visual attention and overshadow more peripheral events, including the location of an off-centered sound. The existence of a relationship between the development of auditory localization responses and visual attention was confirmed by G. K. Humphrey (unpublished), who examined $2\frac{1}{2}$-months-olds' and $4\frac{1}{2}$-months-olds' visual attention and sound localization responses in the same test session. The auditory task involved presenting a recorded rattle sound 90 degrees left and right of midline for 20 seconds or until the infant made a head turn of more than 45 deg. Visual attention was assessed by presenting infants with a centrally located red and black bullseye pattern for a 2-minute inspection period. The order of the visual and auditory tasks was counterbalanced across infants. As shown in figure 11.4a, the $2\frac{1}{2}$-month-olds rarely turned toward the off-centered sound, and head turns had a very long latency (see small figure next to figure 11.4a), while the $4\frac{1}{2}$-month-olds turned rapidly toward the sound source on almost every trial. The nature of the visual inspection behavior also varied with age. As shown in figure 11.4b, younger infants essentially made one or two very long looks at the pattern, fixating it for an average of 112 seconds during the 120-second trial. By contrast, the bullseye elicited many short looks from $4\frac{1}{2}$-month-olds, who also looked at other targets (e.g. their limbs).

Prolonged visual fixation times exhibited by young infants have been noted by others (e.g. Stechler and Latz, 1966). Results, comparable to ours, obtained by Ames and Silfren (1965; quoted in Gibson, 1969, p. 342) led them to remark that "while the older infant may be capturing stimuli with his visual behavior, the young infant is captured by the stimuli." Our results suggested that this "visual capture" is accompanied by diminished auditory localization responsiveness during the second month of life. Indeed, clear evidence for the dominance of visual over auditory stimuli in directing the attention of 2-month-olds was obtained by Field et al. (1979). They presented 2-month-olds with a dynamic, smiling face and tape-recorded voice separately, or simultaneously from the same or different (spatial conflict) locations 45 degrees from the center of the infants' visual field. Infants always turned toward the visual target on the face-vs-voice, spatial-conflict trials.

These visual fixation studies suggest that once young infants fixate a target, they become captured by the stimulus, but by around 4–5 months of age they readily disengage their visual attention. Johnson (1990) and Johnson et al. (1991) hypothesized that the prolonged fixation seen in the infant from 1 to 2 months may occur because of the maturation of neural pathways that inhibit

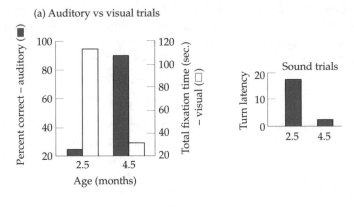

(a) Auditory vs visual trials

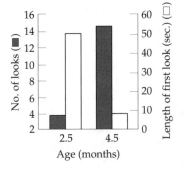

(b) Visual trials

FIGURE 11.4 Composite figures comparing the auditory localization and visual atten-tion behavior of infants $2\frac{1}{2}$ and $4\frac{1}{2}$ months of age. (a) The percentages of correct head turning toward laterally presented sounds at the two ages are shown by filled bars, and the duration of fixation of a bullseye pattern during a 120-second period by open bars. Average response latencies for auditory localization responses of the two age groups are shown in the small, adjacent figure. (b) The number of times infants re-fixated the bullseye pattern after looking away from it during the 120-second period is shown by filled bars, and the length of the first look by the open bars, as a function of age

activity in the superior colliculus. The colliculus plays an important role in eye movements and inhibition of collicular activity may underlie such lengthy fixation. By 3–4 months of age, Johnson suggests that another pathway from the frontal eye fields to the colliculus develops. This pathway is involved in the control of anticipatory eye movements, and may underlie the ability to dis-engage visual fixation.

Age changes in the development of human visual cortex also have been found during the first few months of life. For example, Garey (1984) reports a rapid increase in synapses in the visual cortex when infants are about 4 months of age. His data (abstracted from Garey, 1984, fig. 2) are presented in figure 11.3b to emphasize the parallel timing of visual field expansion, discussed below, and neurogenesis in the visual cortex. More recently, Burkhalter et al. (1993) analyzed the development of local circuits in human visual cortex. They reported that vertical *intra*columnar projections in cortical layers 4B and 5, connecting different points in the visual field, rapidly increase in density from birth to 7 weeks postnatal and form adult-like "blobs" beginning around 8 weeks postnatal. The long-range, horizontal *inter*columnar projections within layer 2/3, emerge around 16 weeks postnatal. Burkhalter et al. suggest "that circuits that process local features of a visual scene [the *intra*columnar connections] develop before circuits necessary to integrate these features into a continuous and coherent neural representation of an image [the *inter*columnar connections – and that] . . . the processing channel for visual motion develops in advance of those that may be more intimately related to the processing of form, color, and precise stereoscopic depth" (p. 1916).

Although the emergence of cortical visual processes may be related to the U-shaped auditory localization function, their actual role in producing the phenomenon is not clear. Intermodal conflict certainly occurs during localization testing in the light, even for neonates (see Muir and Clifton, 1985); however, the presence of conflicting visual input is not sufficient to account for the existence of the auditory U-shaped function. For example, we predicted that 2–3-month-olds given auditory localization tests in complete darkness should exhibit turning towards sound (at least comparable to neonatal performance). However, when infants of this age were tested in the dark, they still made slow, incomplete head-turns and turned in the wrong direction on many trials (e.g. Muir et al., 1979, 1989).

Auditory–visual spatial field integration hypothesis

This explanation involves another aspect of visual processing – the development of an integrated auditory–visual spatial framework which enables infants to perceive the multimodal characteristics of objects in the 3D world. During the first few months of life, a major difference exists in the shapes of the "effective" visual and auditory fields; in other words, in the regions of space over which visual and auditory stimuli can generate an orientation response (Humphrey et al., 1988a). At birth, while orientation towards sounds ±90 degrees from midline is highly reliable, orientation towards sounds within a 45 degree radius of midline is poor (see Muir, 1985); essentially, the effective auditory field may be donut-shaped (rigorous auditory perimetry testing is needed to define its exact shape). By contrast, the effective binocular visual field extends approximately ±20 to ±30 degrees around the midline (Maurer, 1993, personal communication; see review by Maurer and Lewis, 1991). Thus, the two fields appear to have very different extents.

Between 1 and 2 months of age, at approximately the same time as the onset of sustained interest in visual stimuli, discussed above, the temporal visual field begins to expand rapidly and reaches almost adult levels by 4 months of age (Lewis and Maurer, 1992). The nasal visual field expands between 3 and 4 months of age, as plotted in figure 11.3b, after Lewis and Maurer (1992). Thus, these two major shifts in the maturation of visual field size occur at about the same time as the two changes in the U-shaped auditory localization function. Perhaps, during the trough in the auditory U-shaped function, infants reserve their head turning behavior for stimuli within their expanding visual frame of reference, which begins to overlap the neonatal auditory field around 4 months of age.

Neural maturation hypotheses

A classic "cortical maturation hypothesis" was also considered to explain the existence of the U-shaped auditory localization function. McGraw (1943) and others (e.g. Drillien and Drummond, 1977) suggested that as the cortex matures over the first few months of life, it first inhibits subcortically mediated neonatal motor reflexes (e.g. palmar grasp, stepping), and then it directs motor actions in volitional behavior. It was speculated that our infants progressed from turning their heads reflexively towards a sound's general direction, as neonates, to experiencing the sound as an object emanating from a specific location in auditory space (Muir et al., 1979; Field et al., 1980; Muir and Clifton, 1985; Humphrey et al., 1988a).

Three lines of evidence provide indirect support for this cortical maturation hypothesis. First, preterm infants, who were born about $1\frac{1}{2}$ months prematurely and who responded reliably (but with very long latencies – median = 17 seconds) at birth, were correct on 76% of trials when they were tested at full-term (9 months after conception), 40% correct at 3 months post-term, and 91% correct at 6 months post-term. These results suggest that the U-shaped function is dictated by maturational, rather than experiential, factors; if extra-uterine experience was the determining factor, then chance performance should have occurred at full-term, and reliable performance at 3 months post-term.

Secondly, studies have been conducted to compare the developmental course of infants' responses to single source (SS) and "precedence effect" (PE) stimuli, which are thought to be processed at subcortical and cortical levels, respectively. The PE is an illusion produced when identical sounds are played through two loudspeakers, with the output of one delayed by several milliseconds relative to the other. Adults perceive a single sound source emanating from the leading loudspeaker; the suppression of the perception of sound from the lagging loudspeaker (which is related to suppression of echoes in the natural sound environment) depends upon a functional auditory cortex (see Muir et al., 1989, for details). If neonates respond to sound direction using only subcortical processes, they should perceive sounds emanating from both loudspeakers, and might be expected to turn randomly to one side or the other, or not to turn their heads at all, on PE trials. When the cortex matures, around 4–5 months of age, infants should begin to respond to PE stimuli, as they do to single source stimuli.

Muir et al. conducted a cross-sectional study to test these predictions. Infants aged from a few days to 7 months, were presented with SS and PE trials during the same test session. The results are shown in figure 11.3a; as expected, neonates turned correctly toward single sound sources, but failed to turn reliably toward PE sounds. Furthermore, the emergence of correct SS and PE localization responses both occurred around 4–5 months of age. At this age, infants responded faster (1.5–2.5 seconds vs 7–12 seconds when younger), and were much more accurate in pointing their heads towards sound sources at different positions within a hemifield (see Muir, 1985). However, head turning toward the PE target does appear to be slightly inferior at 4 months of age in figure 11.3a, the only age at which there was a statistically significant difference between stimulus conditions. This was because the onset of PE responding by males lagged that of females by 1 month; there was no sex difference in the onset of head turning toward SS sounds. This sex difference parallels one reported by Gwiazda et al. (1989) for visual acuity development. They found no sex difference in the development of grating acuity, but the rapid onset of vernier and stereo acuity between 4 and 6 months of age was 1 month earlier in females than males. Because both stereo and vernier acuity, like the precedence effect, are believed to depend on the functioning of cortical circuitry, it is possible that there is a more rapid development of some aspects of cortical functioning in female than in male infants (see Gwiazda et al., 1989 for speculations on the cause of such differential rates of cortical development).

The third piece of evidence supporting the cortical maturation hypothesis is the coincidence between the time at which the auditory localization response recovers and the onset of a behavior which requires the perception of objects at a particular coordinate position in auditory space. Following Wishart et al. (1978) it was discovered that accurate visually and aurally elicited reaching both emerge at approximately 4 months of age. In a cross-sectional study, Stack et al. (1989) presented a glowing, visible (but silent) object (small wooden egg with fluorescent paint) and an invisible, sounding object (rattle) off midline to infants between 2 and 7 months of age, who were seated on their mothers' laps in the dark. As shown in figure 11.3a, the onset of reliable reaching occurred at 4 months of age, although reaching for the sounding object was not as accurate (more like groping) as the visually elicited reaching. Similar ages of onset of reaching for auditory and visual targets were also found by Clifton et al. (1993) in a longitudinal study of seven infants, tested weekly from 6 to 25 weeks of age.

In conclusion, the relatively sudden appearance of accurate localization responses to both single source and precedence effect stimuli around 4–5 months post-term may reflect a shift from subcortical to the cortical processing of auditory–visual spatial information. The presumed reflexive, directional head turning toward a sound's location, displayed by newborns, may initially be suppressed as cortical structures mature and begin to process spatial information during the infant's second month of life. This appears to be followed by the emergence of a "true" localization response to the sound image's actual location in auditory space, which is reflected by the similar onset times for reliable head turning towards off-centered sounds and reaching for invisible sounds.

DEVELOPMENT OF ABSTRACT VISUAL PATTERN AND FACE PERCEPTION

Cumulative evidence suggests that a major structural maturation of the visual cortex occurs around 4–5 months of age. This is also the age at which infants regain their interest in the location of sounds, suggesting that they are operating within a newly acquired, integrated auditory–visual space. Furthermore, while 1- to 3-month-olds are clearly much more attentive to visual stimuli than newborns, as noted earlier, their visual inspection of a display appears to be more static, when compared with the 4-month-olds' "information-seeking" style of activity in which various elements within a display are sequentially inspected. Thus, we began our studies of early abstract pattern perception using 4-month-olds because their "what" system is clearly operative (see Dodwell et al., 1987, for a review).

Perception of Lie group and Garner patterns

The sensitivity of 4-month-olds to pattern structure can be demonstrated using abstract, "meaningless" patterns. Our technique for studying early pattern perception beyond the neonatal period involved presenting infants with patterns composed of identical elements and varying their configuration, to address the question of whether the infants perceived the global organization of the elements. Generally an habituation procedure was used in which infants were presented, on successive trials, with the same pattern, or the same global pattern made up of different arrangements of the pattern elements. The infants' looking time was measured on each trial, and over trials infants looked less, indicating that they "habituated" to the pattern. After habituation, novel configurations were presented; if looking time increased, a discrimination between old and new patterns was inferred.

Humphrey et al. (1988a, 1988b) habituated separate groups of 4-month-olds to patterns generated from the Lie transformation group model of visual perception (see Dodwell, 1983b), like those shown in figure 11.5. Patterns (a) and (b) have an orderliness or structure lacking in pattern (c). This is because patterns (a) and (b) were generated by a rule that specifies an orientation for each element as a function of its position in the pattern. In pattern (c), the orientation of the elements is random with respect to position. Research with adults has shown that discrimination between such rule-generated patterns is

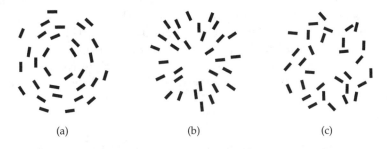

(a)   (b)   (c)

FIGURE 11.5 The vectorpatterns used by Humphrey et al. (1988b) to investigate pattern perception in 4-month-old human infants. Patterns (a) and (b) were generated with regular orientation codes, but with a quasi-random position code. Pattern (c) had both quasi-random orientation and position codes

very acute, but relatively poor for more random patterns (see Dodwell, 1983b; Caelli and Dodwell, 1984). Four-month-olds also perceived the rule-generated patterns differently from the random pattern. After habituation to either of the first two organized patterns (e.g. figure 11.5a), the infants recovered interest to the patterns they had not seen before (e.g. figures 11.5b and c). However, those habituated to the random pattern (e.g. figure 11.5c) did not recover interest to the organized ones (figures 11.5a and b). Possibly, the poorly structured pattern (figure 11.5c) promoted a more local processing strategy (c.f. Vurpillot et al., 1977) and such a strategy could interfere with the perception of a global pattern.

In another study of infants' sensitivity to pattern structure, patterns were generated by another rule-based system. Garner (1974) attempted to devise a system that would capture the Gestalt notion of the goodness of a figure. He defined the goodness of a pattern in terms of the number of different patterns that can be generated from it by the rigid spatial transformations of reflection and 90 degree rotations. The smaller the number of different patterns that can be generated the better he defined the patterns to be. Garner studied dot patterns like those shown in figure 11.6. The top two are "good" patterns because when they are rotated in 90 degree steps in the frontal plane, or reflected about the horizontal, vertical, or diagonal axes, the pattern is the same. The middle two patterns are intermediate (or "medium") in goodness because the same reflection and rotation operations produce four different patterns. The bottom two patterns are "poor" because a different pattern results from each transformation (the number of patterns is eight). Using a variety of tasks, Garner reported that this system of classification predicts adult ratings of pattern goodness, and in information-processing tasks Garner and Sutliff (1974) found that good patterns are processed more efficiently than poor patterns.

Humphrey et al. (1986 – see also, Strauss and Curtiss, 1981; Younger and Gotlieb, 1988) examined infant perception of pattern structure using patterns like those shown in figure 11.6. Separate groups of 4-month-olds were

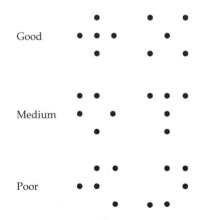

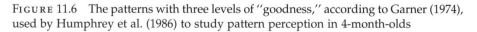

FIGURE 11.6   The patterns with three levels of "goodness," according to Garner (1974), used by Humphrey et al. (1986) to study pattern perception in 4-month-olds

habituated to each of the six patterns. Infants shown the "good" or "medium" patterns habituated more rapidly than those who were shown the "poor" patterns. On test trials, infants habituated to "good" and "medium" patterns recovered interest to a variety of pattern changes, while those habituated to the "poor" patterns did not. Obviously, infants were sensitive to pattern configuration, not just to the elements. We also suggested that infants processed "good" and "medium" patterns more efficiently than "poor" patterns, based on the differences in time to habituate noted above. However, whether processing advantages for "good" and "medium" patterns were due to the ease of perceptual encoding, retrieval, or both, is unknown.

Although the pattern of habituation suggests that well-structured patterns were processed more efficiently than poorly structured patterns, the infants recovered interest on dishabituation trials most reliably to the simple changes in the spatial position, orientation, or size of the patterns. If the novel pattern simply consisted of the habituated pattern at a different position or orientation in the field, or the same pattern enlarged in size, highly reliable increases in looking time were elicited. Indeed, when only configural changes occurred, infants were much less likely to increase their looking time. Thus, although 4-month-olds appear to perceive some aspects of pattern structure, they are most sensitive to the less fine-grained, spatial aspects of the display, which are presumably processed by the "where" system.

Sensitivity to pattern symmetry

The "good" patterns in Garner's system (1974) all have multiple axes of symmetry. In fact, the number of different patterns generated by the reflection and rotation of a pattern is a function of the number of axes of bilateral symmetry it possesses. For example, the "good" patterns in figure 11.6 have bilateral symmetry about the vertical, horizontal, and two diagonal axes. The "medium" patterns have symmetry about one axis, and the "poor" patterns have no axis of bilateral symmetry. Another way to describe these patterns, then, is in terms of the number of axes of bilateral symmetry (Palmer, 1991; but see Garner, 1974). The importance of symmetry in visual pattern perception has long been recognized (e.g. Mach, 1897). Gestalt psychologists emphasized the crucial role symmetry plays as an organizing principle in pattern perception (e.g. Wertheimer, 1938). Also, adults detect bilateral symmetry in otherwise random dot patterns with great efficiency (e.g. Julesz, 1971; Barlow and Reeves, 1979).

Humphrey and Humphrey (1989; also see de Haan and Maurer, 1993) studied the perception of symmetry by 4-month-olds. They used a preference technique to see if increasing the number of axes of symmetry makes it easier for infants to detect symmetry, as it does for adults (Palmer and Hemenway, 1978; Royer, 1981). In each trial, infants were presented with two patterns side by side and looking time to each pattern was recorded. A symmetrical pattern was always paired with an asymmetrical one, as shown in figure 11.7. Patterns with more axes of symmetry should appear more highly structured and attractive. One group of infants were tested with patterns like those shown

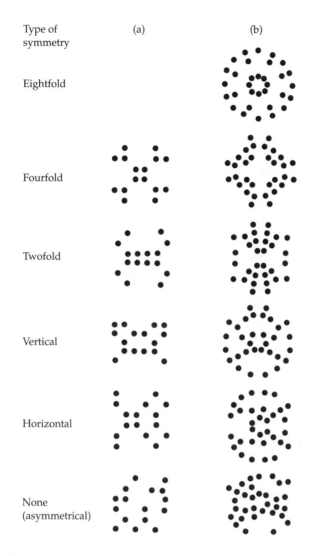

FIGURE 11.7 Examples of the patterns used to study the preference for symmetry in 4-month-olds by Humphrey and Humphrey (1989)

in figure 11.7, column (a); the other group viewed patterns like those in figure 11.7, column (b). The results for the two groups were different in some respects. The infants preferred patterns with multiple axes of symmetry for patterns like those shown in figure 11.7a, but did not show a reliable preference for single-axis vertical symmetry. Infants who viewed patterns like those in figure 11.7b did show a preference for vertical symmetry about a single axis and for patterns with multiple axes of symmetry. The preference for vertical symmetry about a single axis in the latter group was as strong as was the preference for patterns with multiple axes of symmetry. Finally, in both groups, infants never preferred symmetrical over asymmetrical patterns when the axis of symmetry was horizontal.

Generally, then, symmetry is a global configural property of patterns to which young infants are sensitive. Considering single-axis symmetry, it appears that vertically oriented symmetry is an exceptional case in infants, as it is in adults. Bornstein and his colleagues (e.g. Bornstein, 1981; Bornstein et al. 1981; Bornstein and Krinsky, 1985) showed that infants "process" vertical symmetry much more efficiently than symmetry at other orientations. Also, de Haan and Maurer (1993) showed, in an habituation study, that patterns with four axes of symmetry (two diagonals, horizontal and vertical) were not processed any faster than single-axis vertical symmetry (see also Humphrey et al., 1986). Research by Barlow and Reeves (1979) had demonstrated that vertical symmetry is perceived by adults much more efficiently than symmetry at other orientations. The high efficiency with which we detect vertical symmetry led Braitenberg (1990) to suggest that vertical symmetry is an inborn perceptual category. Although it cannot be said whether the perception of vertical symmetry is truly inborn, the results suggest that it is in place by 4 months of age. Several explanations have been given for the high efficiency in detecting vertical symmetry, including the possibility that it depends on a process involving a comparison of homotopic points between symmetrically opposite points in the brain (Julesz, 1971; Braitenberg, 1990; for discussion see Corballis and Beale, 1976, chapter 7).

Sensitivity to dynamic facial configurations

Recently we have looked at infant responses to perturbations in dynamic facial stimuli. We began to study face perception for several reasons. First, we observed that infants continued to be interested in pictures of novel faces we used as controls in our abstract pattern habituation studies, even after habituation (occasionally infants smiled at the face). Pre- and post-habituation presentations of faces were done to ensure that infants' decline in visual interest to an abstract pattern during habituation was not simply due to fatigue (Humphrey et al., 1986). Secondly, Gibsonian theorists, among others, have argued for the need to use ecologically valid, dynamic stimuli in order to engage the perceptual system optimally when we attempt to extract the rules describing its operation. Thirdly, Tronick et al. (1978) conducted a study in which mothers presented a frozen, neutral expression to their 3-month-olds for 2 minutes (called the "still-face" or SF period), interposed between 2-minute periods of normal, face-to-face interactions (which included contingent facial, vocal, and tactile stimulation). The infants' visual fixation and smiling behavior directed at the mothers during the "normal" periods declined dramatically during the SF period (the SF effect). Thus, Tronick et al. (1978) demonstrated that young infants are very sensitive to perturbations of certain "natural" patterns of stimulation.

We replicated and extended Tronick et al.'s work in a series of studies on 3- to 6-month-olds designed to isolate the factors triggering the SF effect (particularly to facial displays). For example, Gusella et al. (1988) found that a large SF effect could be generated when maternal touch was eliminated (at least for older infants) and when mothers and infants engaged in reciprocal interactions

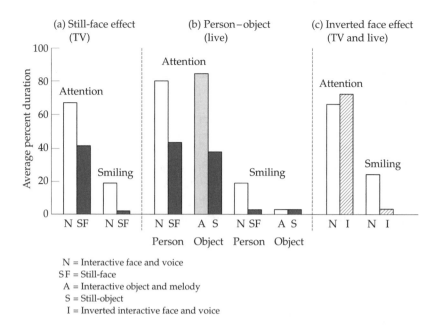

(a) Still-face effect (TV) (b) Person–object (live) (c) Inverted face effect (TV and live)

N = Interactive face and voice
SF = Still-face
A = Interactive object and melody
S = Still-object
I = Inverted interactive face and voice

FIGURE 11.8 Summary figures showing the degree of infant attention and positive affect directed towards adults during 1 1/2-minute periods of normal (N) face-to-face (face plus voice) interactions and various perturbations. (a) The average percentage of time infants spent fixating (two bars to the left) and smiling (two bars to the right) during normal (open bars) and still-face periods (filled bars). (b) The duration of attention (four bars to the left) and smiling (four bars to the right) directed toward a person during normal (open bars) and still-face periods (filled bars) and toward an "interacting" hand-puppet with abstract, non-facial features accompanied by a synthe-sized melodic sound (light gray bar) and the same puppet held stationary (dark gray bar). (c) Attention (two bars on the right) and smiling (two bars on the left) directed toward adults during normal interactions with their faces upright (open bars) and inverted (shaded bars)

over a closed-circuit, color television system (a procedure invented by Murray and Trevarthen, 1985). As shown in figure 11.8a, during the TV procedure, an infant's gaze at the mother's face dropped in duration during the SF period by about 1/3rd, relative to that during normal interactions, while smiling dropped by a factor of ten, almost disappearing in the SF period. The infants' behavior was similar during both "live" and TV procedures; compare the data in figure 11.8a with that for the person (live) in figure 11.8b (also, see Gusella et al., 1988). The TV procedure allowed Gusella et al. (1988) to study the separate contributions of maternal facial and vocal stimulation in the regulation of infant visual attention and smiling directed toward the mothers' faces during face-to-face interactions. They found a strong SF effect was generated when a televised SF was accompanied by an interactive voice, but no SF effect occurred when a silent, but interactive televised face replaced the SF period. Gusella et al. (1988) concluded that infant attention and positive affect are driven primarily by visual, rather than auditory, stimulation during face-to-face interactions. However, it should be noted that the infants' lack of smiling and attention directed toward the SF during the SF–interactive voice period may have been due to the obvious auditory–visual conflict. In recent studies, when an adult presented contingent vocal stimulation while her face was hidden, or inverted, a small amount of infant smiling was generated by the voice – see Muir and Hains (1993).

Next, Ellsworth et al. (1993) showed that the SF effect was not simply due to a shift from dynamic, contingent auditory–visual stimulation to static visual stimulation. A strong SF effect was generated when mothers or strangers interacted with 3- to 6-month-olds, but not when an interactive, cloth hand-puppet was substituted for a person. The puppet had abstract features designed to approximate the number and size, but not the shape of the major facial features. Synthesized melodic sounds accompanied the puppet's movement, which was presented by the experimenter instead of smiling and talking to the infant, in response to the infant's social signals during "face-to-face" interactions. As is illustrated in figure 11.8b, infant visual attention directed towards people and objects was similar. It was higher during dynamic, contingent stimulation and lower during static stimulation. However, while infants smiled at people they rarely smiled at objects. These results demonstrate that duration of visual attention, the dependent measure typically used in infant visual perception studies, can be a relatively insensitive index of an early perceptual competence which is clearly revealed by affect measures, such as smiling.

Finally, the importance of affect measures was emphasized in a series of studies designed to demonstrate that infants actually were "reading" the emotional expressions in the adults' faces during face-to-face interactions, as hypothesized above. It is well known that adults have trouble identifying emotional expressions in inverted faces (see the Margaret Thatcher illusion produced by Thompson, 1980). Because local features are matched in upright and inverted stimuli, inverting an adult's face during a face-to-face interaction with an infant seemed to provide an ideal test of infant sensitivity to emotional expressions per se. Rach-Longman (see Muir and Rach-Longman, 1989; Muir and Hains, 1993) conducted a series of studies in which mothers and female strangers used their faces and voices to interact with 3- and 6-month-olds either in-person or over color TV. The results were unequivocal. Irrespective of age, procedure, and adult identity, as shown in figure 11.8c, infant visual fixation remained high but smiling dropped during interactions when the adult's face was inverted (that is, infants treated the inverted face more like the interacting object used by Ellsworth et al., 1993, than an upright face). To complete the picture, Rach-Longman (1991) produced an orientation tuning curve for this inverted-face effect. She found a systematic decline in smiling as a stranger's live, talking face was rotated more than 45 degrees from upright, while visual attention directed towards the face remained constantly high irrespective of the facial orientation. One might have concluded erroneously that young infants are insensitive to facial orientation, and therefore facial expressions, if attention measures alone had been considered. To conclude, several aspects of our results stand out. First, using socially significant stimuli in an interactive context, we were able to elicit strong responses to various stimulus manipulations (e.g. interactive–static and person–object displays; upright–inverted faces) from virtually every 3- to 6-month-old we tested (striking age effects have not emerged, to date). Secondly, our results underline the importance of using affect as well as attention measures to provide a more complete picture of early perceptual competence in human infants.

SUMMARY AND DISCUSSION

Orientation abilities, as revealed through eye and head turning toward visual, tactual, and auditory stimulation, are evident in human infants at birth. Thus, a primitive "where" system appears to be operative even in the newborn. Indeed, even spatial localization and mapping to motor responses are evident in the prereaching and tracking behavior of neonates. Although these early localization responses are easily engaged by appropriate stimulation, it appears that the very young infant is quite limited in visual pattern analysis (i.e. in analyzing "what" is being displayed). For example, prereaching responses fail to distinguish 3D from 2D objects. However, using a preferential looking procedure, Slater et al., (1984) discovered that newborns consistently fixated a 3D object in preference to its photograph; thus, some depth perception may be functional at birth. Likewise, visual tracking procedures do not always reveal infant pattern preferences. When our schematic face was compared with striped and checkerboard patterns, the neonates showed no preferential tracking. However, when the position of the internal features of a different schematic face was varied by Johnson et al. (1991) and others, newborns tracked the facial configuration further than several scrambled arrangements. The latter work suggests that certain facial configurations may be privileged, but it remains unclear which aspects of face-like stimuli neonates will preferentially track.

As infants progress into their third month of life they show a tendency to fixate and be interested in more complex visual stimuli, even at the expense of orientation. At this developmental point some spatial orientation responses wane while other perceptual abilities wax, particularly interest in visual patterns. Nonlinear functions, such as the U-shaped auditory localization function, are difficult to account for in terms of the "improvement" of a single mechanism underlying the response (for further discussion of such U-shaped functions see Johnson and Morton, 1991). Rather it appears that with the development of new mechanisms, which are likely to be cortically localized, infants reach a new level of spatial perception. The number of neural and behavioral changes that occur from birth to 4 months make it difficult to pinpoint one particular change as the critical one which is responsible for the obvious shifts in spatial responding. Most likely, such U-shaped functions are the result of the confluence of many factors.

By 4 months of age infants can perform quite sophisticated pattern analysis, even with relatively "meaningless" patterns. They appear to be sensitive to

various types of pattern regularities such as symmetry and other global configural properties. The detection of such pattern properties could have important functional consequences. For example, Barlow and Reeves (1979; see also
Attneave, 1954) have argued that a system that detects symmetry and other
regularities can develop a more compact or less redundant representation of
visual input. If one half of an object or pattern is the same as the other half, then
one only needs to describe one half. Thus symmetry detection could lessen the
load on perceptual and memorial systems by allowing an economy of representation. Other theorizing by Witkin and Tenenbaum (1983) suggests that the
perception of such structure plays a central role in vision, just as the Gestalt
psychologists before them argued, and forms a core aspect of human perception, namely, the ability to organize sensory data. It appears that this ability is
present early in life.

Infant responses to dynamic human facial displays also reveal their
sensitivity to certain regularities in the pattern of visual stimulation, although
of a more "meaningful" nature than those embodied in abstract patterns.
At least as early as 3 months of age, infants react differently to objects and
faces, and appear to expect that adult "faces" will respond to their social
signals (e.g. shifts in fixation, smiling, and vocalizing) in a reciprocal inter-
change. Static faces are not of great emotional value to the infant and do not
engage them in the same way as dynamic faces, when changes in expression
are contingent on the infant's behavior (Muir and Hains, 1993). Infants may
also expect that these faces should appear in a particular orientation, relative to
the infant. Three-month-olds perceive differences in the orientation of faces in
the frontal plane; the upright face is the one that babies smile at reliably.
Presumably the infant's smile indicates an attempt at social interaction with
the upright face, or it may simply indicate recognition of a social stimulus.
These studies also emphasize the need for developmental researchers to consider response measures in addition to those concerned with the infant's visual
attention.

This paper has presented a brief, selective review of research on the development of spatial perception during the human infant's first few months of
life. Although the theoretical and empirical contributions of many researchers
have been acknowledged, no attempt was made to provide an exhaustive
review of the literature in this area. Instead, the intention was to highlight
the authors' work over the past 16 years which was influenced in various ways
by Peter Dodwell. His theoretical notions about pattern and spatial perception,
and its development (e.g. Dodwell et al., 1987) served to motivate and guide
many of the studies by the authors. Peter supported much of our work by
acquiring funding, facilitating team-work by post-doctoral fellows and gradu-
ate students, and providing critical reviews of the research, at all stages, with
enthusiasm and wit. His creative insights helped us to interpret puzzling
findings and to extend our work in new directions to improve our understanding of human perception. In closing, we thank him for his invaluable help
over the years.

ACKNOWLEDGMENTS

We thank David Foster, P. C. Dodwell, M. Johnson, J. Morton, and the anonymous reviewers for their critical reading of the manuscript and many valuable suggestions, and D. Maurer for noting that the lack of concordance in visual and auditory spatial fields may contribute to the U-shaped auditory localization function; special thanks go to Larry Symons for his editorial comments and to both him and Monica Hurt for their help with graphics. This work was supported by grants from the Natural Sciences and Engineering Research Council of Canada (NSERC) awarded to G. K. Humphrey and to D. W. Muir.

Notes

1. More recent formulations by Ungerleider and Mishkin (1982) indicate that both the "where" and "what" systems in primates co-exist in the cortex, although the collicular system probably plays a role in the "where" system as well. Goodale and Milner (1992) have suggested another distinction instead of separate "where" vs "what" systems in which the division of labor between the two cortical systems is better characterized by a separation between action and perception. Goodale and Milner propose that both acting and perceiving require information about location as well as object features. While it would be possible to recast the present findings in these more recent notions of visual systems, the original research was guided by the earlier formulations of Held, Schneider, Trevarthen and others.

2. The original formulation by Bronson (1974) of a subcortical to cortical shift in visual processing at about 2 months of age has been questioned by more recent research and theorizing. For example, studies have shown that newborns can discriminate two patterns of lines that differ only in orientation (Atkinson et al., 1988; Slater et al., 1988). Because mechanisms that respond to the orientation of such patterns are only found in the visual cortex, and it is these mechanisms that presumably mediate the discrimination, such results argue for at least some degree of cortical functioning at birth. Anatomical evidence is also consistent with the view that the cortex is at least somewhat functional in the neonate (Burkhalter, 1991). Based on such results several theorists, while acknowledging the immaturity of the cortex very early in life, have proposed models in which such partial cortical functioning plays a limited role before 2 months of age (e.g. Maurer and Lewis, 1979; Atkinson, 1984; Braddick and Atkinson, 1988; Johnson, 1990).

3. There is an important issue here that we do not have space to discuss. The issue is concerned with other ways in which such 2D patterns can be described and how this can be related to infants' responses. We have described patterns in the spatial domain and argue that they were "equated" in terms of their gross luminance characteristics. The patterns can also be described using Fourier analysis to determine the amplitude and phase spectra in the patterns. Some models of early infant pattern preferences suggest that it is only the energy at low spatial frequencies which determines infant responses (i.e. the amplitude spectrum), while others suggest that both the amplitude and phase spectra of the patterns are relevant. Morton (1993, personal communication) noted that a Fourier analysis might reveal why newborns did not prefer our face pattern over the other patterns. For further references and a clear discussion of this issue in relation to pattern preferences in neonates see Johnson and Morton (1991).

REFERENCES

Atkinson, J. (1984). Human visual development over the first 6 months of life: A review and hypothesis. *Human Neurobiol.* **3**, 61–74.

Atkinson, J., Hood, B., Wattam-Bell, J., Anker, S., and Trickelbank, J. (1988). Development of orientation discrimination in infancy. *Perception* **17**, 587–96.

Attneave, F. (1954). Some informational aspects of visual perception. *Psychol. Rev.* **61**, 183–93.

Banks, M. S., and Ginsburg, A. P. (1985). Infant visual preferences: A review and new theoretical treatment. In *Advances in Child Development and Behavior*, vol. 19, H. W. Reese (ed.), Academic Press, New York, pp. 207–46.

Barlow, H. B., and Reeves, B. C. (1979). The versatility and absolute efficiency of detecting mirror symmetry in random dot displays. *Vision Res.* **19**, 783–93.

Bornstein, M. H. (1981). Two kinds of perceptual organization near the beginning of life. In *Minnesota Symposia on Child Psychology*, vol. 14, W. R. Collins (ed.), Erlbaum, Hillsdale, NJ, pp. 39–91.

Bornstein, M. H., Ferdinandsen, K., and Gross, C. (1981). Perception of symmetry in infancy. *Dev. Psychol.* **17**, 82–6.

Bornstein, M. H., and Krinsky, S. J. (1985). Perception of symmetry in infancy: the salience of vertical symmetry and the perception of pattern wholes. *J. Exp. Child Psychol.* **39**, 1–19.

Bower, T. G. R. (1972). Object perception in infants. *Perception* **1**, 15–30.

Braddick, O., and Atkinson, J. (1988). Sensory selectivity, attentional control, and cross-channel integration in early infancy. In *Perceptual Development in Infancy*, vol. 20, A. Yonas (ed.), Erlbaum, Hillsdale, NJ, pp. 105–43.

Braitenberg, V. (1990). Reading the structure of brains. *Network* **1**, 1–11.

Brazelton, T. B. (1980). Neonatal assessment. In *The Course of Life: Psychoanalytic Contributions toward Understanding Personality Development, Vol. 1: Infancy and Early Childhood*, S. I. Greenspan and G. H. Pollack (eds), NIMH Press, Bethesda, MD.

Bronson, G. W. (1974). The postnatal growth of visual capacity. *Child Dev.* **45**, 873–9.

Burkhalter, A. (1991). Developmental status of intrinsic connections in visual cortex of newborn infants. In *The Changing Visual System: Maturation and Aging in the Central Nervous System*, P. Bagnoli and W. Hodos (eds), Plenum Press, New York, pp. 247–54.

Burkhalter, A., Bernardo, K. L., and Charles, V. (1993). Development of local circuits in human visual cortex. *J. Neurosci.* **13**, 1916–31.

Caelli, T. M., and Dodwell, P. C. (1984). Orientation-position coding and invariance characteristics of pattern discrimination. *Percept. Psychophys.* **36**, 159–68.

Clifton, R. K., Muir, D. W., Ashmead, D. H., and Clarkson, M. G. (1993). Is visually guided reaching in early infancy a myth? *Child Dev.* **64**, 1099–110.

Corballis, M. C., and Beale, I. L. (1976). *The Psychology of Left and Right*. Erlbaum, Hillsdale, NJ.

Cynader, M. (1979). Competitive interactions in postnatal development of the kitten's visual system. In *Developmental Neurobiology of Vision*, R. Freeman (ed.), Plenum, New York, pp. 109–20.

de Haan, M., and Maurer, D. (1993). The perception of symmetry by 4-month-olds. Unpublished manuscript.

DiFranco, D. E., Muir, D. W., and Dodwell, P. C. (1978). Reaching in very young infants. *Perception* **7**, 385–92.

Dodwell, P. C. (1983a). Spatial sense of the human infant. In *Spatially Oriented Behavior*, A. Hein and M. J. Jeannerod (eds), Springer, Heidelberg, pp. 197–213.

Dodwell, P. C. (1983b). The Lie transformation group model of visual perception. *Percept. Psychophys.* **34**, 1–16.

Dodwell, P. C., Humphrey, G. K., and Muir, D. W. (1987). Shape and pattern perception. In *Handbook of Infant Perception*, vol. 2, P. Salapatek and L. Cohen (eds), Academic Press, New York, pp. 1–79.

Dodwell, P. C., Muir, D. W. and DiFranco, D. E. (1976). Responses of infants to visually presented objects. *Science* **194**, 209–11.

Drillien, C. M., and Drummond, M. B. (eds) (1977). *Neurodevelopmental Problems in Early Childhood: Assessment and Management*. Blackwell, London.

Ellsworth, C. P., Muir, D. W., and Hains, S. M. J. (1993). Social competence and person–object differentiation: An analysis of the still-face effect. *Dev. Psychol.* **29**, 63–73.

Field, J., DiFranco, D., Dodwell, P., and Muir, D. (1979). Auditory–visual coordination in $2\frac{1}{2}$-month-old infants. *Infant Behav. Dev.* **2**, 113–22.

Field, J., Muir, D., Pilon, R., Sinclair, M., and Dodwell, P. (1980). Infants' orientation to lateral sounds from birth to three months. *Child Dev.* **51**, 295–8.

Garey, L. J. (1984). Structural development of the visual system of man. *Human Neurobiol.* **2**, 75–80.

Garner, W. R. (1974). *The Processing of Information and Structure*. Erlbaum, Hillsdale, NJ.

Garner, W. R., and Sutliff, D. (1974). The effect of goodness on encoding time in visual pattern discrimination. *Percept. Psychophys,* **16**, 426–30.

Gibson, E. J. (1969). *Principles of Perceptual Learning and Development*. Appleton-Century Crofts, New York.

Goodale, M. A., and Milner, A. D. (1992). Separate visual pathways for perception and action. *Trends Neurosci.* **15**, 20–25.

Goren, C. C., Sarty, M., and Wu, P. Y. K. (1975). Visual following and pattern discrimination of face-like stimuli by newborn infants. *Pediatrics* **56**, 544–9.

Gusella, J., Muir, D., and Tronick, E. (1988). The effect of manipulating maternal behavior during an interaction on three- and six-month-olds' affect and attention. *Child Dev.* **59**, 1111–24.

Gwiazda, J., Bauer, J., and Held, R. (1989). From visual acuity to hyperacuity: A 10-year update. *Can. J. Psychol.* **43**, 109–20.

Held, R. (1968). Dissociation of visual functions by deprivation and rearrangement. *Psychol. Forsch.* **31**, 338–48.

Humphrey, G. K., and Humphrey, D. E. (1989). The role of structure in infant visual pattern perception. *Can. J. Psychol.* **43**, 165–82.

Humphrey, G. K., Humphrey, D. E., Muir, D. W., and Dodwell, P. C. (1986). Pattern perception in infants: Effects of structure and transformation. *J. Exp. Child Psychol.* **41**, 128–48.

Humphrey, G. K., Dodwell, P. C., Muir, D. W., and Humphrey, D. E. (1988a). Can blind infants and children use sonar sensory aids? *Can. J. Psychol.* **42**, 94–119.

Humphrey, G. K., Muir, D. W., Dodwell, P. C., and Humphrey, D. E. (1988b). The perception of structure in vectorpatterns by 4-month-old infants. *Can. J. Psychol.* **42**, 35–43.

Johnson, M. H. (1990). Cortical maturation and the development of visual attention in early infancy. *J. Cognitive Neurosci.* **2**, 81–95.

Johnson, M. H., Dziurawiec, S., Ellis, H., and Morton, J. (1991). Newborns' preferential tracking of face-like stimuli and its subsequent decline. *Cognition* **40**, 1–19.

Johnson, M. H., and Morton, J. (1991). *Biology and Cognitive Development: The Case of Face Recognition*. Blackwell, Oxford.

Johnson, M. H., Posner, M. I., and Rothbart, M. K. (1991). Components of visual orienting in early infancy: Contingency learning, anticipatory looking, and disengaging. *J. Cognitive Neurosci.* **3**, 335–44.

Julesz, B. (1971). *Foundations of Cyclopean Perception*. University of Chicago Press, Chicago, IL.

Lewis, T. L., and Maurer, D. (1992). The development of the temporal and nasal visual fields during infancy. *Vision Res.* **32**, 903–11.

Low, J. A., Galbraith, R. S., Muir, D., Killen, H., Karchamr, J., and Campbell, D. (1978a). Intrapartum fetal asphyxia: A preliminary report in regard to long-term morbidity. *Am. J. Obstet. Gynecol.* **130**, 525–33.

Low, J. A., Galbraith, R. S., Muir, D., Killen, H., Karchamr, J., and Campbell, D. (1978b). Intrauterine growth retardation: A preliminary report in regard to long-term morbidity. *Am. J. Obstet. Gynecol.* **130**, 534–45.

Mach, E. (1897). *Contributions to the Analysis of the Sensations*, C. M. Williams (trans.). The Open Court Publishing Co., La Salle, IL. (Original work published in 1886.)

Maurer, D. (1985). Infants' perception of facedness. In *Social Perception in Infants*, T. N. Field and N. Fox (eds), Ablex, Norwood, NJ, pp. 73–100.

Maurer, D., and Lewis, T. L. (1979). A physiological explanation of infants' early visual development. *Can. J. Psychol.* **33**, 232–52.

Maurer, D., and Lewis, T. L. (1991). The development of peripheral vision and its physiological underpinnings. In *Newborn Attention: Biological Constraints and the Influence of Experience*, M. J. Salomon Weiss and P. R. Zelazo (eds), Ablex, Norwood, NJ, pp. 218–55.

Maurer, D., and Young, R. (1983). Newborns' following of natural and distorted arrangements of facial features. *Infant Behav. Dev.* **6**, 127–31.

McGraw, M. B. (1943). *The Neuromuscular Maturation of the Human Infant*. Columbia University Press, New York.

Morton, J., and Johnson, M. H. (1991). CONSPEC and CONLERN: A two-process theory of infant face recognition. *Psychol. Rev.* **98**, 164–81.

Muir, D. W. (1985). The development of infants' auditory spatial sensitivity. In *Auditory Development in Infancy*, S. E. Trehub and B. Schneider (eds), Plenum Press, New York, pp. 51–83.

Muir, D. W., and Clifton, R. (1985). Infants' orientation to the localization of sound sources. In *The Measurement of Audition and Vision during the First Year of Life: A Methodological Overview*, G. Gottlieb and N. Krasnegor (eds), Ablex, Norwood, NJ, pp. 171–94.

Muir, D., and Field, J. (1979). Newborn infants orient to sounds. *Child Dev.* **50**, 431–6.

Muir, D. W., and Hains, S. M. J. (1993). Infant sensitivity to perturbations in adult facial, vocal, tactile, and contingent stimulation during face-to-face interactions. In *Developmental Neurocognition: Speech and Face Processing in the First Year of Life*, de Boysson-Bardies et al. (eds), Kluwer, London, pp. 171–85.

Muir, D., and Rach-Longman, K. (1989). Once more with expression: On de Schonen and Mathivet's (1989) model for the development of face perception in human infants. *Eur. Bull. Cognitive Psychol.* **9**, 103–9.

Muir, D. W., Campbell, D., and Low, J. (1977). Behavioral outcome of babies asphyxiated or growth retarded at birth: Preliminary results. Paper presented at Canadian Psychological Association, Vancouver, B. C.

Muir, D., Abraham, W., Forbes, B., and Harris, L. (1979). The ontogenesis of an auditory localization response from birth to four months of age. *Can. J. Psychol.* **33**, 320–33.

Muir, D., Clifton, R., and Clarkson, M. (1989). The development of a human auditory localization response: A U-shaped function. *Can. J. Psychol.* **43**, 199–216.

Murray, L., and Trevarthen, C. (1985). Emotional regulation of interactions between two-month-olds and their mothers. In *Social Perception in Infants*, T. M. Field and N. Fox (eds), Ablex, Norwood, NJ, pp. 101–25.

Palmer, S. E. (1991). Goodness, gestalt, groups and Garner: Local symmetry subgroups as a theory of figural goodness. In *The Perception of Structure: Essays in Honor of Wendall Garner*, G. R. Lockhead and J. R. Pomerantz (eds), American Psychological Association, Washington, DC, pp. 23–39.

Palmer, S. E., and Hemenway, K. (1978). Orientation and symmetry: Effects of multiple, rotational and near symmetries. *J. Exp. Psychol. Human Percept. Performance* **4**, 691–702.

Rach-Longman, K. (1991). The effect of adult face orientation on human infant affect and attention within the first half year of life. PhD Thesis, Queen's University, Kingston, Ontario.

Royer, F. L. (1981). Detection of symmetry. *J. Exp. Psychol. Human Percept. Performance* **7**, 1186–1210.

Ruff, H., and Halton, A. (1978). Is there directed reaching in the human neonate? *Dev. Psychol.* **14**, 425–6.

Schneider, G. E. (1969). Two visual systems. *Science* **163**, 895–902.

Slater, A., and Morison, V. (1993). Visual attention and memory at birth. In *Newborn Attention: Biological Constraints and the Influence of Experience*, M. J. Salomon Weiss and P. R. Zelazo (eds), Ablex, Norwood, NJ, pp. 256–77.

Slater, A., Morison, V., and Somers, M. (1988). Orientation discrimination and cortical function in the human newborn. *Perception* **17**, 597–602.

Slater, A. M., Rose, D., and Morison, V. (1984). Infants' perception of similarities and differences between two- and three-dimensional stimuli. *Br. J. Dev. Psychol.* **2**, 287–94.

Stack, D., Muir, D., Sherriff, F., and Roman, J. (1989). Development of infant reaching in the dark to luminous objects and "invisible sounds." *Perception* **18**, 69–82.

Stechler, G., and Latz, E. (1966). Some observations on attention and arousal in the human infant. *J. Am. Acad. Child Psychiat.* **5**, 517–25.

Strauss, M. S., and Curtiss, L. E. (1981). Infant perception of patterns differing in goodness of form. Paper presented at the Society for Research in Child Development, Boston, MA.

Thompson, P. (1980). Margaret Thatcher: A new illusion. *Perception* **9**, 483–4.

Trevarthen, C. (1975). Growth of visuomotor coordination in infants. *J. Human Movement Stud.* **1**, 57.

Trevarthen, C. (1986). Form, significance and psychological potential of hand gestures of infants. In *The Biological Foundations of Gestures: Motor and Semiotic Aspects*, J. L. Nespoulos, P. Perron, and A. R. Lecours (eds), Erlbaum, Hillsdale, NJ, pp. 149–202.

Trevarthen, C. B. (1968). Two mechanisms of vision in primates. *Psychol. Forsch.* **31**, 299–337.

Tronick, E., Als, A., Adamson, L., Wise, S., and Brazelton, T. B. (1978). The infant's response to entrapment between contradictory messages in face-to-face interaction. *J. Am. Acad. Child Psychiat.* **17**, 1–13.

Ungerleider, L., and Mishkin, M. (1982). Two cortical systems. In *Analysis of Visual Behavior*, D. J. Ingle, M. A. Goodale, and R. J. Mansfield (eds), MIT Press, Cambridge, MA, pp. 549–86.

Vurpillot, E., Ruel, J., and Castrec, A. (1977). L'organisation perceptive chez le nourrisson: Réponse au tout ou ses éléments. *Bull. Psychologie* **327**, 396–405.

Wertheimer, M. (1938). Laws of organization in perceptual forms. In *A Source Book of Gestalt Psychology*, W. D. Ellis (ed.), Harcourt Brace, New York, pp. 71–88.

Wishart, J. G., Bower, T. G. R., and Dunkeld, J. (1978). Reaching in the dark. *Perception* **7**, 507–12.

Witkin, A. P., and Tenenbaum, J. M. (1983). On the role of structure in vision. In *Human and Machine Vision*, J. Beck, B. Hope, and A. Rosenfeld (eds), Academic Press, New York, pp. 481–543.

Younger, B., and Gotlieb, S. (1988). Development of categorization skills: Changes in the nature or structure of infant form categories. *Dev. Psychol.* **24**, 611–19.

12

IMITATION OF FACIAL AND MANUAL GESTURES BY HUMAN NEONATES*

Andrew N. Meltzoff and M. Keith Moore

EDITORS'
INTRODUCTION

For over 50 years it has been known that 1-year-old infants can imitate facial gestures that they see adults producing. This is not particularly surprising since imitation is one of the ways in which infants, children and adults learn, but it *is* surprising to find that much younger infants can imitate. The first report of newborn infants imitating adult facial gestures was by Olga Maratos, one of Piaget's students, who reported to him that if she stuck out her tongue to a young baby, the baby would respond by sticking its tongue out at her. This goes counter to Piaget's views on imitation – according to his theory it should only emerge from 8 months from birth at the earliest. When Piaget was appraised of his student's findings he apparently sucked contemplatively on his pipe for a few moments and then commented 'How rude.'

The first scientific report of human newborns imitating adult facial (and manual) gestures was by Andy Meltzoff and Keith Moore in 1977, and this paper is reproduced here. When it was published it aroused considerable interest and controversy. The initial debate concerned the question 'Can they do it?', and there were several papers reporting difficulty in replicating the findings. By now, however, at least 25 different studies have confirmed early imitation, and the questions asked have gone beyond 'Can they do it?' (they can), to 'Why is it done?'; 'Does it develop?'; 'Why should we care?'

Meltzoff and Moore, in an invited paper to this selection of readings, bring the debate up to date and consider these questions. Their account is given in their paper 'Resolving the Debate about Early Imitation', which follows their 1977 paper: in the later paper they point the reader to new data

* Previously published in *Science*, **198** (October 1977), pp. 75–8.

and new theories, so that the interested student can chase down the references and be informed about the current debates. Developmental psychology is about development, and about early precursors of later behaviours, and one intriguing suggestion in their paper is that newborn imitation of adult facial gestures is the origin and the foundation for developing a 'theory of mind'. This last topic is discussed in detail in the article by Lee and Homer (article 19), and we have the beginnings of a fascinating developmental story that is yet to be told.

OVERVIEW   Infants between 12 and 21 days of age can imitate both facial and manual gestures: this behavior cannot be explained in terms of either conditioning or innate releasing mechanisms. Such imitation implies that human neonates can equate their own unseen behaviors with gestures they see others perform.

Piaget and other students of developmental psychology consider the imitation of facial gestures to be a landmark achievement in infant development. Infants are thought to pass this milestone at approximately 8 to 12 months of age. Infants younger than this have been postulated to lack the perceptual–cognitive sophistication necessary to match a gesture they see with a gesture of their own which they cannot see.[1] The experiments we report show that the infant's imitative competence has been underestimated. We find that 12- to 21-day-old infants can imitate both facial and manual gestures (plate 12.1). This result has implications for our conception of innate human abilities and for theories of social and cognitive development.

An experimental evaluation of the neonate's imitative competence raises several methodological difficulties. One consists of distinguishing true imitation from a global arousal response. For example, one can conclude nothing about imitation if an infant produces more tongue protrusions in response to a tongue protrusion demonstration than he does to the presentation of a neutral facial expression. It would be more parsimonious simply to conclude that a moving, human face is arousing for the infant and that increased oral activity is part of the infant's arousal response. A second issue involves controlling interactions between adult and infant that might shape the imitative response. We found that if parents were informed of the imitative tasks we planned to examine, they practiced these gestures with their infants before coming into the laboratory so that their baby "would do well on the test." In reviewing films of preliminary work, we also noticed that the examiner tended to alter the rhythm of his tongue protrusion as a function of the response of the infant. These kinds of interactions would expose findings of imitation to a variety of explanations, including the possibility that the infants were merely being conditioned to imitate tongue protrusion. A third issue concerns the scoring of the infant's responses. The movements tested were not generally produced in a discrete, unambiguous fashion, and not surprisingly, there were gross differences in the scoring as a function of whether or not the observer knew which gesture had been demonstrated to the infant.

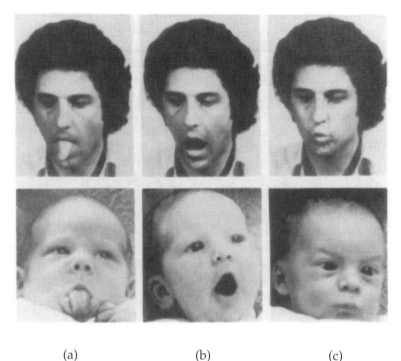

(a)   (b)   (c)

PLATE 12.1 Sample photographs from videotape recordings of 2- to 3-week-old infants imitating (a) tongue protrusion, (b) mouth opening, (c) lip protrusion demonstrated by an adult experimenter

In the experiments we now report, these three issues are addressed as follows. (i) Each infant's response to one gesture is compared with his response to another similar gesture demonstrated by the same adult, at the same distance from the infant, and at the same rate of movement. For instance, we test whether infants produce more tongue protrusions after an adult demonstrates tongue protrusion than after the same adult demonstrates mouth opening, and vice versa. If differential imitation occurs, it cannot be attributed to a mere arousal of oral activity by a dynamic, human face. (ii) Parents were not told that we were examining imitation until after the studies were completed; moreover, the experiments were designed to preclude the possibility that the experimenter might alter the rhythm of his demonstration as a function of the infant's response. (iii) The infant's reactions were videotaped and then scored by observers who were uninformed of the gesture shown to the infant they were scoring.[2]

In experiment 1, the subjects were six infants ranging in age from 12 to 17 days ($\bar{X} = 14.3$ days). Three were male and three female. Testing began with a 90-second period in which the experimenter presented an unreactive, "passive face" (lips closed, neutral facial expression) to the infant. Each infant was then shown the following four gestures in a different random order: lip protrusion, mouth opening, tongue protrusion, and sequential finger movement (opening and closing the hand by serially moving the fingers). Each gesture was demonstrated four times in a 15-second stimulus-presentation period. This period was immediately followed by a 20-second response period for which the experimenter stopped performing the gesture and resumed a passive face. In order to allow for the possibility that the infants might not watch the first stimulus presentation, the procedure allowed a maximum of three stimulus presentations and corresponding response periods for any one gesture. Half the cases required only one stimulus presentation. In those cases necessitating more than one stimulus presentation, the 20-second response period used in assessing imitation was the one following the final presentation of the gesture. A 70-second passive-face period separated the presentation of each new type of gesture from preceding ones.

The videotape recordings of the response periods were scored in a random order by undergraduate volunteers. Two groups of six coders were used. One group scored the infant's facial behavior, the other scored the manual responses. The face coders were informed that the infant in each videotaped segment was shown one of the following four gestures: lip protrusion, mouth opening, tongue protrusion, or passive face. They were instructed to order the four gestures by ranks from the one they thought it most likely the infant in each segment was imitating to the one they thought was least likely. No other training was given. The hand coders were treated identically, except that they were informed that the infant in each segment was presented with one of the following hand gestures: sequential finger movement, finger protrusion, hand opening, or passive hand.

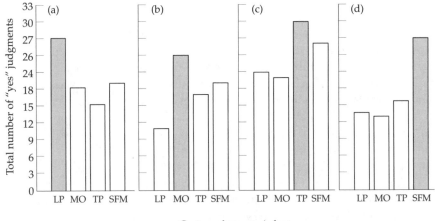

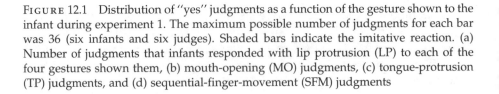

FIGURE 12.1   Distribution of "yes" judgments as a function of the gesture shown to the infant during experiment 1. The maximum possible number of judgments for each bar was 36 (six infants and six judges). Shaded bars indicate the imitative reaction. (a) Number of judgments that infants responded with lip protrusion (LP) to each of the four gestures shown them, (b) mouth-opening (MO) judgments, (c) tongue-protrusion (TP) judgments, and (d) sequential-finger-movement (SFM) judgments

For the purposes of analysis, the two highest ranks and the two lowest ranks were collapsed. This procedure yields dichotomous judgments of whether it was likely or unlikely (hereafter referred to as "yes" or "no") that the infants were imitating a particular gesture. The distribution of "yes" judgments for each infant gesture peaked when the corresponding gesture was demonstrated by the experimenter (figure 12.1). In all four instances, Cochran Q tests[3] reveal that the judged behavior of the infants varies significantly as a function of the gestures they are shown [lip protrusion, $P < .01$ (figure 12.1a); mouth opening, $P < .02$ (figure 12.1b); tongue protrusion, $P < .05$ (figure 12.1c); and sequential finger movement, $P < .001$ (figure 12.1d)]. That this variation is attributable to imitation is supported by the fact that none of these effects is significant when the judgments corresponding to the imitative reaction (shaded columns in figure 12.1) are excluded from the analyses.

Experiment 1 avoided a prolonged stimulus-presentation period during which the experimenter might alter the timing of his gesturing as a function of the infant's responses. However, in adopting a fixed stimulus-presentation period as brief as 15 seconds, it was sometimes necessary to repeat the presentation to ensure that the infants acually saw the gesture they were to imitate. This procedure then opened the possibility that the experimenter might unwittingly have been prefiltering the data by readministering the stimulus presentations until the random behavior of the infant coincided with the behavior demonstrated. A second study was therefore designed which is not open to this potential objection.

The subjects in experiment 2 were 12 infants ranging in age from 16 to 21 days ($\bar{X} = 19.3$). Six were male and six female. They were shown both a mouth-opening and a tongue-protrusion gesture in a repeated-measures design, counterbalanced for order of presentation. The experimental procedure is illustrated in table 12.1. Testing began with the insertion of a pacifier into the infant's mouth. Infants were allowed to suck on it for 30 seconds while the experimenter presented a passive face. The pacifier was then removed, and a 150-second baseline period was timed. After the baseline period, the pacifier was reinserted into the infant's mouth, and the first gesture was demonstrated until the experimenter judged that the infant had watched it for 15 seconds. The experimenter then stopped gesturing, resumed a passive face, and only then removed the pacifier. A 150-second response period, during which the experimenter maintained his passive face, was clocked. Immediately thereafter

TABLE 12.1   Schematic illustration of the pacifier technique for assessing facial imitation in neonates in experiment 2. Half of the infants were exposed to the gestures in the order tongue protrusion, mouth opening; the other half were exposed to the gestures in the reverse order

Condition	Baseline exposure	Baseline period (150 seconds)	Experimental exposure 1	Response period 1 (150 seconds)	Experimental exposure 2	Response period 2 (150 seconds)
Experimenter	Passive face	Passive face	Gesture 1	Passive face	Gesture 2	Passive face
Infant	Pacifier	No pacifier	Pacifier	No pacifier	Pacifier	No pacifier

the pacifier was reinserted, and the second gesture was presented in an identical manner.[4]

Infants did not tend to open their mouths and let the pacifier drop out during the mouth-opening demonstration; nor did they push out the pacifier with their tongues during the tongue-protrusion demonstration. On the contrary, they sucked actively with the pacifier remaining firmly within their mouths during the stimulus-presentation period. Thus, the pacifier technique (i) safeguards against the experimenter's altering his gesturing as a function of the imitative responses of the infant and (ii) permits the experimenter to demonstrate the gesture until the infant has seen it, while ensuring that the experimenter's assessment of this point is uncontaminated by any knowledge of the infant's imitative response.

The 36 videotaped segments (12 infants for 3 periods each) were scored in a random order by an undergraduate assistant who was uninformed of the structure of the experiment. The frequencies of tongue protrusions and mouth openings were tallied for each videotaped segment.[5] The results demonstrate that neonates imitate both tongue protrusion and mouth opening (figure 12.2). As assessed by Wilcoxon matched-pairs signed-ranks tests,[3] significantly more tongue-protrusion responses occurred after that gesture had been presented than during the baseline period ($P < .005$) or after the mouth-opening gesture ($P < .005$). Similarly, there were significantly more mouth-opening responses after that gesture had been demonstrated than during the baseline period ($P < .05$) or after the tongue-protrusion gesture ($P < .05$). It is noteworthy that under the present experimental conditions, the infants had to delay their imitation until after the gesture to be imitated had vanished from the perceptual field.

At least three different mechanisms could potentially underlie the imitation we report.

(1)   It could be argued that the imitation is based on reinforcement administered by either the experimenter or the parents. In order to prevent the

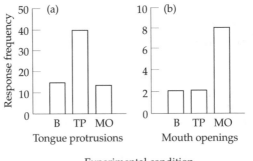

FIGURE 12.2 Total frequency of (a) tongue-protrusion and (b) mouth-opening responses for three conditions in experiment 2. Abbreviations: B = baseline period; TP = tongue-protrusion response period; and MO = mouth-opening response period

experimenter from shaping the infant's imitative responding, the procedure directed that he maintain an unreactive, neutral face during the response period. The experimenter's face was videotaped throughout both experiments in order to evaluate whether this procedure was followed. The videotaped segments were shown to observers whose task it was to score any reinforcements that the experimenter administered. No smiles or vocalizations were noted in any trial. Indeed, the only changes from the passive face occurred in three trials in experiment 1, when the experimenter was judged to "blink extremely rapidly." Considering only experiment 2, then, the experimental procedure does not appear to have been violated, and therefore, differential shaping of the mouth-opening and tongue-protrusion responses during the successive 150-second response periods is an unlikely source of the effects obtained. Since none of the parents were informed about the nature of the study, special practice on imitative tasks at home in preparation for the experiment was avoided. Further, informal questioning revealed that no parent was aware of ever having seen babies imitating in the first 21 days of life; indeed, most were astonished at the idea. Thus, a history of parental reinforcement seems an improbable basis for imitation at this very early age.

(2) This early imitation might be based on an innate releasing mechanism such as that described by Lorenz and Tinbergen.[6] This view would hold that tongue protrusion, mouth opening, lip protrusion, and sequential finger movement are each fixed-action patterns and that each is released by the corresponding adult gesture (sign stimulus). The overall organization of the infant's imitative response, particularly its lack of stereotypy, does not favor this interpretation. In addition, the fact that infants imitate not one, but four different gestures, renders this approach unwieldy.

(3) The hypothesis we favor is that this imitation is based on the neonate's capacity to represent visually and proprioceptively perceived information in a form common to both modalities. The infant could thus compare the sensory information from his own unseen motor behavior with a "supramodal" representation of the visually perceived gesture and construct the match required.[7] In brief, we hypothesize that the imitative responses observed are not innately organized and "released," but are accomplished through an active matching process and mediated by an abstract representational system. Our recent observations of facial imitation in six newborns – one only 60 minutes old – suggest to us that the ability to use intermodal equivalences is an innate ability of humans. If this is so, we must revise our current conceptions of infancy, which hold that such a capacity is the product of many months of postnatal development. The ability to act on the basis of an abstract representation of a perceptually absent stimulus becomes the starting point for psychological development in infancy and not its culmination.

Acknowledgments

A preliminary version of parts of experiment 1 was presented at the Biennial Meeting of the Society for Research in Child Development Denver, Colo., 10 to 13 April 1975.

Portions of this research were reported in A. N. M.'s thesis (Oxford University, 1976). Supported by NSF grant GS42926, the Social Science Research Council, the Washington Association for Retarded Citizens, and the Child Development and Mental Retardation Center of the University of Washington (grant HD02274). This research has greatly benefited from the encouragement and advice provided by Drs J. S. Bruner and G. P. Sackett. We thank Drs D. Holm, S. Landesman-Dwyer, O. Maratos, D. Gentner, and P. Kuhl for helpful suggestions. We are especially indebted to M. DurkanJones for her long and careful work on this project. We also thank W. Barclay, D. Blasius, J. Churcher, D. Clark, A. Gopnik, V. Hanson, R. Hart, M. McCarry, G. Mitchell, and V. Papaioannou. We acknowledge the cooperation of University Hospital of the University of Washington.

References and Notes

1. For example, J. Piaget, *Play, Dreams and Imitation in Childhood* (Norton, New York, 1962); H. Werner and B. Kaplan, *Symbol Formation* (Wiley, New York, 1963); I. Uzgiris and J. Hunt, *Assessment in Infancy* (Univ. of Illinois Press, Chicago, 1975). See D. Parton [*Child Dev.* **47**, 14 (1976)] for a recent review of the literature concerning infant imitation. Some reports are in conflict with these age norms. In the most extensive of these, O. Maratos [thesis, University of Geneva (1973)] noted imitation of two facial gestures by 1- to $2\frac{1}{2}$-month-old infants. However, the interpretation of her work is limited by the fact that the three factors discussed in the text were not controlled.

2. In addition, the following procedural details were held constant for both experiments. All infants were full term (40 ± 2 weeks gestation), of normal birth weight (3400 ± 900 g), and born through an uncomplicated vaginal delivery with a minimum of maternal medication (for example, no general anesthesia). The infants were tested when awake and alert, and they were supported in a semiupright posture by a well-padded infant seat. All the gestures were silently demonstrated 35 cm from the infant's eyes. They were presented against a white cotton backdrop and illuminated by a 20-watt spotlight placed directly above and behind the infant's head. The experimental room was kept as free as possible from auditory distraction and was maintained in subdued, indirect lighting.

3. S. Siegel, *Nonparametric Statistics* (McGraw-Hill, New York, 1956).

4. There was no significant difference ($P > .05$) between the duration of the presentation of the tongue protrusion ($\bar{X} = 67.6$ seconds) and mouth opening ($\bar{X} = 74.8$ seconds) gestures. Preliminary work revealed that infants continued to make sucking movements for about 3 seconds after a pacifier was removed. Therefore, in all cases, a 3-second interval was timed after the pacifier was removed and before the beginning of the 150-second baseline or response period. The infant's oral activity during this interval was not included in the analyses.

5. A tongue protrusion was scored only when the tongue was thrust clearly beyond the lips. A mouth opening was tallied only when the infant fully opened his mouth. Intraobserver agreement (number of agreements divided by the total number of agreements plus disagreements) was high for both tongue protrusion (93 percent) and mouth opening (92 percent).

6. K. Lorenz and N. Tinbergen, *Z. Tierpsychol.* **2**, 1 (1938); N. Tinbergen, *A Study of Instinct* (Oxford Univ. Press, New York, 1951).

7. "Supramodal" is used, following T. Bower [*Development in Infancy* (Freeman, San Francisco, 1974), to denote that the representation is not particular to one sensory modality alone.

12a

RESOLVING THE DEBATE ABOUT EARLY IMITATION

Andrew N. Meltzoff and M. Keith Moore

Facial imitation presents a puzzle. Infants can see an adult's face but cannot see their own faces. They can feel their own faces move, but have no access to the feelings of movement in another person. Developmentalists have known for 50 years that 1-year-olds imitate facial gestures. In 1977, Meltzoff and Moore reported that neonates imitate facial gestures. The report engendered a lively debate, and basic findings of early imitation have now been replicated and extended in 25 different studies from 13 independent laboratories.[1]

The field has now moved on to address four questions: (a) How is it done? (b) Why is it done? (c) Does it develop? (d) Why should we care? A recent review of the literature has identified 10 characteristics of early imitation (table 12a.1).[1] These can be used for addressing the foregoing questions.

TABLE 12a.1   Ten characteristics of early imitation

1. Infants imitate a range of acts
2. Imitation is specific (tongue protrusion leads to tongue not lip protrusion)
3. Newborns imitate
4. Infants quickly activate the appropriate body part
5. Infants correct their imitative efforts
6. Novel acts can be imitated
7. Absent targets can be imitated
8. Static gestures can be imitated
9. Infants recognize being imitated
10. There is developmental change in imitation

Source: Table from Meltzoff and Moore (1997). The paper provides the references reporting each of the 10 characteristics.

How it is done

The 1977 report considered three mechanisms that could potentially underlie early imitation – early learning from social interaction (EL), innate-releasing mechanisms (IRM), or active intermodal mapping (AIM). Further research excluded EL as an account, because studies ·demonstrated that newborns imitated.[1,2,3] The IRM view made three predictions: (a) matching occurs for only a few evolutionarily-privileged gestures, (b) the form of the response is fixed and stereotypic, (c) the matching response is time-locked to the triggering display. Research has disconfirmed each of these. First, although it was once thought that only tongue protrusion was imitated, several new studies have documented imitation for a wide range of gestures, not only tongue protrusion.[1,3] Secondly, the imitative response is not fixed or stereotypic. Infants imitate novel facial acts and correct their initial attempts to home-in on an accurate match.[4] Finally, the response is not rigidly time-locked. Infants can imitate when the model is not perceptually present, with studies documenting deferred facial imitation after delays of up to 24 hours.[4,5]

The new findings support the third view, the AIM account (figure 12a.1). On this view early imitation is intentional, goal-directed intermodal matching. The central notion is that imitation, even early imitation, is a matching-to-target process. The goal or behavioral target is specified visually. Infants' self-produced movements provide proprioceptive feedback that can be compared with the visually-specified target. AIM proposes that such comparison is possible because both perceived and performed human acts are represented within a common framework. This allows correction of imitative attempts toward a more faithful match. A paper elaborating the AIM account provides a detailed description of the metric infants use for establishing the intermodal equivalence of human acts.[1]

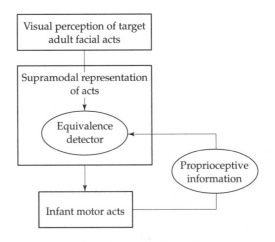

FIGURE 12a.1 The "active intermodal mapping" account (AIM) (reprinted from Meltzoff and Moore, 1997)

WHY IT IS DONE

Any behavior as complex as imitation is multiply determined. However, new findings have suggested that early imitation serves social and communicative functions. In particular, it has been argued that infants deploy imitation to probe whether an encounter with a person is a *re*-encounter with a familiar person or a new encounter with a stranger.[5] Using imitation for this purpose serves a social-identity function.[4] On this view, infants treat a person's non-verbal behavior as an identifier of who the individual is, and use imitation as a means of verifying this identity. The fundamental idea is that the distinctive behavior and special interactive games of people serve as markers of their identity. If infants are uncertain about the identity of a person, they will be motivated to test whether this person has the same behavioral properties as the old one by imitating her behavior and re-creating the previous social interaction. In a recent paper, the social-identity function of early imitation has been articulated in more detail and related to infants' understanding of the identity and permanence of inanimate objects.[6]

DEVELOPMENT

A popular way of assimilating the 1977 article was to treat early imitation as a specialized phenomenon, disconnected from later forms of imitation. The idea was that early imitation existed, but then "dropped out" of the infant's repertoire until about 1 year of age. New empirical findings have shown there is no necessary drop out of early imitation. Studies showed that the apparent drop was not due to change in competence, but rather to performance changes that were easily reversed using novel designs that posed cognitive challenges to these older infants.[5]

Nonetheless, there are important developmental changes in imitation.[1,7] Whereas the newborn is focused on the act ("Can I do that?"), the 6-week-old treats facial displays as posing a problem about the identity of the actor ("Are you the individual who does behavior *x*, not *y*?").[2,4,5] Further development moves infants toward the more abstract notion of a matching relationship between actors. This change is illustrated by studies in which adults purposely imitate the infant, rather than the other way around. Fourteen-month-olds seem to recognize the interaction as a "matching game," and gleefully test whether they are being copied, by abruptly changing acts while staring at the adult to see what he will do.[8] Younger infants show no such testing behavior.

Subsequent development allows imitation of an inferred act. One study presented 18-month-olds with an adult who tried, but failed, to perform an act on an object.[7] Infants imitated what the adult was attempting to do, rather than what he did do. Imitation has developed to the point that infants no longer imitate what they literally see, but what the adult was striving to do. This moves beyond seeing other people solely in terms of behaviors to seeing them at a deeper level – in terms of the goals of their acts and the intentions they hold.[7,9]

Why we should care

Early imitation reveals a more sophisticated initial state than classical theories assumed. The 1977 article suggested that neonates were capable of: cross-modal matching, perceptual–motor coordination, and representation. Although these inferences were considered surprising 20 years ago, empirical discoveries by a host of researchers, using both people and things, has supported them. The modern empirical findings lend increasing support to the most far-reaching conclusion of the 1977 report: "The ability to act on the basis of an abstract representation of a perceptually absent stimulus becomes the starting point for psychological development in infancy and not its culmination" (p. 78).

Current debate in the field now concerns what is implied by such a rich initial state. One popular view is that the innate psychological structures are adult-like – what is built in and available to newborns remains essentially unchanged in the course of development. However, the developmental changes discussed above and elsewhere[6,10,11] do not support the view that infants are born with adult-like knowledge.

We favor an alternative to strong nativism. The notion is that evolution has bequeathed human infants not with adult concepts, but with initial mental structures that serve as "discovery procedures" for developing the more comprehensive and flexible concepts.[6,11] Imitation is deployed as a discovery procedure in understanding persons. Through interactions with others and the concomitant growth in self-understanding, infants are engaged in an open-ended developmental process. If one adopts this developmental view, it becomes tempting to hypothesize that the foundation for developing an "understanding of mind" may be grounded in the initial equivalence of "self" and "other" manifest by early imitation.[1,9] Moreover, the discovery procedures used for understanding of inanimate objects may be deeply connected with those used in the social world.[6,11]

Notes

1. Meltzoff, A. N., and Moore, M. K. (1997). Explaining facial imitation: A theoretical model. *Early Development and Parenting*, **6**, 179–92.
2. Meltzoff, A. N., and Moore, M. K. (1983). Newborn infants imitate adult facial gestures. *Child Development*, **54**, 702–9.
3. Meltzoff, A. N., and Moore, M. K. (1989). Imitation in newborn infants: Exploring the range of gestures imitated and the underlying mechanisms. *Developmental Psychology*, **25**, 954–62.
4. Meltzoff, A. N., and Moore, M. K. (1994). Imitation, memory, and the representation of persons. *Infant Behavior and Development*, **17**, 83–99.
5. Meltzoff, A. N., and Moore, M. K. (1992). Early imitation within a functional framework: The importance of person identity, movement, and development. *Infant Behavior and Development*, **15**, 479–505.

6. Meltzoff, A. N., and Moore, M. K. (1998). Object representation, identity, and the paradox of early permanence: Steps toward a new framework. *Infant Behavior and Development*, **21**, 201–35.

7. Meltzoff, A. N. (1995). Understanding the intentions of others: Re-enactment of intended acts by 18-month-old children. *Developmental Psychology*, **31**, 838–50.

8. Meltzoff, A. N. (1990). Foundations for developing a concept of self: The role of imitation in relating self to other and the value of social mirroring, social modeling, and self practice in infancy. In D. Cicchetti and M. Beeghly (eds), *The Self in Transition: Infancy to Childhood* (pp. 139–64), Chicago: University of Chicago Press.

9. Meltzoff, A. N., and Moore, M. K. (1995). Infants' understanding of people and things: From body imitation to folk psychology. In J. Bermúdez, A. Marcel, and N. Eilan (eds), *The Body and the Self*, Cambridge, MA: MIT Press.

10. Kuhl, P. K., and Meltzoff, A. N. (1996). Infant vocalizations in response to speech: Vocal imitation and developmental change. *Journal of the Acoustical Society of America*, **100**, 2425–38.

11. Gopnik, A., and Meltzoff, A. N. (1997). *Words, Thoughts, and Theories*. Cambridge, MA: MIT Press.

13

INFANTS POSSESS A SYSTEM OF NUMERICAL KNOWLEDGE*

Karen Wynn

EDITORS' INTRODUCTION

Karen Wynn shot to instant fame in developmental psychology with her report in *Nature* (1992) that infants can count! The basic experimental situation was to show the infant a display of a small number of objects, which was then covered by a screen: a hand then removed or added an object (the infant saw the taking away, or adding) and the screen was removed, revealing the display again. She found that young infants were surprised if the number of objects remaining did not match the change that had taken place (they looked more at the unexpected number of objects). This finding has been replicated (e.g., Simon, Hespos and Rochat, 1995), and these reports of infant numerical abilities add to our understanding of the development of children's understanding of number from infancy onwards (this is reviewed by Bryant, 1995). In this paper Wynn gives a detailed account of infants' numerical competence and she suggests that 'a system of numerical competence may be part of the inherent structure of the human mind'.

REFERENCES

Bryant, P. (1995). Children and arithmetic. *Journal of Child Psychology and Psychiatry*, **36**, 3–32.

Simon, T. J., Hespos, S. J., and Rochat, P. (1995). Do infants understand simple arithmetic? A replication of Wynn (1992). *Cognitive Development*, **10**, 253–69.

* Previously published in *Current Directions in Psychological Science*, **4**, 6 (December 1995), pp. 172–7.

A mathematical system can be characterized by a body of mathematical entities, along with a set of procedures for operating upon these entities to yield further information. For example, the system of euclidean geometry is composed of a set of geometrical entities (point, line, plane, angle, etc.), together with a system of inferential reasoning that can be applied over these entities to reveal further geometrical knowledge. Similarly, the natural numbers, in conjunction with arithmetical functions such as addition and multiplication, form another mathematical system.

My colleagues and I have been investigating human infants' numerical abilities. The picture emerging from this research is one of impressive early competence and suggests that a system of numerical knowledge may be part of the inherent structure of the human mind: Infants can mentally represent different numbers and have procedures for manipulating these numerical representations to obtain further numerical information. In this review, I summarize these empirical findings, describe a specific model for how infants might represent and reason about number, and discuss briefly how this initial system of knowledge may relate to later numerical knowledge.

Infants Can Represent Number

Infants can distinguish different small numbers of visual items, such as dots, points of light, and photographs of household objects. In studies showing this capacity, each infant is repeatedly presented with arrays containing a certain number of items, until the infant's looking time to the arrays decreases to a pre-specified criterion (typically to half of his or her initial levels of looking). At this point, the infant is considered to be *habituated* to the stimuli. Following habituation, the infant is presented with new displays, some containing the original number of items and some containing a new number of items. It is well known that infants tend to look longer at things that are new or unexpected to them; therefore, if infants can distinguish between the two numbers, they should look longer at the displays containing the new number of items. It has been found that when infants are habituated to displays of two items, they then look longer when shown three items, and vice versa, showing that they can distinguish the two kinds of arrays. Under some conditions, infants in this type of experiment will also distinguish three items from four.[1]

Infants can enumerate other kinds of entities in addition to visual items. After being habituated to arrays of two objects, infants looked longer at a black disk when it emitted two sequential drumbeats than when it emitted three; infants habituated to arrays of three objects looked longer at the disk when it emitted three drumbeats than when it emitted two.[2] Thus, the infants not only enumerated both the objects and the drumbeats, but also recognized numerical correspondences between them. This finding indicates that infants' numerical representations are abstract ones that can apply to input from different perceptual modalities.

We have recently shown that 6-month-olds can also enumerate physical actions in a sequence.[3] One group of infants was habituated to a puppet

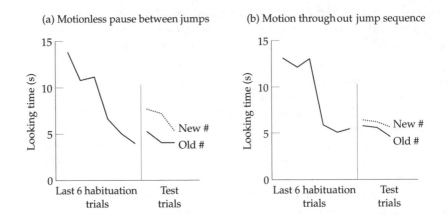

FIGURE 13.1 Six-month-olds' looking times on the last six habituation trials and on old- and novel-number test trials for jump sequences, (a) in which interjump intervals were motionless, and (b) in which the puppet was in continuous motion

jumping two times, another to a puppet jumping three times. On each trial, the puppet jumped the required number of times, with a brief pause between jumps. Upon completing the jump sequence, the puppet stood motionless, and infants' looking time to the stationary puppet was measured. Following habituation, both groups of infants were presented with test trials in which the puppet sometimes jumped two times and sometimes jumped three times. Infants looked reliably longer at the puppet on trials containing the new number of jumps (figure 13.1a). The structure of jump sequences ruled out the possibility that infants were responding on the basis of the tempo or overall duration of the sequences rather than number.

In a second, similar experiment, we asked whether infants could discriminate between two- and three-jump sequences when the puppet remained in constant motion throughout each sequence; between jumps, the puppet's head wagged from side to side in an exaggerated fashion. In these sequences, the individual actions of the puppet could not be defined through a low-level perceptual analysis (on the basis of, e.g., the presence or absence of motion), but required an analysis of the pattern of motion in the sequence. There is, in fact, more than one way to pick out distinct actions in such a sequence; for example, one might pick out the individual jumps as distinct from the head-wagging activity and count them, or one might pick out the repeating pattern of "jumping followed by head wagging" and count its repetitions. Thus, the identification of discrete actions within a continuous sequence of motion is a cognitive imposition. Nonetheless, infants again looked significantly longer at the novel-number test sequences (figure 13.1b), indicating that they are able to parse a continuous sequence of motion into distinct segments on the basis of the structure of motion in the sequence, and to enumerate these segments. Thus, infants can enumerate complex, cognitively determined entities.

Visual items, sounds, and physical actions are all very different kinds of entities. Typically, in experiments of the kind just described, visual items or patterns are presented to infants simultaneously, enduring together through time and occupying different locations in space; thus, the identification of visual items requires primarily an analysis of spatial information. Sounds, in contrast, have no spatial extent (though a sound may emanate from a specific physical location, it is perceived independently of it), but typically occur at different points in time and endure only temporarily, so their identification relies primarily on an analysis of temporal information. Finally, actions consist of internally structured patterns of motion that unfold over time, and so their identification entails an integration of both spatial and temporal information. The fact that infants can enumerate entities with quite distinct properties, presented in different perceptual modalities, indicates that infants possess abstract, generalizable representations of small numbers, and that these representations are independent of the perceptual properties of specific arrays.

INFANTS HAVE PROCEDURES THAT SUPPORT NUMERICAL REASONING

Possessing genuine numerical knowledge entails more than simply the ability to represent different numbers. A numerical system is composed not only of numbers, but also of procedures for manipulating these numbers to yield further numerical information. Infants might be able to determine numbers of entities without being able to reason about these numbers or to use them to make numerical kinds of inferences. If so, we would not want to credit infants with a system of numerical knowledge.

Studies conducted in my laboratory show that 5-month-old infants are able to engage in numerical reasoning: they have procedures for manipulating their numerical representations to obtain information of the relationships that hold between them. In these experiments, the infant is shown a small collection of objects, which then has an object added to or removed from it. The resulting collection of objects that is subsequently shown to the infant is either numerically consistent or inconsistent with the addition or subtraction. Because infants look longer at outcomes that violate their expectations, if they are anticipating the number of objects that should result, they will look longer at inconsistent outcomes than at consistent ones.

In the first experiment,[4] one group of 5-month-old infants was shown an addition situation in which one object was added to another identical object, and another group was shown a subtraction situation in which one object was removed from a collection of two objects. Infants in the $1 + 1$ group saw one item placed into a display case. A screen then rotated up to hide the item, and the experimenter brought a second item into the display and placed it out of sight behind the screen (figure 13.2, top). The $2 - 1$ group saw two items placed into the display. After the screen rotated up to hide them, the experimenter's hand re-entered the display, went behind the screen, and removed one item from the display (figure 13.2, bottom). For both groups, the screen then dropped to reveal either one or two items. Infants' looking times to the displays were then recorded.

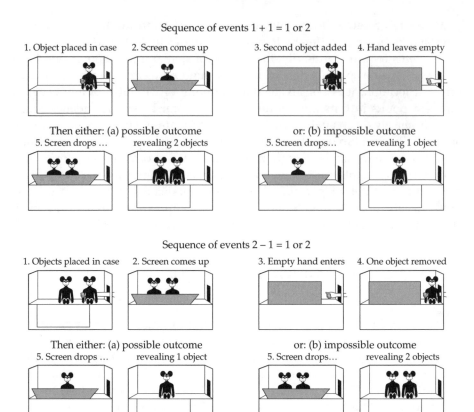

FIGURE 13.2   Sequence of events shown to infants in Wynn (1992), experiments 1 and 2 (courtesy of *Nature*)

Pretest trials, in which infants were simply presented with displays of one and two items to look at, revealed no significant preference for one number over the other, and no significant difference in preference between the two groups. But there was a significant difference in the looking patterns of the two groups on the test trials: Infants in the $1 + 1$ group looked longer at the result of one item than the result of two items; infants in the $2 - 1$ situation looked longer at the result of two items than the result of one item (figure 13.3).

In another experiment, infants were shown an addition of one item to another, and the final number of objects revealed was either two or three. Again, infants looked significantly longer at the inconsistent outcome of three objects than at the consistent outcome of two objects (figure 13.4). (Pretest trials revealed no baseline preference to look at three items over two items.)

These results are robust; they have been obtained in other laboratories, using different stimuli and with variations in the procedure.[5] One study tested the possibility that infants were anticipating certain spatial locations to be filled and others empty, rather than anticipating the number of items in the display. One group of 5-month-old infants was presented with $1 + 1$ situations, and another group was presented with $2 - 1$ situations; for both groups, the

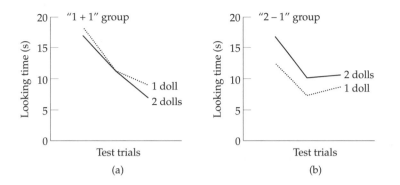

FIGURE 13.3 Five-month-olds' looking times to outcomes of one doll and two dolls following event sequences in which one doll was added to a display of one doll (a), or one doll was taken away from a display of two dolls (b)

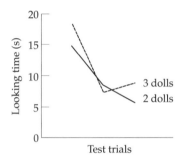

FIGURE 13.4 Five-month-olds' looking times to two versus three dolls after viewing a sequence of events in which one doll was added to a display of one doll

outcome was sometimes one object and sometimes two objects. All the objects were placed on a large revolving plate in the center of the display, which was occluded when the screen was raised. The objects were therefore in continuous motion, so no object retained a distinct spatial location throughout the experimental operation. Nonetheless, infants looked reliably longer at the numerically incorrect outcomes, showing that they were computing over the number of objects, not over the filled-or-empty status of different spatial locations.[6]

A MECHANISM FOR DETERMINING AND REASONING ABOUT NUMBER

The ability to discriminate small numbers of entities precisely, and in some cases to perform numerical operations over these numbers, has been documented in a variety of warm-blooded vertebrate species as well as in human infants. This suggests that a common mechanism may have evolved to perform this function at a distant point in evolutionary history.[7]

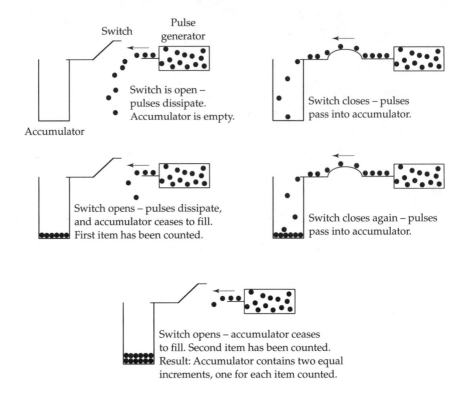

FIGURE 13.5 Schematic diagram of the states of Meck and Church's accumulator mechanism as it enumerates two items. The resulting fullness level of the accumulator is the mental representation for 2 (see note 8)

The *accumulator* is a model of a mental mechanism for representing number, originally proposed to account for numerical abilities in rats.[8] The accumulator mechanism can account for both the ability to represent number and the ability to operate over these numerical representations.[1] This mechanism produces pulses at a constant rate; these pulses can be passed into an accumulator by the closing of a switch. For each entity that is to be counted, the switch closes for a fixed brief interval, passing the pulses into the accumulator during that interval. Thus, the accumulator fills up in equal increments, one increment for each entity counted (figure 13.5). The final fullness level of the accumulator represents the number of items counted. The entire mechanism contains several accumulators and switches to allow the counting of different sets of entities simultaneously.

As the accumulator is a physical mechanism and random variability is inherent to any physical process, the exact fullness level of the accumulator will vary somewhat across different counts of the same number of items. This variability will increase with higher counts; therefore, larger numbers will be less discriminable from their neighbors than smaller numbers. This feature of the model may account for why infants' ability to discriminate adjacent numbers is limited to smaller numbers, and why they less reliably distinguish 3 from 4 than they do 2 from 3.

Because the entire fullness of the accumulator represents the number of the items counted, the magnitudinal relationships between the numbers are specified in these representations. For example, 4 is 2 more than 2, or twice as large; the accumulator's representation for 4 has two more increments than the representation for 2, so the accumulator is twice as full. If the mechanism provides procedures for operating over these representations, infants (and animals) will be able to appreciate some of these numerical relationships. Addition, for example, could be achieved by "pouring" the contents from an accumulator representing one value into an accumulator representing another value. Subtracting one value from another could also be achieved: If Accumulator A represents a given number and Accumulator B represents the value to be subtracted from it, the difference could be obtained by pouring out, one increment at a time, the contents of A into an empty third accumulator, C, until A and B are equally filled. At this point, C will represent the numerical difference of the values originally represented by A and B.

RELATIONSHIP OF THIS INITIAL SYSTEM OF KNOWLEDGE TO LATER NUMERICAL KNOWLEDGE

Although an extensive body of numerical information is in principle accessible by virtue of the magnitudinal structure of the representations produced by the accumulator, access to these facts requires procedures for manipulating the representations in appropriate ways, and there will be practical limits on how the outputs of the mechanism can be manipulated. The kind of procedure required for determining the product of two values, for example, will be much more complex than that for determining the sum of two values; and that required for determining, say, the cube of a value will be more complex still. Infants' knowledge is therefore limited by the procedures they have available for operating over the numerical representations generated by the accumulator mechanism.

There are also limits to the kinds of numerical entities the accumulator mechanism represents. It does not represent numbers other than positive integers. Interestingly, an understanding of numbers other than positive integers emerges only gradually and with much effort, both ontogenetically and culturally.[9] For example, children have great difficulty learning to think of fractions as numerical entities; to do so requires expanding their construal of numbers as values that represent discrete quantities of individual entities. This kind of conceptual expansion has also occurred repeatedly in the historical development of mathematics. Zero, for example, was not initially considered a number, but rather was introduced simply as a place-holder symbol representing an absence of values in a given position in place-value numeral notation (so as to be able to distinguish, e.g., 307 from 37). Only eventually did zero come to be considered a numerical entity in its own right, by virtue of becoming embedded in the number system as rules for its numerical manipulation were developed. The emergences of negative numbers, irrational numbers, complex numbers, and so on have followed similarly gradual progressions.

These facts suggest that the positive integers – the very values that the accumulator model is capable of representing – are psychologically privileged numerical entities. Just as the development of mathematics as a formal system required a conceptualization of numbers that went beyond the positive integers, individual children must undergo a similar (though not necessarily so extensive!) reconceptualization. Gaining a better understanding of how children do this is crucial for ultimately understanding the role that infants' initial foundation of numerical competence plays in the development of later knowledge.

ACKNOWLEDGMENTS

I thank Paul Bloom, Stanislas Dehaene, Randy Gallistel, and Tony Simon for stimulating and invaluable comments on a previous version of this article. Much of the work reported here was supported by an NICHD FIRST Award (Grant No. 1 R29 HD29857) to the author.

NOTES

1. For a comprehensive review of these findings, see K. Wynn, Evidence against empiricist accounts of the origins of numerical knowledge, *Mind and Language*, **7**, 315–32 (1992); K. Wynn, Origins of numerical knowledge, *Mathematical Cognition*, **1**, 35–60 (1995).
2. P. Starkey, E. S. Spelke, and R. Gelman, Numerical abstraction by human infants, *Cognition*, **36**, 97–128 (1990). When, as in this experiment, test stimuli and habituation stimuli are presented in different perceptual modalities, infants typically look longer at the matching stimuli in the new modality rather than the completely novel stimuli, possibly because the correspondence along a single dimension between two very different kinds of stimuli (e.g., pictures and sounds) is inherently interesting to infants.
3. K. Wynn, Infants' individuation and enumeration of actions, *Psychological Science* (in press).
4. K. Wynn, Addition and subtraction by human infants, *Nature*, **358**, 749–50 (1992).
5. We have extended these results, exploring infants' numerical expectations in further situations; see Wynn (1995), note 1. For replications by other researchers, see, e.g., R. Baillargeon, Physical reasoning in young infants: Seeking explanations for impossible events, *British Journal of Developmental Psychology*, **12**, 9–33 (1994); D. S. Moore, *Infant mathematical skills? A conceptual replication and consideration of interpretation*, manuscript submitted for publication (1995); T. Simon, S. J. Hespos, and P. Rochat, Do infants understand simple arithmetic: A replication of Wynn (1992), *Cognitive Development*, **10**, 253–69 (1995).
6. E. Koechlin, S. Dehaene, and J. Mehler, *Numerical transformations in five-month-old human infants*, manuscript submitted for publication (1995).
7. For review and discussion, see chapter 10 of C. R. Gallistel, *The Organization of Learning* (MIT Press, Cambridge, MA, 1990).
8. For a detailed description of the accumulator model and of experimental support for it, see W. H. Meck and R. M. Church, A mode control model of counting and

timing processes, *Journal of Experimental Psychology: Animal Behavior Processes*, **9**, 320–34 (1983); see also C. R. Gallistel and R. Gelman, Preverbal and verbal counting and computation, *Cognition*, **44**, 43–74 (1992).

9. See, e.g., R. Gelman, Epigenetic foundations of knowledge structures: Initial and transcendent constructions, in *The Epigenesis of Mind: Essays on Biology and Cognition*, S. Carey and R. Gelman, eds (Erlbaum, Hillsdale, NJ, 1991); M. Kline, *Mathematical Thought from Ancient to Modern Times*, vol. 1 (Oxford University Press, Oxford, England, 1972).

Part IV

MEMORY, LEARNING AND COGNITION

14

REACTIVATION OF INFANT MEMORY*

Carolyn K. Rovee-Collier, Margaret W. Sullivan, Mary Enright, Debora Lucas and Jeffrey W. Fagen

Carolyn Rovee-Collier and her colleagues consider the intriguing question of 'infantile amnesia' – that is, the well-known inability of adults to remember their infantile experiences. In this paper they suggest that early memories in infancy may not be quickly forgotten, rather that they can be reinstated, with no forgetting, following some sort of 'reactivation treatment'. They demonstrate that memories can be reinstated after intervals as long as 2 and 3 weeks in infants as young as 3 months.

In a more recent paper Rovee-Collier (1996) expands on this view. She argues that adults may not be able to remember the precise circumstances (the 'where' and 'when') in which early memories were formed, but these memories will persist if they are retrieved or updated, perhaps many times, on subsequent occasions: 'Even if a memory that originated in infancy or early childhood has undergone so many transformations that it is no longer recognized as such, it is still the same memory' (1996, p. 397). This leads to the intriguing view – 'Over time, I have come to view the question of infantile amnesia, "Why do adults not remember events from early childhood – before the age of 3 or 4?" as being much like the question, "Have you stopped beating your wife lately?" That is, *the basic premise of the question is wrong*. I propose that *adults actually can and do remember what was experienced early in life*, particularly if they have re-experienced it in the meantime' (1996, p. 395, italics in original).

REFERENCE

Rovee-Collier, C. (1996). Shifting the focus from what to why. *Infant Behavior and Development*, **19**, 385–400.

EDITORS' INTRODUCTION

* Previously published in *Science*, **208**, (6 June 1980), pp. 1159–61.

OVERVIEW   Three-month-old infants learned to activate a crib mobile by means of operant footkicks. Retention of the conditioned response was assessed during a cued recall test with the nonmoving mobile. Although forgetting is typically complete after an 8-day retention interval, infants who received a reactivation treatment – a brief exposure to the reinforcer 24 hours before retention testing – showed no forgetting after retention intervals of either 2 or 4 weeks. Further, the forgetting function after a reactivation treatment did not differ from the original forgetting function. These experiments demonstrate that (i) "reactivation" or "reinstatement" is an effective mechanism by which early experiences can continue to influence behavior over lengthy intervals, and (ii) memory deficits in young infants are best viewed as retrieval deficits.

The pervasive influences of early experiences on later behavior have been extensively documented, as have early memory deficits or "infantile amnesia."[1] Considered jointly, these phenomena pose a major paradox for students of development: How can the effects of early experiences persist into adolescence and adulthood if they are forgotten during infancy and early childhood? Campbell and Jaynes[2] proposed a resolution to this paradox in terms of reinstatement, a mechanism that maintains a memory which would otherwise be forgotten, through occasional re-encounters with the original training conditions over the period of development. Any given re-encounter, however, would be insufficient to promote new learning in organisms lacking the early experience. Spear[3] attributed the efficacy of reinstatement procedures to improved retrieval produced by the reactivation of a sufficient number (or kind) of existing but otherwise inaccessible attributes of the target memory. He hypothesized that re-exposure to stimuli from the original training context, which had been stored as attributes of the memory, could prime or arouse other attributes that represented the original experience, increasing their accessibility and, thus, the probability of their retrieval.

"Reinstatement" or "reactivation" has been demonstrated in young and adult rats[2,4,5] and in grade-school children.[6] We now report that a reactivation treatment can alleviate forgetting in 3-month-old infants after a retention interval as long as 4 weeks and that the forgetting function after a reactivation treatment is similar to the function after original training.

Our procedures were modeled after those of animal memory studies in which the experimenter trains a specific response in a distinctive context and later returns the subject to that context to see if the response is still produced. Because the retrieval cues are contextual and response production is assessed before reinforcement is reintroduced, the procedure is analogous to a test of cued recall.[3]

In our studies, footkicks of 3-month-olds were reinforced by movement of an overhead crib mobile. The infant controlled both the intensity and frequency of the mobile movement by means of a ribbon connecting the ankle (plate 14.1) with the hook from which the mobile hung. This procedure, "mobile conjugate reinforcement," produces rapid acquisition and high, stable response rates

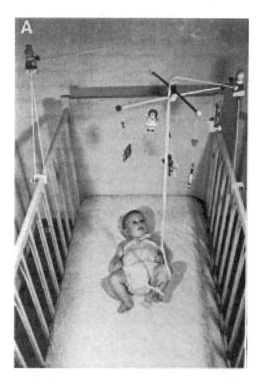

PLATE 14.1   An infant during a reinforcement phase with an ankle ribbon attached to the same suspension bar as that from which a mobile hangs. The empty mobile stand, clamped to the crib rail at the left, will hold the mobile during periods of nonreinforcement (photograph by Breck P. Kent)

attributable to the contingency and not to behavioral arousal.[7] During non-reinforcement phases (baseline, retention tests, extinction), the mobile remained in view but was hung from a second mobile stand with no ribbon attachment and could not be activated by kicks.

Infants received three procedurally identical sessions in their home cribs. The first two were training sessions, spaced by 24 hours; the third followed a lengthy retention interval. Each session consisted of a 9-minute reinforcement phase preceded and followed by a 3-minute nonreinforcement period. In session 1, the initial 3-minute period defined the baseline; in sessions 2 and 3, it was a long-term retention test of the effects of prior training. Total footkicks during this test (B) were expressed as a fraction of the infant's total kicks during the 3-minute nonreinforcement phase at the conclusion of the preceding session (A), which was an immediate retention test. The ratio B/A indexed the extent of an infant's forgetting from one session to the next. Ratios of ≥ 1.00 indicated no forgetting, and < 1.00 indicated fractional loss.[8]

A reactivation treatment was administered 24 hours before session 3. It consisted of a 3-minute exposure to the reinforcer (mobile movement) in a context identical to that of session 2 except that (i) the ribbon was not connected to the ankle but was draped over the side of the crib, where it was

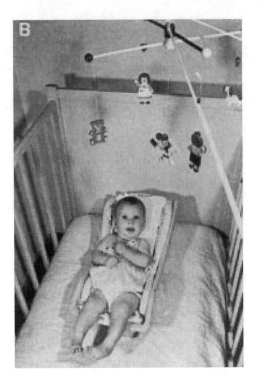

PLATE 14.2   The same infant during a reactivation treatment. The mobile and ribbon are attached to the same suspension hook, but the ribbon is drawn and released by the experimenter (not shown), concealed from the infant's view at the side of the crib. Also not shown is the empty stand, positioned as before. The infant will be exposed to the reinforcer (the moving mobile) for only 3 minutes, 24 hours before retention testing (photograph by Breck P. Kent)

drawn and released by the experimenter at a rate corresponding to each infant's mean response rate during the final 3 minutes of acquisition in session 2; and (ii) the infant was in a reclining seat (plate 14.2), which minimized footkicks and altered the topography of those which did occur.[9] These changes, as well as the brevity of the reminder, precluded the opportunity for new learning or practice during a reactivation treatment. Footkicks were recorded by the experimenter and, independently, by a second observer present for at least a third of the sessions and naive with respect to group assignment and session number. Pearson product-moment reliability coefficients were > .95 for all studies reported here.

In study 1, retention of conditioned footkicks was assessed 2 weeks after training. Infants [mean ($\bar{X}$) age = 88.4 days, standard error (S.E.) = 3.3] were tested in three groups of six each: (i) a reactivation group received a 3-minute reminder 13 days after session 2 (24 hours before session 3); (ii) a no-reactivation group received training but no reactivation treatment prior to session 3; and (iii) a familiarization/reactivation control group received a procedure identical to that of the reactivation group except that infants in this group were removed from their cribs during the reinforcement phases of sessions 1

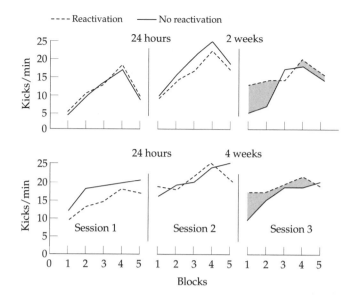

FIGURE 14.1 Mean kicks per minute during training (sessions 1 and 2) and an identical session (session 3) occurring either 2 or 4 weeks after the completion of session 2. Blocks 1 and 5 are nonreinforcement phases: performance during long-term retention tests (block 1, session 2 or 3) is expressed as a fraction of the infant's performance during immediate retention tests (block 5, session 1 or 2, respectively). The reactivation group received a reminder 24 hours before the 2- or 4-week session; the facilitating or priming effect of the reactivation treatment is indicated by the shaded area, session 3

and 2 and thus had no training before session 3. The rates at which their reminders occurred were matched to those of the reactivation group.

Infants in this control group showed no change in response rate either within or across sessions (all $ts < 1$). Thus, infants of this age do not simply become more active over the 2-week interval, and their footkicking during the session-3 cued recall test is not a result of either elicited familiarity reactions or the reactivation treatment per se. The acquisition curve of this group in session 3, when reinforcement was introduced for the first time, was indistinguishable from the session-1 learning curves of the other two groups. An analysis of variance with repeated measures over sessions and blocks confirmed that response rates of the reactivation and no-reactivation groups did not differ during training (figure 14.1). A 2 by 2 analysis of variance over retention ratios yielded a significant group-by-sessions interaction: Although 24-hour retention ratios did not differ, the 14-day retention ratio of the reactivation group significantly exceeded that of the no-reactivation group ($P < .01$), whose ratio reflected a return to baseline performance of session 1 (figure 14.2). The retention ratio of the reactivation group was as high as in the 24-hour measure. Thus, both prior training and a reminder are prerequisite for reactivation.

In study 2, we repeated the procedure with 18 infants ($\bar{X}$ age $= 76.9$ days, S. E. $= 2.0$) but doubled the length of the retention interval. The reactivation group ($N = 9$) received a reminder 27 days after training, and retention was

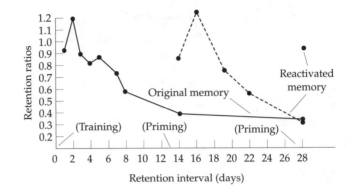

FIGURE 14.2   Retention ratios after 2 days of training (solid line), or 2 days of training plus a reactivation treatment (broken line); priming occurred 13 days after training for all points connected by broken lines or 27 days after training for the single data point at the 28-day retention interval. Each data point represents at least five infants

assessed the next day. A significant group-by-sessions interaction ($P < .03$) again confirmed the superior retention of the reactivation group in session 3 relative to that of the no-reactivation group ($N = 9$), which received no reminder during the retention interval (figure 14.2). As before, the groups had not differed during training (figure 14.1) or in 24-hour retention performance. The 28-day ratio of the no-reactivation group reflected performance equivalent to their session-1 baseline level. The retention ratio (.96) of the reactivation group is remarkable in view of the relatively young age of the infants during training and the relatively large portion of their lives that 4 weeks constitutes.

In study 3, we determined the course of forgetting following a reactivation treatment. Twenty infants ($\bar{X}$ age $= 90.0$ days, S.E. $= 1.3$) received a reactivation treatment 13 days after training as described for study 1; however, session 3 now occurred 3, 6, 9, or 15 days ($N = 5$ per interval) after the reminder. This corresponded to 16, 19, 22, or 28 days, respectively, after the completion of training. The session-3 retention ratios, along with those of the six infants tested 1 day after a reactivation treatment in study 1, were compared with retention ratios describing the original forgetting function. [We had previously obtained this function from 69 infants in a number of different experiments[10] carried out according to the same procedure as that used with the no-reactivation groups of this report.] At least five infants per retention interval contributed data 1, 2, 3, 4, 5, 7, 8, or 14 days after training (figure 14.2). The no-reactivation group of study 2, tested after a 28-day retention interval, was also a control group for the reactivation group tested 15 days after the reminder (28 days after training).

Figure 14.2 is a composite of retention ratios of all groups tested after 2 days of training only ("original memory" function) or after 2 days of training plus a reactivation treatment ("priming") given either 13 (studies 1 and 3) or 27 (study 2) days after training ("reactivated memory" function). A one-way analysis of variance over all data points except that of the study-2 reactivation group indicated that ratios differed reliably as a function of retention interval

$(P < .025)$ and provided the error term for individual comparisons between means (Duncan's multiple range test). The latter indicated that the apparent increase above 1.00 in retention ratios in each function (figure 14.2) was reliable; also, ratios of groups tested 8 (original memory function) and 19 (reactivated memory function) days after training did not differ from ratios of no-reactivation groups tested after retention intervals of 14 and 28 days, respectively. Regression analyses indicated that retention was a linear decreasing function of time elapsed since either training $(P < .005)$ or priming $(P < .005)$. Although the linear model provided a relatively poor fit in each instance, the intercepts and slopes of the two functions did not differ $(ts < 1)$. Thus, forgetting of a reactivated memory followed the same temporal course as forgetting of the original experience.

Our findings confirm Campbell and Jaynes'[2] proposition that reinstatement is a potent mechanism through which experiences of early infancy can continue to influence behavior. An infant's re-encounters with contextual aspects of prior training or an earlier experience can prime or recycle the remaining memory attributes and enhance access to them, alleviating forgetting which otherwise appeared to be complete weeks earlier. Moreover, a re-encounter with the original context can maintain access to the target memory with the same efficacy as original training. Our findings also implicate reinstatement as the mechanism which, during infancy, facilitates the acquisition of the vast amount of learning characteristic of that period of development.

More generally, our findings support a distinction between availability and accessibility of information in memory and imply that failures to observe retention in infants should be discussed in terms of retrieval failures rather than memory deficits.[3,4] We think that procedures that improve accessibility to important retrieval cues will radically alter current views of infant memory[11] and that conditioning procedures, which permit a direct assessment of retention in infants, offer a promising means by which to bridge the gap between human and animal memory research.

Acknowledgment

Study 1 of this research formed a portion of a dissertation submitted by M. W. S. to Rutgers University in partial fulfillment of the requirements for the Ph. D. J. Davis and L. O'Brien assisted in the data collection. Supported by NIMH grant 32307 to C.K.R.-C.

Notes

1. F. A. Beach and J. Jaynes, *Psychol. Bull*, **51**, 239 (1954); E. G. Schachtel, *Psychiatry* **10**, 1 (1947).
2. B. A. Campbell and J. Jaynes, *Psychol. Rev.* **73**, 478 (1966).
3. N. E. Spear, *Psychol. Rev.* **80**, 163 (1973).
4. N. E. Spear and P. J. Parsons, in *Processes of Animal Memory*, D. L. Medin, W. A. Roberts, R. T. Davis, eds (Erlbaum, Hillsdale, NJ, 1976), p. 135.
5. C. F. Mactutus, D. C. Riccio, J. M. Ferek, *Science* **204**, 1319 (1979).

6. K. L. Hoving, L. Coates, M. Bertucci, D. C. Riccio, *Dev. Psychol.* **6**, 426 (1972).
7. C. K. Rovee-Collier and M. J. Gekoski, *Adv. Child Dev. Behav.* **13**, 195 (1979).
8. Because operant levels are typically doubled or tripled during acquisition, retention ratios of .30 to .40 usually indicate performance at operant level. A 3-minute period of nonreinforcement at the conclusion of initial training sessions does not typically extinguish responding in infants 11 to 13 weeks of age.
9. During the reactivation treatment, infants produced responses at a rate of 0 to 2 kicks per minute; operant levels are typically 8 to 11 kicks per minute. In the infant seat, infants rarely exhibit the vertical leg thrusts characteristic of conditioned responding; rather, their movements seem to be postural adjustments or horizontal squirming.
10. C. K. Rovee and J. W. Fagen, *J. Exp. Child Psychol.* **21**, 1 (1976); M. W. Sullivan, C. K. Rovee-Collier, D. M. Tynes, *Child Dev.* **50**, 152 (1979); M. J. Gekoski, paper presented at the meeting of the Eastern Psychological Association, Hartford, Conn., 9 to 12 April 1980.
11. L. B. Cohen and E. R. Gelber, in *Infant Perception: From Sensation to Cognition*, L. B. Cohen and P. Salapatek, eds (Academic Press, New York, 1975), vol. 1, p. 347; J. Kagan, *The Sciences* **19**, 6 (1979); D. S. Ramsay and J. J. Campos, *Dev. Psychol.* **14**, 79 (1978).

15

Rapid Change in the Symbolic Functioning of Very Young Children*

Judy S. DeLoache

One of the fundamental changes in cognitive development in early child-hood is an understanding of symbolic functions. Without this understand-ing many aspects of cognitive growth would not be possible. For instance, language is perhaps the prime example of a symbolic system, and it is only when the child fully appreciates that words are different from the objects and events to which they refer that language development really 'takes off'. In this paper Judy DeLoache charts a remarkable transition that takes place over a six-month period in young children's understanding of scale models – 'from failure to nearly universal success in the space of a few months'.

EDITORS' INTRODUCTION

A remarkable difference in the understanding of the symbolic relation between a scale model and the larger space that it represented was dis-played by two age groups of young children. Three-year-old children who observed an object being hidden in a model knew where to find an analog-ous object hidden in the corresponding location in a room, but 2.5-year-old children did not. The success of the group of older children reveals an advance in their cognitive flexibility: they think of a model in two ways at the same time – both as the thing itself and as a symbol for something else.

OVERVIEW

The results of the research described here reveal the sudden achievement, in a group of children between 2.5 and 3 years of age, of an important develop-mental milestone: the realization that an object can be understood both as a

* Previously published in *Science*, **238** (11 December 1987), pp. 1556–7.

thing itself and as a symbol of something else. Symbolization is a hallmark of human cognition, and the development of symbolic functioning has been assigned a prominent role in many major theories of cognitive development.[1] The specific symbolic relation examined here is that between a scale model and the larger space it represents. It is argued that understanding the representational role of a symbolic object requires thinking about one thing in two different ways at the same time – a crucial aspect of mature, flexible thought.

Previous research has established that very young children are extremely competent at remembering the location of a hidden object.[2] For the research reported here, a young child watched as an attractive toy was hidden within a scale model of a room. (For example, a miniature dog was hidden behind the small couch in the model.) The child was then asked to find an analogous toy that had been concealed in the corresponding place in the room itself (for example, a larger stuffed dog hidden behind the full-sized couch). To succeed, the child had to realize that the model represented the room and that, by remembering the location of the object hidden in the model, he or she could determine the location of the object concealed in the room.

Each experimental session began with an extensive orientation phase highlighting the correspondence between the room (4.80 m by 3.88 m by 2.54 m) and its scale model (71 cm by 65 cm by 33 cm), which was located in an adjoining room. The experimenter explicitly described and demonstrated the correspondence between the two toys to be hidden, between the room and the model, and between the individual items of furniture (the hiding places) within the two spaces.

Immediately after the orientation phase, each child was given four trials, each of which involved three parts. (i) Hiding event – the subject watched as the miniature toy was hidden under or behind an item of furniture in the model. (The toy was hidden in a different place for each trial.) (ii) Retrieval 1 – the child was asked to retrieve the larger toy from the room. On each trial, the child was reminded that the larger toy was hidden in the "same place" as the miniature one. (iii) Retrieval 2 – as a memory check, the child was returned to the model and asked to retrieve the toy that he or she had observed being hidden at the beginning of the trial.[3] Thus, retrieval 2 tapped the child's memory for the original hiding event, and retrieval 1 assessed transfer of that memory to a new context.

The subjects for experiment 1 were 32 children, 16 in a younger group (30 to 32 months; mean age, 31 months) and 16 in an older group (36 to 39 months; mean age, 38 months). The hiding space was counterbalanced with age: half the subjects in each age group watched as the miniature toy was hidden in the model, as described above, and half saw the larger toy being hidden in the room.

The results were dramatic. Figure 15.1 shows the mean number of errorless retrievals of the analogous toy (retrieval 1) and of the original memory object (retrieval 2). The mean level of performance of the older children (old) was better than that of the younger children (young) (old – young = 1.34, SE = 0.17), and overall performance on retrieval 2 (R2) was higher than overall performance on retrieval 1 (R1) (R2 – R1 = 1.59, SE = 0.23). More importantly,

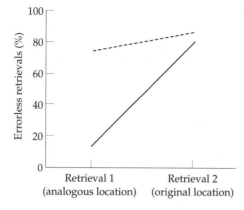

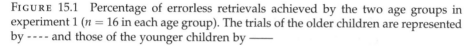

FIGURE 15.1 Percentage of errorless retrievals achieved by the two age groups in experiment 1 ($n = 16$ in each age group). The trials of the older children are represented by - - - - and those of the younger children by ——

the pattern of performance differed for the two age groups. The difference between performance on retrievals 1 and 2 for the older subjects was only 0.27, whereas for the younger children it was 2.69 (SE = 0.32).[4] This difference in the performance of the younger and older children is highly replicable.[5] The results were unaffected by whether the toy was originally hidden in the room or in the model.

For retrieval 2, the younger and older children showed little difference in memory for the original hiding event; their equivalently high performance on the memory check was expected in light of previous memory research.[2] However, the large difference between the two age groups on retrieval 1 – retrieving the analogous object – indicated that they differed dramatically in the use of their memory of one event to reason about another. The older children drew on their knowledge of the location of one hidden object to infer the location of a different object. They were highly adept at making this inference; there was no significant difference between their success as a group in finding the object they had seen and finding the one they had not seen being hidden.

In contrast, the younger children did not use what they knew about the original hiding event to figure out where the other toy had to be. The absence of any systematic pattern to their searching (that is, few correct responses and no identifiable error patterns) suggests that they were unaware that they had any basis for knowing where the toy was without looking for it. Indeed, they gave no evidence, either in their search or in other behavior, that they realized that the two spaces had anything to do with each other.

Why did the younger children in experiment 1 fail to understand the correspondence between the model and the room, to realize that the model represented the room? Experiment 2 evaluated the hypothesis that the problem had to do with a limitation on the symbolic capabilities of the younger children. Success in a model task such as this one requires a dual orientation to the model. On the one hand, it is a real, three-dimensional object (actually, a set of objects) that the child manipulates. On the other hand, the child must realize that the model also stands for or represents something else, in this case, that it is a symbol for the room. Perhaps the younger children think of the model in only one way; the fact that it is a real, three-dimensional object may preclude their realizing that it also stands for something else.

If it is the three-dimensional nature of the model that interferes with the younger children's appreciation of it as a symbol, performance should be better with a purely symbolic medium. A photograph, unlike a real object, typically has no role other than as a symbolic representation of something else[6] and, hence, does not require a dual orientation. Therefore, in experiment 2, the information about where the object was hidden in the room was provided through photographs, rather than through the model, and it was predicted that performance would be better with the photographs than with the model. This prediction is directly contrary to the standard view of the efficacy of pictures versus real objects. Two-dimensional stimuli are generally thought of as less salient and less informative relative to three-dimensional objects. Developmental and cross-cultural studies have repeatedly shown better learning and memory result with real objects than with pictures.[7]

Sixteen children of about the same ages as the younger subjects in experiment 1 (30 to 33 months; mean age, 31.6 months) were observed twice, once in the standard task with the model and once with photographs used in place of the model. Half the children participated in the photograph task first and half in the model task first. For each of the four trials of the photograph task, the child was shown an array of four color photographs (20.3 cm by 25.4 cm), each of which pictured one or more of the hiding places (items of furniture) in the room. On each trial, the experimenter pointed to a different one of the photographs and said, "He's hiding back [under] here." Then the child was taken into the room and encouraged to find the toy.

Figure 15.2 shows the results of experiment 2. Just like the comparable age group in experiment 1, these children were unable to find the toy after seeing it

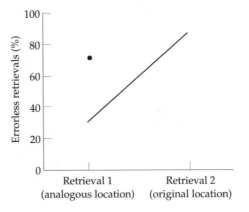

FIGURE 15.2 Percentage of errorless retrievals with photographs and with model, experiment 2 ($n = 16$). The trials using a model room are designated by the solid line and those using a photograph by ●

hidden in the model; they were, however, able to find it after seeing a photograph of its hiding place. Performance in the photograph task (model) was significantly better than performance on retrieval 1 in the model task (model) (photo – model = 1.56, SE = 0.44).[8] Although performance on retrieval 1 was slightly higher for those children who had had the photograph task first, the order effect did not approach significance.

The results of experiment 2 support the hypothesis that the source of 2.5-year-old children's difficulty with the model task was the necessity of maintaining a dual orientation to the model.[9] Although a photograph is a less rich and less salient stimulus than a model, its only function is as a symbol, and even very young children have had substantial experience with pictorial representation. The younger children in this research understood that the photographs represented the room, and they were thus able to apply the pictured information to the room. When faced with a model, they treated it only as a real object. Hence, their knowledge about the location of the hidden object remained specific to that particular toy and that particular space.

One would expect the pattern of developmental change reported here only in domains in which the symbol to be understood is a real object, in line with recent claims that different symbol systems show divergent patterns of development.[10] The current research does not establish the generalizability of these findings; we need to know, for example, to what extent young children's understanding of the relation between a model and a larger space is affected by the degree of difference in scale between the two spaces, the extent of physical similarity between them, and the congruence of the spatial relations among the objects in the spaces.

In conclusion, the failure of 2.5-year-old children to think about a symbolic object both as an object and as a symbol prevented them from generalizing their experience; in other words, it limited their knowledge to the particular instance, rather than the general rule. Understanding the dual role of symbolic objects is thus a crucial developmental step.[11] The possibility of a strongly maturational underpinning for this step is raised by the abrupt nature of the developmental change displayed by the children in these experiments – from failure to nearly universal success in the space of a few months.

ACKNOWLEDGMENTS

Supported in part by grant HD 05951 from the National Institute of Child Health and Human Development and by a Senior International Fellowship from the Fogarty Foundation of the National Institute of Health. I thank R. Baillargeon, P. Harris, G. Clore, and D. Gentner for helpful comments on this work. I also thank the parents and children who participated in the research.

NOTES

1. H. Werner and B. Kaplan, (eds), *Symbol Formation* (Wiley, New York, 1963); L. S. Vygotsky (ed), *Mind in Society* (Harvard Univ. Press, Cambridge, 1978).

2. J. S. DeLoache and A. L. Brown, *Child Dev.* **54**, 888 (1983); *Dev. Psychol.* **20**, 37 (1984); J. S. DeLoache et al., *Child Dev.* **56**, 125 (1985).

3. Retrieval 2 also provided a motivation check; high performance here would rule out low motivation as an explanation of poor performance on retrieval 1.

4. According to an age by hiding space by sex by retrieval mixed analysis of variance (ANOVA) of the number of correct responses, there were statistically significant main effects for age [$F(1, 24) = 62.33$, $P < 0.00001$] and retrieval, [$F(1, 24) = 49.70$, $P < 0.00001$], but no statistically significant effects for sex or for hiding space. The primary result of the analysis was the significant interaction of age by retrieval [$F(1, 24) = 23.41$, $P < 0.0001$].

5. The results of experiment 1 have been replicated several times with the same model and room, as well as with different spaces and with substantial variations in the instructions and orientation procedures. The results are not attributable to differences in verbal skills: the younger children clearly understood every aspect of the instructions except the correspondence between the spaces, and this was in spite of the fact that they did understand the meaning of "the same," as shown in independent comprehension checks.

6. M. C. Potter, in *Symbolic Functioning in Childhood*, N. R. Smith and M. B. Franklin, eds (Erlbaum, Hillsdale, NJ, 1979), pp. 41–65.

7. M. Cole and S. Scribner, *Culture and Thought* (Wiley, New York, 1974); J. S. DeLoache, *Cog. Dev.* **1**, 123 (1986); D. G. Hartley, *Dev. Psychol*, **12**, 218 (1976).

8. There was a significant main effect for task, in a task (photograph versus model, retrieval 1) by order by sex ANOVA [$F(1, 12) = 12.42$, $P < 0.005$].

9. Further support has been provided in subsequent studies. Retrieval 1 performance is the same when a wide-angle photograph or line drawing of the room is used in place of the individual photographs used here. Also, pointing to the correct place in the model produces the same low level of performance that hiding the object in the model does.

10. D. Wolf and H. Gardner, in *Early Language Acquisition and Intervention*, R. Schiefelbusch and D. Bricker, eds (University Park Press, Baltimore, MD, 1981), pp. 286–327.

11. This step may be related to other developmental phenomena involving the appreciation that a single reality can be understood in different and even conflicting ways by one person or by different people, for example, the appearance–reality distinction [J. H. Flavell et al., *Cog. Psychol.* **15**, 95 (1983)]; level 2 perspective taking [J. H. Flavell et al., *Dev. Psychol.* **17**, 99 (1981)]; and understanding false belief [H. Wimmer and J. Perner, *Cognition* **13**, 103 (1983)].

16

DECEPTION IN 3-YEAR-OLDS*

Michael Lewis, Catherine Stanger and Margaret W. Sullivan*

This is a classic study about how children can practise deception, with the interesting finding that truth tellers and deceivers could not easily be differentiated. The reader may wish to compare this study with the next paper, by Ceci and Huffman (article 17), who report that preschool 'children's false statements were quite convincing to professionals' – the professionals were psychiatrists, psychologists, social workers, attorneys, and judges – 'who were unable to distinguish between true and false accounts'.

EDITORS' INTRODUCTION

Children's ability to deceive was examined in order to determine whether they are able to hide their emotional expression intentionally. Three-year-olds were instructed not to peek at a toy while the experimenter left the room. When asked, the great majority either denied that they peeked or would not answer the question. Facial and bodily activity did not differentiate the deceivers from the truth tellers. Boys were more likely than girls to admit their transgression. These results indicate that very young children have begun to learn how to mask their emotional expressions and support the role of socialization in this process.

OVERVIEW

Deception is a frequent activity in the life of individuals. It may take the simple form of agreeing with someone with whose opinion, in fact, we do not agree (e.g., saying we like the color of a tie when we do not) or other forms such as lying about a serious transgression. Deception can be directed toward the self as well, as in the case where we deny that we have a certain feeling when, in

* Previously published in *Developmental Psychincg*, **25**, 3 (1989), pp. 439–43.

fact, we do feel this way (Lewis, in press). Moreover, cultures may have display rules that encourage masking negative emotion (Ekman, Friesen, and Ellsworth, 1972; Izard, 1977). Deception can be observed in all age groups, but the questions of how old a child must be in order to be able to deceive and how well a child can succeed in the deception are largely unexplored.

Anecdotal evidence suggests that very young children may practice deception, for example, young children who deny that they have eaten a cookie when there are signs of the cookie on their mouths. Many other examples of deception exist as well. For example, the 20-month-old child who cries when she scrapes her hand, but only when her mother is present, or the 24-month-old child who knows his name, but when asked what it is playfully responds, "Mommy." In all these examples, the children may respond with verbal or facial–vocal behaviors (or both) that do not reflect what they know to be true. Could these examples reflect the beginning of the ability to deceive? In order to answer this question, it is necessary to be able to infer that there is a known correct response and that the child's behavior is an attempt to hide or avoid that response.

Given that many examples of deception-like behavior appear in the young child, it is surprising that there is very little systematic research on this topic, in terms both of the development of deception and of the individual differences in its use. There are some studies on children's ability to detect deception (DePaulo, Jordan, Irvine, and Laser, 1982; Feldman, Devin-Sheeham, and Allen, 1978; Morency and Krauss, 1982) and children's ability to deceive when instructed to do so (Feldman, Jenkins, and Popoola, 1979; Feldman and White, 1980); however, most of this work has involved children who are 6 years or older. Moreover, little work exists regarding children's ability to hide or mask their emotions or to be deceptive in more naturalistic situations at any age (Saarni, 1984). It has been assumed that both socialization factors and increased cognitive capacity enable children to alter their facial expressions and verbal and nonverbal behaviors in order to mask their underlying emotional state (Ekman et al., 1972; Lewis and Michalson, 1985; Saarni, 1979). The study of deception bears on the development of these capacities.

Saarni (1984) attempted to observe directly developmental differences in children's abilities to use deception in a life-like situation. First, third and fifth graders were placed in a situation where their expectations for a desirable toy were not met. After receiving a desirable gift and the promise of another such gift, the children were given an undesirable gift. The children's facial expression and nonverbal behavior were coded. With increasing age, children demonstrated an increased ability to mask their internal states, and girls showed this ability earlier and to a greater extent than boys. These findings are difficult to interpret, however, because the regulation and dissociation of expressive behavior from the internal state must be inferred. That is, it is unknown whether the children, in fact, were disappointed in not receiving the promised gift and, therefore, used deception to mask their disappointment.

Although the study of children's use of deception is important for our understanding of the socialization of emotion and the relationship between internal states and external expressions, there are few studies on this topic.

Those few that exist provide us with limited information, because the children in them were required to play act, and, thus, were not studied directly in terms of the use of deception in more natural situations. The present study represents an attempt to observe young children engaging in deception under the condition that it is they who chose to deceive. In order to create a natural situation that might induce children to deceive, 3-year-old children were placed in a situation where they were prohibited from looking at a toy. On violating the prohibition, they were asked about their behavior. It was expected that, of the children who violated the rule, some would admit and some would deny their transgression (deception). By observing their actual behavior, we need not infer deception. Moreover, the facial expression of the children was studied prior to as well as after they were asked if they had peeked. In this way, one can judge their emotional expressions to their transgression as well as whether the expressions were a consequence of their denial or admission. Therefore, this study focuses on (a) whether young children engage in both verbal and behavioral deception and (b) how well they deceive by masking their expression.

METHOD

Subjects

Thirty-three subjects, 15 boys and 18 girls, between the ages of 33 and 37 months (M age $= 35.4$ months) were seen in the laboratory. The subjects were from middle- and upper-class Caucasian families and had been seen previously in the same laboratory at 5, 13, and 22 months of age. Data from two additional subjects (1 boy and 1 girl) were omitted from the analysis because they refused to cooperate with the procedure.

Procedure

Subjects were seated in a chair with their back to a small table and told that the experimenter was going to put out a surprise toy. The experimenter then set out a play "zoo."[1] The children were instructed not to peek and that they could play with the toy when the experimenter returned. The experimenter then left the room. The mother was seated with her back to her child, filling out a questionnaire. The children were observed and videotaped through a one-way mirror. The experimenter returned to the room when the children either peeked at the toy or when 5 minutes had passed. The experimenter stood in front and to the right of the child and stared with a neutral expression for 5 seconds, then asked the child, "Did you peek?" If the subject did not respond, she or he was asked again. No subject who did not respond to the first question responded to the second. After waiting 5 seconds the experimenter invited the child to play with the toy and reassured him or her that it was all right to peek.[2]

The verbal and nonverbal responses of the subjects in response to the experimenter's stare and to the question "Did you peek?" were coded from the videotape recording of the session. Verbal responses fell into three categories: (a) saying "yes" or shaking the head "yes"; (b) saying "no" or shaking the head "no"; and (c) giving no verbal or nonverbal response.

A second coder experienced in coding facial expressions using the MAX system (Izard and Dougherty, 1982) also coded facial expressions. Tapes were viewed in both fast and slow motion, and each facial expression was noted as it occurred. Four expressions that occurred with any frequency were coded: *smiling, gaze avert, sober mouth,* and *relaxed-interest mouth.* Also coded was *nervous touching,* which included movement of the hands to touch hair, clothing, face, or other body parts, *startle response,* measured by abrupt body movement with or without breath inhalation, and *body inhibition,* measured by sudden cessation in ongoing activity. Of these three body activities, only nervous touching occurred with sufficient frequency to be analyzed. A second coder scored 10 tapes, and the interobserver reliabilities (agreement/agreement + disagreement) were quite high for facial and bodily activities (93%–98% agreement). The scores ranged from 0 to 2 for the positive behaviors and 0 to 3 for the negative behaviors. Mean scores were obtained by dividing the number of positive behaviors by 2 for the mean positive score and the number of negative behaviors by 3 for the mean negative score.

Results

Verbal response

Subjects were asked whether they had looked at the toy when the experimenter left the room. Four of the 33 subjects did not look, indicating that most children this age will violate such a rule if left alone (sign test, $p < .001$). Of the 29 subjects who violated the rule, 38% said "yes" they did look, 38% said "no" they did not look, and 24% gave no verbal response. The four subjects who did not look said "no". Thus, only 38% of the 3-year-old children were willing to admit to the transgression that they had just performed.[3]

Sex differences in verbal response can be observed, with boys more likely than girls to admit to their transgression. Of the children who said "no," 73% were girls; of those who did not verbally respond, 71% were girls, whereas of those who said "yes," 82% were boys. Whereas 64% of the boys admitted to their transgression (said "yes"), only 13% of girls did so (Fischer's Exact Probability test, $p < .04$). Moreover, girls more often than boys gave no response (28% and 13%, respectively; Fischer's Exact Probability test, $p < .05$). Overall, boys were more truthful (saying "yes" rather than "no" or giving no response) than girls (Fischer's Exact Probability test, $p < .03$).

Facial and bodily response

The facial and bodily response data are presented in table 16.1. The data are presented as the percentage of subjects exhibiting individual behaviors and the mean score of the positive and negative behaviors for the four groups of verbal replies by condition as well as by change in response over the two conditions.

TABLE 16.1   Facial expression by condition and verbal response

| Condition | Subjects who peeked | | | | Subjects who did not peek |
	NR (n = 7)	No (n = 11)	Yes (n = 10)	Total (n = 28)	No (n = 4)
	Stare condition				
Relaxed face	57.1	18.2	20.0	28.6	25.0
Smile	28.6	27.3	40.0	32.1	0.0
M positive behaviors	.429	.227	.300	.304	.125
Sober	42.9	27.3	30.0	32.1	50.0
Avert	100.0	81.8	60.0	78.6	75.0
Nervous touch	57.1	36.4	50.0	46.4	50.0
M negative behaviors	.667	.485	.467	.524	.583

	NR (n = 7)	No (n = 11)	Yes (n = 11)	Total (n = 29)	No (n = 4)
	Question condition				
Relaxed face	28.6	45.5	9.1	27.6	25.0
Smile	14.3	54.5	54.5	44.8	0.0
M positive behaviors	.214	.500	.300	.362	.125
Sober	28.6	18.2	36.4	27.6	50.0
Avert	71.4	81.8	81.8	79.3	75.0
Nervous touch	71.4	45.5	36.4	48.3	50.0
M negative behaviors	.571	.485	.500	.511	.583

	Percentage change over condition				
Relaxed face	−28.5	27.3	10.9	−1.0	0.0
Smile	−14.3	27.5	14.5	12.7	0.0
M positive behaviors	−.215	.279	.000	.051	.000
Sober	−14.3	9.1	6.4	−4.5	0.0
Nervous touch	14.3	9.1	13.6	1.9	0.0
Avert	−28.6	0.0	21.8	0.7	0.0
M negative behaviors	−.096	.000	−.003	−.013	.000

Note: NR = no response. Values represent percentages of subjects.

We conducted a repeated measures analysis of variance (ANOVA) with two within-subject factors (condition: stare vs. ask; affect: positive vs. negative) and a between-subject factor (group: no response, no, yes, and no peek). There were no main effects for group and condition, although there was a significant affect effect, $F(1, 28) = 11.86$, $p < .002$. Over conditions and groups, the mean of the negative behaviors was greater than the mean of the positive behaviors. There was a significant Group × Condition effect, $F(3, 28) = 3.98$, $p < .02$. The Group × Condition effect indicates that the groups differed in their overall responses over the stare and ask conditions. Although not significant, $F(3, 28) = 1.44$, the three-way interaction suggests that the groups differed in their positive behaviors over condition but not in their negative behaviors. Testing each affect separately revealed no changes over condition in the negative behaviors by group, however there were significant changes in the positive behaviors by group, $F(3, 28) = 4.73$, $p < .01$. The no-response group showed a decrease (least significant difference [LSD], $p < .05$), the "no" group showed an increase (LSD, $p < .05$), and the "yes" and no-peek groups showed no change.

Given these overall differences, we next considered observation by condition and groups. In the *stare condition* when the experimenter looked at the child, children who transgressed ($n = 28$) showed more mean negative (.524) than positive (.304) behaviors (LSD, $p < .05$).[4] Children who did not transgress showed a similar pattern (M positive $= .125$ vs. M negative $= .583$). Although children who peeked showed the same mean negative behavior as children who did not peek, the peekers showed greater mean positive behavior than the nonpeekers. For specific positive behaviors this was significant for smile face (test of proportion, $p < .05$). There were no differences among the three groups of peekers, in particular between those who peeked and lied and those who peeked and told the truth.

In the *question condition* the children who transgressed again showed more mean negative than positive behaviors (LSD, $p < .05$). Children who did not transgress also showed this pattern. The children who transgressed showed more mean positive behavior than the children who did not transgress, although there was no difference in the mean of negative behaviors. Smiling behavior was greater for those subjects who transgressed than for those who did not (test of proportion, $p < .05$). Among the children who transgressed, "no" subjects showed the most mean positive behavior and the no-response subjects showed the least (LSD, $p < .05$). Although the deceivers showed a larger mean positive behavior than the truth tellers, this difference was not significant (LSD, $p < .10$). There were no differences among groups for the mean negative behaviors.

Of interest is the examination of the 11 subjects who said "no" they did not peek but did and the four subjects who said "no" and did not peek. The truthful "no" subjects showed smaller mean positive behaviors than the deceivers (LSD, $p < .05$); specifically, they smiled less ($z = 1.90, p < .06$). There was no difference in the mean negative behaviors between these two groups.

Change in behavior

These scores reflect, in part, the effect of deceiving, telling the truth, or not answering the question posed by the experimenter. There were no differences in either the mean positive or negative behaviors when subjects who peeked were compared with those who did not peek, partly because the three groups of subjects who transgressed differed markedly in the degree of positive behavior change that they expressed. Subjects who transgressed and said "no" showed more mean positive behavior change than the other two groups. Although the mean of the positive behaviors increased for the "no" group they declined for the no-response group (LSD, $p < .01$) and stayed the same for the "yes" group. The comparison of deceivers and truth tellers was also significant

(LSD, $p < .05$). A comparison between the two "no" groups revealed more mean increase in positive behavior for the deceivers than for those telling the truth (Fischer's Exact Probability test, $p < .10$).

DISCUSSION

When 3-year-old children transgress a rule and are asked about it, they are capable of deception. Only 38% in this study admitted to looking at a toy that they had been instructed not to look at. By 3 years of age, children do use verbal deception. Thus, we have some evidence to support the hypothesis that deception strategies are adopted at early ages. This is not surprising given early socialization factors. Although parents tell their children not to lie, they also inform them both directly and indirectly that deception is socially appropriate. For example, children are directly informed to pretend that they like a gift even though they do not ("Remember to thank grandmother for the sweater even though you wanted a toy"). Indirectly, children watch the behaviors of others and observe the same type of behavior. For example, mother pretends that she is happy to see her neighbor, when immediately before the neighbor arrived she had expressed her desire not to see her.

Given these different and, at times, contradictory social messages, the task of the young child is to learn the rules of masking emotional expression. Why, then, do findings with children past 6 years indicate only moderate success in accomplishing this task? It may be because in previous studies the children were asked to *pretend* that they liked or did not like a drink. Play acting may require cognitive skills beyond those necessary for deception that make this experimental type of deception more difficult.[5] When experimental situations are used that are more naturalistic and are familiar to children in relation to their daily lives, children may show more competence.

Although almost all 3-year-olds succumb to the temptation to look when told not to, not all subjects do so. In this study, about 15% of the children did not peek, even after 5 minutes of being left alone in the room with an attractive toy. Individual differences in young children's ability to inhibit forbidden action may be a function of the cognitive strategy that they adopt while confronted with the transgression. For example, Mischel and Ebbesen (1970) reported that mental distraction is one of the strategies that leads to successful inhibition of action. Individual differences in resisting temptation may also reflect differences in socialization or in temperament. Socialization differences in response to inhibiting action have been discussed by many (e.g., Aronfreed, 1976; Parke and Slaby, 1983). In regard to temperament, Mowrer (1950) reported a study by Solomon where specific differences in puppy dogs' ability to inhibit a forbidden action were found. He claimed that these individual differences, at least in dogs, were related to biological rather than socialization differences because all of the animals were trained in exactly the same way. Further studies are required to examine whether differences in cognitive ability, socialization, temperament, or a combination of these are related to individual differences in resisting temptation.

Given that young children transgress and are capable of verbal deception, how successful are they in masking their expressive behavior? One way to answer this is by observing their facial and bodily behavior. Facial differences that occurred when the subjects were questioned appear to co-vary with the nature of their verbal response. The differences among the groups, as seen in the change scores, reveal that the truth tellers (children who said "yes" when they did peek and those who said "no" when they did not peek) showed little behavior change when they responded verbally. On the other hand, the deceivers showed change in their positive behavior; the children who said "no" and peeked showed an increase in smiling and relaxed face, and the no-response children showed a decrease in these behaviors and an increase in nervous touching. These results suggest that for the children who deceive, verbal and facial deception are organized and integrated. That is, these children hide their verbal deception with increased positive rather than negative behaviors. The no-response children also failed to admit their transgression – however, they were less organized and integrated. First, they could not directly lie (i.e., say "no") but chose not to answer the question. Secondly, their facial/bodily responses showed an increase in nervous touching. In both ways, then, their deception was less developed than that of the children who said "no." These children either may represent the transitional phase from truth telling to deception or may be poor deceivers (see Saarni, 1979). Only longitudinal investigation can reveal whether deception ability passes through such phases.

Exact analysis of behavior allows us in retrospect to observe differences in those 3-year-olds who deceive in comparison with those who tell the truth. However, the analysis is retrospective, that is, we know already who the deceivers are and look for differences. Given that it is an increase in mean positive (and not negative) behaviors that differentiates the groups, how would the naive observer react to these facial and bodily changes, and are observers able to discriminate these subtle cues? Sixty adult subjects, varying in age from 21 to 25 years, were asked to view the videotapes in order to determine whether they could identify the subjects who told the truth. Only those segments of the tape in which the subject was asked about peeking were presented (approximately 5 seconds), one at a time, to the adults. The adults had to indicate whether they thought the particular child peeked or did not peek or that they did not know if the child peeked. Because children shook their heads as they gave their verbal response it was not possible to include those subjects who admitted to their transgression, because it would make little sense for children to say "yes" to something they did not do. Therefore, only subjects who said "no" or gave no response were rated. There were 15 subjects who said "no" (11 who had peeked and 4 who had not) and 7 subjects who gave no response. The adult judges were not able to differentiate between the groups, particularly between subjects who said "no" and peeked and subjects who said "no" and did not peek, as well as between those who said "no" and those who gave no response. Thus, although the number of subjects was few, the adult judges did not appear to be able to discriminate the children on the basis of their behavioral differences during the questioning period, even though some differences exist when careful measurement is applied. Such findings do not disagree with the recent work by Ekman, Friesen, and O'Sulli-van (1988), who found that deceptive smiling can be detected. In their study, observers who were trained on facial coding were used, and, as such, this situation does not relate to naive observers looking at facial behavior.

The adult judges in this study were not able to see the changes in behavior from the stare to questioning conditions, and this change may be what is important for more accurate judgments. Just looking at children's response to questioning may not be sufficient for making accurate judgments. Even in the question condition, however, the children differ in their responses. Alternatively, the judges may have been able to observe the differences in expression but interpreted them differently. If the adults believed that smiling and relaxed face do not reference guilt, their judgment would result in the findings obtained. Smiling and relaxed face are not usually believed to reference guilt (Izard, 1977).

Sex differences indicate that girls show more verbal deception than boys, a finding consistent with other studies using facial expression (Feldman and White, 1980; Saarni, 1984). Specifically, females use deception earlier, and their use of deception is less detectable than in males. Why should such group differences appear? In the present study, girls show no more transgression than boys, yet they are significantly more apt to deny their transgression than boys. There appear to be at least two possible reasons for this. First, females may be more ashamed/embarrassed about their transgression than males and, thus, would be less likely to admit the transgression to the experimenter. H. Lewis (1971) reported that females show more shame than males in interpersonal relationships, and Lewis, Sullivan, Stanger, and Weiss (1989) have shown that 2-year-old girls show more embarrassment than boys. Such findings indicate sex differences in some emotional responses and, thus, may contribute to sex differences in the likelihood of admitting to transgression. If this difference in the emotional response to transgression is true, it remains a puzzle why there are no differences in the likelihood of violating a rule, because the violation of the rule should evoke more upset for females than for males. In fact, although not significant, there were three females to one male who did not peek. Thus, there is some tendency for females not to transgress as much as males.

A second reason for these sex differences is possible, one which may have more to do with social pressure than with emotional differences. It may be the case that females, being more interested in social approval (Block, 1978; Huston, 1983), are less likely to admit to a transgression because such an admission might result in the displeasure of the adult experimenter. In this case, sex differences in the need for social desirability and, perhaps, the fear of punishment are what motivate the female children's deception. Why sex differences in deception occur remains an important question and one related to the socialization of children within the first 3 years of life.

NOTES

1. Manufactured by Fisher-Price, 1984 (Copyright 916).

2. Parents were debriefed and informed that the study was designed so that *all* subjects were expected to peek. Parents appeared satisfied that their children did not show any deviant behavior and all agreed to participate in a second study.
3. It is difficult to assign a significance level to these data because it is not reasonable to give an equally likely probability to each of the three types of response. Thus, only descriptive data are presented here.
4. One subject's tape was unavailable for measurement during the stare condition.
5. Play acting deception is a complex skill in the manner of a meta-decept skill, whereas deception itself is a simple skill; that is, play acting a deception requires a "play acting of a play acting."

ACKNOWLEDGMENTS

This research was supported in part by a grant from the W. T. Grant Foundation. Special appreciation is given to Andree-Maryse Duvalsaint and Phillip Barone for data collection and to John Jaskir for data analysis.

REFERENCES

Aronfreed, J. (1976). Moral development from the standpoint of a general psychological theory. In T. Lickona (ed.), *Moral Development and Behavior* (pp. 21–36), New York: Holt, Rinehart & Winston.

Block, J. H. (1978). Another look at sex differentiation in the socialization behaviors of mothers and fathers. In J. Sherman and F. L. Denmark (eds), *The Psychology of Women: Future Directions of Research* (pp. 54–68), New York: Psychological Dimensions.

DePaulo, B., Jordan, A., Irvine, A., and Laser, P. (1982). Age changes in the detection of deception. *Child Development*, **53**, 701–9.

Ekman, P., Friesen, W., and Ellsworth, P. (1972). *Emotion in the Human Face*. New York: Pergamon.

Ekman, P., Friesen, W. V., and O'Sullivan, M. (1988). Smiles when lying. *Journal of Personality and Social Psychology*, **54**, 414–20.

Feldman, R., Devin-Sheeham, L., and Allen, V. (1978). Nonverbal cues as indicators of verbal dissembling. *American Education Research Journal*, **15**, 217–31.

Feldman, R., Jenkins, L., and Popoola, O. (1979). Detection of deception in adults and children via facial expressions. *Child Development*, **50**, 350–55.

Feldman, R., and White, J. (1980). Detecting deception in children. *Journal of Communication*, **30**, 121–9.

Huston, A. C. (1983). Sex typing. In P. H. Mussen (series ed.) and E. M. Hetherington (vol. ed.), *Handbook of Child Psychology: Vol. 4. Socialization, Personality, and Social Development* (4th edn, pp. 387–468), New York: Wiley.

Izard, C. (1977). *Human Emotions*. New York: Plenum Press.

Izard, C., and Dougherty, L. (1982). Two complementary systems for measuring facial expressions in infants and children. In C. E. Izard (ed.), *Measuring Emotions in Infants and Children* (pp. 97–126), New York: Cambridge University Press.

Lewis, H. (1971). *Shame and Guilt in Neuroses*. New York: International University Press.

Lewis, H., Sullivan, M. W., Stanger, C., and Weiss, M. (1989). Self-development and self-conscious emotions. *Child Development*, **60**, 146–56.

Lewis, M. (in press). Thinking and feeling – The elephant's tail. In C. A. Maher, M. Schwebel, and N. S. Faley (eds), *Thinking about Problem Solving in the Developmental Process: International Perspectives*, New Brunswick, NJ: Rutgers Press.

Lewis, M., and Michalson, L. (1985). Faces as signs and symbols. In G. Zivin (ed.), *Development of Expressive Behavior: Biology–environmental Interaction* (pp. 153–82), New York: Academic Press.

Mischel, W., and Ebbesen, E. B. (1970). Attention in delay of gratification. *Journal of Personality and Social Psychology*, **16**, 329–37.

Morency, N., and Krauss, R. (1982). Children's nonverbal encoding and decoding of affect. In R. S. Feldman (ed.), *Development of Nonverbal Behavior in Children* (pp. 181–202), New York: Springer-Verlag.

Mowrer, O. H. (1950). *Learning Theory and Personality Dynamics*. New York: Ronald.

Parke, R. D., and Slaby, R. G. (1983). The development of aggression. In P. H. Mussen (series ed.) and E. M. Hetherington (vol. ed.), *Handbook of Child Psychology: Vol. 4. Socialization, Personality, and Social Development* (4th edn., pp. 547–641), New York: Wiley.

Saarni, C. (1979). Children's understanding of display rules for expressive behavior. *Developmental Psychology*, **15**, 424–9.

Saarni, C. (1984). An observational study of children's attempts to monitor their expressive behavior. *Child Development*, **55**, 1504–13.

17

How Suggestible are Preschool Children? Cognitive and Social Factors*

Stephen J. Ceci and
Mary Lyn Crotteau Huffman

OVERVIEW   *Objectives*: In this series of studies, the authors sought to determine some of the cognitive and social boundary conditions that can undermine the accuracy of young children's reporting. Care was taken to include events and interviewing variables that more accurately reflect the experiences of children in real-world investigations of alleged sexual abuse. Videotaped interviews with preschool children were presented to experts to determine how adept they are at distinguishing between true and false accounts. *Method*: All the studies were designed to investigate the susceptibility to suggestion in young preschool children. The difference between studies was the form of that suggestion and the nature of the event to which the children were exposed. All studies measured recall accuracy, false assent rate, and the change in these outcomes over time and/or successive interviews. *Results*: Very young preschool children (aged 3 and 4 years) were significantly more vulnerable to suggestions than were older preschool children (aged 5 and 6 years). The number of interviews and the length of the interval over which they were presented resulted in the greatest level of suggestibility. *Conclusions*: While some types of events (negative, genital, salient) were more difficult to implant in children's statements, some children appeared to internalize the false suggestions and resisted debriefing. These children's false statements were quite convincing to professionals, who were unable to distinguish between true and false accounts.

* Previously published in the *Journal of the American Academy of Child and Adolescent Psychiatry*, **36**, 7 (July 1997), pp. 948–58.

Sexual abuse of children is a serious societal problem. In 1991 there was an incident rate of just under 1% of all children younger than the age of 18. Although this may appear to be a small number, in actuality it translates into nearly a half million reported allegations, 129,697 of which were substantiated cases of sexual abuse (National Center on Child Abuse and Neglect, 1993). In the latest survey data, this number had nearly doubled (National Center on Child Abuse and Neglect, 1996). This number may be an underestimation of the prevalence of child sexual abuse because many cases go unreported (Ceci and Bruck, 1993a).

Because of the large number of sexual abuse allegations, there has been a large increase in the number of children involved in the juvenile and criminal justice systems. It seems that preschool children are not only disproportionately more likely to be abused, but also more likely to have their case come to trial (Ceci and Bruck, 1993b). In this article we will describe some recent research on factors that may influence the accuracy of a child's report. Of particular interest in our research are the effects of suggestibility and stereotypes on a child's testimony, particularly when they are presented repeatedly over long intervals.

Before describing our research on suggestibility and source misattributions, it is important to distinguish between the interviewing procedures of researchers on the one hand and those of forensic, law enforcement, and mental health professionals on the other. In traditional laboratory experiments, children are usually interviewed once, within minutes or hours of witnessing an event; interviewers know the "ground truth," and no attempt is made to mislead the child. In actual court cases, however, children are interviewed many times by many different people (e.g., attorneys, psychologists, social workers, police, etc.) over the course of weeks, months, and even years after the event. The average child in the courtroom has been interviewed formally 3.5 to 11 times before his or her court appearance (Gray, 1993; McGough, 1993). (While reliable data are unavailable on the number of informal interviews by parents, therapists, and friends, it is undoubtedly greater than the number of formal ones.) In response to this difference, our research has incorporated these real-world factors.

The creation of a false belief   Not all children who take the witness stand tell the truth. Though some may be motivated to lie, others may genuinely believe they are telling the truth, despite making errors. When a child believes a false event to have occurred, what has happened? There are two possibilities, one having to do with suggestions and the other with source misattributions: (1) the child's original memory has been changed by information provided either before, during, or after the event such that the initial memory trace has been erased or overwritten; or (2) the child has confused the source of the information, recognizing an event as "familiar" while failing to remember whether the source of the familiarity is internal (e.g., imagined) or external (e.g., actually observed).

What would cause a child to harbor a false belief? Numerous volumes have been written on this very topic, and it is beyond the scope of this article to review them. Extensive reviews have been provided by Ceci and Bruck (1993a, 1995), Stein et al. (1996), Zaragoza (1995), and Fivush and Hudson (1990). In this article we shall focus on the work done at the Cornell laboratory as it is representative of the work being done across the United States and Canada and has been designed to mimic the procedures that bring many children into contact with the juvenile and criminal justice systems.

In a recent set of experiments (Ceci et al., 1994a, b), we have identified three factors that appear to contribute to children's false reports: (1) being suggestively interviewed about an event repeatedly over a long interval (usually several months), (2) telling the child that some authority source (e.g., a parent) said the event was true, or (3) being asked to create mental images of a fictitious event repeatedly. In what follows, we will explain why these three activities are detrimental to a child's report accuracy.

Suggestibility   Before beginning a general discussion of the effects of suggestibility, it is important to define the term. Narrowly defined, suggestibility refers to "the extent to which individuals come to accept and subsequently incorporate post-event information into their memory recollections" (Gudjonsson, 1986, p. 195). This definition implies that suggestions are incorporated unconsciously into the memory system, as a result of suggestions made after an event is witnessed (i.e., postevent). Ceci and Bruck (1993b) have argued for a broader definition of suggestibility, however: one that entails not only unconscious processing of suggestions but conscious processing of information provided before, during, and after the event, and social (e.g., bribes and threats) as well as cognitive (i.e., memory) factors. According to these authors, "suggestibility concerns the degree to which children's encoding, storage, retrieval, and reporting of events can be influenced by a range of social and psychological factors" (Ceci and Bruck, 1993b, p. 404).

Individual differences   No formula can predict how different internal and external factors will affect an individual child. Some children may be more influenced by social cues such as bribes and threats by significant others, while others may be resilient to these factors. Other children may be particularly susceptible to cognitive cues such as suggestive and leading questions. The vast differences between children in their vulnerability to a host of cognitive and social factors has only recently begun to receive the attention of experimentalists (Goodman and Quas, 1996; Ornstein et al., 1996). Although we have known for some time that individual differences are pronounced, with some young children actually being more resistant to suggestions than some older ones, we have little understanding of the reasons for such differences.

Source-misattribution error   Researchers have repeatedly shown that children can have trouble distinguishing between actual and imagined events, that is, actions they actually performed and actions they just imagined performing (Foley et al., 1989; Johnson and Foley, 1985). Young children can confuse their memories when the same actor is involved in the actions. Markham (1991) found that 6-year-old children had trouble distinguishing between actions they imagined performing and actions they actually did perform. Lindsay et al. (1991) found that 8-year-olds also had difficulty distinguishing between actions they saw another perform and actions they imagined that same person performing. They did not have trouble, however, distinguishing between an observed and an imagined action when different actors were involved in each, thus leading Lindsay and Johnson (1989) to conclude: "In a series of experiments, source-monitoring errors were found to be more frequent when potential memory sources were similar to one another in terms of their perceptual properties, modality of presentation, semantic content, or cognitive operations (orienting task)" (p. 350).

When a child experiences an event, he or she may simultaneously see it, think about it, hear it, possibly read about it, and thus store information from all of these sources. If children are not able to differentiate between different sources of their knowledge, they will be more susceptible to misattribution error and suggestions.

CURRENT LABORATORY AND FIELD RESEARCH

As noted above, recent research has attempted to incorporate factors known to be relevant in forensic contexts, such as repeated suggestions over long intervals. Because it is ethically impermissible to experiment with actual sexual abuse, researchers have turned their attention to naturally occurring analogs of abuse. Thus, it is increasingly common for these factors to be embedded in naturalistic situations where there is a high level of stress, a loss of control, the possibility of embarrassment, and active participation. Finally, current research has expanded the focus to include the role of the interviewer as well as the child. This constellation of factors and context is illustrated in the following synopses of seven recently completed experiments.

Study 1: Effects of induced stereotypes and repeated suggestions

The purpose of this study was to determine whether pairing the induction of stereotypes in a child's mind with repeated misleading suggestions would affect both the accuracy and credibility of the child's testimony.

To accomplish this, a mythical character named "Sam Stone" visited nursery schools for 2 minutes. Children were randomly assigned to one of four groups, each composed of 40 to 50 preschool children (see Leichtman and Ceci, 1995, for details).

After Sam Stone's 2-minute visit to their classroom, control group children were interviewed four times over the next 10 weeks about Sam Stone's visit, using nonsuggestive techniques ("Tell me what happened"). During the fifth and final interview, these children were first asked for a free narrative ("Tell me everything that happened the day Sam Stone visited your classroom"), then they were probed about two nonevents involving a book and a teddy bear (e.g., "Did Sam Stone rip a book?" "Did he spill anything on a teddy bear?").

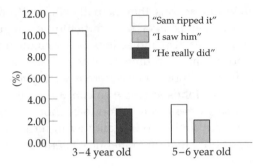

FIGURE 17.1   Children's report accuracy: no suggestion; no stereotype

These control group children did very well, correctly recalling most of what actually transpired during Sam Stone's visit and refraining from answering the misleading probe questions incorrectly (figure 17.1). Only 10% of the youngest children (3- to 4-year-olds) assented to these events, and only 5% continued to assent when asked whether they actually *saw* him do these things as opposed to hearing about it. None of the older preschool children (5- to 6-year-olds) said they had seen Sam Stone do anything to the book or the teddy bear.

A second group of preschool children was given a stereotype about Sam Stone before he came into their classroom. For a month before his visit, these children were told once a week of something clumsy Sam had done. After the same 2-minute visit, these children were interviewed (nonsuggestively) four times over the subsequent 10 weeks about Sam's visit; the fifth interview was the final one. Of these children, 42% of younger ones said Sam Stone did these things, and 19% claimed they *saw* him do them (figure 17.2). But only 11% of these 3- to 4-year-olds maintained their false claims when gently challenged ("Tell me what he really did, OK?"). Again, the older preschool children were more resistant, with error rates about half of the younger children's.

A third group was not given a stereotype about Sam Stone's being clumsy, but this group was interviewed four times over 10 weeks in a highly suggestive manner ("Do you remember that time Sam Stone visited your classroom and ripped that book? Did he do it on purpose or was it an accident?" "When Sam

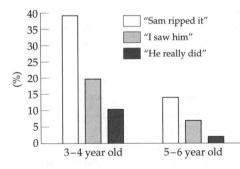

FIGURE 17.2   Report accuracy: no suggestion; + stereotype

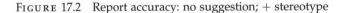

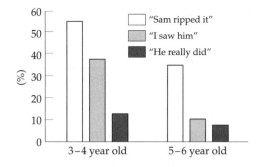

FIGURE 17.3   Report accuracy: + suggestion; no stereotype

Stone spilled ice cream on the teddy bear, was he being silly or angry?"). During the fifth and final interview, 52% of the younger children and 38% of the older children claimed that Sam Stone either ripped the book or hurt the teddy bear (figure 17.3). Even when gently challenged, 10% of the youngest · preschool children continued to insist that they actually had observed him doing this. The false claim rate for the older children was 8%.

The final group of children was given a stereotype about Sam Stone's clumsiness before he visited their classroom *plus* they were interviewed in a highly suggestive manner during the 10 weeks. During the final interview, 72% of the younger children stated that Sam had done things to the book and teddy bear. This figure dropped to 44% when they were asked whether they had *seen* Sam do these things (figure 17.4). Even after being challenged, 20% of the younger preschool children and 11% of the older ones maintained that they saw Sam do these things.

To assess whether the children's claims might be viewed as convincing to experts, 1,000 researchers and clinicians (psychiatrists and psychologists) were shown videotapes of the final interviews and asked to judge which of the events had actually transpired as well as to rate each child's credibility. Overall, most of the professionals were inaccurate. Despite their confidence in their judgments, experts could not reliably determine the accuracy of a child's testimony. The overall credibility ratings were significantly lower than chance,

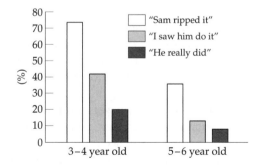

FIGURE 17.4   Report accuracy: + suggestion; + stereotype

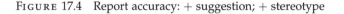

indicating that experts applied invalid indices (e.g., child avoids eye contact) but in a reliable manner. As a rule, the least accurate children were considered to be the most accurate by experts. This shows how difficult it is, even for trained professionals, to separate fact from fiction when the children have been repeatedly interviewed in a suggestive manner, especially when the interviews have been accompanied with congruent stereotypes.

Study 2: Effects of interviewer bias on a child's report

In the previous study we saw how children's report accuracy was diminished when interviewers misled them with erroneous suggestions and stereotypes. But what happens if the interviewers themselves are misled; will this also compromise children's accuracy? Will interviewers use incorrect information to form erroneous hypotheses about what a child experienced and pursue the child in a single-minded and suggestive manner?

In this study, Ceci et al. (in press) examined the effects of an interviewer's bias on the accuracy of a child's report. Usually, interviewers are not blind to relevant information about a case and they proceed to test only those hypotheses that are consistent with their hunch. Thus, they do not test every conceivable hypothesis. The purpose of this experiment was to examine whether the failure of an interviewer to test a rival hypothesis could result in a reporting error.

To accomplish this aim, preschool children were exposed to a gamelike event and then interviewed about it 1 month later. The interviewer, an experienced social worker, was given information about events that *might* have occurred. While some of the information supplied to the interviewer was accurate (e.g., she was told that there was a good chance that the child had put a marble in another child's ear), some of the information given to her was inaccurate (e.g., she was told that there was a good chance that another child licked this child's elbow).

When the interviewer was correctly informed about the events, she got the children to recall 93% of the events correctly. The only errors made were "errors of omission," occasionally leaving out correct information. None of the children made false accusations when interviewers were correctly informed.

However, as can be seen in figure 17.5, when the interviewer was misinformed about what might have happened, 34% of the 3- and 4-year-olds and 18% of the 5- and 6-year-olds assented to inaccurate leading questions about the events the interviewer believed to be true ("Didn't Tara lick your elbow?"). In this condition, the errors were "errors of commission," providing false answers.

Two months later, another interviewer was supplied with the social worker's notes from the first interview to see whether these would result in the second interviewer forming both accurate and inaccurate hypotheses. The second interviewer not only got the children to continue to assent to false events that she assumed had occurred (figure 17.6), but the children did so with increased confidence levels and perceptual embellishments. These

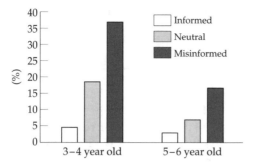

FIGURE 17.5   One-month interview

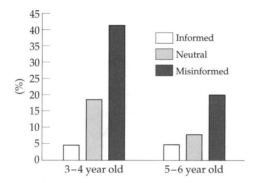

FIGURE 17.6   Three-month interview

findings, if replicated and extended, would seem to have relevance for front-line interviewers who are charged with interviewing children after the receipt of an allegation. If the report given to interviewers leads them to hypothesize incorrectly, then these results suggest that their false hypotheses may lead young preschool children to make false assents. The interviewers rarely posed and tested alternative hypotheses.

Study 3:   Effects of repeated interviewing on a child's free narrative

The two prior studies showed that persistent suggestions over long periods can have baleful consequences on preschool children's report accuracy. The purpose of this study was to determine whether repeatedly interviewing a child without suggestive techniques also posed risks. Of particular interest was whether a child's recollections were influenced by techniques that encouraged the formation of mental imagery.

Perhaps asking a child each week over extended periods of time to think about or imagine fictitious scenarios will have the effect of increasing famili-arity with fictitious events to the point where the child cannot discriminate between events that are fictitious and those that are real. Such an expectation is consistent with source-monitoring theory; each time an event is probed, the child may generate an image and check it against a stored representation to decide whether it is familiar. With subsequent attempts, the image may seem increasingly familiar, not because it was actually experienced but merely because the child had previously created images that are now familiar.

Young children are disproportionately prone to source amnesia, meaning that they may be especially likely to forget the basis of the event's familiarity, falsely attributing it to actual experience when it is due to imaging.

Ceci et al. (1994a) studied the effects of repeatedly interviewing children about the same event, each time asking the child to "think real hard" about both real and fictitious events. One hundred and twenty-four preschool children (3 to 6 years old) were asked each week for 10 to 12 consecutive weeks to think about different events, some which did happen and some which did not. They were asked to "think real hard before answering" whether they remembered the event happening. The procedure is alluringly simple: "Think real hard. Did you ever get your hand caught in a mousetrap and go to the hospital to get it off?"

In the initial interview, twice as many 3- and 4-year-old children assented to false events compared with 5- and 6-year-old children (44% versus 25%). So, even without repeated enjoinders to "think real hard," some children already were assenting to false events. After 10 weeks of repeating this exercise, more than one-fourth of both the younger and older children claimed that they had experienced the majority of the false events and often provided elaborate narratives describing their experiences. Although they had correctly identified the fictitious events as untrue in the earliest interviews, 58% of all the children assented to at least one of the false events during the final interview (figure 17.7).

The most surprising result was not that the children remembered the false events as true, but rather their ability to provide a detailed and coherent narrative about these false events. So compelling did the children's narratives appear that we suspected that some of the children had come to truly believe they had experienced the fictitious events. Neither parents nor researchers

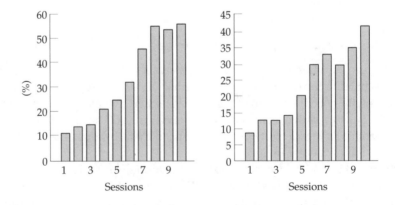

FIGURE 17.7   False assents over 11 sessions: *left panel*: 3- to 4-year-olds; *right panel*: 5- to 6-year-olds

were able to convince 27% of the children that the events never happened. (For example, one child who tenaciously clung to his story that his hand had been caught in a mousetrap and taken to the hospital to get it removed, argued against his mother's debriefing: "But it did happen! You were not in the room when it happened. It was at our old house." His mother was unsuccessful in convincing him that they never had a mousetrap in their old house, and at any rate he had been 6 months old when they moved from it.)

The videotapes of some of these interviews were shown to experts in the area of children's testimony. These professionals were no better than chance at predicting which of the children were accurate. Because it appears that a subset of the children had come to truly believe these events occurred, they express the appropriate affective cues and show none of the signs of lying or deception.

Study 4: Effects of repeated visualization on a child's free narrative

In a follow-up to the above study, Ceci et al. (1994b) were interested in the effect of repeatedly asking a child to visualize fictitious events. They asked children not only to "think real hard" about the false events, but also to create a visual picture in their head. They also varied the type of suggestive event (i.e., positive or negative). Finally, these researchers were interested in whether the children would cling to their false statements if they were told by a new interviewer that the old interviewer was trying to trick them and that some of the events never happened.

Forty-eight preschool children were interviewed once a week for 11 weeks. Over time, these children increasingly assented to the false events, but the rates of false assent differed for the different types of events (figure 17.8). Neutral events ("Do you remember seeing X in a red bus?"), and to a lesser degree positive events ("Do you remember making paper boats at X's birthday party?"), were easier to bias than were negative events ("Do you remember falling off your bike and getting three stitches in your face at the hospital?"). However, although negative events were the most resistant to suggestion, they nevertheless significantly increased over the 11 weekly sessions.

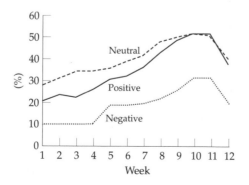

FIGURE 17.8 False assents to positive and negative vignettes

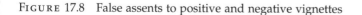

As can be seen, during the terminal session when the new interviewer informed the children that the previous interviewer had confused children and they had made mistakes, many of the children did relent on their claims. False assents decreased significantly, though importantly they did not return to baseline levels at the first session. This is consistent with the interpretation that children truly believed some of the events had occurred.

Ceci et al. (1994b) also asked clinicians to view the videotaped interviews with the children and distinguish between the accurate and inaccurate testimonies. Videotapes of 10 children from study 1 were shown to professionals, who were asked to use a 7-point rating procedure, with 1 indicating extreme confidence that the event did not occur and 7 indicating extreme confidence that it did occur (Leichtman and Ceci, 1995). Professionals were no better than chance at distinguishing between the children's accurate and inaccurate narratives: There were as many professionals who were reliably worse than chance at detecting which events were real as there were professionals above chance (overall $p = .60$, for two-tailed test, $\alpha = .025$ each tail). A static Bernoulli sampling process specifies the likelihood of correctly judging a real claim (p) and the likelihood of achieving precisely x correct in N independent trials $= (N/x) px qN - x$, where the probabilities for $x = 0$ to 10 correct guesses, $N = 10$ trials, and $p = .5$ and $q = .5$. (A two-tailed test was preferred in view of our interest in the number of raters who performed above as well as below chance.) This result accords with Horner and colleagues' (1993) finding using a different methodology. In their study, clinical psychologists' and social workers' predictions of the accuracy of children's sexual abuse reports were disturbingly unreliable, spanning the full range of estimated probabilities (from 0 to 1.0) of the child's having been abused.

Thus, these professionals were no better than chance at distinguishing between accurate and inaccurate reports. Even clinical and research psychologists who specialize in interviewing children performed at chance.

Study 5:   Influencing a child's report of a pediatric visit

Critics of the first three studies might argue that children would act differently and be more resilient to interviewers' false suggestion if the events in question were more salient, perhaps ones that involve their own body and participation (Rudy and Goodman, 1991). To examine such claims, Bruck et al. (1995) studied preschool children's ability to remember the events of a pediatric visit after repeated postevent suggestions over a 1-year interval.

In the first phase of the experiment, 5-year-old children visited their pediatrician and received their annual checkup. After this routine checkup, a female research assistant entered the room and discussed a poster on the wall with the child. The pediatrician then proceeded to give the child an oral polio vaccine and a DPT inoculation. After this, the child was given either neutral or pain-denying feedback by another research assistant. Children in the neutral group were told the shot was over ("It's over now. You can get ready to go home."), and the pain-denying group were told, "You were so brave that the shot hardly hurt you." Then, regardless of feedback condition, the research assistant gave the child a treat and read a story to him or her.

A week later, the children were visited by a different assistant and asked how much the shot had hurt and how much they had cried. They were given a developmentally appropriate scale to make their ratings, with a happy face anchoring one pole and a frowning face anchoring the other.

The results showed that the children's answers were not influenced by their assigned feedback condition. Therefore, from this phase of the experiment, we concluded that children cannot be readily influenced about events involving their own bodies.

In the second phase of the experiment, the children were reinterviewed four more times during the following year, using suggestive questions consistent with their feedback condition. During each of these interviews, the children in the pain-denying condition were given consistent feedback (e.g., "Remember when you got your shot at Dr Emmet's office? You hardly cried!"), and the children assigned to the neutral condition were simply asked, "Remember when you got your shot at Dr Emmet's office?"

At the final interview, the children were again asked to rate how much the shot had hurt and how much they had cried. Large suggestibility effects were observed, with children in the pain-denying condition reporting significantly less crying and pain than the children in the neutral condition.

The children in the pain-denying condition had also been misled about who performed certain tasks – the doctor, the nurse, or the research assistant. Of those children given misleading information, 67% assented that the doctor had shown them the poster, had given them the treat, or had read them a story. Only 27% of those in the control group made the same mistakes. Of the children who were falsely told that the research assistant had given them the oral vaccine and the shot, 50% (versus 16% of the control group) assented to at least one of these suggestions. Thirty-eight percent of these children who were given misinformation about the research assistant also said nonevents happened which, while not suggested, were congruent with false suggestions. For example, children in the pain-denying condition were falsely told that the female research assistant had been the person who inoculated them (it had always been a male pediatrician), and one-third of these children later claimed that the female assistant had checked their eyes, ears, and throat. Thus, the misled children not only assented to false information that had been supplied by the interviewer (less pain, female inoculation), but also added fictitious events that were consistent with the script if the doctor had been a female.

On the basis of these findings, we can conclude that under certain circumstances, suggestibility effects can be observed for stressful events involving a child's own body. Although the nature of the inoculation event is quite different from the nature of the event in the "Sam Stone" experiment, the results are similar. As was the case in the Sam Stone study, the two crucial factors leading to heightened report errors were the repetition of misleading suggestions and the long intervals over which the suggestions were made. These two factors often occur in forensic cases when a child is repeatedly interviewed and there is a large time lag between the event and the child's testifying in court (Ceci and Bruck, 1995).

Study 6: Suggestibility effects of anatomically correct dolls

So far, we have seen that very young preschool children are disproportionately more susceptible to suggestions than older children and that such effects extend to painful, personally experienced bodily events. But what about genital events? Are young preschool children also suggestible about genital touching, or is this off limits? While it is ethically impermissible for experimentalists to induce genital touching, it is possible to explore this question by taking advantage of naturally occurring doctor visits.

Bruck et al. (1995) took advantage of 70 naturally occurring pediatric visits to study the effects of using anatomically correct dolls during a postevent interview. The visits included an examination in which 35 three-year-olds were given a genital examination and 35 others were given a nongenital examination. Unlike the former group, none of the latter group had their underclothing removed or had their genitalia or buttocks touched during their examination. All children were interviewed with their mother present 5 minutes after the examination. Initially, they were asked to explain, without using the doll, where the doctor touched them. Then, the children were given an anatomical doll and asked to show where the doctor touched them.

Before the doll was presented, only 45% of the children receiving a genital examination correctly reported that they had been touched on the buttocks or genitals. On the other hand, only 50% of the children receiving a nongenital examination said that they had *not* been touched on the buttocks or genitals. When the dolls were presented, the children became even less accurate. Only 25% of the children given a genital examination correctly demonstrated on the doll where they had been touched, and 55% of the children who received a nongenital examination incorrectly demonstrated genital insertion and other inappropriate sexual actions. This form of "commission error" was more prevalent among the girls in this group; 75% of the female subjects who did not receive a genital examination demonstrated that the pediatrician touched their buttocks or their genitals.

What are we to make of these findings? Anatomically detailed dolls are often used by professionals who investigate claims of child sexual abuse. A recent survey indicated that 90% of professionals use these dolls at least occasionally (Conte et al., 1991). Although some would argue that use of the dolls enables a child to overcome embarrassment, shyness, and linguistic limitations and helps cue her memory about genital events, others contend that their use is inherently suggestive.

Cognitive-developmental research is replete with evidence that children younger than 28 to 36 months are unable to engage in symbolic representation. For example, children below this age cannot use a scale model of a house to symbolize its referent; when asked to hide an object in the small scale model, the children are unable to find it in the larger house (see DeLoache and Marzolf, 1995, for details).

There is some research that indicates that older children rarely make such errors with dolls (Saywitz et al., 1991). Bruck and colleagues' (1995) findings are currently being explored with 4-year-old children, and preliminary results appear to indicate that errors are approximately half the magnitude observed with 3-year-olds. Pending evidence to the contrary, these findings raise cautions about the use of dolls *diagnostically* (as opposed to devices to get children to label anatomical parts) with very young preschool children. In keeping with their general symbolic limitations, very young preschool children appear confused about the representational use of all props, including dolls.

Study 7: Validity of content-based criteria analysis

In all but two of the preceding six studies, videotapes of the children's behaviors and statements were shown to professionals, and they were asked to judge their authenticity. The results of these demonstrations indicated that it is extremely difficult to distinguish between actual and suggested events when children have been pursued with repeated suggestions over long intervals.

Although the modal professional in these demonstrations could not accurately determine which statements were valid, some experts contend that content-based criteria analysis (CBCA) can successfully determine the validity of a child's statement.

Along with an interview technique and a validity checklist, CBCA is one of the three components of statement validity analysis. Specifically, CBCA consists of 18 criteria which assess the general characteristics, the specific content, and the motivation-related content of a statement. The presence or absence of these criteria is a clue to the accuracy of the testimony. Certain psychologists contend that by conducting a structured interview and applying these criteria to the transcript, a researcher can accurately distinguish between real and fabricated accounts by both adults and children. The specific criteria are explained in depth in a number of studies (e.g., Horowitz, 1991; Raskin and Esplin, 1991; Raskin and Yuille, 1989).

To determine whether experts could distinguish between the true and false reports, transcripts were made of the final interviews from study 3 and sent to four leading experts on statement validity analysis (Crotteau, 1994). The transcripts of 20 stories (10 true and 10 fictitious) were assessed on the 18 criteria of CBCA. Since each criterion was scored either 0 (not present), 1 (present), or 2 (strongly present), each of the 20 transcripts could receive a score ranging between 0 and 36.

Although an independent t test showed a significant difference between the means of the true and false stories, the magnitude of the difference was quite small. While the mean for the false stories was 1.79, ranging from 0 to 6 (SD = 1.82), the mean for true stories was only 3.89, ranging from 2 to 7 (SD = 1.65). The mean of the true stories is much lower than one would expect.

It was also unclear which combination of the criteria is the most useful in determining the accuracy of a child's account. Of the 18 criteria, 5 were not found in any of the accounts. Only 6 of the 18 criteria were predictive of whether the story was true or false, and two criteria ("superfluous details" and "admitting lack of memory or knowledge") actually led to reverse predictions (Crotteau, 1994).

More research is needed to determine how CBCA should be used when children have been repeatedly exposed to suggestions over long intervals, since some subset of them may come to harbor false beliefs that are quite unlike the deliberate lies that CBCA was developed to detect. Until more is known, professionals should exercise caution when using CBCA to assess the validity of a preschool child's account.

Conclusions

The findings from these seven studies would seem to have some relevance for "front-line" professionals charged with the difficult task of obtaining disclosures from preschool children. Below we summarize the main implications.

First, these results, taken together, make clear that it is possible to mislead a subset of the children into believing they experienced fictitious events. There are several indications that this is so, most importantly our inability to debrief 27% to 35% of the children in studies 3 and 4. No matter how hard their parents and we tried, this subset of children refused to accept the explanation that the fictitious events never occurred. Professionals watching these children were essentially at chance in deciding whether the event really occurred, another indication that the children believed what they were reporting, since it is quite difficult for a 3-year-old to lie consistently and convincingly, especially in the face of countersuggestions. In addition, results from other methodologies not described here are consistent with the view that a subset of children's false assents appear to be memory-based rather than the result of social compliance. Finally, techniques designed to detect deliberate lies (CBCA) are not notably successful in distinguishing fictitious from true accounts in these children (study 7).

Secondly, although there are pronounced age differences in these findings, with the youngest preschool children at greatest risk for errors, even the 3-year-old children are not as hypersuggestible and coachable as some contend (nor, for that matter, are they as resistant to suggestion as some others would have us believe). In those studies that used an untreated control group (studies 2 and 4), even 3-year-olds did quite well when they were not interviewed suggestively, often recalling 90% accurately. *Thus, when the adults who have access to preschool children do not attempt to usurp their memories through repeated suggestions over long intervals, even very young children do very well.* The suggestibility of any particular child is dependent on a host of cognitive and social factors, and future research is needed to narrow the uncertainties related to individual differences.

A likely causal mechanism underlying false assents is "source misattributions." False beliefs appear to arise when children misattribute the basis of an event's perceived familiarity, incorrectly confusing familiarity due to imagining the event with that due to actual perception. If this account is correct, then the question becomes why the youngest children become amnestic for source information faster than older children, hence leading to source misattributions. A number of speculations have been put forward, including the lagged development of brain structures involved in separating and monitoring sources of information (frontal lobes), age-related differences in metacognitive awareness, and less stable and integrated memory traces (Ceci, 1994). Once again, future research is needed to decide among these possibilities (or some other).

One very robust finding was the thrice-replicated demonstration, with different stimulus materials, that professionals can be fooled about the accuracy of a child's report when the child has been exposed to repeated suggestions over long delays. In contrast to professionals' professed confidence, they were no better than chance at distinguishing between true and false accounts in these studies. Of the several thousand psychiatrists, psychologists, social workers, attorneys, and judges who watched the videotapes, many expressed deep surprise to learn that their judgments were so incorrect.

In closing, it is worth nothing that the suggestive techniques used in these studies (repeated suggestions, stereotypes, visually guided imagery) did not always have baleful consequences on children's report accuracy. When the child actually experienced the event in question, these techniques led to high levels of correct disclosure. The problem is that they also led to high levels of false assents when the event was not experienced. Results of research reported elsewhere suggest that the pursuit of at least one feasible alternative hypothesis while testing a favored hypothesis seems to lessen the reliability risks due to suggestions. Hence, interviewers of young children ought to be encouraged to generate and test alternative hunches at the same time that they attempt to elicit statements consistent with their favored hypothesis.

REFERENCES

Bruck, M., Ceci, S. J., Francouer, E., Barr, R. (1995), "I hardly cried when I got my shot!" Influencing children's reports about a visit to their pediatrician. *Child Dev.* **66**: 193–208.

Ceci, S. J. (1994), Cognitive and social factors in children's testimony. In *APA Master Lectures: Psychology in Litigation and Legislation*, Sales, B., Vanden Bos, G., eds. Washington, DC: American Psychological Association, pp. 14–54.

Ceci, S. J., Bruck, M. (1993a), Child witness: Translating research into policy. *Social Policy Report: Society for Research in Child Development* (Fall).

Ceci, S. J., Bruck, M. (1993b), The suggestibility of the child witness: A historical review and synthesis. *Psychol. Bull.* **113**: 403–39.

Ceci, S. J., Bruck, M. (1995), *Jeopardy in the Courtroom: A Scientific Analysis of Children's Testimony*. Washington, DC: American Psychological Association.

Ceci, S. J., Huffman, M. L. C., Smith, E., Loftus, E. W. (1994a), Repeatedly thinking about non-events: Source misattributions among preschoolers. *Consciousness Cognition* **3**: 388–407.

Ceci, S. J., Leichtman, M., White, T. (in press), Interviewing preschoolers: Remembrance of things planted. In *The Child Witness in Context: Cognitive, Social, and Legal Perspectives*, Peters, D. P., ed., The Netherlands: Kluwer.

Ceci, S. J., Loftus, E. F., Leichtman, M. D., Bruck, M. (1994b), The possible role of source misattributions in the creation of false beliefs among preschoolers. *Int. J. Clin. Exp. Hypn*, **42**: 304–20.

Conte, J. R., Sorenson, E., Fogarty, L., Rosa, J. D. (1991), Evaluating children's reports of sexual abuse: results from a survey of professionals. *J. Orthopsychiatry* **78**: 428–37.

Crotteau, M. L. (1994), Can criteria-based content analysis discriminate between accurate and false reports of preschoolers? A validation attempt. Master's thesis, Cornell University, Ithaca, NY.

DeLoache, J. S., Marzolf, D. P. (1995), The use of dolls to interview young children: Issues of symbolic representation. *J. Exp. Child Psychol*, **60**: 155–73.

Fivush, R., Hudson, J., eds (1990), *Knowing and Remembering in Young Children*, New York: Cambridge University Press.

Foley, M. A., Santini, J., Sopasakis, M. (1989), Discriminating between memories: Evidence for children's spontaneous elaboration. *J. Exp. Child Psychol* 48: 146–69.

Goodman, G. S., Quas, J. (1996), Trauma and memory: Individual differences in children's recounting of a stressful experience. In *Memory for Everyday and Emotional Events*, Stein, N. L., Brainerd, C., Ornstein, P. A., Tversky, B., eds, Mahwah, NJ: Erlbaum, pp. 267–94.

Gray, E. (1993), *Unequal Justice: The Prosecution of Child Sexual Abuse*. New York: Macmillan.

Gudjonsson, G. (1986), The relationship between interrogative suggestibility and acquiescence: Empirical findings and theoretical implications. *Personality Individual Differences* **7**: 195–99.

Horner, T. M., Guyer, M. J., Kalter, N. M. (1993), Clinical expertise and the assessment of child sexual abuse. *J. Am. Acad. Child Adolesc. Psychiatry* **32**: 925–31.

Horowitz, S. W. (1991), Empirical support for statement validity assessment. *Behav. Assess.* **13**: 293–313.

Johnson, M. K., Foley, M. A. (1985), Differentiating fact from fantasy: The reliability of children's memory. *J. Soc. Iss.* **40**: 33–50.

Leichtman, M. D., Ceci, S. J. (1995), The effects of stereotypes and suggestions on preschoolers' reports. *Dev. Psychol.* **31**: 568–78.

Lindsay, D. S., Johnson, M. K. (1989), The eyewitness suggestibility effect and memory for source. *Memory Cognition* **17**: 349–58.

Lindsay, D. S., Johnson, M. K., Kwon, P. (1991), Developmental changes in memory source monitoring. *J. Exp. Child Psychol.* **52**: 297–318.

Markham, R. (1991), Development of reality monitoring for performed and imagined actions. *Percept. Mot. Skills* **72** (3, part 2): 1347–54.

McGough, L. (1993), *Fragile Voices: The Child Witness in American Courts*. New Haven, CT: Yale University Press.

National Center on Child Abuse and Neglect (1993), *National Child Abuse and Neglect Data System, 1991: Summary Data Component*. Gaithersburg, MD: US Department of Health and Human Services.

National Center on Child Abuse and Neglect (1996), *Third National Incidence Study of Child Abuse and Neglect*. Washington, DC: US Department of Health and Human Services.

Ornstein, P. A., Shapiro, L. B., Clubb, P. A., Follmer, A., Baker-Ward, L. (1996), The influence of prior knowledge on children's memory for salient medical experiences. In *Memory for Everyday and Emotional Events*, Stein, N. L., Brainerd, C., Ornstein, P. A., Tversky, B., eds, Mahwah, NJ: Erlbaum, pp. 83–111.

Raskin, D. C., Esplin, P. W. (1991), Statement validity assessment: Interview procedures and content analysis of children's statements of sexual abuse. *Behav. Assess.* **13**: 265–91.

Raskin, D. C., Yuille, J. C. (1989), Problems in evaluating interviews of children in sexual abuse cases. In *Perspectives on Children's Testimony*, Ceci, S. J., Ross D. F., Toglia, M. P., eds, New York: Springer-Verlag, pp. 184–207.

Rudy, L., Goodman, G. S. (1991), Effects of participation on children's reports: Implications for children's testimony. *Dev. Psychol.*, **27**: 527–38.

Saywitz, K., Goodman, G., Nicholas, G., Moan, S. (1991), Children's memory for genital exam: Implications for child sexual abuse. *J. Consult. Clin. Psychol.* **59**: 682–91.

Stein, N. L., Brainerd, C., Ornstein, P. A., Tversky, B., eds (1996), *Memory for Everyday and Emotional Events*. Mahwah, NJ: Erlbaum.

Zaragoza, M. (1995), *Memory and Testimony in the Child Witness*. Beverly Hills, CA: Sage.

18

The Development of Children's Knowledge about the Appearance–Reality Distinction*

John H. Flavell

OVERVIEW   Recent research on the acquisition of knowledge about the important and pervasive appearance–reality distinction suggests the following course of development. Many 3-year-olds seem to possess little or no understanding of the distinction. They fail very easy-looking tests of this understanding and are unresponsive to training. At this age level, skill in solving simple appearance–reality tasks is highly correlated with skill in solving simple visual perspective-taking tasks. This and other findings are consistent with the hypothesis that what helps children finally grasp the distinction is an increased cognizance of the fact that people are sentient subjects who have mental representations of objects and events. It does so by allowing them to understand that the selfsame stimulus can be mentally represented in two different, seemingly contradictory ways: (a) in the appearance–reality case, how it appears to the self versus how it really is; and (b) in the perspective-taking case, how it presently appears to self versus other. In contrast to young preschoolers, children of 6 to 7 years manage simple appearance–reality tasks with ease. However, they have great difficulty reflecting on and talking about such appearance–reality notions as "looks like," "really and truly," and especially, "looks different from the way it really and truly is." Finally, children of 11 to 12 years, and to an even greater degree college students, give evidence of possessing a substantial body of rich, readily available, and explicit knowledge in this area.

Suppose someone shows a three-year-old and a six-year-old a red toy car covered by a green filter that makes the car look black, hands the car to the

* Previously published in *American Psychologist*, **41**, 4 (April 1986), pp. 418–25.

children to inspect, puts it behind the filter again, and asks, "What color is this car? Is it red or is it black?" (Flavell, Green, and Flavell, 1985; cf. Braine and Shanks, 1965a, 1965b). The three-year-old is likely to say "black," the six-year-old, "red." The questioner is also apt to get the same answers even if he or she first carefully explains and demonstrates the intended difference in meaning, for illusory displays, between "looks like to your eyes right now" and "really and truly is," and then asks what color it "*really* and *truly* is." At issue in such simple tasks is the distinction between how things presently appear to the senses and how or what they really and enduringly are, that is, the familiar distinction between appearance and reality. The six-year-old is clearly in possession of some knowledge about this distinction and quickly senses what the task is about. The three-year-old, who is much less knowledgeable about the distinction, does not.

For the past half-dozen years my co-workers and I have been using these and other methods to chart the developmental course of knowledge acquisition in this area. That is, we have been trying to find out what children of different ages do and do not know about the appearance–reality distinction and related phenomena. In this article I summarize what we have done and what we think we have learned (Flavell, Flavell, and Green, 1983; Flavell et al., 1985; Flavell, Zhang, Zou, Dong, and Qi, 1983; Taylor and Flavell, 1984). The summary is organized around the main questions that have guided our thinking and research in this area.

Why is this Development Important to Study?

First, the distinction between appearance and reality is ecologically significant. It assumes many forms, arises in many situations, and can have serious consequences for our lives. The relation between appearance and reality figures importantly in everyday perceptual, conceptual, emotional, and social activity – in misperceptions, misexpectations, misunderstandings, false beliefs, deception, play, fantasy, and so forth. It is also a major preoccupation of philosophers, scientists, and other scholars; of artists, politicians, and other public performers; and of the thinking public that tries to evaluate what they say and do. It is, in sum, "the distinction which probably provides the intellectual basis for the fundamental epistemological construct common to science, 'folk' philosophy, religion, and myth, of a real world 'underlying' and 'explaining' the phenomenal one" (Braine and Shanks, 1965a, pp. 241–2).

Secondly, the acquisition of at least some explicit knowledge about the appearance–reality distinction is probably a universal developmental outcome in our species. This knowledge seems so necessary to everyday intellectual and social life that one can hardly imagine a society in which normal people would not acquire it. To cite an example that has actually been researched, a number of investigators have been interested in the child's command of the distinction as a possible developmental prerequisite for, and perhaps even mediator of, Piagetian conservations (e.g., Braine and Shanks, 1965a, 1965b; Murray, 1968).

Thirdly, knowledge about the distinction seems to presuppose the explicit knowledge that human beings are sentient, cognizing *subjects* (cf. Chandler and Boyce, 1982; Selman, 1980) whose mental representations of objects and events can differ, both within the same person and between persons. In the within-person case, for example, I may be aware both that something appears to be A and that it really is B. I could also be aware that it might appear to be C under special viewing conditions, or that I pretended or fantasized that it was D yesterday. I may know that these are all possible ways that I can *represent* the very same thing (i.e., perceive it, encode it, know it, interpret it, construe it, or think about it – although inadequate, the term "represent" will have to do). In the between-persons case, I may be aware that you might represent the same thing differently than I do, because our perceptual, conceptual, or affective perspectives on it might differ. If this analysis is correct, knowledge about the appearance–reality distinction is but one instance of our more general know-ledge that the selfsame object or event can be represented (apprehended, experi-enced, etc.) in different ways by the same person and by different people. In this analysis, then, its development is worth studying because it is part of the larger development of our conscious knowledge about our own and other minds and, thus, of metacognition (e.g., Brown, Bransford, Ferrara, and Campione, 1983; Flavell, 1985; Wellman, 1985) and of social cognition (e.g., Flavell, 1985; Shantz, 1983). I will return to this line of reasoning in another section of the article.

How can Young Children's Knowledge about the Appearance–Reality Distinction be Tested?

The development of appearance–reality knowledge in preschool children has been investigated by Braine and Shanks (1965a, 1965b), Daehler (1970), De Vries (1969), Elkind (1966), King (1971), Langer and Strauss (1972), Murray (1965, 1968), Tronick and Hershenson (1979) and, most recently and system-atically, by our research group. In most of our studies we have used variations of the following procedure to assess young children's ability to think about appearance and reality (Flavell, Flavell, and Green, 1983). First, we pretrain the children briefly on the meaning of the distinction and associated terminology by showing them (for example) a Charlie Brown puppet inside a ghost cos-tume. We explain and demonstrate that Charlie Brown "*looks like* a ghost to your eyes right now" but is "*really and truly* Charlie Brown," and that "some-times things look like one thing to your eyes when they are really and truly something else." We then present a variety of illusory stimuli in a nondecept-ive fashion and ask about their appearance and their reality. For instance, we first show the children a very realistic looking fake rock made out of a soft sponge-like material and then let them discover its identity by manipulating it. We next ask, in random order: (a) "What is this *really* and *truly*? Is it *really* and *truly* a sponge or is it *really* and *truly* a rock?" (b) "When you look at this with your eyes right now, does it *look like* a rock or does it *look like* a sponge?" Or we show the children a white stimulus, move it behind a blue filter, and similarly ask about its real and apparent color. (Of course its "real color" is now blue, but only people who know something about color perception realize this.) Similar procedures are used to assess sensitivity to the distinction between real and apparent size, shape, events, and object presence.

How do Young Children Perform on Simple Appearance–Reality Tasks?

Our studies have consistently shown that three- to four-year-old children presented with tasks of this sort usually either answer both questions correctly, suggesting some ability to differentiate appearance and reality representations, or else give the same answer (reporting either the appearance or the reality) to both questions, suggesting some conceptual difficulty with the distinction. Incorrect answers to both questions occur only infrequently, suggesting that even the children who err are not responding randomly. There is a marked improvement with age during early childhood in the ability to solve these appearance–reality tasks: Only a few three-year-olds get them right consistently, whereas almost all six- to seven-year-olds do (Flavell et al., 1985).

 Some illusory stimuli tend to elicit appearance answers to both questions (called a *phenomenism* error pattern), whereas others tend to elicit reality answers to both (*intellectual realism* pattern). The intellectual realism pattern is the more surprising one, because it contradicts the widely held view that young children respond only to what is most striking and noticeable in their immediate perceptual field (Flavell, 1977, pp. 79–80; for a review of other research on intellectual realism, see Pillow and Flavell, 1985). If the task is to distinguish between the real and apparent properties of color, size, and shape, phenomenism errors predominate. Thus, if an object that is really white or small or straight is temporarily made to look blue, big, or bent by means of filters or lenses, young children are very likely to say the object really *is* blue, big, or bent. If, instead, the task is to indicate what object(s) or event is present, really versus apparently, intellectual realism errors are likelier to predominate. For example, the fake rock is incorrectly said to look like a sponge rather than a rock; a tiny picture of a cup is incorrectly said to look like a cup rather than a spot when viewed from afar; an array consisting of a small object completely occluded by a large one is incorrectly said to look like it contains both objects rather than only the visible one; an experimenter who appears from the child's viewing position to be reading a large book, but who is known by the child really to be drawing a picture inside it, is incorrectly said to look like she is drawing rather than reading (Flavell, Flavell, and Green, 1983). Indeed, Taylor and Flavell (1984) found that significantly more phenomenism errors occurred when illusory stimuli were described to children in terms of their properties (e.g., "white" vs. "orange" liquid) than when the same stimuli were described to the same children in terms of identities ("milk" vs. "Koolaid"). We do not know yet exactly why the appearance usually seems to be more cognitively salient for young children in these property tasks and (less dependably) the relaity more salient in the object/event identity tasks, although we have proposed some possible explanations (Flavell, Flavell, and Green, 1983).

How can we Find Out whether Young Children's Difficulties with this Distinction are Real or Only Apparent?

Much of our research has focused on the appearance–reality knowledge and related skills that three-year-olds possess and lack, because the early emergence of knowledge in any domain is of particular interest. (We have not yet found effective ways to test for possible cognitive precursors in children younger than three, but we hope to eventually.) As just mentioned, the evidence is now clear that many three-year-olds perform poorly even on what seem like very simple and straightforward appearance–reality tasks. Exactly how this poor performance should be interpreted is an important issue. Perhaps these tasks are valid and sensitive measures of young children's basic competence in this area, and their poor performance on them simply means that they really lack such competence. On the other hand, it is more than possible that the tasks we have been using significantly underestimate three-year-olds' capabilities. If there is one lesson to be learned from the recent history of the field of cognitive development, it is that the cognitive capabilities of young children are often seriously underestimated by the tasks developmentalists initially devise to assess those capabilities (e.g., Flavell, 1985; Flavell and Markman, 1983, pp. viii–x; Gelman, 1979). It is quite possible, therefore, that children aged three or even younger really do understand the distinction. It is even imaginable that humans are in some sense born with a sensitivity to the distinction. What could one do to try to find out whether three-year-olds really lack competence in this area or only appear to?

Try cross-cultural replication

We repeated as exactly as possible one of our early experiments (Flavell, Flavell, and Green, 1983, experiment 2) in a different language and culture, namely, using Mandarin in the People's Republic of China (Flavell, Zhang, Zou, Dong, and Qi, 1983). The American children were three- to five-year-olds from Stanford University's laboratory preschool. The Chinese children were three- to five-year-olds from Beijing (Peking) Normal University's laboratory preschool. Pretraining and testing procedures, and the illusory stimuli, were the same for the two samples. We worked closely with Chinese colleagues on the translation of instructions and key terms and in the pilot testing. Error patterns, age changes, and even absolute levels of performance at each age level proved to be remarkably similar in the two subject samples. These results suggest that previously observed difficulties with our tasks cannot be due solely to some sort of simple and developmentally inconsequential misunderstanding by young American children of the English expressions "really and truly" and "looks like to your eyes right now." Rather, they suggest, as such cross-cultural replications usually do (e.g., of Piagetian phenomena), that our tasks may in fact be assessing a real and robust conceptual acquisition.

Try making the tasks easier

In three recent studies (Flavell et al., 1985) we compared the difficulty for three-year-olds of "standard" and "easy" appearance–reality tasks. Standard tasks were the object-identity (fake objects) and color (objects placed behind colored filters) ones used in our previous investigations. Easy tasks were created by thinking of possible obstacles to good performance posed by the standard ones and devising tasks that eliminated or reduced these obstacles. We tried to invent tasks that still demanded some genuine if minimal knowledge of the appearance–reality distinction but that, by virtue of being stripped of certain knowledge-irrelevant processing demands, came closer than the standard ones to demanding *only* that knowledge. In short, we tried to create more sensitive assessment procedures in hopes of coaxing out nascent, hard-to-elicit appearance–reality competence.

We constructed five putatively easy color tasks using this method.

(1) A small part of the target object was left uncovered when the color filter was placed over it. Consequently, visible evidence of the object's real color was still available to the children when the appearance and reality questions were asked; they did not have to remember what its real color was.

(2) A liquid (milk) whose real color (white) is well known to young children was caused by use of a filter to temporarily appear to be a color (red) that they would never see in reality. We thought this might help the children both keep the real color in mind and recognize the bizarre apparent color to be a mere appearance.

(3) The device that changed the object's apparent color was a familiar one known by children to have just that function (sun-glasses rather than a filter). In addition, its effect on the children's momentary color experience (appearance) rather than on the object's enduring surface color (reality) was highlighted by placing it next to the children's eyes rather than next to the object.

(4) The device was itself an object that possessed its own real color (a blue filter cut into the shape of a large fish) distinct from that of the object whose apparent color it changed (a small white fish that temporarily became blue-looking by chancing to "swim" behind the large one). This setup might help young children distinguish between the little fish's real color and its accidental apparent color, which really "belongs" to the big fish.

(5) It is possible that the repeated juxtaposition of two different questions, one about appearance and one about reality, confuses or overtaxes three-year-olds; they might do better if simply asked what color the object behind the filter "is." Therefore, at the very beginning of the testing session, prior to any talk about appearances and realities, we asked the single "is" question about a toy car's color described in the opening sentence of this article.

The same strategy was used to create three easier object-identity tasks.

(1) After a brief conversation about dressing up for Halloween in masks and costumes, the children were questioned about the real and apparent

identity of one of the experimenters after she had conspicuously put on a mask disguise. We assumed that young children would be more knowledgeable about this sort of appearance–reality discrepancy through Halloween and play experiences than with those presented by the fake objects and filters used in standard tasks.

(2)   The apparent identity of each object was conveyed by its sound, and its real identity by its visual appearance. To illustrate, a small can (real identity) sounded like a cow (apparent identity) when turned over, the children were then asked if it sounded like a can or like a cow, and whether it really and truly was a can or a cow. We thought that appearance and reality might be easier for young children to attend to separately, and keep straight, if the two were presented via different sense modalities. In an attempt to make the task easier still, at the moment the reality question was asked the reality was perceptible (the can was still visible), but the appearance was not (the can was not still making mooing sounds) – the opposite of what happens in all standard tasks.

(3)   Task 3 was the same as 2, except that the nonvisual modality used was smell rather than sound. For example, one of the objects used was a cloth (real identity) that smelled like a lemon (apparent identity).

These efforts to bring to light underlying appearance–reality competence by using easier, seemingly less demanding probes for this competence were surprisingly unsuccessful. Of the five easy color tasks, only Task 1 elicited better performance than did the standard color and object-identity tasks. Children performed significantly better on the three easy object-identity tasks than on the standard object-identity tasks, but not better than on the standard color ones. Moreover, their absolute level of performance on these three tasks was not very high. Thus, the results of these studies do not support the view that the typical young preschooler can differentially represent and think about appearances and realities if only the eliciting conditions are made sufficiently facilitative and "child-friendly."

Try teaching appearance–reality knowledge

Finally we (Flavell, Green, and Flavell, 1985) have recently tried to probe for hidden competence by assessing children's response to training: in effect, to use training as a diagnostic tool (Flavell, 1985, pp. 277–8). We selected a group of 16 three-year-olds who performed very poorly on color and object-identity (fake object) pretests, trained them intensively for five to seven minutes on the meaning of real versus apparent color, and then readministered the same pretests. In this training we demonstrated, explained, defined terms, helped the child demonstrate, and gave corrective feedback on the theme that the real, true color of an object stays the same despite repeated, temporary changes in its apparent color due to the interposition of different color filters. Although we fully expected that this training would be helpful, in fact it was not. Only one of the 16 children performed well on the post-test, and he did so only on the color tasks, showing no transfer to the object-identity tasks. Braine and Shanks (1965a) had likewise been largely unsuccessful in training three-year-olds on the distinction between real and apparent size, although they used a less conceptually oriented training procedure. These results present a striking contrast to the results of the scores of studies that have tried to train conservation and other Piagetian concepts (Kuhn, 1984). Many of these studies have at least succeeded in inducing young nonconservers to behave like conservers; what remains controversial is the extent to which that trained conservation behavior reflects a real gain in genuine understanding. In contrast, the children in our study and in Braine and Shanks' (1965a) study could not be induced even to *behave* like children who understand the appearance–reality distinction. It seems reasonable to conclude, therefore, that they really did not understand it.

In summary, we have used three different research strategies to find out whether young children's difficulties with the appearance–reality distinction are real or only apparent. The results of this research strongly suggest that these difficulties are very real indeed.

What Relevant Competencies do Young Children Possess and Lack?

We can identify some relevant-seeming competencies that young children who fail simple appearance–reality tasks have already acquired. Although not sufficient in themselves to ensure understanding of the appearance–reality distinction, these competencies might be either necessary or helpful to its acquisition. By the age of three, children have become quite proficient at creating discrepancies between real and pretend identities (Bretherton, 1984; Rubin, Fein, and Vandenberg, 1983). As examples, they can pretend that a toy block is a car or make believe that they themselves are animals. Consistent with these skills in symbolic play, Estes and Wellman (H. M. Wellman, personal communication, 1984) and we (Flavell et al., 1985) have shown that most three-year-olds can consistently identify nonfake objects as being "real" and fake ones as being "not real" or "pretend," even without pretraining. We also presented three-year-olds with standard color appearance–reality task situations: that is, first show an object, then place it behind a filter that changes the object's apparent color. However, we then asked the children, not the usual appearance and reality questions, but simply whether the object will look A (its apparent color) or R (its real color) when the filter is removed. We found that many three-year-olds who performed well on this task nevertheless performed poorly on the standard color appearance–reality task. These results cannot be taken to imply that three-year-olds always maintain the object's original color in focal attention when answering reality questions, nor that they represent the object as being that color while it is behind the filter. However, these results do suggest that young children's abilities to (a) realize that the experimenter is talking about the object's color rather than the filter's color, (b) remember what color the object was before the filter was put over it, and (c) understand that it will look that same color again when the filter is removed, are not sufficient to ensure good performance on color appearance–reality tasks, although they are no doubt necessary. There are undoubtedly other competencies not yet identified that also play this sort of developmental role of being necessary and facilitative but not sufficient.

What developing competencies might actually be sufficient or nearly sufficient to enable young children to grasp the appearance–reality distinction? We really do not know, but we have a hypothesis. The hypothesis is derived from the third-mentioned reason why we think this development is important to study, as described earlier in this article.

Consider the conceptual demands of appearance–reality tasks. In reality, an object cannot simultaneously be, for instance, both all blue and all white, or both a rock and a sponge. Nevertheless, to solve these tasks we have to attribute such mutually incompatible and contradictory properties and identities to the same object at the same moment in time. As adults, we easily resolve the seeming contradiction by identifying one representation of its property or identity with its present appearance and the other with its reality. We identify the one with what we see and the other with what we know. This resolution is easy for us because we are well aware that people are sentient, cognizing subjects who have internal representations of external things and can represent singular things in multiple ways. Although we are aware that external objects themselves cannot simultaneously be two different things at once, we are also aware that we can represent them as simultaneously looking like the one thing ("that's what it looks like") and really being the other ("that's what it really is").

In contrast, everything we know about metacognitive and social-cognitive development (e.g., Brown et al., 1983; Flavell, 1985; Shantz, 1983) suggests that young children are less cognizant of these facts about subjectivity and mental representation than older children and adults are. This is not to claim that they are wholly incognizant of these facts (see Shatz, Wellman, and Silber, 1983, and Wellman, 1985, for evidence of some early knowledge of this kind) but only to claim that they are less cognizant of them. Therefore, they might not be aware of the ongoing role of subjectivity and representational activity as they inspect the target object. Instead, they may try only to decide what single thing the object "is," as an entity out there in the world. That the object can be represented as having more than one "is," inside our heads, may be a possibility that does not, or perhaps even cannot, occur to them. (Note that identifying a fake rock as a "pretend rock," which we have just said that young children can do, does *not* require representing that object as having more than one "is" – as looking like a rock but really being a sponge.) As they become increasingly cognizant of these facts in the course of development, according to this hypothesis, the distinction between appearance and reality should become increasingly meaningful to them.

Although this hypothesis has not yet been tested directly (we are still trying to formulate it clearly), there are two pieces of evidence that are at least consistent with it. One is the fact, mentioned above, that children who err on our tasks usually do so by giving the same answer to both the appearance and the reality questions, even though the two questions sound quite different and we stress the fact during both pretraining and testing that we are asking them two different questions. It is as if, despite all efforts to help them do otherwise, they decide what the object identity or property "is" and just say it twice.

The other piece of evidence is our recent finding (Flavell et al., 1985), obtained in two separate studies using three-year-old subjects, of high positive correlations (.67 to .87) between the ability to distinguish between appearance for the self and reality (appearance–reality ability) and the ability to distinguish between appearance for the self and appearance for another person (visual perspective-taking ability). We take this finding to be supportive of our hypothesis because both tasks require the previously discussed awareness that the same object can be simultaneously represented in two different ways: appearance and reality in the appearance–reality task and two different appearances to two differently situated observers in the perspective-taking task. In the more elaborate of the two studies, 40 three-year-olds were tested in two sessions. In one session they were given five color and five shape appearance–reality tasks (standard type); in the other they saw the same 10 task displays but were asked perspective-taking questions about them. Appropriate pretraining was given at the beginning of each session. To illustrate, one of the five shape displays consisted of a bent straw that looked straight to the child who viewed it through a bottle of liquid but bent to the experimenter who, seated opposite, did not view it through the distorting bottle. As in all our studies, the child initially saw the straw without the distorting device, in its real shape. In the appearance–reality session, the three-year-olds were asked whether the straw looked bent or straight to them and whether it was really and truly bent or straight. In the perspective-taking session, they were asked whether it looked bent or straight to them and whether it looked bent or straight to the experimenter. The correlations between appearance–reality and perspective-taking scores were .67 for the color displays and .72 for the shape displays. These correlations are as high as those between color and shape appearance–reality scores (.73) and those between color and shape perspective-taking scores (.69), despite the fact that the appearance–reality and perspective-taking abilities were assessed in different experimental sessions separated by several days.

In summary, I have suggested some cognitive competencies that may variously be facilitative, necessary, or sufficient for a beginning understanding of the appearance–reality distinction. One competency hypothesized to be sufficient or nearly sufficient is an increased cognizance of subjectivity and mental representation; this competency may allow children to construe an illusory stimulus as simultaneously possessing two seemingly incompatible properties or identities – one identified with its appearance and the other with its reality. Although the hypothesis has not yet been tested directly, there exist some data that make it seem plausible.

What Is the Subsequent Course of Development in this Area?

According to the hypothesis proposed in the previous section, as children become increasingly cognizant of subjectivity and mental representation, both simple appearance–reality tasks and simple perspective-taking tasks should begin to make sense to them and become easily soluble. Whether this explanation of development proves to be the correct one, there is considerable evidence that tasks of both kinds do become increasingly easy to manage as youngsters approach the middle childhood years. For example, children of four and five years are much more competent at simple visual perspective-taking tasks than children of three (Flavell, Flavell, Green, and Wilcox, 1980, 1981). There is even empirical support for the more general claim that "around the ages of 4 to 6 years the ability to represent the relationship between two or more persons' epistemic states emerges and becomes firmly established" (Wimmer and Perner, 1983, p. 104). Likewise, performance on standard appearance–reality tasks improves significantly between three and five years in both American and Chinese (People's Republic of China) children (Flavell, Flavell, and Green, 1983; Flavell, Zhang et al., 1983). Finally, we have recently found that six- to seven-year-olds perform almost errorlessly on simple tasks of both types (Flavell et al., 1985). Unlike the majority of three-year-olds, six- to seven-year-olds can consistently report realities when realities are requested and appearances when appearances are requested, whether the appearances are from their own or another person's viewing position. Consistent with these results with real and apparent object identities and object properties, Harris, Donnelly, Guz, and Pitt-Watson (1985) have recently found that children of this age are also capable of understanding the distinction between real and apparent emotion.

However, our investigations (Flavell et al., 1985) also show that development is by no means complete at this age. Using groups of six- to seven-year-olds, we administered two types of more demanding tests of the ability to think and talk about appearances, realities, and appearance–reality relations: identification tasks and administration tasks. In identification tasks, they were presented with a wide variety of stimuli and were asked to identify those that exhibited discrepancies or nondiscrepancies between appearance and reality and to explain their selections. In two studies, for example, they were shown a series of 23 pairs of stimuli. Within each pair, the stimuli differed from one another in degree of discrepancy between appearance and reality or in other ways relevant to the distinction. The subjects' job was to choose the member(s) of each pair, if any, that best exemplified an appearance–reality discrepancy and to explain their choice. In one of these studies, for instance, subjects were initially pretrained and given corrective feedback on what they were to look for. In addition, each new stimulus pair was introduced with the instruction: "Remember, we are trying to find things that don't look like what they really and truly are. Here are two things. Which one is better for the kind of things we are trying to find – this one, or this one, or are they both just about as good for the kinds of things we are trying to find?" The following items illustrate the variety of stimulus pairs used: (a) a real piece of candy and a magnet that looked like a piece of candy; (b) a bottle of cologne that looked like a tennis ball when its green base was not visible; the bottle was held so that the telltale base either was or was not visible; (c) a realistic-looking fake rock and a fake-looking fake water faucet; (d) two real flowers, one of them (an antherium) fake-looking. In the administration tasks, six- to seven-year-olds were asked to administer standard appearance–reality tasks, after having had experience taking them and following brief training on how they should be given.

The data from the identification tasks showed that the ability to identify on request stimuli exhibiting appearance–reality discrepancies and nondiscrepancies is still fragile and task dependent at the beginning of middle childhood. On one particularly easy-looking identification task, six- to seven-year-olds did perform well but on three others, including the 23-pairs task described above, identification performance was surprisingly poor. Furthermore, they seemed to find it even more difficult to talk about appearances, realities, and appearance–reality relations. They often failed to refer to them even when asked to explain their correct stimulus choices, that is, stimuli correctly chosen as best exhibiting an appearance–reality disparity. The same difficulty was evident in the administration task data. That is, six- to seven-year-olds also tended not to mention appearances, realities, and relations between them when asked to administer the very sorts of standard appearance–reality tasks they, as subjects, found so easy to solve – even after the experimenter had explained and repeatedly demonstrated the administration procedure.

We believe that these difficulties in nonverbal identification and verbal labeling reflect genuine conceptual difficulties. Many children of this age simply seem unable to think about such notions as "looks like," "really and truly," and "looks different from the way it really and truly is" in an abstract, metaconceptual way. Although they are able to identify concrete examples of the first and second notions quite easily and of the third with considerably more difficulty, they seem to lack the knowledge and ability to reflect on and talk about, indeed, often even briefly mention, the notions themselves.

We also administered an identification task involving the 23 pairs of stimuli to 11- to 12-year-olds and college students (Flavell, Green, and Flavell, 1985). The data gave evidence of considerable knowledge development in this area subsequent to early middle childhood. They suggest that 11- to 12-year-olds, and to an even greater extent college students, have acquired a substantial body of knowledge that is both richly structured and highly accessible.

As to rich structure, older subjects seem to possess abstract and general schemas for appearances, realities, and possible relations between the two. For example, they may make abstract, general statements such as "This doesn't look like what it really is" when confronted with an appearance–reality discrepancy. These schemas permit them to identify as possible instances of the abstract category, "appearance different from reality," many different types of appearance–reality discrepancies, including unusual and marginal ones. They can similarly identify instances of the category, "appearance same as reality," and can discriminate these from instances of the former category. They can also recognize subtle distinctions among appearance–reality task displays. In particular, they are able to identify and differentiate, with respect to these two categories, among realistic-looking nonfake objects, realistic-looking fake objects ("good fakes"), nonrealistic-looking fakes ("poor fakes"), and even fake-looking nonfakes. Consistent with our findings suggesting that appearance–reality and perspective-taking competencies are psychologically related, older subjects often draw upon their perspective-taking knowledge when thinking and talking about appearance–reality phenomena. For example, they comment spontaneously on how the appearance of a given stimulus (and therefore, perhaps, the observable appearance–reality relation) may vary with the observer's prior knowledge, previous viewing experience, or present viewing position. Finally, they can not only identify the appearances and appearance–reality discrepancies presented to them, but they can also reproduce these discrepancies, change them, or even create new ones. That is, their knowledge in this area is generative and creative as well as rich.

The appearance–reality knowledge of older subjects is also more accessible than that of younger ones, in the sense of being both (a) easily elicited by instructions and task materials, and (b) readily available to conscious reflection and verbal elaboration (metaconceptual). In terms of (a), vague instructions and a few concrete examples suffice to activate their appearance–reality knowledge; they require little help from the task materials or the experimenter. In terms of (b), older subjects can describe in detail what they know and think about appearance–reality phenomena. They readily talk about their own and other people's mental events, including the expectations and inferences an object's appearance would stimulate in an observer.

In summary, the subsequent course of development in this area seems to be both lengthy and substantial. Although 6- to 7-year-olds can easily manage the simple appearance–reality tasks that 3-year-olds fail, their ability to reflect on and talk about appearances, realities, and appearance–reality relations remains very limited. In contrast, the appearance–reality and related knowledge of 11- to 12-year-olds and especially college students is both richly structured and highly accessible. In an early article on this topic, Langer and Strauss (1972) hypothesized "that the cognition of the appearance and the reality of things follows a long and varied course" (p. 106). Our evidence certainly supports their hypothesis.

WHAT NEXT?

As always, there is much more to do. One obvious task for future research in this area is to find effective ways to probe for prerequisites, protoforms, and precursors in infants and very young children. Another is to make direct tests of our current hypothesis about what mediates an elementary understanding of the appearance–reality distinction. A third is to search for other abilities that seem to require the same general type of dual representation as appearance–reality and perspective-taking ones and that may for that reason be developmentally linked to them. A possible candidate we are currently examining is the ability to represent explicitly the selfsame object as simultaneously having a real identity (e.g., that of a small piece of wood) and a temporary pretend identity (e.g., that of a car, in the child's pretend play activity).

We think linking appearance–reality and perspective-taking abilities as we have done may shed new light on both. Similarly, trying to relate pretend play to these two might further illuminate all three. Continuing in this integrative vein, there seems to be a whole family of distinctions that have a similar "feel" to them. In each, one thing is represented in two ways, and the two ways have some kind of adversative, "but" type relation between them. Familiar examples: This is x but it seems or appears (perceptually, conceptually, affectively, etc.) to be y. This seems or appears x to me but seems or appears y to you. This is x but I can imagine or pretend that it is y. Further examples: This is x but it should be y (on moral, conventional, practical, aesthetic, or other grounds). I meant x but, being an imprecise communicator, said y (Beal and Flavell, 1984; Bonitatibus and Flavell, 1985; Olson, 1981; Robinson, Goelman and Olson, 1983). I know it is x but, deliberately lying, say it is y (Wimmer, Gruber and Perner, 1984). I thought of doing x, but I did not actually do it (Wellman and Estes, in press). We have just begun to think about these distinctions but find them intriguing. They appear to require similar processing and therefore seem as if they might be developmentally related. But a lot more hard thinking and research will be needed to find out whether they *are – really* and *truly*.

Acknowledgment

The work described in this article was supported by National Institute for Child Health and Human Development (NICHD) Grant HD 09814. I am very grateful to my research collaborators, Eleanor Flavell and Frances Green, and to Carole Beal, Gary Bonitatibus, Susan Carey, Sophia Cohen, Rochel Gelman, Suzanne Lovett, Eleanor Maccoby, Ellen Markman, Bradford Pillow, Qian Man-jun, Marjorie Taylor, Zhang Xiao-dong, and other colleagues and students for their invaluable help with this research.

Notes

This article is based on a Distinguished Scientific Contribution Award address presented at the meeting of the American Psychological Association, Los Angeles, California, August 1985.

References

Beal, C. R., and Flavell, J. H. (1984). Development of the ability to distinguish communicative intention and literal message meaning. *Child Development*, **55**, 920–8.

Bonitatibus, G. J. and Flavell, J. H. (1985). The effect of presenting a message in written form on young children's ability to evaluate its communicative adequacy. *Developmental Psychology*, **21**, 455–61.

Braine, M. D. S., and Shanks, B. L. (1965a). The development of conservation of size. *Journal of Verbal Learning and Verbal Behavior*, **4**, 227–42.

Braine, M. D. S., and Shanks, B. L. (1965b). The conservation of a shape property and a proposal about the origin of the conservations. *Canadian Journal of Psychology*, **19**, 197–207.

Bretherton, I. (1984). *Symbolic Play: The Development of Social Understanding*. New York: Academic Press.

Brown, A. L., Bransford, J. D., Ferrara, R. A., and Campione, J. C. (1983). Learning, remembering, and understanding. In J. H. Flavell and E. M. Markman (eds), *Handbook of Child Psychology: Cognitive Development* (vol. 3, pp. 77–166), New York: Wiley.

Chandler, M., and Boyce, M. (1982). Social-cognitive development. In B. B. Wolman (ed.), *Handbook of Developmental Psychology* (pp. 387–402), Englewood Cliffs, NJ: Prentice-Hall.

Daehler, M. W. (1970). Children's manipulation of illusory and ambiguous stimuli, discriminative performance, and implications for conceptual development. *Child Development*, **41**, 225–41.

DeVries, R. (1969). Constancy of generic identity in the years three to six. *Society for Research in Child Development Monographs*, **34** (3, Serial No. 127).

Elkind, D. (1966). Conservation across illusory transformations in young children. *Acta Psychologica*, **25**, 389–400.

Flavell, J. H. (1977). *Cognitive development*. Englewood Cliffs, NJ: Prentice-Hall.

Flavell, J. H. (1985). *Cognitive development* (rev. edn). Englewood Cliffs, NJ: Prentice-Hall.

Flavell, J. H., Flavell, E. R., and Green, F. L. (1983). Development of the appearance–reality distinction. *Cognitive Psychology*, **15**, 95–120.

Flavell, J. H., Flavell, E. R., Green, F. L., and Wilcox, S. A. (1980). Young children's knowledge about visual perception: Effect of observer's distance from target on perceptual clarity of target. *Developmental Psychology*, **16**, 10–12.

Flavell, J. H., Flavell, E. R., Green, F. L., and Wilcox, S. A. (1981). The development of three spatial perspective-taking rules. *Child Development*, **52**, 356–8.

Flavell, J. H., Green, F. L., and Flavell, E. R. (1985). *Development of knowledge about the appearance–reality distinction*. Unpublished manuscript, Stanford University, Department of Psychology.

Flavell, J. H., and Markman, E. M. (eds) (1983). *Handbook of Child Psychology: Cognitive Development* (vol. 3), New York: Wiley.

Flavell, J. H., Zhang, X.-D., Zou, H., Dong, Q., and Qi, S. (1983). A comparison between the development of the appearance–reality distinction in the People's Republic of China and the United States. *Cognitive Psychology*, **15**, 459–66.

Gelman, R. (1979). Preschool thought. *American Psychologist*, **34**, 900–5.

Harris, P. L., Donnelly, K., Guz, G. R., and Pitt-Watson, R. (1985). *Children's understanding of the distinction between real and apparent emotion*. Unpublished manuscript, University of Oxford, Department of Experimental Psychology, Oxford, England.

King, W. L. (1971). A nonarbitrary behavioral criterion for conservation of illusion-distorted length in five-year-olds. *Journal of Experimental Child Psychology*, **11**, 171–81.

Kuhn, D. (1984). Cognitive development. In M. H. Bornstein and M. E. Lamb (eds), *Developmental Psychology: An Advanced Textbook* (pp. 133–80), Hillsdale, NJ: Erlbaum.

Langer, J., and Strauss, S. (1972). Appearance, reality and identity. *Cognition*, **1**, 105–28.

Murray, F. B. (1965). Conservation of illusion-distorted lengths and areas by primary school children. *Journal of Educational Psychology*, **56**, 62–6.

Murray, F. B. (1968). Phenomenal–real discrimination and the conservation of illusion-distorted length. *Canadian Journal of Psychology*, **22**, 114–21.

Olson, D. R. (1981, August). *A conceptual revolution in the early school years: Learning to differentiate intended meaning from the meaning in the text*. Paper presented at the meeting of the International Society for the Study of Behavioural Development.

Pillow, B. H., and Flavell, J. H. (1985). Intellectual realism: The role of children's interpretations of pictures and perceptual verbs. *Child Development*, **56**, 664–70.

Robinson, E. J., Goelman, H., and Olson, D. R. (1983). Children's understanding of the relation between expressions (what was said) and intentions (what was meant). *British Journal of Developmental Psychology*, **1**, 75–86.

Rubin, K. H., Fein, G. G., and Vandenberg, B. (1983). Play. In E. M. Hetherington (ed.), *Handbook of Child Psychology: Vol. 4. Socialization, Personality, and Social Development* (pp. 693–774), New York: Wiley.

Selman, R. L. (1980). *The Growth of Interpersonal Understanding*, New York: Academic Press.

Shantz, C. U. (1983). Social cognition. In J. H. Flavell and E. M. Markman (eds), *Handbook of Child Psychology: Vol. 3. Cognitive Development* (pp. 495–555). New York: Wiley.

Shatz, M., Wellman, H. M., and Silber, S. (1983). The acquisition of mental verbs: A systematic investigation of the first reference to mental states. *Cognition*, **14**, 301–21.

Taylor, M., and Flavell, J. H. (1984). Seeing and believing: Children's understanding of the distinction between appearance and reality. *Child Development*, **55**, 1710–20.

Tronick, E., and Hershenson, M. (1979). Size–distance perception in preschool children. *Journal of Experimental Child Psychology*, **27**, 166–84.

Wellman, H. M. (1985). The origins of metacognition. In D. L. Forrest-Pressley, G. E. MacKinnon, and T. G. Waller (eds), *Metacognition, Cognition, and Human Performance*, New York: Academic Press.

Wellman, H. M., and Estes, D. (in press). Early understanding of mental entities: A reexamination of childhood realism. *Child Development*.

Wimmer, H., Gruber, S., and Perner, J. (1984). Young children's conception of lying: Lexical realism – moral subjectivism. *Journal of Experimental Child Psychology*, **37**, 1–30.

Wimmer, H., and Perner, J. (1983). Beliefs about beliefs: Representation and constraining function of wrong beliefs in young children's understanding of deception. *Cognition*, **13**, 103–28.

19

Children as Folk Psychologists: The Developing Understanding of the Mind

Kang Lee and Bruce Homer

EDITORS' INTRODUCTION

The term Theory of Mind has been used to describe our everyday understanding of the mind, or *folk psychology*. As we interact with others we take account of their feelings, desires, motivations, intentions, and so on. We try to understand why people say and do the things they do, and predict what they are likely to do in the future. Clear evidence of this type of awareness is in our everyday language: questions such as 'What do you think?', 'I'm sure you'll like this', 'Why was she upset?', refer to other people's thoughts, desires, beliefs, intentions, and other mental states.

The development of a theory of mind in childhood is currently one of the most active research areas, and Kang Lee and Bruce Homer give a comprehensive review of this research. Dennett (1978) suggested that the minimal criterion for crediting an individual with a theory of mind is that they should be able to appreciate that others have beliefs of a simple factual nature. For example, if I give my friend Mary a box of Smarties for her birthday, she will believe that the content is Smarties from looking at the exterior of the box. But if I trick her and put something else in the box, I will understand that she has a *false belief* – Mary thinks there are Smarties in the box, but there are not!

An understanding of false belief is seen as a crucial landmark in developing a theory of mind, and Lee and Homer begin their account by describing its development. They continue to review many other aspects of research that have implications for a theory of mind, and comment on the origins of a theory of mind in infancy. Their comprehensive review ends by discussing likely areas of future research. It has been persuasively argued that autistic children fail to develop a theory of mind, and an account of this is given in the article by Frith (article 37).

REFERENCE

Dennett, D. C. (1978). Beliefs about beliefs. *Behavioral and Brain Sciences*, 1, 568–70.

Let us suppose that you and your friend Amy are interested in a lecture on children's theory of mind. The lecture was originally scheduled for Room A and is now moved to Room B owing to an unexpectedly large audience turnout. Your friend Amy is a bit late and does not know about the last-minute location change. Now, which room do you think Amy will go to first?

"Room A of course," you reply.

But why?

Without hesitation, you answer, "Because Amy *thinks* the lecture is in Room A."

Notice that you made a causal prediction about Amy's action based on her false belief about the location of the lecture. In daily life, we adults frequently and readily make assumptions about others' mental states in order to predict and explain their actions. For example, Mike orders food in a restaurant because he *wants* to eat; Mary is *upset* because her purse is stolen; Susan *knows* whether it is raining because she just came in from outside. Philosophers and psychologists believe that the reason that adults are able to make such predictions and explanations is because they are folk psychologists. That is, adults, though not professionally trained, have a commonsense theory about how the mind works, or a theory of mind.

Adults hold three fundamental assumptions about the mind that are the cornerstones of a commonsense theory of mind. First, adults believe that the mind exists, although its activities are invisible and private (the existence assumption); secondly, they believe the mind consists of various mental states and processes such as intention, knowledge, emotion, desire, and belief (the component assumption); thirdly, they believe there exist various causal links between an individual's mind, external environments, and actions (the causality assumption). For example, "seeing leads to knowing," "desire leads to an intent to act," and "false belief leads to misguided action." Adults use these assumptions to make mentalistic explanations and predictions. Although using these assumptions frequently, adults may not be aware of their existence. This is because, according to D'Andrade (1987), commonsense mentalistic assumptions are knowledge inter-subjectively shared by all members in a social group. As a result, these assumptions are taken as obvious facts of the world. Individuals in the social group do not normally make explicit, nor see the need to make explicit, these assumptions when using them. In this respect, psychologists are an odd breed as they are "obsessed" with making explicit and scrutinizing such assumptions. (The present paper is an obvious case in point!)

While agreeing that adults have a set of shared commonsense assumptions about the mind, theorists and researchers are divided as to the ontogeny and development of a theory of mind, that is, the age at which children begin to understand mental activities and how this understanding emerges and progresses with age. In the last two decades, work in this area has occurred with unprecedented alacrity: hundreds of studies have been conducted; more than a dozen books are written; and a score of theories are proposed (for reviews, see Astington, 1993; Perner, 1991; Taylor, 1996; and Wellman, 1990). All these activities are a result of developmental psychologists' heated pursuit of the answer to a deceptively simple, but truly complex question: Do young children understand that a person has a mind?

The difficulty lies in the fact that young children's knowledge about the existence of the mind is as private and unobservable as the mind itself. The challenge that developmental researchers face is how to use children's overt behaviors, for example, their verbal statements, to reveal such covert knowledge, while ruling out more parsimonious interpretations. A child may display an overt behavior that appears to be "mentalistic," that is, derived from some knowledge about, or directed at, the mind (e.g., empathy, lying). To confirm this, however, researchers must first rule out that (a) the child behaves egocentrically (e.g., the child may report that another person *wants* something, basing this not on her understanding of that person's desire but rather on her own desire for it), and (b) the child responds simply by reverting to past experience instead of using mentalistic knowledge. In addition, if children fail a task designed to test their understanding of the mind, researchers must rule out that the failure is due to unrelated factors (e.g., fatigue, boredom, or information overload). In the past two decades, much research has been devoted to devising tasks to meet these requirements and to ascertain whether or not a child indeed has an understanding of the mind.

To test for an understanding of the mind, a task must require children to utilize one of the three fundamental assumptions about the mind (i.e., existence, component, and causality). Note that each assumption rests on the prior assumption: To understand that there are components of the mind, the child must first accept the existence of the mind, and to understand the causal nature of mind, the child must have some knowledge about the components of mind (e.g., beliefs and desires) and how they interact.

This chapter provides a review of current research on children's understanding of the components of mind and their causal effects. We begin in the same way that theory of mind research began, by focusing on children's understanding of beliefs. Being able to reason about beliefs, particularly false beliefs, is of primary importance because this ability has been identified by many theorists as being the sine qua non of possessing a theory of mind. However, children's understanding of the mind does not begin with an understanding of beliefs. Hence, the subsequent sections of this paper cover some of the earlier conceptual developments that relate to theory-of-mind understanding. First, children's understanding of perception, knowledge, and desire is considered. Then, two preverbal behaviors, namely pretense and joint attention, that require a rudimentary understanding of the mind are discussed. We conclude with some suggestions as to the direction that future research in the field will take.

Belief and False Belief

A belief is a mental representation of a proposition about the world. One of the tenets of our folk psychology is that a person's beliefs are formed directly from their experience with the world, but are independent of the world. In other words, beliefs are representations of the world that can be true or false. A belief is false when the representation does not correspond to reality. Being able to represent another person's false belief has been viewed by many researchers as a clear indication of understanding the existence of the mind and its basic properties. Some researchers even go as far as to say that understanding false belief is the "marker" or "litmus test" of children's theory of mind (e.g., Wellman, 1990). This is because the ability to represent another person's false belief correctly requires individuals to realize that what they themselves believe may differ from what another person believes. While knowing what the true belief should be, they must also be aware of what is falsely represented in the person's mind, what leads to such a false belief (e.g., ignorance), and what is the consequence of such a false belief (e.g., misguided behavior). In other words, to succeed in representing another person's false belief, one must have a fundamental understanding of the existence, component, and causality assumptions.

Take the room-change scenario given at the beginning as an example. The reason you can infer that Amy is going to Room A is because you represent in your mind the following propositions: (1) Amy *wants* to go to the talk, (2) Amy does not *know* the change of venue, (3) Amy *thinks* that the talk is being held in Room A, and finally (4) Amy is likely to base her action on what she believes. An egocentric or reality-based response would be that Amy will go to "Room B," which would be based on your knowledge of the true state of affairs. For this incorrect response, you do not need to know Amy's mental states at all. You simply use what you know in order to respond to the question. It is possible, however, for you to give a correct response without any mentalistic understanding. For example, past experience indicates to you that Amy always goes to Room A for a child development talk, regardless of whether the talk is actually held in Room A or B. However, this explanation is very unlikely as long as the child development talk in Room B is a novel event rather than a constant, ever present situation in Amy's life. For these reasons, if you respond "Room A," it would be evident to developmental researchers that you indeed have some basic understandings of the mind.

Do young children have an understanding of the mind like yours? In the last two decades, this has been the major question hotly pursued by many developmental researchers. A number of paradigms have been developed for this purpose. The first paradigm is a *search task*, which is similar to the location-change scenario described above (e.g., Wimmer and Perner, 1983). Variations in details notwithstanding, this paradigm commonly involves a story book or a puppet show in which a story character, "A," leaves a candy in one location. In her absence, another story character, "B," moves the candy from that location to a new location (see figure 19.1 for an example). The child participant is then

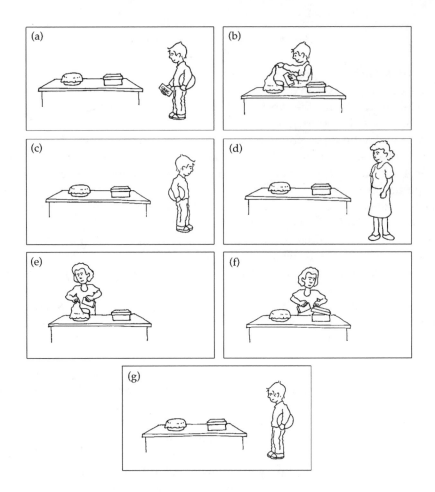

FIGURE 19.1 A sample false-belief task. (a) This is Mark. Mark has a chocolate bar and a basketball. He says to himself: "First, I want to play basketball and then I will eat my chocolate bar. I am going to put the chocolate bar in the basket while I play"; (b) So, Mark puts the chocolate bar in the basket; (c) Then Mark goes outside to play basketball; (d) While Mark is outside, Mother comes into the kitchen; (e) She finds the chocolate bar in the basket. She says: "Hey! Why is the chocolate bar in the basket? It should be in the candy box"; (f) So, Mother takes the chocolate bar out of the basket and puts it in the candy box; (g) Now, Mark returns.

The search question: Where will Mark look for his chocolate bar?
The think question: Where does Mark think his chocolate is?
The knowledge question: Does Mark know that his mother moved his chocolate?

asked the key "belief question": "Where will A look for the candy when she returns?" In addition, the child participant is asked a control "knowledge question": "Does A know that B moved her candy?" Studies using this paradigm (for a review, see Astington and Gopnik, 1991) show that most 3-year-olds and nearly all 4-year-olds correctly answer the knowledge question. However, most 3-year-olds fail the false-belief question, while only a small portion of 4-year-olds do the same. The children who fail the false-belief questions, always give a reality-based response (i.e., they say that A will look for the candy in its actual location). It should be pointed out that this response is unlikely to be an egocentric response because most of the children who give such an answer tend to respond correctly to the knowledge question. That is, they report that A does not know that the candy has been moved, although they themselves know this information.

While the search question requires the child not only to represent a false belief but also to make a causal prediction about someone's action based on a false belief, a *Think Paradigm* (e.g., Gopnik and Astington, 1988) asks the child: "Where does A *think* the candy is?" This paradigm is presumed only to probe children's representation of another person's false belief without asking them to make causal inferences (or inferences about the belief's attitude in philosophical terms). Despite this simplification, similar results are obtained: Most 3-year-olds continue to have difficulty in providing a correct answer. Another paradigm taps into children's representations of their own false beliefs. The so-called *Representational Change Paradigm* (e.g., Gopnik and Astington, 1988) involves a familiar container (e.g., a Smarties box), with the conventional content (i.e., Smarties) replaced with an unconventional one (e.g., crayons). The child is first asked about the contents of the box before the actual contents are revealed. Normally, an incorrect response results (i.e., reporting the box's conventional content, Smarties). Then, after being shown the true contents of the box, the child is asked: "What did you think was in the box when I first showed it to you?" (the self-belief question). In addition, the child is sometimes asked what another person would think is in the box before they see its true contents (the other-belief question). This latter question is assumed to be the same as the false-belief question in the Think Paradigm. Again, most 3-year-olds are found to have difficulty similar to their problems with the self-belief question. Although they reported just a few seconds previously that there were Smarties in the box, they claim that they *thought* there were crayons in the Smarties box. They also predict that another person will think there are crayons in the Smarties box without being shown its actual contents (see figure 19.2 for examples of testing results).

Results obtained in the above paradigms have led several researchers to propose a "cognitive deficit" theory (e.g., Perner, 1992; Perner, Leekam, and

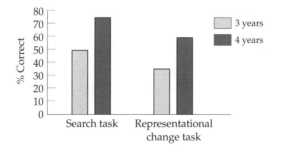

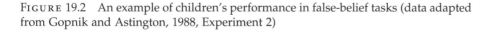

FIGURE 19.2   An example of children's performance in false-belief tasks (data adapted from Gopnik and Astington, 1988, Experiment 2)

Wimmer, 1987). This theory claims that 3-year-olds' difficulty with false-belief tasks reflects a deep-seated cognitive deficit in representing beliefs and false beliefs. Further, there was even suggestion that 3-year-olds may be lacking a theory of mind altogether. Additional evidence regarding autism seems to support this cognitive deficit theory. A number of studies (e.g., Baron-Cohen, Leslie, and Frith, 1985; Leslie and Frith, 1988; for a review, see Frith, 1989) have reported that autistic children, in addition to a host of problems related to interpersonal interaction, tend to fail false-belief tasks, while their IQ-matched Down's Syndrome counterparts succeed with flying colors.

Many researchers, however, disagree with the cognitive-deficit theorists' conclusions. Several alternative interpretations of the findings have been offered. These researchers claim that the above paradigms have methodological shortcomings and are not sensitive enough to assess young children's genuine understanding of false beliefs in specific cases and theories of mind in general (Chandler, Fritz, and Hala, 1989; Siegal, 1996). The first methodological problem lies in the way in which probe questions are asked. Siegal (1996) suggests that the commonly used questions in false-belief tasks may conflict with children's understanding of conversational rules. Their failure in false-belief tasks demonstrates children's misunderstanding of conversational implicatures involved in testing situations. For example, in the Search Paradigm, when children are asked, "Where will A look when she returns?" they may take the question as asking, "Where *should* A look?" or "Where *will* A look and find the candy?" Siegal and Beattie (1991) tested 2- and 3-year-olds on this possibility. Indeed, when children were asked, "Where will A look *first* when she returns?" most of them reported that A would look first in the original location, a correct answer. By contrast, another group who received the typical question, "Where will A look when she returns?" performed substantially worse. Children's sensitivity to forms of the probe questions is also found in the representational-change task. Lewis and Osborne (1990) compared children's correct-response rates in two conditions: in the first, children were asked, "When I opened the box, what did you think was in it?" and in the second, the word "when" was replaced with the word "before." The experimenters found that the use of "before" significantly improved 3-year-olds' performance. The findings of both studies illustrate that "minor" wording changes may yield very different assessments of young children's understanding of false belief. It seems that before methodological problems are sorted out, the notion of cognitive deficit seems to be a premature one.

The belief verb used in the probe question has also been found to affect young children's performance in both false-belief paradigms. In English, there are several verbs that can be used to describe beliefs (e.g., "think," "believe," "assume"). The word "think" is often used in a typical false-belief task due to its early emergence and use in young English-speaking children's vocabulary. In contrast, by about 3 years of age, Chinese-speaking children have three belief verbs at their disposal which can be used to describe their own or another person's beliefs: "xiang," "yiwei," and "dang." While all three words are appropriate for false beliefs, they have different connotations regarding the likelihood of a belief being false, with "xiang," which is most similar in meaning and usage to the English word "think," being more neutral than either "yiwei" or "dang." Lee, Olson, and Torrance (1996) administered a series of typical false-belief and representational-change tasks to Chinese-speaking preschool children with belief-probe questions that differed only in the belief verb used. They found that younger Chinese children, particularly 3-year-olds, performed significantly better when "yiwei" and "dang" were used in belief questions that when "xiang" was used. Lee et al. (1996) suggested that the use of verbs appropriate for the false-belief situation highlighted the possibility that the belief in question could be false and helped the children who were able to represent false beliefs give a correct response.

In addition to the effect of the nature of probe questions, many researchers suggest that the context in which a false-belief event takes place also plays an important role in revealing young children's understanding of false beliefs. Deception is considered to be an ideal context for testing children's theory-of-mind understanding as it is thought to involve an individual's deliberate intent to manipulate another person's belief system. In order to succeed in deception, one must be able to carry out actions to instill false belief into another person's mind. Studies have shown that children seem to be familiar with deception at a rather young age: children as young as 3 years of age engage in deceptive acts (e.g., lying) and some of them are even able to deceive naive adults (e.g., Lewis, Stanger, and Sullivan, 1989), although it is unclear whether the deceptive acts are learned behaviors or a result of children's deliberate attempt to instill false beliefs into another person's mind (Peskin, 1992; Ruffman, Olson, Ash, and Keenan, 1993).

To examine this issue, Chandler, Fritz, and Hala (1989) asked children of 2,3, and 4 years of age to help a doll hide "treasures" in one of four containers. During the hiding process, the doll left a trail of footprints leading to the baited container. Children were instructed to do something so that an adult who was not present during hiding would not be able to locate the treasures. Most of the children of all age groups employed various deceptive strategies, including: (1) withholding evidence (80%, 90%, and 100% for 2-, 3- and 4-year-olds respectively), (2) destroying evidence (i.e., wiping off a trail leading to the hiding place, 50%, 60%, and 80% for 2-, 3- and 4-year-olds respectively), (3) producing false information without destroying evidence (20%, 35%, and 20% for 2-, 3- and 4-year-olds respectively), and (4) the deadliest of all strategies: producing false information and destroying evidence! (50%, 25%, and 50% for 2- and 4-year-olds respectively). In addition, about 30% of 2-year-olds, 60% of 3-year-olds, and 55% of 4-year-olds lied about the whereabouts of the treasures. Chandler et al. (1989) claimed that children as young as 2 years of age not only employed deceptive tactics, but also engaged in deception with the *intent* to create "false beliefs" in others' minds. This would mean that very young children in fact have a fledgling understanding of false beliefs, contrary to what is suggested by the cognitive-deficit theory. This conclusion was highly controversial. Several researchers (e.g., Sodian, 1991) have suggested that the seemingly deceptive behaviors seen in Chandler et al.'s study (e.g., wiping off a trail leading to the hiding place) were merely sabotage tactics that did not need to take into consideration another's belief system: removing trails was very much like removing the tracks of a toy train. Further, some of those young children in Chandler et al.'s study might just enjoy wiping off or adding trails, with no intent to deceive at all.

To answer Sodian's (1991) criticisms, Hala, Chandler, and Fritz (1991) conducted a follow-up study which included the standard Wimmer and Perner (1983) false-belief task (i.e., the search task). Children were also asked to indicate where the competitor "thinks the treasure is," a question comparable to the standard false-belief question. Interestingly, while 3-year-olds consistently failed the standard false-belief task, 75% of them succeeded in answering the false-belief questions about the treasures. This indicates that the 3-year-olds understood that deceptive strategies led others into a false belief. Further, when using a cooperative condition similar to Sodian's (1991), Hala et al. found young children did not lay false tracks, which was in contrast to what was seen in the competitive condition. Again, this indicates that young children understood the deceptive implication of their actions. This finding was consistent with the findings of Sullivan and Winner (1993), who situated the standard representational-change task in a deceptive context. Their children also performed significantly better in a deceptive condition than in a cooperative condition.

Despite these recent findings, the controversy regarding the exact timing of the emergence of false-belief understanding remains. Researchers on both sides of the debate are still challenging the empirical validity of each other's findings and disputing about how these findings should be interpreted. Disagreement notwithstanding, most researchers do agree that by the end of preschool years, children have acquired some important understandings about the mind that are fundamental constituents of an adult-like theory of mind. Of course, it will take several more years for the child to acquire a more detailed theory of mind prescribed by D'Andrade (1987). Nevertheless, somewhere between the ages of 3 and 5 years, preschool children demonstrate behaviors that can only be parsimoniously interpreted as based on an understanding of the mind. Their success in false-belief tasks meets the stringent requirement put forth by many philosophers and psychologists and serves as unequivocal evidence that children have a basic understanding of the three mentalistic assumptions: the existence of the mind, its components (belief/false belief as opposed to knowledge/ignorance), and the causal relations between people's mind and their actions (e.g., a relation between false belief and misguided action).

It should be noted that it would be an error to construe an all-or-nothing notion of children's developing theory of mind based on whether they succeed or fail a false-belief task. A folk theory of mind consists of many mentalistic constructs. Belief and false belief are just two of these constructs. Among the other mentalistic constructs are perception, desire, knowledge, and intention. Also, there exist a host of causal links between people's mental states, their actions, and the environment around them (e.g., the relation between seeing and knowing and that between desire and action). Again, the causal relation between a false belief and a misguided behavior is simply one such link. Assumptions about the existence of the mind, its components, and its causal links are also about other aspects of the mind. The understanding of beliefs and false beliefs is only a milestone in children's long journey towards a mature folk theory of mind. This milestone is not the end and certainly not the beginning of the development in children's understanding of the mind. The understanding of false belief is important only in an empirical sense as it provides unequivocal evidence to researchers about whether a child has a basic understanding of the intentional nature of the mind. From a functional point of view, the understanding of beliefs and false beliefs, for all its practical purposes, is no more important than understanding desire, knowledge/ignorance, perception, and intention. This point is unfortunately often lost during heated debate.

PERCEPTION, KNOWLEDGE, AND DESIRE

Perception

Children's understanding of the other aspects of the mind emerge either concurrently or prior to the development of false-belief understanding. One of the concurrent developments is the appearance–reality distinction, that is, knowing that an object or person may appear to be one thing when in reality it is another (Flavell, 1986). Appearance–reality understanding requires the child to hold concurrently two contradictory representations of the object, one being the object's apparent identity and the other being the object's true identity. In this sense, appearance–reality understanding is similar to that of false belief as both require dual representations of conflicting ideas. However, the appearance–reality distinction calls for a different understanding of the mind, namely that perception is the source of the object's apparent identity. In a false-belief situation, the source of misconception is lack of knowledge, or ignorance.

Flavell and his associates (e.g., Flavell, Flavell, and Green, 1983) are the main contenders of appearance–reality research, and have devised numerous tasks to assess children's appearance–reality understanding. A typical appearance–reality task involves presenting children with a deceptive object (e.g., a sponge that looks like a rock) that appears to be one thing (e.g., a rock) but in reality is another (e.g., a sponge). After revealing the object's true identity, children are asked about its appearance (What does it look like?) and identity (What is it really?). Most studies to date consistently revealed a developmental pattern: 3-year-olds have great difficulty in making such distinctions while 4-year-olds are generally successful in an appearance–reality task. Three-year-olds tend to make two types of errors, an intellectual-realism error (e.g., reporting that the sponge/rock looks like and is a sponge) or a phenomenism error (e.g., reporting that the sponge/rock looks like and is a rock). This pattern of results was replicated with various deceptive objects in both physical (e.g., deceptive objects) and social domains (e.g., disguise). Training, and simplifying appearance–reality tasks, generally failed to produce any improvement. Further, the same results were also found with Chinese-speaking children. On the basis of these findings, Flavell (1988) concluded that 3-year-olds have a deep-seated intellectual inability to hold a dual representation for deceptive objects.

Recent findings have strongly challenged this conclusion. In addition to findings that suggest an earlier development of dual representation of non-deceptive objects (e.g., pictures and toys; Woolley and Wellman, 1990), several recent studies (Sapp, Lee, and Muir, 1997; Siegal and Share, 1990; Rice, Koinis, Sullivan, Tager-Flusberg, and Winner, 1997) show that 3-year-olds and even some 2-year-olds have rather consolidated understanding of the difference between an object's appearance and reality. This successful performance was obtained when the appearance–reality task was situated in a deceptive situation with which young children are rather familiar (Rice et al., 1997), in an ecologically significant context (e.g., a glass of milk that was contaminated by a cockroach but appeared to be drinkable; Siegal and Share, 1990), and in a task in which children only need to give a nonverbal response (Sapp, Lee, and Muir, 1997). For example, Sapp et al. (1997) followed the same procedure as did Flavell and his associates with one modification: instead of asking children to respond to the appearance-and-reality probe questions, researchers in this study made two requests that required the child to engage in nonverbal behaviors. One nonverbal request concerned a deceptive object's reality property (e.g., in the Sponge/Rock task, children were asked to give the experimenter something to clean up spilled water), and the other concerned its appearance (e.g., children were asked to bring something that looked like a rock for picture taking). Nearly all 3-year-olds correctly responded, nonverbally, to requests concerning deceptive objects' real and apparent properties. By contrast, most of the same children, when asked the typical Flavellian appearance-and-reality questions, performed as poorly as the children in Flavell and his associates' studies. Sapp et al. (1997) suggested that, in addition to the factor of context and ecological significance, linguistic constraints (Markman, 1987, 1991; Merriman, Jarvis, and Marazita, 1995) also play a critical role in children's performance in the typical appearance–reality tasks. These factors may contribute significantly to young children's apparent "inability" to succeed in a typical appearance–reality task. In this sense, it is the developmental psychologists who are making appearance–reality errors!

Knowledge

Children's understanding of knowledge involves three different levels of understandings of knowing: one is understanding the difference between knowledge and ignorance and reasons for knowing or not knowing; the second is the representation of the content of one's own and others' knowledge, which is in fact, the representation of belief or false belief; the third is the understanding of the origin and process of knowledge acquisition.

There is a consensus in the literature that children's understanding of knowledge/ignorance precedes that of belief and false belief (Wellman, 1990; Perner, 1992). As said earlier, in most false-belief studies, although they fail the false-belief question, a majority of 3-year-olds correctly report that the individual is ignorant of the displacement of the hidden object. Children's success with the knowledge question is probably due to their understanding of the causal relation between the individual's absence during the object's displacement and the individual's knowledge, or more generally, the link between perception and knowledge. Earlier studies by Flavell and his associates (Lempers, Flavell, and Flavell, 1977) established that children after 2 years of age begin to understand that the lack of visual access to information often leads to ignorance (Level 1 perspective taking). Recent studies by Pillow (1989) and Pratt and Bryant (1990) further demonstrated that by 3 years of age children also understand the other side of the causal relationship between perception and knowledge; that seeing leads to knowing. For example, 3-year-olds know that a person must look inside a box, not just be physically near it, to know its content (Pillow, 1989). O'Neil (1996) demonstrated that even 2-year-olds were aware of their mothers' knowledge or ignorance of an object's displacement. They tended to name the object and indicate its location more frequently when the mother did not witness the displacement than when the mother was present. A recent study by Shwe and Markman (1997) further revealed that children as young as 30 months of age were even sensitive to an adult's misunderstanding of their verbal request. They appeared to be more concerned about whether the adult received information accurately rather than whether their verbal request achieved its goal. They tended to clarify the misunderstanding for the adult even when the adult with misunderstanding actually gave them the requested toys.

Despite these remarkable early accomplishments in the understanding of knowledge and ignorance, 2-year-olds' understanding of knowledge is still rather rudimentary. Although they are aware of basic conditions (e.g., seeing or not seeing) that lead an individual to have or not to have knowledge, they have yet to come to grips with the content of the individual's knowledge under these conditions. In the literature, before the current theory-of-mind research, there was extensive research on children's representation of knowledge content or, as it was often referred to, perspective taking. The pioneering work by Piaget suggested that preoperational children were unable to take others' perspectives and often egocentrically assumed that information available to them was also available to others who were located elsewhere. Many ensuing studies, however, failed to confirm this conclusion. Preschoolers may have difficulty inferring what others might know from a different perspective but they make no more egocentric errors than any other possible type of error (Liben, 1978). Some studies (Borke, 1975; Donaldson, 1978) further demonstrated that older preschoolers were able to represent others' perspectives when information from different perspectives was marked by distinctive landmarks or the task was situated in a child-friendly context (Donaldson, 1978).

Preschool children in general seem to have the most difficulty with the third aspect of knowledge understanding. That is, they often fail to pinpoint when, how, and from which source a particular piece of knowledge is acquired. For example, young children cannot answer *why* they do or do not know a particular piece of information, even though they can report correctly whether they have the information (Perner and Ogden, 1988; Taylor, 1988). They have difficulty distinguishing between information that is provided by others and information that they obtain themselves (Foley and Johnson, 1985; Gopnik and Graf, 1988). They sometimes fail to attribute specific knowledge (e.g., color) to specific sensory experience (e.g., seeing; O'Neil and Gopnik, 1991). They also do not understand that one can gain knowledge via inference, that is, "thinking/reasoning leads to knowing" (Sodian and Wimmer, 1987).

Preschool children are possibly not alone in having difficulty with understanding the origin and acquisition process of knowledge. Older children and adults may also find it difficult to explain how and why certain knowledge is acquired: empirical evidence is scanty on this issue. Many tasks used in the above-mentioned studies are often not administered to children beyond the first grade, perhaps owing to a common assumption that older individuals should have correct understanding of the origin and process of knowledge acquisition and those tasks would be too easy for them. This, of course, is a dangerous assumption (Chandler, 1988). As illustrated by Mitchell and his colleagues (Mitchell, Robinson, Isaacs, and Nye, 1996), under certain conditions, even adults can make mistakes in their judgment. In their study, children and adults were told a story (based on Perner and Davies, 1991) in which a character is told something, namely the location of an ice-cream van, which either agrees with or contradicts the character's prior belief. The subjects, who knew the actual location of the van, were asked whether the character would believe either the message or what he or she had previously seen. In both cases, knowing if the message is true or false should not affect the subjects' answers as the experience is the same for the story character. Mitchell et al. found that 5-year-olds put more weight on what the protagonist had seen and were not influenced by the true location of the van. In contrast, adults' judgments of the character's beliefs were affected by their own knowledge of the van, resulting in erroneous responses. In other words, 5-year-olds in their study were in fact better than adults at predicting someone's belief! It is unclear, however, whether adults also have difficulties with explaining the knowledge-acquisition process, which should be clarified in future research. It should be noted that certain processes of knowledge acquisition may be inherently unexplainable without formal philosophical or psychological training (just try to explain why seeing leads to knowing or why misperceptions or illusions occur). Hence, the third aspect of the understanding of knowing may be a cognitive task that requires extensive learning, and its development may extend well beyond childhood.

Desire

To be able to understand someone's actions, it is not enough to know their beliefs; we must also know what they want. I may know that you think that there are cookies in the cupboard and apples in the refrigerator, but unless I know what you want to eat, it will be impossible for me to predict where you will look for food. Hence, it is "wanting" that makes linkages between the mind and action. In other words, desire drives action.

Even young infants are quite good at indicating what they want, for example, by using pointing and other nonverbal gestures. By the time they are

2 years old, children can use language to indicate their desires. As any parent will know, the word "want" is a big part of 2-year-olds' vocabulary. At this age, children understand that people will act in ways that fulfill desires. For example, Wellman and Woolley (1990) investigated 2-year-olds' understanding of how desire predicts a character's actions. Children were told a story in which a character wanted to find an object that was in one of two locations. The character then looked in one of the locations and did not find the object. The children were asked whether or not the character would continue to search. A majority of the 2-year-olds correctly predicted that the character would continue to search until they found the desired object. A recent study by Lee, Eskritt, Symons, and Muir (in press) further revealed that children as young as 2 years of age were sensitive to an individual's nonverbal attentional cues (eye gaze, head direction, and pointing). They readily used these cues to infer which object was desired by the individual.

Although 2-year-olds demonstrate an understanding of the causal nature of desires, according to Wellman (1990), they have difficulty with making predictions and explanations based on their representations of beliefs. This is because 2- and 3-year-olds are desire psychologists. They tend to use another individual's desire, rather than belief, as the primary cause for explaining and predicting the individual's actions. In their folk theory of mind, belief does not play an important role. By contrast, adults and children above 4 years of age are thought to be belief psychologists as they attach greater importance to belief than to desire in their causal reasoning.

PREVERBAL EXPRESSIONS OF THEORY OF MIND

Much of our knowledge about children's developing understanding of the mind derives from research paradigms that more or less require the child to have some basic language abilities. Many tasks require children to both comprehend narratives and produce verbal reports. Some of them (e.g., the Think Paradigm) even require children to understand and use the words that in and of themselves are mentalistic. For example, probe questions often use the words "think" and "know." To understand and use these words appropriately, children must have some understanding of the mind in the first instance, which is paradoxically the very issue that such paradigms are designed to examine. This paradoxical situation makes it difficult to ascertain whether children's success or failure in such paradigms is due to their knowledge of the mind or their knowledge of the language about the mind. Further, although the language about the mind is clearly related to, and may play an important role in, children's acquisition of a theory of mind (Jenkins and Astington 1996), it is certainly possible that certain mentalistic understandings do exist beyond the linguistic domain. From an empirical point of view, behaviors in nonlinguistic domains are equally as useful indicators of mentalistic understandings as verbal reports, so long as more parsimonious explanations can be ruled out. The advantage of examining nonlinguistic behaviors is that it allows us to glean information about the emergence of mentalistic knowledge in children who are at early stages of language development, namely children around and under 2 years of age, and these might give information about the precursors of a theory of mind.

Pretense

Several behaviors have been identified to be indicative of children's mentalistic understanding. One such behavior is pretense. Children begin to engage in pretend play around the age of 1 year (Leslie, 1987). Their pretend play activities increase greatly over the next two years. In a typical pretend play, children use "props" to simulate objects or situations that do not currently exist. For example, the child pretends that a banana is a telephone and acts as if she is making a phone call; or the child acts out a dinner scene with a toy tea set. To developmental researchers, what is remarkable about pretense is that children are able to both engage in elaborate fantasies and keep a strong footing in reality. Children clearly do not confuse a pretend telephone (e.g., a banana) with a real telephone. While pretending a banana is a telephone, they have no hesitation in eating it if they so choose!

In order to pretend successfully, according to some researchers, children must be able to carry out simultaneously factual and counter-factual representations. That is, they have to represent a prop both as what it is in reality (e.g., a banana) and as what it is pretended to be (e.g., a telephone). Also, they must be able to differentiate between the world of reality and the realm of imagination. They must understand that the "pretend" representation is the creation of the mind, which should not be confused with what is truly out there in the physical world. Failure to make such distinctions makes it difficult to engage in pretend play as evidenced by studies with autistic children, who are thought to be impaired in understanding mental activities (Leslie, 1992; Leslie, 1994; Baron-Cohen, Leslie, and Frith, 1985). It could even be dangerous to fail to understand the source of pretense. Just imagine that at snack time, the child confuses a telephone with a banana! For this reason, children's pretend play indicates that children at least understand the existence of the mind (the existence assumption). Leslie (1987, 1988) pushes the point even further. According to his computational model, having dual representations during pretense demands similar cognitive processing requirements as representing beliefs and false beliefs. For this reason, he argues that 2-year-olds have already achieved a basic form of theory of mind.

Leslie's (1987, 1988) interpretation is challenged by several researchers. Harris (1994) suggests that children's pretense differs qualitatively from belief/false-belief representation. He argues that children can simply use their knowledge about the world to create make-believe acts with their imaginations, and then quarantine it from reality by representing it as "not true." By contrast, false-belief representation requires the child to contrast an untruthful representation with a truthful one. Lillard (1993) further agues that children may not need to base their pretense on mental representation at all. Sessions of pretend play among young children are simply "acting-as-if" acts. In other words, children carry out pretend acts to mimic the behaviors of the to-be-pretended. They do not have a conceptual understanding that pretense involves the mind.

To test her argument, Lillard presented children with stories in which a character engaged in an act (e.g., hopping like a rabbit). Children were told that the character either knew or did not know what a rabbit was. When asked if the character was or was not pretending to be a rabbit, 63% of 4-year-olds claimed that he was pretending to be a rabbit even though they were told that the character did not know what a rabbit was. By contrast, 68% of 5-year-olds correctly indicated that the character was not pretending because he did not know what a rabbit was. Lillard concluded that under 5 years of age, children do not consider pretense to involve mental states. Rather, they view pretending as action or "acting-as-if."

To date, this debate has not been resolved (for a review, see Woolley, 1995). However, an important distinction should be made between Lillard's findings and Leslie's theory. Leslie focuses on *the action of pretense* and argues that the action of pretense requires both a representation of the reality and that of nonreality ("metarepresentation" in his term). Lillard's task, by contrast, focuses on children's understanding of *the concept of pretense*, or more precisely the word "pretend." Further, her task also requires children to understand the causal relations between knowing or not knowing and one's action. It is unclear whether 4-year-olds' difficulty in Lillard's study was due to their lack of understanding of pretense or their failure to understand the mature meaning of the word "pretend." Moreover, the children might also have difficulty understanding the causal relation between pretending and knowledge/ignorance. It seems that Lillard's findings do not fundamentally challenge Leslie's account of the development of pretense in terms of its relation to theory of mind.

Joint attention

Another mentalistic understanding is the understanding of another's focus of attention. This knowledge can be observed in infants' joint attentional activities with adults. There are two types of joint attentional activities. One is dyadic joint attention. It occurs during the face-to-face interaction between children and adults. Research in the last two decades has consistently shown that infants as young as 3 months of age are skilled at monitoring and conducting "dance-like" interactions with adults (for a review, see, Muir and Nadel, in press). They are very sensitive to changes in adult interactors' behaviors and perceptual properties. For example, when the adult stops interacting with them and poses a still face, infants' behaviors change dramatically. Their attention to the caregiver decreases significantly, and their smiling, a common occurrence during normal interaction, reduces to almost nonexistence. Some infants even become upset. This is the so-called "still-face effect" (Muir, Humphrey, and Humphrey, 1994). Less drastic changes in the appearance and behavior of the adult also produce significant results. For example, when the caregiver's face is presented upside down to infants, their attention to the caregiver is maintained but smiling decreases significantly. Apparently, the upside down display of an adult is treated as an asocial stimulus (Muir and Hains, 1993). It would be imprudent to suggest that these results reflect that infants are sensitive to the presence or absence of adults' intention for interaction and already understand the critical role of attention in face-to-face interaction. Rather, they can be parsimoniously attributed to the reduction of stimulation during still-face manipulation or disruption of natural face information processing when the face is presented upside down.

However, some recent evidence makes a reductionist explanation less plausible. For example, Hains and Muir (1996a) found that in a modified still-face paradigm, when interactors' behavior becomes noncontingent (e.g., the interactor interacts with an instant replay of the infant's behavior or a taped sequence of another infant's behavior), infants show near normal level of attention while their smiling is infrequent. Interestingly, these same patterns of attention and smiling behaviors are observed when a puppet interacts with them *contingently*, while their contingent interaction with a human interactor produces high frequencies of smiling and attentional behaviors (Ellsworth, Muir, and Hains, 1993). Moreover, infants between 3 and 6 months of age are extremely sensitive to whether the adult's eye gaze is directed at them. When the adult's gaze is averted as little as 5 degrees (e.g., when the adult looks at the infant's ear), even though the interaction is contingent, infant's smiling decreases significantly while gazing remains at normal levels (Hains and Muir, 1996b; Symons, Hains, Dawson, and Muir, 1996). Clearly, infants by 3 to 6 months are already selective about to whom their social interactions are directed as well as sensitive to whether adults' interaction is directed at them.

Infants' knowledge regarding others' attention is more evident in a triadic joint attentional situation. Triadic joint attention (which is often referred to simply as joint attention in the literature) involves a third party (an object or a person). Current evidence suggests that triadic joint attention emerges later than dyadic joint attention. Before 8 or 9 months of age, infants often treat adults' averted focus of attention as an insignificant or irrelevant signal and simply ignore it. Sometimes, they may notice it but seem not to know how to use the information. For example, in a study by Butterworth and Grover (1990), infants at 6 months of age orient their gaze to the same side as their mother's, but are confused about which object to attend to when several objects are present on the same side. Recent evidence suggests that infants can briefly follow adults' head orientation (D'Entremont, Hains, and Muir, in press). It is, however, unclear whether these infants treat the gaze signal as a cue to a third party, or simply engage in motion following.

Infants' understanding of the role of attention for regulating triadic interaction emerges around 12 months of age. At this age, infants have been reported to attempt to initiate triadic joint attention. For example, they begin to use their own eye gaze to engage their mothers while pointing to objects in the environment (Desrochers, Morissette, & Ricard, 1995; Morissette, Ricard and Decarie, 1995). Butterworth (1991) also reported that infants at the same age begin to use adults' gaze to establish joint attention with them, and by about 18 months, they can accurately determine others' focus of attention (Butterworth, 1991; Butterworth and Jarrett, 1991). At 18 months of age, young children also begin to use triadic eye gaze and other directional cues (e.g., pointing and head orientation) for referential communicative purposes. For example, they use adults' attentional cues to learn new words (Baldwin, 1993, 1995). By about 24 months of age, children even use adults' gaze to gain information about another's desire (Lee, et al., in press) and knowledge (Eskritt, Lee, Symons, and Muir, 1996). From here, children seem to have crossed a critical threshold. Now, they have entered a new realm of the mind where they must learn to master the notions of belief, knowledge, perception, and desire, and use these mental constructs to organize their experiences, to explain, and to predict actions.

SUMMARY

Research on the development of theory of mind is one of the most significant advancements in developmental psychology in the last two decades. In this brief review, we surveyed studies that address several major issues regarding young children's developing understanding of the fundamental aspects of the mind, namely, belief/false belief, knowledge/ignorance, desire, perception, and attention. The landscape of the mind is, however, much broader than these mentalistic constructs, and the causal links between them are more complex than the ones we have explored. Despite the explosive upsurge of research in the area in the last twenty years, our current knowledge of children's developing understanding of the mind is still rather limited. According to D'Andrade (1987), the mind is composed of a variety of mental processes and states, including perception, beliefs, feelings, desires, intentions, and resolutions; each of the mental states has various characteristics such as the locus of cause (e.g., feelings are caused internally while perception is caused externally), the agent of the mental state (e.g., a self-induced mental state vs a mental state effected by an external force), whether the mental state requires simple objects or propositional objects, and whether the state is controllable. In addition, various mental states and processes are inter-linked to form a complex web of causal relationships. A critical research task in the near future is to expand our theories to account for the development of theory of mind beyond the simple relationships that we have explored.

We propose a few critical directions of future research that may greatly advance our understanding of the development of a theory of mind. They include the investigation of (a) the development of a theory of mind beyond early preschool years, (b) the relation between theory of mind and other psychological constructs (e.g., personality, executive control), (c) universality and cultural specificity of children's theory of mind, and (d) finding applications for theory-of-mind research.

A few researchers have begun to take steps in these directions. First, with regard to milestones of theory of mind after preschool years, researchers have explored children's understanding of beliefs about beliefs, or second-order beliefs (i.e., "John thinks that Mary thinks that the ice-cream van is in the park"). The recursive representation of beliefs is a development that occurs after the age of 4 years and which has been the focus of some recent research, and is presumed built upon the first-order understanding of belief and false belief (e.g., Wimmer and Perner, 1983; Sullivan, Zaitchik, and Tager-Flusberg, 1994; Homer and Astington, 1997). Research has also shifted from the current emphasis on children's report of mental states and their action-predictions to explore the development of psychological explanation (e.g., Schult and Wellman, 1997). Adults' understanding of belief formation and the types of errors adults make when attributing beliefs and desires is also being investigated (e.g., Mitchell et al., 1996; Harvey, 1992). Research on adults' and older children's theories of mind should provide a more comprehensive developmental picture as well as a benchmark on which preschool children's performance can be empirically compared.

Secondly, developments in theory of mind need to be related to the development of other psychological constructs. For example, tentative links have been made between children's understanding of beliefs and understanding personality traits such as "nice" and "mean" (e.g., Yuill, 1992; Peskin, Ramsay, and Olson, 1997; Ramsay, 1997). Theory of mind has also been found to be related to children's understanding of various forms of communications such as mistakes, lies, jokes and ironies (Lucariello and Mindolovich, 1995; Sullivan, Winner, and Hopfield, 1995). Other researchers have explored the relation between the development of "executive function" and that of theory of mind (e.g., Ozonoff, Pennington, and Rogers, 1991; Frye, Zelazo, and Palfai, 1995; Zelazo, Burack, Benedetto, and Frye, 1996).

For example, Frye et al. (1995) found that children's performance in a false-belief task was correlated with their performance in "executive control" tasks that did not require reasoning about mental states, but did require children to switch between two conflicting sets of rules to make a judgment. It is suggested that 3-year-olds' difficulty with the false-belief task may be due to a more general inability to switch between two conflicting judgments, that is, switching between thinking about their own belief and about another individual's false belief.

The third issue concerns cross-cultural investigation of the development of theory of mind. Almost all of the research to date has been done with Western children. Cross-cultural research will address this bias and have implications for the cultural universality and specificity of children's understanding of the mind. In the few studies that have examined the effects of culture, some cultural differences have been found (e.g., Vinden, 1996; Lee, Olson, and Torrance, 1996; Wahi and Johri, 1994). However, more research is needed before any definite conclusions can be made regarding this complex issue.

Finally, some researchers have begun to examine the implications of theory of mind research for more applied domains. Particular attention has been paid to educational implications. Lalonde and Chandler (1995), for example, found that children's success on a theory-of-mind task was correlated with teachers' ratings of social–emotional skills and behaviors. Also, Astington and her colleagues (Astington, 1997; Astington and Pelletier, 1997; Astington and Pelletier, 1996) have found that, controlling for general intelligence, theory-of-mind understanding predicts early school success. Relations between social understanding and different types of learning may also exist (Tomasello, Kruger, and Ratner, 1993). Future research should examine other implications of theory of mind, for example, in the areas of treating children with autism, using young children as witnesses in court cases (Ceci and Huffman, 1997), and predicting and remedying aggression in children (Lochman and Dodge, 1994; Crick and Dodge, 1996).

References

Astington, J. W. (1993). *The Child's Discovery of the Mind*. Cambridge, MA: Harvard University Press.

Astington, J. W. (1997). Reflective teaching and learning: Children's and teachers' theories of mind. *Teaching Education*, **9**, 95–103.

Astington J. W., and Gopnik, A. (1991). Theoretical explanations of children's understanding of the mind. *British Journal of Developmental Psychology*, **9**, 7–31.

Astington, J. W., and Pelletier, J. (1996). The language of mind: Its role in learning and teaching. In D. R. Olson and N. Torrance (eds), *The Handbook of Education and Human Development: New Models of Learning, Teaching and Schooling* (pp. 593–619), Oxford: Blackwell.

Astington, J. W., and Pelletier, J. (1997, April). *Young children's theory of mind and its relation to their success in school*. Paper presented at the Biennial Meeting of the Society for Research in Child Development, Washington, DC.

Baldwin, D. (1993). Infants' ability to consult the speaker for clues to word reference. *Journal of Child Language*, **20**, 395–418.

Baldwin, D. (1995). Understanding the link between joint attention and language. In C. Moore and P. J. Dunham (eds), *Joint Attention: Its Origins and Role in Development* (pp. 131–58), Hillsdale, NJ: Lawrence Erlbaum Associates.

Baron-Cohen, S., Leslie, A., and Frith, U. (1985). Does the autistic child have a "theory of mind?" *Cognition*, **21**, 37–46.

Borke, H. (1975). Piaget's mountains revisited: Changes in the egocentric landscape. *Developmental Psychology*, **11**, 240–3.

Butterworth, G. (1991). The ontogeny and phylogeny of joint visual attention. In A. Whiten (ed.), *Natural Theories of Mind: Evolution, Development and Simulation of Everyday Mindreading* (pp. 223–32), Oxford: Basil Blackwell.

Butterworth, G., and Grover, L. (1988). The origins of referential communication in human infancy. In L. Weiskrantz (ed.), *Thought without Language* (pp. 5–25), Oxford: Oxford University Press.

Butterworth, G., and Grover, L. (1990). Joint visual attention, manual pointing and preverbal communication in human infancy. In M. Jeannerod (ed.), *Attention and Performance, XII* (pp. 605–24), Hillsdale, NJ: Erlbaum.

Butterworth, G., and Jarrett, N. L. M. (1991). What minds have in common is space: Spatial mechanisms serving joint visual attention in infancy. *British Journal of Developmental Psychology*, **9**, 55–72.

Ceci, S. J., and Huffman, M. (1997). How suggestible are preschool children? Cognitive and social factors. *Journal of the American Academy of Child and Adolescent Psychiatry*, **36** (7), 948–58.

Chandler, M. J. (1988). Doubt and developing theory of mind. In J. W. Astington, P. L. Harris, and D. R. Olson (eds), *Developing Theories of Mind* (pp. 387–413), Cambridge: Cambridge University Press.

Chandler, M. J., Fritz, A. S., and Hala, S. (1989). Small-scale deceit: Deception as a marker of 2-, 3-, and 4-year-olds' early theories of mind. *Child Development*, **60**, 1263–77.

Crick, N. R., and Dodge, K. A. (1996). Social information-processing mechanisms on reactive and proactive aggression. *Child Development*, **67** (3), 993–1002.

D'Andrade, R. (1987). A folk model of the mind. In D. Holland and N. Quinn (eds), *Cultural Models in Language and Thought*, (pp. 112–50), New York: Cambridge University Press.

D'Entremont, B., Hains, S. M. J., and Muir, D. W. (in press). A demonstration of gaze following in 3- to 6-month-olds. *Infant Behavior and Development*.

Desrochers, S., Morissette, P., and Ricard, M. (1995). Two perspectives on pointing in infancy. In C. Moore and P. J. Dunham (eds), *Joint Attention: Its Origins and Role in Development* (pp. 85–101), Hillsdale, NJ: Lawrence Erlbaum Associates.

Donaldson, M. (1978). *Children's Minds*. New York, NY: W. W. Norton.

Ellsworth, C. P., Muir, D. W., and Hains, S. M. J. (1993). Social competence and person–object differentiation: An analysis of the still-face effect. *Developmental Psychology*, **29**, 63–73.

Eskritt, M., Lee, K., Symons, L., and Muir, D. (1996). Can children spontaneously use eye gaze for "mind-reading"? *Proceedings of the XIVth Biennial Meeting of the International Society for Studies in Behavioral Development*, 553.

Flavell, J. (1986). The development of children's knowledge about the appearance–reality distinction. *American Psychologist*, **41**, 418–25.

Flavell, J. (1988). The development of children's knowledge about the mind: From cognitive connections to mental representations. In J. W. Astington, P. L. Harris, and D. R. Olson (eds) *Developing Theories of Mind* (pp. 244–70), Cambridge: Cambridge University Press.

Flavell, J. H., Flavell, E. R., and Green, F. L. (1983) Development of the appearance–reality distinction. *Cognitive Psychology*, **15**, 95–120.

Foley, M. A., and Johnson, M. K. (1985). Confusions between memories for performed and imagined actions: A developmental comparison. *Child Development*, **56** (5), 1145–55.

Frith, U. (1989). *Autism: Explaining the Enigma*. Oxford: Blackwell.

Frye, D., Zelazo, P. D., and Palfai, T. (1995). Theory of Mind and rule-based reasoning. *Cognitive Development*, **10**, 483–527.

Gopnik, A., and Astington, J. W. (1988). Children's understanding of representational change and its relation to the understanding of false belief and the appearance–reality distinction. *Child Development*, **59**, 26–37.

Gopnik, A., and Graf, P. (1988). Knowing how you know: Young children's ability to identify and remember the sources of their beliefs. *Child Development*, **59** (5), 1366–71.

Hains, S. W. J., and Muir, D. W. (1996a). Effects of stimulus contingency in infant–adult interactions. *Infant Behavior and Development*, **19**, 49–61.

Hains, S. W. J., and Muir, D. W. (1996b). Infant sensitivity to adult eye direction. *Child Development*, **67**, 1940–51.

Hala, S., Chandler, M., and Fritz, A. S. (1991). Fledgling theories of mind: Deception as a marker of three-year-olds' understanding of false belief. *Child Development*, **62** (1), 83–97.

Harris, P. (1994). Thinking by children and scientists: False analogies and neglected similarities. In L. A. Hirschfeld and S. A. Gelman (eds), *Mapping the Mind* (pp. 294–315), New York, NY: Cambridge University Press.

Harvey, N. (1992). Wishful thinking impairs belief–desire reasoning: A case of decoupling failure in adults? *Cognition*, **45**, 141–62.

Homer, B., and Astington, J. W. (1997). The development of children's understanding of second-order beliefs [Abstract]. *Canadian Psychology*, **38** (2a), 89.

Jenkins, J., and Astington, J. W. (1996). Cognitive factors and family structure associated with theory of mind development in young children. *Developmental Psychology*, **32** (1), 70–78.

Lalonde, C. E., and Chandler, M. J. (1995). False belief understanding goes to school: On the social–emotional consequences of coming early or late to a first theory of mind. *Cognition and Emotion*, **9** (2–3), 167–85.

Lee, K., Olson, D., and Torrance, N. (1996). Chinese children's understanding of false beliefs: The effect of language. *Proceedings of the XIVth Biennial Meeting of the International Society for Studies in Behavioral Development*, 354.

Lee, K., Eskritt, M., Symons, L., and Muir, D. (in press). Children's use of triadic eye gaze information for "mind reading," *Developmental Psychology*.

Lempers, J. D., Flavell, E. R., and Flavell, J. H. (1977). The development in very young children of tacit knowledge concerning visual perceptions. *Genetic Psychology Monographs*, **95**, pp. 3–53.

Leslie, A. (1987). Pretense and representation: The origins of "theory of mind." *Psychological Review*, **94**, 412–26.

Leslie, A. (1988). Some implications of pretence for mechanisms underlying the child's theory of mind. In J. W. Astington, P. L. Harris, and D. R. Olson (eds), *Developing Theories of Mind* (pp. 19–46), Cambridge: Cambridge University Press.

Leslie, A. (1992). Pretense, autism, and the theory-of-mind module. *Current Directions in Psychological Science*, **1** (1), 18–21.

Leslie, A. (1994). Pretending and believing: Issues in the theory of ToMM. *Cognition*, **50** (1–3), 211–38.

Leslie, A., and Frith, U. (1988). Autistic children's understanding of seeing, knowing and believing. *British Journal of Developmental Psychology*, **6** (4), 315–24.

Lewis, M., and Osborne, A. (1990). Three-year-olds' problem with false-belief: Conceptual deficit or linguistic artifact? *Child Development*, **61**, 1514–19.

Lewis, M., Stanger, C., Sullivan, M. W. (1989). Deception in 3-year-olds. *Developmental Psychology*, **25** (3), 439–43.

Liben, L. S. (1978). Perspective-taking skills in young children: Seeing the world through rose-colored glasses. *Developmental Psychology*, **14**, 87–92.

Lillard, A. (1993). Young children's conceptualisation of pretense: Action or mental representational state? *Child Development*, **64**, 372–86.

Lochman, J. E., and Dodge, K. A. (1994). Social-cognitive processes of severely violent, moderately aggressive, and nonaggressive boys. *Journal of Consulting and Clinical Psychology*, **62** (2), 366–74.

Lucariello, J., and Mindolovich, C. (1995). The development of complex metarepresentational reasoning: The case of situational irony. *Cognitive Development*, **10** (4), 551–76.

Markman, E. M. (1987). How children constrain the possible meanings of words. In U. Neisser (ed.), *Concepts and Conceptual Development: Ecological and Intellectual Factors in Categorization* (pp. 255–87), New York: Cambridge University Press.

Markman, E. M. (1991). The whole-object, taxonomic, and mutual exclusivity assumptions as initial constraints on word meanings. In S. A. Gelman and J. P. Byrnes (eds), *Perspectives on Language and Thought: Interrelations in Development*, New York: Cambridge University Press.

Merriman, W., Jarvis, L., and Marazita, J. (1995). How shall a deceptive thing be called? *Journal of Child Language*, **22**, 129–49.

Mitchell, P., Robinson, E. J., Isaacs, J. E., and Nye, R. M. (1996). Contamination in reasoning about false belief: An instance of realist bias in adults but not children. *Cognition*, **59**, 1–21.

Morissette, P., Ricard, M., and Decarie, T. G. (1995). Joint visual attention and pointing in infancy: A longitudinal study of comprehension. *British Journal of Developmental Psychology*, **13**, 163–75.

Muir, D. W., and Hains, S. M. J. (1993). Infantile sensitivity to perturbations in adult facial, vocal, tactile, and contingent stimulation during face-to-facing interactions. In B. de Boysson-Bardies et al. (eds), *Developmental Neurocognition: Speech and Face Processing the First Year of Life*, Netherlands: Kluwer Academic Publishers.

Muir, D. W., Humphrey, D., and Humphrey, G. K. (1994). Pattern and space perception in young infants. *Spatial Vision*, **8**, 141–65.

Muir, D. W., and Nadel, J. (in press). Infant social perception. In A. Slater (ed.), *Perceptual Development: Visual, Auditory, and Language Perception*, UK: Psychology Press.

O'Neil, D. (1996). Two-year-old children's sensitivity to a parent's knowledge state when making requests. *Child Development*, **67** (2), 659–77.

O'Neil, D., and Gopnik, A. (1991). Young children's ability to identify the sources of their beliefs. *Developmental Psychology*, **27**, 390–7.

Ozonoff, S., Pennington, B., and Rogers, S. (1991). Executive function deficits in high-functioning autistic individuals: Relationship to theory of mind. *Journal of Child Psychology and Psychiatry*, **32**, 1081–105.

Perner, J. (1991). *Understanding the Representational Mind*. Cambridge, MA: Bradford Books/MIT Press.

Perner, J. (1992). Grasping the concept of representation: Its impact on 4-year-olds' theory of mind and beyond. *Human Development*, **35** (3), 146–55.

Perner, J., and Davies, G. (1991). Understanding the mind as an active information processor: Do young children have a "copy theory of mind"? *Cognition*, **39**, 51–69.

Perner, J., Leekam, S., and Wimmer, H. (1987). Three-year-olds' difficulty with false belief: The case for a conceptual deficit. *British Journal of Developmental Psychology*, **5**, 125–37.

Perner, J., and Ogden, J. E. (1988). Knowledge for hunger: Children's problem with representation in imputing mental states. *Cognition*, **29** (1), 47–61.

Peskin, J. (1992). Ruse and representations: On children's ability to conceal information. *Developmental Psychology*, **9**, 331–49.

Peskin, J., Ramsay, J. T., and Olson, D. R. (1997, April). *Children's understanding of misleading appearances in characterization*. Paper presented at the Biannual meeting of the Society for Research in Child Development, Washington, DC.

Pillow, B. H. (1989). Early understanding of perception as a source of knowledge. *Journal of Experimental Child Psychology*, **47** (1), 116–29.

Pratt, C., and Bryant, P. E. (1990). Young children understand that looking leads to knowing (as long as they are looking into a single barrel). *Child Development*, **61** (4), 973–82.

Ramsay, J. T. (1997, April). *First- and second-order belief understanding and trait term use in children*. Poster presented at the Annual Convention of the American Psychological Association, Chicago, IL.

Rice, C., Koinis, D., Sullivan, K., Tager-Flusberg, H., and Winner, E. (1997). When 3-year-olds pass the appearance–reality test. *Developmental Psychology*, **33**, 54–61.

Ruffman, T., Olson, D., Ash, T., and Keenan, T. (1993). The ABCs of deception: Do young children understand deception in the same way as adults? *Developmental Psychology*, **29** (1), 74–87.

Sapp, F., Lee, K., and Muir, D. (1997). *Three-year-olds' difficulty with the appearance–reality distinction: Is it apparent or real*. Poster presented at the Society for Research in Child Development, Washington, DC.

Schult, C. A., and Wellman, H. M. (1997). Explaining human movements and actions: Children's understanding of the limits of psychological explanation. *Cognition*, **62** (3), 291–324.

Shwe, H. I., and Markman, E. I. (1997). Young children's appreciation of the mental impact of their communicative signals. *Developmental Psychology*, **33** (5), 630–6.

Siegal, M. (1996). Conversation and cognition. In E. Carterette and M. Friedman (eds), *Handbook of Perception and Cognition: Perceptual and Cognitive Development* (vol. eds: R. Gelman and T. K. Au), 2nd edition (pp. 244–82), New York: Academic Press.

Siegal, M., and Beattie, K. (1991). Where to look first for children's knowledge of false beliefs. *Cognition*, **1**, 1–12.

Siegal, M., and Share, D. L. (1990). Contamination sensitivity in young children. *Developmental Psychology*, **26** (3), 455–8.

Sodian, B. (1991). The development of deception in young children. *British Journal of Developmental Psychology*, **9** (1), 173–88.

Sodian, B., and Wimmer, H. (1987). Children's understanding of inference as a source of knowledge. *Child Development*, **58** (2), 424–33.

Sullivan, K., and Winner, E. (1993). Three-year-olds' understanding of mental states: The influence of trickery. *Journal of Experimental Child Psychology*, **56**, 135–48.

Sullivan, K., Winner, E., and Hopfield, N. (1995). How children tell a lie from a joke: The role of second-order mental state attributions. *British Journal of Developmental Psychology*, **13** (2), 191–204.

Sullivan, K., Zaitchik, D., and Tager-Flusberg, H. (1994). Preschoolers can attribute second-order beliefs. *Developmental Psychology*, **30** (3), 395–402.

Symons, L. A., Hains, S. M. J., Dawson, S., and Muir, D. W. (1996). 5-month-olds' sensitivity to adult eye direction in dyadic interactions (Abstract). *Infant Behavior and Development*, **19**, 770.

Taylor, M. (1988). The development of chidlren's understanding of the seeing–knowing distinction. In J. W. Astington, P. L. Harris, and D. R. Olson (eds), *Developing Theories of Mind* (pp. 207–25), Cambridge: Cambridge University Press.

Taylor, M. (1996). A theory of mind perspective on social cognitive development. In E. Carterette and M. Friedman (eds), *Handbook of Perception and Cognition: Perceptual and Cognitive Development* (vol. eds: R. Gelman and T. K. Au), 2nd edition (pp. 283–332), New York: Academic Press.

Tomasello, M., Kruger, A. C., and Ratner, H. H. (1993). Cultural learning. *Behavioral and Brain Sciences*, **16** (3), 495–511.

Vinden, P. G. (1996). Junin Quechua children's understanding of mind. *Child Development*, **67** (4), 1707–16.

Wahi, S., and Johri, R. (1994). Questioning a universal theory of mind: Mental–real distinctions made by Indian children. *Journal of Genetic Psychology*, **155** (4), 503–10.

Wellman, H. (1990). *The Child's Theory of Mind*. Cambridge, MA: MIT Press/Bradford Books.

Wellman, H. and Woolley, J. D. (1990). From simple desires to ordinary beliefs: The early development of everyday psychology. *Cognition*, **35**, 910–23.

Wimmer, H., and Perner, J. (1983). Beliefs about beliefs: Representation and constraining function of wrong beliefs in young children's understanding of deception. *Cognition*, **13**, 103–28.

Woolley, J. (1995). The fictional mind: Young children's understanding of imagination, pretense, and dreams. *Developmental Review*, **15**, 172–211.

Woolley, J., and Wellman, H. (1990). Young children's understanding of realities, non-realities and appearances. *Child Development*, **61**, 946–61.

Yuill, N. (1992). Children's conception of personality traits. *Human Development*, **35**, 265–79.

Zelazo, P. D., Burack, J. A., Benedetto, E., and Frye, D. (1996). Theory of Mind and rule use in individuals with Down's Syndrome: A test of the uniqueness and specificity claims. *Journal of Child Psychology and Psychiatry and Allied Disciplines*, **37** (4), 479–84.

20

Development of Intuitive Theories of Motion: Curvilinear Motion in the Absence of External Forces*

Mary Kister Kaiser, Michael McCloskey and Dennis R. Proffitt

EDITORS' INTRODUCTION

Imagine the following situation. A person is holding a stone at shoulder height while walking forward at a brisk pace. What will happen if the person drops the stone? What kind of path will the stone follow as it falls?' McCloskey (1983) begins his article on 'Intuitive Physics' with this question. In reality, the forward momentum of the person, interacting with gravity, mean that the stone will move forwards as it falls from the dropping point, landing some inches beyond the release point. Many adults will claim that the stone will simply drop straight down, and others will make the curious claim that it will actually travel *backwards* and land behind its point of release.

This finding alerts us to the fact that there is often a discrepancy between physical reality and our intuitive beliefs about what might happen, with the latter often being quite different from what does happen. The paper by Kaiser, McCloskey and Proffitt explores children's and college students' understanding of the path that a ball would take on exiting from a curved tube – many children and students get it quite wrong!

Can you beat Oppenheimer?

It is usually found that those who have had formal training in physics are able to solve these 'intuitive physics' problems without error, because of their formal training. The great theoretical nuclear physicist J. Robert Oppenheimer (1904–67) was once presented the following problem at a cocktail party:

---

* Previously published in *Developmental Psychology*, **22**, 1 (1986), pp. 67–71.

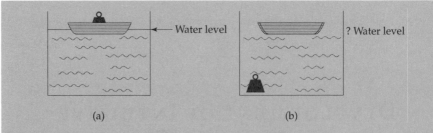

FIGURE 20.1 Oppenheimer's problem

> There is a weight placed in a boat that is floating on a very small pond. The
> water level is indicated by the arrow in (a). The weight is then taken out of the
> boat and placed in the pond (b). The question is, what will happen to the level
> of the water – will it rise, fall, or stay the same?

Oppenheimer got it wrong, demonstrating that expertise in physics is not a
guarantee of success in simple physics problems! The correct solution (with
explanations!) is given at the end of the article (p. 263).

REFERENCE

McCloskey, M. (1983). Intuitive Physics. *Scientific American*, **248** (4), 114–21.

OVERVIEW College students and children between the ages of 4 and 12 were asked to
draw the path a ball would take upon exiting a curved tube. As in previous
studies, many subjects erroneously predicted curvilinear paths. However, a
clear U-shaped curve was evident in the data: Preschoolers and kindergartners performed as well as college students, whereas school-aged children
were more likely to make erroneous predictions. A second study suggested
that the youngest children's correct responses could not be attributed to
response biases or drawing abilities. This developmental trend is interpreted to mean that the school-aged children are developing intuitive theories of motion that include erroneous principles. The results are related to
the "growth errors" found in other cognitive domains and to the historical
development of formal theories of motion.

People encounter moving objects in almost every facet of their daily lives.
Recent research suggests that people develop from these encounters a systematic intuitive theory of motion that is inconsistent with fundamental principles
of Newtonian mechanics and resembles instead the pre-Newtonian theory of
impetus popular in the 14th through 16th centuries (Champagne, Klopfer, and
Anderson, 1980; Clement, 1982; McCloskey, 1983; McCloskey, Caramazza, and
Green, 1980). The intuitive theory holds that the act of setting an object in
motion (e.g., by throwing or pushing it) imparts to the object an internal force,

or impetus, that serves to keep the object moving for some time after it is no longer in contact with the original mover. However, the impetus steadily dissipates, and the object gradually slows to a stop.

The intuitive impetus theory incorporates a number of striking misconceptions about how moving objects behave in seemingly simple situations. One such misconception was revealed by McCloskey et al.'s (1980) study in which college students were shown the drawing in figure 20.2a and told that it represented a thin curved tube lying on a flat surface. The students were asked to imagine that a metal ball was put into the end of the tube indicated by the arrow and shot out of the other end at a high speed. The students' task was to draw the path the ball would follow after emerging from the tube.

It is a basic principle of Newtonian mechanics than an object moves in a straight line in the absence of a net applied force. Hence, the correct answer to the problem is that the ball will follow a straight path, as shown in figure 20.2b. However, half of the students to whom the problem was presented indicated that the ball would continue to curve after leaving the tube, as shown in figure 20.2c. The students' explanations for their responses suggested that the curved trajectories reflected a belief that an object can acquire impetus for curvilinear as well as rectilinear motion. One student explained, for example, that "the momentum from the curve of the tube gives the ball the arc. The force that the ball picks up from the tube eventually dissipates and it will follow a normal straight line."

It is perhaps not surprising that people develop the basic concept of impetus from their experience with motion; this concept provides a straightforward explanation for the fact that an inanimate object set in motion usually continues moving for some time and then stops. How, though, do people come to have misconceptions of the sort revealed by the curved-tube problem, erroneous beliefs that are clearly at variance with the way in which objects actually move? In an attempt to gain insight into the development of ideas concerning curvilinear motion, Experiment 1 examined children's responses to the curved-tube problem across a wide range of ages.

Experiment 1

Method

Subjects Ninety-six middle-class children, ranging in age from 4.5 to 12 years, and 20 college students participated in the study. Three additional subjects, all of whom were preschool children, were excluded because they did not understand the task. Children were classified into four groups according to grade. There were 23 preschoolers and kindergartners (12 males, 11 females; mean age, 5 years 10 months); 23 first- and second-graders (13 males, 10 females; mean age, 7 years 11 months); 28 third- and fourth-graders (12 males, 16 females; mean age, 10 years 1 month); and 22 fifth- and sixth-graders (11 males, 11 females; mean age, 12 years 1 month). The college sample consisted

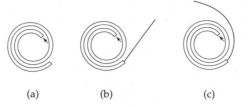

(a)   (b)   (c)

FIGURE 20.2   The curved tube problem (a), its correct solution (b), and the most common incorrect response (c)

of 10 men and 10 women, all but 2 of whom had taken high school or college physics courses.

Materials and procedure   Three tubes were mounted on an 85-cm by 105-cm plywood board that lay flat on a level table. The tubes were 2.2 cm in diameter and were made of clear plastic. One end of each tube was elevated such that a 1-cm steel ball placed in the elevated end would roll through the tube at a moderate speed. The first tube ran in a straight line for 40 cm, the second formed a C-shaped curve with an interior diameter of 25 cm, and the third formed a spiral of 540° rotation with an interior diameter of 20 cm (similar to the tube in figure 20.2). Subjects were given the following instructions:

> Suppose I take this ball and put it in this end of the tube. It will go through the tube like this (experimenter traces the path through the tube) and come out here (experimenter indicates the mouth of the tube). What I want you to do is take this marker and draw for me the path the ball will take when it comes out of the tube. Start here where it comes out and draw the path here on the paper.

Subjects made their drawings on a 28-cm by 55-cm piece of paper placed on the board at the mouth of the tube. The straight-tube problem was always presented first, as a pretest to ensure that the subject understood the task. The order of presentation for the C-curve and spiral was counterbalanced across subjects. After a subject had responded to all three tubes, he or she was asked to justify and explain the responses. The subjects' drawings were coded as straight or curved by criteria similar to that employed in earlier studies (e.g., McCloskey et al., 1980). Generally, paths that curved less than 10° per foot were scored as straight.

Results

All subjects gave correct straight-line responses for the straight tube. For the curved tubes, however, 41% of the responses were curved paths of the sort shown in figure 20.2c. As in the previous studies, the likelihood of a curved response was related to the degree of curvature of the tube: the spiral tube elicited more curved paths than the C-tube. Errors other than paths curved in the direction of the tube curvature were rare, occurring on only 4% of the trials.

Examination of age trends on the curved-tube problems revealed a striking pattern of results. The percentage of correct responses was approximately the same for the youngest subjects (preschool and kindergarten children) and the oldest subjects (college students) but was considerably worse for the intermediate-age subjects (first-through sixth-graders). For example, for the spiral-tube problem the percentage of correct responses was 61% for the preschool and kindergarten children, 60% for the college students, but only 25% for the third- and fourth-graders.

The U shape of the function relating age and performance is evident in figure 20.3. Log-linear analyses confirmed the presence of significant quadratic trends in both the C-tube and spiral-tube data. For the C-tube data, a model with only a linear age trend did not fit the data, $G^2(7) = 14.076$, $p < .05$, $R^2 = .017$, whereas a model including a quadratic term fit quite well, $G^2(6) = 6.668$, $p > .25$, $R^2 = .457$.[1] Similarly, a linear age model did not fit the spiral-tube data, $G^2(7) = 15.694$, $p < .05$, $R^2 = .022$, but a model containing a quadratic term fit well, $G^2(6) = 9.226$, $p > .10$, $R^2 = .425$.

In their verbal explanations, most children who predicted curved paths justified their responses as based on the curvature of the tube. Generally, comments related the degree of path curvature to "how much the tube turns." Hence, children who predicted a curved trajectory from the spiral tube and a straight trajectory from the C-tube explained that the C-tube "didn't turn enough."

Older children who predicted straight trajectories commented that the curvature of the tube had no effect on the ball once it exited the tube. When queried, none could imagine a tube configuration that would result in a nonlinear trajectory. The younger children (preschool and kindergarten) who predicted straight trajectories did not produce very informative justifications. They tended to respond that "balls roll straight" and seemed confused at the suggestion of a curvilinear path.

Experiment 2

Although the preschool and kindergarten children gave as many correct responses as college students in Experiment 1, the basis of their predictions was not clear from their explanations. Generally, there seemed to be at least three possible explanations for their seemingly precocious responses. First, these children could be unable or unwilling to draw curved lines. Thus, although they might actually believe that the ball would continue to curve, they might be unable to represent this outcome in their drawing because of a production deficiency (Flavell, 1977).

The second possibility is that these children would predict a straight trajectory for any object, even when a linear path is inappropriate. That is, it could be that the youngest children employ a very simple heuristic: Objects move in straight paths. If this were true, then these children should predict a straight path even in inappropriate cases, for example, when asked to predict the trajectory of a toy car with its wheels turned. This sort of rule-application

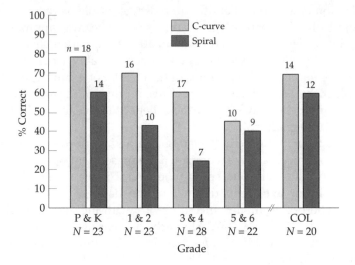

FIGURE 20.3 Proportion of correct predictions on the C-curve and spiral tube problems by age group (P = preschool, K = kindergarten, COL = college)

strategy has been observed to lead to U-shaped curves in other domains (Richards and Siegler, 1982).

The final explanation holds that the children who gave a correct response to the curved-tube problem deal with motion on the level of particular cases and have no overarching theory of motion. If this were the case, these children should predict the path of the car correctly on the basis of their experiences with toy vehicles, just as they correctly answered the curved-tube problem on the basis of their experiences with rolling balls. Such a "particular case" competence is similar to that demonstrated by young children's proper use of irregular verbs (Brown, 1973).

In an attempt to determine which of these three explanations best accounted for the children's correct responses in Experiment 1, we assessed young children's drawing ability and their predictions for situations in which a curvilinear path is appropriate.

Method

Subjects Twenty-four children attending a university preschool participated in the study. There were 12 males and 12 females (mean age, 5 years 2 months).

Materials and procedure Children were administered three tasks. The first employed the straight and spiral tubes employed in Experiment 1; the procedure for eliciting children's trajectory predictions was the same as in that study.

The second task required the child to predict the path a spring-driven toy car would take under two conditions: with its front wheels straight and with its front wheels turned at an angle. In each condition, the child saw the car travel along a drawn path (the circular path was a C-curve 10 cm in diameter) and encounter a barrier. The child was asked to draw the path the car would take if the barrier was removed.

The final task was a copying task that required the child to draw copies of two sample paths, one straight and one curved. This task was always administered last. The order of the two prediction tasks was counterbalanced across subjects. All drawings were coded as straight or curved by the same criteria used in Experiment 1.

Thus, these three tasks help differentiate among the three possible explanations for young children's correct responses in Experiment 1. If children of this age are unable to draw curved lines, they should not produce them on either prediction task or on the copying task. If children are able to produce curved responses on the copying task yet persist in predicting linear trajectories for both the car with turned wheels and the ball in the curved tube, we would conclude that these children employ a simple "objects roll straight" rule to all situations, even when inappropriate. The third possibility is that children who predict a linear path for the ball would recognize that the car continues to curve, reflecting their ability to deal correctly with the motion of specific objects.

Results

Children's responses on the copying task indicated that all of them were capable of drawing curved lines as well as straight, at least when provided with a model. In the two trajectory-prediction tasks, all but 2 children produced straight paths for the straight-tube and the car-with-wheels-straight problems. These 2 children's predictions were uncodable and will not be considered further. The 24 children's patterns of predictions for the curved-tube and car-with-wheels-turned problems are as follows: Ten of the children predicted a straight path for the ball and a curved path for the car (Pattern 1); 10 predicted that both the ball and car would curve (Pattern 2); 2 predicted straight paths for both the ball and car (Pattern 3); and 2 predicted the ball would curve but the car would go straight (Pattern 4). Predictions were not related to gender.

Of the 12 children who predicted a straight path for the curved-tube problem (Patterns 1 and 3), 10 of them recognized that the car would continue to curve (Pattern 1). These children justified their differential predictions by citing the tube as the cause of the ball's curvilinear motion (which then ceases) and contrasting it with the turned wheels, which would maintain the car's curvilinear motion. Most of the children who predicted a curved path for the curved-tube problem (Patterns 2 and 4) likewise predicted a curved path for the car (Pattern 2). The children producing Pattern 2 responses justified the ball's and car's curved paths in terms of the objects' previous curvilinear motion. One of the 2 children exhibiting Pattern 4 responses explained that the car would roll straight because the barrier had altered its motion. Both of the Pattern 3 children explained that the car would not curve because it had not moved in a circular path as long as the ball had ($180°$ vs. $540°$ rotation).

Discussion

The results of this study suggest that the younger children's correct responses in Experiment 1 cannot be attributed to an inability to draw curved lines, or to a tendency to predict straight trajectories in all situations. Eighteen of the children properly responded that the car with wheels turned would continue on a curved path. That 10 of the children predicted the car would continue to curve but the ball would roll straight, despite the ball's undergoing greater circular rotation, suggests that many children clearly differentiate the two situations.

GENERAL DISCUSSION

U-shaped developmental trends have been reported in many cognitive domains. Strauss (1982) distinguished several possible underlying mechanisms for U-shaped behavioral growth. These include (a) short-term, unstable behavior patterns that may appear U-shaped because of assessment techniques (Strauss, 1972); (b) artifactual U-shaped curves resulting from a Strategy X Task interaction (Richards and Siegler, 1982); (c) U-shaped curves resulting from an interaction between systems of representation (Bower, 1978); and (d) U-shaped curves resulting from the reorganization of knowledge from experience-based, case-specific understanding to general knowledge schemes (McNeill, 1970).

Previous studies of children's understanding of motion have noted the variance in children's competencies in sensorimotor and representational domains (e.g., Piaget, 1976). However, none has postulated the existence of U-shaped behavioral growth of the fourth kind. This may be explained by the fact that this sort of U-shaped growth is most evident when the general knowledge scheme requires the recognition of special cases and exceptions, as is the case for English grammar and impetus theories. Because the role impetus models play in adults' understanding of motion has only recently been realized (McCloskey, 1983), children's "growth errors" in this domain would not have been recognized.

We believe our subjects' performance on the curved-tube problem exemplifies this fourth type of U-shaped growth. The youngest children generally deal with the problem on a concrete level, perhaps thinking about other situations in which they observed a ball rolling across a table or other surface. Consequently, they draw straight paths for the ball. Older children, however, have begun to think about motion on a higher, theoretical level. They have begun to abstract from their experiences general principles that help them to understand and predict events involving motion. In particular, the children may have developed a "persistence of motion" principle, a primitive precursor to the concept of inertia. In their attempt to consolidate particular experiences into a single, overarching scheme of motion, children may arrive at a general principle like "an object that is set in motion tends to keep moving for some time in the way it was set going." This overly general persistence principle is then applied to instances involving curvilinear as well as rectilinear motion, leading to the prediction that the ball moving through the curved tube will continue in curvilinear motion for some time after it emerges. Thus, the curvilinear motion misconception may arise as a by-product of the development of a general persistence of motion principle that, for the most part, is very useful in predicting and understanding motion.

Many people eventually come to realize (through everyday experience or formal physics instruction) that curvilinear motion, unlike rectilinear motion, occurs only when an external force acts continually on the moving object. These individuals reformulate their persistence of motion principles accordingly, and this reformulation leads to improved performance on the curved-tube problems among the older subjects. The considerably less than perfect performance of the college students suggests, however, that some people retain the principle that both straight-line and curved motions tend to continue once started.

The cognitive developmental process we have postulated, in which a general principle concerning the persistence of motion in the absence of external forces is formulated and subsequently refined, finds parallels in the historical development of the science of mechanics. Aristotelian physics explicitly denied the natural persistence of motion; Aristotle held that objects remain in motion only so long as they are in direct contact with an external mover (Clagett, 1959; Crombie, 1952). With the advent of the medieval theory of impetus came the idea that motion may continue in the absence of external forces; impetus impressed in an object keeps it moving. Like the persistence-of-motion principle developed by our subjects, however, the assumptions of the impetus theory were overly general. According to the theory, an object could be impressed with impetus for circular as well as straight-line motion, so that curvilinear as well as rectilinear motions tended to continue once started. For example, Jean Buridan, the 14th-century Parisian philosopher, stated that

> a mover in moving a body impresses on it a certain impetus, a certain power capable of moving this body in the direction in which the mover set it going, whether upwards, downwards, sideways or in a circle.... It is by this impetus that the stone is moved after the thrower ceases to move it.   (Crombie, 1952)

The concept of circular impetus, and hence the persistence of circular motion, went largely unquestioned for nearly three centuries. It was not until the mid-17th century, shortly before the publication of Newton's *Principia* in 1686, that Descartes and Gassendi explicitly articulated the principle that only rectilinear motion persists in the absence of external forces (Crombie, 1952).

Caution must be taken in drawing too strong a parallel between historical developments in physical theory and the child's developing models of motion. Further research is needed to better substantiate our claim that the school-aged children's errors resulted from the systematic overextension of a general motion concept. Nonetheless, it does seem feasible to suggest that, on both historical and ontological levels, an impetus-like conception of motion is appealingly intuitive and may represent a natural early attempt at a cogent, overarching explanation of inanimate motion.

ACKNOWLEDGMENTS

This research was supported by National Institute of Mental Health Training Grant T32-MH16892 to the first author and National Institute for Child Health and Development Grant HD-16195 to the third author.

We would like to thank David Larabell, principal of West Willow Elementary School, Steven Sternberg, director of the University of Michigan Children's Center, and their staffs for their hospitality and cooperation.

NOTE

1. The G^2 index of goodness of fit is asymptotically equivalent to the chi-square statistic but is considered preferable for smaller samples. For a discussion of the G^2 statistic and the meaning of R^2 in the context of model fitting, the reader is referred to Haberman (1978).

REFERENCES

Bower, T. G. R. (1978). Concepts of development. In *Proceedings of the 21st International Congress of Psychology* (pp. 1020–32), Paris: Presses Universitaires de France.

Brown, R. (1973), *A First Language: The Early Stages*. Cambridge: Harvard University Press.

Champagne, A. B., Klopfer, L. E., and Anderson, J. H. (1980). Factors influencing the learning of classical mechanisms. *American Journal of Physics*, **48**, 1074–79.

Clagett, M. (1959), *The Science of Mechanics in the Middle Ages*. Madison: University of Wisconsin Press.

Clement, J. (1982). Students' preconceptions in introductory mechanics. *American Journal of Physics*, **50**, 66–71.

Crombie, A. C. (1952). *Augustine to Galileo: The History of Science A. D. 400–1650*. London: Falcon Press.

Flavell, J. H. (1977), *Cognitive Development*. Englewood Cliffs, NJ: Prentice-Hall.

Haberman, S. J. (1978), *Analysis of Qualitative Data*. New York: Academic Press.

McCloskey, M. (1983). Intuitive physics. *Scientific American*, **248** (4), 122–30.

McCloskey, M., Caramazza, A., and Green, B. (1980). Curvilinear motion in the absence of external forces: Naive beliefs about the motion of objects. *Science*, **210**, 1139–41.

McNeill, D. (1970). *The Acquisition of Language*. New York: Harper & Row.

Piaget, J. (1976). *The Grasp of Consciousness*. Cambridge, MA: Harvard University Press.

Richards, D. D., and Siegler, R. S. (1982). U-shaped behavioral curves: It's not whether you're right or wrong, it's why. In S. Strauss (ed.), *U-shaped Behavioral Growth* (pp. 37–61), New York: Academic Press.

Strauss, S. (1972). Inducing cognitive development and learning: A review of short-term training experiments. I: The organismic developmental approach. *Cognition*, **1**, 329–57.

Strauss, S. (1982), *U-shaped Behavioral Growth*. New York: Academic Press.

SOLUTION TO 'OPPENHEIMER'S PROBLEM'

When the weight is in the boat it will displace its weight of water. But when it is placed in the water it will displace its *volume* and not its *weight*. Since the weight, volume for volume, is heavier (or denser) than water (i.e., its specific gravity is greater than 1, which is why it sinks to the bottom) it will displace *less* water when it is in the pond than when it is in the boat. Thus, when it is placed in the pond the water level will fall.

Part V

LANGUAGE AND COMMUNICATION

21

Babbling in the Manual Mode: Evidence for the Ontogeny of Language*

Laura Ann Petitto and Paula F. Marentette

EDITORS' INTRODUCTION

We are accustomed to thinking of language as a speech-based phenomenon, and it has often been claimed that thinking can be understood as subvocal activity. It has been reported on innumerable occasions that language development is severely delayed in the deaf, perhaps because of their inability to hear and to comprehend spoken language. Petitto and Marentette give a remarkable demonstration that speech, per se, is not critical to language acquisition, and that deaf children are able to acquire language using manual (signed) gestures. Here, they report that there are similarities between deaf and hearing children in the time course, structure, and use of manual babbling, which 'suggest that there is a unitary language capacity that underlies human signed and spoken language'.

Thus, humans' language capacity is flexible with regard to the expressive modality it can adopt to realize this capacity (signed or spoken). In a short paper later in this reader (article 34) Alan Slater gives a brief account of the life, and of the language abilities, of Helen Keller, who was both blind and deaf and for whom language was learned from neither signing (seeing) nor hearing.

OVERVIEW

Infant vocal babbling has been assumed to be a speech-based phenomenon that reflects the maturation of the articulatory apparatus responsible for spoken language production. Manual babbling has now been reported to occur in deaf children exposed to signed languages from birth. The similarities between manual and vocal babbling suggest that babbling is a product

* Previously published in *Science*, **251** (22 March 1991), pp. 1493–6.

of an amodal, brain-based language capacity under maturational control, in which phonetic and syllabic units are produced by the infant as a first step toward building a mature linguistic system. Contrary to prevailing accounts of the neurological basis of babbling in language ontogeny, the speech modality is not critical in babbling. Rather, babbling is tied to the abstract linguistic structure of language and to an expressive capcity capable of processing different types of signals (signed or spoken).

A key feature of human development is the regular onset of vocal babbling well before infants are able to utter recognizable words.[1] Vocal babbling is widely recognized as being continuous with later language acquisition.[2] The prevailing view is that the structure of vocal babbling is determined by development of the anatomy of the vocal tract and the neural mechanisms subserving the motor control of speech production.[3,4] In brain-based theories of language representation, it is argued that the human language capacity has a unique link to innate mechanisms for producing speech;[5] it has also been argued that human language has been shaped by properties of speech.[6]

Although there is general agreement that humans possess some innately specified knowledge about language,[7] the maturation of the human language capacity may not be uniquely tied to the maturation of speech-specific production mechanisms. Naturally evolved human signed languages exist that are organized identically to spoken languages (for example, phonology, morphology, syntax, and semantics).[8] If babbling is due to the maturation of a language capacity and the articulatory mechanisms responsible for speech production, then it should be specific to speech. However, if babbling is due to the maturation of a brain-based language capacity and an expressive capacity capable of processing different types of signals, then it should occur in spoken and signed language modalities.

Hearing infants between 7 and 10 months of age begin to produce a type of vocalization described as reduplicated or syllabic babbling, for example, "dadadada" or "babababa."[9] Syllabic vocal babbling is characterized by (i) use of a reduced subset of possible sounds (phonetic units) found in spoken languages,[10] (ii) syllabic organization (well-formed consonant–vowel clusters),[11] and (iii) use without apparent meaning or reference.[12] Other properties include reduplication, well-defined age of onset, characteristic stages,[12] and continuity of phonetic form and syllabic type within an individual child's babbling and first words.[2]

In this study, experimental and naturalistic data were collected from five infants, each videotaped at three ages (approximately 10, 12, and 14 months). Two subjects were profoundly deaf infants of deaf parents (D1 and D2), acquiring American Sign Language (ASL) as a first language. Three control subjects were hearing infants of hearing parents (H1, H2, H3), acquiring spoken language with no exposure to a signed language.[13,14]

In studies of vocal babbling, investigators typically transcribe all acoustic forms or sounds produced over a period of time[15] and analyze all acoustic forms that are not words to see if they have any systematic organization. If systematic organization is found, the investigator determines whether the organization has phonetic and syllabic features common to spoken languages.[2]

We analyzed the deaf and hearing infants' manual activities in an identical manner. First, all of the infant's manual activities were transcribed and entered into a computer database[16] with a transcription system that we had devised and tested.[17] In this system, the precise physical form of the child's every manual activity is coded with diacritics that represent internal features of the hand or hands, such as its handshape and location in space. The precise manner of use is also coded for each manual activity, including whether the form was used with or without objects in hand, used referentially, used communicatively, had conventional meaning, or was a standard sign in ASL (a sign has identical linguistic properties to a word in spoken languages).[18] Secondly, we further analyzed all manual activities that were not ASL signs and were not pointing to objects, to determine whether they had any systematic organization. If so, we analyzed these activities to determine whether they had unique organizational properties or whether they shared phonetic and syllabic organization common to signed languages.[19,20] Attribution of manual babbling was applied only to forms that fulfilled the same criteria as vocal babbling. This transcription system permitted direct comparisons of the manual activities of the deaf and hearing infants. The reliability of rating for two independent coders ranged from 82 to 95%.[21]

The results yielded two types of manual activity: syllabic manual babbling and gestures (for example, raising arms to be picked up and holding a cup to lips as if to drink). Both types were observed in deaf and hearing infants. The manual activities identified as syllabic manual babbling (i) were produced with a reduced subset of combinatorial units that were members of the phonetic inventory of signed languages,[20] (ii) demonstrated syllabic organization seen only in signed languages, and (iii) were produced without meaning or reference. By contrast, gestures were not constructed from a restricted set of combinatorial units, had no principled internal organization, and were used referentially.[22]

Hearing and deaf infants produced similar types and quantities of gestures during the three sessions. However, they differed in their production of manual babbling (table 21.1). Manual babbling accounted for 32 to 71% of manual activity in deaf infants and a mere 4 to 15% of the manual activity of hearing infants (figure 21.1).

In manual babbling, the deaf infants used a reduced subset of the phonetic units found in ASL:[23] 32% (13/40) of the handshapes[20] that make up the phonetic inventory of adult ASL (plate 21.1). Of these 13 handshapes, 6 were used 75% of the time: 5, 52, A, A2, O, and G.[24] The deaf infants produced 54% (13/24) of ASL's movements;[20] the three most frequently used were the closing of a handshape, movement toward the body, and an up-and-down movement. Most of the deaf children's manual babbling (98%, 188/191) was produced within a restricted space in front of the body. In addition, each infant had an individual preference regarding the location:[20] most of D1's manual babbling was produced in the space in front of the mid-torso (neutral space), whereas the majority of D2's manual babbling involved contact with the head, ears, and

TABLE 21.1   Tokens of gestures and manual babbling
produced by each child over the three taping sessions

Child	Gesture	Manual babbling
Hearing		
H1	98	10
H2	195	8
H3	121	14
Deaf		
D1	101	80
D2	122	111

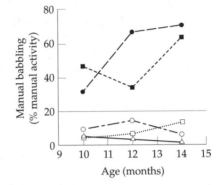

FIGURE 21.1   Manual babbling as a percent of manual activity [manual babbling /
(manual babbling + gesture)]. Open symbols represent the hearing children and closed
symbols represent the deaf children (□, H1; △, H2; ○, H3; ●, D1; and ■, D2). The
required syllabic ratio is 20% (line) syllabic to total vocal utterances for children to be
classed in the syllabic vocal babbling stage of language acquisition (see Chomsky, 1980;
Gleitman, 1981; note 7). The deaf children met and surpassed this ratio in their manual
babbling, but the hearing children did not

face region. Similarly, hearing infants demonstrate clear individual preferences
in the phonetic content of their vocal babbling.[25]

The manual babbling of the deaf infants contained four syllable types,[20] a
subset of which were used more frequently (plate 21.2). D1 predominantly
produced syllables involving secondary movement in the form of handshape
change (69%). D2 predominantly produced syllables involving path movement
(69%).

The deaf infants' manual babbling demonstrated four other properties
observed in hearing children's vocal babbling. First, reduplication occurred
in 47% of the tokens of sign babbling produced by the deaf infants.[26] Second,
by age 10 months, the deaf infants were well into the syllabic manual babbling
stage, which occurred at the same time as in hearing infants (ages 7 to 10
months). Third, the deaf infants progressed through stages of manual babbling
similar to the stages of vocal babbling observed in hearing infants, and on a

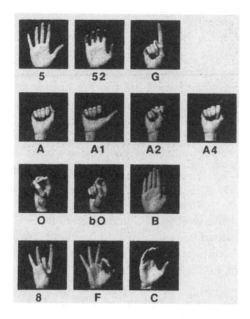

PLATE 21.1 The 13 handshape primes produced by deaf children in their manual babbling. The handshape A4 does not occur in adult ASL; it is a possible but nonexistent phoneme

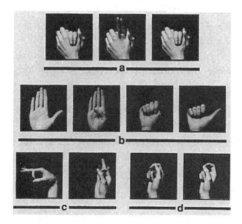

PLATE 21.2 Examples of syllable types in manual babbling. In real time these are continuous forms; in order to demonstrate the handshapes that occur, the forms have been presented as sequences of static pictures. All forms were reduplicated; only the basic unit is presented here. (a) A two-handed handshape-change syllable. (b) A unimanual, bisyllabic, handshape-change production involving four distinct handshapes. (c) An orientation-change syllable produced by a flexing of the wrist. (d) A handshape-change syllable typically produced by the hearing children, which is much less complex than that shown in example (b)

similar time course. Hearing children produced vocal jargon babbling (meaningless babbling sequences that sound like sentences; onset 12 to 14 months);[12] similarly, the deaf infants produced manual jargon babbling (onset 12 to 14 months). They produced phonologically possible, but nonexisting, forms in the ASL lexicon; the forms maintained the rhythm and duration of rudimentary ASL sentences and were similar to hearing infants' use of stress and intonation in vocal jargon babbling.[12] Fourth, there was a continuity between the phonetic and syllabic forms used in the deaf infants' manual babbling and their first signs. For each infant, the most frequent phonetic units in his or her manual babbling were also the most frequent in his or her first signs: the 5 handshape was most frequent for both D1 [manual babbling (m.b.) $= 27\%$, signs (s.) $= 43\%$] and D2 (m.b. $= 29\%$, s. $= 54\%$); the most frequent movement type produced by D1 was the closing of a handshape (m.b. $= 55\%$, s. $= 36\%$), and D2's most frequent movement type was movement toward the signer (m.b. $= 29\%$, s. $= 40\%$); D1 continued to produce signs in neutral space (m.b. $= 82\%$, s. $= 59\%$), and D2 maintained a preference for locations in the head and face area (m.b. $= 51\%$, s. $= 53\%$). As for syllables, D1 continued to prefer handshape-change syllables (m.b. $= 69\%$, s. $= 44\%$), and D2 continued to prefer location-change syllables (m.b. $= 69\%$, s. $= 58\%$). Thus, like hearing infants,[2] deaf infants produce their first signs from the pool of phonetic and syllabic types rehearsed in their babbling. Further, the deaf infants' first signs and the hearing infants' first words occurred at similar ages: D1 (10 months, 10 days), D2 (11 months, 28 days), H1 (11 months, 6 days), H2 (12 months, 11 days), H3 (12 months, 14 days).

The hearing infants in this study produced few instances of manual babbling (table 21.1). They used an even smaller subset of phonetic units than did deaf infants, displaying only three handshapes (F, O, bO; 80%, 28/35),[27] one movement (thumb to digit contact plus repeated rub; 84%, 27/32) and one location (neutral space; 100%, 32/32). Further, they used primarily one syllable type (handshape change; 88%, 28/32). This is similar to deaf infants' limited production of syllabic vocal babbling, which also shows little variation in form and a very reduced set of consonants and vowels.[11,28]

Our data do not support the notion that babbling is determined by motor developments of the articulatory mechanisms subserving speech production.[4] Instead, babbling is an expression of an amodal, brain-based language capacity that is linked to an expressive capacity capable of processing speech and sign. Despite radical differences between the motoric mechanisms that subserve signed and spoken languages, deaf and hearing infants produce identical babbling units. Both manual and vocal babbling contain units and combinations of units that are organized in accordance with the phonetic and syllabic properties of human language. Thus, the form and organization of babbling is tied to the abstract linguistic structure of language.

Infants appear to be innately predisposed to discover the particular patterned input of phonetic and syllabic units,[29,30] that is, particular patterns in the input signal that correspond to the temporal and hierarchical grouping and rhythmical characteristics in natural language phonology. We suggest that this predisposition is a property of an amodal language capacity. Patterned input in either the signed or spoken modalities with phonetic and syllabic organization can serve as the vehicle for language production and reception, thereby triggering a babbling stage.[31] Babbling is thus the mechanism by which infants discover the map between the structure of language and the means for producing this structure. The production of babbling units helps infants to identify the finite inventory of basic units, and the permissible combination of these units, from which language will be constructed.[29] By attending to particular patterned input, infants can begin to acquire the basic forms of language well before they have mastered adult knowledge of language structure and meaning.

Similarities in the time course, structure, and use of manual and vocal babbling suggest that there is a unitary language capacity that underlies human signed and spoken language acquisition. Like other systems identified in evolutionary biology,[32] the language capacity appears to be both constrained and flexible. It is internally constrained with regard to the structures that it can realize (phonetic and syllabic units), yet, in the face of environmental variation, it appears to be flexible with regard to the expressive modality it can adopt to realize this capacity (signed or spoken).

ACKNOWLEDGMENTS

We thank K. Dunbar, M. Bruck, S. Waxman, R. Wise, and anonymous reviewers for comments on versions of this paper. Supported by the Natural Sciences Engineering Research Council of Canada, McGill IBM Cooperative Project, and McDonnell-Pew Centre Grant in Cognitive Neuroscience.

NOTES

1. E. H. Lenneberg, *Biological Foundations of Language* (Wiley, New York, 1967).
2. M. M. Vihman et al., *Language* **61**, 397 (1985).
3. J. L. Locke, *Phonological Acquisition and Change* (Academic Press, New York, 1983).
4. J. M. Van der Stelt and F. J. Koopmans-van Bienum, in *Precursors of Early Speech*, B. Lindblom and R. Zetterstrom, eds (Stockton, New York, 1986), pp. 163–73.
5. A. M. Liberman and I. G. Mattingly, *Cognition* **21**, 1 (1985); *Science* **243**, 489 (1989).
6. P. Lieberman, *The Biology and Evolution of Language* (Harvard Univ. Press, Cambridge, MA, 1984).
7. N. Chomsky, *Behav. Brain Sci.* **3**, 1 (1980); L. Gleitman, *Cognition* **10**, 103 (1981).
8. E. S. Klima and U. Bellugi, *The Signs of Language* (Harvard Univ. Press, Cambridge, MA, 1979).
9. D. K. Oller, in *Production*, vol. 1 of *Child Phonology*, G. Yeni-Komshian, J. F. Kavanagh, C. A. Ferguson, eds (Academic Press, New York, 1980), pp. 93–112.
10. Cross-linguistic evidence suggests that infants use a universal subset of possible consonants during babbling (see note 3).
11. D. K. Oller and R. E. Eilers, *Child Dev.* **59**, 441 (1988).
12. L. Elbers, *Cognition* **12**, 45 (1982).
13. Subjects' gender, native language, and age at each taping were as follows: D1 (female, ASL, 10 months, 10 days; 12 months, 0 days; 14 months, 17 days); D2

(male, ASL, 9 months, 26 days; 11 months, 29 days; 13 months, 23 days);
H1 (female, French, 9 months, 27 days; 11 months, 27 days; 14 months, 14 days);
H2 (female, French, 10 months, 10 days; 12 months, 14 days; 15 months, 7 days);
H3 (male, English, 11 months, 9 days; 12 months, 8 days; 13 months, 29 days).

14. Videotaped sessions commenced with a period in which the infant and parent played freely. Then there was an elicitation task, in which common baby toys were held in the infant's sight but out of reach for 10 seconds and then were given to the infant. Finally, each infant was observed in solitary play. Sessions were conducted in the infant's native language (signed or spoken).

15. Vegetative sounds, such as crying or belching, are not transcribed because they are unrelated to an infant's prelinguistic development.

16. Manual activities such as scratching or eye-rubbing were not transcribed (see note 15).

17. L. A. Petitto, in *The Development of Language and Language Researchers: Essays in Honor of Roger Brown*, F. S. Kessel, ed. (Erlbaum, Hillsdale, NJ, 1988), pp. 187–221.

18. "Used referentially" refers to manual activity that was used in relation to a referent in the world. "Used communicatively" refers to manual activity that was produced with clear communicative intent (fixed eye gaze at adult). The term "has conventional meaning" refers to manual activity with established cultural meaning that was not the standard sign in ASL. For example, the manual activity used to convey the concept "quiet" (index to pursed lips while producing a "shhh" sound) is used by children and adults (deaf and hearing) to indicate "quiet," but the sign QUIET in ASL is produced with an entirely different handshape and movement.

19. We further transcribed the data utilizing a notational system analogous to the International Phonetic Alphabet for spoken languages (W. C. Stokoe, D. C. Casterline, C. G. Croneberg, *A Dictionary of American Sign Language on Linguistic Principles*, Linstok Press, Silver Spring, MD, 1976).

20. As in spoken languages, signed languages are constructed from a finite set of meaningless units (phonetic units); the subset of units used for production of a particular language is its phonetic inventory. ASL's phonetic inventory is drawn from the four parameters of a sign – handshape, movement, location, and palm orientation – each of which contains a restricted set of phonetic units (for example, a set of handshapes, a set of movements). Phonetic units are further organized into structured units called syllables [S. K. Liddell, *Language* 60, 372 (1984)]. A well-formed syllable has a handshape, a location, and a path movement (change in location) or secondary movement (change in handshape or orientation). This yields at least four syllable types: (i) path movement, (ii) secondary movement (handshape change), (iii) secondary movement (orientation change), and (iv) path and secondary movement combined.

21. One of each infant's three videotapes (selected across all three ages) was transcribed by two coders. Reliability was calculated based on coders' percent agreement on whether a manual activity had occurred and on the precise content of a manual activity; thus, the full range of infant manual activity is represented in the figures provided.

22. Unlike words or signs, gestures (i) had unrestricted forms; (ii) violated natural-kind boundaries (events, objects, possessions, and locations) typically observed in hearing [J. Huttenlocher and P. Smiley, *Cognit. Psychol.* 19, 63 (1987)] and deaf infants; (iii) were used in communicatively restricted contexts (typically requests); and (iv) showed no semantic or structural developmental progression (see note 17).

23. Just as hearing infants do not babble in specific languages (see note 10), deaf infants do not babble in ASL or any other sign language. Deaf infants acquiring two distinct sign languages (ASL and Langue des Signes Québécoise) also use a common subset of possible phonetic units [L. A. Petitto and P. F. Marentette, in preparation; L. A. Petitto, *Cognition* **27**, 1 (1987)].

24. These symbols represent the meaningless alphanumeric labels used for notation of the restricted set of handshapes in signed languages (see note 20).

25. M. M. Vihman, C. A. Ferguson, M. Elbert, *Appl. Psycholinguist.* **7**, 3 (1986).

26. Percent reduplicated vocal babbling has not been reported to our knowledge.

27. This ratio is divided by 35 instead of 32 because some instances of manual babbling involved more than one handshape.

28. That infants produce occasional babbling forms in the modality that does not carry linguistic input appears to be the vestige of their potential to have produced language in either modality. This babbling is unproductive because of the lack of systematic input.

29. P. W. Jusczyk, in *Invariance and Variability in Speech Processes*, J. Perkell and D. H. Klatt, eds (Erlbaum, Hillsdale, NJ, 1986), pp. 1–19.

30. J. Mehler, G. Lambertz, P. Jusczyk, C. Amiel-Tison, *C. R. Acad. Sci. Ser. III Sci. Vie* **303** (no. 15), 637 (1986).

31. Hearing children of deaf parents, acquiring both signed and spoken languages, produce babbling and other linguistic milestones in both modalities on an identical time course (P. F. Marentette and L. A. Petitto, in preparation).

32. M. Shatz, *Merrill-Palmer Q.* **31**, 211 (1985).

22

The Role of Discourse Novelty in Early Word Learning*

Nameera Akhtar, Malinda Carpenter and Michael Tomasello

EDITORS' INTRODUCTION

Nameera Akhtar, Malinda Carpenter and Michael Tomasello describe studies which have demonstrated that young children can be sensitive to the informational needs, or understanding, of others in their early language production. They suggest that 'it is plausible to assume that they make use of this sensitivity in their comprehension and learning of language'. They demonstrate this with two ingenious experiments. In the first, 2-year-olds played with three objects with adults (two experimenters and their mother), but none of these objects was named, only being referred to by pronouns (it, that, this). Thus, the objects became familiar, but nameless. Then the objects were placed in a clear plastic box, together with a new object. An experimenter then grasped the box and said in an excited tone, 'Look, I see a modi! A modi! I see a modi in there!' The parent then added 'Look a modi! I see a modi!' The children were then likely to select the novel object when asked to give the experimenter the modi. Thus, the children were using the novelty of the object, and the coincidence of the adults' excitement and their production of the word 'modi', to assume that the word referred to the new object and not to one of the familiar ones.

In their second experiment the new object was a 'gazzer'. The first part of the procedure was the same as in Study 1 – the two experimenters and the parent played with the three 'familiar' objects. Then one experimenter and the parent left the room and the child was introduced to the new object. The experimenter and the parent then returned to the room: thus, on their return, one object was new to them and three familiar. Then the experimenter who had returned looked in the box that contained all four objects, and

* Previously published in *Child Development*, **67** (1996), pp. 635–45.

said in an excited tone, 'Look, I see a gazzer! A gazzer! I see a gazzer in there!' The parent then added 'Look, a gazzer! I see a gazzer!' The children then assumed that 'gazzer' referred to the novel object, even though it was familiar to them but unfamiliar to the mother, and the child had never heard her say the word before!

These two studies are ingenious in demonstrating that young children are sensitive to discourse novelty in their earliest productions of language, and that they are using their understanding of others' intentions and beliefs (i.e., they assume that the experimenters' and their mother's excitement is because they have seen the novel object, and therefore that the novel word, 'modi' or 'gazzer', names that object) in interpreting their linguistic world; thus '24-month-old children demonstrate an ability to use a broad range of pragmatic cues in determining adults' referential intentions in a wide variety of discourse situations... and... it is, this understanding that forms the foundation of the process of language acquisition.'

OVERVIEW

Two studies of word learning are reported. In Study 1, 24-month–old children and 2 adults played with 3 nameless objects. These objects were placed in a clear box along with a novel nameless object. The adults then displayed excitement about the contents of the box and modeled a new word. Comparison with a control condition indicated significant learning of the new word for the novel object. Study 2 followed the same procedure with one difference: the children played with the novel object while the adults were absent. Thus, at the time of the language model the target object was novel only to the adults, not to the children. Again subjects displayed significant learning of the new word. This last finding suggests that 24-month-old children understand that adults use language for things that are novel to the discourse context and that this novelty is determined from the speaker's point of view.

From early infancy children preferentially attend to novel or changing stimuli, as evidenced by the well-known phenomenon of dishabituation (e.g., Fantz, 1964). A number of researchers have argued and presented evidence that, from its inception, the use of language is coordinated with this characteristic of the attentional system. It has been found, for example, that the vocalizations of prelinguistic infants tend to occur at points of attentional change (Furrow and James, 1985; Hilke, 1988). Moreover, when children begin to use conventional language itself, their first words and utterances are used to report on new or changing elements in their environments as part of a larger orienting response (Lempert and Kinsbourne, 1985). Greenfield and her colleagues have shown that slightly older children, who have at their command a number of linguistic choices, tend to verbalize that element that is new to the situation. For example, if a child has been watching a sibling place blocks in a box, and the sibling suddenly places a ball in the box, the child is likely to verbalize "ball" at that point in the interaction (Greenfield, 1979, 1982; Greenfield, Reilly, Leaper, and Baker, 1985). Greenfield and Zukow (1978) and Baker and Greenfield (1988) have provided experimental confirmation for this finding by manipulating elements in scripted situations and demonstrating that young children tend to talk about what is new in the current discourse context.

It does not necessarily follow, however, that children are talking about what is new or most informative for the *listener*. Verbalizing the new element in a given context may simply reflect the fact that children speak about what is new from their own perspective; that is, they may egocentrically talk about whatever new thing captures their attention. Greenfield's data do not address this issue, as the experimental studies have involved situations in which the critical elements were new to both the speaker and listener. However, a separate body of research on the communicative abilities of young speakers suggests that they may indeed be attuned to the perspectives of their listeners. Golinkoff (1993) has recently reviewed evidence that young children adjust their language for different situations and interlocutors; for example, they respond differently to requests for clarification depending on the familiarity of the person making the request (Tomasello, Farrar, and Dines, 1984; also see O'Neill, 1993).

Thus, it appears that young children can demonstrate sensitivity to the informational needs of others in their early language production. If this is true, it is plausible to assume that they make use of this sensitivity in their comprehension and learning of language as well. There is only scant evidence for this hypothesis, however. The only available data are observations that children learn words for variable or changing phenomena. For example, Greenfield (1973) reported that her daughter learned her first word *dada* not when her father was a static presence, but only when the word was said as her father was entering the room, that is, when he was a novel perceptual stimulus. Along these same lines, Nelson (1973) reported that children learn their first words mostly for variable phenomena – salient activities or objects that change or move (e.g., baths and people) – and not for things that remain constant (e.g., breathing and walls). There are to our knowledge no experimental tests of the hypothesis that *novelty* itself aids children in word learning. Such a test would involve a situation in which an adult uses a new word in the presence of a number of unnamed but potentially nameable referents, only one of which is novel to the situation. If children were able to attach the new word to the novel referent in this situation, it would indicate that they rely on novelty in word learning.

The fact that children can use novelty to learn a new word, however, does not address the issue of whether children understand that adults tend to talk about the elements in a situation that are novel or changing *for the adults themselves*. Even if a child was to learn a new word for the novel element in the above-described situation, it would be unclear whether she was able to understand the perspective of the adult uttering the new word or whether her attention was simply automatically (egocentrically) drawn to the novel element, resulting in the pairing of that element with the new word. Some lexical training studies would seem to support the egocentric interpretation, demonstrating that it is easier for a child to learn a new word when adults follow into the child's already established focus of attention than when adults use a new word for something at their own focus of attention (Dunham, Dunham, and Curwin, 1993; Tomasello and Farrar, 1986). Baldwin (1991, 1993) has replicated this result but has also shown that children as young as 19 months of age are able to learn new words when they are required to shift their attention away from an object they are looking at to one the adult is looking at. In this "discrepant labeling" situation children almost never associated the new word with what they were looking at when they heard it. This finding demonstrates children's knowledge that an adult's focus of attention may be different from their own and is supported by studies showing that children are able to use a variety of cues to determine an adult's focus at around this same age (Akhtar and Tomasello, in press–a; Tomasello and Barton, 1994). None of these studies of language learning, however, has directly addressed the question of whether children know what is new for another person in the situation and that the new element is what the other person is likely to be talking about. The only way to address this question is in an experimental paradigm in which the element being named is new for the adult but is not new for the child.

Two experiments were conducted. The first addressed the question of whether children assume that a new word is being used to refer to the novel element in a situation. Twenty-four-month-old children heard a new word modeled (with an excitement consistent with the adult having spied a new and interesting thing) in the presence of four objects for which they had no name. None of these objects was singled out by gaze direction or any other immediate cues. Three of the objects were familiar in that they had been played with previously; one was new to the discourse context. If children use novelty as a cue in object label learning, they should be more likely to choose the novel object in a subsequent comprehension test than a control group of subjects who experienced the same procedures but did not hear a new word. Such a result would suggest that novelty aids young children in acquiring object labels, but it would not necessarily imply an understanding that adults tend to talk about things that are new *to them*. The second study, therefore, modified the procedures of the first study so that children played with all four nameless objects, but the mother and an experimenter only played with three of them, leaving the room before the fourth object was introduced. Therefore, when the language model was given, no object was new to the child but one object was new to the adults. If in a subsequent comprehension test, children were more likely than their control counterparts to choose the object that was new from the adults' perspective, this would imply that they understand not only that adults use language for things that are new to the situation but also that this newness is determined from the speaker's point of view.

Study 1

Method

Subjects   Potential subjects were recruited by telephone from a list of mostly white, middle-class parents who had volunteered to participate in studies of

TABLE 22.1   Mean estimates of vocabulary and noun vocabulary for children in the experimental and control conditions of each study

Condition	Vocabulary	Nouns
Study 1:		
Experimental ($N = 16$)	63.9 (32.0)	32.2 (15.7)
Control ($N = 16$)	67.4 (31.4)	34.8 (15.1)
Study 2:		
Experimental ($N = 24$)	67.1 (32.4)	34.5 (15.0)
Control ($N = 24$)	70.3 (30.8)	36.0 (15.0)

Note: Vocabulary and Noun Vocabulary was assessed by a short checklist, Reznick and Goldsmith, 1989. Standard deviations are in parentheses.

child development. Only children whose parents reported that they were using some productive language were invited to participate, and parents also completed a productive vocabulary checklist after the experimental session (Form A of the short version of the MacArthur Communicative Development Inventory; Reznick and Goldsmith, 1989). Data from three children were deleted due to noncompliance or inattention (two boys) or procedural error (one girl). The final sample consisted of 16 boys (10 firstborns) and 16 girls (9 firstborns), ranging in age from 2–0.8 to 2–1.6 ($M = 2$–0.22). The children were randomly assigned to the experimental or control condition such that there were approximately equal numbers of males and females and firstborns and laterborns in each condition. The mean values for parental estimates of vocabulary and noun vocabulary as a function of condition are shown in the first two rows of table 22.1. There is a total of 123 words on the checklist and 65 words that were categorized as object labels. As a check on random assignment, the estimates of vocabulary size were compared across conditions and revealed no significant differences; $t < 1$ in both cases.

Materials   Four novel objects were used: a liquid timer, a novelty yo-yo, a small kalimba, and an object that made noises when buttons on it were pressed. Each of the four objects occurred as the target object for four children in each condition. Parents were shown the objects and asked to indicate if their child would produce or comprehend a name for any one of them. A reserve set of unfamiliar objects (e.g., wallpaper roller, beanbag frisbee) was used to replace any object for which a given child already had a label. An additional set of familiar objects (a plastic Barney figure, a ball, a cup, and a spoon) was used in a warm-up comprehension task.

Training procedure   Children came with a parent to a playroom at the psychology department. All sessions were videotaped. Sessions began with a warm-up period during which children played with one of the experimenters (E1) while the other experimenter (E2) explained the procedure to the parent. Parents were asked not to label any of the objects and not to request labels from their children. Then E1, E2, the child, and the parent played together on the floor with three of the four experimental objects as follows. E1 took one object (in random order) out of an opaque bag and demonstrated an action on it, for example, played the kalimba. E1 then gave the object to the child, encouraging the child, and then the parent and E2, to examine the object and perform the demonstrated action on it. Each participant then took turns dropping the object down a plastic chute. All of the objects were referred to by pronouns (it, that, this) and none was labeled at any time. This procedure was repeated with each of the remaining two nontarget objects so that the child and all three adults became familiar with the first three objects, but the objects all remained nameless. The fourth object, the target object, remained in the bag out of sight of the child, the parent, and E2.

After playing with the first three objects, E2 and the parent distracted the child while E1 placed the three familiar objects, along with the fourth, novel object, in random positions in a clear plastic box. E1 covered the box with a transparent lid and put it on the floor. For children in the experimental condition, E2 grasped the box from both ends and said in an excited tone, "Look, I see a modi! A modi! I see a modi in there!" The parent then added, "Look, a modi! I see a modi!" for a total of five models of the novel label in the experimental condition. Children in the control group experienced the same procedures with the exception that no novel word was modeled. Instead, for this group, E2 exclaimed "Look! Look at that! Look at that in there!" and the parent added, "Look at that! Look at that!" It is important to note that in both conditions adults spoke without pointing or looking at any one object; their focus was on the box as a whole. Thus, in the immediate physical context there were no transparent cues to the referential intent of the adults; the only cue available was the novelty of one object in the discourse context. As a check to ensure that the adults had not provided inadvertent cues, a blind coder made judgments as to which object was the target of the adult's exclamations. She chose the novel (target) object on only six out of 30 judgments (20%), which is not significantly different from chance (25%) by a binomial test ($p = .67$).

All participants then played with all four objects for 3–4 minutes; again, no labels were provided. The purpose of this phase of the procedure was to provide the child with the opportunity to examine and interact with the new object without singling it out. The objects were not withdrawn at the end of this period if the child indicated a desire to continue playing with them. The final play period thus ensured that children's choice on the comprehension task (see below) would not be biased by their not having had sufficient opportunity to play with the target object. This period also allowed for spontaneous production of the novel word; if a child did produce the word spontaneously, no feedback was provided.

Testing procedure All children in both conditions experienced the same testing procedures as follows. After the language models and play period, E2 first administered a practice comprehension test with four familiar objects. She placed all four objects (a cup, a ball, a spoon, and a plastic Barney figure) in a box and asked the child to show/give each object to her in turn (e.g., "Can you show me the cup?"), replacing each object after the child had chosen it and correcting any errors. The four familiar objects were then exchanged with the four experimental objects (presented in random positions) and the child was asked to show/give E2 the "modi" as a test of comprehension of the novel word. The request was repeated, if necessary, until the child distinctly chose an object (almost always by pointing to it or giving it to E2). E2 maintained eye contact with the child during the test so as not to single out any object by means of gaze direction. (To ensure that E2 had not provided any inadvertent cues, a blind coder subsequently made forced-choice judgments as to which object was the target. She was correct on only 9 out of 28 judgments; binomial probability $= 0.51$.) E1 recorded the object chosen by the child live on a code sheet. An independent, blind coder subsequently scored 25% of the comprehension trials, randomly chosen from the videotapes, and achieved 100% agreement with the live coder as to which object was chosen.

E1 recorded throughout the session any instances of spontaneous productions by the children. An elicited production test was also administered. For this test, E2 removed the nontarget objects from sight, held up the target object, and asked the child to name it (e.g., "What is this? What is this called?"). This request was repeated, if necessary, by E2 and/or the child's parent. Two blind coders subsequently independently coded all instances of production of the target word (spontaneous and elicited) as to which of the four objects the child was referring to, based on which object they were looking at, pointing to, or holding up (coders also could code a production as "ambiguous"). The coders agreed on 100% of their decisions. A third individual then used these codings, along with information about which object was the target for a given child, to determine whether a given use of the target word was appropriate, that is, was used in reference to the target object. Children were given credit for production only if they were clearly referring to the target object when they uttered the experimental word.

Results

The analysis of results is in terms of the number of children who comprehended, produced, or showed any learning (comprehension and/or production) of the target word. Where expected frequencies were high enough (> 5), chi-square tests of significance were used; where they were not, Fisher exact probabilities were calculated. Because we had directional predictions in all cases, one-tailed tests of significance were employed.

The first row of table 22.2 shows the number of children who evidenced comprehension of the novel word by choosing the target object when asked to give E2 the "modi." Two children in the control group and eight of the experimental subjects chose the target object. The distribution of frequencies in these two groups was significantly different, $\chi^2 = 5.24$, $p < .02$, indicating that more experimental subjects chose the target object in the comprehension test than did control subjects.

As shown in the second row of table 22.2, five experimental subjects appropriately produced the novel word, either spontaneously or in the elicited production task; no control subjects did so. The two groups were significantly different from each other (Fisher exact probability $= .02$). It could be argued

TABLE 22.2 Number of children in each condition comprehending, producing, and displaying any learning (comprehension and/or production) of the target word in Study 1

	Experimental (N = 16)	Control (N = 16)
Comprehension	8	2
Production	5	0
Any Learning	10	2

that the procedure used in the elicited production task – holding the target object up and asking for a label – may have induced the children to use the novel word they had just heard regardless of which object was held up. However, it is important to note that (1) no child in the experimental group produced the novel word for an incorrect referent at any time during the experiment and (2) of the five children who produced the novel word appropriately, three did so spontaneously and a fourth was successful on the comprehension task (in addition to producing the word in the elicited production task). There is thus only one child for whom the sole evidence of word learning is elicited production.

As a final comparison between the experimental and control groups, subjects were classified as either learners or nonlearners on the basis of whether they were successful in the comprehension task and/or produced the word appropriately (shown in table 22.2 as "Any Learning"). Ten experimental subjects showed evidence of some form of learning, whereas only two control subjects showed such evidence. The groups were statistically different, $\chi^2 = 8.53$, $p < .01$. No differences were found between learners and nonlearners on the basis of gender, birth order, or vocabulary size.

Discussion

These results demonstrate that 24-month-old children can use novelty to the discourse context as a cue in learning a novel object label. Procedural factors other than newness to the discourse context that might have differentially enhanced the target object (e.g., playing with it last) cannot explain the comprehension performance of children in the experimental group, since children in the control group experienced the same procedures but chose the target object significantly less than their experimental counterparts. It is important in this context to be clear about what children in the control group were doing. In the comprehension test when the control children were asked "Show me the modi," this was the first time they had heard the word, and some time had passed (with intervening play with all four objects) since the adult had shown excitement upon seeing the target object by saying "Look at that!" It is possible, indeed likely, that when control children first heard the adults saying "Look at that!" they assumed it was the new object (the target) they were excited about. Nevertheless, when later the child was asked for the modi, she had no reason to assume it was the object the adults had singled out some time previously. The same reasoning applies to the elicited production task – even if the control children knew at the time of initial exposure to the novel object which one the adult was excited about, they had no reason to suppose that the novel word (which they only heard much later in the comprehension test) was connected to that object. The comparison between the control and experimental groups would seem to suggest, therefore, that the children in the experimental group were indeed processing the linguistic model as an act of linguistic reference at the time it was given, and that their performance on the comprehension and production tasks was not due to some procedural artifact. Although only 10 of 16 experimental subjects showed signs of word learning, it is important to recall that there was only a single exposure to the novel object accompanied by the target word (of which there were five tokens) – due to the fact that the object could be new to the discourse situation on only one occasion.

There are at least two possible explanations for how the novelty of the target object might have aided the experimental children in attaching the label to it. First, the egocentric account would be that the children's attention was automatically attracted to the novel object at the same time as they encountered the novel word, and they formed an association as a result – without paying any attention to the adult at all. On the other hand, the nonegocentric account would be that the children understood something about how the adults were using the new word. Thus, it could be that they realized that if the adults were going to label one of the nontarget objects they would have done so during the initial play session; they could have then ruled out the nontargets as potential referents of the novel word. Another possibility along these lines is that the experimental subjects knew that adults tend to get excited about new things, which would also lead them to the target object as the referent of the new word. The egocentric and nonegocentric explanations cannot be distinguished in the current study. What is needed to distinguish them is a situation in which what is new to the adult is not new to the child. This was the rationale for Study 2.

STUDY 2

Method

Subjects Subjects from Study 1 also participated in Study 2. Five children (four males) were noncompliant or inattentive, and two (one male) were dropped due to procedural errors. Twenty-one additional subjects from the same pool were recruited for participation in Study 2 for a final sample consisting of 24 males (14 firstborns) and 24 females (16 firstborns), ranging in age from 2–0.5 to 2–1.20 ($M = 2 - 0.21$). Children who had been randomly assigned to the experimental condition in Study 1 were assigned to the control condition in Study 2 and vice versa. The reason for this assignment was to avoid having any child participate in two control conditions (as parents had been invited for participation in a study of word learning, we felt it would be inappropriate to then not teach their children a new word in either of the two studies). The additional subjects also participated in the procedures of Study 1 to ensure that they would have had the same experience before starting Study 2. There were approximately equal numbers of males and females and firstborns and laterborns in each condition. The mean values for parental estimates of vocabulary and noun vocabulary as a function of condition are shown in the last two rows of table 22.1. As a check on random assignment, these estimates of vocabulary size were compared across conditions and revealed no significant differences; $t < 1$ in both cases.

Materials   Four novel objects were used: a brightly colored wooden ratchet, a novelty top, a set of connected blocks with bells inside, and a wooden toy that wobbled when rolled on the floor. Each of the four novel objects occurred as the target object for six children in each condition. As in Study 1, experimenters ascertained that objects were novel to children by parental report and replaced any objects for which parents said children already had labels (back-up objects were the same as in Study 1).

Training procedure   Study 2 employed all the same procedures as Study 1 with one critical difference: the children were first exposed to the target object while their parent and E2 were out of the room. Thus, as in Study 1, E1, E2, the child, and the parent played together with three of the experimental objects. In each case, E1 took an object in random order out of a bag, demonstrated an action on it, and gave it to the other participants. Each participant had a chance to examine the object and perform the demonstrated action on it. They also took turns catapulting it from a plastic launcher. After the child and each adult were familiar with the three nontarget objects, E2 and the parent left the room (or, in the case of a very few children who protested, sat in chairs at the end of the room with their backs turned to E1 and the child). While E2 and the parent were outside, E1 and the child played with the fourth, novel object in a manner similar to that in which they had played with the other three: E1 demonstrated an action on the object, gave the child a chance to examine it and perform the action, and then both took turns catapulting the object. In introducing the object, E1 said, "Look at this new one" and once while playing with it, "Mommy can't see this one."

Before calling E2 and the parent back, E1 placed the four objects (the three objects with which all participants had played and the object only E1 and the child had seen) in a clear plastic box[1] and put the box on the floor in the middle of the room. Thus, when E2 and the parent returned, one object was new to them, but no object was new to the child. For children in the experimental condition, E2 said in an excited tone, "Look, I see a gazzer! A gazzer! I see a gazzer in there!" The parent then added "Look, a gazzer! I see a gazzer!" for a total of five models of the novel label in the experimental condition. Children in the control group experienced the same procedures with the exception that no novel word was modeled. Instead, for this group, E2 exclaimed, "Look! Look at that! Look at that in there!" and the parent added,

"Look at that! Look at that!" It is important to note that in both conditions adults spoke without pointing or looking at any one object; their focus was on the box as a whole. Thus, in the immediate physical context there were no transparent cues to the referential intent of the adults; the only cue available was the novelty of one object in the discourse context for the adults. Again, as a check to ensure that the adults had not provided inadvertent cues, a blind coder made forced-choice judgments as to which object was the target of the adults' exclamations; she chose the target object on only nine out of 44 judgments (20%; binomial probability $= .60$).

All participants then played with all four objects for 3–4 minutes; no labels were provided. This period allowed for spontaneous production of the novel word.

Testing procedure The testing procedures were basically identical to those of Study 1. The comprehension test involved E2 placing the four experimental objects in random position in a box and asking the child to give her the "gazzer." The request was repeated, if necessary, until the child distinctly chose an object (almost always by pointing to it or giving it to E2). E2 maintained eye contact with the child during the test so as not to single out any object by means of gaze direction. A blind coder was correct at guessing which object was the target on only 8 out of 41 trials (binomial probability $= .53$). E1 recorded the object chosen by the child live on a code sheet. An independent, blind coder subsequently scored 25% of the comprehension trials, randomly chosen from the videotapes, and achieved 100% agreement with the live coder as to which object was chosen.

After comprehension testing, an elicited production test was administered. For this test, E2 removed the nontarget objects from sight, held up the target object, and asked the child to name it (e.g., "What is this? What is this called?"). This request was repeated, if necessary, by E2 and/or the child's parent. Two independent, blind coders subsequently coded all instances of production of the target word (spontaneous and elicited) as to which of the four objects the children were referring to, based on which object they were looking at, pointing to, or holding up (coders also could code a production as "ambiguous"). The coders agreed on 100% of their decisions. A third individual then used these codings to determine whether a given use of the target word was appropriate (i.e., clearly referred to the target object), and the children were given credit only for appropriate uses.

Results

The first row of table 22.3 shows the number of children who evidenced comprehension of the novel word by choosing the target object when asked to give E2 the "gazzer." Four children in the control group and 10 children in the experimental group chose the target object. The distribution of frequencies in these two groups was significantly different, $\chi^2 = 3.63$, $p < .03$, indicating that experimental subjects chose the target object in the comprehension test more often than did control subjects.

TABLE 22.3 Number of children in each condition comprehending, producing, and displaying any learning (comprehension and/or production) of the target word in Study 2

	Experimental (N = 24)	Control (N = 24)
Comprehension	10	4
Production	7	0
Any Learning	11	4

As shown in the second row of table 22.3, seven of the experimental subjects appropriately produced the novel word, either spontaneously or in the elicited production task; no control subjects did so. The two groups were significantly different from each other on this measure of learning (Fisher exact probability = .005). Again, it is important to note that (1) no child in the experimental group produced the novel word inappropriately and (2) of the seven children who produced the novel word appropriately, six did so spontaneously and the other comprehended it correctly in addition to producing it in the elicited production task. There is thus no child for whom the sole evidence of word learning is elicited production.

As a final comparison between the experimental and control groups, subjects were classified as either learners or nonlearners on the basis of whether they were successful in the comprehension task and/or produced the word appropriately (shown in table 22.3 as "Any Learning"). Eleven experimental subjects showed evidence of some form of learning, whereas only four control subjects showed such evidence. The groups were significantly different, $\chi^2 = 4.75$, $p < .02$. No differences were found between learners and nonlearners on the basis of gender, birth order, or vocabulary size.

Control analysis During the play period in both the experimental and the control conditions, the target object was always the last one presented. Whereas the control condition described above controlled for recency in that comparisons in both groups were based on the rate of selection of the final object presented, there existed the possibility that the combination of recency and exposure to the novel word gave some advantage to children in the experimental group. We thus included an additional control for the effects of recency and word exposure. In this condition, 12 additional children played with three adults with all four objects in turn. These children ranged in age from 1–1.25 to 2–1.10 ($M = 2$–0.20) and had means of 68.0 ($SD = 33.0$) and 36.8 ($SD = 15.42$) on total vocabulary and noun vocabulary, respectively.

The objects were placed in the transparent box, and then children heard the experimenter and their mother exclaim, "Look, I see a gazzer! A gazzer! I see a gazzer in there!" Only one of these 12 subjects later chose the last object played with when asked to "find the gazzer" in the comprehension test (this is significantly different from the experimental subjects' performance, Fisher exact probability=$p < .05$). Thus, in both control groups there appeared to be a tendency (although not statistically significant) *away* from choosing the last object presented; only five of the combined 36 control subjects chose the most recent object in the comprehension test whereas nine (25%) would have been expected to do so. The performance of the experimental group is therefore all the more compelling because it appears these children may have had to overcome a bias in order to show evidence of word learning.

Discussion

These results suggest that 24-month-olds can use novelty to the discourse context *from the adult's perspective* as a cue in learning a novel object label. As in Study 1, procedural factors other than newness to the discourse context that might have differentially enhanced the target object (e.g., playing with it last) are ruled out by the performance of children in the control groups. Also as in Study 1, it is very possible that control children identified the object that was new to the adult at the time the adults first saw it and became excited; indeed, E1 tried to ensure that all subjects – experimental and control – noticed that their parent was not in the room and could not see the last object they played with. But the control subjects had no reason to associate the novel word – heard later in another context – with that object; thus, any enhancement of the target object that might have occurred when E1 and the child were alone did not influence the control subjects to choose that object in the subsequent comprehension test. The experimental subjects, on the other hand, clearly identified the element in the situation that was new for the adults, but they understood in addition that the new word the adults were using was being used for that new thing. These results thus demonstrate not only that children are sensitive to what is experientially new for an adult in a given situation but also that they understand that adults are likely to talk about things that are new to them in that situation – a basic principle of the pragmatics of language use.

In contrast to Study 1, the egocentric explanation is not possible in this study. The target object was not new to the children at the time of the language model, and no other cues served to make it stand out for them. Both of the two nonegocentric interpretations of how the novelty of the target object (from the adults' perspective) might have aided the children in attaching the label to it are still viable, however. It is possible that the children could have ruled out the nontargets as potential referents of the novel word because they had seen E2 and their parent play with these objects without labeling any of them; thus, they could have attached the word to the appropriate referent by a process of elimination. Alternatively, they might have registered the fact that the adults did not see the target object and they knew that adults tend to get excited about and talk about new things; both of these pieces of information would have enabled them to associate the new word with the target object. These two explanations are not mutually exclusive, and, in any case, they both imply some understanding on the part of the children of which object was new to the adults. Again the fact that only about half of our experimental subjects learned the word is most likely due to the single exposure episode, but it may also be the case that this is an emerging skill for 24-month-old children.

General Discussion

The studies reported here complement and extend the findings of Green-field and colleagues who found that young children are sensitive to discourse novelty in their earliest productions of language. In the current studies we have demonstrated that 24-month-old children are also sensitive to discourse novelty in their comprehension and learning of language. These findings are related to the well-known phenomenon of "fast mapping," in which children of this age learn a novel label for a novel object, without having the referent explicitly designated; they can do this because they already know names for all except one of the potential referents (Clark, 1990; Mervis and Bertrand, 1994). In the current studies, children did not have names for any of the objects present at the time of the language model, but all of the objects except one were familiar from past interactions. In this case, therefore, they discerned the adult's intended referent not from their knowledge of which objects already had names but, rather, from an understanding of which objects were old and which were new to the discourse context. Study 2 established that 24-month-old children engage in this process not egocentrically but, rather, from the point of view of the adult. Their performance in this study indicates that they understood that what was being labeled was the element in the situation that was new for the adults.

These findings are consistent with a number of recent studies showing that young children are able to learn words in a wide variety of pragmatic contexts. The situations simulated in these studies – situations in which there are a number of potential referents present – are presumably common in the lives of children just beginning to learn language. In these potentially ambiguous situations, however, children accurately pick out adults' intended referents by using pragmatic cues such as adult gaze direction (Baldwin, 1993); affective cues indicating the fulfilling or thwarting of an adult's announced intention (Tomasello and Barton, 1994, Study 4); behavioral cues associated with intentional versus accidental actions (Tomasello and Barton, 1994, Study 3); and knowledge of what is likely to happen next in a situation, based on previous experience (Akhtar and Tomasello, in press–a). The current study adds to this list children's understanding of what is new in the discourse context from the adult's perspective.

The findings of these studies have important implications for theories of word learning. In the way in which the problem of lexical acquisition is most commonly posed, the child's task is to discover the adult's intended referent from a theoretically infinite set. To reduce the possibilities, Markman (1989, 1992) has proposed the Whole Object and Mutual Exclusivity assumptions. According to this view, young children initially assume that a new word refers to a whole object that does not already have a name. In the current studies, however, such assumptions could not help children as they were confronted with four potential referents, all of which were whole objects and all of which were nameless. In such situations, they must rely on some pragmatic cue to tell them which *one* of the nameless objects the adult is talking about. In the current studies, they could not do this using some simple, easily programmable cue such as adult gaze direction because gaze direction was not diagnostic. Instead, children in these studies were using a cue, discourse novelty, which depended on their understanding of the entire situation as it unfolded over time. Specifically, they had to be sensitive to what they and the adults had already experienced, and they had to know that adults tend to use language to comment on new things. Thus, in the current studies, and in the studies cited above, 24-month-old children demonstrate an ability to use a broad range of pragmatic cues in determining adults' referential intentions in a wide variety of discourse situations. This ability indicates a deep and flexible understanding of the behavior of other persons and their referential intentions. In our view, it is this understanding that forms the foundation of the process of language acquisition (Tomasello, 1992).

We thus would argue that young children know more about the behavior and cognition of other persons than previously believed. They may not have an adult-like "theory of mind" in the sense of an explicit understanding of the thoughts and beliefs of others. For example, our 2-year-old subjects may not be aware that speakers sometimes talk about things that they believe to be new for others. However, 1–2-year-old children understand a great deal about other persons in terms of their attention and intentions (Baron-Cohen, 1993; Tomasello, 1995; Tomasello, Kruger, and Ratner, 1993); indeed, language acquisition would not be possible without such understanding (Akhtar and Tomasello, in press – b; Bruner, 1983). Situations such as those constructed in the current study highlight this social understanding and demonstrate how children use it to learn linguistic conventions from others.

Acknowledgments

This research was supported in part by an NSERC postdoctoral fellowship to the first author and a grant to the last author from the Spencer Foundation. Thanks to the parents and children who participated in the study, to Laura Rekau, Michelle Rothstein, Danielle Weir, and Josep Call for assistance with coding and analyses, and to three anonymous reviewers for their helpful comments on a previous draft.

Note

1. The first half of the subjects (12 experimental subjects, 12 control subjects) saw the toys on a window sill out of reach but in view. Because this procedure caused some behavioral problems, the plastic box was used for the second half of the subjects. As these two groups of children were identical in their performance on the tests of learning, they were not distinguished in any further analyses.

References

Akhtar, N., and Tomasello, M. (in press – a). Two-year-olds learn words for absent objects and actions. *British Journal of Developmental Psychology.*

Akhtar, N., and Tomasello, M. (in press – b). Intersubjectivity in early language learning and use. In S. Braten (ed.), *Intersubjective Communication and Emotion in Ontogeny: Between Nature, Nurture, and Culture*, Oslo: Norwegian, Academy of Science and Letters.

Baker, N. D., and Greenfield, P. M. (1988). The development of new and old information in young children's early language. *Language Sciences*, **10**, 3–34.

Baldwin, D. A. (1991). Infants' contribution to the achievement of joint reference. *Child Development*, **62**, 875–90.

Baldwin, D. A. (1993). Early referential understanding: Young children's ability to recognize referential acts for what they are. *Developmental Psychology*, **29**, 832–43.

Baron-Cohen, S. (1993). From attention–goal psychology to belief–desire psychology: The development of a theory of mind, and its dysfunction. In S. Baron-Cohen, H. Tager-Flusberg, and D. J. Cohen (eds), *Understanding other Minds: Perspectives from Autism* (pp. 59–82), Oxford: Oxford University Press.

Bruner, J. S. (1983). *Child's Talk: Learning to Use Language*. New York: Norton.

Clark, E. V. (1990). On the pragmatics of contrast. *Journal of Child Language*, **17**, 417–31.

Dunham, P. J., Dunham, F. S., and Curwin, A. (1993). Joint attentional states and lexical acquisition at 18 months. *Developmental Psychology*, **29**, 827–31.

Fantz, R. (1964). Visual experience in infants: Decreased attention to familiar patterns relative to novel ones. *Science*, **146**, 668–70.

Furrow, D., and James, P. (1985). Attentional change and vocalization: Evidence for a relation. *Child Development*, **56**, 1179–83.

Golinkoff, R. M. (1993). When is communication a "meeting of minds"? *Journal of Child Language*, **20**, 199–207.

Greenfield, P. M. (1973). Who is Dada? Some aspects of the semantic and phonological development of a child's first words. *Language and Speech*, **16**, 34–43.

Greenfield, P. M. (1979). Informativeness, presupposition, and semantic choice in single-word utterances. In E. Ochs and B. B. Schieffelin (eds), *Developmental Pragmatics* (pp. 159–66), New York: Academic.

Greenfield, P. M. (1982). The role of perceived variability in the transition to language. *Journal of Child Language*, **9**, 1–12.

Greenfield, P. M., Reilly, J., Leaper, C., and Baker, N. (1985). The structural and functional status of single-word utterances and their relationship to early multi-word speech. In M. D. Barrett (ed.), *Children's Single-word Speech* (pp. 233–67), London: Wiley.

Greenfield, P. M., and Zukow, P. (1978). Why do children say what they say when they say it? An experimental approach to the psychogenesis of presupposition. In K. E. Nelson (ed.), *Children's Language* (vol. 1), New York: Gardner.

Hilke, D. D. (1988). Infant vocalizations and changes in experience. *Journal of Child Language*, **15**, 1–15.

Lempert, H., and Kinsbourne, M. (1985). Possible origin of speech in selective orienting. *Psychological Bulletin*, **97**, 62–73.

Markman, E. (1989). *Categorization and Naming in Children: Problems of Induction*. Cambridge, MA: MIT Press.

Markman, E. (1992). Constraints on word learning: Speculations about their nature, origins, and domain specificity. In M. R. Gunnar and M. P. Maratsos (eds), *Modularity and Constraints in Language and Cognition: The Minnesota Symposia on Child Psychology* (pp. 59–101), Hillsdale, NJ: Erlbaum.

Mervis, C. B., and Bertrand, J. (1994). Acquisition of the Novel Name–Nameless Category (N3C) principle. *Child Development*, **65**, 1646–62.

Nelson, K. (1973). Structure and strategy in learning to talk. *Monographs of the Society for Research in Child Development*, **38** (1–2, Serial No. 149).

O'Neill, D. (1993). *Two-year-olds' ability to make informative requests*. Unpublished doctoral dissertation, Stanford University.

Reznick, J. S., and Goldsmith, L. (1989). A multiple form word production checklist for assessing early language. *Journal of Child Language*, **16**, 91–100.

Tomasello, M. (1992). The social bases of language acquisition. *Social Development*, **1**, 67–87.

Tomasello, M. (1995). Joint attention as social cognition. In C. Moore and P. J. Dunham (eds), *Joint Attention: Its Origins and Role in Development* (pp. 103–30), Hillsdale, NJ: Erlbaum.

Tomasello, M., and Barton, M. (1994). Learning words in nonostensive contexts. *Developmental Psychology*, **30**, 639–50.

Tomasello, M., Farrar, M. J. (1986). Joint attention and early language. *Child Development*, **57**, 1454–63.

Tomasello, M., Farrar, J., and Dines, L. (1984). Children's speech revisions for a familiar and an unfamiliar adult. *Journal of Speech and Hearing Research*, **27**, 359–63.

Tomasello, M., Kruger, A. C., and Ratner, H. H. (1993). Cultural learning. *Behavioral and Brain Sciences*, **16**, 495–552.

23

Young Children's Appreciation of the Mental Impact of their Communicative Signals*

Helen I. Shwe and Ellen M. Markman

EDITORS' INTRODUCTION

In this ingenious study 30-month-olds were shown two objects, a car and a sock, and then asked by the experimenter which of the two they wanted – they all wanted the car, the sock is boring! As soon as the child requested the car Shwe and Markman were able to put him or her into one of four conditions:

1. *Understanding/Wrong Object*: 'You asked for the *car*. Here's the *sock*.'
2. *No Understanding/Wrong Object*: 'You asked for the *sock*. Here's the *sock*.'
3. *Understanding/Correct Object*: 'You asked for the *car*. Here's the *car*.'
4. *No Understanding/Correct Object*: 'You asked for the *sock*. Here's the *car*.'

What they found was that the children persisted in clarifying their communicative signals more when the listener expressed misunderstanding (2 and 4) than when she understood (1 and 3). An interesting comparison is between the two conditions where the children received the correct toy, but in one the adult understood the request (3), and in the other she appeared to misunderstand (4). In 3 the children *never* repeated the request, but in 4 the common response was to repeat the label of the requested object – the children were aware their communicative attempts had been misunderstood. Shwe and Markman conclude 'Thus, young children monitor their communicative partner's knowledge state and care about their listener's comprehension over and above getting what they requested.'

* Previously published in *Developmental Psychology*, **33**, 4 (1997), pp. 630–36.

OVERVIEW   This work addresses whether 30-month-olds appreciate that their communicative signals are being understood (or not) by another person. Infants produce a range of behaviors, such as repairing their failed signals, that have been construed as evidence that they have an implicit theory of mind. Such behavior could be interpreted as attempts to obtain some desired goal rather than as attempts to gain listener understanding. This study was designed to separate listener comprehension from obtaining a material goal. In 4 conditions, children either did or did not get what they wanted and the experimenter understood or misunderstood their request. As predicted, children clarified their signal more when the experimenter misunderstood compared with when she understood. Regardless of whether young children achieved their overt goal, they engaged in behaviors to ensure their communicative act had been understood.

Adults understand that one important function of language is to influence the thoughts, desires, intentions, and beliefs of others. They are aware that their communicative signals have an impact on their listener's mind. With respect to development, some authors argue that young children's communicative acts indicate that they too appreciate the mental impact of their signals, whereas others interpret these behaviors as only persistent efforts to achieve a material goal. Existing studies do not convincingly resolve this issue. The present work attempted to clarify whether young children (30-month-olds) recognize that their signals can affect the mental states of others.

Recent research by Baldwin (1991, 1993) and Tomasello (1995; Tomasello and Barton, 1994; Tomasello and Kruger, 1992) on infants' early communicative abilities suggests that infants understand that others' attentional cues provide necessary information about the intended referent of a novel word. For example, Baldwin presented young infants with a scenario in which they could potentially map a novel label to the wrong referent – this might occur when an adult utters a novel object label at a time when the infant is looking at something other than the correct object. She found that infants (16 months and up) had the ability to gather information about a speaker's focus of attention and thus avoided mapping errors. Moreover, by around 2 years of age, children can discriminate between intentional and unintentional actions that signal the speaker's communicative intent.

In summary, Baldwin and Tomasello (Baldwin, 1991, 1993; Tomasello and Barton, 1994; Tomasello and Kruger, 1992) have shown that infants seem to be aware of the mental lives of others and can use the attentional focus of others to interpret the meaning of a novel word. It is still not clear, however, whether young children use their own communicative signals to influence the mental life of others. One line of early research that begins to address this question is the work on intentional signals. Researchers have used the term *intention signal* to describe a range of behaviors that infants begin producing at about 1 year of age (e.g., Bates, Benigni, Bretherton, Camaioni, and Volterra, 1979; Bretherton and Beeghly, 1982; Bretherton, 1984; Golinkoff, 1986, 1993). For example, infants request help from others in obtaining objects, give and show objects to others, and reject objects that others offer them. According to these researchers, such behaviors indicate that infants are aware of other people's mental lives and are trying to influence others' mental experience.

These claims, however, go well beyond the data. Shatz (1983) argued that infants may be engaging in *magical thinking* when they produce intentional signals. She proposed that children may create the "illusion" of trying to influence the mental life of others by persisting in their attempts to achieve certain goals. That is, Shatz claimed that infants' intentional signals are used to manipulate their listeners' behavior and not to influence the mental processes underlying those behaviors.

In opposition to Shatz, Golinkoff (1986, p. 456) argued that certain behaviors that infants produce in events she called the "negotiation of failed messages" suggest that infants are intentionally communicating. She claimed that prelinguistic children are communicating to get their point across and not just to gain material ends. To support this claim, Golinkoff drew upon findings from a longitudinal study of communicative episodes between preverbal infants (12- and 18-month-olds) and their mothers. By analyzing the distribution of various types of behaviors that infants produced in negotiation episodes (i.e., at least one comprehension failure by mother), Golinkoff provided three types of evidence that she interpreted as indicating that infants appreciate the mental impact of their signals: (a) infants initiate negotiation episodes, (b) infants reject incorrect interpretations of signals, and (c) infants creatively repair their failed signals. These findings do not, however, provide compelling evidence for the claim that infants appreciate the mental impact of their signals because they can all be explained by alternative behavioral explanations. For example, infants may reject incorrect interpretations of their signals because they want to change another person's behavior (e.g., removing an undesired object) not because they want their listener to understand their initial signal.

In response to Golinkoff's (1986) claim that infants appreciate the mental processes that underlie certain behavioral responses, Shatz and O'Reilly (1990) conducted an observational study that examined miscommunication episodes between children (age 2 years 6 months) and their parents in free play sessions. Shatz and O'Reilly concluded from the results of their study that Golinkoff seriously overestimated infants' and young children's ability to understand the mental aspect of communicative signals. Shatz and O'Reilly classified child utterances eliciting parental requests for clarification into one of two categories: (a) request for action or information, or (b) assertion. They hypothesized that children would persist more in achieving mutual understanding with their parent when their original utterance was a request rather than an assertion because this would indicate that children use communicative signals mainly to achieve behavioral goals. Shatz and O'Reilly found that children responded to requests for clarification made of their own requests significantly more frequently than they responded to clarification requests made of their own assertions (means of 94% and 84%, respectively). They interpreted these results to support their claim that young children use communicative signals mainly to get things.

Golinkoff (1993) responded to Shatz and O'Reilly's (1990) criticisms by arguing that the high rate (84%) at which children clarified their assertions supports her claim that children communicate for the sake of being understood. Furthermore, Golinkoff pointed out that even adults will provide more repairs when they are trying to obtain an overt goal and not just providing some information to others.

In summary, although Golinkoff (1993) argued that infants' early gestural behaviors demonstrate their appreciation of the mental component of communicative interactions, there are alternative explanations for these findings. A weaker claim that is supported by these findings is that infants and young children have goals and persist in their attempts to achieve them. In line with Golinkoff's work, a handful of observational studies in the theory-of-mind literature suggest that 2-year-olds are aware of the mental lives of others (Garvey, 1984; Keenan and Schieffelin, 1976). These studies have documented the active attempts of children to ensure that they and their communicative partners are attuned to the same topic. Garvey investigated young children's attempts to inform another person about an object or event by recording their conversations with adults and peers at home and school. These observations showed that 2- and 3-year-olds persisted in establishing a common label for an object for the purposes of talking about that object or helping a communicative partner recall something to talk about a previous event. In addition, Keenan and Schieffelin observed 3 children (during the period from 16 to 35 months of age) and recorded their attempts to initiate and sustain topics of conversation. These children used a number of verbal (e.g., verbs such as *see* and *look*, deictic particles such as *there*) and nonverbal (e.g., pointing, eye contact) devices to focus the attention of their listeners on present objects or events. These observations of young children's persistence in establishing a common label for an object or event suggest that they monitor the attentive focus of their listener.

These observational studies, however, do not provide clear evidence to answer whether young children use communicative signals to influence the cognitive state of their listener or simply to manipulate the listener's behavior. This question must be addressed by using a method that can separate the factors of gaining overt goals from influencing the cognition of others. The present study was designed to address this issue by creating a situation in which children's persistence could be interpreted only as trying to obtain listener understanding.

In a set of recent studies with 2-year-olds, O'Neill (1996) introduced experimental manipulations to investigate whether toddlers take into account their mothers' knowledge states when communicating with them. Children had to ask their mothers for help in retrieving an object in two different conditions. In one condition, mothers had witnessed the object's placement; in the other condition, the mother had not witnessed the object's placement (e.g., she was out of the room or covered her eyes). As predicted, O'Neill found that 2-year-olds named the object, named its location, and gestured to its location significantly more often when their mother had not witnessed the object's placement than when she had witnessed its placement. Thus, young children altered their verbal and nonverbal communication according to the knowledge state of their communicative partner.

Thus, under some circumstances, 2-year-olds monitor their listener's knowledge state and can tailor their signals appropriately. Yet we still do not know whether young children care that their goal oriented requests are understood or whether they only care that they achieve their goal. When young children are faced with a situation in which they desire an object, the motivation to achieve their goal might swamp any incipient ability they have to monitor their listener's comprehension.

To address whether children are able to monitor their listener's comprehension when a salient goal is at stake, we must distinguish between efforts to be understood per se and efforts to achieve a goal. Refusal of a child's request is one situation in which the components of listener comprehension and obtaining some goal are distinguishable. For example, a child requests a ball and the listener responds by saying "You want the ball? You may not have the ball now." In this scenario, the listener conveys to the child that she understood the child's request, but at the same time does not satisfy the request for the object. So in this case, the elements of listener understanding and obtaining a material goal are not confounded.

In the present study, we investigated young children's understanding of the mental aspect of their communicative signals by presenting children with situations in which their listener conveys either misunderstanding or comprehension of their request for an object. In one set of conditions, children were presented with two situations in which they did not get what they wanted. In one of those conditions, the experimenter expressed understanding; in the other, she conveyed misunderstanding of the request for an object. In another set of conditions, children obtained what they wanted: one in which the experimenter conveyed understanding of their request and one in which she did not. If children persist in their attempts to get their point across to their listener even after their goal has been achieved, then the hypothesis that children appreciate the mental component of their signals would have even stronger support. In summary, if young children care whether their signals are being understood per se, then they should persist in clarifying their signals more when the listener misunderstands compared with when the listener understands their request, regardless of whether they achieve their overt goal.

METHOD

Participants

Twenty-two healthy children (M age = 30 months 17 days, range = 30 months 2 days to 31 months 7 days, 11 boys and 11 girls) participated in this study. They were recruited through ads in local parent newspapers and magazines and received either a small object or $5 for their participation. Eight additional children participated in the study but were not part of the final data set because of failure to choose objects consistently or failure to complete the procedure.

Materials

Stimuli Each child saw 10 objects that were presented in pairs. Every child in the study was presented with a duck, a car, a train, a ball, a turtle, a plane, a boat, and a pig paired with either a shirt or a sock in the eight experimental trials. The duck toy was a mother with her baby attached to her stomach. When the baby duck was pulled away from the mother, the mother flapped its wings and walked across the table. The car was a battery-powered car that made noise and drove in circles on the table when a button was pushed. The train and turtle moved across the table when pushed. The ball was soft, somewhat bouncy, and bright pink. The plane had Big Bird sitting in it and was a children's flashlight that made noise and lit up when you pushed it. The pig talked when its stomach was pushed. In the filler trial (first trial), children were presented with an additional set of familiar objects.

On each trial, the child was presented with one action object and one boring object (shirt or sock). Pilot studies indicated that children found the action objects (duck, car, train, ball, turtle, plane, boat, and pig) very attractive. The shirt and sock were both blue with no interesting features. Pilot work indicated that children typically did not request these objects and were noticeably dissatisfied when handed a shirt or sock instead of an interesting object. An action toy was paired with a less interesting object in the hope that children would consistently choose the same object in the experimental conditions and would care which object the experimenter gave them. We expected children to request the action toy and be somewhat dissatisfied when the experimenter handed them the sock or shirt.

Equipment A video camera equipped with a stopwatch function was used to tape each session.

Design

There were two experimental conditions in which children did not get the object they requested but that differed in terms of whether the experimenter indicated she understood their request or not. These two conditions were Understanding/Wrong Object and No Understanding/Wrong Object. In addition, there were two experimental conditions in which children obtained the requested object. These two conditions were Understanding/Correct Object and No Understanding/Correct Object.

Each child participated in all four conditions with two trials of each. The order of each set of test trials was random so that children got one trial of each condition in the first block of four trials and the same for the second block of trials. Children were presented with a different pair of objects on each of the eight experimental trials. The test trials were preceded by one filler trial in which the experimenter simply gave the requested object to the child (i.e., no verbal response from experimenter). This filler trial was used to familiarize the baby with the game that involved requesting only one object instead of both.

To make the game more interesting for the children, the experimenter often used a puppet to retrieve the objects from the child.

Procedure

In all of the conditions, children were shown two objects and were prompted to request one of the objects from an experimenter. After the child clearly requested one of the objects by pointing, reaching, or labeling, the experimenter placed one of the objects in a bucket on the far corner of the table leaving only one object in front of the child. For example, in the two conditions in which children obtained the requested object, the other (undesired) object was taken away and placed in the bucket. The object was placed in a bucket on the table instead of removing it from the table so that children's responses (i.e., persistence in requesting an object) would be clear for coding purposes. That is, if children persisted in requesting an object, they would have a specific referent at which to direct their verbal requests. The opaque bucket was used to make the procedure less frustrating for the children – having the desired object in their direct line of sight would have been upsetting. After the experimenter gave a verbal response to the child's request, she handed the object on the table to the child.

Gestural forms of requests by the child were coded as requests in this study. We did not require a verbal request from young children because in pilot work we had to eliminate too many children on the basis of their low frequency of verbal requests. However, simply by placing the two objects on the table in front of the children but out of reach we were able to reliably elicit gestures. That is, children clearly indicated the desired object by pointing or reaching. These gestures were often accompanied by eye gaze and verbalizations such as "that" or "want that one," which made coding gestural requests clear and straightforward in most cases. The test trials of 12 participants were coded independently by two coders, and they agreed 100% of the time on which object the child requested. Although gestural requests indicated which object the child desired, verbalizations were coded as the dependent measure after children's initial request for an object. Thus, children's original requests could be gestural, but their rerequests were only coded if they were verbal.

Listener comprehension was conveyed by having the experimenter correctly repeat the label of the object that the child requested. In contrast, misunderstanding was conveyed by having the experimenter incorrectly repeat the label of the unrequested object. In all four conditions, the same carrier phrases and intonation were used when the experimenter expressed understanding or misunderstanding of the child's request and refused or complied with the child's request (e.g., "You asked for the *object label 1*. I think you want the *object label 1*. I'm going to give you the *object label 2*. Here's the *object label 2*."). For example, in the Understanding/Wrong Object condition, if the child requested the duck, the experimenter said, "You asked for the *duck*. I think you want the *duck*. I'm going to give you the *shirt*. Here's the *shirt*." These carrier phrases were used so that the experimenter would convey her understanding or misunderstanding of the child's request and nothing more.

Children were seated at a table, with their parent seated next to them and the experimenter seated across the table. The experimenter presented the child with two objects by placing them approximately 60 cm apart on the table in front of the child but out of reaching distance. The experimenter then prompted the child to request one of the objects (if necessary) by saying, "Which object do you want to see? Would you like to see the —— or the ——?" After the child clearly requested one of the objects, the experimenter placed one of the objects in a bucket on the far corner of the table, gave the appropriate verbal response, and then handed the object left on the table to the child. The following examples of each condition pertain to a trial where the experimenter presents a car and sock, and the child requests the car.

For the two conditions in which children did not get the requested object, the experimenter placed the requested object (car) in the bucket on the corner of the table. Thus, the boring object was in front of the child just out of reach, and the requested object was put away out of sight. At this point the experimenter then gave the relevant verbal response:

1. Understanding/Wrong Object: "You asked for the *car*. I think you want the *car*. I'm going to give you the *sock*. Here's the *sock*."

2. No Understanding/Wrong Object: "You asked for the *sock*. I think you want the *sock*. I'm going to give you the *sock*. Here's the *sock*."

After the experimenter gave a verbal response to the child's request, she handed the child the other object (sock). Then the experimenter waited approximately 10 seconds until she retrieved the object and began the next trial.

For the two conditions in which children obtained the requested object, the experimenter placed the other object (sock) in the bucket on the corner of the table. Thus the desired object was in front of the child just out of reach, and the boring object was put away out of sight. At this point the experimenter gave the appropriate verbal response for the condition:

1. Understanding/Correct Object: "You asked for the *car*. I think you want the *car*. I'm going to give you the *car*. Here's the *car*."

2. No Understanding/Correct Object: "You asked for the *sock*. I think you want the *sock*. I'm going to give you the *car*. Here's the *car*."

After the experimenter gave a verbal response to the child's request, she handed the child the requested object (car). Then the experimenter waited approximately 10 seconds until she retrieved the object and began the next trial.

RESULTS

If young children appreciate the mental component of their signals, then they should persist in clarifying their signal more when their listener misunderstands them than when their listener understands their request. This comparison can be made between two sets of conditions when children did not receive what they requested (Understanding/Wrong Object vs. No Understanding/Wrong Object) and when they did obtain the requested object (Understanding/Correct Object vs. No Understanding/Correct Object). Children's verbalizations were coded to determine whether they followed the predicted pattern. We predicted that children would repeat the label of the requested object and verbally reject the undesired object more when the experimenter conveyed misunderstanding than when she conveyed understanding of their request.

Coding

Children's reactions were compared in the four conditions by coding two types of verbalizations – repetitions of the requested object label and rejections of the undesired object. Children's nonverbal responses (e.g., looking, touching, reaching for objects) were not coded in this study because pilot work indicated that these data were difficult to interpret, and only a few trends in the predicted direction were observed.

The number of repetitions was calculated for children's request of the desired object and their rejection of the undesired object. The verbalizations of children's request for the desired object included phrases such as "Want duck," "Give me the duck," and "Please duck," in addition to repetitions of the other object label in isolation. Children rejected the unrequested object by using a number of different verbalizations: "I don't want that," "No sock," and "I don't like it."

Each trial started when the experimenter placed one of the objects in a bucket on the far corner of the table. At this point one of the objects had been removed, leaving only one object visible to make it clear which object the experimenter was about to hand over to the child. Thus, the verbal data is not open to a behavioral explanation because the coding started at the point when children should know which object they were going to get. That is, in pilot versions of the study, children did not know which toy the experimenter was going to hand them until after she provided a verbal response to their request. Children may have persisted more when they heard the label of the undesired toy because they recognized that as a sign that they were not going to get what they wanted. In the present study, the experimenter provided a verbal response to the children's requests only after the children knew which to they were going to get. The trial ended when the experimenter retrieved the object from the child.

The test trials of all 22 participants were coded independently by two coders. Reliability was calculated with Cohen's (1960) kappa. The two coders showed relatively strong agreement (94%, $\kappa = .89$) in their judgments of the number of times each participant requested the desired object but somewhat weaker agreement (82%, $\kappa = .72$) in their judgments of the number of times each participant rejected the unrequested object. Each discrepancy was carefully re-examined by both coders, at which time they came to an agreement about what the child had said or done. All of the disagreements resulted from one of the coders' failing to record a behavior that the child exhibited. That is, each coder had failed to notice some verbalization on a small number of trials. The final coding used in the data analyses was the agreed-upon responses from both coders.

All Conditions

A first set of analyses was conducted to compare all four conditions: Understanding/Wrong Object, No Understanding/Wrong Object, Understanding/Correct Object, and No Understanding/Correct Object. Children's verbalizations were analyzed in a 2 (object: correct, incorrect) × 2 (response: understanding, misunderstanding) × 2 (trial: trial 1, trial 2) × 2 (gender: male, female) analysis of variance (ANOVA). Two such analyses were conducted: one analysis with the requested object (requesting the object in the bucket) verbalization measure and the second with the no (rejecting the object given by the experimenter) response measure. As predicted, these analyses revealed a significant main effect of response for the number of repetitions of the requested object, $F(1, 20) = 27.69$, $p < .001$. That is, children repeated the label of the requested object more when the experimenter expressed misunderstanding ($M = .63$ repetitions) than when she conveyed understanding ($M = .08$ repetitions). Furthermore, these omnibus ANOVAs revealed a significant main effect of response for verbally rejecting the object given by the experimenter, $F(1, 20) = 6.96$, $p < .01$. Children verbally rejected the given object more when the experimenter misunderstood their signal ($M = .49$ repetitions) than when she understood ($M = .09$) their request. In addition to the predicted main effects of response, these analyses revealed a significant Object × Response interaction for the number of repetitions of the requested object and a significant main effect of object for verbally rejecting the given object. To better understand these findings, we will first consider the responses of children when they did not obtain the requested object and then examine their responses in the conditions in which they obtained the requested toy.

Understanding/Wrong Object versus No Understanding/Wrong Object

We compared children's verbalizations in the conditions in which children did not get the requested object but were understood in one condition and misunderstood in the other. The two categories of verbalizations analyzed were requested object (requesting the object in the bucket) and no (rejecting the object given by the experimenter). Children's verbalizations were analyzed in a series of 2 (condition) × 2 (gender) × 2 (trial) ANOVAs. As predicted, children who did not get the desired object tended to repeat the requested object label more when the experimenter expressed misunderstanding ($M = .48$ repetitions) than when she conveyed understanding ($M = .16$ repetitions) of the children's request, $F(1, 20) = 5.03$, $p < .05$ (see table 23.1 for summary of results). Eight of the children repeated the label of the requested object more

TABLE 23.1   Repetitions of requested object

Condition	Wrong object	Correct object
Understanding		
M	.16	0.00
SD	.43	0.00
No understanding		
M	.48	.77
SD	.88	.86

TABLE 23.2   Rejections of undesired object

Condition	Wrong object	Correct object
Understanding		
M	.18	0.00
SD	.54	0.00
No understanding		
M	.70	.27
SD	1.11	.58

when their listener conveyed misunderstanding than when she expressed understanding, whereas 3 children showed the opposite pattern. This difference, however, did not reach significance (binomial test, $p = .11$). Children verbally rejected the given (undesired) object more when the experimenter expressed misunderstanding ($M = .70$ repetitions) than when she conveyed understanding ($M = .18$ repetitions) of their request, $F(1, 20) = 8.94$, $p < .01$ (see table 23.2 for summary of results). Thirteen of the children verbally rejected the undesired object more when their listener expressed misunderstanding than when she conveyed understanding, but none of the children showed the opposite response pattern (binomial test, $p < .001$).[1]

Understanding/Correct Object versus No Understanding/Correct Object

In addition to comparing the two conditions in which children did not get the object they requested, we compared children's verbalizations in the two conditions in which children obtained the requested object. Children who obtained the requested object repeated the label of the desired object more when the experimenter expressed misunderstanding than when she conveyed understanding of their request. Children repeated the label of the requested object a mean of .77 times when she conveyed misunderstanding, whereas they never uttered the label of the requested object when the experimenter expressed understanding of their request, $F(1, 20) = 28.47$, $p < .001$. Seventeen (of the 22) children who obtained the requested object repeated the label of the desired object more when the experimenter conveyed misunderstanding than when she expressed understanding of their request, whereas none of the children showed the opposite pattern (binomial test, $p < .001$). Furthermore, children who obtained the desired object verbally rejected the unrequested object more when the experimenter expressed misunderstanding of their request. Children verbally rejected the undesired object a mean of .27 times when the experimenter conveyed misunderstanding, whereas they never verbally rejected the undesired object when she expressed understanding of their request, $F(1,20) = 6.15, p < .05$. Seven children verbally rejected the undesired object more when their listener conveyed misunderstanding than when she expressed understanding of their request, but none showed the opposite response pattern (binomial test, $p < .01$).

In summary, when children did not get the requested object, they tended to repeat the label of the other object and verbally rejected the given object more when the experimenter expressed misunderstanding than when she conveyed understanding of their request. Furthermore, even when children obtained the requested object, they showed an analogous pattern of responses. That is, they repeated the label of the requested object and verbally rejected the undesired object significantly more when the experimenter conveyed misunderstanding than when she expressed understanding of their request for an object.

Receiving the Desired Object versus Rejected Object

Turning back to the findings from the omnibus ANOVAs, a significant interaction between response and object was found for the number of repetitions of the requested object. As expected, children never repeated the label of the requested object when the experimenter conveyed understanding of their signal and they obtained the requested toy. Also as expected, children persisted to clarify their signal at a relatively low rate ($M = .16$ repetitions) when the experimenter expressed understanding but they did not get what they wanted. The puzzling finding, however, is the comparison between the two cases in which the experimenter expressed misunderstanding; in one case the children obtained the requested toy, and in the other they did not. That is, children persisted to clarify their signal more when they got what they wanted but the experimenter misunderstood ($M = 0.77$ repetitions) than when they got the wrong object and the adult misunderstood ($M = 0.48$ repetitions). Although this finding is somewhat counterintuitive, one possible explanation is that when children are faced with a situation in which they are misunderstood and, on top of that, do not get what they want, they may be too frustrated or upset to clarify their signal. In the case in which they at least get what they want (but are still misunderstood), children can devote some of their resources to clarifying their signal.

The omnibus ANOVAs also revealed a significant main effect for object for children's verbal rejection of the toy given by the experimenter. That is, children verbally rejected (e.g., "No"; "Don't want it") the undesired toy more than the requested toy ($Ms = 0.44$ and 0.14 repetitions, respectively). Part of this main effect can be attributed to the obvious expectation that when children were understood, they verbally rejected the wrong object more than the requested object ($Ms = 0.18$ and 0.00, respectively). More interestingly, even when children were misunderstood, they verbally rejected the wrong object more ($M = 0.70$ repetitions) than the correct object ($M = 0.27$ repetitions).

Although this main effect for object was not one of the main predictions, it makes sense given the different responses children could give to clarify their signal. On the one hand, when children did not obtain the requested toy, they could either repeat the label of the requested toy or verbally reject the undesired toy to clarify their signal. On the other hand, when children obtained the requested toy, it made more sense for them to repeat the label of the requested toy to clarify their signal when the experimenter misunderstood them. That is, it did not make much sense for children to clarify their signal by saying "No" or "I don't want it" when they obtained the requested toy but the experimenter misunderstood them. Thus, these young children were showing some signs of modulating their corrections to be appropriate for the kind of misunderstanding the experimenter expressed (i.e., whether children obtained the requested or rejected toy).

DISCUSSION

The results of this study suggest that young children are aware that their communicative signals have an impact on the mental state of their listeners. Children persisted in clarifying their signals more when their listener expressed misunderstanding than when she conveyed understanding in situations in which children did not fulfill their goal of obtaining an attractive object. Furthermore, the predicted pattern of differences in children's verbalizations was found even when children obtained the object they requested.

These findings provide evidence that young children appreciate the mental component of their signals and treat their listeners as more than just manipulable objects. In reference to the debate between Golinkoff (1986) and Shatz and O'Reilly (1990), our results are consistent with Golinkoff's claim that young children are communicating to get their point across and not just to get things they want. Our findings do not support Shatz and O'Reilly's interpretation of the results from their study on miscommunication episodes with 2-year-olds. Our findings indicate that young children care whether their signals are being understood, regardless of whether their request is successful. This work helps to resolve the debate between Golinkoff and Shatz and O'Reilly by providing a controlled experiment that distinguishes between intentions and overt goals. It remains to be seen, however, whether babies as young as 18–24 months old appreciate the mental impact of their signals.

Our results also help clarify the issue of exactly how to characterize 2-year-olds' understanding of the mental world. These findings support the conclusions of Garvey (1984) and Keenan and Schieffelin (1976) regarding young children's ability to ensure that they and their communicative partners are focused on the same topic of conversation. More specifically, in a request scenario, it is vital for children to ensure that their listener is attuned to the same topic. Our results indicate that young children use verbal devices to focus the attention of their listener on the correct (requested) object.

Furthermore, our results corroborate O'Neill's (1996) finding that 2-year-olds take into account their communicative partner's knowledge state and can adjust their level of informativeness accordingly. Although O'Neill's procedure differs markedly from ours in many respects, the two procedures tap some of the same basic communicative abilities in young children. For example, in O'Neill's procedure, children had to monitor their mothers' knowledge state (inferred from what the mother witnesses) and then adjust their level of informativeness accordingly to obtain a desired object. Similarly, in our procedure, children had to monitor their listener's knowledge state (inferred from what label she used) to determine whether a higher level of persistence was required to obtain listener comprehension. Discussions of attention in infancy have focused on infants' abilities to take into account the direction of the gaze of another person (Baldwin, 1991, 1993; Baldwin and Moses, 1993). O'Neill suggested that children in her task were not simply monitoring the direction of their mothers' eye gaze but rather assessing which events their mothers were jointly attending to with them. She suggested that although the ability to determine an adult's gaze is useful for infants in many situations, as children grow older their understanding of joint attention must incorporate other factors as well.

A similar conclusion can be made in relation to our findings – children could not simply monitor the eye gaze or other attentional cues of their listener to determine whether she understood them or not. That is, in all of the experimental conditions, the listener looked at the child (and not at one of the objects) when giving the verbal response to the children's request. Children in our task were clearly using their receptive language comprehension to determine whether the experimenter understood their request or not. Thus, 2-year-olds' understanding of attention goes beyond monitoring specific attentional cues such as eye gaze and pointing, in communicative interactions. Our findings support the conclusion that 2-year-olds are not limited to these sorts of information about an adult's attentional focus but, rather, have a number of resources at their disposal to monitor the focus of attention and knowledge state of their listener. Furthermore, these findings suggest that when they are misunderstood, young children tailor their clarification responses to accommodate the context of the misunderstanding (i.e., whether they received the desired object). Our results, in combination with O'Neill's (1996) findings, suggest that 2-year-olds are broadening their understanding of attention, which, in turn, will help them monitor the knowledge state of their listener across an increasingly wide range of situations.

In conclusion, young children's persistence in clarifying their communicative signals regardless of whether they achieve their goal is striking, given their strong desire for an interesting object. Children were presented with attractive toys and encouraged to request them from an experimenter in the present procedure. Young children's strong desire for a toy easily could have masked their communicative competence, resulting in no difference between the conditions. In fact, when children were misunderstood, they tended to clarify their signal more when they obtained the requested toy. Yet when children did not get what they wanted, their disappointment did not completely overshadow their ability to clarify their communicative intent to their listener. Thus, young children monitor their communicative partner's knowledge state and care about their listener's comprehension over and above getting what they requested.

Acknowledgments

Portions of these findings were presented at the March 1995 biennial meeting of the Society for Research in Child Development in Indianapolis, Indiana. This research was supported in part by National Science Foundation Grant BNS-9109236. We would like to express our appreciation to the parents and infants who generously participated in this research. We thank Judith Wascow for administrative help and Nancy Lin, Amy Jones, and Cindy Lupin for their diligence in coding videotapes.

Note

1. We replicated these findings in a previous study with 24 children who were 30 months old. Children repeated the other object label significantly more in the No Understanding/Wrong Object than the Understanding/Wrong Object trials. Furthermore, the boys also verbally rejected the given toy more in the No Understanding/Wrong Object than in the Understanding/Wrong Object trials. The girls showed no difference between the two conditions.

References

Baldwin, D. A. (1991). Infants' contribution to the achievement of joint reference. *Child Development*, **62**, 875–90.

Baldwin, D. A. (1993). Infants' ability to consult the speaker for clues to word reference. *Journal of Child Language*, **20**, 395–418.

Baldwin, D. A., and Moses, L. J. (1993). In C. Lewis and P. Mitchell (eds), *Origins of an Understanding of Mind*, Hillsdale, NJ: Erlbaum.

Bates, E., Benigni, L., Bretherton, I., Camaioni, L., and Volterra, V. (1979). *The Emergence of Symbols: Cognition and Communication in Infancy*. New York: Academic Press.

Bretherton, I. (1984). Social referencing and the interfacing of minds: A commentary on the views of Feinman and Campos. *Merrill-Palmer Quarterly*, **30**, 419–27.

Bretherton, I., and Beeghly, M. (1982). Talking about internal states: The acquisition of an explicit theory of mind. *Developmental Psychology*, **18**, 906–21.

Cohen, J. (1960). A coefficient of agreement for nominal scales. *Educational and Psychological Measurement*, **20**, 37–46.

Garvey, C. (1984). *Children's Talk*. Cambridge, MA: Harvard University Press.

Golinkoff, R. M. (1983). The preverbal negotiation of failed messages: Insights into the transition period. In R. M. Golinkoff (ed.), *The Transition from Prelinguistic to Linguistic Communication*, Hillsdale, NJ: Erlbaum.

Golinkoff, R. M. (1986). "I beg your pardon?": The preverbal negotiation of failed messages. *Journal of Child Language*, **13**, 455–76.

Golinkoff, R. M. (1993). When is communication a "meeting of minds"? *Journal of Child Language*, **20**, 199–207.

Keenan, E. O., and Schieffelin, B. B. (1976). Topic as a discourse notion: A study of topic in the conservations of children and adults. In C. N. Li (ed.), *Subject and Topic* (pp. 335–84), New York: Academic Press.

O'Neill, D. K. (1996). Two-year-old children's sensitivity to a parent's knowledge state when making requests. *Child Development*, **67**, 659–77.

Shatz, M. (1983). Communication. In P. H. Mussen (series ed.) and J. Flavell and E. Markman (vol. eds), *Handbook of Child Psychology: Vol. 3. Cognitive Development* (4th edn, pp. 841–89), New York: Wiley.

Shatz, M., and O'Reilly, A. (1990). Conversation or communicative skill? A reassessment of two-year-olds' behavior in miscommunication episodes. *Journal of Child Language*, **17**, 131–46.

Tomasello, M. (1995). Joint attention as social cognition. In C. Moore and P. Dunham (eds), *Joint Attention: Its Origins and Role in Development* (pp. 103–30), Hillsdale, NJ: Erlbaum.

Tomasello, M., and Barton, M. (1994). Learning words in nonostensive contexts. *Developmental Psychology*, **30**, 639–50.

Tomasello, M., and Kruger, A. (1992). Joint attention on actions: Acquiring verbs in ostensive and non-ostensive contexts. *Journal of Child Language*, **19**, 311–33.

24

Rules of Language*

Steven Pinker

Language and cognition have been explained as the products of a homo-geneous associative memory structure or, alternatively, as a set of geneti-cally determined computational modules in which rules manipulate symbolic representations. Intensive study of one phenomenon of English grammar and how it is processed and acquired suggests that both theories are partly right. Regular verbs (*walk–walked*) are computed by a suffixation rule in a neural system for grammatical processing; irregular verbs (*run–ran*) are retrieved from an associative memory.

OVERVIEW

Every normal human can convey and receive an unlimited number of discrete messages through a highly structured stream of sound or, in the case of signed languages, manual gestures. This remarkable piece of natural engineering depends upon a complex code or grammar implemented in the brain that is deployed without conscious effort and that develops, without explicit training, by the age of four. Explaining this talent is an important goal of the human sciences.

Theories of language and other cognitive processes generally fall into two classes. Associationism describes the brain as a homogeneous network of interconnected units modified by a learning mechanism that records correlations among frequently co-occurring input patterns.[1] Rule-and-representation theories describe the brain as a computational device in which rules and principles operate on symbolic data structures.[2,3] Some rule theories further propose that the brain is divided into modular computational systems that

---

* Previously published in *Science*, **253** (2 August 1991), pp. 530–5.

have an organization that is largely specified genetically, one of the systems being language.[3,4]

During the last 35 years, there has been an unprecedented empirical study of human language structure, acquisition, use, and breakdown, allowing these centuries-old proposals to be refined and tested. I will illustrate how intensive multidisciplinary study of one linguistic phenomenon shows that both associationism and rule theories are partly correct, but about different components of the language system.

MODULES OF LANGUAGE

A grammar defines a mapping between sounds and meanings, but the mapping is not done in a single step but through a chain of intermediate data structures, each governed by a subsystem. Morphology is the subsystem that computes the forms of words. I focus on a single process of morphology: English past tense inflection, in which the physical shape of the verb varies to encode the relative time of occurrence of the referent event and the speech act. Regular past tense marking (for example, *walk–walked*) is a rulelike process resulting in addition of the suffix *-d*. In addition there are about 180 irregular verbs that mark the past tense in other ways (for example, *hit–hit, come–came, feel–felt*).

Past tense inflection is an isolable subsystem in which grammatical mechanisms can be studied in detail, without complex interactions with the rest of language. It is computed independently of syntax, the subsystem that defines the form of phrases and sentences: The syntax of English forces its speakers to mark tense in every sentence, but no aspect of syntax works differently with regular and irregular verbs. Past tense marking is also insensitive to lexical semantics:[5,6] the regular–irregular distinction does not correlate with any feature of verb meaning. For example, *hit–hit, strike–struck*, and *slap–slapped* have similar meanings, but three different past tense forms; *stand–stood, stand me up–stood me up*, and *understand–understood*, have unrelated meanings but identical past tense forms. Past marking is also independent of phonology, which determines the possible sound sequences in a language: the three pronunciations of the regular suffix (in *ripped, ribbed*, and *ridded*) represent not three independent processes but a single suffix *-d* modified to conform with general laws of English sound patterning.[5]

RULELIKE PROCESSES IN LANGUAGE

English inflection can illustrate the major kinds of theories used to explain linguistic processes. Traditional grammar offers the following first approximation: Regular inflection, being fully predictable, is computed by a rule that concatenates the affix *-d* to the verb stem. This allows a speaker to inflect an unlimited number of new verbs, an ability seen both in adults, who easily create past forms for neologisms like *faxed*, and in preschoolers, who, given a novel verb like *to rick* in experiments, freely produced *ricked*.[7] In contrast, irregular verb forms are unpredictable: compare *sit–sat* and *hit–hit*, *sing–sang* and *string–strung*, *feel–felt* and *tell–told*. Therefore they must be individually memorized. Retrieval of an irregular form from memory ordinarily blocks application of the regular rule, although in children retrieval occasionally fails, yielding "overregularization" errors like *breaked*.[8,9,10]

The rule-rote theory, although appealingly straightforward, is inadequate. Rote memory, if thought of as a list of slots, is designed for the very rare verbs with unrelated past tense forms, like *be–was* and *go–went*. But for all other irregular verbs, the phonological content of the stem is largely preserved in the past form, as in *swing–swung*.[5,11] Moreover, a given irregular pattern such as a vowel change is typically seen in a family of phonetically similar items, such as *sing–sang*, *ring–rang*, *spring–sprang*, *shrink–shrank*, and *swim–swam*, or *grow–grew*, *blow–blew*, *throw–threw*, and *fly–flew*.[5,9,11] The rote theory cannot explain why verbs with irregular past forms come in similarity families, rather than belonging to arbitrary lists. Finally, irregular pairs are psychologically not a closed list, but their patterns can sometimes be extended to new forms on the basis of similarity to existing forms. All children occasionally use forms such as *bring–brang* and *bite–bote*.[5,9] A few irregular past forms have entered the language historically under the influence of existing forms. *Quit, cost, catch* are from French, and *fling, sling, stick* have joined irregular clusters in the last few hundred years;[12] such effects are obvious when dialects are compared (for example, *help–holp*, *rise–riz*, *drag–drug*, *climb–clome*[13]). Such analogizing can be demonstrated in the laboratory: faced with inflecting nonsense verbs like *spling*, many adults produce *splung*.[6,7,14,15]

The partial systematicity of irregular verbs has been handled in opposite ways by modern rule and associationist theories. One version of the theory of Generative Phonology[11] posits rules for irregular verbs (for example, change *i* to *a*) as well as for regular ones. The theory is designed to explain the similarity between verb stems and their past tense forms: if the rule just changes a specified segment, the rest of the stem comes through in the output untouched, by default, just as in the fully regular case. But the rule theory does not address the similarity among different verbs in the input set and people's tendency to generalize irregular patterns. If an irregular rule is restricted to apply to a list of words, the similarity among the words in the list is unexplained. But if a common pattern shared by the words is identified and the rule is restricted to apply to all and only the verbs displaying that pattern (for example, change *i* to *a* when it appears after a consonant cluster and precedes *ng*), the rule fails because the similarity to be accounted for is one of family resemblance rather than necessary or sufficient conditions:[5,9,14,18] such a rule, while successfully applying to *spring, shrink, drink*, would incorrectly apply to *bring–brought* and *fling–flung* and would fail to apply to *begin–began* and *swim–swam*, where it should apply.

Associationist theories also propose that regular and irregular patterns are computed by a single mechanism, but here the mechanism is an associative memory. A formal implementation in neural net terms is the "connectionist" model of Rumelhart and McClelland,[16] which consists of an array of input units, an array of output units, and a matrix of modifiable weighted links between every input and every output. None of the elements or links corresponds exactly to a word or rule. The stem is represented by turning on a subset of input nodes, each corresponding to a sound pattern in the stem. This sends a signal across each of the links to the output nodes, which represent the sounds of the past tense form. Each output node sums its incoming signals and turns on if the sum exceeds a threshold; the output form is the word most compatible with the set of active output nodes. During the learning phase, the past tense form computed by the network is juxtaposed with the correct version provided by a "teacher," and the strengths of the links and thresholds are adjusted so as to reduce the difference. By recording and superimposing associations between stem sounds and past sounds, the model improves its performance and can generalize to new forms to the extent that their sounds overlap with old ones. This process is qualitatively the same for regular and irregular verbs: *stopped* is produced because input *op* units were linked to output *opped* units by previous verbs; *clung* is produced because *ing* was linked to *ung*. As a result such models can imitate people's analogizing of irregular patterns to new forms.

The models, however, are inadequate in other ways.[5,17] The precise patterns of inflectional mappings in the world's languages are unaccounted for: the network can learn input–output mappings found in no human language, such as mirror-reversing the order of segments, and cannot learn mappings that are common, such as reduplicating the stem. The actual outputs are often unsystematic blends such as *mail–membled* and *tour–tourder*. Lacking a representation of words as lexical entries, distinct from their phonological or semantic content, the model cannot explain how languages can contain semantically unrelated homophones with different past tense forms such as *lie–lied* (prevaricate) and *lie–lay* (recline), *ring–rang* and *wring–wrung*, *meet–met* and *mete–meted*.

These problems call for a theory of language with both a computational component, containing specific kinds of rules and representations, and an associative memory system, with certain properties of connectionist models.[5,6,10] In such a theory, regular past tense forms are computed by a rule that concatenates an affix with a variable standing for the stem. Irregulars are memorized pairs of words, but the linkages between the pair members are stored in an associative memory structure fostering some generalization by analogy:[9,14,18] although *string* and *strung* are represented as separate, linked words, the mental representation of the pair overlaps in part with similar forms like *sling* and *bring*, so that the learning of *slung* is easier and extensions like *brung* can occur as the result of noise or decay in the parts of the representation that code the identity of the lexical entry.

Because it categorically distinguishes regular from irregular forms, the rule-association hybrid predicts that the two processes should be dissociable from virtually every point of view. With respect to the psychology of language use, irregular forms, as memorized items, should be strongly affected by properties of associative memory such as frequency and similarity, whereas regular forms should not. With respect to language structure, irregular forms, as memory-listed words, should be available as the input to other word-formation processes, whereas regular forms, being the final outputs of such processes, should not. With respect to implementation in the brain, because regular and irregular verbs are subserved by different mechanisms, it should be possible to find one system impaired while the other is spared. The predictions can be tested with methods ranging from reaction time experiments to the grammatical analysis of languages to the study of child development to the investigation of brain damage and genetic deficits.

LANGUAGE USE AND ASSOCIATIVE LAWS

Frequency

If irregular verbs are memorized items, they should be better remembered the more they are encountered. Indeed, children make errors like *breaked* more often for verbs their parents use in the past tense forms less frequently.[9,10,19] To adults, low-frequency irregular past tense forms like *smote, bade, slew,* and *strode* sound odd or stilted and often coexist with regularized counterparts such as *slayed* and *strided*.[5,18,20] As these psychological effects accumulate over generations, they shape the language. Old English had many more irregular verbs than Modern English, such as *abide–abode, chide–chid, gild–gilt;* the ones used with lower frequencies have become regular over the centuries.[18] Most surviving irregular verbs are used at high frequencies, and the 13 most frequent verbs in English – *be, have, do, say, make, go, take, come, see, get, know, give, find* – are all irregular.[21]

Although any theory positing a frequency-sensitive memory can account for frequency effects on irregular verbs (with inverse effects on their corresponding regularized versions),[20] the rule-associative-memory hybrid model predicts that regular inflection is different. If regular past tense forms can be computed on-line by concatenation of symbols for the stem and affix, they do not require prior storage of a past tense entry and thus need not be harder or stranger for low-frequency verbs than higher ones.[22]

Judgments by native English speakers of the naturalness of word forms bear this prediction out. Unlike irregular verbs, novel or low-frequency regular verbs, although they may sound unfamiliar in themselves, do not accrue any increment of oddness or uncertainty when put in the past tense: *infarcted* is as natural a past tense form of *infarct* as *walked* is of *walk*.[5] The contrast can be seen clearly in idioms and clichés, because they can contain a verb that is not unfamiliar itself but that appears in the idiom exclusively in the present or infinitive form. Irregular verbs in such idioms can sound strange when put in the past tense: Compare *You'll excuse me if I forgo the pleasure of reading your paper before it's published* with *Last night I forwent the pleasure of reading student papers,* or *I don't know how she can bear the guy* with *I don't know how she bore the guy*. In contrast, regular verbs in nonpast idioms do not sound worse when put in the past: compare *She doesn't suffer fools gladly* with *None of them ever suffered fools gladly*. Similarly, some regular verbs like *afford* and *cope* usually appear with *can't*, which requires the stem form, and hence have common stems but very low-frequency past tense forms.[21] But the uncommon *I don't know how he afforded it (coped)* does not sound worse than *He can't afford it (cope)*.

These effects can be demonstrated in quantitative studies:[20] Subjects' ratings of regular past tense forms of different verbs correlate significantly with their ratings of the corresponding stems ($r = 0.62$) but not with the frequency of the past form (-0.14, partialing out stem rating). In contrast, ratings of irregular past tense forms correlate less strongly with their stem ratings (0.32), and significantly with past frequency (0.29, partialing out stem rating).

Experiments on how people produce and comprehend inflected forms in real time confirm this difference. When subjects see verb stems on a screen and must utter the past form as quickly as possible, they take significantly less time (16- to 29-msec difference) for irregular verbs with high past frequencies than for irregular verbs with low past frequencies (stem frequencies equated), but show no such difference for regular verbs (< 2-msec difference).[23] When recognizing words, people are aided by having seen the word previously on an earlier trial in the experiment; their mental representation of the word has been "primed" by the first presentation. Presenting a regular past tense form speeds up subsequent recognition of the stem no less than presenting the stem itself (181-versus 166-msec reduction), suggesting that people store and prime only the stem and analyze a regular inflected form as a stem plus a suffix. In contrast, prior presentation of an irregular form is significantly less effective at priming its stem than presentation of the stem itself (39-versus 99-msec reduction), suggesting that the two are stored as separate but linked items.[24]

Similarity

Irregular verbs fall into families with similar stems and similar past tense forms, partly because the associative nature of memory makes it easier to memorize verbs in such families. Indeed, children make fewer overregularization errors for verbs that fall into families with more numerous and higher frequency members.[5,8–10,25] As mentioned above, speakers occasionally extend irregular patterns to verbs that are highly similar to irregular families (*brang*), and such extensions are seen in dialects.[13] A continuous effect of similarity has been measured experimentally: subjects frequently (44%) convert *spling* to *splung* (based on *string*, *sling*, etc.), less often (24%) convert *shink* to *shunk*, and rarely (7%) convert *sid* to *sud*.[14]

The rule-associative-memory theory predicts that the ability to generate regular past tense forms should not depend on similarity to existing regular verbs: The regular rule applies as a default, treating all nonirregular stems as equally valid instantiations of the mental symbol "verb." Within English vocabulary, we find that a regular verb can have any sound pattern, rather than falling into similarity clusters that complement the irregulars:[5] for example, *need–needed* coexists with *bleed–bled* and *feed–fed*, *blink–blinked* with *shrink–shrank* and *drink–drank*. Regular–irregular homophones such as *lie–lay*, *lie–lied*; *meet–met*, *mete–meted*; and *hang–hung*, *hang–hanged* are the clearest examples. Moreover verbs with highly unusual sounds are easily provided with regular pasts. Although no English verb ends in *-ev* or a neutral vowel,[21] novel verbs with these patterns are readily inflectable as natural past tense forms, such as *Yeltsin out-Gorbachev'ed Gorbachev* or *We rhumba'd all night*. Children are no more likely to overregularize an irregular verb if it resembles a family of similar regular verbs than if it is dissimilar from regulars, suggesting that regulars, unlike irregulars, do not form attracting clusters in memory.[10,25] Adults, when provided with novel verbs, do not rate regular past forms of unusual sounds like *ploamphed* as any worse, relative to the stem, than familiar sounds like *plipped* (similar to *clip, flip, slip*, etc.), unlike their ratings for irregulars.[15,26] In contrast, in associationist models both irregular and regular generalizations tend to be sensitive to similarity. For example the Rumelhart–McClelland model could not produce any output for many novel regular verbs that did not resemble other regulars in the training set.[5,15,17]

Organization of Grammatical Processes

Grammars divide into fairly autonomous submodules in which blocks of rules produce outputs that serve (or cannot serve) as the input for other blocks of rules. Linguistic research suggests an information flow of lexicon to derivational morphology (complex word-formation) to regular inflection, with regular and irregular processes encapsulated within different subcomponents.[27, 28] If irregular past tense forms are stored in memory as entries in the mental lexicon, then like other stored words they should be the input to rules of complex word formation. If regular past tense forms are computed from words by a rule acting as a default, they should be formed from the outputs of complex word formation rules. Two phenomena illustrate this organization.

A potent demonstration of the earlier point that regular processes can apply to any sound whatsoever, no matter how tightly associated with an irregular pattern, is "regularization-through-derivation": verbs intuitively perceived as derived from nouns or adjectives are always regular, even if similar or identical to an irregular verb. Thus one says *grandstanded*, not *grandstood*; *flied out* in baseball [from a fly (ball)], not *flew out*; *high-sticked* in hockey, not *high-stuck*.[5, 6,28] The explanation is that irregularity consists of a linkage between two word roots, the atomic sound-meaning pairings stored in the mental lexicon; it is not a link between two words or sound patterns directly. *High-stuck* sounds silly because the verb is tacitly perceived as being based on the noun root (*hockey*) *stick*, and noun roots cannot be listed in the lexicon as having any past tense form (the past tense of a noun makes no sense semantically), let alone an irregular one. Because its root is not the verb *stick* there is no data pathway by which *stuck* can be made available; to obtain a past tense form, the speaker must apply the regular rule, which serves as the default. Subjects presented with novel irregular-sounding verbs (for example, *to line-drive*) strongly prefer the regular past tense form (*line-drived*) if it is understood as being based on a noun ("to hit a line drive"), but not in a control condition for unfamiliarity where the items were based on existing irregular verbs ("to drive along a line"); here the usual irregular form is preferred.[6]

The effect, moreover, occurs in experiments testing subjects with no college education[6] and in preschool children.[29] This is consistent with the fact that many of these lawful forms entered the language from vernacular speech and were opposed by language mavens and guardians of "proper" style.[6, 13] "Rules of grammar" in the psycholinguists' sense, and their organization into components, are inherent to the computational systems found in all humans, not just those with access to explicit schooling or stylistic injunctions. These injunctions, involving a very different sense of "rule" as something that ought to be followed, usually pertain to minor differences between standard written and nonstandard spoken dialects.

A related effect occurs in lexical compounds, which sound natural when they contain irregular noun plurals, but not regular noun plurals: Compare *mice-infested* with *rats-infested*, *teethmarks* with *clawsmarks*, *men-bashing* with *guys-bashing*.[28] Assume that this compounding rule is fed by stored words. Irregulars are stored words, so they can feed compounding; regulars are computed at the output end of the morphology system, not stored at the input end, so they do not appear inside lexical compounds. This constraint has been documented experimentally in 3- to 5-year-old children:[30] when children who knew the word *mice* were asked for a word for a "monster who eats mice," they responded with *mice-eater* 90% of the time; but when children who knew *rats* were asked for a word for "monster who eats rats," they responded *rats-eater* only 2% of the time. The children could not have learned the constraint by recording whether adults use irregular versus regular plurals inside compounds. Adults do not use such compounds often enough for most children to have heard them: the frequency of English compounds containing any kind of plural is indistinguishable from zero.[21, 30] Rather, the constraint may be a consequence of the inherent organization of the children's grammatical systems.

Developmental and Neurological Dissociations

If regular and irregular patterns are computed in different subsystems, they should dissociate in special populations. Individuals with undeveloped or damaged grammatical systems and intact lexical memory should be unable to compute regular forms but should be able to handle irregulars. Conversely, individuals with intact grammatical systems and atypical lexical retrieval should handle regulars properly but be prone to overregularizing irregulars. Such double dissociations, most clearly demonstrated in detailed case studies, are an important source of evidence for the existence of separate neural subsystems. Preliminary evidence suggests that regular and irregular inflection may show such dissociations.

Children

Most of the grammatical structure of English develops rapidly in the third year of life.[31] One conspicuous development is the appearance of overregularizations like *comed*. Such errors constitute a worsening of past marking with time;

for months beforehand, all overtly marked irregular past forms are correct.[10] The phenomenon is not due to the child becoming temporarily overwhelmed by the regular pattern because of an influx of regular verbs, as connectionist theories[16] predict.[5, 10, 32] Instead it accompanies the appearance of the regular tense marking process itself: overregularizations appear when the child ceases using bare stems like *walk* to refer to past events.[8, 10] Say memorization of verb forms from parental speech, including irregulars, can take place as soon as words of any kind can be learned. But deployment of the rule system must await the abstraction of the English rule from a set of word pairs juxtaposed as nonpast and past versions of the same verb. The young child could possess memorized irregulars, produced probabilistically but without overt error, but no rule; the older child, possessing the rule as well, would apply it obligatorily in past tense sentences whenever he failed to retrieve the irregular, resulting in occasional errors.

Aphasics

A syndrome sometimes called agrammatic aphasia can occur after extensive damage to Broca's area and nearby structures in the left cerebral hemisphere. Labored speech, absence of inflections and other grammatical words, and difficulty comprehending grammatical distinctions are frequent symptoms. Agrammatics have trouble reading aloud regular inflected forms: *smiled* is pronounced as *smile*, *wanted* as *wanting*. Nonregular plural and past forms are read with much greater accuracy, controlling for frequency and pronounceability.[33] This is predicted if agrammatism results from damage to neural circuitry that executes rules of grammar, including the regular rule necessary for analyzing regularly inflected stimuli, but leaves the lexicon relatively undamaged, including stored irregulars which can be directly matched against the irregular stimuli.

Specific language impairment (SLI)

SLI refers to a syndrome of language deficits not attributable to auditory, cognitive, or social problems. The syndrome usually includes delayed onset of language, articulation difficulties in childhood, and problems in controlling grammatical features such as tense, number, gender, case, and person. One form of SLI may especially impair aspects of the regular inflectional process.[34] Natural speech includes errors like "We're go take a bus"; "I play musics"; "One machine clean all the two arena." In experiments, the patients have difficulty converting present sentences to past (32% for SLI; 78% for sibling controls). The difficulty is more pronounced for regular verbs than irregulars. Regular past forms are virtually absent from the children's spontaneous speech and writing, although irregulars often appear. In the writing samples of two children examined quantitatively, 85% of irregular pasts but 30% of regular pasts were correctly supplied. The first written regular past tense forms are for verbs with past tense frequencies higher than their stem frequencies; subsequent ones are acquired one at a time in response to teacher training, with little transfer to nontrained verbs. Adults' performance improves and their speech begins to sound normal but they continue to have difficulty inflecting nonsense forms like *zoop* (47% for SLI; 83% for controls). It appears as if their ability to apply inflectional rules is impaired relatively normally, enjoying their advantage of high frequencies; regular forms are memorized as if they were irregular.

SLI appears to have an inherited component. Language impairments have been found in 3% of first-degree family members of normal probands but 23% of language-impaired probands.[35] The impairment has been found to be 80% concordant in monozygotic twins and 35% concordant in dizygotic twins.[36] One case study[34] investigated a three-generation, 30-member family, 16 of whom had SLI; the syndrome followed the pattern of a dominant, fully penetrant autosomal gene. This constitutes evidence that some aspects of use of grammar have a genetic basis.

Williams syndrome

Williams syndrome (WS), associated with a defective gene expressed in the central nervous system involved in calcium metabolism, causes an unusual kind of mental retardation.[37] Although their Intelligence Quotient is measured at around 50, older children and adolescents with WS are described as hyperlinguistic with selective sparing of syntax, and grammatical abilities are close to normal in controlled testing.[37] This is one of several kinds of dissociation in which language is preserved despite severe cognitive impairments, suggesting that the language system is autonomous of many other kinds of cognitive processing.

WS children retrieve words in a deviant fashion.[37] When normal or other retarded children are asked to name some animals, they say *dog, cat, pig*; WS children offer *unicorn, tyrandon, yak, ibex*. Normal children speak of *pouring water*; WS children speak of *evacuating a glass*. According to the rule-associative-memory hybrid theory, preserved grammatical abilities and deviant retrieval of high-frequency words are preconditions for overregularization. Indeed, some WS children overregularize at high rates (16%), one of their few noticeable grammatical errors.[38, 39]

CONCLUSION

For hundreds of years, the mind has been portrayed as a homogeneous system whose complexity comes from the complexity of environmental correlations as recorded by a general-purpose learning mechanism. Modern research on language renders such a view increasingly implausible. Although there is evidence that the memory system used in language acquisition and processing has some of the properties of an associative network, these properties do not exhaust the computational abilities of the brain. Focusing on a single rule of grammar, we find evidence for a system that is modular, independent of real-world meaning, nonassociative (unaffected by frequency and similarity), sensitive to abstract formal distinctions (for example, root versus derived, noun versus verb), more sophisticated than the kinds of "rules" that are explicitly taught, developing on a schedule not timed by environmental input, organized by principles that could not have been learned, possibly with a distinct neural substrate and genetic basis.

Acknowledgments

I thank my collaborators A. Prince, G. Hickok, M. Hollander, J. Kim, G. Marcus, S. Prasada, A. Senghas, and M. Ullman, and thank T. Bever, N. Block, N. Etcoff, and especially A. Prince for comments. Supported by NIH grant HD 18381.

Notes

1. D. Hume, *Inquiry Concerning Human Understanding* (Bobbs-Merril, Indianapolis, 1955); D. Hebb, *Organization of Behavior* (Wiley, New York, 1949); D. Rumelhart and J. McClelland, *Parallel Distributed Processing* (MIT Press, Cambridge, 1986).
2. G. Leibniz, *Philosophical Essays* (Hackett, Indianapolis, 1989); A. Newell and H. Simon, *Science* **134**, 2011 (1961).
3. J. Fodor, *Modularity of Mind* (MIT Press, Cambridge, 1983).
4. N. Chomsky, *Rules and Representations* (Columbia Univ. Press, New York, 1980); E. Lenneberg, *Biological Foundations of Language* (Wiley, New York, 1967).
5. S. Pinker and A. Prince, *Cognition* **28**, 73 (1988).
6. J. Kim, S. Pinker, A. Prince, S. Prasada, *Cognitive Science* **15**, 173 (1991).
7. J. Berko, *Word* **14**, 150 (1958).
8. S. Kuczaj, *J. Verb. Learn. Behav.* **16**, 589 (1977).
9. J. Bybee and D. Slobin, *Language* **58**, 265 (1982).
10. G. Marcus, M. Ullman, S. Pinker, M. Hollander, T. Rosen, F. Xu, *Ctr. Cog. Sci. Occ. Pap.* **41** (Massachusetts Institute of Technology, Cambridge, 1990).
11. N. Chomsky and M. Halle, *Sound Pattern of English* (MIT Press, Cambridge, 1990).
12. O. Jespersen, *A Modern English Grammar on Historical Principles* (Allen and Unwin, London, 1961).
13. H. Mencken, *The American Language* (Knopf, New York, 1936).
14. J. Bybee and C. Moder, *Language* **59**, 251 (1983).
15. S. Prasada and S. Pinker, unpublished data.
16. D. Rumelhart and J. McClelland, in *Parallel Distributed Processing*, J. McClelland and D. Rumelhart, eds (MIT Press, Cambridge, 1986), pp. 216–71.
17. J. Lachter and T. Bever, *Cognition* **28**, 197 (1988). More sophisticated connectionist models of past tense formation employing a hidden layer of nodes have computational limitations similar to those of the Rumelhart–McClelland model (D. Egedi and R. Sproat, unpublished data).
18. J. Bybee, *Morphology* (Benjamins, Philadelphia, 1985).
19. In speech samples from 19 children containing 9684 irregular past tense forms (see note 10), aggregate overregularization rate for 39 verbs correlated $- 0.37$ with aggregate log frequency in parental speech. All correlations and differences noted herein are significant at $p = 0.05$ or less.
20. M. Ullman and S. Pinker, paper presented at the Spring Symposium of the AAAI, Stanford, 26 to 28 March 1991. Data represent mean ratings by 99 subjects of the

naturalness of the past and stem forms of 142 irregular verbs and 59 regular verbs that did not rhyme with any irregular, each presented in a sentence in counter-balanced random order.

21. N. Francis and H. Kucera, *Frequency Analysis of English Usage* (Houghton Mifflin, Boston, 1982).

22. Such effects can also occur in certain connectionist models that lack distinct representations of words and superimpose associations between the phonological elements of stem and past forms. After such models are trained on many regular verbs, any new verb would activate previously trained phonological associations to the regular pattern and could yield a strong regular form; the absence of prior training on the verb itself would not necessarily hurt it. However, the existence of homophones with different past tense forms (*lie–lay* versus *lie–lied*) makes such models psychologically unrealistic; representations of individual words are called for, and they would engender word familiarity effects.

23. S. Prasada, S. Pinker, W. Snyder, paper presented at the 31st Annual Meeting of the Psychonomic Society, New Orleans, 16 to 18 November 1990. The effects obtained in three experiments, each showing 32 to 40 subjects the stem forms of verbs on a screen for 300 msec and measuring their vocal response time for the past tense form. Thirty to 48 irregular verbs and 30 to 48 regular verbs were shown, one at a time in random order; every verb had a counterpart with the same stem frequency but a different past tense frequency (see note 21). In control experiments, 40 subjects generated third person singular forms of stems, read stems aloud, or read past tense forms aloud, and the frequency difference among irregulars did not occur; this shows the effect is not due to inherent differences in access or articulation times of the verbs.

24. R. Stanners, J. Neiser, W. Hernon, R. Hall, *J. Verb Learn. Verb Behav.* **18**, 399 (1979); S. Kempley and J. Morton, *Br. J. Psychol.* **73**, 441 (1982). The effect was not an artifact of differences in phonological or orthographic overlap between the members of regular and irregular pairs.

25. For 17 of 19 children studied (see note 10), the higher the frequencies of the other irregulars rhyming with an irregular, the lower its overregulation rate (mean correlation − 0.07, significantly less than 0). For the corresponding calculation with regulars rhyming with an irregular, no consistency resulted and the mean correlation did not differ significantly from zero.

26. Twenty-four subjects read 60 sentences containing novel verbs, presented in either stem form, a past form displaying an English irregular vowel change, or a past form containing the regular suffix. Each subject rated how good the verb sounded, with a 7-point scale; each verb was rated in each of the forms by different subjects. For novel verbs highly similar to an irregular family, the irregular past form was rated 0.8 points worse than the stem; for novel verbs dissimilar to the family, the irregular past form was rated 2.2 points worse. For novel verbs resembling a family of regular verbs, the regular past form was rated 0.4 points better than the stem; for novel verbs dissimilar to the family, the regular past form was rated 1.5 points better. This interaction was replicated in two other experiments.

27. M. Aronoff, *Annu. Rev. Anthropol.* **12**, 355 (1983); S. Anderson, in *Linguistics: The Cambridge Survey* (Cambridge Univ. Press, New York, 1988), vol. 1, pp. 146–91.

28. P. Kiparsky, in *The Structure of Phonological Representations*, H. van der Hulst and N. Smith, eds (Foris, Dordrecht, 1982).

29. J. Kim, G. Marcus, M. Hollander, S. Pinker, *Pap. Rep. Child Lang. Dev.*, in press.

30. P. Gordon, *Cognition* **21**, 73 (1985). The effect is not an artifact of pronounceability, as children were willing to say *pants-eater* and *scissors-eater*, containing *s*-final nouns that are not regular plurals.

31. R. Brown, *A First Language* (Harvard Univ. Press, Cambridge, 1973).

32. The proportion of regular verb tokens in children's and parents' speech remains unchanged throughout childhood, because high frequency irregular verbs (*make*, *put*, *take*, etc) dominate conversation at any age. The proportion of regular verb types in children's vocabulary necessarily increases because irregular verbs are a small fraction of English vocabulary, but this growth does not correlate with overregularization errors (see notes 3, 8).

33. O. Marin, E. Saffran, M. Schwartz, *Ann. N. Y. Acad. Sci.* **280**, 868 (1976). For example, regular *misers*, *clues*, *buds* were read by three agrammatic patients less accurately than phonologically matched plurals that are not regular because they lack a corresponding singular, like *trousers*, *news*, *suds* (45% versus 90%), even though a phonologically well-formed stem is available in both cases. In another study, when verbs matched for past and base frequencies and pronounceability were presented to an agrammatic patient, he read 56% of irregular past forms and 18% of regular past forms successfully (G. Hickok and S. Pinker, unpublished data).

34. M. Gopnik, *Nature* **344**, 715, (1990); *Lang. Acq.* **1**, 139 (1990); M. Gopnik and M. Crago, *Cognition*, in press.

35. J. Tomblin, *J. Speech Hear. Disord.* **54**, 287 (1989); P. Tallal, R. Ross, S. Curtiss, ibid., p. 167.

36. J. Tomblin, unpublished data.

37. U. Bellugi, A. Bihrle, T. Jernigan, D. Trauner, S. Doherty, *Am. J. Med. Genet. Suppl.* **6**, 115 (1990).

38. S. Curtiss, in *The Exceptional Brain*, L. Obler and D. Fein, eds (Guilford, New York, 1988).

39. E. Klima and U. Bellugi, unpublished data.

25

Children's Understanding of Notations as Domains of Knowledge versus Referential-Communicative Tools*

Liliana Tolchinsky Landsmann and Annette Karmiloff-Smith

OVERVIEW

Previous research has suggested that young children confound writing and number notation with drawing. We present two studies; a sorting task that required children to establish constraints on notational forms for writing and for numbers, and a production task that asked them to invent numbers, letters, and words that do not exist. The latter task was aimed at discovering whether the constraints used in the sorting task were implicitly represented in the structure of children's behavior, or were explicitly represented and therefore available for purposeful manipulation. We draw a distinction between notations as domains of knowledge to be explored as formal objects, and notations in their function as referential-communicative tools. Our results show that children as young as 4 do not confuse writing and number notation with drawing when considered as a domain of knowledge. However, it is not until about 6 years of age that children clearly separate the notational domains in their function as referential-communicative tools.

Most species generate *internal* representations, but there is something about the architecture of the human mind that enables us also to produce *external* representations, that is, notations of various forms. Humans use natural and cultural artifacts to record speech, quantities, information about different domains of knowledge, and to symbolize religious and mythical beliefs. The use of external notations extends human memory and communication. But, apart from being useful referential–communicative tools, the artifacts, products, and processes involved in notational activities constitute potential domains of knowledge in their own right.

* Previously published in *Cognitive Development*, 7 (1992), pp. 287–300.

Children's environments are pervaded by notations. Family homes and public places display pictures, written signs, clocks, calendars, and maps. These notations have different domains of reference and fulfill different referential-communicative functions. The pictures are *of* something: they depict objects, animals, scenes, and so forth. The maps display spatial locations from given perspectives. The written signs are *about* something: they encode and transmit linguistic messages. The figures and tallies in analog clocks refer to hours and minutes and regulate people's daily activities. Obviously, young children do not understand what these notations refer to or what they are used for. None the less, it is possible that even before they fully understand these notations, young children are sensitive to the formal differences between drawing, writing, and numerals.

Most studies of the development of writing and number notation have concentrated on children's ability to use them to interpret or express meanings (Bialystock, 1992; Gardner and Wolf, 1983). The focus of the present article is different. We raise the issue of whether or not the notational domain is a formal problem space for young children. In other words, do children relate to notational systems as domains of knowledge, or do children first understand notations in their function as referential-communicative tools? Are children sensitive to the different constraints inherent in each system, or do they consider all notations simply as drawings?

What Characterizes Notational Systems?

The particular ways that notations can be considered symbolic, and the similarities and differences between notational forms, have been the subjects of philosophical, anthropological, and historical enquiry (e.g., Cassirer, 1946; Coulmas, 1989; Goodman, 1976, 1978; Koch, 1955). Notations can be iconic or noniconic. Drawing is usually thought of as iconic, whereas writing and numerals are considered noniconic. However, all attempts to define differences between drawing and writing/number notation in terms of distinctions between realistic depictions of reality, versus arbitrary links to reality, turn out to be problematic (Goodman, 1976). We propose three distinguishing features for notation systems that go beyond the realism/arbitrary distinction. They are: *relative-closure constraint, element-string constraint*, and *referential-communicative constraint*.

The first feature concerns the *relative closure* of the conventional systems of writing and number notation versus the domain of drawing. Drawing constitutes a comparatively open system because it is always possible to invent and include new elements. By contrast, writing and number notation are relatively closed systems. Although new combinations of elements are infinite, the *elements* within each system are finite; invention and inclusion of new elements is exceedingly rare. This distinction is similar to the one made in linguistics between open-class categories (e.g., nouns and verbs) that admit new members, and closed-class categories (e.g., articles, prepositions, etc.) that do not.

A second feature that distinguishes drawing from notational systems is the *element-string constraint*. In both writing and number notation, strings are segmentable into discrete elements and retain separate meanings. In Goodman's terminology, notational systems are articulated into characters, and characters must be disjoint (Goodman, 1976). By contrast, in drawing it is difficult to define the equivalent of an element, that is, a segmentable graphic unit (see Willats, 1977, and Freeman, 1987, for interesting discussions in this respect).

The third feature concerns the *referential-communicative constraint*. Notational systems allow for what Goodman calls "authoritative identification of a work from performance to performance" (Goodman, 1976). In other words, there is a formal mapping both from the notation to the referent, and from the referent to the notation. For example, a musical score has a referential relationship with a piece of music and, conversely, a musical piece determines its notation. In writing, certain marks refer to a limited range of phonological segments and, conversely, given the pronunciation of a phonological segment, its written notation falls within a limited number of alternatives. This dual direction of referential mapping is exclusive to notational systems. It does not apply to drawing and other pictorial depictions.

A distinction must also be drawn between *writing* and *written language*. Although in the literature the two terms are often used interchangeably, a distinction should be made between the written notational system (writing), and the forms of discourse that have resulted from using the system in different circumstances and epochs (Biber, 1988; Halliday, 1989; Tannen, 1982). A text, that is, a piece of written language, is open to multiple interpretations, whereas writing, or, the actual string of written elements, is not.

DEVELOPMENTAL STUDIES OF NOTATIONAL SYSTEMS

Some studies of emergent literacy have shown that the differentiation between iconic and noniconic forms of notation is developmentally precocious. Furthermore, once the initial iconic/noniconic distinction is established, children impose a number of formal constraints on what qualifies as writing, for example, linearity, number of elements in a string, intrastring variety of elements, and so forth (Ferreiro and Teberosky, 1979; Lavine, 1977). Studies using sorting tasks have shown that preliterate children consider a notation "good for reading" if it contains more than two and less than eight or nine elements, and provided adjacent elements are not identical. Moreover, these constraints appear to be general across different orthographic systems (Tolchinsky Landsmann, 1990, in press). Thus far, however, no research has compared the constraints young children impose on written notation with those they impose on number notation.

The early iconic/noniconic differentiation and the formal constraints children use to sort written notation, both found in these studies, stand in sharp contrast with the popular view that young children confound drawing and writing. Such a conclusion has also been drawn from experimental studies that instruct young children to "write a letter to a friend" or to "leave a message for another addressee"; the children often produce drawings (McLane and McNamee, 1991; Sulzby, 1986). In our view, this apparent contradiction has to do with the fact that the former studies focused on children's understanding of notation as a domain of knowledge, whereas the latter studies concentrated on children's use of notation as a referential-communicative tool. What the different groups of studies suggest is that these two aspects of notational competence do not develop synchronously. The distinction between notation as a domain of knowledge and notation as a referential-communicative tool may also help to account for discrepant findings in studies focused on number notation (Allardice, 1977; Hughes, 1986; Sastre and Moreno, 1976; Sinclair and Sinclair, 1984). In experiments where number notation was used as a referential-communicative tool, it was again shown that young children frequently resort to drawing when asked to represent number.

The studies to be reported below raised two issues: (a) whether children impose different constraints on written notation versus number notation when these are focused on as domains of knowledge, and (b) whether the constraints that children impose on different notational systems are merely implicit in the structure of their sorting behaviors, or whether they are explicitly represented and therefore available for purposeful manipulation (see Karmiloff-Smith, 1986, 1991, 1992, for detailed discussion of the issue of representational flexibility and the passage from implicit to explicit representations). We present here two sorting tasks (writing and number) based on techniques used in earlier work on the written system (Ferreiro and Teberosky, 1979; Tolchinsky Landsmann, 1990), and a production task based on an earlier study of changes in children's capacity to manipulate their drawing procedures (Karmiloff-Smith, 1990).

STUDY 1

The purpose of Study 1 was to ascertain how children decide which combinations of elements belong to specific notational domains and which do not.

Method

Subjects Seventy-six children between the ages of 3;8 and 6;6 years (twenty-seven 4-year-olds, twenty-five 5-year-olds, and twenty-four 6-year-olds) participated in the study. All were from the same school in a lower-middle-class urban neighborhood of Barcelona. The school language was Catalan, but 40% of the subjects also spoke Spanish at home. All the children had attended the school since kindergarten. The pilot studies, carried out on monolingual English-speaking children, yielded similar findings, thereby suggesting that the bilingualism of our subjects did not affect the results.

Materials The materials consisted of two sets of 15 cards to be sorted. One set of cards was used for the written notation task, the other for the number

Number	Writing
09070	OBOLO
2222	*mmmm*
243727879	*bocabadats*
35240	METRO

243727879	BOCABADAT
15346	CLAUS
44444	TTTTT
$M¤6®	ΩTΔ8©
$7^0 3^5 1$	$P^0 M^E S$
iconic	iconic
9	P
00899070	*prlcst*
∥∥∥	∥∥∥
TAULA	*348*

FIGURE 25.1 Cards used in the two sorting tasks

notation task. Several criteria were varied to pin down the types of constraints children impose on sorting cards into different notational categories. These included: presence or absence of iconicity, presence or absence of linearity, variety of different letters/numbers versus a string of identical ones, long versus short strings (including single elements), separate versus cursively-linked elements, strings using conventional letters/numbers versus a string of abstract lines, and for the written domain, strings that are pronounceable versus a string of consonants only. The sets of cards for each notational domain are illustrated in figure 25.1. The variation of these different features made it possible to determine whether children impose different constraints on the domains of writing and number notation, and to compare the two.

Design Each child participated in both sorting tasks. Order of presentation was counterbalanced across children.

Procedure Children were tested individually in a room outside their classroom. For each task, the cards were randomly spread across the table in front of each child. Each child was then instructed as follows: "We are going to look at these cards together. Look carefully at each card and then put all those that are *not good for writing* on one side." Similar instructions were given for the number notation set. For each task, after three cards had been selected by the child, the experimenter asked for justifications for the choices or rejections. Note that the instruction to select negative exemplars of a class is more difficult than to select positive exemplars. However, this is an advantage for the researcher in that it ensures that children's choices cannot be based on mere recognition of prototypical members of the positive class.

Results and discussion

The results are analyzed in terms of the percentage of children spontaneously choosing particular cards as "not good for writing" who maintained their choices in the face of the experimenter's countersuggestions. Children who changed their minds or who rejected a card after a countersuggestion are not included. The same criteria were used for the number notation set.

The age groups have been collapsed because, except for two of the cards in the writing domain (a single letter and an unpronounceable string), results for the rest of the cards in the writing set and all of those in the number set showed no age differences. The results were clear. More than 95% of children at all ages distinguished between strings belonging to writing or number notation and those belonging to drawing: in both cases they overwhelmingly selected iconic cards as not good for either writing or number. They also selected, in 85% of cases, mixtures of elements from different systems as being not good exemplars of either domain. Furthermore, children drew a clear distinction between writing and number notation. Eighty percent of subjects at all ages chose strings with repeated identical elements as not good for writing, but did not do so for number notation with respect to strings of identical numerals. They clearly imposed a constraint on writing stipulating that strings must include a variety of different elements, but knew that for number notation such a constraint does not pertain. Moreover, they chose linked elements as bad exemplars of number notation, but accepted cursive writing for written notation. Table 25.1 summarizes the results in terms of whether or not children imposed particular constraints on each of the domains.

As mentioned above, two of the cards did produce age differences in the domain of writing. These were the single letter "P" and the unpronounceable string of consonants "prlcst." Whereas 67% of the 4-year-olds chose "P" as not good for writing, by 5 and 6 years of age 92% considered a single letter inadequate for writing. By contrast, a single number was almost never chosen

TABLE 25.1 Constraints imposed by children as a function of notational system

Features accepted	Number	Writing
Drawing	no	no
Mixture of systems	no	no
Single element	yes	no
Repetition of identical elements	yes	no
Linkage between elements	no	yes
Limited range for length of string	no	yes

327

as not good for number notation at any age. By 5 or 6 years old children think of writing in terms of strings rather than isolated elements.

The age trend with respect to the string of consonants showed an opposite trend to that of the single letter. At 4 years of age, only 28% of children chose "prlcst" as not good for writing, whereas by 5 and 6 years of age, 55% selected this card as not good for written notation. For most of the youngest subjects, it seems that the string of consonants is considered good for writing because it obeys the constraint of nonidentity of adjacent elements in a string. For the older children, by contrast, whether or not a string obeys vowel/consonant alternation affected their choices. Thus, "OBOLO," an unusual Spanish word that they did not know, but that obeys such regularities, was almost never selected as not good for writing.

In general, the results of the sorting tasks demonstrate how successful young children are at differentiating both writing and number notation from drawing, and at using different formal constraints to distinguish the domain of writing from that of number notation. Iconicity and cross-system mixtures are not considered to be good for writing or for number notation. Nonrepetition of identical elements is a constraint imposed on the writing system but not on the number system. Length is a constraint that applies more to written strings than to numerical strings. Linkage between elements is permissible for writing but not for number notation. These constraints hold true at all ages. However, while 4-year-olds consider strings to be appropriate for written notation if they obey the above constraints, 5- to 6-year-olds impose a further constraint on the written system: that the string obey the consonant/vowel regularities of the conventional written system. Thus, all children focus on differences between notational systems as domains of knowledge, but it is only the older children who start to become sensitive to the function of notations as potentially meaningful referential-communicative tools.

STUDY 2

Study 1 showed that children discriminate between notational systems according to specific constraints. The purpose of the second study was to ascertain whether the constraints that children used in the sorting tasks are embedded implicitly in the structure of their behavior, or whether they are explicitly represented and thus available for purposeful manipulation.

Method

Subjects Fifty-six children between the ages of 3;6 and 6;6 (with 20 subjects in each of the 4- and 5-year-old groups, and 16 in the 6-year-old group) were tested individually. All came from the same school as in Study 1, but had not participated in that study. All spoke Catalan at school, but this time 60% of the subjects also spoke Spanish at home. Again, they had all attended the school since kindergarten.

Materials   Children were given a selection of pencils and paper.

Design and procedure   Children were interviewed individually as in the previous experiment. They were first asked to write on paper their own name, as well as other names, words, letters, and numbers that they knew. These instructions were given irrespective of whether children could yet use the conventional systems. The experimenter then pointed to one of the child's productions, for example, a number, and said: "Here you made a number, now make a number that doesn't exist." The same procedure was used with children's productions of words and letters. Several different expressions were used to ensure that children understood the instructions: "an X (number, letter, word) that doesn't exist," "an X that you invent," "an X that no-one has ever seen before," "an X that is not an X," and so forth. When the instruction was to produce a letter or a word that doesn't exist, the experimenter used the verb "to write." However, when it concerned a number that doesn't exist, the experimenter used the expressions "to make a number that doesn't exist," or "to put a number here that doesn't exist," in order to avoid actually suggesting the use of elements from the written system. For the word category, the term "name" was sometimes used because this is the term children frequently used to refer to written words.

The order of the three categories (number, letter, word) was randomly varied across subjects.

Results and discussion

Protocols were first analyzed with respect to the features displayed when children produced real numbers, letters, and words, and then with respect to the types of change children introduced in order to produce non-numbers, non-letters, and non-words. On the basis of the analysis of these graphic differences, as well as of the process of production and the spontaneous oral comments that children made, the following four categories were used to classify children's productions of nonexistent categories:

1. *No violation:* Children in this category produced exemplars for the non-existent numbers, letters, and words that were barely distinguishable from those they produced for existing ones. Subjects who refused to produce nonexistent exemplars, despite having produced existing ones, were also included in this category.
2. *Violation of relative closure constraint:* Children in this category produced nonexistent numbers, letters, and words, by violating the feature of relative closure between open and closed systems. In other words, they transgressed the intersystem boundaries and used parts of the drawing system to make non-letters, non-numbers, and non-words. They also used elements of the number system to make non-words and non-letters, and vice versa.
3. *Violation of the element/string constraint:* Children in this category violated the specific constraints on strings of elements in a particular notational

system. If they had produced a string of different letters for a real word, they used a string of repeated identical letters for a non-word. If they had produced a single numeral for a real number, they offered a very lengthy string of numbers for a number that doesn't exist. For non-letters, they deformed the graphic shape by duplicating parts or changing the contour. A few children blurred the boundaries between elements and invented new units by amalgamating two letters or two numerals to produce non-letters and non-numbers.

4. *Violation of referential-communicative constraint:* Children in this category focused on the function of notations as referential-communicative tools. Thus, for non-words they announced that they would write "words that cannot be said," or "words that aren't anything"; for non-numbers they announced that they would produce "numbers so large that they couldn't possibly exist," or containing multiple zeros.

We illustrate each of the four categories below in figures 25.2 through 25.5. Figure 25.2 shows pairs of productions for a word and for a non-word, and a number and a non-number. Both come from Category 1 subjects who manifested no violations. It is important to note that children in Category 1 who displayed no capacity to produce nonexistent exemplars, none the less clearly distinguish between notational domains in their productions. They use, for example, a form of simile writing for written notation and ill- or well-formed numerals for the number domain.

Apart from those in Category 1, all other subjects, even some as young as 4 years of age, produced violations. Figure 25.3 shows two examples of violations of the relative closure constraint (Category 2), figure 25.4 provides several examples of how children violate the element/string constraint (Category 3), and figure 25.5 illustrates violations of the referential-communicative constraint (Category 4).

Table 25.2 shows the breakdown as a function of age and of violation category for productions of non-letters. Four-year-olds are relatively evenly distributed across the first three categories, producing drawings, numerals or deformed shapes for non-letters. Only at 5 years old do children start to violate the element/string constraint more consistently and, by 6 years of age, 73% of

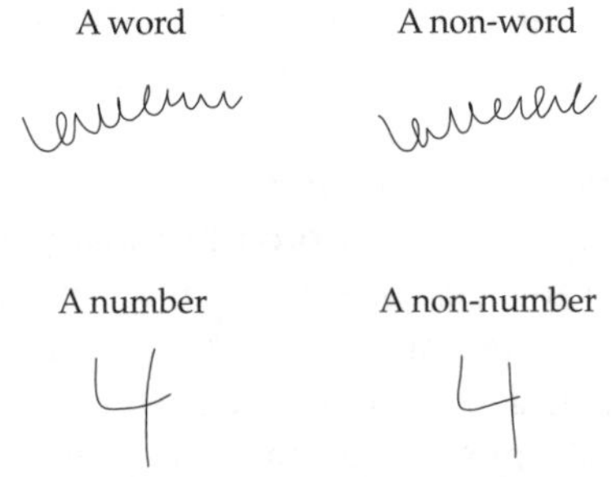

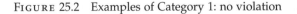

A word   A non-word

A number   A non-number

FIGURE 25.2   Examples of Category 1: no violation

A letter   A non-letter

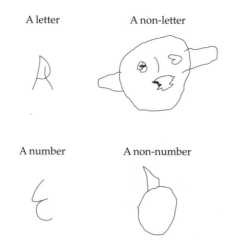

A number   A non-number

FIGURE 25.3   Examples of Category 2: violations of relative closure constraint

A word   A non-word

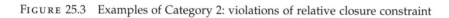

A number   A non-number

A letter   A non-letter

FIGURE 25.4   Examples of Category 3: violations of element/string constraint

A number   A non-number

A word   A non-word

A word   A non-word

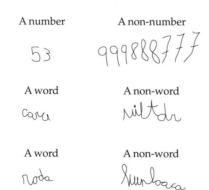

FIGURE 25.5   Examples of Category 4: violations of referential-communicative constraint

TABLE 25.2   Production of non-letters as a function of violation category and age

Age (Yrs)	No violation (%)	Violation of relative closure constraint (%)	Violation of element/ string constraint (%)	Violation of referential constraint (%)
4	30	35	35	0
5	25	25	50	0
6	13	14	73	0

children opt for this solution. No age group violated the referential-commun-icative constraint for producing non-letters (Category 4). To produce a non-letter under this category, they would have had to invent a novel sound and propose a novel graphic notation for it, something even a much older child or adult might find difficult. None the less, one 5-year-old did appear to be aiming for just that. She started voicing different sounds out loud, as if she were exploring their range, but halted when she spontaneously concluded that "all the letters already exist."

Table 25.3 gives the distribution of subjects' responses to the request for non-numbers. Again, they are categorized into the four categories outlined earlier. Unlike the case of non-letters, as many as 74% of 6-year-olds used violation of referential-communicative constraint as a means to produce non-numbers. Otherwise, responses were more or less evenly distributed across the remaining three categories at all ages.

Finally, table 25.4 shows the percentage of subjects who used each of the four violation categories to produce non-words. For non-words, 4- and 5-year-olds tended to use mainly the violation of the element/string constraint, whereas 87% of 6-year-olds again used the violation of the referential-communicative constraint.

TABLE 25.3   Production of non-numbers as a function of violation category and age

Age (Yrs)	No violation (%)	Violation of relative closure constraint (%)	Violation of element/ string constraint (%)	Violation of referential constraint (%)
4	25	35	30	10
5	15	30	20	35
6	13	0	13	74

TABLE 25.4   Production of non-words as a function of violation category and age

Age (Yrs)	No violation (%)	Violation of relative closure constraint (%)	Violation of element/ string constraint (%)	Violation of referential constraint (%)
4	30	25	45	0
5	10	15	45	30
6	0	0	13	87

General Discussion

Most developmental studies of emergent literacy and numeracy have focused on the referential and communicative function of writing and number notation. The questions we have addressed in this article are different, but complementary. Our work suggests that prior to becoming useful referential-communicative tools for children, writing and number notation are formal problem spaces in their own right for young children. Not only are the formal similarities and differences between notational systems a subject of philosophical enquiry, they are also something that young children are particularly sensitive to. The results of the sorting tasks in Study 1 show that from a very early age, the constraints that children impose on notational forms are domain specific. In other words, children do not treat notations as a single general domain of knowledge, nor do they confound number notation or writing with drawing. Rather, each specific manifestation of external notational systems (drawing, number notation, writing) is explored according to its own particular constraints. Moreover, a few children as young as 4, and the majority of 5- and 6-year-olds, have explicit representations of the constraints they impose on different notational systems as domains of knowledge, such that they can purposefully violate the constraints in order to produce nonexistent exemplars, as illustrated in Study 2.

Although it has been shown that many preschoolers resort to drawing when asked to "write a letter to a friend" or to "leave a message for an addressee," the distinction we have introduced between notation as a domain of knowledge and notation as a referential-communicative tool provides an explanation for the discrepancies in the results from different studies. When children use notations as referential-communicative tools, they focus on the *content* that they wish to convey, and may at young ages use drawing to express it. But, this is a far cry from confounding different notational systems as domains of knowledge. Our studies suggest that, unlike the view that writing and number notation are derived ontogenetically from drawing (e.g., Vygotsky, 1976), very early on children are sensitive to the domain-specific constraints operating on each notational domain.

References

Allardice, B. (1977). The development of written representation for some mathematical concepts. *Journal of Children's Mathematical Behavior*, **2**, 135–48.

Bialystok, E. (1992). Symbolic representation of letters and numbers. *Cognitive Development*, **7**, 301–16.

Biber, D. (1988). *Variations across Speech and Writing*. New York: Cambridge University Press.

Cassirer, E. (1946). *Language and Myth*. New York: Harper.

Coulmas, F. (1989). *The Writing Systems of the World*. Oxford: Blackwell.

Ferreiro, E., and Teberosky, A. (1979). *Los sistemas de escritura en el desarollo del niño* [Writing systems in ontogeny]. Mexico: Siglo XXI.

Freeman, N. H. (1987). Current problems in the development of representational picture production. *Archives de Psychologie*, **55**, 127–52.

Gardner, H., and Wolf, D. (1983). Waves and streams of symbolization. In D. R. Rogers and J. A. Sloboda (eds), *The Acquisition of Symbolic Skills*, London: Plenum.

Goodman, N. (1976). *Language of Arts*. Cambridge, England: Hackett.

Goodman, N. (1978). *Ways of Worldmaking*. Cambridge, England: Hackett.

Halliday, M. A. K. (1989). El linguage y el orden natural. In N. Fabb, D. Attridge, A. Durant, Y. Durant, and C. MacCabe (eds), *La linguística de la escritura: Debates entre linguage y literatura* [The linguistics of writing: Debates between language science and literature], Madrid: Visor.

Hughes, M. (1986). *Children and Number Difficulties in Learning Mathematics*. Oxford: Blackwell.

Karmiloff-Smith, A. (1986). From metaprocesses to conscious access: Evidence from children's metalinguistic and repair data. *Cognition*, **23**, 95–147.

Karmiloff-Smith, A. (1990). Constraints on representational change: Evidence from children's drawing. *Cognition*, **34**, 57–83.

Karmiloff-Smith, A. (1991). Beyond modularity: Innate constraints and developmental change. In S. Carey and R. Gelman (eds), *Epigenesis of Mind: Essays in Biology and Knowledge*, Hillsdale, NJ: Erlbaum.

Karmiloff-Smith, A. (1992). *Beyond Modularity: A Developmental Perspective on Cognitive Science*. Cambridge, MA: MIT Press/Bradford Books.

Koch, R. (1955). *The Book of Signs*. New York: Dover Books.

Lavine, L. (1977). Differentiation of letterlike forms in prereading children. *Developmental Psychology*, **23**, 89–94.

McLane, J. B., and McNamee, G. D. (1991). *Early Literacy*. Cambridge, MA: Harvard University Press.

Sastre, G., and Moreno, M. (1976). Représentation graphique de la quantité [Graphic representation of quantity]. *Bulletin de Psychologie*, **30**, 355–66.

Sinclair, A., and Sinclair, H. (1984). Preschoolers' interpretation of written numerals. *Human Learning*, **3**, 173–84.

Sulzby, E. (1986). *Emergent Writing and Reading in 5–6-year-olds: A Longitudinal Study*. Norwood, NJ: Ablex.

Tannen, D. (1982). The oral/literature continuum in discourse. In D. Tannen (ed.), *Spoken and Written Language: Exploring Orality and Literacy*, Norwood, NJ: Ablex.

Tolchinsky Landsmann, L. (1990). Early writing development: Evidence from different orthographic systems. In M. Spoolders (ed.), *Literacy Acquisition*, Norwood, NJ: Ablex.

Tolchinsky Landsmann, L. (in press). *El escribir y lo escrito* [Writing and the written word]. Barcelona: Anthropos.

Vygotsky, L. (1976). *Mind in Society*. Cambridge, MA: Harvard University Press.

Willats, J. (1977). How children learn to draw realistic pictures. *Quarterly Journal of Experimental Psychology*, **29**, 367–82.

26

Categorizing Sounds and Learning to Read – A Causal Connection*

L. Bradley and P. E. Bryant

Children who are backward in reading are strikingly insensitive to rhyme and alliteration.[1] They are at a disadvantage when categorizing words on the basis of common sounds even in comparison with younger children who read no better than they do. Categorizing words in this way involves attending to their constituent sounds, and so does learning to use the alphabet in reading and spelling. Thus the experiences which a child has with rhyme before he goes to school might have a considerable effect on his success later on in learning to read and to write. We now report the results of a large-scale project which support this hypothesis.

Our study combined two different methods. The first was longitudinal. We measured 403 children's skills at sound categorization before they had started to read, and related these to their progress in reading and spelling over the next 4 years: at the end of this time the size of our group was 368. The second was intensive training in sound categorization or other forms of categorization given to a subsample of our larger group. We used both methods because we reasoned that neither on its own is a sufficient test of a causal hypothesis and that the strengths and weaknesses of the two are complementary. Properly controlled training studies demonstrate cause–effect relationships, but these could be arbitrary; one cannot be sure that such relationships exist in real life. On the other hand, longitudinal studies which control for other variables such as intelligence do demonstrate genuine relationships; but it is not certain that these are causal. For example, simply to show that children's skills at categorizing sounds predict their success in reading later on would not exclude the possibility that both are determined by some unknown *tertium quid*. Thus the

---

* Previously published in *Nature*, **301**, 5899 (3 February 1983), pp. 419–21.

strength of each method makes up for the weakness of the other. Together they can isolate existing relationships and establish whether these are causal.

This combination of methods has not been used in studies of reading or, as far as we can establish, in developmental research in general.

Initially we tested 118 4-year-olds and 285 5-year-old children (table 26.1) on categorizing sounds. None of the children could read (that is, were able to read any word in the Schonell reading test). Our method, as before[1] was to say three or four words per trial, all but one of which shared a common phoneme (table 26.2): the child had to detect the odd word. There were 30 trials. In such a task the child must remember the words as well as categorize their sounds. To control for this we also gave them 30 memory trials: the child heard the same words and had to recall them straightaway. In addition we tested verbal intelligence (EPVT).

At the end of the project (as well as at other times) we gave the children standardized tests of reading and spelling, and we also tested their IQ (WISC/R)

TABLE 26.1 Details of sample tested on categorizing sounds

	Children initially tested at age 4 yr	Children initially tested at age 5 yr
N at end of project	104	264
Initial tests		
Mean age (months)	58.62	65.52
Mean EPVT	110.62	109.39
Final tests		
Mean age (months)	101.85	101.42
Mean IQ (WISC)	113.38	106.79
Mean reading age (months)		
Schonell	103.13	100.03
Neale	105.13	101.30
Mean spelling age (months)		
Schonell	97.27	93.94

TABLE 26.2 Examples of words used in initial sound categorization tests and mean scores on these tests

	4-yr group				5-yr group				
	Words given to children			Mean correct (out of 10)	Words given to children				Mean correct (out of 10)
Sounds in common									
First sound	hill	pig	pin	5.69 (1.90)	bud	bun	bus	rug	5.36 (2.29)
	bus	bun	rug		pip	pin	hill	pig	
Middle sound	cot	pot	hat	7.53 (1.96)	lot	cot	hat	pot	6.89 (2.35)
	pin	bun	gun		fun	pin	bun	gun	
End sound	pin	win	sit	7.42 (2.09)	pin	win	sit	fin	6.67 (2.33)
	doll	hop	top		doll	hop	top	pop	

Standard deviations given in parentheses.

to exclude the effects of intellectual differences. To check that our results were specific to reading and spelling and not to educational achievement in general we also included a standardized mathematical test (MATB-NFER), which we administered to 263 of our total sample of 368.

There were high correlations between the initial sound categorization scores and the children's reading and spelling over 3 years later (table 26.3). Stepwise multiple regressions established that these relationships remained strong even when the influence of intellectual level at the time of the initial and the final tests and of differences in memory were removed (table 26.3). In every case categorizing sound accounted for a significant proportion of the variance in reading and spelling with these other factors controlled.

So a definite relationship does exist between a child's skill in categorizing sounds and his eventual success in reading and spelling. The design of the project, for the reasons just given, included a training study as a check that any such relationship is a causal one: 65 children were selected from our sample and divided into four groups closely matched for age, verbal intelligence and their original scores on sound categorization. These children were drawn from those with lower scores on sound categorization (at least two standard deviations below the mean); they could not read when the training began. Starting in the second year of the project two of the groups (I and II) received intensive training in categorizing sounds. The training involved 40 individual sessions which were spread over 2 years. With the help of coloured pictures of familiar objects the children were taught that the same word shared common

TABLE 26.3 Correlations between initial sound categorization and final reading and spelling levels

Correlations between initial scores and final scores

| | Initial scores: | | | | | |
	Sound categorization		EPVT		Memory	
Final scores	4	5	4	5	4	5
Reading: Schonell	0.57	0.44	0.52	0.39	0.40	0.22
Reading: Neale	0.53	0.48	0.52	0.44	0.40	0.25
Spelling: Schonell	0.48	0.44	0.33	0.31	0.33	0.20

Multiple regressions testing relationship of initial sound categorization to final reading and spelling levels

	Schonell reading		Neale reading		Schonell spelling	
	4	5	4	5	4	5
% Of total variance accounted for by all variables	47.98	29.88	47.55	34.52	33.59	24.77
% Of total variance accounted for by sound categorization*	9.84†	4.06†	6.24†	4.56†	8.09†	5.59†

* IQ, EPVT, final CA and memory controlled.
† $P < 0.001$.

beginning (hen, hat), middle (hen, pet) and end (hen, man) sounds with other words and thus could be categorized in different ways. Group I received this training only, but group II in addition was taught, with the help of plastic letters, how each common sound was represented by a letter of the alphabet (see note 2 for further details of this method). The other two groups were controls. Group III was also taught over the same period in as many sessions and with the same pictures how to categorize but here the categories were conceptual ones; the children were taught that the same word could be classified in several different ways (for example, hen, bat (animals); hen, pig (farm animals)). Group IV received no training at all.

The training had a considerable effect which was specific to reading and spelling (table 26.4). At the end of the project group I (trained on sound categorization only) was ahead of group III (trained on conceptual categorization only) by 3–4 months in standardized tests of reading and spelling. This suggests a causal relationship between sound categorization and reading and spelling. Group II (trained with alphabetic letters as well as on sound categorization) succeeded even better than group I (trained on sound categorization only) in reading and particularly in spelling. This suggests that training in sound categorization is more effective when it also involves an explicit connection with the alphabet. That the relationship is specific to these two skills is shown by the mathematics results, where the differences were a great deal smaller.

Analyses of covariance, in which the covariates were the children's final IQ scores and their age at the time of the final reading and spelling tests, established that the group differences were significant in the case of reading (Schonell: $F = 5.23$; d.f.3,58; $P < 0.003$. Neale: $F = 7.80$; d.f.3,58; $P < 0.001$) and of spelling ($F = 12.18$; d.f.3,58; $P < 0.001$)) but not in the case of mathematics ($F = 1.64$; d.f.3,39; P, not significant). Post tests (Tukey's HSD) showed that

TABLE 26.4 Training study: details of groups and mean final reading, spelling and mathematics levels

		Mean scores			
		Experimental groups		Control groups	
Groups		I	II	III	IV
N		13	13	26	13
Aptitude tests					
Initial EPVT		103.00	103.00	102.34	102.69
Final IQ (WISC/R)		97.15	101.23	102.96	100.15
Final educational tests					
Schonell: reading age (months)		92.23	96.96	88.48	84.46
Neale: reading age (months)		93.47	99.77	89.09	85.70
Schonell: spelling age (months)		85.97	98.81	81.76	75.15
	N	9	8	20	7
Maths MATB (ratio score)		91.27	91.09	87.99	84.13

Reading, spelling and mathematics mean scores are adjusted for two covariates: age and IQ.

group II was significantly better than both control groups (groups III and IV) in Schonell and in Neale reading ($P < 0.05$) and in Schonell spelling ($P < 0.01$). There was no significant difference between groups I and II (the two groups trained in sound categorization) in the two reading tests but group II did surpass group I in spelling ($P < 0.05$). Although reading and spelling scores in group I were always ahead of those of group III this difference did not reach significance in the post tests. But the consistent 3–4-month superiority of group I over group III does strongly suggest that training in sound categorization affects progress in reading and spelling. Group I was significantly better than group IV (the untrained control group) in the two reading tests and in the spelling test ($P < 0.05$). On the other hand there were no significant differences at all between the two control groups (III and IV).

Put together, our longitudinal and training results provide strong support for the hypothesis that the awareness of rhyme and alliteration which children acquire before they go to school, possibly as a result of their experiences at home, has a powerful influence on their eventual success in learning to read and to spell. Although others have suggested a link between phonological awareness and reading,[3-5] our study is the first adequate empirical evidence that the link is causal. Our results also show how specific experiences which a child has before he goes to school may affect his progress once he gets there.

ACKNOWLEDGEMENTS

We thank Morag Maclean for help with gathering and analysing the data, the Oxford Education Authority and the schools for their cooperation, and the SSRC for supporting our research.

NOTES

1. Bradley, L., and Bryant, P. E. *Nature* **271**, 746–7 (1978).
2. Bradley, L. *Assessing Reading Difficulties* (Macmillan, London, 1980).
3. Goldstein, D. M. *J. Educ. Psychol.* **68**, 680–8 (1976).
4. Liberman, I., et al. in *Toward a Psychology of Reading*, eds Reber, A., and Scarborough, D. (L. Erlbaum Association, Hillsdale, New Jersey, 1977).
5. Lunderg, I., Olofsson, A., and Wall, S. *Scand. J. Psychol.* **21**, 159–73 (1980).

Part VI

EMOTIONAL AND SOCIAL DEVELOPMENT

27

SELF DEVELOPMENT AND SELF-CONSCIOUS EMOTIONS*

Michael Lewis, Margaret Wolan Sullivan, Catherine Stanger and Maya Weiss

<table>
<tr><td>

Lewis and his colleagues distinguish different types of emotion. Primary emotions include joy, fear, anger, sadness, disgust, and surprise, and these are all found in early infancy. As infancy progresses, an understanding of the self emerges, and with it self-conscious emotions. These secondary emotions include embarrassment, empathy, and perhaps envy, and they are characterized by self-referential behaviour – the ability to recognize oneself. The classic test of self-recognition is the 'rouge on the nose test'. In this, a spot of rouge is applied to the infant's nose, usually by the mother, but the infant is unaware of the application (the mother pretends to wipe her infant's face). The infant is then placed in front of a mirror and the most reliable indicator of self-recognition is mark-directed behaviour such as touching the spot on the nose. Lewis et al. report that those infants who recognize themselves (shown either by touching their nose, or by other behaviours) are able to show embarrassment, but it does not occur unless self-referential behaviour exists. Infants can discriminate themselves from others in early infancy, but it is the ability to *consider* one's self that allows for self-conscious emotions to emerge.

</td><td>

EDITORS' INTRODUCTION

</td></tr>
</table>

<table>
<tr><td>

In each of 2 studies, the mirror-rouge technique was used to differentiate children into those who showed self-recognition and those who did not. In Study 1, 27 children (aged 9–24 months) were observed in 2 experimental situations thought to differentially elicit fear and embarrassment behaviors. In Study 2, 44 children (aged 22 months) were seen in the situations of Study

</td><td>

OVERVIEW

</td></tr>
</table>

* Previously published in *Child Development*, **60** (1989), pp. 146–56.

1 and in 3 additional contexts thought to elicit embarrassment behavior. The results of both studies indicate that embarrassment but not wariness was related to self-recognition.

This article explores the relation between self development as measured by self-recognition and the expression of fear and embarrassment. Fear, but not embarrassment, has been considered a primary emotion (Tomkins, 1963). Our general hypothesis is that specific cognition skills are necessary for the emergence of the secondary emotions, although they are not necessary for the primary emotions. In particular, self-referential behavior is not necessary for the emergence of fear but is necessary for the emergence of embarrassment.

The current literature on emotions in the first 2 years focuses on the appearance of what has been called the fundamental or primary emotions (Lewis and Michalson, 1983). These emotions are characterized both by their early appearance and by having prototypic and universal facial expressions. Beyond the appearance of these early emotions, the emergence of other emotions remains relatively uncharted, although some empirical work on pride and guilt, especially within an achievement situation, has recently appeared (Geppert and Kuster, 1983; Heckhausen, 1984).

Theories regarding the origins of the secondary emotions and their dynamics and relation to one another are largely untested, perhaps because measurement methods, operational definitions, and a catalog of possible emotions are not well developed. The appearance of some emotions after the emergence of the primary ones has led to their classification as secondary or derived emotions (Lewis and Michalson, 1983; Plutchik, 1970). The use of the terms primary, secondary, or derived promotes a number of alternative views regarding the course of emotional development. One model presumes that these later emotions are derived from the earlier ones and are composed of combinations of the primary emotions, as all colors are composed from the three primary ones (Plutchik, 1970). Another model considers that these secondary emotions follow the primary ones but are not constructed from these earlier ones (Izard, 1977). Still another model holds that emotions are tied to cognitive processes; those needing the least cognitive support emerge first, and those needing more emerge later (Lewis and Michalson, 1983). To the degree that the earlier, primary emotions contribute to cognitive development, it can be said that they are indirectly related to the secondary or derived emotions (Lewis, Sullivan, and Michalson, 1984).

Although the sequence of emergence of primary emotions has yet to be fully articulated, it seems that by 12 months of age, they all have appeared. Even so, it is not until the middle of the second year that the secondary emotions are observed (Borke, 1971; Lewis and Brooks-Gunn, 1979a; Stipek, 1983). More elaborate cognitive abilities either are necessary for, or occur prior to, the emergence of this new class of emotions – abilities that appear between the end of the first year and the middle of the second year of life.

Figure 27.1 presents a general developmental model. In Stage 1, the primary emotions appear. The timing of the emergence of particular primary emotions is undetermined as yet; interest, joy, physical distress, and disgust expressions appear to be present at or shortly after birth (Izard, 1977).[1] Anger expressions have been observed as early as 4 months (Stenberg, Campos, and Emde, 1983), surprise by 6 months (Charlesworth, 1969), and given the appropriate eliciting circumstances, surprise, anger, fear, and sad expressions can be observed in 10-week-old infants (Sullivan and Lewis, in press).

In Stage 2, self-referential behavior emerges, although the self system has been undergoing development over the first 2 years of life. Self–other differentiation appears first, followed by object permanence, which appears around 8 months, even though permanence is not consolidated until 18 months or so (Piaget, 1954). Self-referential behavior has a developmental course and appears between 15 and 24 months of age (Bertenthal and Fischer, 1978; Lewis and Brooks-Gunn, 1979b).

The appearance and consolidation of these cognitive skills provide the underpinning for the emergence of Stage 3, the first class of secondary emotions. Self-conscious emotions are characterized by self-referential behavior and include embarrassment, empathy, and perhaps envy. These emotions appear before or around the second birthday. At the same time, children

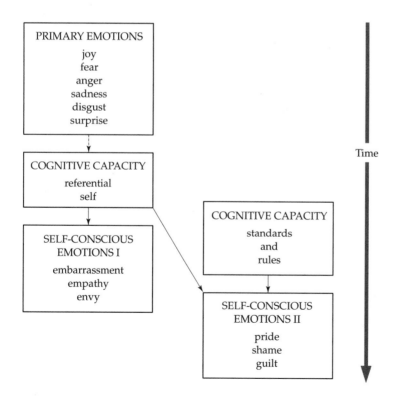

FIGURE 27.1 A general model of the interface between cognition and the development of self-conscious emotions

learn about other aspects of their social world, including emotional scripts (Michalson and Lewis, 1985) and rules of conduct that allow them to evaluate their own production and behavior (Kagan, 1981). This leads to the second class of self-conscious emotions – self-evaluative emotions, such as guilt, shame, and pride. Self-evaluative emotions emerge after the self-conscious emotions since they require more cognitive capacity.

In order to observe the relation between self-referential behavior and these secondary emotions, it is necessary (1) to observe the development of two classes of emotion, one associated with primary, the other with self-conscious emotions, and (2) to study their relation to self-referential behavior. The primary emotion of fear (or wariness) will appear early and not require self-referential behavior, while embarrassment should emerge with or following self-referential behavior.

Study 1

Method

Subjects The subjects were 27 infants divided into three age groups: nine were between 9 and 12 months ($\bar{X}$ age: 10.5 months); 10 were aged 15–18 months ($\bar{X}$ age: 17 months); and eight were aged 21–24 months ($\bar{X}$ age: 22.5 months). Data from three additional subjects were omitted from analysis because of an uncooperative child, a videotape problem, and failure of the mother to follow instructions.

Apparatus and procedure Each subject was given a Bayley Test of Mental Maturity in addition to the three experimental conditions, the order of which was counterbalanced across all subjects. All conditions were videotaped.

FACING THE STRANGER The child was seated in a high chair while the mother sat close by in a laboratory room (3 × 4 m). At a signal, an unfamiliar woman appeared in the door and slowly walked toward the child, taking about 15 seconds to reach the infant, whereupon she touched the subject's hand, turned, and left the room.

FACING THE MIRROR The same infants received two different procedures using a mirror. In both situations, the infant was placed in front of a one-way mirror (46 × 89 cm) mounted on a large (1.22 × 2.44 cm) sheet of plywood behind which a videocamera was placed.

In the first procedure, on the experimenter's signal the infant was placed in front of the mirror by the mother. The child's facial and gestural response in front of the mirror was obtained from the videotape. In the second procedure, nonscented rouge was applied to the infants' noses by their mothers, who pretended to wipe their child's face. The children were placed in front of the mirror and their behavior toward the marked nose was observed (see Lewis and Brooks-Gunn, 1979a, for a more specific description).

Measures

SELF-RECOGNITION   Mark-directed behavior (touching of the spot on the nose) during the mirror-rouge episode has been found to be the most reliable indicator of self-recognition in numerous studies (Lewis and Brooks-Gunn, 1979a), and served as the index of self-referential behavior. Nose touching was scored from videotape for all subjects by two coders; reliability was 100%. Coding of self-recognition was carried out independently of coding the emotions and was done by different coders.

FEAR/WARINESS   The prototypic situation for studying fear in young children has been the approach of a stranger. The appearance of full-blown fear or distress reactions to the stranger approach is not a universal reaction (Rheingold and Eckerman, 1973); however, mild negative reactions and inhibited behavior have been noted and termed wariness (Lewis and Rosenblum, 1974).

Wariness was defined as an attentive look characterized by a neutral or sober facial expression accompanied by a sudden inhibition of ongoing vocal or other behavior and was followed by gaze aversion. All three components were required to be present in the designated sequence in order for wariness to be scored. Whenever they occurred, fear expressions and crying were coded. A fear face was defined as it is described in the MAX coding system (Izard and Dougherty, 1982). Crying also was scored. Interobserver reliability, the number of agreements over number of agreements plus number of disagreements, was (90%) fear, (92%) wariness, and (98%) cry.

EMBARRASSMENT   Darwin (1872/1965) was the first to describe self-conscious emotions, including the phenomenon of blushing, although he used self-conscious emotion terms somewhat interchangeably. Izard (1977) and Tomkins (1963) treated shame and embarrassment as behaviorally identical. Embarrassment has been defined to include blushing (originally identified by Darwin in 1872) and a 'silly smile' and/or laughter, particularly giggling (Buss, 1980). Hand gestures and body movements also have been implicated as components of embarrassment and serve to distinguish it from amusement (Edelman and Hampson, 1981; Geppert, 1986).

A prototypical eliciting situation does not exist for embarrassment. Buss (1980) has discussed several situations, including breaches of privacy, public self-consciousness, and overpraise. Public self-consciousness, which may be a quite useful procedure with young children, may be elicited by viewing the self in a mirror as others watch. Although it may seem counterintuitive to expect a mirror to elicit embarrassment (it is not a social situation, for example), viewing oneself in a mirror is an attentional manipulation, and one which can direct attention to specific aspects of the self. Amsterdam (1972), Dixon (1957), and Schulman and Kaplowitz (1977) all reported instances of self-conscious behavior in young children viewing themselves in mirrors.

The behavioral criteria for embarrassment were selected by relying primarily on the descriptions of Buss (1980), Edelman and Hampson (1981), and

Geppert (1986). The behaviors necessary to score embarrassment were a smiling facial expression followed by a gaze aversion and movement of the hands to touch hair, clothing, face, or other body parts. These hand gestures appear to capture the nervous movements previous investigators state are characteristic of embarrassment. Such body touching could accompany smiling/gaze avert, or follow it immediately. All three behaviors were required for a person to be scored as having shown embarrassment, although very similar findings as those to be reported were found when only smiling and gaze aversion were used as the criteria. Blushing was not used as a criterion for embarrassment since it appears to be an infrequent response, even in older preschool children (Buss, 1980). Interobserver reliability for embarrassment was 85%.

Results

A dichotomous (yes/no) score for self-recognition, crying, fear, wariness, and embarrassed faces was obtained. Table 27.1 presents these data by age and condition.

STRANGER CONDITION   Few subjects cried or showed a fear face, although most showed a wary face. There was a significant difference between wary (and cry) and embarrassed faces ($Z = 4.83$, $p < .01$) and cry and embarrassed faces ($Z = 5.00$, $p < .01$). While there were no age differences in wary face, there were age differences in the cry face, $\chi^2(2) = 12.02, p < .01$, with the younger subjects showing the most cry.

MIRROR CONDITION   No subjects showed wariness (two showed crying), but 10 subjects showed embarrassment (Wilcoxon $T = 2.00$, $p < .005$). Nine subjects cried and five showed a fear face in the stranger approach, but only two subjects cried, and one showed a fear face in the mirror condition ($Z = 4.89, p < .01, Z = 3.77, p < .01$, respectively). While 10 subjects showed

TABLE 27.1   Distribution of subjects at each age who exhibit various emotional behaviors during stranger approach and before a mirror

AGE (in months)	N	Cried (n)	Fear (n)	Wary (n)	Embarrassed (n)
Stranger:					
9–12	9	7	1	7	1
15–18	10	1	3	10	1
21–24	8	1	1	6	0
Total	27	9	5	23	2
Mirror:					
9–12	9	2	1	0	2
15–18	10	0	0	0	3
21–24	8	0	0	0	5
Total	27	2	1	0	10

embarrassment in the mirror condition, only two showed it in the stranger approach $(Z = 2.74, p < .01)$. The number who showed embarrassment increased with age, $\chi^2(2) = 9.90, p < .01$.

SELF-RECOGNITION BEHAVIOR   Ten of 27 children showed mark-directed behavior. None touched their noses during either the non-rouge mirror situation or the stranger condition. Age changes were significant, $\chi^2(2) = 5.5, p < .01$, and consistent with prior findings (Lewis, Brooks-Gunn, and Jaskir, 1985).

Relationship between self-recognition and emotional expression   A chi-square ana-lysis was conducted to determine the relation of both wariness and embarrass-ment to self-recognition. Yates's corrected chi squares for the total sample $(n = 27)$ and Fischer's exact probability, when the data for the 15–24-month-olds were examined $(n = 18)$, were used. Wariness was not significantly asso-ciated with self-recognition; touchers and nontouchers were equally likely to exhibit wariness, 80% versus 82%, respectively. Embarrassment was more likely to occur for subjects who touched their noses than for those who did not, $\chi^2(1) = 5.32, p < .02$.[2] Of these subjects who showed embarrassment, 80% also touched their noses. Thus, despite the low level of embarrassment exhibited in the study, almost all subjects who exhibited embarrassment touched their noses.

Relationship between self-recognition, emotional expression, and general cognitive ability   The significant relation between self-recognition and embarrassment and the lack of relation between self-recognition and wariness might be due to a third factor, that is, the child's general cognitive ability. To test for this, we examined children's scores on the Bayley Scales of Infant Development and found no relation between the MDI scores and their performance on any of the three tasks.

Discussion

Infants' responses to the stranger approach situation were consistent with the literature (Rheingold and Eckerman, 1973). Infants showed wariness more than fear. Wariness was expressed when infants faced a stranger and not when they were exposed to a mirror. Wariness, like fear, theoretically need not involve a referential self, although it does require detection of the familiar versus novel and possibly self–other discrimination.

Embarrassment was seen in the mirror, but not in the stranger situation. Mirrors direct the child's attention to itself and result in embarrass-ment (Amsterdam, 1972). The relatively moderate frequency of embarrassment may be attributable to the situation used to elicit it. Even so, embarrassment in the older two age groups (15–24-month-olds) was moderately high; 44% of the subjects exhibit this behavior.

The relation between self-recognition ability and embarrassment but not wariness was supported. The overwhelming number of subjects who showed embarrassment also touched their noses in self-recognition. No evidence was found for a relation between recognition and wariness or the effects of general cognitive ability on these associations.

STUDY 2

A second study was undertaken to further pursue these results. Besides seeking to replicate the findings, Study 2 addressed some of the specific issues raised. Age changes in self-recognition and embarrassment may have produced a spurious association between self-referential behavior and embarrassment. Use of more subjects all of the same age would not confound the age variable. Although other variables may affect the relation between self-recognition and embarrassment, the results of Study 1 indicate that general cognitive ability is not one of these factors.

The use of more than one situation to elicit embarrassment provides an opportunity to explore situations likely to elicit this emotion. Since Buss (1980) has suggested that exposure and overpraise may elicit embarrassment, we chose, besides the mirror situation, to look at three other conditions likely to lead to embarrassment. Moreover, looking at four situations as elicitors of embarrassment permits an assessment of the amount of embarrassment each child shows by looking at the number of times the child exhibited this emotion.

Method

Subjects The subjects were 44 children, 19 females and 25 males, who were part of a short-term longitudinal study of emotional development. The mean age of the sample was 22 months (±2 weeks).

Procedures Each subject received five emotion-eliciting situations administered in a random order. Each was videotaped, and close-up views of the child's face and upper body were obtained. The situations were as follows.

THE STRANGER SITUATION The situation was conducted as in Study 1 except that a small table and chair were used in lieu of the high chair. An unfamiliar female other than the experimenter served as the stranger during the approach sequence.

THE MIRROR SITUATION The mirror procedure was the same as in Study 1 and included two segments – one without rouge, which served as the embarrassment situation, and one with rouge, which provided the index of self-referential behavior.

OVERCOMPLIMENT SITUATION The experimenter initiated interaction with the child, during which she lavishly complimented the child in an effusive manner. A series of four to five compliments were made about the child or his or her appearance. For example, the child was told he was smart, cute, had beautiful hair, and had lovely clothes, etc.

REQUEST-TO-DANCE SITUATIONS (MOTHER AND EXPERIMENTER) In these two situations, the experimenter handed the mother a small tambourine and asked the mother to coax the child to dance, or did so herself. They each said, "Let's see you dance, dance for me, I'll sing 'Old MacDonald' [or a song familiar to the child]." The dance situation was utilized since conspicuousness is thought to be an elicitor of embarrassment (Buss, 1980). The episode terminated either when the child complied and danced, or upon direct refusal.

Measures Fear, cry, wariness, and embarrassment, along with self-recognition, were defined and coded as in Study 1. Interobserver reliabilities were fear face (92%), wariness (92%), cry (95%), embarrassment (87%), and self-recognition (100%).

Results

Table 27.2 presents the numbers and percentage of subjects by sex showing fear face, crying, wariness, and embarrassment for each of the five conditions. Given the frequencies, only wariness and embarrassment were analyzed.

TABLE 27.2 Emotional expression by experimental condition

					Expression				
		Wary		Fear		Cried		Embarrassed	
Condition	N	n	%	n	%	n	%	n	%
Stranger:									
Total	44	24	55	0	0	2	5	2	5
Males	25	19	76	0	0	2	8	2	8
Females	19	5	26	0	0	0	0	0	0
Mirror:									
Total	44	2	5	2	5	4	9	11	25
Males	25	1	4	1	5	3	12	6	24
Females	19	1	5	1	4	1	5	5	26
Compliment:									
Total	41	4	10	0	0	1	2	13	32
Males	22	4	18	0	0	0	0	5	23
Females	19	0	0	0	0	1	5	8	42
Dance for mother:									
Total	41	0	0	0	0	4	9	10	23
Males	22	0	0	0	0	3	12	3	13
Females	19	0	0	0	0	1	5	7	37
Dance for experimenter:									
Total	41	2	5	0	0	2	5	13	32
Males	23	2	9	0	0	0	0	4	17
Females	18	0	0	0	0	2	5	9	50

Wariness showed an overall condition effect (Cochran Q test, $Q = 30.15$, $p = < .001$) such that wariness is more likely in the stranger situation than in any of the others: stranger versus mirror, $\chi^2(1) = 50.22, p < .001$; stranger versus compliment, $\chi^2(1) = 17.3$, $p < .001$; stranger versus dance/m, $\chi^2(1) = 60.00$, $p < .001$; stranger versus dance/e, $\chi^2(1) = 22.38$, $p < .01$. Wariness, rather than embarrassment, was seen in the stranger condition ($Z = 4.08, p < .01$).

Embarrassment also shows an overall condition effect (Cochran Q test, $Q = 14.04$, $p < .01$) and was less likely to occur in the stranger situation than in any of the others: stranger versus mirror, $\chi^2(1) = 5.78, p < .02$; stranger versus compliment, $\chi^2(1) = 8.99, p < .003$; stranger versus dance/m, $\chi^2(1) = 4.92, p < .025$; stranger versus dance/e, $\chi^2(1) = 8.99, p < .003$. Embarrassment did not differ by condition.

Self-recognition and emotional behavior   Across conditions, an aggregate count of the number of subjects who showed a range of behavior was obtained (see Table 27.3). This range varies from never showing the emotion on any of the four conditions to showing the emotion on each condition.[3] Table 27.4 presents by condition the number and percentage of subjects who showed wary and embarrassed behavior as a function of self-recognition. It was predicted that while there would be no difference between touchers and nontouchers for wary behavior, touchers would show significantly more embarrassed behavior than nontouchers.

The first analysis looked at the numbers of subjects who did and did not show the two emotions across conditions as a function of self-recognition.

TABLE 27.3   Number of times embarrassment and wariness were observed over the situations used to elicit them

	Embarrassment (Mirror, Compliment, Dance/m, Dance/e Conditions)				
	0	*1*	*2*	*3*	*4*
Total	20	9	7	5	3
Males	14	6	2	2	1
Females	6	3	5	3	2
Touchers	7	7	6	4	2
Nontouchers	13	2	1	1	1

	Wariness (Stranger Condition)	
	0	*1+*
Total	17	27
Males	4	21
Females	13	6
Touchers	10	16
Nontouchers	7	11

Dance/m: mother; Dance/e: experimenter

Of the touchers, 7 did not show any embarrassment, while 19 showed embarrassment on at least one condition. Likewise, there were 13 nontouchers who showed no embarrassment, while there were only 5 nontouchers who showed embarrassment, a significant difference, $\chi^2(1) = 8.08, p < .005$. Of those subjects who showed at least one occasion of embarrassment, approximately 80% touched their noses. Moreover, 32 out of 44 subjects showed the predicted relation between embarrassment and self-recognition. Observation of the number who showed wary behavior as a function of self-recognition revealed no significant differences; only self-recognition is related to embarrassment.

A condition analysis (see Table 27.4) revealed that for the stranger condition, there was no significant difference in wariness as a function of self-recognition, while there were several significant (or near significant) effects for embarrassment. Subjects who showed self-recognition also exhibited more embarrassment in the compliment (Fischer's exact, $p < .055$), dance/m (Fischer's exact, $p < .11$), and dance/e (Fischer's exact, $p < .02$) conditions. Thus, the overall effect was replicated by observing each of the conditions individually.

Sex differences   Two classes of sex differences can be observed: first, sex differences in embarrassment and wariness independent of self-recognition; and second, sex differences in the relation between self-recognition and embarrassment. Table 27.3 allows us to observe these effects. With respect to wariness, four males showed none, while 21 subjects showed at least one occasion of wariness, while for females the numbers were 13 versus 6, respectively, $\chi^2(1) = 10.32, p < .002$. Across all four conditions, females showed more embarrassment than males. For males, 15 showed none, while 10 showed at least one occasion of embarrassment, while for females the numbers were 6 versus 13, respectively, $\chi^2(1) = 2.60, p < .10$. Of the subjects who showed two or more occasions of embarrassment, 20% of males and 52% of females showed this effect ($p < .001$). When the same analysis is performed by condition, similar findings appear, especially for the conditions on which there was a high degree of wariness observed. For the stranger and compliment

TABLE 27.4   For total sample, those who have attained self-referential behavior (touchers) and those who have not (nontouchers)

	% of Subjects Showing Wariness or Embarrassment									
	Stranger		Mirror		Compliment		Dance-Exp		Dance-Mother	
	W	E	W	E	W	E	W	E	W	E
Total	55	5	5	25	10	32	5	32	0	23
Touchers	54	8	4	31	4	42	8	44	0	27
Nontouchers	56	0	6	17	18	18	0	13	0	18
	No. of Subjects Showing Wariness or Embarrassment									
Total	24	2	2	11	4	13	2	13	0	10
Touchers	14	2	1	8	1	10	2	11	0	7
Nontouchers	10	0	1	3	3	3	0	2	0	3

conditions, there is a significant sex difference, with males showing more wariness than females, $\chi^2(1) = 10.74, p < .005; \chi^2(1) = 3.84, p = .05$, respectively. Sex differences in embarrassment by condition indicated that females showed more embarrassment than males for the dance/e condition, $\chi^2(1) = 3.57, p < .05$.

Observation of the relation between embarrassment and self-recognition by sex indicates that both sexes show a strong relation between this cognitive milestone and emotional development. Of males who showed embarrassment, 10 out of 11 touched their noses, while of the females who showed embarrassment, nine of 13 touched their noses. Likewise, there was no relation between wariness and self-recognition for either sex.

Discussion

The general discussion will consider three issues: (1) situations eliciting emotions and measures, (2) the interface of cognition and emotion, and (3) individual and sex differences in the development of embarrassment.

Situations and measures   The data from both studies agree, even though Study 1 varied age. Embarrassment, but not wariness, was related to self-recognition when observed either by looking at age changes in the ability to recognize oneself in the mirror or by looking at individual differences in this ability during the period of time when it is being acquired.

The approach of a stranger has long been used as a situation to elicit fear, although wariness rather than fear is usually observed (see Lewis and Rosenblum, 1974). Embarrassment is elicited by situations that produce exposure of the self, although Buss (1980) describes embarrassment also as being elicited by impropriety or lack of social competence, as well as conspicuousness. There are many situations that might be used to elicit this emotion, and we found that four were successful: viewing oneself in the mirror (in both studies), being complimented, and being asked to perform (to dance). Self-conspicuousness is the central feature of these situations. While these situations are different in terms of the amount of embarrassment elicited, they did not produce much wariness/fear. Likewise, few subjects showed embarrassment during stranger approach. These situations, therefore, are adequate to observe embarrassment.

Although the measurement of wariness/fear has been well established, the measurement of embarrassment has received less attention, although since Darwin (1872/1965) it has been described and seen in young children (Amsterdam, 1972; Dixon, 1957; Lewis and Brooks-Gunn, 1979a; Schulman and Kaplowitz, 1977). In this study, the measurement approach used provides easy criteria for observing its presence.

One problem with using nervous touching as part of the criteria is that this is a behavior also used in the self-recognition measure. In order to eliminate any confusion, we limited our definition of embarrassment to smiling and gaze averting, a procedure used by some (Buss, 1980). Using this new measure to compare embarrassment with self-recognition resulted in findings quite similar to those when nervous touching is included. Under this measurement procedure, many more subjects would be said to show embarrassment. For example, in Study 1, 21 rather than 10 subjects showed embarrassment. Although the numbers of subjects increase, the percentage of subjects who show embarrassment, without using nervous touching as a criterion, and who show self-recognition is 78%, while 22% show embarrassment and no self-recognition. These figures are similar to the findings using nervous touching; thus, there is no reason to believe that our definition of embarrassment affects the results reported.

The role of cognition and affect   We have suggested that in order for all secondary emotions, both self-conscious and self-evaluative, to emerge, a referential self is necessary. It is important to note that a self system and its development consists of several features (Lewis and Brooks-Gunn, 1979b). While details of this system are still being worked out (see, e.g., Pipp, Jennings, and Fischer, 1987), self–other differentiation, self-permanence, and the ability to consider the self as a separate entity are some of the features of this system. The ability to consider one's self – what has been called self-awareness or referential self – is one of the last features of self to emerge, occurring in the last half of the second year of life. The ability to consider one's self rather than the ability to differentiate or discriminate self from other is the cognitive capacity that allows for all self-conscious emotions such as embarrassment and empathy, although the development of standards is also needed for self-conscious evaluative emotions such as shame, guilt, and pride. Self-referential behavior has been defined operationally as the ability of the child to look at its image in the mirror and to show, by pointing and touching its nose, that the image in the mirror *there* is located in space *here* at the physical site of the child itself. In the results reported in both studies, embarrassment, in general, does not occur unless self-referential behavior exists.[4]

While a third factor may be related to our findings, given the observed relation between embarrassment, but not wariness, and self-referential behavior, it would seem that self-recognition behavior represents an important milestone in the child's development of a self system and in its general cognitive and emotional development.

The relation between the primary emotions and the development of the self has been suggested (Lewis et al., 1985; Schneider-Rosen and Cicchetti, 1984; Stern, 1985), but little empirical work has been conducted relating these two systems. The mother–child relationship has been proposed to affect the development of self, but only two studies have shown any relation (Lewis et al., 1985; Schneider-Rosen and Cicchetti, 1984). While it appears likely that socioemotional behavior and its socialization affect the child's developing self system, there is only weak evidence to indicate any direct effect of early emotional life on the referential self. Nevertheless, the development of the self system impacts on the child's subsequent emotional life.

Sex differences   While males are more wary than females in the stranger approach situation, females are more embarrassed than males. Sex differences in fear/wariness, when they appear, indicate that females are more wary than males (Maccoby and Jacklin, 1974). For embarrassment, there are still fewer data, unless we look to variables such as sociability or shyness, where there is some evidence that at adolescence females are more shy and less sociable than males (see Crozier, 1979; Gould, 1987). It is difficult to determine exactly why these sex differences appear. Differential socialization practices might account for differences in emotional expressivity (Brooks-Gunn and Lewis, 1982; Malatesta and Haviland, 1982). Although there are few studies in this regard, data from the classroom indicate that teachers are more apt to direct their comments pertaining to the self's action (how well or poorly a problem was handled) to boys than to girls, while they are more apt to direct comments pertaining to the self (good or bad child) to girls than to boys (Cherry, 1975). Differential socialization may produce these sex differences.

Individual differences were determined by obtaining a total score of embarrassment over four conspicuous situations. While most children exhibited either no embarrassment or one embarrassment over the four situations, there were eight children who showed embarrassment 75% or more of the time. Maternal reports confirm that these children are most easily embarrassed. Data collected on these same children at 3 years indicate that these eight children remain easily embarrassed (Lewis, Stanger, and Sullivan, in press). The etiology of individual differences in embarrassment has not been studied; some have suggested, however, that besides differences in parental behavior, temperament differences might play some role (Kagan, Garcia-Coll, and Reznick, 1984; Jones, Check, and Briggs, 1986; Zimbardo, 1977). Clearly, more work, on both individual as well as sex differences, needs to be undertaken. Given an adequate measurement system and situations now available to elicit these emotions, such an undertaking is possible.

ACKNOWLEDGMENT

This research is supported from a grant by W. T. Grant Foundation to Michael Lewis and by HD 17205 to Margaret W. Sullivan.

NOTES

1. The distinction between emotional state, expression, and experience has been made (Lewis and Michalson, 1983; Lewis and Rosenblum, 1974). Here we refer to emotional states and expressions. Emotional experiences require more elaborate cognitive ability (Lewis and Brooks-Gunn, 1979b; Lewis and Michalson, 1983).
2. When the 15–24-month-olds were combined in an attempt to unconfound age, which is related both to self-recognition and embarrassment, embarrassment was associated with recognition (Fischer's exact probability, $p < .02$).
3. Table 27.3 also shows the aggregate score for wary behavior. However, since wariness was exhibited so seldom in the other conditions, the aggregate scores of more than 1 occurred for only five subjects, and we have combined them into the 1+ category.

4. The relation between embarrassment display and self-referential behavior is not perfect. In both studies, a very few subjects showed embarrassment but did not show self-referential behavior. We cannot explain why this occurred, except to point out that very few subjects did so and that the measurement systems, for either self-recognition or embarrassment, are not perfect. It may be the case that a child was scored as embarrassed and was not, or the children did not touch their noses during the test for some reason and should have, given that they possess self-referential ability. The latter seems more likely, since we had only one situation of self-recognition but four situations in which to measure embarrassment. In fact, in Study 2 there were five children who showed embarrassment but did not touch their noses. Review of their behavior before the mirror indicates that four of the five can be said to have recognized themselves. One subject labeled her image by name. The utterance was unintelligible but apparently was accepted by the mother as her name. Three other children showed concern over the rouge on their noses and appeared to be upset by its appearance. Although those four subjects did not touch their noses when they looked in the mirror, they appeared to recognize themselves since they complained about the rouge on their noses. If this is so, then of the subjects who showed embarrassment ($n = 24$), 96% had some type of self-referential behavior.

References

Amsterdam, B. K. (1972). Mirror self image reactions before age two. *Developmental Psychology*, **5**, 297–305.

Bertenthal, F. I., and Fischer, K. W. (1978). The development of self-recognition in the infant. *Developmental Psychology*, **11**, 44–50.

Borke, H. (1971). Interpersonal perception of young children: Egocentrism or empathy. *Developmental Psychology*, **5**, 263–9.

Brooks-Gunn, J., and Lewis, M. (1982). Affective exchanges between normal and handicapped infants and their mothers. In T. Field and A. Fogel (eds), *Emotions and Early Interaction* (pp. 161–88), Hillsdale, NJ: Erlbaum.

Buss, A. H. (1980). *Self-consciousness and Social Anxiety*. San Francisco: W. H. Freeman.

Charlesworth, W. R. (1969). The role of surprise in cognitive development. In D. Elkind and J. H. Flavell (eds), *Studies in Cognitive Development: Essays in Honor of Jean Piaget* (pp. 257–314), London: Oxford University Press.

Cherry, L. (1975). The preschool child–teacher dyad: Sex differences in verbal interaction. *Child Development*, **46**, 532–5.

Crozier, W. R. (1979). Shyness as anxious self-preoccupation. *Psychological Reports*, **44**, 959–62.

Darwin, C. (1965). *The Expression of Emotion in Animals and Man*. Chicago: University of Chicago Press (Original edition 1872).

Dixon, J. C. (1957). The development of self-recognition. *Journal of Genetic Psychology*, **91**, 251–6.

Edelman, R. J., and Hampson, S. E. (1981). The recognition of embarrassment. *Personality and Social Psychology Bulletin*, **7**, 109–16.

Geppert, U. (1986). *A Coding System for Analyzing Behavioral Expressions of Self-evaluative Emotions*. Munich: Max-Planck Institute for Psychological Research.

Geppert, U., and Kuster, U. (1983). The emergence of 'wanting to do it oneself': A precursor of achievement motivation. *International Journal of Behavioral Development*, **6**, 355–70.

Gould, S. J. (1987). Gender differences in advertising response and self-conscious variables. *Sex Roles*, **5/6**, 215–25.

Heckhausen, H. (1984). Emergent achievement behavior: Some early developments. In J. Nicholls (ed.), *The Development of Achievement Motivation* (pp. 1–32), Greenwich, CT: Jai.

Izard, C. E. (1977). *Human Emotions*. New York: Plenum.

Izard, C. E., and Dougherty, L. M. (1982). Two complementary systems for measuring facial expressions in infants and children. In C. E. Izard (ed.), *Measuring Emotions in Infants and Children* (pp. 97–126), New York: Cambridge University Press.

Jones, W. H., Check, T. M., and Briggs, S. R. (eds). (1986). *Shyness*. New York: Plenum.

Kagan, J. (1981). *The Second Year: The Emergence of Self-awareness*. Cambridge, MA: Harvard University Press.

Kagan, J., Garcia-Coll, C., and Reznick, J. S. (1984). Behavioral inhibition in young children. *Child Development*, **55**, 1005–19.

Lewis, M., and Brooks-Gunn, J. (1979a). *Social Cognition and the Acquisition of Self*. New York: Plenum.

Lewis, M., and Brooks-Gunn, J. (1979b). Toward a theory of social cognition: The development of self. In I. Uzgiris (ed.), *New Directions in Child Development: Social Interaction and Communication in Infancy* (pp. 1–20), San Francisco: Jossey-Bass.

Lewis, M., Brooks-Gunn, J., and Jaskir, J. (1985). Individual differences in early visual self-recognition. *Developmental Psychology*, **21**, 1181–7.

Lewis, M., and Michalson, L. (1983). *Children's Emotions and Moods: Developmental Theory and Measurement*. New York: Plenum.

Lewis, M., and Rosenblum, L. (eds), (1974). *The Origins of Fear*. New York: Wiley.

Lewis, M., and Rosenblum, L. (1978). Introduction: Issues in affect development. In M. Lewis and L. Rosenblum (eds), *The Development of Affect: The Genesis of Behavior* (vol. 1, pp. 1–10); New York: Plenum.

Lewis, M., Stanger, C., and Sullivan, M. W. (in press). Deception in three-year-olds. *Developmental Psychology*.

Lewis, M., Sullivan, M. W., and Michalson, L. (1984). The cognitive–emotional fugue. In C. E. Izard, J. Kagan, and R. B. Zajonc (eds), *Emotions, Cognition and Behavior* (pp. 264–88), London: Cambridge University Press.

Maccoby, E. E., and Jacklin, C. N. (eds), (1974). *The Psychology of Sex Differences*. Stanford, CA: Stanford University Press.

Malatesta, C. Z., and Haviland, J. M. (1982). Learning display rules: The socialization of emotional expression in infancy. *Child Development*, **53**, 991–1003.

Michalson, L., and Lewis, M. (1985). What do children know about emotions and when do they know it? In M. Lewis and C. Saarni (eds), *The Socialization of Emotions* (pp. 117–40), New York: Plenum.

Piaget, J. (1954). *The Origins of Intelligence in Children* (M. Cook, trans.). New York: Norton.

Pipp, S., Jennings, S., and Fischer, K. W. (1987). Acquisition of self and mother knowledge in infancy. *Developmental Psychology*, **23**, 86–96.

Plutchik, R. (1970). Emotions, evolution and adaptive processes. In M. Arnold (ed.), *Feelings and Emotion* (pp. 384–402), New York: Academic Press.

Rheingold, H. L., and Eckerman, C. O. (1973). Fear of the stranger: A critical examination. In H. Reese (ed.), *Advances in Child Development and Behavior* (vol. 8, pp. 186–223), New York: Academic Press.

Schneider-Rosen, K., and Cicchetti, D. (1984). The relationship between affect and cognition in maltreated infants: Quality of attachment and the development of visual self-recognition. *Child Development*, **55**, 648–58.

Schulman, A. H., and Kaplowitz, C. (1977). Mirror-image response during the first two years of life. *Developmental Psychology*, **10**, 133–42.

Stenberg, C., Campos, J., and Emde, R. (1983). The facial expression of anger in seven-month-old infants. *Child Development*, **54**, 178–84.

Stern, D. N. (1985). *The Interpersonal World of the Infant*. New York: Basic.

Stipek, D. J. (1983). A developmental analysis of pride and shame. *Human Development*, **26**, 42–54.

Sullivan, M. W., and Lewis, M. (in press). Emotion and cognition in infancy: Facial expressions during contingency learning. *International Journal of Behavioral Development*.

Tomkins, S. S. (1963). *Affect, Imagery and Consciousness: Vol. 2. The Negative Affect*. New York: Springer.

Zimbardo, P. G. (1977). *Shyness: What it is, What I do about it*. New York: Addison-Wesley.

28

Recent Developments in Attachment Theory and Research*

Susan Goldberg

OVERVIEW　The history and development of attachment theory are reviewed. Research has focused on four major patterns of attachment in infancy: one pattern of secure attachment and three patterns of insecure attachment (avoidant, resistant, and disorganized). These patterns have been shown to reflect different histories of parent–child interaction and affected subsequent development up to age eight. More recently, methods have been developed for identifying similar patterns of attachment in preschoolers, five- to seven-year-olds and adults. Future research is likely to focus on the development of attachment patterns and their transmission from one generation to another. New data on the relationship between attachment and behaviour problems has generated mutual respect and collaboration between clinicians and researchers.

It is widely accepted that the parent–child relationship plays a central role in a child's development, but empirical data to support this hypothesis are very recent and remarkably scant. The most common theoretical approaches to the study of parent–child relationships are psychoanalytic theory (object relations), social learning theory (dependency), and attachment theory. There has been research into each of these, but it is attachment theory that has given rise to a recent wave of empirical studies that has excited both clinicians and researchers. The goal of this article is to review the basic constructs of attachment theory and empirical research.

* Previously published in *Canadian Journal of Psychiatry*, **36**, 6 (August 1991), pp. 393–400.

A Capsule View of Attachment Theory

Attachment theory was originally described by Bowlby,[1-4] combining ideas from psychoanalysis and ethology. Bowlby argued that affectional ties between children and their caregivers have a biological basis which is best understood in an evolutionary context. Since children's survival depends on the care they receive from adults, there is a genetic bias among infants to behave in ways which maintain and enhance proximity to caregivers and elicit their attention and investment. A complementary evolutionary history biases adults to behave reciprocally. Thus, while psychoanalytic theory emphasizes the caregivers' initial roles in reducing physiological arousal, and social learning theory emphasizes the caregivers as teachers, attachment theory focuses on parents as protectors and providers of security. (All three theories acknowledge that parents play multiple roles, those of teacher, caregiver, playmate, etc.; they differ with respect to which role is considered most influential.) Furthermore, while the psychoanalytic and learning theories view children as initially passive, Bowlby's view credited infants with active participation. Prior theories considered infants to be dependent on caregivers, and dependency as a state which must be outgrown. Attachment theory, however, considers it possible for individuals to be reciprocally attached. Attachment is therefore a quality of relationships which lasts one's lifetime. The nature of attachments may be transformed as children develop, but an attachment can endure.

The concept of attachment includes social components (it is a property of social relationships), emotional components (each participant in the relationship feels emotional bonds with the other), cognitive components (each participant forms a cognitive scheme – a 'working model' of the relationship and its participants), and behavioural components (participants engage in behaviours that reflect and maintain the relationship). It is the nature and interrelationship of these components that reflect developmental change.

Over the first year, the infant's proximity-promoting behaviours (orienting signals such as cries and vocalizations, and direct actions such as approaching and clinging to the caregiver) become organized into a goal-oriented system focused on a specific caregiver. The mother is usually the first such figure, but others can play this role. When the attachment system is in its goal state (i.e., there is adequate proximity and contact), attachment behaviours subside; when the goal state is threatened, attachment behaviours are activated. Furthermore, because the attachment system operates in the context of other related systems (for example, exploration), the goal is adjusted to fit the context. For a healthy infant in a familiar (safe) environment, the goal may be to remain in the same room with the attachment figure; if the infant is tired or ill or the environment is unfamiliar, the goal becomes greater proximity and contact.

As the child's locomotor, linguistic and social skills develop, the goals of the attachment system are modified to allow for longer separations over greater distances. Cognitive components play a more dominant role and proximity plays a less important role in moderating attachment behaviour.

Individuals' working models of particular relationships include concepts of themselves and others. A more general 'working model' of relationships also develops which reflects individuals' experiences in relationships. The quality of both early and later attachments influences self-concepts as well as expectations and attitudes toward social relationships. Individuals whose primary attachment relationships in childhood were satisfying and provided emotional security view themselves as lovable, expect positive interactions with others, and value intimate relationships. Individuals who experienced rejection or harsh treatment as children view themselves as unworthy of love, expect further rejections, and act in ways that elicit rejections. These predictions may not differ radically from those of other theoretical approaches to relationships; however, the evaluation of a theory depends on its ability to be empirically tested.

History of Research into Attachment: An Overview

Attachment theory has generated 25 years of productive empirical research. Empirical research was made possible by Ainsworth and her students,[5, 6] who classified infant–parent attachment between 12 and 18 months of age into three distinct patterns. The first ten to 15 years of research based on this method were devoted to collecting normative data and documenting the precursors and sequelae of different patterns of attachment. Initial efforts to study patterns of attachment in clinical populations followed (for example, maltreated infants, medically ill infants, infants of depressed mothers). These efforts resulted in the addition of a fourth pattern of attachment, which was thought to be potentially more pathological.[7,8] However, the inability to examine patterns of attachment beyond infancy soon became a recognized limitation, and more recent work has included the development and validation of methods for assessing attachment in preschoolers,[9] five- to seven-year-olds,[10] and adults.[11] An outline of these schemes is shown in table 28.1. This conceptual scheme is likely to be completed in the future.

TABLE 28.1   Patterns of attachment at different stages of life

Age	Assessment Method	Patterns of Attachment			
		Secure (B)	Dismissing (A)	Preoccupied (C)	Disorganized (D)
12 to 18 months	Structured observation (Strange Situation)	Secure	Avoidant	Ambivalent/ resistant	Disorganized
$2\frac{1}{2}$ to four years	Structured observation (reunions)	Secure	Avoidant	Dependent	Controlling/ disorganized
Five to seven years	Structured observation (reunions)	Secure	Avoidant	Dependent	Controlling
Adult	Interview	Autonomous/ secure	Dismissing	Preoccupied	Unresolved mourning (loss)

PATTERNS OF ATTACHMENT

Since theories of infant–parent attachment were developed before other age groups were looked at and have been most extensively studied, they will be reviewed in detail as a prelude to introducing the analogues for other age groups. The assessment of infant–mother attachment developed by Ainsworth et al. is based on their hypothesis that the infant's feelings of security are the ontogenetic function of the attachment system. Bowlby acknowledged both the phylogenetic goal of protection from predators and external danger, and the ontogenetic function of psychologically perceived security. Ainsworth elaborated on the latter in the Strange Situation. The procedure involves observing the infant, caregiver (usually the mother) and a friendly but unfamiliar adult in a series of eight semi-structured episodes in a laboratory playroom.[5, 6] It relies on the observation of the balance of attachment and exploratory behaviours in response to the manipulations in the eight episodes. The crux of the procedure is a standard sequence of separations and reunions between the infant and each of the two adults. It is felt that over the course of the eight episodes the child experiences increasing distress and a greater need for proximity. The extent to which children cope with these needs and the strategies they use to do so are considered to indicate the quality of attachment.

Scoring depends on a detailed review of videotapes. The infant is rated on behaviour directed at the caregiver: seeking contact, maintaining contact, distance interaction, avoidance, and resistance to contact. From this information, the dyad is classified into one of eight subtypes that fall into three broad categories. Although behaviour during the entire session is considered, reunion behaviours have been shown to be the most salient feature distinguishing between these patterns.[6]

These three patterns reflect strategies used by the infant to manage affective arousal during interactions with, separations from, and reunions with the caregiver. In the secure strategy, the attachment system is activated only when the infant's security is threatened (for example, the caregiver departs and the child is left in an unfamiliar place) and subsides to give the exploratory system free rein when the attachment figure (the secure base) returns. In the avoidant (dismissing) strategy, the attachment system is defensively suppressed so that the child appears to be exploring without concern for security, although he carefully monitors the attachment figure. In the ambivalent/resistant (preoccupied) strategy, the attachment system is continuously activated at the expense of the exploratory system, even when to all outward appearances the child should be safe and comfortable (i.e., the attachment figure is present). Another way of understanding this is to consider the threshold for activating attachment behaviour: in the avoidant strategy the threshold is very high, while in the ambivalent/resistant strategy, it is very low. In both insecure strategies, the threshold is set primarily to meet internal needs and is not adapted to the environment. However, in the secure strategy, the threshold is both moderate and sensitive to environmental conditions.

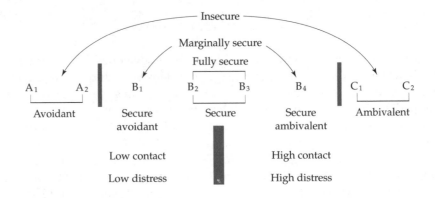

FIGURE 28.1   Attachment classifications

In Ainsworth's original study,[5] 65% of the babies exhibited a secure pattern of attachment, 21% an avoidant pattern and 14% an ambivalent/resistant pattern.[6] A recent meta-analysis of nearly 2,000 infants from 39 studies conducted in eight different countries showed almost exactly the same distribution, although there were some cultural variations.[12] Furthermore, under stable life conditions, patterns of attachment are relatively stable over both the short term (six months)[13] and the long term (up to five years).[10] These data refer to attachment to the same caregiver assessed on different occasions.

A number of studies have shown that patterns of attachment to the mother and to the father are independent.[14–16] This demonstrates that attachment patterns derived from the Strange Situation reflect qualities of distinct relationships rather than a trait of the child. In a recent meta-analysis of 11 studies of attachment to the mother and the father. Fox and his colleagues[17] found a high degree of concordance between patterns of attachment to mother and father, which raises some questions about the trait-versus-relationship interpretation of attachment inferred from the Strange Situation. These findings can be better understood if we consider the relationship between temperament and attachment.

There has been an ongoing discussion in the literature over the extent to which the infant's temperament affects attachment.[18–22] It would seem the infant's propensity to become distressed is the primary determinant of behaviour during the Strange Situation. However, the most salient behaviours for classification are not the presence or absence of distress, but the infant's style of coping with distress: in particular, use of the attachment figure as a source of comfort. Studies of parent reports of temperament have generally found little association between scores on questionnaires of temperament and security of attachment.[22] However, more careful examination of the full classification scheme (including all the subgroups) suggests that there is a temperament dimension inherent in the scheme. Figure 28.1 illustrates the full classification scheme. Avoidant babies and some secure babies who are slightly avoidant (B_1) are less easily distressed than resistant babies, very secure babies (B_3), and secure babies who are slightly resistant (B_4). If we divide infants according to the degree to which they are likely to become distressed (high/low distress groups), infants in the high distress group are more likely to be reported as temperamentally 'difficult' by parents, and those in the low distress group are more likely to be reported as 'easy'.[18] Thus, the distress experienced during the Strange Situation is related to the type of security or insecurity, not to security per se.

In the meta-analysis conducted by Fox et al.[17] a high degree of concordance was found between the infant's attachment to the mother and father in the high distress (A_1–B_2) and low distress (B_3–C_2) groups. However, within each of these groups, security to the mother and the father were not concordant. Thus, if an infant falls into the A_1–B_2 group with one parent, s/he is likely to fall into the same group with the other parent, but within the A_1–B_2 group, having an A (avoidant) or B (secure) pattern of attachment with one parent does not predict security or insecurity with the other parent. These findings show an association between temperament and behaviour on the Strange Situation Test, but they also indicate that security is a characteristic of relationships, rather than an individual trait.

Patterns of attachment behaviour during the Strange Situation are related to both prior and current behaviour in the home. Mothers of secure infants have been rated as being more sensitive, responsive, accessible and cooperative during the first year than mothers of insecure infants.[23–26] Although there is some evidence that characteristics and/or behaviours of the infant may also predict the quality of attachment, these findings have been less consistent than those on maternal behaviour. This suggests that the mother plays a more influential role than the infant in shaping the quality of the relationship.

An increasing number of studies have found that secure infants are more competent than insecure infants in a variety of subsequent cognitive and social skills.[27–33] The most ambitious undertaking in this domain is the longitudinal research conducted by Sroufe and his colleagues[31–6] at the Institute for Child Study in Minneapolis. A large sample of children in whom attachment was assessed in infancy are now reaching puberty. Published reports of data up through the early school years consistently document the influences of early attachment on social skills in later life.

Coherent relationships between behaviour at home and attachment assessed in the laboratory and between the latter and subsequent development in normative samples have been demonstrated. This has led researchers to use the Strange Situation to explore possible 'derailing' of the infant–mother relationship under unusually stressful conditions (for example, premature birth, maltreatment, maternal depression). It was thought that there would be fewer infants with secure attachment relationships with the parent in these populations at-risk. In general, medically ill infants are not more likely to develop insecure patterns of attachment.[24,37,38] Some early studies found that maltreated infants are less likely to develop secure attachment relationships.[38,39] However, it seems implausible that the majority of maltreated infants or even a substantial minority should be securely attached.[7] These studies of 'atypical' populations provided the first indication that there might be potential problems in attachment theory or in the assessment methodology. Another intriguing finding was that while there had been a small number of cases that could not be classified into the three-pattern scheme, Crittenden's observations of maltreated toddlers[39] and Radke-Yarrow's assessments of preschoolers of depressed mothers[40] uncovered a substantial number of children who seemed to be both avoidant and ambivalent/resistant. In both studies infants with a mixed pattern of attachment were from the most potentially damaging conditions.

Subsequently Main and Solomon[7,8] reviewed a large number of cases which had not previously been classified or were anomalous (for example, securely attached infants who had been maltreated), by studying videotapes, and identified a fourth pattern, which they called 'disorganized'.

Unlike the previous patterns, which could be described as strategies, the infants in the 'disorganized' group did not have a coherent strategy for coping with the separations and reunions during the Strange Situation. In addition, they engaged in unusual and inexplicable behaviours which only made sense if interpreted to reflect confusion or fear of the caregiver. The 'mixed' pattern described by Crittenden[39] and Radke-Yarrow[40] was also included in this new disorganized group. Subsequent studies of maltreated children using this new category indicated a high proportion of disorganized attachment.[38,41,42] These data lead to the speculation that disorganization is a very insecure pattern of attachment and that some children in previous risk populations who were actually disorganized were initially 'misclassified' as secure. This is one area where we can expect further development, and it seems likely that disorganization of attachment may have implications for subsequent psychopathology. However, some observed 'disorganization' may also reflect transient responses to events that are normally stressful to a young child (for example, the birth of a sibling). Studies of the disorganized pattern of attachment are needed to provide normative data on the precursors and sequelae of disorganization. Psychiatric populations have not been widely used in studies of attachment. Such studies may make major contributions to both clinical understanding and attachment theory.

Beyond Infancy

While a few studies used the Strange Situation on children up to age four,[39,41] the absence of methodology for assessing attachment beyond infancy has limited the development of attachment theory. What Bowlby had intended to be a life-span construct became an infancy construct because infancy was the only developmental period in which attachment could be measured. Although it is important to study the sequelae of early attachment in later development, it is equally important to study the development of attachment itself.

The most important new directions concern the development of assessment methods for preschoolers, five- to seven-year-olds, and adults (see table 28.1). As with the procedures used for infants, those for preschoolers and five- to seven-year-olds rely on videotaped observations of reunions. (The nature and duration of separations are not specified, but typically the child is engaged in a series of tasks with an experimenter.) Adult procedure relies on interviews about the individual's early attachments. A detailed transcript of the interview is scored. The goal is not to make an objective determination of the nature of these relationships, but rather to assess the individual's current working model of attachment. As shown in table 28.1, the four patterns previously described for infants can be applied to the other age periods. These classification schemes are relatively new, and research to validate them is only beginning. Nevertheless, these preliminary descriptions provide some sense of the developmental continuity in attachment patterns which might be possible.

Secure/autonomous

Secure preschoolers and five- to seven-year-olds, like secure infants, greet a returning parent happily and are able to coordinate attention to the parent and exploration. Separation is less stressful to these children than to infants because their cognitive schemas, which include recognition of parents as independent individuals, are more sophisticated. Older children may engage in enjoyable and absorbing activities during the separation. Thus greeting, while happy, is casual and children usually continue their activities but find a way to involve the parent either by inviting the parent to join the activity or by volunteering information about what they have been doing. Conversation is fluent, and both participants are relaxed. There is comfortable eye contact, and children may initiate physical proximity or contact.

Secure adults (described as autonomous) value attachments and are able to talk coherently and realistically about them. If they had positive relationships with their parents, they can acknowledge and accept their parents' imperfections. If they had a difficult or harsh childhood, they can acknowledge the unhappiness, have come to some understanding of it, and can establish new and important relationships for themselves.

Avoidant/dismissing

Avoidant preschoolers and five- to seven-year-olds, like avoidant infants, appear to be more interested in other activities than in the parent's return. However, they have learned that social conventions require greetings as well as responses to initiations by the parent. Avoidance in older children is therefore more subtle and is shown by a lack of eye contact, lack of social initiatives and a minimal response to parental overtures. The strategy of avoidance is to maintain neutrality – to do nothing either positive or negative that would draw attention to the relationship.

Avoidant or 'dismissing' adults likewise downplay the importance of intimate relationships. They may idealize their childhood experiences without being able to supply supporting details, or, in fact, give contradictory examples. Some may speak of negative experiences but do not acknowledge the effects of these experiences. They attempt to limit the influences of attachments on themselves. The reader of the interview transcript can infer a history of lack of closeness or support, or significant rejections.

Dependent/preoccupied

Among older children, the insecure/ambivalent pattern is labelled 'dependent' and, like the infant pattern, its hallmark is preoccupation with the relationship at the expense of other activities. The parent and child may be engaged in a constant struggle for control, the conversation marked by 'put-downs' and disagreements. The child is whiny and contentious. Alternatively, the child may emphasize his dependence with extreme coyness (for example, whispering) and feigned helplessness. Even at this age, dependent children are more likely to be visibly upset at the parent's departure than children in other groups.

The adult analogue of this pattern is labelled 'preoccupied'. These individuals are caught in old struggles with parents, lack a sense of personal identity apart from family or parents, and are unable to evaluate their own role within relationships. They are unable to move beyond details of early memories or current interactions with parents to an objective overview.

Disorganized/controlling/unresolved mourning

This is the least consistent category. Some signs of disorganization similar to those in infants can be seen in preschoolers, especially the youngest preschoolers. However, in older children the disorganized pattern seems to emerge as disorganization in the relationship rather than the individual. The child takes control of the parent in one of two ways. The first is related to caregiving. The child appears to feel responsible for making the parent happy and is overly bright and enthusiastic at reunions. The child works hard to engage the parent. The second is punitive. The child is directly hostile toward the parent in a style that conveys assurance that the parent will comply or meet demands. The child may also ignore the parent when it is clear that such ignoring is a flagrant violation of the social conventions.

The significant feature of adults in the 'disorganized' category is unresolved mourning over the loss of an attachment figure. The loss may be a death or loss through divorce or a loss of trust through abuse or neglect. Initial mourning is typically characterized by disorganizing and disorienting experiences. Unresolved mourning is inferred from interview transcripts where signs of continuing cognitive disorganization are shown when the attachment figure is discussed (for example, disbelief in the loss, persisting inappropriate guilt).

At all ages, disorganized individuals are also given an alternative or 'forced' classification of one of the other three alternatives (avoidant, secure, ambivalent).

DEVELOPMENT OF ATTACHMENT

We have already noted that a core group of studies on infants found prior observations in the home to be predictors of attachment status based on the

Strange Situation. Indeed, behaviour during the Strange Situation is a marker or indicator of the relationship history. Since the "disorganized" classification was developed, studies of maltreated children have consistently shown that disorganized attachment is more common in maltreated infants than in controls.[38–40,42] In addition, initial data from an ongoing longitudinal study of the children of clinically, depressed mothers document a high rate of 'mixed insecure' attachment (A/C, now considered a form of disorganized attachment) among children with mothers who have major bipolar affective disorder.[40] These studies support the assertion that secure attachment is the result of appropriately responsive parental care and that inadequate care is the result of very insecure attachment. Furthermore, in the Minnesota longitudinal study,[43] it was shown that when infants are tested in the Strange Situation, at 12 and 18 months, changes in quality of attachment are related to changes in family environment. If the mother's quality of life improves, the infant–mother relationship is more likely to become more secure; if the mother's quality of life deteriorates, infant–mother attachment is likely to become less secure.

Now that methods are available to assess attachment in preschool and early school years, it is possible to evaluate stability and change in attachment relationships over a longer period of time. In the first such study, Main and her associates[10] found that the correlation between security of attachment to the mother at one year and security of attachment to the mother at six years was $r = .76(p < .001)$; the analogous correlation for attachment to the father at 18 months and six years was $r = .30(p < .05)$. Several other studies of this type are under way. From these we can expect to learn about factors contributing to stability and change in attachment status.

TRANSMISSION OF ATTACHMENT PATTERNS BETWEEN GENERATIONS

With the development of the Adult Attachment Interview (AAI),[11] it is also possible to test whether individuals' experiences of nurturing determine their ability to nurture their own children. Indeed, the first studies of this type show a high degree of concordance between adult 'states of mind' regarding attachment and the attachment status of their infants;[44–6] parents who are 'secure/ autonomous' tend to have securely attached infants, those who are 'dismissing' tend to have avoidant infants, and those who are preoccupied tend to have ambivalent/resistant infants. While disorganized attachment in infants has been associated with maltreatment and maternal bipolar affective disorder, it also occurs among infants in low-risk families. In these circumstances, the initial indications are that disorganized attachment in the infant is associated with unresolved mourning in the parent.[46] Although it has not yet been clearly demonstrated, it is possible that parents who maltreat children have experienced traumatic and unresolved loss as a result of inadequate care as children.

The AAI does not purport to provide an accurate picture of childhood. It represents the adult's working model (i.e., present attitudes and feelings) of important relationships during their childhood. Even the preliminary data now available indicate that a significant number of adults with unhappy childhoods are secure/autonomous adults.[10] Likewise, some adults who are insecure were probably securely attached during earlier periods of life. The indications from the current generation of studies are that an adult's cognitions and emotions (i.e., working models) about relationships influence their caregiving, which in turn affects their children's attachment status. While those who had secure childhoods clearly have a better chance of becoming secure adults than those whose initial experiences were harsh and rejecting, intervening experiences can change working models of attachment and lead to behaviour consistent with the new model. This is good news for clinicians, whose goal is to bring about a positive change through therapeutic intervention. The availability of a method for assessing adult attachment now makes possible the use of pre- and post-therapy assessments to ascertain whether therapy has resulted in changes in working models of attachment.

IMPLICATIONS FOR CHILD PSYCHIATRY

The methods developed by researchers studying attachment can be applied to studies of the relationship between attachment (particularly in infancy) and behaviour problems. Most of the existing studies have looked at relatively large cohorts of normally developing children. The number of children likely to have behaviour disorders that can be diagnosed would be small in this group. Therefore, the measure of outcome is generally a parent or teacher report checklist[47-9] or a composite score on experimental observation and standardized social competence measures.[34-6]

The findings of these studies are equivocal. For example, Sroufe and his colleagues[34-6] have shown that the quality of early attachment is related to later behaviour problems in children up to early school age. However, this relationship is stronger in boys than in girls. Lewis and his colleagues[48] reported similar findings, but two other studies[47,49] failed to find such an association.

In our own recent preliminary data, we have found that while there is no consistent relationship between quality of attachment in infancy and scores on the Achenbach's Child Behavior Checklist (CBCL), a different pattern emerges if we consider only children whose parental report scores were high enough to place them in the clinical range. For example, at three years of age, 7 per cent of children who had had insecure attachment relationships as infants were scored in the clinical range of the CBCL by their mothers, compared with 2 per cent of securely attached infants. Figures based on the fathers' reports were similar: 12 per cent of insecurely attached infants in the clinical range and 5 per cent of securely attached infants. The relative odds of scoring in the clinical range were therefore 2.4 to 3.5 times higher if the child had had an early insecure attachment than if the child had had a secure attachment.

Thus, measures of outcome are important in this type of study. When the actual number of diagnosable cases is expected to be small, a full psychiatric assessment for each child in a large cohort is difficult to justify. Standardized parent and teacher reports, however, do not provide psychiatric diagnoses. It may be that differences in scores below the clinical cutoff are not clinically relevant measures.

An alternative approach, and one that may be of greater use in associating specific diagnoses with particular attachment patterns, is the use of measures of attachment on an experimental basis as part of routine assessment of children referred to clinics for behaviour problems. When attachment was measured (using the measure used to assess preschoolers) in 25 children referred for one of the DSM-III-R disruptive behaviour disorders and 25 children who were not referred, 84% of the clinic children were classified insecure compared with only 25% of the non-clinic group.[50] Furthermore, a significantly greater proportion of the children who were referred to the clinic fell into the insecure/controlling category (40% versus 12%). This is the first study to demonstrate an association between clinic status and attachment quality and between a specific diagnosis and a specific form of attachment.

COLLABORATION BETWEEN RESEARCHERS AND CLINICIANS

Much of the work reviewed above has been carried out by psychologists studying child development who communicate with each other and publish their work in journals not routinely read by psychiatrists. Many developmental psychologists remain cautious and sceptical of this work.[51] Yet, whenever psychiatrists, particularly child psychiatrists, have been exposed to these ideas, methods and findings, there has been enthusiastic reception. Why is this so?

First, the concepts of attachment theory are familiar to many child psychiatrists. John Bowlby was a psychiatrist and wrote from a psychiatric perspective. However, there is now considerable empirical evidence to support what child psychiatrists always knew: experiences with a primary caregiver influence important aspects of personality. There is the promise in these new findings of a firm scientific basis for some aspects of common belief and practice.

Secondly, research on attachment combines clinical and experimental techniques. These methods rely on standard manipulations or probes and evaluation of resulting behaviour by schemes that can be objectively described and replicated. However, an important component of this evaluation is clinical in nature – reliance on detailed sensitive observations of the patterning and organization of behaviour. The training of coders, whether to score reunions from videotape or to review interview transcripts, is primarily training in clinical judgement. Detailed descriptions of salient behaviours are provided, but the coder must also learn how to use clinical intuitions. Thus, developmental psychologists working in this field are gaining more appreciation of clinical approaches to human behaviour.

Clinicians have been quick to see the possible applications of the methods used in research on attachment to clinical practice. Such efforts could lead to important clinical insights as well as information relevant to attachment theory. However, caution is warranted. These experimental methods are time consuming and costly in clinical practice. Furthermore, the available data are group data, not individual data. We do not know, for example, how frequently classification errors are made or what factors influence them. This is less important for group research data than for the clinical assessment or treatment of individuals. In addition, all but the methods used with infants must be considered to be in a very early stage of development. Nevertheless, a number of projects supported by research funding are using these methods in clinical settings as part of assessment and treatment,[50,52] and these projects promise to provide insight into the developmental history of psychopathology.

The result of this research has been a growing collaboration between researchers and clinicians, and between psychologists and psychiatrists. The history of attachment research is short but it has shown early promise. These interdisciplinary collaborations are a necessary step in making that future a reality.

References

1. Bowlby, J. The nature of the child's tie to his mother. *Int. J. Psychoanal.* (1958), **39**: 350–73.
2. Bowlby, J. *Attachment and loss: Attachment.* New York: Basic Books, 1969.
3. Bowlby, J. *Attachment and loss: Separation.* New York: Basic Books, 1973.
4. Bowlby, J. *Attachment and loss: Loss, sadness and depression.* New York: Basic Books, 1980.
5. Ainsworth, M. D. S., Wittig, B. A. Attachment and exploratory behavior of one-year-olds in a strange situation. In Foss, B. M. (ed.), *Determinants of infant behavior,* London: Methuen, 1969.
6. Ainsworth, M. D. S., Blehar, M. C., Waters, E., et al. *Patterns of attachment: A Psychological Study of the Strange Situation.* Hillsdale, NJ: Erlbaum, 1978.
7. Main, M., Solomon, J. Discovery of an insecure-disorganized/disoriented attachment pattern. In Brazelton, T. B., Yogman, M. W. (eds), *Affective Development in Infancy,* Norwood, NJ: Ablex, 1986.
8. Main, M., Solomon, J. Procedures for identifying infants as disorganized/disoriented during the Ainsworth Strange Situation. In Greenberg, M. T., Cicchetti, D., Cummings, E. M. (eds), *Attachment in the Preschool Years,* Chicago, IL: University of Chicago Press, 1990.
9. Cassidy, J., Marvin, R. S. Attachment organization in three- and four-year-olds: Coding guidelines (unpublished manual). Charlottesville, VA: Department of Psychology, University of Virginia, 1990.
10. Main, M., Kaplan, N., Cassidy, J. Security in infancy, childhood and adulthood: A move to the level of representation. *Monogr. Soc. Res. Child Dev.* (1985) **50**, (1–2, Serial no. 209): 6–104.
11. George, C., Kaplan, N., Main, M. The Berkeley Adult Attachment Interview (unpublished protocol). Berkeley, CA: Department of Psychology, University of California, 1985.
12. Van Ijzendoom, M. H., Kroonenberg, P. M. Cross cultural patterns of attachment: A meta-analysis of the strange situation. *Child Dev.* (1988), **59**: 147–56.

13. Waters, E. The stability of individual differences in infant–mother attachment. *Child Dev.* (1978), **49**: 483–94.
14. Grossmann, K. E., Grossmann, K. Parent–infant relationships in Bielefeld. In Immelman, K., Barlow, G., Petrinovich, L., et al. (eds), *Behavioral Development: The Bielefeld Interdisciplinary Project*, New York: Cambridge University Press, 1981.
15. Lamb, M. E. Qualitative aspect of mother–infant and father–infant attachments. *Infant Behav. Developm.* (1978), **1**: 265–75.
16. Main, M., Weston, D. R. The quality of the toddler's relationship to mother and to father: Related to conflict behavior and readiness to establish new relationships. *Child Dev.* (1981), **52**: 932–40.
17. Fox, N., Kimmerly, N. L., Schafer, W. D. Attachment to mother/attachment to father: A meta-analysis. *Child Dev.* (1991), **62**: 210–25.
18. Belsky, J., Rovine, M. Temperament and attachment security in the strange situation: An empirical rapprochement. *Child Dev.* (1987), **8**: 787–95.
19. Chess, S., Thomas, A. Infant bonding: Mystique and reality. *Am. J. Orthopsychiatry* (1982), **52**: 213–22.
20. Crockenberg, S. B. Infant irritability, mother responsiveness, and social support influences on security of infant–mother attachment. *Child Dev.* (1981), **52**: 857–65.
21. Goldsmith, H. H., Alansky, J. A. Maternal and infant temperamental predictors of attachment: A meta-analytical review. *J. Consult. Clin. Psychol.* (1987), **55**: 806–16.
22. Sroufe, L. A. Attachment classification from the perspective of infant–caregiver relationships and infant temperament. *Child Dev.* (1985), **56**: 1–14.
23. Belsky, J., Rovine, M., Taylor, D. G. The Pennsylvania Infant and Family Development Project. III: The origins of individual differences in infant–mother attachment: Maternal and infant contributions. *Child Dev.* (1984), **55**: 718–28.
24. Goldberg, S., Perrotta, M., Minde, K., et al. Maternal behavior and attachment in low birthweight twins and singletons. *Child Dev.* (1986), **57**: 34–46.
25. Grossmann, K., Grossmann, K. E. Maternal sensitivity and newborns' orientation responses as related to quality of attachment in northern Germany. *Monogr. Soc. Res. Child Dev.* (1985), **50** (1–2, Serial no. 209): 233–56.
26. Main, M., Tomasini, L., Tolan, W. Differences among mothers of infants judged to differ in security. *Dev. Psychol.* (1979), **15**: 472–3.
27. Arend, R., Gove, F., Sroufe, L. A. Continuity of individual adaptation from infancy to kindergarten: A predictive study of ego resiliency and curiosity in preschoolers. *Child Dev.* (1979), **50**: 950–59.
28. Bell, S. The development of the concept of object as related to infant–mother attachment. *Child Dev.* (1970), **41**: 291–311.
29. Lieberman, A. Preschooler's competence with a peer: Relations with attachment and peer experience. *Child Dev.* (1977), **48**: 1277–87.
30. Londerville, S., Main, M. Security of attachment, compliance, and maternal training methods in the second year of life. *Dev. Psychol.* (1981), **17**: 289–99.
31. Matas, L., Arend, R. A., Sroufe, L. A. Continuity and adaptation in the second year. The relationship between quality of attachment and later competence. *Child Dev.* (1978), **49**: 549–56.
32. Sroufe, L. A., Fox, N., Pancake, V. Attachment and dependency in developmental perspective. *Child Dev.* (1983), **54**: 1335–54.
33. Waters, E., Wippman, J., Sroufe, L. A. Attachment, positive affect, and competence in the peer group: Two studies in construct validation. *Child Dev.* (1979), **50**: 821–9.
34. Erickson, M. F., Sroufe, L. A., Egeland, B. The relationship between quality of attachment and behavior problems in a preschool high-risk sample. *Monogr. Soc. Res. Child Dev.* 1985; **50** (1–2, Serial no. 209): 147–66.

35. Renken, B., Egeland, B., Marvinney, D., et al. Early childhood antecedents of aggression and passive-withdrawal in early elementary school. *J. Pers.* (1989) **57**: 257–81.

36. Sroufe, L. A., Egeland, B., Kreutzer, T. The fate of early experience following developmental change: Longitudinal approaches to individual adaptation in childhood. *Child Dev.* (1990), **61**: 1363–73.

37. Goldberg, S. Risk factors in attachment. *Can. J. Psychol.* (1988), **42**: 173–88.

38. Spieker, S. J., Booth, C. Maternal antecedents of attachment quality. In Belsky, J., Nezworski, T. (eds), *Clinical Implications of Attachment*, Hillsdale, NJ: Erlbaum, 1988.

39. Crittenden, P. Maltreated infants: Vulnerability and resilience. *J. Child Psychol. Psychiatry* (1985), **26**: 85–96.

40. Radke-Yarrow, M., Cummings, E. M., Kuczynski, L., et al. Patterns of attachment in two- and three-year-olds in normal families and families with paternal depression. *Child Dev.* (1985), **56**: 591–615.

41. Lyons-Ruth, C., Connell, D., Zoll, D., et al. Infants at social risk: Relations among infant maltreatment, maternal behavior, and infant attachment behavior. *Dev. Psychol.* (1987), **23**: 223–32.

42. Carlson, V., Cicchetti, D., Barnett, D., et al. Disorganized/disoriented attachment relationships in maltreated infants. *Dev. Psychol.* (1989), **25**: 525–31.

43. Egeland, B., Farber, E. A. Infant–mother attachment: Factors related to its development and changes over time. *Child Dev.* (1984), **55**: 753–71.

44. Levine, L., Ward, M., Carlson, B. Attachment across three generations: Grandmother, mother, and infants. Paper presented at the World Association of Infant Psychiatry and Allied Disciplines, Lugano, Switzerland, 1989.

45. Van Ijzendoom, M. H. Intergenerational transmission of parenting: A review of studies in non-clinical populations. *Developm. Rev.* (in press).

46. Main, M., Hesse, E. Parents' unresolved traumatic experiences are related to infant disorganized attachment status: Is frightened or frightening behavior the linking mechanism? In Greenberg, M., Cicchetti, D., Cummings, E. M. (eds), *Attachment in the Preschool Years: Theory, Research and Intervention*, Chicago, IL: University of Chicago Press, 1990: 161–84.

47. Goldberg, S., Corter, C., Lojkasek, M., et al. Prediction of behavior problems in 4-year-olds born prematurely. *Developmental Psychopath.* (1990), **2**: 15–30.

48. Lewis, M., Feiring, C., McGuffog, C., et al. Predicting psychopathology in six-year-olds from early social relations. *Child Dev.* (1984), **55**: 123–36.

49. Bates, J. E., Bayles, K. Attachment and the development of behavior problems. In Belsky, J., Nezworski, T. (eds), *Clinical Implications of Attachment*, Hillsdale, NJ: Erlbaum, 1988.

50. Speltz, M. L. The treatment of preschool conduct problems: An integration of behavioral and attachment concepts. In Greenberg, M., Cicchetti, D., Cummings, E. M. (eds), *Attachment in the Preschool Years: Theory, Research and Intervention*, Chicago, IL: University Press, 1990: 399–426.

51. Lamb, M. E., Thompson, R. A., Gardner, W.P., et al. Security of infantile attachment as assessed in the 'strange situation': Its study and biological interpretation. *Behav. Brain Sci.* (1984), **7**: 127–47.

52. Lieberman, A. Pawl, J. Clinical applications of attachment theory: In Belsky, J., Nezworski, T. (eds), *Clinical Implications of Attachment*, Hillsdale, NJ: Erlbaum, 1988: 327–51.

29

AMERICAN CHILD CARE TODAY*

Sandra Scarr

Child care has two purposes: mothers' employment and children's devel- **OVERVIEW**
opment. These are conflicting goals, because the first focuses on the quantity
and affordability of child care whereas the second favors expensive quality
services. Affordable child care fosters maternal employment and gender
equality. With welfare reform demanding more child-care places to move
mothers from welfare to work, the pressure for larger quantities of child
care is great. Demanding regulations raise the quality of care and give more
assurance of children's well-being, but they also increase the cost. More
expensive regulations price more working parents out of licensed care and
force them to use unregulated home care. Widely varying qualities of child
care have been shown to have only small effects on children's current
development and no demonstrated long-term impact, except on disadvantaged children, whose homes put them at developmental risk. Parents have
far greater impact on their children's development through both the genes
and environments they provide. Thus, greater quantities of affordable,
regulated child care may be possible.

Care of American children by anyone other than their own mothers needs to
have a name. Even care of children by their own fathers is counted by the US
Labor Department as "other relative care." Cultural anxiety about nonmaternal child care is revealed in every aspect of research, practices, and policies that
are reviewed in this article.

Terms for the care of children by people other than mothers include *child
care, family day care, home care, center care, nanny care, babysitting, preschool*

* Previously published in *American Psychologist*, **53**, 2 (February 1998), pp. 95–108.

education, after-school care, and others. *Day care* is probably the most frequently used term, although early childhood professionals prefer the term *child care*, because "we take care of *children*, not *days*" (M. Guddemi, personal communication, July 6, 1996). Different terms relate to the age of the child (infant, toddler, preschool or school age), the setting (e.g., home versus center), and the primary purpose (babysitting, when the focus is on working mothers' needs, versus preschool education, when the focus is on benefits to the child). The term *child care* is used throughout this article to include all varieties of nonmaternal care of children who reside with their parent(s) or close family members; it excludes foster care and institutional care.

The assumption of all the nomenclature is that child care provided by anyone other than the child's mother deserves special notice, because it is a nonnormative event that needs definition. In fact, shared child care is the normative experience for contemporary American children, the vast majority of whose mothers are employed. More than half the mothers of infants under 12 months of age are in the labor force; three-quarters of school-age children's mothers are working (Behrman, 1996).

HISTORY OF CHILD CARE

Nonmaternal shared child care is, in fact, normative for the human young, both historically and worldwide: "Nonparental care is a universal practice with a long history, not a dangerous innovation representing a major deviation from species-typical and species-appropriate patterns of child care" (Lamb, in press). Exclusive maternal care of infants and young children is a cultural myth of an idealized 1950s, not a reality anywhere in the world either now or in earlier times. Child care has always been shared, usually among female relatives. Until recently, most American children of working parents were cared for by other female relatives, but high rates of female employment have reduced that source of babysitters. What has changed over time and varies crossnationally is the degree to which child care is bought in the marketplace rather than shared among female relatives.

Today, more American children are cared for by paid providers than by relatives. Relatives have, presumably, some emotional commitment to the health and safety of relatives' offspring; therefore, quality of care was seldom raised as an issue of concern. The predominance of nonrelative care in the last decade has alerted consumers, governments, and the research community to the possibly damaging effects of poor quality care on children's development; the zeitgeist called for critical appraisal of nonmaternal care (Scarr, 1985).

In agricultural societies, infants are typically left in the care of siblings, grandmothers, or female neighbors, who are also caring for their own children. In industrialized societies, mothers' employment outside the home has necessitated nonmaternal care of various types. Demand for child care is driven entirely by the economic need for women in the labor force (Lamb, Sternberg, Hwang, & Broberg, 1992), although occasional subgroups, such as upper-class mothers with heavy social schedules, may use extensive nonmaternal child care (Lamb, in press). Tracing historical changes in maternal employment provides a guide to the demand for and use of nonmaternal child care.

Employment moved out of the home and into the workplace

Prior to the Industrial Revolution, and in nonindustrial parts of the world today, women are both economically productive workers and primary child-caregivers. When employment moved outside the home and into the factory and office, men followed work into new settings, and women generally remained at home, without a direct economic role.

In a correlated development, mothers' roles as knowledgeable caregivers began to be stressed. In the late 19th and early 20th centuries, child rearing was no longer a natural species response but a role that required extensive education and knowledge. Children began to have tender psyches that required maternal attention to develop well. Mothers were given an important emotional role in the home that complemented fathers' economic productivity (Kagan, 1980; Scarr, 1984).

Prior to World War II, few women remained in the labor force after childbearing. The need for industrial workers during the war brought many mothers into factories and offices to replace men away at war. Mothers' employment was culturally sanctioned and supported by the government provision of child-care centers attached to war factories. Mothers, as Rosie the Riveter, took on the many paid work roles that had previously been denied them.

After the war, government and cultural supports for mothers' employment were withdrawn, child-care centers were closed, and mothers were told to go home to make way in the workplace for returning veterans. The birthrate soared and new suburbs were built as federally sponsored highway programs fueled a boom in housing outside of cities. All of this was a direct result of government policy that held as ideal a two-parent family with a working father and a nonworking mother, ensconced in single-family dwelling.

Erroneous predictions about an economic recession after the war, which became instead an economic boom fueled by unfulfilled consumer demand for cars, refrigerators, and housing, left many jobs open to women. Many mothers did not follow official advice to go home, and female employment has grown steadily since. Goods and services that used to be homemade (e.g., clothing, canned goods, and cleaning) came to be increasingly purchased, requiring additional family income. As the divorce rate and single motherhood soared, more mothers needed jobs to support their families. Today most mothers are employed.

In 1995, 62% of mothers with children under six years were employed. This rate was up more than 2% from 1994 and nearly 5% from 1993. Among mothers with children under two years, 58% were working in March 1995, up 4% from 1993 (1996 Green Book, as cited in Hofferth, 1996). The ideal of a nonemployed mother remained strong, however. One legacy for working mothers of the baby-boom generation and beyond is guilt about their employment.

Purposes of child care

Three major, often conflicting, purposes for child care create the child-care dilemma we as a society suffer today (Scarr and Weinberg, 1986; Stoney and Greenberg, 1996). First, child care supports maternal employment, which for individual families and for the economy has become a necessity. It is assumed that US working families will pay for their own child-care services. Secondly, child care serves children's development, which can be enhanced by high-quality early childhood programs, whether or not children's mothers are employed. Again, families are expected to pay for early childhood programs, unless they are poor. Thirdly, child care has been used throughout this century to intervene with economically disadvantaged and ethnic minority children to socialize them to the cultural mainstream. Poor and immigrant children could be fed, immunized, given English language experience, behaviorally trained, given an orderly schedule, and so forth (Scarr and Weinberg, 1986; Stoney and Greenberg, 1996). Taxpayers have paid for these services to the poor.

The roots of child care are in the welfare and reform movements of the 19th century. Day nurseries, which evolved into the child-care centers of today, began in Boston in the 1840s to care for the children of widows and working wives of seamen, two groups of women who had to work outside the home. Reformers, such as Jane Addams, founded day nurseries to care for poor and immigrant children, whose mothers had to work (Scarr and Weinberg, 1986). Preteen school-age children required adult supervision in order to be safely occupied and kept out of trouble. The primary purpose of day nurseries was to keep children safe and fed while their poor mothers worked. Other benefits, such as early education, were secondary.

By contrast, kindergartens and nursery schools began in the early 20th century to enhance the social development of middle- and upper-class children. For a few hours a week, the children could play with others and experience an enriched learning environment under the tutelage of trained early childhood teachers. Nursery schools existed to serve the developmental needs of middle- and upper-class children, whose mothers were not employed (Scarr and Weinberg, 1986).

By the late 1960s, educators and child-development researchers recognized the value of nursery schools for poor children, who needed the stimulation and learning opportunities that such early childhood settings afforded children from affluent families. Head Start was designed, in large part, to enhance the learning of poor and minority children – to provide the same kinds of early childhood opportunities that middle-class children had enjoyed for decades. Because many of their mothers were supported by welfare, Head Start could involve mothers in early childhood programs and serve children's developmental needs. As part-day, part-year programs, Head Start did not serve the child-care needs of working mothers.

These three purposes for child care set quite different priorities for the services to be offered and have different assumptions about who will pay for them. Thus, disputes continue about whose goals are to be served by child-care services, who shall pay for them, and what form child care should take. Conflicting advocacy for (a) high-quantity, low-cost caregiving, versus (b) high-quality, high-cost, child-centered preschool education, versus (c) intervention and compensation for poor children continues to compete for attention in debates about American child care.

Varieties of child-care arrangements

When the focus is on early childhood education, whether for higher or lower income children, the setting is usually a center or preschool. When the focus is on care while parents work, the setting is often a home. In fact, these distinctions have blurred in recent years, as more and more children move from homes to center-based programs, where they receive both extended care and early education.

Family day care versus center care   Family day-care providers care for children in their own homes. The providers' own children are often included in the mix of children, which can include infants through school-age children who come before and after school. Most family day-care homes accommodate 6 or fewer children and have one caregiver. Some larger homes care for 6 to 20 children and employ aides to assist the family day-care providers. States generally regulate larger homes. Family day-care homes are for-profit independent providers.

Child-care centers provide group care for children from infancy to school age in age-segregated groups, with smaller ratios of children, at younger ages, to adults. Facilities vary from church basements to purpose-built centers with specialized spaces and equipment. The most notable differences between homes and centers are educational curricula and staff training, which centers are required to provide and homes are not. Parents prefer center-based care for preschool children and home care for infants and toddlers.

Licensed versus unlicensed care   In all states, child-care centers must be licensed by a state department of social services or its equivalent.[1] Licensure includes regulations on health and safety, ratios of children to adults, group sizes, staff training, and often required play materials. Regular inspections are done semiannually or annually, or more frequently if problems have been noted.

Family homes that care for more than six children are usually required to be licensed, although regulations vary considerably from state to state. Most family day-care providers care for fewer than six children and are therefore exempt from any state regulation or inspection. Availability of federal food subsidies to licensed homes, however, has encouraged more family day-care homes to seek licensure or registration. Family day-care homes are rarely visited by state regulators.

Nonprofit versus for-profit centers   In the United States, child-care centers are sponsored by churches, nonprofit community groups, public schools, Head Start, employers, for-profit independent providers, and corporations. Public schools and Head Start serve older preschool children only, whereas other centers usually include younger children as well. Only about half of all centers, however, provide infant care, because the required low ratios of infants to providers make infant care prohibitively expensive.

The mix of public provision and private enterprise in US child care reflects the ambivalence Americans feel about whether child care should be primarily a publicly supported service for children or a business expense for working families (partially offset by tax credits). Should tax dollars be used to supply child care only to poor children, or should all children be eligible for publicly supported child care? Should family day care and privately owned centers profit from the child-care business, or should child care be a nonprofit service (as in Hawaii) like primary education?

Where are children today?

In 1995, there were nearly 21 million children under the age of five years who were not yet enrolled in school. Of these, about 40% were cared for regularly by parents, 21% by other relatives, 31% in child-care centers, 14% in family day-care homes, and 4% by sitters in the child's home. These figures total more than 100% because 9% of children have more than one regular care arrangement, such as enrollment in a part-time preschool program and parental care at home during other hours (Hofferth, 1996). The distribution of center sponsorship is shown in figure 29.1.

Over the last 30 years, children have been shifted gradually from home to center-based care. In 1965, only 6% of children were cared for in centers; by 1995, 31% were. Use of family day care and care by parents, other relatives, and sitters all declined. Figure 29.2 shows historical trends in use of different forms of child care. By 1990, in families with employed mothers (three-fifths of families with young children), only 37% of infants and 32% of children from one to two years of age were cared for primarily by parents. Of three- to four-year-olds, only 25% were primarily in parental care, and 37% were in child-care centers (Hofferth, 1996).

In surveys by *Working Mother* magazine in 1995 and 1996, readers expressed strong preferences for center-based care over home care, whether by relatives

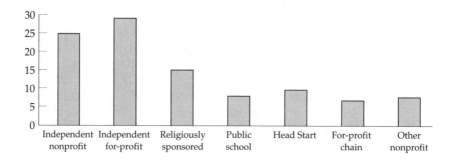

FIGURE 29.1 Administrative auspices of child-care centers (by percentage) in the United States, 1990 (Willer et al., 1991)

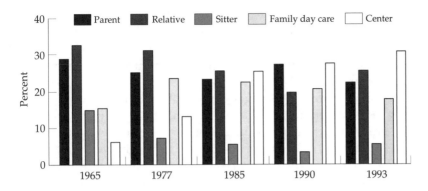

FIGURE 29.2 Primary care for youngest preschool child of employed mothers, 1965–93 (Hofferth, 1996)

or not. Child safety and parental control over the arrangement were prominent reasons for the preference. Home care is unsupervised and usually unlicensed. Television exposés of abuse and neglect in day-care homes have appeared regularly over the last decade. Relatives do not always abide by parents' child-rearing preferences, such as toilet-training techniques and feeding routines. Paid help is more dependable and controllable. Child-care centers are open even if one caregiver is ill or on vacation (Mason and Kuhlthau, as cited in Mason and Duberstein, 1992).

Relative care is, in general, less costly than other care (Hofferth, 1996). About half of relative care involves payment, but the rates tend to be lower than market rates. Although 23% of parents express a preference for relative care, 77% of mothers prefer another kind of child care (Mason and Kuhlthau, as cited in Mason and Duberstein, 1992). Economic factors play the major role in use of relative care. The more preschool children in the family, the more likely it is that relatives will supply the care, because market discounts for multichild families do not substantially reduce the total cost of child care. The higher the family income, the less likely parents are to choose relative care (Blau and Robbins, 1990).

Older preschool children are more likely than infants and toddlers to be enrolled in center care, but from 1965 to 1995, the use of center care for infants and toddlers grew exponentially, from about 3% in 1965 to 23% in 1993. Parental care of infants and toddlers declined dramatically across that period. School-age care has lagged behind the need for this service and enjoys little public support.

Children from more affluent families and those from families on welfare are most likely to be enrolled in centers rather than cared for in homes. Families with an annual income of more than $50,000 can afford center-based programs; those below the poverty line receive subsidies for child care and enroll their children without charge in Head Start. Working families with annual incomes below $25,000 but above the poverty line are the least likely to be able to afford and to use center-based child care.

Nearly 10% of mothers work nonstandard hours; they have fewer choices of child-care arrangements. Only 3% of centers and about 17% of family day-care homes provide evening and weekend care (Hofferth, 1996). In two-parent families, children of evening-shift and weekend workers may be cared for by the other parent, or by another relative in the case of single-parent families. Father care is a seldom recognized choice that minimizes costs of child care in a dual-income family.

Presser's data from Detroit suggest that child-care preferences often determine whether mothers work shifts other than 9-to-5. Fully one-third of dual-income families have one parent working nonstandard hours to offset child-care costs (Presser, 1992b). When mothers work nights and weekends, and when they have more than one preschool child, fathers are more likely to supply some of the child care. As child-care costs rise, parents are more likely to arrange schedules to provide the care themselves (Mason and Duberstein, 1992).

Much has been said about the shortage of child-care spaces in the United States (Hofferth, 1992). With annual increases in the percentage and numbers of working mothers (soon to increase dramatically with welfare reform), the child-care supply is not growing sufficiently to meet the demand for the care of infants and toddlers, of mildly sick children, or of children whose parents work nonstandard hours. Infant and toddler care are scarce nationally; because of low ratio requirements of children to staff, infant and toddler care are very expensive and therefore in particularly short supply. Preschool and after-school care are less costly and more readily available. It is also difficult to find suitable care for disabled children. Even with the Americans With Disabilities Act to encourage nondiscrimination, few facilities can provide competent care for disabled children, particularly those with severe behavior disorders and multiple physical handicaps.

The primary problem is that the market for child care is poorly funded, both by limited parental incomes and by low state subsidies. The price of child care cannot be set high enough in many communities to encourage investment in new facilities or quality programs. Low-income communities have a smaller child-care supply than more affluent ones because of parents' inability to pay for care.

Child-care regulations

The 50 states and the District of Columbia display amazing differences in the regulations they have developed to affect cost and quality of child care. Ratios of children to adults in some states (e.g., Maryland, Massachusetts) are less than half of those approved in other states (e.g., Ohio, Texas). Permissible ratios for children under 12 months of age range from 3 to 8 per caregiver. For children ages 12 to 35 months, the range among states is from 4 to 13 children per caregiver! Teacher training requirements vary from none (e.g., Georgia, Alabama) to college degrees or advanced credentials (e.g., Illinois, New Jersey). Group sizes permitted for younger children vary from 4 or 6 children, to 20 children, to legally unlimited numbers.

There is a significant cultural and economic gradient from North to South, whereby parents and state regulators in the Northern tier of states demand better quality preschool and child-care programs and are willing to pay more for lower ratios and more highly trained staff. However, in some Northern states with very low ratios and high training requirements, few parents can afford center-based care. Massachusetts, for example, has less than one-third the number of child-care center spaces per capita than Texas, a high-ratio, low-training state, has. Low ratios and teacher training requirements raise the cost of center care to such levels that the vast majority of parents in Massachusetts are forced to use unregulated family day care. By contrast, parents in Texas have the highest provision of center-based programs in the country. The trade-off of quantity and quality in center-based care is a recurring dilemma.

A LABOR FORCE PERSPECTIVE ON CHILD-CARE RESEARCH

Despite national ambivalence about maternal employment, the US economy could not function without women employees and enterpreneurs. Today, 48% of workers are women. It is inconceivable that the 80% of these women who are mothers could stay home. Seldom do developmental psychologists consider the economic legitimacy of child care to serve the goal of maternal employment.

There are two major reasons for maternal employment: (a) economic well-being of the family, and (b) gender equality (Scarr, 1996). "Child care policies in many countries have been designed at least in part to promote female employment and to equalize potential employment opportunities of men and women" (Lamb, in press).

First and foremost, mothers (and fathers) are employed because their families need or want the income to enhance their standard of living. In today's economy, it is most often a necessity to have two employed parents to support a family with children. Two-thirds of mothers are working to keep their families out of poverty (Scarr, Phillips, and McCartney, 1990). With welfare reform, this proportion will increase.

The second reason for maternal employment – to promote economic, social, and political gender equality – is a more complicated issue. The major reason for discrepancies in men's and women's work compensation and career achievements is that family responsibilities fall more heavily on women, especially when there are small children in the home (Scarr, 1996). Most mothers do not maintain full-time employment or have the same commitment to careers that childless women have or that men have, whether they are fathers or not. Unequal child-care responsibilities lead mothers to be less invested in career development and less motivated to maintain continuous, full-time employment. As several commentators have noted, there cannot be gender equality in the work-force until men take more responsibility for child care. According to Supreme Court Justice Ruth Bader Ginsburg, "Women will not be truly liberated until men take equal care of children. If I had an affirmative action plan to design, it would be to give men every incentive to be concerned about the rearing of children" ("Justice Ginsburg Takes On," 1995, p. A4).

Although mothers in the Western industrialized world have increased their economic activity, the gendered division of responsibility and work involved in child-care provision is still the norm in families with young children. When tested for anxiety about leaving their children in child care, fathers expressed more anxiety than mothers, but when asked to rate how their wives felt about leaving children in care, fathers greatly exaggerated their wives' worries about employment and child care (Deater-Deckard, Scarr, McCartney, and Eisenberg, 1994). By inference, fathers think it is the mother's job to worry more about child care, even today. Men's collective choice of nonparticipation in child care helps to maintain men's privileged position in society and in relation to the market and the state (Leira, 1992; Presser, 1992a).

Child care and other family supports

One often hears liberal policy analysts yearn for the federal government to provide more family-friendly policies that make balancing work and family life less stressful. Corporations vie each year to be on the *Working Mother* magazine list of the top 100 most family-friendly companies. The world's role models of countries with the most family-friendly policies are the Nordic countries.

Family-friendly government policies in the Nordic countries (Sweden, Norway, Finland, Denmark, and Iceland) help mothers to balance work and family life by granting paid, job-guaranteed maternity and parental leaves, child allowances to supplement family income, and part-time work for mothers when their children are young. Although parental leave and part-time employment opportunities can be used by either fathers or mothers, mothers take more than 95% of the leave time and make up virtually all of the part-time workers.

The collective effect of these family-friendly policies is to increase gender inequality to such an extent that Swedish women earn only half of men's wages (in the United States, women earn 77% of men's wages; "Women's Figures," 1997) and hold virtually none of the top jobs in corporations or universities (Cherlin, 1992; Leira, 1992; Scarr, 1996).

Government policies that support maternal absences from the labor force, such as paid parental leaves and child allowances, make balancing work and family life easier for mothers of young children, but they have long-term deleterious consequences for mothers' careers (Scarr, 1996). Although many admire the Swedish system of extensive supports for working parents, including part-time work opportunities when children are young, Cherlin (1992) cited some of the disadvantages:

> Note that you cannot make Partner in a Stockholm law firm working six hours a day. The cost of the system is that its solutions may impede the ability of well-educated mothers to rise up the managerial and professional hierarchies.... That still leaves the problem that women ... may lose experience and continuity in the labor force and the associated promotions and wage increases.   (p. 213)

In the United States, where there are few family supports, mothers are more often employed full-time even when their children are infants, thus maintaining more continuous labor-force participation, which leads to career advancement, higher incomes, retirement benefits, and other markers of gender equality. Most mothers want to be employed for a variety of reasons. Women's labor-force participation is associated with higher family income, greater personal satisfaction, and more social support. However, the double burdens of home and family also lead to role overload and excessive work hours for young mothers in the United States (Scarr, Phillips, and McCartney, 1989). Although working mothers experience greater time stress and role strain (Staines & Pleck, 1983), they express greater satisfaction with their multiple roles than stay-at-home mothers (Scarr, Phillips, & McCartney, 1989).

Significant problems with child-care arrangements and high child-care costs discourage mothers' labor-force participation and can lead to depression and marital problems (Ross and Mirowsky, 1988; White and Keith, 1990). If child-care costs were more reasonable, national surveys show that 10–20% more mothers would return to the labor force after giving birth (Mason and Duberstein, 1992). Child-care problems impair women's long-term earning prospects by limiting their participation in the labor force (Cherlin, 1992; Collins and Hofferth, 1996; Mason and Duberstein, 1992; Scarr, 1996).

Income inequalities between men and women are largely explained by the lower labor-force participation of mothers in their childbearing years. In 1995, childless women in their 20s and 30s earned 98% of men's wages ("Women's Figures," 1997). In addition, women are less likely than men to be given advanced training opportunities, promotions, and managerial responsibility because they are perceived to have less commitment to careers (Scarr, 1996). Subsidized child care is the one family-friendly government policy that supports gender equality and women's career achievements.

Welfare reform, or Why shouldn't poor mothers work too?

The idea that mothers should be paid to stay at home with children arose during the 1930s, when widows and a few divorcees needed support to rear their children at least to school age. Aid to Families with Dependent Children (AFDC) was the last in a series of programs that was initiated to accomplish this goal. Support levels were generally low, so that a mother and her children could live at the poverty level, but they were provided with medical insurance, food stamps, often housing and clothing allowances, and social services. Gradually, over the past 50 years, welfare (AFDC) recipients came to be identified with never-married minority women and poor White women who had children in their teens and early 20s and were never employed.

As the majority of middle-class mothers entered the labor force in the 1980s, there was a sea-change in thinking about AFDC. By the early 1990s, the majority of middle-class mothers of infants and young children were employed: two-thirds when their children were under six years of age and three-quarters by the time their children were school age, with most of these mothers working full-time. Married mothers were working at the same rate as single mothers (Scarr, Phillips, and McCartney, 1989). Public empathy for mothers supported by AFDC to stay home with their children evaporated. Why should the taxes of working mothers go to support poor mothers to enjoy the privilege of staying home with their children? Reform of the welfare system rose to the top of the political agenda and was passed in 1996. Welfare will no longer be an open-ended, lifetime entitlement. It will provide time-limited support in emergencies, but mothers of children over three years of age can expect to be employed. Child-care assistance for low-income mothers is the key to welfare reform, because single low-income mothers cannot pay market rates for child care.

'Workfare means day care'

Child care is the essential ingredient in welfare reform and mothers' employment, as indicated by the above heading taken from a recent *Time* magazine article (1996). State by state, policies are being developed to provide child care to permit poor mothers to work. The major intent is to care for children while their mothers are employed, but what quality of care will be afforded by the states? There are no necessary quality assurances, beyond basic health and safety, in the provision of child care that allows mothers to work. Only when one is concerned about the children's development do other qualities of the child-care experience matter.

The quality/cost/affordability dilemma

Child care is critical to working parents' well-being (Mason and Duberstein, 1992). The availability and affordability of child care of acceptable quality directly affect parents' ability to manage both work and family life. Location, hours of operation, and flexibility (with respect to rules, mildly ill children, and the like) are major factors in the perceived availability of child care. Many parents find their choices quite limited (Galinsky, 1992).

Cost in relation to family income is the major affordability issue (Scarr, 1992b). As in any market-driven service, quality depends on what consumers are willing and able to pay for child care, which economists refer to as the *cost per quality unit of care* (Mason and Duberstein, 1992; Morris and Helburn, 1996). Consumers who are able to pay a high price will find someone willing to provide the service. Low-income families struggle to find acceptable quality care at a price they can afford, although they pay a higher percentage of their income for child care (23% versus 6% in high-income families). The trade-off of cost and quality of services is a major dilemma in American child care (Morris and Helburn, 1996).

Accessibility and cost of child care per quality unit are overriding issues in evaluating the impact of child care on parents (Prosser and McGroder, 1992). Ease of access, measured in travel time to a child-care center, directly affects how likely a mother is to stay in the labor force (Collins and Hofferth, 1996). Middle- and upper-income mothers are much more likely to keep their jobs if they use formal child-care arrangements (day-care centers) than if they have informal or no stable arrangements. Labor force participation among low-income mothers is more sensitive to the availability of relatives to care for children, because they cannot afford to pay market rates for child care (Collins and Hofferth, 1996).

Absenteeism and productivity effects

Mothers with secure child care are absent from work and tardy less often and are more productive in the workplace.

> When child care arrangements break down, employed parents are more likely to be absent, to be late, to report being unable to concentrate on the job, to have higher levels of stress and more stress-related health problems, and to report lower parental and marital satisfaction. (Galinsky, 1992, p. 167)

Breakdowns in child-care arrangements are frequent and stressful; in a Portland, Oregon, study, 36% of fathers and 46% of mothers who used out-of-home care reported child-care-related stress. Leading causes of child-care breakdown are child illness and a provider who quits (Galinsky, 1992). The greater the number of child-care arrangements, the more likely they are to break down and the greater the parental stress. Stable, reliable child care of acceptable quality is clearly related to mothers returning to work and staying in the labor force; this is especially true of middle- and high-income mothers (Collins and Hofferth, 1996; Phillips, 1992).

A CHILD DEVELOPMENT PERSPECTIVE ON CHILD-CARE RESEARCH

Three waves of research

The ecology of child-care research has undergone some important changes in the past two decades. Three waves of child-care research have been identified (Belsky, 1984; Clarke-Stewart, 1988; McCartney and Marshall, 1989). In the 1970s, the first wave compared maternal care with any kind of nonmaternal care, without assessment of the quality of either setting in which the care took place. The implicit research question was "How much damage is done to infants and young children by working mothers?" There was no consideration of whether variation in child development depended on variation in kind and quality of care, at home or in other child-care settings.

The second wave examined the quality and variety of child-care settings and introduced the idea that children's responses to child care may be individually different. In the 1980s, many child-care studies actually observed child care in process, evaluated quality of care, and assessed children individually.

The third wave of research included not only proximal influences on the child but distal influences as well. McCartney and Marshall (1989) suggested the inclusion of three systems to describe a true ecological study of the child-care experience: first, variation of child-care quality and type; second, family characteristics; and, third, individual differences among children. Although considerable attention has been devoted to evaluating child-care settings, characteristics of parents and family settings have seldom been integrated into child-care research.

A special note should be made on child-care-as–intervention with children from low-income and disadvantaged families. The best studied interventions, such as the Carolina Abecedarian Project (Ramey, Bryant, Sparling, and Wasik, 1985), used child care to enrich poor children's lives with positive results both concurrently and into primary school. Children with poor learning opportunities at home and without sufficient emotional support are particularly benefited by early childhood programs (McCartney, Scarr, Phillips, and Grajek, 1985), and the more intensive the intervention, the better the results (Ramey and Ramey, 1992).

Dimensions of quality

There is an extraordinary international consensus among child-care researchers and practitioners about what quality child care is: It is warm, supportive interactions with adults in a safe, healthy, and stimulating environment, where early education and trusting relationships combine to support individual children's physical, emotional, social, and intellectual development (Bredekamp, 1989).

Although quality of care is a multifaceted concept, the most commonly used measures of center quality are remarkably similar in the dimensions of quality they stress and in their measurement characteristics (Scarr, Eisenberg, and Deater-Deckard, 1994). Determinations of child-care quality are based on a number of criteria, but the most commonly agreed on are health and safety requirements, responsive and warm interaction between staff and children, developmentally appropriate curricula, limited group size, age-appropriate caregiver:child ratios, adequate indoor and outdoor space, and adequate staff training in either early childhood education or child development (Bredekamp, 1989; Kontos and Fiene, 1987). Caregivers with specific training in child care and child development provide more sensitive and responsive care than do those without such training. In sum, the quality of child care is affected by lower ratios, smaller group sizes, and better qualified teachers (Cost, Quality, and Child Outcomes Study Team, 1995; Scarr, Eisenberg, and Deater-Deckard, 1994; Whitebook, Howes, and Phillips, 1991).

Staff turnover is another common measure of the quality of care. High turnover means that children have fewer opportunities to develop stable, affectionate relationships with caregivers. Stability of care appears to be especially important for infants and toddlers, who display more appropriate social behaviors in stable than in unstable care arrangements (Howes and Stewart, 1987; Suwalsky, Zaslow, Klein, and Rabinovich, 1986). Recently, a tri-state study has shown that quality of care is more closely related to teacher wages than to other structural center-care variables (Phillips, Mekos, Scarr, McCartney, and Abbott-Shim, in press; Scarr, Eisenberg, and Deater-Deckard, 1994).

Variations in quality of care

Few experienced observers would doubt that center quality in the United States varies from excellent to dreadful and is, on average, mediocre (Cost, Quality, and Child Outcomes Study Team, 1995; Hofferth, Brayfield, Deich, and Holcomb, 1991; National Institute of Child Health and Human Development [NICHD] Early Child Care Research Network, 1996; Scarr, Phillips, McCartney, and Abbott-Shim, 1993). Quality in child-care centers is measured, by observation and interview, in units that are regulated (such as ratios of teachers to children, group sizes, and teacher training) and in dimensions that are process-oriented (such as adult–child interactions and developmentally appropriate activites; Phillips, 1987). In European studies, child-care quality also varies but not as dramatically as in the United States (Lamb, Sternberg, Hwang, and Broberg, 1992).

Family day-care homes have seldom been studied, and those that have been sampled may not be representative of the enormous number of unlicensed, unregulated homes. Studies of family day care have found quality to be highly variable (Galinsky, Howes, Kontos, and Shinn, 1994). In the recent NICHD study (NICHD Early Child Care Research Network, 1996), day-care home quality was, on average, fair to good but again highly variable.

Poor quality child care has been reported to put children's development at risk for poorer language and cognitive scores and lower ratings of social and emotional adjustment (for reviews, see Lamb, in press; Scarr and Eisenberg, 1993). Studies of center quality and child outcomes, which controlled statistically for family background differences, have found that overall quality has small but reliable effects on language and cognitive development (Goelman and Pence, 1987; McCartney, 1984; Wasik, Ramey, Bryant, and Sparling, 1990), social competence, and social adjustment (McCartney et al., 1997). Parents and caregivers rated children as more considerate, sociable, intelligent, and task-oriented when caregivers engaged in more positive verbal interactions with the children.[2] Other studies have found that children with involved and responsive caregivers display more exploratory behaviors, are more positive (Clarke-Stewart, Gruber, and Fitzgerald, 1994; Holloway and Reichhart-Erickson, 1989), and display better peer relations (Howes, Phillips, and Whitebook, 1992) than children with uninvolved, unresponsive caregivers. The inferences from these findings are not straightforward, however.

Predictably, quality of care selected by parents has been found to be correlated with parents' personal characteristics (Bolger and Scarr, 1995), thereby complicating interpretations of any effects of child care per se. The confound of family and child-care characteristics leads to overestimation of child-care effects that result instead from family differences. For example, children from families with single employed mothers and low incomes were more likely to be found in lower-quality care (Howes and Olenick, 1986). Children in high-quality care had parents who were more involved and interested in compliance than parents of children in lower quality care, and behavioral differences were evident in the center. Parents who use more punitive forms of discipline and hold more authoritarian attitudes toward children were found to choose lower-quality care for their children (Bolger and Scarr, 1995; Scarr et al., 1993).

In a recent large study, less sensitive mothers who value work more chose poorer-quality child care in the infants' first six months, enrolled their infants in centers at earlier ages for more hours per week, and were more likely to have insecurely attached infants (NICHD Early Child Care Research Network, in press). Of course, variations in parents' interactions with their children and in parents' personality, intelligence, and attitudes determine the characteristics that will be transmitted to children genetically as well as environmentally (Scarr, 1992a; 1993). How can these confounds be sorted out?

Many studies statistically co-vary out measured family characteristics from associations between child care and child outcomes and look at residual associations. When family and child-care qualities are truly confounded, however, it is impossible to co-vary out all family effects, because one has only a limited set of measures of the families – typically parents' education, income, and occupation, and some personality, cognitive, or attitudinal test scores. Parents who differ on any one of these measures are very likely to differ on many other unmeasured traits that affect associations between child care and child outcomes. Thus, the small, statistically reliable associations that have been found between child-care quality and child outcomes are exceedingly difficult to interpret.

Nonmaternal Care

Nonmaternal infant care has been the most controversial issue in the entire child-care research field, but it may soon be laid to rest. Throughout the 1980s and early 1990s, dramatic claims were made about the damaging effects of early entry into "day care" (not defined or measured) on infants' attachments to their mothers (Belsky, 1986, 1988, 1992; Belsky and Rovine, 1988). Reanalyses of data on day-care versus "home-reared" infants revealed a slight difference in rates of insecure attachments as measured by the Strange Situation: 37% versus 29% (Clarke-Stewart, 1988, 1989; Lamb, Sternberg, and Prodromidis, 1992). Other measures of attachment showed no relationship to age at entry or amount of infant child care.

Arguments swirled in the public press and developmental literature about whether the results applied only to boys; to infants with insensitive mothers; to infants who experience more than 20, 30, or 35 hours of nonmaternal care a week; or to infants who experience poor-quality care (Phillips, McCartney, Scarr, and Howes, 1987). Working mothers were tormented with doubt and guilt (Bowman, 1992). Finally, the NICHD Early Child Care Research Study (NICHD Early Child Care Research Network, in press) of more than 1,000 infants has shown no relationship between age at entry or amount of infant care, and attachments as measured by the Strange Situation (for a full review, see Lamb, in press). Naturally, less sensitive, less well-adjusted mothers were much more likely to have insecurely attached infants (NICHD Early Child Care Research Network, in press). Several interaction effects suggested that higher-quality care may help to offset poor mothering. Let us hope that is the end of the early child-care controversy.

Lack of long-term effects

Researchers have explored the possible long-term effects of day-care experiences in different qualities of care for children from different kinds of backgrounds. Children from low-income families are definitely benefited by quality child care, which has been used as an intervention strategy (Field, 1991; Ramey et al., 1985; Ramey and Ramey, 1992). Poor children who experience high-quality infant and preschool care show better school achievement and socialized behaviors in later years than similar children without child-care experience or with experience in lower-quality care. For poor children, quality child care offers learning opportunities and social and emotional supports that many would not experience at home.

For children from middle- and upper-income families, the long-term picture is far less clear. With a few exceptions that can be explained by the confounding of family with child-care characteristics in the United States, research results show that the impact on development from poorer versus better care within a broad range of safe environments is small and temporary. Given the learning opportunities and social and emotional supports that their homes generally offer, child care is not a unique or lasting experience for these children.

Long-term effects of day-care quality were reported in longitudinal studies by Vandell, Henderson, and Wilson (1988) and by Howes (1988). The former researchers reported that children who attended better-quality day-care centers in the preschool period were better liked by their peers and exhibited more empathy and social competence at age eight than children from poorer-quality preschool centers. Howes found that after controlling for the effects of some family characteristics, good school skills and few behavior problems were predicted by high-quality care for both boys and girls. However, age at entry and amount of day care were not related to later academic achievement or to social behaviors, so that one suspects that family effects, confounded with child-care quality (Bolger & Scarr, 1995), accounted for the long-term results.

In contrast to the US findings, the results of two longitudinal studies conducted in Sweden indicated that early age of entry into day care was associated with better school performance and positive teacher ratings from childhood to early adulthood (Andersson, 1989; Hartmann, 1995). Of the many differences in family background that could be only partially controlled, early entrants into child care had better educated mothers who returned to work earlier than less achieving mothers. Again, one suspects that unmeasured family effects account for the long-term positive effects of child care in the Swedish study, as they did for negative effects in the US studies.

A more thorough Swedish study (Broberg, Hwang, and Chace, 1993) reported no long-term effects of differences in child-care environments on children's adjustments or achievements at eight to nine years of age. It should be noted, however, that Sweden's uniformly high-quality child-care centers

(Hennessy and Melhuish, 1991) do not really test for the effects of poor child care on later development.

No effects of quality of preschool care on school-age development were also reported in a Dutch retrospective study (Goosens, Ottenhoff, and Koops, 1991). However, there was very little variance in the measure of quality in this study, which may account for that finding.

Four studies of long-term impact of varied child-care quality

Study 1   In a large US study of highly varied child-care centers (McCartney et al., 1997; Scarr et al., 1993), 720 young children (ages 12 to 60 months) who were enrolled in 120 child-care centers in three states were evaluated for social adjustment. Quality of care in the centers and family characteristics were used to predict differences in parents' and teachers' ratings of children's adjustment and observations of social behaviors.

Both structural (e.g., staff to child ratios, teachers' wages, education, training) and process (interactions, programs) measures were used to evaluate quality of care in the centers. Family structural characteristics (e.g., income, educational levels, race, number of children) and processes (e.g., parenting stress, work–family interference, parental attitudes, separation anxieties) represented family effects. Children's own characteristics of age, gender, and child-care history were also used to predict adjustment and social behavior. Thus, center-care quality, family, and child characteristics were jointly used to predict children's social adjustment and social behaviors.

Results showed substantial effects of child and family characteristics on both teachers' and parents' ratings of children's adjustment and social behaviors and very small, but statistically reliable, effects of quality of child care on social adjustment ratings. In a four-year follow-up study of 141 children, Deater-Deckard, Pinkerton, and Scarr (1996) reported no long-term effects of differences in quality of preschool child care on these school-age children's social, emotional, or behavioral adjustment.

Study 2   A study of day-care centers in Bermuda (McCartney, 1984; McCartney et al., 1985; Phillips, McCartney and Scarr, 1987) emphasized the importance of quality care for infants, toddlers, and preschool children. The major question addressed longitudinally was whether or not the effects of differences in quality of child care in the preschool years continue to be seen at ages five through nine years.

In a follow-up study (Chin-Quee and Scarr, 1994), teacher ratings of social competence and academic achievement were obtained from 127 of the children at ages five, six, seven, and eight years. In hierarchical and simultaneous regressions, family background characteristics, not child-care amounts or qualities, were found to be predictive of social competence and academic achievement in the primary grades. By the school-age years, the effects of infant and preschool child-care experiences were no longer influential in children's development, but family background continued to be important.

Study 3   In another longitudinal study in Bermuda (Scarr, Lande, and McCartney, 1989), the child-care experiences of 117 children, who had been assessed for cognitive and social development at two and four years of age, were examined for long-term effects. At 24 months of age, children in center-based care, where the ratio of infants to caregivers was 8:1, had poorer cognitive and language development than children in family day care or at home with their mothers (who did not differ from each other). These results persisted after controlling for maternal education, IQ, income, and occupational status. However, at 42 to 48 months, no differences were found between children in center care and other children.

Study 4   In Bermuda, an islandwide screening, assessment, and treatment program was implemented to help children with developmental problems (Scarr, McCartney, Miller, Hauenstein, and Ricciuti, 1994). Child-care histories were also ascertained. Two samples were studied: a population sample of 1,100 Bermudan children and a smaller subsample of children, most of whom were considered to be at risk for developmental problems.

To assess the effects of maternal employment (Scarr and Thompson, 1994), infants with mothers who worked 20 or more hours a week were compared with infants with mothers who worked less than 20 hours a week. To assess the effects of entry into nonmaternal care before the age of one, infants who were placed in regular nonmaternal care before the age of one were compared with infants who did not experience regular nonmaternal care before the age of one. Teacher ratings of social competence and academic achievement were obtained for the children at ages five, six, seven, and eight years.

Results revealed that family background variables frequently predicted child social competence and academic achievement measures in both samples. After controlling for family characteristics, no differences in school-age outcomes were found between children whose mothers worked 20 or more hours a week when they were infants and children with mothers who worked less than 20 hours a week, in either sample. In addition, age of entry into nonmaternal care before the age of one did not significantly predict any child outcome measures.

Conclusions

In studies in Sweden and Holland, in a large study of child-care centers in the United States, and in three separate studies in Bermuda, differences in child-care experience, both qualitative and quantitative, did not have persistent effects on children's development. In these studies, child-care centers in Bermuda and the United States included both good- and poor-quality care, whereas centers in Sweden and Holland included only good-quality care. Research to date on quality differences does not show a major impact on the development of children from ordinary homes. These results may differ for the children from socioeconomically disadvantaged homes, for whom quality child-care programs may supply missing elements in their lives.

PUBLIC POLICY AND THE QUALITY/COST TRADE-OFF

Quality/cost/affordability trade-off

In general, higher-quality child care costs more than lower-quality care. Fifty to seventy percent of the cost is in staff salaries, and higher-quality centers spend proportionately more on labor (Morris and Helburn, 1996). For example, center-based child care costs twice as much in Massachusetts, which has among the most demanding regulations in the United States, as in Georgia, which has more lenient regulations. In a study of 120 centers in three states, centers in Massachusetts had higher-quality care, on average, than those in Georgia, but comparisons of costs of living and incomes showed that families in Massachusetts are economically disadvantaged by the high cost of child care (Hancock, Eisenberg, and Scarr, 1993). Whereas the 1990 median family income for Georgia parents who used center-based care was $50,000, in Massachusetts the median income of families who could afford center care was nearly $80,000. Massachusetts families with an annual income of less than about $60,000 were unable to afford state-regulated quality care.

The more stringent the child-care regulations, the less licensed child care will be available and the more families will be forced to use unregulated care for their children. When regulations become so stringent that most families are priced out of the regulated child-care market, one has to wonder about the wisdom of having such expensive regulations.

Unfortunately, regulations have only tangential effects on the actual quality of care. States cannot legislate warm, sensitive interactions or rich learning opportunities provided by talented teachers. Aside from safety and health considerations, which can be effectively regulated, observed quality of child care is correlated only .30 to .40 with regulated variables, such as ratios and teacher qualifications (Scarr, Eisenberg, and Deater-Deckard, 1994). Therefore, regulations directly produce higher costs but only indirectly improve quality of care.

In addition, parents may not agree that quality defined by professionals is what they want or are willing to pay for in the child care they choose (Cost, Quality, and Child Outcomes Study Team, 1995; Haskins, 1992). Whereas early-childhood professionals value discovery learning and hands-on experience, many working-class and more traditional parents prefer structured learning and direct instruction for their preschool children. Individual attention to each child requires more staff than a classroom organized for group instruction. Lower ratios equal higher staff costs, which some parents are not willing to support, especially if the program is not what they want anyway.

States should examine the cost:benefit ratio of their regulations and their impact on making child care affordable, available, and of sufficient quality to support good child development without driving most families into the underground market of unregulated care. Surely, we all expect state regulations to protect children and to assure them a supportive environment in child care. That is the minimum governmental responsibility. Given the wide variation in regulations among the states, however, it should be possible to examine the benefits of greater and lesser costs of child care.

Equity in child care

In the United States, a two-tier system is evolving – a higher-quality one for both affluent families and the poor, who get public support for child care, and a lower-quality one for middle- and lower-income working families, who cannot pay for high-quality care (Maynard and McGinnis, 1992; Whitebook et al., 1991). In my opinion and in that of many other child advocates, public support for child care should make quality services available to all children of working families.

To make this dream a reality, we must spend tax moneys efficiently. Government-provided services are the least cost-effective means to provide quality child care. Compare Head Start expenditures per child with those of a typical child-care center with excellent early educational programs. Head Start spends approximately $5,000 per child annually for part-day (typically three to four hours), part-year (public school calendar) programs.[3] For exactly the same amount of money, the government could give poor parents vouchers to purchase quality child care and education in full-day, full-year child-care programs (Cost, Quality, and Child Outcomes Study Team, 1995). Another benefit of vouchers is the reduction in socioeconomic segregation, which results from programs that only poor children may attend. In most nonprofit and for-profit centers, between 5% and 40% of the children are on child-care assistance, whereas in Head Start centers, nearly 100% of the children are on child-care assistance.

Edward Zigler (Zigler and Finn-Stevenson, 1996) has proposed that public schools, well-entrenched institutions in all communities, be used to implement child-care services for preschool children (not infants or toddlers). With varying mixes of federal, state, local, and private funding, including parental fees, Zigler has prompted more than 400 schools to incorporate child care in their educational programs. Public schools can be one mechanism to increase the child-care supply for older children, but critics complain that most schools need to focus exclusively on improving their existing educational programs, which international surveys show to be of poor quality.

States are currently setting child-care reimbursement rates under the new welfare-reform legislation. If they are pressured to serve more children, their rates will be too low to give poor parents access to quality care. If they set rates high enough to give poor parents access to quality care, they may not be able to serve all eligible families. Inadequate funding drives states to make Solomonic choices.

Whither child care in America?

Repeatedly, international research results have shown only small concurrent effects of child care on children's development and no evidence for long-term effects, unless the children are seriously disadvantaged. Observations about the small effects on children of differences in quality of care can be enhanced beyond their practical importance by liberal politicians and child advocates, who may demand high-quality child care regardless of cost. Conservatives, however, will ask the logically obvious question: What is the minimal expense for child care that will allow mothers to work and not do permanent damage to children? Conservative politicians will find the research results conveniently permissive of mediocre quality. Mediocre is not the same as deleterious, unsafe, and abusive care, however, and there is some of that in the United States that must be eliminated. Government standards that prevent terrible care are essential for our nation's well-being.

Debates about welfare reform, working mothers, and child care reflect broad societal conflicts about women, families, and children.

- Is child care in America primarily meant to serve the needs of working parents, with little regard for the education of preschoolers, especially disadvantaged children?
- Will nonwelfare working families have to pay for the child care they need, discouraging many women from entering the labor force, or will the public decide that, like primary education, child care is a public service that deserves broad taxpayer support?
- Will regulations on licensed care be made so expensive that most parents will be priced out of the center-care market and forced to use unregulated care in homes? Or, will state regulations be so lax that American child care will be little better than custodial warehousing?

In summary, I hope the United States will decide that child care is both an essential service for working families and an important service to America's children, especially to the poorest among them. Governments have the responsibility to make child care affordable for all working parents and to regulate child care to assure that children are afforded opportunities to develop emotionally, socially, and intellectually. Regardless of who their parents are, children are the next generation for all of us.

NOTES

1. In 11 states, church-sponsored child care is exempt from all but health and safety licensure.
2. Paradoxically, in one study, children's social adjustment was positively related to poorer quality care, but this finding has not been replicated and is probably sample-specific (Phillips, McCartney, and Scarr, 1987).
3. Costs of medical, dental, and social-service programs are additional.

REFERENCES

Andersson, B. E. (1989). Effects of public day care – A longitudinal study. *Child Development*, **60**, 857–66.

Behrman, R. E. (ed.) (1996). Financing child care. *The Future of Children*, **6** (2).

Belsky, J. (1984). Two waves of day care research: Developmental effects and conditions of quality. In R. C. Ainslie (ed.), *The Child and the Day Care Setting* (pp. 24–42), New York: Praeger.

Belsky, J. (1986). Infant day care: A cause for concern? *Zero to Three*, **6**, 1–9.

Belsky, J. (1988). The 'effects' of infant day care reconsidered. *Early Childhood Research Quarterly*, **3**, 235–72.

Belsky, J. (1992). Consequences of child care for children's development: A deconstructionist view. In A. Booth (ed.), *Child Care in the 1990s: Trends and Consequences* (pp. 83–94), Hillsdale, NJ: Erlbaum.

Belsky, J., and Rovine, M. J. (1988). Nonmaternal care in the first year of life and the infant – parent attachment. *Child Development*, **59**, 157–67.

Blau, D. M. and Robbins, P. K. (1990, April). *Child care demand and labor supply of young mothers over time.* Paper presented at the annual meeting of the Population Association of America, Toronto, Ontario, Canada.

Bolger, K. E., and Scarr, S. (1995). Not so far from home: How family characteristics predict child care quality. *Early Development and Parenting*, **4** (3), 103–12.

Bowman, B. (1992). Child development and its implications for day care. In A. Booth (ed.), *Child Care in the 1990s: Trends and Consequences* (pp. 95–100), Hillsdale. NJ: Erlbaum.

Bredekamp, S. (1989, November). *Measuring quality through a national accreditation system for early childhood programs.* Paper presented at the annual meeting of the American Educational Research Association, San Francisco, CA.

Broberg, A. G., Hwang, C. P., and Chace, S. V. (1993, March). *Effects of day care on elementary school performance and adjustment.* Paper presented at the biennial meetings of the Society for Research in Child Development, New Orleans, LA.

Cherlin, A. (1992). Infant care and full-time employment. In A. Booth (ed.), *Child Care in the 1990s: Trends and Consequences* (pp. 209–14), Hillsdale, NJ: Erlbaum.

Chin-Quee, D., and Scarr, S. (1994). Lack of longitudinal effects of infant and preschool child care on school-age children's social and intellectual development. *Early Development and Parenting*, **3** (2), 103–12.

Clarke-Stewart, A. (1988). The 'effects' of infant day care reconsidered: Risks for parents, children, and researchers. *Early Childhood Research Quarterly*, **3**, 293–318.

Clarke-Stewart, K. A. (1989). Infant day care: Maligned or malignant? *American Psychologist*, **44**, 266–73.

Clarke-Stewart, K. A., Gruber, C. P., and Fitzgerald, L. M. (1994). *Children at Home and in Day Care.* Hillsdale, NJ: Erlbaum.

Collins, N., and Hofferth, S. (1996, May). *Child care and employment turnover.* Paper presented at the annual meeting of the Population Association of America, New Orleans, LA.

Cost, Quality, and Child Outcomes Study Team (1995), *Cost, quality, and child outcomes in child care centers* (Public Report, 2nd ed), Denver: University of Colorado at Denver, Economics Department.

Deater-Deckard, K. Pinkerton, R. and Scarr, S. (1996). Child care quality and children's behavioral adjustment: A four-year longitudinal study. *Journal of Child Psychology and Psychiatry*, **37** (8), 937–48.

Deater-Deckard, K., Scarr, S., McCartney, K., and Eisenberg, M. (1994). Paternal separation anxiety: Relationships with parenting stress, child-rearing attitudes, and maternal anxieties. *Psychological Science*, **5** (6), 341–6.

Field, T. (1991). Quality infant day-care and grade school behavior and performance. *Child Development*, **62**, 863–70.

Galinsky, E. (1992). The impact of child care on parents. In A. Booth (ed.), *Child Care in the 1990s: Trends and Consequences* (pp. 159–71), Hillsdale, NJ: Erlbaum.

Galinsky, E., Howes, C., Kontos, S., and Shinn, M. (1994). *The Study of Children in Family Child Care and Relative Care.* New York: Families and Work Institute.

Goelman, H., and Pence, A. R. (1987). Effects of child care, family and individual characteristics on children's language development: The Victoria Day Care Research Project. In D. Phillips (ed.), *Quality in Child Care: What does Research tell us? Research monographs of the National Association for the Education of Young Children* (pp. 43–56), Washington, DC: National Association for the Education of Young Children.

Goosens, F. A., Ottenhoff, G., and Koops, W. (1991). Day care and social outcomes in middle childhood: A retrospective study. *Journal of Reproductive and Infant Psychology,* **9**, 137–50.

Hancock, T., Eisenberg, M., and Scarr, S. (1993, March). *Cost of child care and families' standard of living.* Paper presented at the biennial meetings of the Society for Research in Child Development, New Orleans, LA.

Hartmann, E. (1995). *Long-term effects of day care and maternal teaching on educational competence, independence and autonomy in young adulthood.* Unpublished manuscript, University of Oslo, Oslo, Norway.

Haskins, R. (1992). Is anything more important than day-care quality? In A. Booth (ed.), *Child Care in the 1990s: Trends and Consequences* (pp. 101–15), Hillsdale, NJ: Erlbaum.

Hennessy, E., and Melhuish, E. C. (1991). Early day care and the development of school-age children: A review. *Journal of Reproductive and Infant Psychology,* **9**, 117–36.

Hofferth, S. (1992). The demand for and supply of child care in the 1990s. In A. Booth (ed.), *Child Care in the 1990s: Trends and Consequences* (pp. 3–25), Hillsdale, NJ: Erlbaum.

Hofferth, S. (1996). Child care in the United States today. *The Future of Children,* **6**(2), 41–61.

Hofferth, S., Brayfield, A., Deich, S., and Holcomb, P. (1991). *National Child Care Survey 1990.* Washington, DC: The Urban Institute.

Holloway, S. D., and Reichhart-Erickson, M. (1989). Child care quality, family structure, and maternal expectations: Relationship to preschool children's peer relations. *Journal of Applied Developmental Psychology,* **4**, 99–107.

Howes, C. (1988). Relations between early child care and schooling, *Developmental Psychology,* **24**, 53–7.

Howes, C., and Olenick, M. (1986). Family and child care influences on toddlers' compliance. *Child Development,* **57**, 202–16.

Howes, C., Phillips, D. A., and Whitebook, M. (1992). Thresholds of quality; Implications for the social development of children in center-based child care, *Child Development,* **63**, 449–60.

Howes, C., and Stewart, P. (1987). Child's play with adults, toys, and peers: An examination of family and child-care influences. *Developmental Psychology,* **23**, 423–30.

Justice Ginsburg Takes On Affirmative Action. (1995, April 17), *The Washington Post,* p. A4.

Kagan, J. (1980). Perspectives on continuity. In O. G. Brim and J. Kagan (eds), *Constancy and Change in Human Development* (pp. 1–15), Cambridge, MA: Harvard University Press.

Kontos, S., and Fiene, R. (1987). Child care quality, family background, and children's development. *Early Childhood Research Quarterly,* **6**, 249–62.

Lamb, M. (in press). Nonparental child care: Context quality, correlates, and consequences. In W. Damon (series ed.) and I. E. Sigel and K. A. Renninger (vol. eds), *Handbook of Child Psychology: Child Psychology in Practice* (4th ed), New York: Wiley.

Lamb, M., Sternberg, K. J., Hwang, P., and Broberg, A. (eds), (1992). *Child Care in Context* Hillsdale, NJ: Erlbaum.

Lamb, M., Sternberg, K. J., and Prodromidis, M. (1992). The effects of day care on infant–mother attachment: A re-analysis of the data. *Infant Behavior and Development*, **15**, 71–83.

Leira, A. (1992). *Welfare States and Working Mothers*. Cambridge, England: Cambridge University Press.

Mason, K., and Duberstein, L. (1992). Consequences of child care for parents' well-being. In A. Booth (ed.), *Child Care in the 1990s: Trends and Consequences* (pp. 127–58), Hillsdale, NJ: Erlbaum.

Maynard, R., and McGinnis, E. (1992). Policies to enhance access to high-quality child care. In A. Booth (ed.), *Child Care in the 1990s: Trends and Consequences* (pp. 189–208), Hillsdale, NJ: Erlbaum.

McCartney, K. (1984). The effect of quality of day care environment upon children's language development. *Developmental Psychology*, **20**, 244–60.

McCartney, K., and Marshall, N. (1989). The development of child care research, *Newsletter of the Division of Children, Youth, and Family, Services*, **12** (4), 14–15.

McCartney, K., Scarr, S., Phillips, D., and Grajek, S. (1985). Day care as intervention: Comparisons of varying quality programs. *Journal of Applied Developmental Psychology*, **6**, 247–60.

McCartney, K., Scarr, S., Rocheleau, A., Phillips, D., Eisenberg, M., Keefe, N., Rosenthal, S., and Abbott-Shim, M. (1997). Social development in the context of typical center-based child care. *Merrill-Palmer Quarterly*, **43** (3), 426–50.

Morris, J., and Helburn, S. (1996, July). How centers spend money on quality. *Child Care Information Exchange*, 75–9.

National Institute of Child Health and Human Development Early Child Care Research Network. (1996). Characteristics of infant child care: Factors contributing to positive caregiving, *Early Childhood Research Quarterly*, **11**, 269–306.

National Institute of Child Health and Human Development Early Child Care Research Network. (in press). The effects of infant child care on infant–mother attachment security: Results of the NICHD Study of Early Child Care. *Child Development*.

Phillips, D. (ed). (1987). *Quality in Child Care: What does Research Tell Us? Research monographs of the National Association for the Education of Young Children*, Washington, DC: National Association for the Education of Young Children.

Phillips, D. (1992). Child care and parental well-being: Bringing quality of care into the picture. In A. Booth (ed.), *Child Care in the 1990s: Trends and Consequences* (pp. 172–9), Hillsdale, NJ: Erlbaum.

Phillips, D., McCartney, K., and Scarr, S. (1987). Child care quality and children's social development. *Developmental Psychology*, **23**, 537–43.

Phillips, D., McCartney, K., Scarr, S., and Howes, C. (1987). Selective review of infant day care research: A cause for concern. *Zero to Three*, **7**, 18–21.

Phillips, D., Mekos, D., Scarr, S., McCartney, K., and Abbott-Shim, M. (in press). Paths to quality in child care: Structural and contextual influences on classroom environments. *Early Childhood Research Quarterly*.

Presser, H. (1992a). Child care and parental well-being: A needed focus on gender trade-offs. In A. Booth (ed.), *Child Care in the 1990s: Trends and Consequences* (pp. 180–85), Hillsdale, NJ: Erlbaum.

Presser, H. (1992b). Child-care supply and demand: What do we really know? In A. Booth (ed.), *Child Care in the 1990s: Trends and Consequences* (pp. 26–32), Hillsdale, NJ: Erlbaum.

Prosser, W., and McGroder, S. (1992). The supply and demand for child care: Measurement and analytic issues. In A. Booth (ed.), *Child Care in the 1990s: Trends and Consequences* (pp. 42–55), Hillsdale, NJ: Erlbaum.

Ramey, C., Bryant, D., Sparling, J., and Wasik, B. (1985). Project CARE: A comparison of two early intervention strategies to prevent retarded development. *Topics in Early Childhood Special Education*, **5** (2), 12–25.

Ramey, C., and Ramey, S. (1992). Early educational intervention with disadvantaged children – to what effect? *Applied and Preventive Psychology*, **1**, 131–40.

Ross, C. E., and Mirowsky, J. (1988). Child care and emotional adjustment to wives' employment. *Journal of Health and Social Behavior*, **29**, 127–38.

Scarr, S. (1984). *Mother Care/Other Care*. New York: Basic Books.

Scarr, S. (1985). Constructing psychology: Making facts and fables for our times. *American Psychologist*, **40**, 499–512.

Scarr, S. (1992a). Developmental theories for the 1990s: Development and individual differences. *Child Development*, **63**, 1–19.

Scarr, S. (1992b). Keep our eyes on the prize: Family and child care policy in the United States, as it should be. In A. Booth (ed.), *Child Care in the 1990s: Trends and Consequences* (pp. 215–22), Hillsdale, NJ: Erlbaum.

Scarr, S. (1993). Biological and cultural diversity: The legacy of Darwin for development. *Child Development*, **64**, 1333–53.

Scarr, S. (1996). Family policy dilemmas in contemporary nation-states: Are women benefited by family-friendly governments? In S. Gustavsson and L. Lewin (eds), *The Future of the Nation State: Essays on Cultural Pluralism and Political Integration* (pp. 107–29), London: Routledge.

Scarr, S., and Eisenberg, M. (1993). Child care research: Issues, perspectives, and results, *Annual Review of Psychology*, **44**, 613–44.

Scarr, S., Eisenberg, M., and Deater-Deckard, K. (1994). Measurement of quality on child care centers. *Early Childhood Research Quarterly*, **9**, 131–51.

Scarr, S., Lande, J. and McCartney, K. (1989), Child care and the family: Cooperation and interaction. In J. Lande, S. Scarr, and N. Guzenhauser (eds), *Caring for Children: Challenge to America* (pp. 21–40), Hillsdale, NJ: Erlbaum.

Scarr, S., McCartney, K., Miller, S., Hauenstein, E., and Ricciuti, A. (1994). Evaluation of an islandwide screening, assessment and treatment program. *Early Development and Parenting*, **3** (4), 199–210.

Scarr, S., Phillips, D., and McCartney, K. (1989). Working mothers and their families, *American Psychologist*, **44**, 1402–9.

Scarr, S., Phillips, D., and McCartney, K. (1990). Facts, fantasies, and the future of child care in the United States. *Psychological Science*, **1**, 26–35.

Scarr, S., Phillips, D., McCartney, K. and Abbott-Shim, M. (1993). Quality of child care as an aspect of family and child care policy in the United States. *Pediatrics*, **91** (1), 182–8.

Scarr, S., and Thompson, W. (1994). Effects of maternal employment and nonmaternal infant care on development at two and four years. *Early Development and Parenting*, **3** (2), 113–23.

Scarr, S., and Weinberg, R. A. (1986). The early childhood enterprise: Care and education of the young. *American Psychologist*, **41**, 1140–6.

Staines, G. L. and Pleck, J. H. (1983). *The Impact of Work Schedules on the Family*. Ann Arbor, MI: Institute for Social Research, Survey Research Center.

Stoney, L., and Greenberg, M. H. (1996). The financing of child care: Current and emerging trends. *The Future of Children*, **6**, 83–102.

Suwalsky, J., Zaslow, M., Klein, R. and Rabinovich, B. (1986, August). *Continuity of substitute care in relation to infant – mother attachment*. Paper presented at the 94th Annual Convention of the American Psychological Association, Washington, DC.

Vandell, D. L., Henderson, V. K., and Wilson, K. S. (1988). A longitudinal study of children with day-care experiences of varying quality. *Child Development*, **59**, 1286–92.

Wasik, B. H., Ramey, C. T., Bryant, D. M., and Sparling, J. J. (1990). A longitudinal study of two early intervention strategies: Project CARE, *Child Development*, **61**, 1682–96.

White, L., and Keith, B. (1990). The effect of shift work on the quality and stability of marital relations. *Journal of Marriage and the Family*, **52**, 453–62.

Whitebook, M., Howes, C., and Phillips, D. (1991). *Who Cares? Child care teachers and the quality of care in America*. Final Report of the National Child Care Staffing Study. Oakland, CA: Center on Child Care Staffing.

Willer, B., Hofferth, S., Kisker, E. E., et al. (1991). *The Demand and Supply of Child Care in 1990*. Washington, DC: National Association for the Education of Young People.

Women's figures. (1997, January 15). *Wall Street Journal*, p. A15.

Workfare means day care, (1996, December 23). *Time*, 38–40.

Zigler, E. F., and Finn-Stevenson, M. (1996). Funding child care and public education. *The Future of Children*, **6**, 104–21.

30

Chinese and Canadian Children's Evaluations of Lying and Truth Telling: Similarities and Differences in the Context of Pro- and Antisocial Behaviors*

Kang Lee, Catherine Ann Cameron, Fen Xu, Genyao Fu and Julie Board

EDITORS' INTRODUCTION

Consider the following stories:

A.   A little boy (or a little girl) goes for a walk in the street and meets a big dog who frightens him very much. So then he goes home and tells his mother that he has seen a dog that is as big as a cow.
B.   A child comes home from school and tells his mother that the teacher has given him good marks, but it was not true; the teacher had given him no marks at all, either good or bad. Then his mother was very pleased and rewarded him.

Piaget (1932) used pairs of stories like these in order to investigate children's understanding of lying. Each story contains either a lie with plausible content, and told with manifest intention to deceive (*B*), or a mere inaccuracy devoid of any ill intentions, but being a clear departure from fact (*A*). Having heard the stories, children were then asked to say which was the bigger lie, and which should be punished. Here is a 6-year-old's reply to Piaget's questions:

FEL (6) repeats the two stories correctly (asking the child to repeat the stories checks that she has understood them): 'Which of these two children is the naughtiest? – *The little girl who said she saw a dog as big as a cow.* – Why is she the naughtiest? – *Because it could never happen.* – Did her mother believe her? – *No, because they never are* [dogs are never as big as cows]. – Why did she say that? – *To exaggerate.* – And why did the other one tell a lie? – *Because she wanted to make people believe that she had a good report.* – Did her mother believe her? – *Yes.* –

* Previously published in *Child Development*, **68**, 5 (October 1997), pp. 924–34.

Which would you punish most if you were the mother? – *The one with the dog because she told the worst lies and was the naughtiest.'* (Piaget, 1932, p. 144)

This example illustrates Piaget's finding that many of the younger children they questioned evaluated the lies according to the greater or lesser like-lihood of the lying statement, and not according to the intentions of the liar.

There has been a recent upsurge of interest in children's understanding, and evaluation, of truth telling and lying. Lee et al. describe the reasons for this in their introduction, and in this article they describe an intriguing cultural difference between Chinese and Canadian children's evaluations of lying and truth telling in prosocial and antisocial situations.

REFERENCE

Piaget, J. (1965). *The Moral Judgement of the Child*. New York: Macmillan (original work published 1932).

The present study compared Chinese and Canadian children's moral eva-luations of lie and truth telling in situations involving pro- and antisocial behaviors. Seven-, 9-, and 11-year-old Chinese and Canadian children were presented 4 brief stories. Two stories involved a child who intentionally carried out a good deed, and the other 2 stories involved a child who intentionally carried out a bad deed. When story characters were questioned by a teacher as to who had committed the deed, they either lied or told the truth. Children were asked to evaluate the story characters' deeds and their verbal statements. Overall, Chinese children rated truth telling less posit-ively and lie telling more positively in prosocial settings than Canadian children, indicating that the emphasis on self-effacement and modesty in Chinese culture overrides Chinese children's evaluations of lying in some situations. Both Chinese and Canadian children rated truth telling posit-ively and lie telling negatively in antisocial situations, reflecting the empha-sis in both cultures on the distinction between misdeed and truth/lie telling. The findings of the present study suggest that, in the realm of lying and truth telling, a close relation between sociocultural practices and moral judgment exists. Specific social and cultural norms have an impact on children's developing moral judgments, which, in turn, are modified by age and experience in a particular culture.

OVERVIEW

INTRODUCTION

Children's understanding and moral judgment of lying and truth telling was an early topic of investigation in developmental psychology (Binet, 1896; Hall, 1891; Piaget, 1932/1965; for a review, see Hyman, 1989). Since the early 1980s, developmental psychologists have shown a renewed interest in children's understanding and moral judgments of lying and truth telling, after neglecting the topic for nearly half a century (Bussey, 1992; Peterson, 1995; Peterson, Peterson, and Seeto, 1983; Strichartz and Burton, 1990; Wimmer, Gruber, and Perner, 1984). This recent upsurge of interest is mainly due to the fact that the study of the development of lying and truth telling bears theoretical significance for current debates about children's theory of mind (Wimmer et al., 1984) as well as the universality of moral development (Boyes and Walker, 1988; Shweder, Mahapatra, and Miller, 1987) and has practical implications for the controversy about using children as witnesses in courts of law (Burton and Strichartz, 1991; Goodman, 1984).

In his pioneering work, Piaget (1932/1965) presented children with pairs of scenarios in which protagonists engaged in various forms of verbal communication such as lying, guessing, and exaggeration. Children were asked to judge the "naughtiness" of verbal statements that deviated from the truth. He found that young children's moral judgments about lying and truth telling primarily relied on the extent to which a verbal statement differed from factuality and whether or not the lie was punished. Not until around 11 years of age did children begin to use the protagonist's intention as the key factor in their moral judgments.

Recently, researchers have begun to use a single scenario, instead of Piaget's moral-dilemma choice-paradigm, to simplify task demands (Bussey, 1992; Peterson, 1995; Peterson et al., 1983). In general, the studies replicated Piaget's findings regarding the dominant role of factuality in children's moral judgment of lying and truth telling. However, whether or not a lie is punished was found to have little effect on children's moral judgement, at least at the elementary school level. On one hand, most studies confirmed that the role of intention is relatively limited for young school-aged children in determining a statement to be a lie or the truth. On the other hand, researchers disagreed with Piaget's claim that the use of intention emerges only around 11 years of age. Although researchers are still debating the role of intention (Peterson, 1995; Peterson et al., 1983; Wimmer et al., 1984), there is a general consensus in the literature that preschool and young school-aged children are distinctly capable of distinguishing lying from behavioral misdeeds and making consistent and accurate moral judgments. In particular, most studies have consistently shown that young children's moral judgment is similar to that of older children and adults when both the falsity of a statement and the speaker's intention to deceive are highlighted (Wimmer et al., 1984).

Despite the advances of research in recent years, our understanding of the development of children's moral judgments of lying is still rather restricted. One of the limitations is that all of the above-mentioned studies were conducted with children in Western countries. These children were raised in industrialized environments that emphasize individualism, self-assertion/promotion, and competition. It is unclear whether the findings with these children can be generalized to children of other sociocultural backgrounds. Recently, Sweetser (1987) proposed a folkloristic model of lying. She suggested that the concept of lying is not simply a cognitive construct defined by such key semantic features as factuality (whether a statement reflects the truth), intention (whether the speaker intends to deceive), and belief (whether the speaker believes the statement) alone, but it is also a sociocultural construct. She argued that the understanding of lying is greatly influenced by the cultural norms and moral values in which individuals are socialized. Although some anthropological studies and anecdotal reports (Gilsenan, 1976; Ochs Keenan, 1976) seem to support Sweetser's model, little systematic developmental evidence has been advanced (see Lee and Ross, 1997).

The present study was conducted to bridge this gap in the literature by directly testing the posited effect of culture on children's moral evaluations of lying and truth telling. Specifically, the present study focused on the lying and truth-telling situations that have derived the most consistent research findings from both past and recent studies (Bussey, 1992; Peterson, 1995; Peterson et al., 1983; Strichartz and Burton, 1990; Wimmer et al., 1984). These situations involve a speaker telling a lie or the truth while the speaker's intention and the true state of affairs are prominently indicated. The moral judgments of Canadian children and Chinese children from the People's Republic of China (PRC) were compared in situations in which pro- and antisocial actions were denied or acknowledged.

The choice of using Chinese children in the PRC as participants of this study was not accidental. In contrast to Canada, the People's Republic of China is a communist-collectivist society that cherishes communitarianism over individualism and promotes personal sacrifice for the social good (Bond, 1986; Dien, 1982; Ho and Chiu, 1994). Chinese children are systematically educated in the tenets of this ideology as early as the kindergarten years (Davin, 1991; Domino and Hannah, 1987; Hayhoe, 1984). For example, in addition to advancing collectivism and patriotism, the central government specifically requires schools at all levels to incorporate the promotion of honesty and modesty into their political-moral education programs (Davin, 1991; Lo, 1984; Price, 1992; Zhu, 1982). In fact, honesty and modesty are among the major "Five Virtues" (Price, 1992) that are strongly emphasized in the Chinese school curriculum, and these twin virtues are central criteria used to assess children's school comportment. In school settings, modesty and honesty are expected both in behavioral conduct and in academic achievement. With regard to honesty, children are encouraged to report misdeeds committed by themselves or others, not to misrepresent themselves to gain approval, and not to cheat or steal. To promote honesty, children are repeatedly taught specific rules and slogans that exemplify honesty, such as "Be an honest, good child" and "One must be brave to admit wrong-doing."

With regard to modesty, children are specifically taught to avoid self-aggrandizement, not to brag about personal achievements, including high marks and good deeds, and not to seek the teacher's explicit praise. As part of the endeavor to promote modesty, self-effacement is directly encouraged. Children are encouraged to minimize their own good behaviors and grades. They are taught to revere "unsung heroes" who commit good deeds and do not leave their names. In fact, school textbooks are replete with stories that condone "lying" in conjunction with good deeds (e.g., the stories of Lei Feng and Jiao Yulu, two communist heroes whose altruistic and philanthropic deeds were told only after their deaths). Furthermore, both Chinese Confucian and Taoist traditions support this teaching (Bond, 1986; Bond, Leung, and Wan, 1982; Ma, 1988). Bond et al. (1982) pointed out that in China, the humility of individual members is a priority for maintaining harmonious interpersonal relationships in a collectivity (also see Ma, 1988). This and other traditional moral rules are deeply rooted in the Chinese culture. They are also reflected in the Chinese communist ideology (i.e., Maoism), and legitimized in the Chinese Communist Party's platforms (Hayhoe, 1984; Price, 1992). Hence, admitting a good deed is viewed as a violation both of traditional Chinese cultural norms and of communist-collectivist doctrine.

In Western culture, whereas "white lies" or deceptions to avoid embarrassment or hurt are tolerated, concealing laudable behavior is not explicitly encouraged, especially in the early school years. Self-aggrandizement, a part of the practice of individualistic self-promotion, is not considered a character flaw in the Western culture as it is in the Chinese culture. In fact, self-promotion is thought to enhance self-esteem, independence, and even achievement (Bond et al., 1982) and, hence, is encouraged in schools in North America (see, e.g., California Task Force to Promote Self-Esteem and Personal and Social Responsibility, 1990; Early Childhood Consultants in Collaboration with Members of the Kindergarten Curriculum Advisory Committee, 1991; Seligman, 1996).

Whereas China's political and cultural rules regarding lying about good deeds differ quite dramatically from those in Canada and other Western countries, for whom self-effacement is not so strong a motive, both Western and Chinese parents and teachers stress the distinction between misdeeds and lying. Whereas lying about a misdeed is strictly prohibited, confessing a misdeed is encouraged in both cultures, although perhaps from different ideological bases: In the West, contractual assumptions between individuals, personal rights to information, and individual freedom all assume truth-telling principles (Bok, 1978; Grice, 1975; Kupfer, 1982; Sweetser, 1987); in China, the individual is held accountable for social disruption and therefore must admit a misdeed to be reintegrated into the group and maintain collective harmony (Bond, 1986).

Given the differences between Chinese and Western cultures regarding the moral significance of lying and truth telling in good-deed and misdeed situations, the comparison between Chinese and Canadian children's moral judgment offers an opportunity for examining the extent to which cultural practices affect the development of children's understanding and moral evaluations of lying. In addition, this comparison provides insight into questions of universality in moral development (Boyes and Walker, 1988; Shweder et al., 1987).

In the present study, 7-, 9-, and 11-year-old Chinese and Canadian children were assigned to two conditions in each of which they were presented four brief stories. The stories were constructed in such a way that the situations depicted were familiar to school children in both cultures. Two stories involved a child who intentionally carried out a good deed (a deed valued by adults in both cultures), whereas the other two stories involved a child who intentionally carried out a bad deed (a deed viewed negatively in both cultures). Then, when the story character was questioned by a teacher as to who had done the deed, she or he either lied or told the truth. Sweetser (1987) suggests that the word "lying" often carries a negative connotation. Henceforth, "lying" behavior will be referred to as "lie telling," a neutral term. To delineate further situational effects and to ascertain the generalizability of the stories, half of the children were presented stories that depicted a child conducting a deed directly affecting another child (the social story condition), and the other half received stories that depicted a child carrying out a deed involving only physical objects, although also having social implications (the physical story condition). Children were asked to rate both the story character's deed and verbal statement as "naughty" or "good." Based on Sweetser's (1987) model and the above analyses, a cultural effect was expected on the ratings of lie telling and truth telling involving prosocial behaviors. Chinese children were predicted to rate truth telling in prosocial situations less positively and lie telling in the same situations less negatively than Canadian children. This difference was expected to increase with age as a result of the increased exposure to and experience with cultural norms. By contrast, based on the current literature (Berndt and Berndt, 1975; Bussey, 1992; Wimmer et al., 1984), children of both cultures were expected to show similar moral evaluations of lie telling and truth telling related to antisocial behaviors. All were expected to rate lie telling negatively and truth telling positively in antisocial behavioral situations.

Method

Participants

One hundred and twenty Chinese children participated in the study: 40 7-year-olds (M age = 7.5 years, 20 male and 20 female), 40 9-year-olds (M age = 9.4 years, 20 male and 20 female), and 40 11-year-olds (M age = 11.3, 20 male and 20 female). They were recruited from elementary schools in Hangzhou, Zhejiang Province, a medium-sized city (provincial capital) in the People's Republic of China. Hangzhou is one of the main cultural, educational, and commercial centers in China. Information regarding the socioeconomic status of the children's families was not available, as the means to categorize families by social group standing still does not exist in the People's Republic of China, nor is it encouraged by the government. Half of the children participated in the social story condition, and the other half were placed in the physical story condition. The children were assigned to the conditions randomly.

One hundred and eight Canadian children also participated in the study: 36 7-year-olds (M age = 7.4 years, 20 male and 16 female), 40 9-year-olds (M age = 9.6 years, 24 male and 16 female), 32 11-year-olds (M age = 11.5 years, 14 male and 18 female). They were recruited from elementary schools in Fredericton, New Brunswick, Canada. Like Hangzhou, Fredericton is also a provincial capital, but its population is considerably smaller than that of Hangzhou. Neither city involved in this research is a heavy industrial center. Most of the

Canadian children were from middle-class families. Nineteen 7-year-olds, 20 9-year-olds, and 17 11-year-olds were randomly assigned to the social story condition, and the other children were assigned to the physical story condition.

Material

Children were read four scenarios accompanied by illustrations. The English versions of the scenarios are shown in the Appendix. The following example illustrates the story used in the physical story condition that involves lie telling in a prosocial situation:

> Here is Alex. Alex's class had to stay inside at recess time because of bad weather, so Alex decided to tidy up the classroom for his teacher.
> *(Question 1: Is what Alex did good or naughty?)*
> So Alex cleaned the classroom, and when the teacher returned after recess, she said to her students, "Oh, I see that someone has cleaned the classroom for me." The teacher then asked Alex, "Do you know who cleaned the classroom?" Alex said to his teacher, "I did not do it."
> *(Question 2: Is what Alex said to his teacher good or naughty?)*

Procedures

Children were seen individually. They were first instructed about the meaning of the words and the symbols on a 7-point rating chart. The words and symbols are: very very good (three red stars), very good (two red stars), good (one red star), neither good nor naughty (a blue circle), naughty (one black cross), very naughty (two black crosses), and very very naughty (three black crosses). Children were then read either four social stories or four physical stories. A story's "deed" section was first read to children, which contained the information regarding the child story character's pro- or antisocial behaviors. Children were asked, "Was what she (he) did good or naughty?" They were asked to indicate their rating either verbally, or nonverbally, or both, on the rating chart. The meaning of each symbol was repeated every time the question was asked. Then, children were read the second section of the story and asked, "Was what she (he) said good or naughty?" Again, the symbols' meanings on the chart were indicated and children were requested to rate the story character's verbal statement on the chart. The words, "good" and "naughty," in the two questions, were alternated within subjects. To control for an order effect, for each condition, two orders of the four stories were first determined using a randomization table. About half of the children in each condition were read the stories in one predetermined order, and the other half were read them in the other order.

RESULTS

Children's ratings were converted according to the following scale: very very good $= 3$, very good $= 2$, good $= 1$, neither good nor naughty $= 0$, naughty = −1, very naughty = −2, and very very naughty = −3. Preliminary analyses of the effects of order and gender yielded no significant differences. Hence, the data on these two dimensions were combined for subsequent analyses.

Tables 30.1 and 30.2 show the means and standard deviations of both Chinese and Canadian children's ratings of the story characters' pro- or anti-social behaviors and verbal statements, respectively, in the four situations of social and physical story conditions.

Prosocial behavior/truth-telling situations

A planned 2 (culture: Canadian and Chinese) ×2 (condition: physical and social stories) ×3 (age: 7, 9, 11 years) analysis of covariance with the ratings of deeds as covariates was conducted on children's ratings of truth telling. The use of the ratings of deeds as covariates was to control for the effect of children's moral evaluations of prosocial behaviors on their subsequent ratings of truth telling. The covariate was not significant, $t(1) = .34$, ns, indicating that children of both cultures rated the prosocial behaviors similarly. The age and culture main effects were significant, $F(2, 215) = 9.79$, $p < .001$, and $F(1, 215) = 20.65, p < .001$, respectively. The condition main effect was not significant, $F(1, 215) = .82$, ns. The only significant interaction was the one between age and culture, $F(2, 215) = 5.75, p < .01$. As shown in figure 30.1, the significant interaction was due to the fact that Canadian children at each age gave similar ratings to truth telling whereas Chinese children's ratings became less positive as age increased.

TABLE 30.1 Means and standard deviations of Chinese and Canadian children's ratings of good and bad deeds

	China			Canada		
	Social	Physical	Combined	Social	Physical	Combined
Story 1: good deed situation:						
7 years	2.45 (.69)	1.60 (1.73)	2.03 (1.37)	1.90 (.88)	2.35 (.79)	2.13 (.85)
9 years	1.25 (1.77)	2.50 (.61)	1.88 (1.45)	1.80 (1.36)	2.35 (.67)	2.08 (1.10)
11 years	1.20 (1.32)	2.15 (.67)	1.68 (1.14)	2.29 (.85)	2.33 (.82)	2.31 (.82)
Story 2: good deed situation:						
7 years	2.45 (.69)	1.65 (1.50)	2.05 (1.22)	2.00 (.82)	2.35 (.79)	2.18 (.81)
9 years	1.25 (1.74)	2.55 (.61)	1.90 (1.45)	1.75 (1.37)	2.10 (1.07)	1.93 (1.23)
11 years	1.65 (1.27)	1.85 (.81)	1.75 (1.06)	2.06 (1.14)	1.93 (.80)	2.00 (.98)
Story 3: bad deed situation:						
7 years	−2.15 (.81)	−1.65 (1.46)	−1.90 (1.19)	−1.95 (.62)	−2.35 (.86)	−2.15 (.76)
9 years	−2.35 (.59)	−2.80 (.41)	−2.58 (.55)	−1.85 (1.18)	−2.50 (.76)	−2.18 (1.04)
11 years	−2.30 (1.38)	−2.40 (.68)	−2.35 (1.08)	−2.53 (.72)	−2.67 (.49)	−2.60 (.61)
Story 4 bad deed situation:						
7 years	−2.40 (.75)	−1.35 (1.50)	−1.88 (1.28)	−1.63 (.68)	−2.12 (.86)	−1.88 (.80)
9 years	−2.60 (.50)	−2.25 (.72)	−2.43 (.64)	−1.60 (1.23)	−2.30 (.73)	−1.95 (1.06)
11 years	−2.65 (.49)	−2.25 (.55)	−2.45 (.55)	−2.47 (.62)	−2.27 (.70)	−2.37 (.66)

Note: Standard deviations are in parentheses.

TABLE 30.2 Means and standard deviations of Chinese and Canadian children's ratings of lie and truth telling in good and bad deed situations

	China			Canada		
	Social	Physical	Combined	Social	Physical	Combined
Story 1: truth telling (good deed situation):						
7 years	1.75 (1.68)	1.90 (1.02)	1.83 (1.38)	2.11 (.74)	2.35 (.79)	2.23 (.76)
9 years	1.65 (1.90)	.85 (1.42)	1.25 (1.71)	1.45 (1.43)	1.70 (.92)	1.58 (1.20)
11 years	.55 (1.54)	.10 (1.07)	.33 (1.33)	2.06 (.83)	1.80 (.78)	1.93 (.80)
Story 2: lie telling (good deed situation):						
7 years	−.50 (2.01)	−.70 (1.87)	−.60 (1.92)	−1.26 (1.10)	−1.47 (.72)	−1.37 (.93)
9 years	−1.00 (1.89)	1.05 (1.93)	.03 (2.15)	−.95 (1.43)	−.95 (1.15)	−.95 (1.28)
11 years	.85 (1.79)	1.10 (1.17)	.98 (1.49)	−1.12 (.93)	−.87 (1.30)	−1.00 (1.11)
Story 3: truth telling (bad deed situation):						
7 years	1.95 (.83)	1.90 (.79)	1.93 (.80)	1.79 (.86)	1.77 (1.52)	1.78 (1.20)
9 years	2.00 (.80)	2.10 (.91)	2.05 (.85)	1.90 (.79)	1.90 (1.07)	1.90 (.93)
11 years	1.75 (.72)	1.90 (.91)	1.83 (.81)	2.18 (.81)	2.13 (.64)	2.16 (.72)
Story 4: lie telling (bad deed situation):						
7 years	−2.40 (.75)	−1.80 (1.28)	−2.10 (1.08)	−1.84 (.77)	−2.59 (.62)	−2.22 (1.79)
9 years	−2.60 (.60)	−2.65 (.59)	−2.63 (.59)	−2.35 (.81)	−2.25 (.55)	−2.30 (.69)
11 years	−2.90 (.45)	−2.35 (.81)	−2.63 (.70)	−2.53 (.62)	−2.67 (.49)	−2.60 (.56)

Note: Standard deviations are in parentheses.

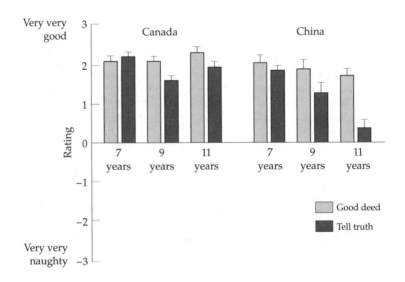

FIGURE 30.1 Chinese and Canadian children's ratings of truth telling in prosocial situations (social and physical story conditions combined)

Prosocial behavior/lie-telling situations

A planned 2 (culture: Canadian and Chinese) × 2 (condition: physical and social stories) × 3 (age: 7, 9, 11 years) analysis of covariance with the ratings of deeds as covariates was conducted on children's ratings of lie telling in the prosocial behavior/lie-telling situations. The covariate was significant, $t(1) = 2.88, p < .01$, indicating that children from the two cultures rated the prosocial behaviors differently both in different age groups and in the two conditions. However, after partialing out the effect of the covariates, the age and culture main effects remained significant, $F(2, 215) = 8.80, p < .001$, and $F(1, 215) = 40.64, p < .001$, respectively. The condition main effect was not significant, $F(1, 215) = 2.27$, ns. Only the interaction between age and culture was significant, $F(2, 215) = 3.59, p < .05$. As shown in figure 30.2, Canadian children overall rated lie telling in this situation negatively. As age increased, their ratings became somewhat less negative. By contrast, Chinese children's ratings of lie telling in the prosocial situation changed from negative to positive as age increased.

Antisocial behavior/truth-telling situations

A planned 2 (culture: Canadian and Chinese) ×2 (condition: physical and social stories) ×3 (age: 7, 9, 11 years) analysis of covariance with the ratings of deeds as covariates was conducted on children's ratings of truth telling in the antisocial behavior/truth-telling situations. The covariate was not significant, $t(1) = -1.51$, ns, indicating that children from both cultures rated the

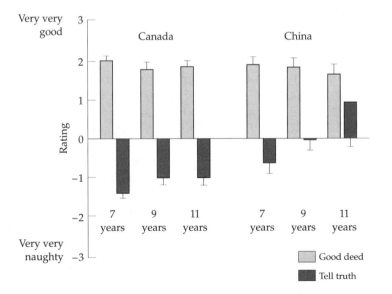

FIGURE 30.2   Chinese and Canadian children's ratings of lie telling in prosocial situations (social and physical story conditions combined)

antisocial behaviors similarly. No main effect or interaction was significant. As shown in table 30.2, children from the two cultures rated truth telling in the antisocial situations very positively.

Antisocial behavior/lie-telling situations

A planned 2 (culture: Canadian and Chinese) $\times$ 2 (condition: physical and social stories) $\times$ 3 (age: 7, 9, 11 years) analysis of covariance with the ratings of deeds as covariates was conducted on children's ratings of lie telling in the antisocial behavior/lie-telling situations. The covariate was significant, $t(1) = 4.96, p < .01$, indicating that children of both cultures rated the antisocial behaviors differently in different age groups in the two conditions. However, after partialing out the effect of the covariates, the age main effect remained significant, $F(2, 215) = 3.50, p < .05$. The culture and condition main effects were not significant, $F(1, 215) = .08$, ns, and $F(1, 215) = .02$, ns. Only the interaction between age, culture, and condition was significant, $F(2, 215) = 5.18, p < .01$. As shown in table 30.2, both Chinese and Canadian children rated lie telling in the antisocial situations negatively. Overall, negative ratings increased with age irrespective of culture. However, Chinese 7-year-old children rated lie telling less negatively than older children in the physical story condition, whereas Canadian 7-year-old children rated lie telling less negatively than older children in the social story condition. The reason for the specific interaction was unclear. No interpretation was attempted here.

DISCUSSION

The present study compared Chinese and Canadian children's moral evaluations of truth and lie telling in situations involving pro- and antisocial behaviors. The predicted cultural differences were found. Chinese children differed from Canadian children in their evaluations of truth and lie telling in prosocial situations. Chinese children generally rated truth telling in prosocial settings less positively than Canadian children. Even more interestingly, Chinese children rated lie telling in the same situations more positively than Canadian children. As age increased, Chinese children's ratings went from negative to positive. This particular trend with Chinese children suggests that the emphasis on self-effacement and modesty in Chinese culture increasingly asserts its impact on Chinese children's moral judgment. As the children's experience with these moral rules increased through schooling and other means of socialization (e.g., mass media, extra-curricular political–moral educational activities), their moral judgment regarding truth and lie telling about prosocial behaviors became increasingly consistent with Chinese society's moral rules.

This is consistent with Chinese children's comments during post-experimental discussions. With regard to the prosocial behavior/truth-telling situations, 8% of 7-year-olds, 28% of 9-year-olds, and 48% of 11-year-olds gave negative ratings (-1 to -3) to the child story character who told the truth. When asked why they gave negative ratings, nearly half of them commented that they gave a negative rating because the child was "wanting" or "begging for" the teacher's praise, a behavior specifically discouraged by teachers in the Chinese schools (Zhu, 1982). One-third of the children indicated that one "should not leave his (her) name after doing a good deed." The rest of the children stated that the story character should not admit the good deed or tell the teacher about the deed. With regard to the prosocial behavior/lie-telling situations, 25% of the 7-year-olds, 43% of the 9-year-olds, and 70% of the 11-year-olds gave positive ratings (+1 to +3 scores) to the child story character who "lied" to the teacher. Most of those children justified their positive ratings of lie telling by either stating that one should not leave one's name after doing a good deed (54%) or indicating that one should not tell the teacher about the good deed (36%). These comments are consistent with the specific social rules regarding modesty explicitly taught in the Chinese schools. The Chinese children, however, did not offer further explanations about the rationales for following these rules. This may be due to the fact that these social rules, like any other cultural rules, are intersubjectively shared (D'Andrade, 1987; Grice, 1975; Sweetser, 1987). Whereas the moral rules themselves are explicitly known to the members of a specific culture, the rationale for following the moral rules is assumed to be self-evident and need not be made explicit (D'Andrade, 1987; Sweetser, 1987; Weinreich-Haste, 1984). Hence, the Chinese children might be able to explain the rationale underlying the rule, but they did not see the need to do so. This possibility, however, needs to be tested empirically with specific paradigms that require explicit explanations about social and moral norms, such as direct questioning and/or dialectical discussion about the rationale underlying the norms.

Chinese and Canadian children also made similar responses under certain conditions. First, children in both cultures clearly distinguished verbal statements from deeds. They gave differentiated moral evaluations of a deed and a verbal statement regarding the deed. Second, children in both cultures gave very negative ratings to lie telling in antisocial situations, as both cultures discourage such verbal behavior and seem to see it as compounding the error. Third, both Chinese and Canadian children rated truth telling in antisocial situations very positively, while giving antisocial behaviors negative ratings. This finding is in line with Bussey (1992), who found that Western children as young as 5 years of age were able to provide differential ratings for lie telling/ truth telling and misconduct. For instance, children in the Bussey (1992) study, like those in the present study, not only rated truth telling about a misdeed positively but also reported a sense of pride in doing so. The findings of the present study as well as those of others (e.g., Bussey, 1992; Peterson, 1995; Peterson et al., 1983) suggest that, although a mature understanding of the concept of lying, per se, is achieved later in childhood, the distinction between lie telling and misconduct and the appropriate moral evaluations of them develop much earlier. However, it may be inappropriate to conclude that the response similarities between Chinese and Canadian children regarding confessing a misdeed are due to similar cultural practices in the two cultures. As indicated earlier, confession may serve different purposes for individuals in different cultures. For example, in the Chinese culture, confessional behavior is valued because it serves to maintain group harmony (Bond, 1986), whereas the Western culture encourages children to confess a misdeed to teach them the importance of fulfilling one's contractual commitment to one's partner in interpersonal communication and respecting the person's right to information (Bok, 1978; Grice, 1975; Kupfer, 1982; Sweetser, 1987). Whether Chinese and Canadian children's similar ratings of confessional behaviors stem from the two contrasting cultural orientations remains to be examined in future research.

Overall, the present findings indicate that, in the realm of lie telling, children acquire specific social and cultural norms, which in turn have a direct impact on moral development. This specifically results in differences in both Chinese and Canadian children's moral judgment. This close relation between socio-cultural practices and moral development also exists in other areas related to the development of lying. Studies have shown that children's early formation of the concept of a lie is strongly influenced by external rules (Bussey, 1992; Peterson et al., 1983; Piaget, 1932/1965; Strichartz and Burton, 1990). For example, young preschool children tend to label verbal statements that are prohibited by adults as lies. They are also more inclined to label an intention-ally false statement punished by adults as lie than the same statement that goes unpunished, although recent evidence shows that this tendency disappears after around 6 years of age (Bussey, 1992; Peterson et al., 1983). Nevertheless, social norms apparently play an important role in young children's acquisition of the concept of lying. Older children and adults have also been reported to use social rules such as the Gricean communicative maxims (Grice, 1975) for interpersonal communication (e.g., "To help; not to harm," and "To inform; not to misinform"; for definitions, see Sweetser, 1987) to define lying. For example, they are reluctant to label an intentionally false statement that the speaker tells to help the hearer, as a lie (Coleman and Kay, 1981; Lee and Ross, 1997; Peterson et al., 1983). The evidence presented here in conjunction with the existing evidence in the literature suggests that Sweetser's folklorist model of lying may not only be applicable to the development of the concept of lying but also can be extended to account for moral development in the behavioral area of lie telling.

The present study also contributes new evidence to the debate regarding the issue of the universality of moral development. Several earlier studies suggested that moral development is a universal phenomenon and is mainly determined by children's levels of cognitive development rather than social and situational factors (e.g., Colby, Kohlberg, Gibbs, and Lieberman, 1983; Edwards, 1981; Kohlberg, 1964; Turiel, Edwards, and Kohlberg, 1978). However, recent findings (for reviews, see Boyes and Walker, 1988, and Shweder et al., 1987), in line with the present results, indicated that moral development is a highly contextualized process (Baumrind, 1978; Gilligan, 1982; Harari and McDavid, 1969; Snarey, 1985; Walker, 1989; Walker, de Vries, and Trevethan, 1987; Walker and Taylor, 1991) and is affected by the culture and/or social environment in which children are socialized (Dien, 1982; Haidt, Koller, and Dias, 1993; Harkness, Edwards, and Super, 1981; Ma, 1988; Miller and Goodnow, 1990; Shweder, Jensen, and Goldstein, 1990; Tietjen and Walker, 1985). In light of the current evidence, it seems reasonable to propose that, although children's cognitive ability plays an undeniable role, cultural and social factors are also key determinants in children's moral development (Shweder et al., 1987).

Appendix: Stories

1. Prosocial Behavior/Truth-Telling Stories

A. The physical story

Here is Jenny. When Jenny was out at recess, she saw that the school yard was littered with garbage, so she picked up all the pieces she could find and threw them in the litter bin.
(Question 1: Is what Jenny did good or naughty?)
So Jenny cleaned the school yard, and at the end of recess, the teacher said to her students, "I notice that the school yard is now nice and clean." The teacher then asked Jenny, "Do you know who cleaned the yard?" Jenny said to her teacher, "I did it."
(Question 2: Is what Jenny said to her teacher good or naughty?)

B. The social story

Here is Mark. Mark knew that his friend, Timmy, had lost his lunch money on the way to school and now had no money to buy his lunch. When Timmy left his desk, Mark secretly put some of his own money in Timmy's desk so Timmy could buy some lunch.
(Question 1: Is what Mark did good or naughty?)
So Mark left some money for Timmy, and when Timmy found the money and told his teacher, the teacher said to the class, "Timmy just told me that someone has given him money so he can now buy his lunch." The teacher then asked Mark, "Do you know who left the money for Timmy?" Mark said to his teacher, "I did it."
(Question 2: Is what Mark said to his teacher good or naughty?)

2. Prosocial Behavior/Lie-Telling Stories

A. The physical story

Here is Alex. Alex's class had to stay inside at recess time because of bad weather, so Alex decided to tidy up the classroom for his teacher.
(Question 1: Is what Alex did good or naughty?)
So Alex cleaned the classroom, and when the teacher returned after recess, she said to her students, "Oh, I see that someone has cleaned the classroom for me." The teacher then asked Alex, "Do you know who cleaned the classroom?" Alex said to his teacher, "I did not do it."
(Question 2: Is what Alex said to his teacher good or naughty?)

B. The social story

Here is Kelly. Kelly knew that her friend, Anne, had lost her money for the class trip and now could not go on the trip with the rest of her class. When Anne hung up her coat, Kelly secretly put some of her own money in Anne's pocket so Anne could go on the trip.
(Question 1: Is what Kelly did good or naughty?)

So Kelly left the money for Anne, and when Anne found the money and told her teacher, the teacher said to the class, "Anne just told me that someone has given her money so she can now go on the trip." The teacher then asked Kelly, "Do you know who left the money for Anne?" Kelly said to her teacher, "I did not do it." *(Question 2: Is what Kelly said to her teacher good or naughty?)*

3. Antisocial Behavior/Truth-Telling Stories

A. The physical story

Here is Ryan. Ryan wanted to make paper airplanes so he tore some pages out of a storybook from the library.
(Question 1: Is what Ryan did good or naughty?)
   So Ryan tore the pages from a storybook, and when the teacher noticed the missing pages in the book, she said to the class, "I see that someone has torn some pages from this book." The teacher then asked Ryan, "Do you know who tore out the pages?" Ryan said to his teacher, "I did it."
(Question 2: Is what Ryan said to his teacher good or naughty?)

B. The social story

Here is Katie. Katie wanted to play with the skipping rope during gym class but discovered that one of her classmates, Sherry, was already playing with it. Katie told Sherry that she wanted the skipping rope, and when Sherry said no, Katie pushed her to the ground and made her cry.
(Question 1: Is what Katie did good or naughty?)
   So Katie pushed Sherry and made her cry, and when the teacher came over to see if Sherry was alright, she said, "Oh dear, Sherry's been hurt." The teacher then asked Katie, "Do you know who just hurt Sherry?" Katie said to her teacher, "I did it."
(Question 2: Is what Sherry said to her teacher good or naughty?)

4. Antisocial Behavior/Lie-Telling Stories

A. The physical story

Here is Shelly. Shelly wanted to draw some pictures, so she took one of the story books from the library and scribbled all over the pages.
(Question 1: Is what Shelly did good or naughty?)
   So Shelly drew pictures all over the pages in the story book, and when the teacher noticed the scribbled pages, she said to the class, "I see that someone has scribbled all over the pages in this book." The teacher then asked Shelly, "Do you know who scribbled on the pages?" Shelly said to her teacher, "I did not do it."
(Question 2: Is what Shelly said to her teacher good or naughty?)

B. The social story

Here is Paul. A new boy, named Jimmy, had just joined Paul's class, and Paul decided that he did not like him. Paul went over to Jimmy, and when the teacher was not looking, Paul pushed Jimmy to the ground and made him cry.
(Question 1: Is what Paul did good or naughty?)

So Paul pushed Jimmy and made him cry, and when the teacher came over to see if Jimmy was all right, she said, "Oh dear, Jimmy's been hurt." The teacher then asked Paul, "Do you know who just hurt Jimmy?" Paul said to his teacher, "I did not do it." *(Question 2: Is what Paul said to his teacher good or naughty?)*

Acknowledgments

We would like to thank the participating children, their parents, and their schools for their cooperation and support. We are also very grateful to Dr Richard A. Shweder and two anonymous reviewers for their constructive suggestions. This research was supported by grants to the first and second authors from the Social Sciences and Humanities Research Council of Canada.

References

Baumrind, D. (1978). A dialectical materialist's perspective on knowing social reality. In W. Damon (ed.), *New Directions for Child Development: Moral Development* (No. 2, pp. 61–82), San Francisco: Jossey-Bass.

Berndt, T. J., and Berndt, E. G. (1975). Children's use of motives and intentionality in person perception and moral judgment. *Child Development*, **46**, 904–12.

Binet, A. (1896). Psychology of prestidigitation. *Annual Report of the Board of Regents of Smithsonian Institution, 1894*, 555–71.

Bok, S. (1978). *Lying: Moral Choice in Public and Private Life*. New York: Random House.

Bond, M. H. (1986). *Lifting one of the Last Bamboo Curtains: Review of the Psychology of the Chinese People*. Hong Kong: Oxford University Press.

Bond, M. H., Leung, K., and Wan, K-C. (1982). The social impact of self-effacing attributions: The Chinese case. *Journal of Social Psychology*, **118**, 157–66.

Boyes, M. C., and Walker, L. J. (1988). Implications of cultural diversity for the universality claims of Kohlberg's theory of moral reasoning. *Human Development*, **31**, 44–59.

Burton, R. V., and Strichartz, A. F. (1991). Children on the stand: The obligation to speak the truth. *Developmental and Behavioral Pediatrics*, **12**, 121–8.

Bussey, K. (1992). Lying and truthfulness: Children's definitions, standards, and evaluative reactions. *Child Development*, **63**, 129–37.

California Task Force to Promote Self-Esteem and Personal and Social Responsibility. (1990). *Toward a State of Esteem*. Sacramento: California State Department of Education.

Colby, A., Kohlberg, L., Gibbs, J., and Lieberman, M. (1983). A longitudinal study of moral development. *Monographs of the Society for Research in Child Development*, **48** (1–2, Serial no. 200).

Coleman, L., and Kay, P. (1981). Prototype semantics: The English word *lie*. *Language*, **57**, 26–44.

D'Andrade, R. (1987). A folk model of the mind. In L. Holland and N. Quinn (eds), *Cultural Models in Language and Thought* (pp. 112–50), Cambridge: Cambridge University Press.

Davin, D. (1991). The early childhood education of the only child generation in urban China. In I. Epstein (ed.), *Chinese Education: Problems, Policies, and Prospects* (pp. 42–65), New York: Garland.

Dien, D. S. (1982). A Chinese perspective on Kohlberg's theory of moral development. *Developmental Review*, **2**, 331–41.

Domino, G., and Hannah, M. T. (1987). A comparative analysis of social values of Chinese and American children. *Journal of Cross-Cultural Psychology*, **18**, 58–77.

Early Childhood Consultants in Collaboration with the Members of the Kindergarten Curriculum Advisory Committee. (1991). *Young Children Learning: A Teacher's Guide to Learning* (2nd edn). Fredericton: New Brunswick Department of Education.

Edwards, C. P. (1981). The development of moral reasoning in cross-cultural perspective. In R. H. Monroe and B. B. Whiting (eds), *Handbook of Cross-cultural Human Development*, New York: Garland.

Gilligan, C. (1982). *In a Different Voice: Psychological Theory and Women's Development*. Cambridge, MA: Harvard University Press.

Gilsenan, M. (1976). Lying, honor, and contradiction. In B. Kapferer (ed.), *Essays in Social Anthropology: Vol. 1. Transaction and Meaning: Directions in the Anthropology of Exchange and Symbolic Behavior* (pp. 191–219), Philadelphia: Institute for the Study of Human Issues.

Goodman, G. S. (1984). Children's testimony in historical perspective. *Journal of Social Issues*, **40**, 9–31.

Grice, H. P. (1975). Logic and conversation. In P. Cole and J. L. Morgan (eds), *Syntax and Semantics: Vol. 3. Speech Acts* (pp. 41–58), New York: Academic Press.

Haidt, J., Koller, S. H., and Dias, M. G. (1993). Affect, culture, and morality, or is it wrong to eat your dog? *Journal of Personality and Social Psychology*, **65**, 613–28.

Hall, G. S. (1891). Children's lies. *Pedagogical Seminary*, **1**, 211–18.

Harari, H., and McDavid, J. W. (1969). Situational influence on moral justice: A study of "finking." *Journal of Personality and Social Psychology*, **11**, 240–4.

Harkness, S., Edwards, C. P., and Super, C. M. (1981). Social roles and moral reasoning: A case study in a rural African community. *Developmental Psychology*, **17**, 595–603.

Hayhoe, R. (1984). The evolution of modern Chinese educational institutions. In R. Hayhoe (ed.), *Contemporary Chinese Education* (pp. 26–46), Armonk, NY: Sharp.

Ho, D. Y. F., and Chiu, C. Y. (1994). Component ideas of individualism, collectivism, and social organization: An application in the study of Chinese culture. In U. Kim, H. C. Triandis, C. Kagitcibasi, S. C. Choi, and G. Yoon (eds), *Individualism and Collectivism: Theory, Method, and Applications* (pp. 137–56), London: Sage.

Hyman, R. (1989). The psychology of deception. *Annual Review of Psychology*, **40**, 133–54.

Kohlberg, L. (1964). Development of moral character and moral ideology. In M. Hoffman and L. Hoffman (ed.), *Review of Child Development Research*, New York: Harper & Row.

Kupfer, J. (1982). The moral presumption against lying. *Review of Metaphysics*, **36**, 103–26.

Lee, K., and Ross, H. (1997). The concept of lying in adolescents and young adults: Testing Sweetser's folkloristic model. *Merrill-Palmer Quarterly*, **43**, 255–70.

Lo, B. L. C. (1984). Primary education: A two-track system for dual tasks. In R. Hayhoe (ed.), *Contemporary Chinese Education* (pp. 47–64), Armonk, NY: Sharp.

Ma, H. K. (1988). The Chinese perspective on moral development. *International Journal of Psychology*, **23**, 201–27.

Miller, P. J., and Goodnow, J. J. (1990). Cultural practices: Toward an integration of culture and development. In J. J. Goodnow, P. J. Miller, and F. Kessel (eds), *Cultural Practices as Contexts for Development* (pp. 5–16, New Directions for Child Development, No. 67), San Francisco: Jossey-Bass.

Ochs Keenan, E. (1976). On the universality of conversational implicatures. *Language in Society*, **5**, 67–80.

Peterson, C. C. (1995). The role of perceived intention to deceive in children's and adults' concepts of lying. *British Journal of Developmental Psychology*, **13**, 237–60.

Peterson, C. C., Peterson, J. L., and Seeto, D. (1983). Developmental changes in ideas about lying. *Child Development*, **54**, 1529–35.

Piaget, J. (1965). *The Moral Judgement of the Child*. New York: Macmillan (original work published 1932).

Price, R. (1992). Moral-political education and modernization. In R. Hayhoe (ed.), *Education and Modernization: The Chinese Experience* (pp. 211–38), New York: Pergamon.

Seligman, M. E. P. (1996). *The Optimistic Child*. Boston: Houghton Mifflin.

Shweder, R. A., Jensen, L. A., and Goldstein, W. M. (1990). Who sleeps by whom revisited: A method for extracting the moral goods implicit in practice. In J. J. Goodnow, P. J. Miller, and F. Kessel (eds), *Cultural Practices as Contexts for Development* (pp. 5–16, New Directions for Child Development, No. 67), San Francisco: Jossey-Bass.

Shweder, R. A., Mahapatra, M., and Miller, J. (1987). Culture and moral development. In J. Kagan and S. Lamb (eds), *The Emergence of Morality in Young Children*, Chicago: University of Chicago Press.

Snarey, J. R. (1985). Cross-cultural universality of social-moral development: A critical review of Kohlbergian research. *Psychological Bulletin*, **97**, 202–32.

Strichartz, A. F., and Burton, R. V. (1990). Lies and truth: A study of the development of the concept. *Child Development*, **61**, 211–20.

Sweetser, E. E. (1987). The definition of lie: An examination of the folk models underlying a semantic prototype. In D. Holland (ed.), *Cultural Models in Language and Thought* (pp. 43–66), New York: Cambridge University Press.

Tietjen, A. M., and Walker, L. J. (1985). Moral reasoning and leadership among men in a Papua New Guinea society. *Developmental Psychology*, **21**, 982–92.

Turiel, E., Edwards, C. P., and Kohlberg, L. (1978). Moral development in Turkish children, adolescents, and young adults. *Journal of Cross-Cultural Psychology*, **9**, 75–86.

Walker, L. J. (1989). A longitudinal study of moral reasoning, *Child Development*, **60**, 157–66.

Walker, L. J., de Vries, B., and Trevethan, S. D. (1987). Moral stages and moral orientations in real-life and hypothetical dilemmas. *Child Development*, **58**, 842–58.

Walker, L. J., and Taylor, H. H. (1991). Family interactions and the development of moral reasoning. *Child Development*, **62**, 262–83.

Weinreich-Haste, H. (1984). Morality, social meaning, and rhetoric: The social context of moral reasoning. In W. M. Kurtines and J. L. Gewirtz (eds), *Morality, Moral Behavior, and Moral Development* (pp. 325–47), New York: Wiley & Sons.

Wimmer, H., Gruber, S., and Perner, J. (1984). Young children's conception of lying: Lexical realism – moral subjectivism. *Journal of Experimental Child Psychology*, **37**, 1–30.

Zhu, Z. X. (ed.). (1982). *Issues in Child Developmental Psychology* (in Chinese). Beijing: Beijing Normal University Press.

31

The Relationship between Parenting Types and Older Adolescents' Personality, Academic Achievement, Adjustment and Substance Use*

Laura H. Weiss and J. Conrad Schwarz

EDITORS' INTRODUCTION

Over the last 30 years Diana Baumrind has carried out some of the most extensive studies of the effects of parenting styles on children's development. She has identified seven different parenting styles, finding that the best adjusted children are from homes where parents use firm, consistent discipline, and who are warm and supportive – the 'Authoritative style'. In this paper Laura Weiss and Conrad Schwartz explore differences between parenting styles and their effects on adolescents' personality, academic achievement, adjustment, and substance abuse. They find results supportive of Baumrind's classification, though not as large as the effects reported by Baumrind. It seems possible that this is because Weiss and Schwarz have examined a fairly homogeneous adolescent population (they were all students), and their results are important both in confirming Baumrind's classification of parenting styles, and in successfully predicting relations between these parenting styles and their adolescent children's behaviour.

OVERVIEW

The purpose of the present study was to examine Baumrind's T3 conceptual framework using a multiple informant design and an older adolescent population. With 178 college students and their families as participants, the present study found many of the predicted relations between parents' child-rearing style (Authoritative, Democratic, Nondirective, Nonauthoritarian-Directive, Authoritarian-Directive, and Unengaged) and their adolescent children's behavior in the four domains assessed: personality, adjustment, academic achievement, and substance use. The differences

* Previously published in *Child Development*, **67** (1996), pp. 2101–14.

between parenting types on the criterion measures were not as large as reported in Baumrind's study, and significant effects were predominantly due to the poor scores from children with Unengaged and Authoritarian-Directive parents. The results are discussed in terms of their implications for the Authoritative parenting type, the utility of using a typology, and areas for future research.

Diana Baumrind (1968, 1971, 1989a, 1989b, 1991a, 1991b) conducted one of the most comprehensive longitudinal studies examining the effects of parenting style on the development of children ages 3 to 15. In her most recent report (1989a, 1991a, 1991b), at Time 3 (15-year-olds), she identified seven parenting types: Authoritative, Democratic, Nondirective, Authoritarian-Directive, Nonauthoritarian-Directive, Unengaged, and Good Enough. The results she observed were consistent with her theory and with her results from past waves. Baumrind found that good adjustment in children was associated with parents who use firm, consistent discipline and who are warm and supportive – a combination she labeled Authoritative (Baumrind, 1989a, 1991b). Adolescent children from Democratic homes (where the parents are unconventional and modestly firm) had substantially higher drug use than children from Authoritative homes, but were otherwise similar. Adolescents from Nondirective homes (where the parents are supportive, unconventional, and lax, also known as "Permissive") were less competent, achievement oriented, and self-regulated than adolescents from Authoritative or Democratic homes.

Adolescents from Directive homes (where parents are controlling, firm, rejecting, and traditional) lacked social responsibility, were conforming, and opposed drug use. Children from Authoritarian-Directive homes (the one of two Directive subtypes in which parents are highly intrusive) had slightly worse outcomes than children from Nonauthoritarian-Directive homes (the other Directive subtype, in which parents were not as intrusive). The children who had the lowest achievement scores and were the least adjusted were from Unengaged homes (where the parents are rejecting and neglecting). Lastly, those children from Good-Enough homes (where parents had moderate scores on all parenting dimensions) were, as expected, moderately competent.

Baumrind's results have been supported by a series of studies by Steinberg, Mounts, Lamborn, Dornbusch, and colleagues that have specifically addressed the utility and generality of Baumrind's conceptual framework (Dornbusch, Ritter, Leiderman, Roberts, and Fraleigh, 1987; Lamborn, Mounts, Steinberg, and Dornbusch, 1991; Steinberg, Elmen, and Mounts, 1989; Steinberg, Lamborn, Darling, Mounts, and Dornbusch, 1994; Steinberg, Mounts, Lamborn, and Dornbusch, 1991). These attempts at replicating her findings have added to the growing evidence that the Authoritative parenting style is associated with children who perform well scholastically, exhibit few internalizing or externalizing problem behaviors, and are prosocial. Furthermore, since these studies have used large, diverse samples, they have been able to show the consistency of these effects across gender, ethnicity, socioeconomic status, family structure, and time. After a 1-year interval, they found that children from Authoritative homes maintained their high level of performance, while children from neglectful or unengaged parents were performing worse on follow-up (Lamborn et al., 1991; Steinberg et al., 1994).

Yet, as strong as these studies are, they have been criticized for their single-informant design. Their exclusive use of student reports to assess both parent behavior and filial adjustment allows for the possibility that associations between the two are due to shared methods variance (e.g., socially desirable responding) and not to a true relation between the constructs. Using a multi-informant design, as in the present study, or direct observation, as in Baumrind's study, largely eliminates this threat to internal and external validity.

Another potential difficulty with their methodology is that they operationalize their parenting types differently than does Baumrind while applying Baumrind's names for the resulting typology. Since a type serves as a shorthand to refer to an entire constellation of attributes, an incomplete assessment of the attributes that define a single type will change its meaning, rendering a comparison between types difficult. A case in point is Dornbusch and colleagues' study (1987) in which Baumrind's type name, Permissive, was used, but their measure assessed only the absence of parental intervention and not Baumrind's second component, supportiveness.

Furthermore, these studies have assessed only a subset of Baumrind's typology. A great deal of attention has been given to Authoritative, Authoritarian-Directive, and Unengaged, while others (e.g., Nonauthoritarian-Directive, Democratic) have been neglected. Since previous investigations have focused on a few select types (e.g., Steinberg et al., 1991), these types included as comparisons to the Authoritative parenting type may not have provided an adequate challenge to the Authoritative parenting type; therefore, results that show superiority of the Authoritative parenting type may overestimate its positive impact.

Lastly, most of Baumrind's research and other studies have focused on high-school-aged adolescents or younger children. The good outcomes found to be associated with Authoritative parenting during the high school years may not necessarily continue into the college years, a time when parental support and prohibitions are less ubiquitous. Attributional theorists posit that strong external control hinders the operation of intrinsic reward systems that may support the internalization of standards by children. In other words, while the imminent threat of parental disapproval may suppress unwanted behaviors, there may be no lasting suppression in the absence of the parents (Lepper, 1981; Lewis, 1981; Martin, 1987).

The distinguishing attributes of the present study are that we used a multi-informant design, constructed the typology in a manner similar to that used by Baumrind, examined six of Baumrind's seven types, and assessed the generalizability of her relations to a college-age population. The present study included reports by the student, the mother, the father, and one sibling. Where relevant, reports by the student's roommate were also used. The ratings of multiple informants were averaged for analysis. Aggregating ratings decreases method variance, and in the case of parenting behavior increases the reliability and validity of measurements (see Schwarz, Barton-Henry, and

Pruzinsky, 1985; Schwarz and Mearns, 1989). In particular, this methodology corrects for "correlational bias" – the tendency for raters to assume greater similarity between mother's and father's child-rearing behavior than actually exists (Kenny and Berman, 1980). As a result, our ratings of mothers' and fathers' behaviors are more independent than those reported for other studies where a single-informant design or single observer was used.

Although, like other investigators, we have departed from Baumrind's methodology by using questionnaires, we have taken more effort to duplicate Baumrind's constructs of parenting behavior and her procedures for creating typological categories of families. To this end, we included scales that had content and emphasis similar to Baumrind's T3 study, solicited Baumrind's comments on their composition, and revised the parenting scales in accordance with her suggestions.

The final objective of the present study was to examine the generalizability of Baumrind's findings to an older, more independent, college-age population. This population provided an opportunity to examine offspring at a developmental stage in which parents' direct influence had diminished substantially and peers' influence had heightened. The combination of age and environmental context provides a good test for the internalization of parental standards.

Method

Subjects

Participants were 178 students from the University of Connecticut and their roommates, mothers, fathers, and one sibling. The sample was a subset selected from the Family Dynamics Study (FDS) database, consisting of data on 369 families who were recruited for the purposes of examining family conflict and its influence on adjustment in late adolescence (Schwarz, 1992; Schwarz, Barton-Henry, and Pruzinsky, 1985; Schwarz and Mearns, 1989). In keeping with this primary objective, students selected for the FDS met the following criteria: (a) freshman status; (b) a sibling within 3 years of the student's age; (c) a mother and a father with whom the student had lived until at least age 16; (d) willingness of the sibling, mother, and father to participate in the study; and (e) a college roommate or friend who was also willing to participate in the study. Thus each family was intact and included at least two children, one of whom was a college fresh-person at the University of Connecticut at the outset of the study. To obtain an equal number of low- and high-conflict families, the original sampling procedure overselected for high-conflict families, which was defined by a score above the seventy-fifth percentile on the Schwarz Inter-Parental Conflict Scale (IPC: Schwarz, 1990).

Procedure

Families who qualified for the study were admitted when all members of the study unit agreed in writing to participate. Student participants completed questionnaires in groups of 15 to 20. They attended four sessions spaced at 2-week intervals. Roommates also attended the second and third sessions. Two packets of questionnaires were then mailed separately to the mother, father, and sibling. Upon return of the first packet, a second packet of similar length was mailed to the correspondent. In an attempt to prevent family members from influencing each other, participants were asked to fill out the questions independently and to mail them in separate envelopes. Pronoun changes were made on the instructions and the items of each questionnaire to make them appropriate for a given informant type; otherwise questionnaires were identical. Three years later, during the students' senior year, the students were asked to participate in a follow-up study. Seventy-five percent of the original sample agreed to participate and completed questionnaires pertaining to adjustment and to alcohol and drug use.

Parenting typology

Measures used   The FDS data set includes a number of measures that assess parenting behavior. The Children's Report of Parental Behavior Inventory (CRPBI: Schaefer, 1965; Schludermann and Schludermann, 1970) and the Parental Behavior Form (PBF: Worell and Worell, 1974) were designed to assess child-rearing behavior by requiring the respondent to complete items descriptive of maternal and paternal behavior toward the student subject. The CRPBI has 18 subscales, and the PBF has 13 subscales and two validity scales. The number of items on each subscale ranges from five to eight. Using the CRPBI and the PBF, both the mother and the father were rated by four types of informant: mother, father, sibling, and student. Informants' scores were aggregated within subscales of the CRPBI and the PBF (see Schwarz et al., 1985; Schwarz and Mearns, 1989, for intercorrelation between informants).

A third measure, the Social Attitude Questionnaire (SAQ), was composed of items from the Monitoring the Future project of the Institute for Social Research (Bachman, O'Malley, and Johnston, 1979). It examined attitudes toward substance use, politics, religion, and gender roles and was administered as a self-report to both the mother and father. Also included in the SAQ was a seven-item likert scale measuring parental attitude toward sexual permissiveness (Meyer, 1977). Since a student report of both the mother's and father's sexual permissiveness was also available, an aggregate score based on two informants, student and parent, was computed for each parent.

Measuring Baumrind's four dimensions of parental control   The initial selection of scales and items from the FDS to assess parenting behavior was made on the basis of content similarity to measures from Baumrind's study. In keeping with Baumrind's methodology, four composite measures of parenting behavior were constructed: Assertive Control, Supportive Control, Directive/Conventional Control, and Intrusive Control (Baumrind, 1989a, 1991b). Wherever possible, scales and subscales were used, as opposed to individual items, because scales typically have greater reliability than single items. Scales pertaining to each of Baumrind's parenting dimensions were intercorrelated, and those that did not correlate significantly with the majority of remaining scales for each dimension were deleted. Additional revisions were made based on the judgments of four expert raters. As a final check, candidate scales for each dimension were submitted to Dr Baumrind (personal communication, Sept. 5, 1990) for her judgment of relevance and appropriateness to the construct. Baumrind's suggestions for refinement were followed except in those cases where other important psychometric objectives would have been seriously compromised. Finally, before averaging, the scales assessing each of Baumrind's four dimensions of parental control were standardized and weighted to approximate the emphasis and overall thrust of each dimension. A separate score for both mother and father was calculated for each dimension of control.

Supportive control   Our measure of Baumrind's Supportive Control dimension consisted of three CRPBI subscales – Acceptance of Individuation, Positive Involvement, and Rejection (reversed) – and five PBF subscales – Curiosity, Active Involvement, Rejection (reversed), Cognitive Independence, and Cognitive Encouragement. Table 31.1 shows the intercorrelations for eight subscales. The weight of those subscales that dealt with cognitive stimulation was doubled to approximate the emphasis given in Baumrind's construct. For fathers and mothers, the alpha coefficients for the Supportive Control measure (treating subscale scores as item scores) were .91 and .89, respectively.

Assertive control   Our measure of Baumrind's Assertive Control dimension consisted of five CRPBI subscales – Extreme Autonomy, Control, Enforcement, Nonenforcement (reversed), and Lax Discipline (reversed) – and one PBF subscale, Lax Control (reversed). Table 31.2 shows the intercorrelations for the six subscales. For fathers and mothers, the alpha coefficients for the Assertive Control measure were .88 and .87, respectively.

Directive/conventional control   Constructing our index of Baumrind's Directive Control dimension was slightly more complicated, given its dual emphasis on

TABLE 31.1   The intercorrelation of subscales on Supportive Control

Scales	Acc	Cur	CI	CC	AI	PI	Rej(C)	Rej(P)
Acceptance of individuation	...	.39	.58	.36	.48	.69	−.70	−.49
Curiosity	.47	...	.75	.71	.46	.42	−.28	−.32
Cognitive independence	.73	.73	...	.62	.59	.52	−.44	−.49
Cognitive competency	.41	.71	.60	...	.36	.36	−.22	−.27
Active involvement	.59	.46	.64	.38	...	.74	−.45	−.47
Positive involvement	.73	.43	.62	.38	.83	...	−.61	−.44
Rejection (CRPBI)	−.74	−.32	−.58	−.30	−.53	−.66	...	.60
Rejection (PBF)	−.55	−.30	−.56	−.30	−.54	−.59	.68	...

Note: The correlations on the upper right side of the matrix pertain to mothers and the correlations on the lower left side of the matrix pertain to fathers. All correlations are significant at $p < .0001$.

TABLE 31.2 The intercorrelation of subscales on Assertive Control

Scales	Control	Enforce	Ext. Aut	Lax Con	Nonenf	Lax Dis
Control	...	.79	−.38	−.54	−.43	−.59
Enforcement	.73	...	−.36	−.52	−.40	−.65
Ext. autonomy	−.42	−.40	...	.65	.48	.46
Lax control	−.52	−.50	.63	...	.65	.70
Nonenforcement	−.40	−.45	.40	.59	...	.61
Lax discipline	−.49	−.58	.41	.62	.60	...

Note: The correlations on the upper right side of the matrix pertain to fathers and the correlations on the lower left side of the matrix pertain to mothers. All correlations are significant at $p < .0001$.

traditional values and overcontrolling child-rearing style. Traditional attitudes were assessed by a six-item scale that measured parents' attitudes toward their child's drug use (Bachman et al., 1979), a seven-item scale that measured parents' attitudes toward sexual permissiveness (Meyer, 1977), and a single question concerning conservatism of political beliefs (Bachman et al.,) 1979). The correlations among these three measures were .04, .18, and .26 for fathers and .10, .26, and .26 for mothers. Even though parents' political beliefs were not significantly correlated with their attitudes on sexuality, we felt that these were all-important components of and relevant to assessing traditional attitudes. We standarized and aggregated the three measures to form a single *traditional attitudes* composite, which made up one-fourth of our Directive Control measure. The PBF subscale, Conformity, which also relates to traditional values, made up another one-fourth of our Directive Control. The remaining half of Directive Control was composed of a single subscale from the PBF, Strict Control, which assesses a highly controlling and directive child-rearing style. The correlations among the traditional attitudes composite, the Conformity subscale, and the Strict Control subscale are presented in table 31.3. For fathers and mothers, the alpha coefficients for our Directive Control measure were .56 and .62, respectively. The concept of Directive Control, with its dual emphasis on control and traditional child rearing, is not a homogeneous concept, which is reflected in its slightly lower alpha coefficient.

TABLE 31.3 The intercorrelation of subscales on Directive Control

Scales	Tradition	Conformity	Strict Control
Traditional attitude	...	.31[**]	.15[*]
Conformity	.37[**]	...	.43[**]
Strict control	.19[*]	.51[**]	...

Note: The correlations on the upper right side of the matrix pertain to fathers and the correlations on the lower left side of the matrix pertain to mothers.
[*] $p < .01$.
[**] $p < .0001$.

Intrusive control Our measure of Baumrind's Intrusive Control dimension consisted of one subscale from the CRPBI, Intrusiveness.

Construction of the typology The scores of mothers and fathers on the dimensions of Supportive, Assertive, Directive Conventional, and Intrusive Control were used to qualify the family for one of six parenting types. If one parent's score fell a half standard deviation or more above the mean and the other parent's score fell a half standard deviation or more below the mean on any of the four dimensions, the parental dyad was deleted. On this basis, 46 families were excluded. While loss of subjects means a loss of power, the cost seemed justified and necessary to attain a pure representation of each parenting type. For remaining families, the scores of the two parents on each of Baumrind's four parenting dimensions were averaged.[1]

Following Baumrind's procedures, the Assertive, Supportive, and Directive/Conventional Control dimensions were each divided into four categories: high, midhigh, midlow, and low (Baumrind, 1989a, 1991a, 1991b). All parental dyads with average scores greater than a half a standard deviation from the mean were put in the two extreme categories; the remaining dyads were placed in the two middle categories. Intrusive Control was divided at the mean into two categories: high intrusiveness and low intrusiveness.

Six parenting types – Authoritative, Democratic, Nondirective, Nonauthoritarian-Directive, Authoritarian-Directive, and Unengaged – were then constructed according to Baumrind's formulas at T3 (Baumrind, 1989a, 1991a, 1991b). The Authoritative type was defined by parental dyads who were high on Assertive Control and high on Supportive Control. The Democratic type was defined by parental dyads who were high on Supportive Control, not high on Directive Control, and midhigh or midlow on Assertive Control. The Nondirective type was defined by parental dyads who were low on Directive Control, low on Assertive Control, and midhigh or high on Supportive Control. The Unengaged type was defined by parental dyads who were low on Assertive Control and low on Supportive Control. Directive type was defined by parental dyads who were high on Directive Control, high on Assertive Control, and midlow or low on Supportive Control. The two subtypes of the Directive parenting type were the Nonauthoritarian-Directive type, which was defined by a low score on Intrusive Control, and Authoritarian-Directive, which was defined by a high score on Intrusive Control.[2] Table 31.4 shows the breakdown of adolescent subjects by parenting type and gender. Analyses showed no significant association between type and gender, $\chi^2(5) = 2.66$, $p < .75$.

Criterion variables

Concerning the behavior of the late-adolescent sons and daughters, there were four categories of criterion variables: (*a*) personality, (*b*) academic achievement, (*c*) adjustment, and (*d*) substance use. The validity and reliability of scores were enhanced by aggregating the reports of multiple informants. Aggregation

TABLE 31.4   Number of adolescents by parenting type and gender

	Gender		
Parenting Type	Male	Female	Total N
Authoritative	14	18	32
Democratic	15	17	32
Nondirective	16	17	33
Nonauthoritarian-directive	10	15	25
Authoritarian-directive	18	12	30
Unengaged	12	14	26
Total N	85	93	178

over raters and instruments increases the generalizability of the measurements.

Personality measures   Personality traits was assessed by the five scales developed by Schwarz, Weiss, Wheeler, and Taren (1995) from the Gough–Heilbrun Adjective Check List (ACL: Gough and Heilbrun, 1983). These scales were empirically derived to measure the "Big Five" model of personality, namely, Agreeableness, Extroversion, Conscientiousness, Neuroticism, and Openness to Experience. These scales displayed good psychometric properties. Internal consistencies ranged from .87 to .93. They were completed by all five raters: subject, mother, father, sibling, and roommate.

Academic achievement measures   With the student's consent, grade point averages (GPA) and Standardized Aptitude Test (SAT) scores were obtained from university records upon graduation.

Adjustment measures   Four composite measures were used to assess adjustment: Social Nonconformity, General Maladjustment, Neurotic Symptoms, and Severe Depression (Schwarz, 1989). The measure of Social Nonconformity, which reflects the subject's inclination toward antisocial attitudes and behavior, is composed of two measures: the Social Nonconformity Scale from Lanyon's (1973) Psychological Screening Inventory (PSI), rated by self and roommate, and a self-report measure of teenage misconduct (TMS: West and Farrington, 1973; Campbell, 1977). The General Maladjustment Score, which reflects personal discomfort or dissatisfaction, is composed of two scales from the Gough–Heilbrun Adjective Check List (ACL; Gough and Heilbrun, 1983) – the Personal Adjustment Scale (reversed) and the Ideal-Self Scale (reversed); the PSI's Discomfort Scale, which assesses anxiety, depression, and feeling badly about oneself; and the Negativistic/Unstable Scale from Millon's (1983) Clinical Multiaxial Inventory (MCMI) rated by self and roommate. The Neurotic Symptoms Score is composed of four strongly intercorrelated MCMI scales: the Anxiety Scale, the Somatoform Scale, the Dysthymic or Neurotic Depression Scale, and the Borderline/Cycloid Scale. The Depressive Episodes Score, which is an index of the severity of past depressive episodes, is composed of three measures: self-ratings of the student's worst and second worst past depression, assessed with the Beck Depression Inventory (BDI: Beck, Rial, and Rickels, 1974), and the score from the Psychotic Depression Scale Score of the MCMI, rated by self and roommate.

Substance use measures   Freshman and Senior Drug and Alcohol measures fell under the heading of Substance Use indices. Both drug and alcohol measures were derived from items on the Cigarettes, Alcohol, and Other Drugs (CAD) Questionnaire, which contained items that were developed by Bachman et al. (1979) for the "Monitoring the Future" project. Both the freshman year and senior alcohol scores reflected subjects' average daily alcohol consumption and self-perceived problems with alcohol (Schwarz and Wheeler, 1990). The drug scores were computed from questions that required the subjects to rate, for each drug or class of drugs mentioned (total of nine drugs or drug classes), the amount used in their lifetime, during the last 12 months, and during the last 30 days.

RESULTS

Parenting type (six levels), gender of subject (two levels), and the interaction term, parenting type × gender, were used as predictor variables in 15 separate simultaneous multiple-regression analyses.[3] The multiple regressions were performed using SAS's General Linear Model (GLM) procedure, which transforms each level of a nominal predictor into separate variables, dummy coded as 0 and 1 (for more detailed information see SAS Institute, Inc., 1990, pp. 928–32). This method takes into account possible correlations between gender and parenting type in this nonrandom design (Cohen and Cohen, 1975). It tests the significance of the independent contributions of gender, parenting type, and their interaction to the prediction of each criterion variable. Significant F ratios ($p < .05$) involving parenting type were followed by Duncan's multiple-range tests to assess the significance of differences between pairs of individual means ($p < .05$).

Since the purpose of the present study was to examine the effects of parenting type on adolescent outcome, main effects of gender will not be reported. However, significant effects for parenting type and interaction effects of parenting type and gender will be fully explained below. The F ratios for main-effect tests of parenting type on all criterion variables are presented in table 31.5, along with associated p values, mean scores for six of the criterion variables by parenting type, and a code indicating the significant differences between the means, based on Duncan's test. In cases where the interaction term is significant, comparable statistics by gender are provided. Within table 31.5, variables are grouped into four categories: personality, academic achievement and aptitude, adjustment, and substance use. For ease of comparison, all criterion variables are presented in T score form ($M = 50$ and $SD = 10$), as standardized on the study sample of 178 students.

TABLE 31.5 Means of personality, achievement, adjustment, and substance use measures by parenting type

Adolescent	F	p	Parenting Types						Comparisons
			1 (Aut)	2 (Dem)	3 (Nond)	4 (N-Dir)	5 (A-Dir)	6 (Unen)	
Personality:									
Agreeableness	2.89	.02	53.3	53.2	51.2	50.0	48.8	45.4	1, 2, 3 > 6
Extroversion	.72	N.S.	51.9	52.2	49.0	51.4	49.8	48.9	
Conscientiousness	1.58	.17	52.5	50.9	50.2	52.9	48.0	46.6	
Open to experience	3.79	.002	52.2	51.8	54.2	51.0	47.9	45.0	1, 2, 3, 4 > 6; 3 > 5
Neuroticism	3.55	.0002	48.8	45.6	48.1	49.0	53.0	50.7	5 > 2
Academic:									
SAT total	2.33	.05	51.0	50.0	54.2	51.5	47.2	50.7	3 > 5, 2
GPA*	2.08	N.S.	53.1	49.8	53.2	51.2	46.1	49.0	
Male	2.95	.01	52.7	51.4	46.9	50.8	44.0	49.7	1 > 5
Female	...	...	53.3	47.8	58.7	51.5	49.7	48.5	3 > 2, 5, 6
Adjustment:									
Depression	1.53	N.S.	47.0	49.1	49.2	48.8	53.9	49.7	
Neuroticism	1.05	N.S.	46.7	47.3	48.6	51.3	51.3	49.4	
Maladjustment*	2.92	.01	46.3	45.6	47.6	49.6	52.2	53.1	
Male	2.80	.02	43.6	49.8	45.2	47.8	54.7	52.6	5, 6 > 1; 5 > 3
Female	...	...	48.4	41.8	49.9	50.8	48.4	53.5	3, 4, 6 > 2
Nonconformity	2.93	.01	45.8	49.8	47.1	48.7	50.4	53.6	6 > 1, 3, 4
Substance use:									
Freshman alcohol	1.78	N.S.	47.8	50.7	48.8	47.5	51.0	53.6	
Freshman drug	1.09	N.S.	47.9	49.4	50.5	48.7	46.7	53.0	
Senior alcohol	3.97	.002	47.8	54.4	48.6	45.8	51.0	57.3	6 > 1, 3, 4; 2 > 1, 4
Senior drug*	1.58	N.S.	46.7	52.2	48.0	50.7	46.4	54.0	
Male	1.93	.09	45.3	58.0	47.4	51.2	43.3	53.8	
Female	...	...	47.9	47.9	48.8	50.3	53.6	54.2	

Note: Underscored numbers in the Comparison column refer to significant gender differences. Aut = Authoritative, Dem = Democratic, Nond = Nondirective, N-Dir = Nonauthoritarian-Directive; A-Dir = Authoritarian-Directive; Unen = Unengaged.
* Significant or marginally significant interaction.

Personality

A significant main effect for parenting type was found for three of the five personality measures: Agreeableness, Openness to Experience, and Neuroticism. Children from Unengaged homes had the most extreme, low scores on Agreeableness and Openness to Experience and were significantly different from children from most other homes, with the exception of Authoritarian-Directive. Consequently, these children could be characterized as dominant, rude, stubborn, and lacking in creativity. With poor but less extreme scores, children from Authoritarian-Directive homes were found to be significantly less open to experience than children from Nondirective homes, and significantly more neurotic or temperamental than those from Democratic homes.

Academic achievement and aptitude

Children from Nondirective homes had significantly higher SAT scores than children from Authoritarian-Directive and Democratic homes. The parenting type × gender interaction on GPA revealed that sons with Authoritative parents had a significantly higher GPA than sons with Authoritarian-Directive parents. On the other hand, for daughters, it was those children from Nondirective homes that had an exceedingly high GPA, almost 1 standard deviation above the mean. Their mean GPA was significantly higher than the GPA of females from all other parenting types, except Authoritative and Nonauthoritarian-Directive. In addition, daughters from Nondirective homes had a significantly higher GPA than sons from the same home type. Thus, the academic aptitude and achievement results suggested that children, particularly females, from Nondirective homes, excelled scholastically.

Drug and alcohol use

Models predicting Freshman-Year Substance Use were not significant, whereas one of two models predicting Senior-Year Substance Use was significant despite shrinkage in sample size by the senior-year assessment. It was hypothesized that alcohol and drug use at freshman year were related to situational influences, such as the increased freedom and availability of drugs and alcohol in college, which would impact strongly upon all subjects and suppress family-type differences. The significant model with Senior-Year Alcohol Use and nonsignificant model with a parallel trend for Senior-Year Drug Use are consistent with the hypothesis that by the senior year, the novelty of college had decreased and family-type effects had re-emerged.

The main effect of Senior-Year Alcohol Use revealed that children from Nonauthoritarian-Directive or Authoritative parents had the lowest alcohol use by their senior year, and their alcohol use was significantly lower than that of individuals from Democratic or Unengaged homes. The interaction effect on Senior-Year Drug Use approached but did not reach significance and therefore should be treated with caution. However, it is worth noting that the group with the most deviant score – almost a standard deviation above the mean – was sons from Democratic households.

Adjustment

Of the four adjustment measures, two, Nonconformity and Maladjustment, were significantly predicted by parenting type or a parenting type × gender interaction. The examination of the significant main effect for parenting type on Nonconformity revealed that children from Authoritative, Nondirective, or Nonauthoritarian-Directive homes were significantly more conforming than those from Unengaged homes. Similarly, examination of the significant inter-action effect on Maladjustment showed that sons from Authoritative homes were significantly less maladjusted than sons from Authoritarian-Directive or Unengaged homes. Sons from the Nondirective homes differed only from sons from Authoritarian-Directive homes. Daughters with Democratic parents had the lowest maladjustment scores and had, in fact, lower scores than females from all other parenting types except the Authoritarian-Directive and Author-itative. Furthermore, the interaction between parenting type and gender showed a general trend for sons to be less maladjusted than daughters, with the exception of children from Democratic and Authoritarian-Directive homes. For the latter family types, the opposite pattern was observed (i.e., sons being more maladjusted than daughters), however, only the differences between sons and daughters of Democratic parents attained significance.

DISCUSSION

The results of this study present a mixed finding. Although the patterning of the means across criterion measures was remarkably similar to Baumrind's T3 results, the magnitude of the differences was smaller than reported by Baum-rind (1989a, 1991b). In general, our models achieved significance predomin-antly because of the extreme scores obtained by children from Unengaged homes and, to a lesser extent, the scores of children from Authoritarian-Directive homes, a finding characteristic of previous studies (Baumrind, 1989a, 1991b; Dornbusch et al., 1987; Lamborn et al., 1991; Steinberg et al., 1994). The present results depart from their predecessors, however, in that while children from Authoritative homes received the most or second most favorable scores in the majority of instances, they did not achieve scores with significant magnitude to set them apart or to distinguish them from children from all other family types.

The smaller magnitude of differences between parental types observed here may be a consequence of range restriction inherent in a sample pooled from a university. The sample was restricted at the low end by the absence of late-adolescent participants with achievement motivation and academic aptitude near or below the mean of the general population. Such individuals either do not apply or are unlikely to be accepted to the university. At the upper end, the sample was probably restricted by a dearth of very high achievers, who would have been chosen to attend yet more prestigious universities. In addition, if late-adolescent outcomes are correlated with parenting type, and it is likely that they are, and if outcomes affect college admission, then the range of parenting behaviors in this sample would also have been restricted.

Nevertheless, the differences in outcome between the present study and others are, for the most part, of degree but not of kind. The characteristics reported in Baumrind's T3 study that distinguished the children raised with different parenting styles are present also in this older, late-adolescent, college-age sample. Like Baumrind, we found that our Unengaged parenting style was associated with a variety of negative sequelae in children. Children from Unengaged homes were significantly more nonconforming, maladjusted, dominating, selfish, and unoriginal and had a higher consumption of alcohol than children from most other homes.

The results for children of Nonauthoritarian- and Authoritarian-Directive parents were also similar to the results found by Baumrind. As in Baumrind's study (1989a, 1991a, 1991b), no significant differences were found between our children of Nonauthoritarian- and Authoritarian-Directive parents, but the two groups did display different strengths and weaknesses when compared with children from other types of homes, particularly the Unengaged type. The children from Authoritarian-Directive homes tended to cluster with those from Unengaged homes in that they did not differ significantly on the criterion measures, whereas children from Nonauthoritarian-Directive homes were significantly more open to experience and conforming than children from Unengaged homes. Furthermore, children from Nonauthoritarian-Directive homes consumed less alcohol in their senior year than those from Democratic or Unengaged homes, a characteristic that distinguished them in Baumrind's study as well. Also congruent with Baumrind, children from Authoritarian-Directive homes had a particular weakness in academic aptitude and achievement compared with children from Nondirective or Authoritative homes.

The mean scores from our Nonauthoritarian-Directive group tended to cluster with the Authoritative, Democratic, and Nondirective group. Outside of a few select areas, the differences between these groups were minor and mostly of degree, with the adolescents from the Authoritative and Nondirective homes having the highest scores. Alcohol consumption was one of those areas in which differences were apparent. Adolescents from Nonauthoritarian-Directive homes distinguished themselves by their low alcohol consumption, whereas children from Democratic homes distinguished themselves from the Nonauthoritarian-Directive and Authoritative groups by their high consumption of alcohol. Consistent with Baumrind's T3 study, high alcohol use in this parenting type did not translate into greater psychological distress (i.e., Neuroticism and Maladjustment), as it had for the Unengaged group. This suggests that, in contrast to the Unengaged group, the alcohol use of the Democratic group, with its greater peer affiliation and nontraditional parental beliefs, was indicative of experimentation in the context of peer relations and not of an overall pattern of deviance.

Moreover, daughters from Democratic homes were more psychologically adjusted than children from most other homes, including the sons of

Democratic parents. The only other gender × parenting type interaction found in the present study was for GPA: children from Nondirective homes had the most discrepant findings across gender. Baumrind found a similar gender difference for children from Nondirective homes on Maths and Verbal Achievement, but her sample size was too small to test for a significant difference in gender. For both Democratic and Nondirective groups, the results favored daughters over sons, suggesting that sons may require more rules and limitsetting than daughters to reach their full potential.

In the present study, the most divergent finding from Baumrind's was the favorable outcome for our children with Nondirective parents; whereas Baumrind found that the Nondirective group scored moderately to poorly, in our study the Nondirective group rivaled the Authoritative group in positive outcomes. The age difference between samples in the present study and other studies may be one explanation to account for the discrepancy in the results. Parents may change their child-rearing strategy as their children mature. Parents who are highly autonomy-granting when the children are younger may be providing too much freedom, whereas parents who appropriately reduce direct control over their children in late adolescence may be helping their children to develop self-esteem and autonomy. Although a plausible explanation, research evidence points to the contrary, namely, that both parents' and children's behaviors are relatively stable over time. McNally, Eisenberg, and Harris (1991) found few changes in maternal child-rearing practices over an 8-year period. Similarly, longitudinal studies examining the impact of child rearing on children's development also suggest relatively stable associations between parenting type and filial outcome (Lamborn et al., 1991; Steinberg et al., 1994).

Methodological differences may be a more likely explanation for the discrepant results. Baumrind had a small Nondirective sample, which consisted of only seven parental dyads. In contrast, the present study identified 33 Nondirective homes, a number equivalent to that observed for other parental types. In all but one of Baumrind's seven dyads, the parents were divorced, a confounding factor that can directly affect children's adjustment regardless of parenting style (Amato and Keith, 1991). Baumrind's results (1991a) also indicate that, as compared with Democratic or Authoritative mothers, Nondirective mothers were not in fact highly supportive.

Although the superiority of Authoritative parenting is more ambiguous in the present study than in previous ones, children from Authoritative homes did distinguish themselves favorably in several ways. Unlike their Nondirective and Democratic counterparts, children from Authoritative homes had high favorable scores that were never reliably inferior to those of children from other parenting subtypes, and they also performed equally well regardless of gender. This is, of course, a less than unqualified victory for Authoritative parenting.

The clustering of positive outcomes for children from Authoritative, Nondirective, and Democratic homes seems to suggest that parental supportiveness is the distinguishing factor in late-adolescent outcome; Authoritative, Nondirective, and Democratic types were each high on supportiveness and were each associated with positive outcomes, whereas Authoritarian-Directive, Nonauthoritarian-Directive, and Unengaged types were each low on supportiveness, and each of these types tended to be associated with less positive outcomes. However, the fact that children from Democratic homes had slightly different outcomes than those from Authoritative and Nondirective homes suggests that assertive control does have an impact on outcome, albeit a smaller one; Democratic style was defined as moderately assertive, whereas Authoritative and Nondirective were at the extremes of parental assertiveness.

Just as the examination of parenting types solely according to their level of supportiveness might lead one to ignore potentially meaningful distinctions concerning assertiveness, so the merging of groups to form fewer types risks the loss of other nuances and the possibility of another parenting type providing a good challenge to hegemony of the Authoritative parenting style. Steinberg et al. (1994) and Lamborn et al. (1991) used a fourfold typology derived from Macoby and Martin's theories. Their low-control-but-high-supportiveness parenting group (i.e., the Indulgent group), which corresponds somewhat with both Democratic and Nondirective subtypes, was associated with children who were prosocial, competent, and psychologically adjusted, but who also had a poor work orientation and used drugs heavily. The Steinberg et al. and Lamborn et al. results are more similar to those reported for children from our Democratic type, who performed moderately, than for children from our Nondirective type, who performed more favorably. The academic striving, low drug use, and work ethic of their Authoritarian group (which corresponds to our Nonauthoritarian and Authoritarian-Directive groups) were more similar to the favorable outcomes of our Nonauthoritarian-Directive group than to the less favorable outcomes of our Authoritarian-Directive group. In these cases, it would appear that the possibility of more extreme results, both positive (for Nondirective) and negative (for Authoritarian-Directive), were diluted by the failure to separate potentially predictive parenting subtypes.

Since the use of a typology restricts the ability to discern which of the defining components are contributing the predominant effects, future research should also focus on and assess the effects of the parent-behavior dimensions used to form the typology. Grolnick and Ryan (1989) and Steinberg et al. (1989) are examples of studies that have examined simultaneously the effect of more than one continuous dimension of parenting behavior on adolescent outcome. In both of these studies, however, interactions between the parenting variables were not examined because the studies lacked a sufficient number of subjects for these additional terms to be included in the regression models. Keeping the measures of parenting behavior in their continuous form would permit one (a) to utilize all subjects, (b) to address questions of linearity, (c) to provide more detailed information on how each component of parental behavior affects adolescent outcome, as well as (d) to examine the effects of interactions between multiple parenting dimensions.

APPENDIX: SAMPLE ITEMS FROM THE PARENTING SCALES

Supportive Control

CRPBI: Acceptance of individuation	Likes me to choose own way of doing things.
CRPBI: Positive involvement	Tells me how much she loves me.
CRPBI: Rejection (reversed)	Makes me feel I'm not loved.
PBF: Curiosity	Encourages me to fool around with new ideas.
PBF: Active involvement	Gives me a lot of care and attention.
PBF: Cognitive independence	Likes me to assert my own ideas with her.
PBF: Cognitive competency	Wants me to find out answers for myself.
PBF: Rejection (reversed)	Doesn't show that she loves me.

Assertive Control

CRPBI: Control	Has a lot of rules and sticks to them.
CRPBI: Enforcement	Sees to it that I obey [rules].
CRPBI: External autonomy (reversed)	Lets me do anything I like to do.
CRPBI: Nonenforcement (reversed)	Doesn't pay much attention to my misbehavior.
CRPBI: Lax discipline (reversed)	Excuses my bad conduct.
PBF: Lax control (reversed)	Does not bother to enforce rules.

Directive/Conventional Control

SAQ: Drugs	How would you feel about your UCONN student trying LSD once or twice?
SAQ: Permissiveness	Most men do not want to marry virgins.
SAQ: Politics	How would you describe your political beliefs (very conservative – radical)?
PBF: Conformity	Tells me that hard work will make life worthwhile.
CRPBI: Strict control	Wants to control whatever I do.

Intrusive Control

CRPBI: Intrusiveness	Asks me to tell everything that happens when I'm away from home.

ACKNOWLEDGMENTS

The development of the data base employed in the study was supported by PHS grant RO1 MH31750-01-6, by PHS grant 5R01 AA06754-01-02, and by funds from the University of Connecticut Research Foundation and Computer Center. The first author was supported in part by the National Institute of Mental Health Prevention Research Branch and Office on AIDS Research Training Grant T32MH19933 to Roger Weissberg. The authors thank Diana Baumrind for her advice and consultation regarding the composition of our parenting measures. We also thank the following individuals for their assistance in developing the database: George Goldsmith, Sterling Green, Jack Mearns, Sharla Rausch, Bob Upson, and David Wheeler.

NOTES

1. Baumrind typed each parent separately and favored the mother's type when it differed from the father's. Since ratings of mothers' and fathers' behaviors were relatively independent because the "correlational bias" was reduced by our use of aggregated ratings, it was frequently the case that parents within a dyad fell into slightly different categories. Thus in this study we used the average score of the two parents on each of the four control measures. Even so, because her typology did not assess all combinations of the four control measures and we did not include one of her types, 145 parental dyads were dropped for failing to fall within the defining criteria for any of the six parenting types assessed. The deletion of cases made the sample more representative because the high-conflict families were dropped at a 3:2 ratio to low-conflict families. This is not to say that the child-rearing style of these 145 parental dyads (whose behaviors were more moderate) are unworthy of investigation in a future study, but rather that these moderate parenting styles did not fulfill our present purpose of examining Baumrind's more extreme parenting types.
2. One of Baumrind's types, Good-Enough, was not included in this study owing to an insufficient number of cases. This category is somewhat tangential and of less theoretical importance than the others.
3. When conflict (as measured by the IPC) was added to the model as a covariate, it did not change the observed relations between parenting style, gender, and the criterion measures.

REFERENCES

Amato, P., and Keith, B. (1991). Parental divorce and the well-being of children: A meta-analysis. *Psychological Bulletin*, **110**, 26–46.

Bachman, J. G., O'Malley, P. M., and Johnston, L. D. (1979). *Developing composite measures of drug use: Comparisons among lifetime, annual, and monthly reports for thirteen classes of drugs*. Monitoring the Future Occasional Paper No. 5. Ann Arbor: Institute for Social Research.

Baumrind, D. (1968). Child care practices anteceding three patterns of preschool behavior. *Genetic Psychology Monographs*, **75**, 43–88.

Baumrind, D. (1971). Current patterns of parental authority. *Developmental Psychology Monographs* (Part 2), **4**, 99–102.

Baumrind, D. (1989a, August). *The influence of parenting style on adolescent competence and problem behavior*. Paper presented at the APA's "Science Weekend," New Orleans, LA.

Baumrind, D. (1989b). Rearing competent children. In W. Damon (ed.), *New Direction for Child Development: Child Development, Today and Tomorrow* (pp. 349–78), San Francisco: Jossey-Bass.

Baumrind, D. (1991a). The influence of parenting style on adolescent competence and substance use. *Journal of Early Adolescence*, **11**, 56–95.

Baumrind, D. (1991b). Parenting styles and adolescent development. In R. Learner, A. C. Petersen, and J. Brooks-Gunn (eds), *The Encyclopedia on Adolescence* (pp. 746–58), New York: Garland.

Beck, A., Rial, W., and Rickels, K. (1974). Short form of depression inventory: Cross-validation. *Psychological Reports*, **34**, 1184–6.

Campbell, A. C. (1977, December). *Self-reported delinquency among English adolescent girls*. Paper delivered to the British Sociological Society: Criminology Section, Department of Experimental Psychology, South Parks Road, Oxford, England.

Cohen, J., and Cohen, P. (1975). *Applied Multiple Regression/Correlation Analysis for the Behavioral Sciences*. Hillsdale, NJ: Erlbaum.

Dornbusch, S., Ritter, P., Leiderman, P., Roberts, D., and Fraleigh, M. (1987). The relation of parenting style to adolescent school performance. *Child Development*, **58**, 1244–57.

Gough, H. G., and Heilbrun, A. B. (1983). *Manual for the Adjective Check List*. Palo Alto, CA: Consulting Psychologists Press.

Grolnick, W., and Ryan, R. (1989). Parent styles associated with children's self-regulation and competence in school. *Journal of Educational Psychology*, **81**, 143–54.

Kenny, D. A., and Berman, J. S. (1980). Statistical approaches to the correction of correlational bias. *Psychological Bulletin*, **88**, 288–95.

Lamborn, S. D., Mounts, N. S., Steinberg, L., and Dornbusch, S. M. (1991). Patterns of competence and adjustment among adolescents from authoritative, authoritarian, indulgent, and neglectful families. *Child Development*, **62**, 1049–65.

Lanyon, R. I. (1973). *Psychological Screening Inventory: Manual*. Goshen, NY: Research Psychologist Press.

Lepper, M. R. (1981). Social control processes, attributions of motivation, and the internalization of social values. In E. T. Higgins, D. N. Rubie, and W. W. Hartup (eds), *Social Cognition and Social Behavior: Developmental Perspectives*, San Francisco: Jossey-Bass.

Lewis, C. (1981). The effects of parental firm control: A reinterpretation of findings. *Psychological Bulletin*, **90**, 547–63.

Martin, B. (1987). Developmental perspectives on family theory and psychopathology. In T. Jacob (ed.), *Family Interaction and Psychopathology Theories, Methods, and Findings*, New York: Plenum.

McNally, S., Eisenberg, N., and Harris, J. D. (1991). Consistency and change in maternal child-rearing practices and values: A longitudinal study. *Child Development*, **62**, 190–8.

Meyer, R. M. (1977). *Parent–daughter relationship and daughters' sexual self-concept, sexual behavior, and sexual values*. Unpublished doctoral dissertation, Yale University.

Millon, T. (1983). *Millon Multiaxial Clinical Inventory Manual*. Minneapolis, MN: National Computer Systems, Inc.

SAS Institute, Inc. (1990). *SAS/STAT user's guide: Vol. 2. GLM-VARCOMP*, 4th edn. Cary, NC: SAS Institute, Inc.

Schaefer, E. S. (1965). Children's Report of Parental Behavior: An inventory. *Child Development*, **36**, 413–24.

Schludermann, E., and Schludermann, S. (1970). Replicability of factors in the Children's Report of Parent Behavior (CRPBI). *Journal of Psychology*, **76**, 239–49.

Schwarz, J. C. (1989, August). *Family dynamic predictors of coalition, maladjustment, and substance abuse*. Paper presented at the First European Congress of Psychology, Amsterdam, Netherlands.

Schwarz, J. C. (1990). Schwarz Inter-Parental Conflict Scale (IPC) (abstract). In J. Touliatos, B. Perlmutter, and M. Straus (eds), *Handbook of Family Measurement Techniques* (pp. 485–6), Thousand Oaks, CA: Sage.

Schwarz, J. C. (1992, August). Parenting, marital conflict, coalition, and maladjustment in sons and daughters. In J. C. Schwarz (Chair), *Parenting and family dynamic in the prediction of late-adolescent adjustment*, Symposium conducted at the 100th annual convention of the America Psychological Association, Washington, DC.

Schwarz, J. C., Barton-Henry, M., and Pruzinsky, T. (1985). Assessing child-rearing behaviors: A comparison of ratings made by mother, father, child, and sibling on the CRPBI. *Child Development*, **56**, 462–79.

Schwarz, J. C., and Mearns, J. (1989). Assessing parental childrearing behaviors: A comparison of parent, child, and aggregate ratings from two instruments. *Journal of Research in Personality*, **23**, 450–68.

Schwarz, J. C., Weiss, L. H., Wheeler, D. S., and Taren, P. (1995). *Searching for the Big Five in the Adjective Check List: Factor analysis and scale development*. Manuscript submitted for publication.

Schwarz, J. C., and Wheeler, D. S. (1990). *Predicting alcohol and drug use: Conjoint effects of five personality traits*. Unpublished manuscript, University of Connecticut, Storrs.

Steinberg, L., Elmen, J., and Mounts, N. (1989). Authoritative parenting, psychosocial maturity, and academic success among adolescents. *Child Development*, **60**, 1424–36.

Steinberg, L., Lamborn, S. D., Darling, N., Mounts, N. S., and Dornbusch, S. M. (1994). Over-time changes in adjustment and competence among adolescents from authoritative, authoritarian, indulgent, and neglectful families. *Child Development*, **65**, 754–70.

Steinberg, L., Mounts, N., Lamborn, S., and Dornbusch, S. (1991). Authoritative parenting and adolescent adjustment across varied ecological niches. *Journal of Research on Adolescence*, **1**, 19–36.

West, D., and Farrington, D. P. (1973). *Who Becomes Delinquent?* London: Heinemann.

Worell, L., and Worell, J. (1974). *The Parent Behavior Form*. Unpublished manuscript, University of Kentucky, Lexington.

32

Understanding Bullying from a Dynamic Systems Perspective

Debra Pepler, Wendy M. Craig and Paul O'Connell

EDITORS' INTRODUCTION

Bullying is an antisocial behaviour that can have awful effects on those who are bullied, resulting in unhappiness, fear, truancy, and in extreme circumstances, suicide. Pepler, Craig and O'Connell consider some of the causes of bullying, and the ways in which the social situation can promote and maintain bullying and victimization. They argue that bullying is best seen in the context of a social dynamic system, in which all parts of the system are involved – the victim and the bully are only part of the system.

Dynamic systems theory is a theoretical perspective that describes relations between systems and, as such, can be applied to an understanding of the development, acceleration, maintenance and perhaps termination of bullying among school children. Although dynamic systems theory was originally conceived to explain physical phenomena (e.g., chemical reactions, bridge stresses), it provides a useful framework to consider the very complex relations between people. In the physical sciences, researchers have used dynamic systems theory to describe how random events or uncoordinated phenomena are gradually pulled into a synchronous unit. A physical example of this is the Tacoma Narrows Bridge near Seattle, Washington. Parts of the bridge were vibrating randomly, but the vibrations gradually merged into a smooth harmonic in heavy winds, resulting in undulations along the roadway of up to three metres in height. The bridge eventually collapsed as it was unable to sustain the stresses generated by the coordinated harmonic wave. In human interaction, dynamic systems theory provides an explanation for how relations can be stable and changing at the same time. For example, dynamic systems theory would explain the coercive process model of social learning theory proposed by Patterson (1982). The somewhat random aversive behaviours of a parent and a child gradually become coordinated and accelerate in a non-linear fashion. In this chapter, we will explore the utility of dynamic systems theory as it relates to bullying and victimization. First, however, we will explain some key concepts in dynamic systems theory.

FRAME

The concept of a frame is central to dynamic systems theory as it applies to social relations (Fogel, 1993). A frame is a pattern of interactions that becomes established as people interact. These frames are emergent (i.e., they develop over time) and they are dynamic (i.e., they are constantly changing). For example, parents establish a bedtime routine with their young children – they have a fairly consistent pattern of behaviours that serves to settle the child down after an active day. The mother or father have certain 'prescribed' behaviours such as reading a story and singing a song; the child has a set of complementary behaviours – to snuggle close and listen.

In the case of bullying, there is a 'dance macabre' or ritual that develops between the bully and the victim, which has a certain stable form but may vary slightly from time to time. Similar to the parent–child frame, both the bully and the victim have 'prescribed' roles – to attack and to be attacked. These frames can be found at a dyadic, group, or broader cultural level. For example, at a group level, gangs have ritual greetings or behaviours that serve to bring the group together with common expectations of how to behave. At a cultural level, the French culture has the greeting frame of kissing twice, once on each cheek. Frames provide predictability in interactions because of their stability over time.

POSITIVE FEEDBACK

Two processes account for self-organization within dynamic systems theory according to Lewis (1995): positive feedback and coupling. Positive feedback promotes the development of a frame. In the case of the bedtime ritual, there are likely to be several positive feedback loops: the child settles when the parent reads and sings, thereby encouraging the parent to continue this behaviour pattern. Similarly, the parent may become relaxed and content as the child nestles in and listens to the story. The two participants' behaviours influence each other in a reciprocally enhancing fashion. In this way, the bedtime ritual becomes an emergent form. A similar positive feedback process may operate in the development of a bully–victim relationship between school children. As the bully repeatedly threatens and harasses the victim, the victim may become more submissive or upset, which may fuel the bully's motivation to experience the power of domination. Conversely, the victim may experience increased fear and distress as the attacks of the bully continue. A feature of the positive feedback process is that the emerging frame or form is sensitive to small differences because these are amplified through the positive feedback. In an emerging bully–victim relationship, the bully may change his or her tormenting slightly to include threats at the end of recess. These threats may set the victim into a state of distress during class time in anticipation of what might unfold during the next recess.

COUPLING

The second process in Lewis's (1995) account of a social dynamic system is coupling. This refers to the coordination of particular behaviours or elements in the reciprocal interaction processes. These are the behaviours that emerge together in the frame and distinguish that interactional unit from others. The coupling of behaviours (e.g., when parent starts to sing, child lies down) constitutes the emerging coherence in the interactional frame. Because the coupling promotes coherence and consolidation of the interactions within a frame, the system becomes resistant to change. In the case of bully–victim interactions, a victim may develop a fear response to the bully's gathering friends around and looking in the victim's direction. The victim's emotional response may extend to situations in which the bully is always talking to friends, and not looking in the victim's direction. When the victim's fear becomes coupled with the bully's behaviour, their relationship becomes predictable, consolidated, and increasingly difficult to break.

STABILITY

Frames form when people come together for some purpose, such as settling a child down for the night, or establishing dominance in the case of the bully and victim. The players' interactions comprise dynamic processes. Through repeated interactions, roles and behaviour patterns become established. The behaviours of one individual are complementary to those of the other. The bedtime routine requires both a parent and a child and it is the parent's role to provide the quiet activities and security in order to settle the child for sleep. In the case of bullies and victims, the bully becomes established as the individual with more power who harasses the victim. Conversely, the victim adopts a style of submission or avoidance in the face of the bully's negative behaviours.

Cognitive and emotional factors also continue to comprise the emergent frames (Lewis, 1995). In the case of parent–child interactions, bedtime routines provide the child with security and a sense of love and belonging. Emotions also play a significant role in bully–victim interactions. Bullies may, for example, enjoy the sense of power and become increasingly confident in their position of dominance as their victims continue to submit. As in other forms of abuse, the victim may gradually come to define him/herself as worthless and deserving of the abuse. The victim may experience increased fear of the bully as the relationship becomes firmly established. The anxiety the victim experiences often interferes with school performance. You can imagine the victim's difficulty in attending to challenging academic tasks when the bully has cast a glance that indicates trouble during the upcoming lunch hour.

A basic principle of dynamic systems theory is that a system must lose stability for the behavioral pattern to change (Thelen and Smith, 1994). As we will discuss later, this principle is extremely important in our attempts to reduce the problems of bullying at school. We turn now to a consideration of change within dynamic systems theory.

CHANGE

Frames (or interactional patterns within relationships) are dynamic and evolve over time. Whereas stability comes about with, or despite, gradual fluctuations in feelings, change occurs when fluctuations become amplified such that the feelings are extreme and disrupt the frame (Fogel, 1993). The parent–child bedtime routine might change, for example, if the child started to experience fear of the dark. The parent would alter his/her behaviour to reassure the child that there is nothing to be concerned about and to refocus the child on more positive thoughts. In the case of bully–victim relationships, change might occur if the victim's reactions shift to high distress or to avoidance. In the case of extreme reactions, the bully might become concerned about the amount of distress being caused (although this may be unlikely with some children) and/or others close to the victim may intervene to change the power imbalance and disrupt the bully–victim frame.

SYSTEMS THEORY MEETS DYNAMIC SYSTEMS THEORY

Human interactions are very complex and, as such, present a formidable challenge to those of us who seek to describe and understand them. In our field, there is a move away from unidimensional theoretical models to models that are multidimensional, and take into account that interactions between two individuals most often unfold within a broader system. For example, the interactions between a mother and child are affected by and affect the interactions between other members of the family. This understanding is central to systemic family therapy. The family is also embedded in a broader system of the community. Bronfenbrenner (1979) has identified this as the ecological approach. Cairns and Cairns (1991) have identified the multiple systems in which we need to study the development of aggressive behaviour problems. Their research has pointed to the peer group as a particularly important factor in the development of antisocial behaviour. Through playground observations of bullying, we learned that the peer group is present in 85 per cent of the episodes. We are now struggling to identify and describe the influences of the peer group on bully–victim interactions. This struggle has brought us to the consideration of dynamic systems theory which forms the basis of this review.

Whereas dynamic systems theory describes the process, systems theory indicates the contexts in which the process unfolds. Therefore, a theoretical

---

School

1. Cognitions, behaviours, and emotions of teachers, administrators.
   Awareness of attitudes that promote bullying.
   Sensitivity to the needs of victims.
   Explicit school policy that addresses bullying.
   Policy states interventions that should occur in the case of bullying.

Peer Group Processes

1. Cognitions, behaviours, and emotions of peer group serve to:
   Maintain reputations of the bully and victim (fear of bully and perceived weakness of victim).
   Attract peers to bullying interactions.
   Reinforce the bully and victim by providing attention or by observing and joining in.
   Heighten emotions of excitement and arousal because of aggression.

Dyadic Level

1. Interaction of the bully's and victim's cognitive and behavioural tendencies.
2. Emergence of a frame or interaction pattern.
3. Positive feedback loop to bully and victim.
4. Coupling in interactions.
5. Maintenance of relationship and perhaps increase in intensity.

Bullies	**Victims**
1. Cognitions ("I am dominant")	1. Cognitions (e.g.,"I cannot fight back")
2. Behaviours	2. Behaviours
• Aggressive personality	• Physical weakness
• Physical strength	• Timidity
• History of harsh punishment at home	• Anxious personality
• Lack of warm relationships at home	• Overprotected by families
• Aggressiveness at home	

FIGURE 32.1   A dynamic systems perspective on bullying and victimization

model for bullying must comprise an explanation of the developing interactional processes at numerous levels or systems. In the following section, we describe the features of the dynamic systems at the dyadic, group and broader contextual level of the school. See figure 32.1 for a diagram of our model.

INDIVIDUAL LEVEL

The first factor that we must consider in developing a theoretical framework for bullying is the individual. The work of Dan Olweus, which emerged from a personality perspective, has been fundamental in identifying the characteristics of boys who are bullies and victims. Olweus (1991) describes bullies as having an antisocial personality combined with physical strength. These boys are often from homes with harsh punishment and a lack of warmth. Their bullying behaviour is often manifested in the home environment in physical attacks on their parents and siblings. Victims, on the other hand, are typically physically weak, timid, and with an anxious personality. They are often over-protected within their families. These descriptions imply numerous foundations for the behaviour patterns of bullies and victims. Their behaviours may be determined by genetic factors such as temperament (impulsivity or inhibition), early experience in the family environment, and influences from other systems such as the sibling or peer systems. These influences converge to establish a behavioural and cognitive tendency to become involved as the aggressor or victim within a bully–victim relationship.

DYADIC LEVEL

When a bully and victim with these behavioural and cognitive tendencies come face-to-face, their interactions comprise a dynamic system. A frame or interaction pattern begins to emerge based on changing cognitions, emotions, and behaviours. Positive feedback loops develop which contribute to the coupling of these components within the bully and victim and to their emerging relationship. When they first come together, the direction that their relationship will take is undetermined and depends on the behaviours, cognitions, and emotions of both the bully and the victim. The course of the relationship unfolds like the branches of a tree, with high potential for change at the transition points.

The bully's cognitions might be: 'I'm dominant. He is asking for a beating', his/her emotions might be such that to bully is arousing, exciting, fun, and/or risky. The bully's behaviour occurs as some form of attack on the victim. The feedback for the bully's actions comes both from within the bully (that feeling of power and control was exciting) and from the victim, who may submit and reinforce the bully's sense of dominance. Alternatively, the bully's behaviour patterns may take a different course if the victim stands up to the attack, if the bully experiences empathy for the victim and remorse for the aggression, or if a teacher or peers provide a negative message about the bullying behaviour. The more advanced the bully–victim relationship, the less likely it is that these deterrents will have an effect.

The victim's cognitions, behaviours and emotions also determine the direction of the frame or system. If the victim is generally anxious and intimidated, s/he may feel ineffective in standing up to the bully's attack. The corresponding emotional response may comprise fear, anxiety and helplessness. Under these conditions, the victim's behavioural response is likely to be to submit to the bully's attack. Conversely, if the child who has been targeted for an attack is generally confident and possesses the verbal and behavioural skills to stand up to the bully, the interaction is likely to take a different course. The victim will have cognitions that support a positive self concept (I'm okay, I'm effective). The corresponding emotional response to an attack might be anger or annoyance, with the resultant behaviour being to fight back or to ignore the bully's attack.

Together the cognitions, emotions and behaviours of both the bully and the victim determine the course of their relationship. If there is positive feedback and coupling in their interactions, the bullying is likely to continue and perhaps increase in intensity. Conversely, if their behaviours are not synchronous (i.e., mutually reciprocating), a bully–victim relationship will not develop between these two individuals. The determinants for the emerging bully–victim relationship reside within the individuals, but also within the context in which the bullying unfolds. A central feature of the context is the peer group, which is embedded in a larger school and societal context.

Peer Group Processes

Our observational research suggests that the peer group provides an important context for bullying interactions. We placed remote microphones on children and filmed them from inside the school building while they went out for recess and lunch. This technology enables us to capture the verbalizations as well as the behaviours of children during unstructured play. (For a review of this methodology, see Pepler and Craig, 1995.) On the playground and in the classroom, peers were present in 85% of the bullying episodes that we observed (Craig and Pepler, 1995). The peers play various roles in the bullying episode from simply providing an audience to becoming actively involved in the interaction between the bully and the victim. We are currently in the early stages of examining peer involvement in bullying from a dynamic systems perspective.

Prior to our introduction to dynamic systems theory, our theoretical understanding of the peer groups' role was based in social learning theory. From a social learning perspective, the reinforcement contingencies can be identified. For example, the peers may be providing positive reinforcement to the bully through attention, favourable comments, joining in the attack, or deference to the bully. The peer group may also influence the victim's behaviour by taunting, ignoring the attack, or distancing. In 12% of the episodes, peers came to the support of the victim, so they may also assist the victim (Craig and Pepler, in press). Social learning theory provides substantial insight into the interrelatedness of the behaviours of the bully, the victim and the peer group. The traditional models, however, have been unidimensional and therefore cannot fully account for the dynamic (stable and changing) nature of bully–victim interactions in the context of peers. Currently, we are looking at how relatively uncoordinated peers become drawn into a bully–victim interaction and how their behaviours serve to maintain, accelerate, and occasionally decelerate bully–victim interactions. That is to say: does orderliness emerge spontaneously or is it just the summation of the effects of pre-established reinforcement schedules.

We are limited in our observations by taking a brief slice out of children's playground activities. Our experience of working in the schools with particular problems of bullying within a peer group context indicates that the bullying develops over a period of time, as dynamic systems theory would suggest.

Although we know that any interactions we observe derive from a history of past interactions between the individuals, we are not able to assess that history. Nevertheless, we can describe the participants' interactions as they unfold in the microcosm of a single episode on the playground.

In the initial stages of an episode, the behaviours of the bully, victim and peer group are relatively heterogeneous or uncoordinated. The bully then decides to attack the victim (either alone or with a peer: 90% of our playground episodes involved only one bully) (Craig and Pepler, in press). As the bully's behaviour intensifies, it appears to attract the attention of peers (a positive attractor in dynamic systems theory language). We have struggled to understand the draw of bullying for the peer group. In trying to understand it, consider the multi-billion dollar industry of violent films and television programming, or the millions that boxing or wrestling matches attract. We humans, at least some of us, are very attracted to violence and will pay heavily to be the audience for a violent encounter.

But what about children on the playground? Their experience is not an 'as if' or fantasy created by special effects in the film industry. The combatants are not relatively equal and consenting to the theatre of violence as in wrestling or boxing. In contrast, there is a power differential with the victim being at high risk of being hurt (psychologically, if not physically) by the bully. What is it that draws children into the limelight of a bullying theatre? Excitement probably plays a major role and often children are seeking some excitement during unstructured and inactive playground time. It seems that humans find violence arousing and exciting. One need only witness a fight at a hockey or rugby game to experience the excitement of violence. But the playground is different. The players aren't padded; there isn't a referee to break up the fight. In discussing this dilemma with Martin Daily (an evolutionary psychologist), he suggested a survival value in attending to a bullying episode. Perhaps the peers are drawn in and are paying close attention in order to determine who is doing what to whom in what way, and with whom they should align in order to avoid being the victim. Whatever the underlying mechanisms, our observations of bullying on the school playground suggest that bullying does not occur in a vacuum, but most often in the context of a peer group. The behaviours of those peers, who are somehow attracted to the bullying episode, gradually become coordinated in a frame through positive feedback and coupling. In this way, the peer group may play a very significant role in the frequency and intensity of bullying observed on the school playground.

As described earlier for the development of the dyadic frame, the peers' cognitions, emotions, and behaviour are all likely to play a part in sustaining bullying. Having observed the behaviour of the bully and victim over time, the peers probably develop perceptions of the bully as dominant, someone to be feared, and perhaps respected in some way (so as not to become the next victim). Peers are likely to develop perceptions of the victim as weak, vulnerable, and perhaps deserving of the abuse. There is a high risk for peers who side with the victim: they place themselves in danger of becoming victimized as well. As these cognitions develop, they organize the peers' attentions and provide feedback to the bully and the victim that serves to stabilize and/or accelerate the bully–victim frame.

The emotions in the peer group also play a role. In addition to the excitement and arousal described above, peers may fear or revere the bully (either way it is enhancing attention to the bully). In either case, they are unlikely to intervene to stop the bully's attacks on the victim. They may develop a dislike, or conversely empathy and concern, for the victim. In the latter case, peers may be distressed by the repeated attacks on the victim, which may lead them to intervene on the victim's behalf. As mentioned earlier, the stability of a frame is disrupted when emotions are extreme (when strong emotions are incongruent with other participating elements). Our work with peers, and that of other researchers, focuses on developing empathy for the victim. Our experience is that it is only when peers can understand the distress of the victim, that they are moved to intervene or change their behaviours.

The cognitions and emotions are coupled with the behaviours of the peer group in response to bullying episodes. The peers' behaviours generally serve to promote bullying: they stand around, watch, comment, make an occasional kick, or verbally taunt the victim themselves, and for the most part do not intervene to stop the interaction. Since bullying interactions, especially those that have developed over a long period of time, are very stable, it requires considerable energy to disrupt the system. On the other hand, it is possible to change the bully–victim frame. If alliances within the peer group shift from the bully to the victim, it is less likely that the peers will provide the reinforcement necessary to maintain bullying. Our experience in working with children suggests that adult intervention is required to shift alliances within the peer group. In the case of bullying, where the bully has considerable power over the victim, the victim is by definition unable to shift the balance. Peers are also unlikely to change spontaneously given the dynamics that have been described above. So another system, the teacher–children system, must be brought into play to disrupt the bully–victim frame and the peer frame that surrounds the bully–victim interaction.

BROADER CONTEXT OF CLASSROOM AND SCHOOL

In our original observational study, there were large differences in the frequency of bullying on the two school playgrounds: one school had 70% of the observed episodes, the other school had 30% (Craig and Pepler, in press). In other words, there are school differences in the prevalence of bullying. Although we did not measure school climate, we gained some insights into the school differences when we asked whether the schools would be willing to participate in a further study of bullying. The principal of the school with 70% of the episodes said that there was no bullying at his school and that they were certainly not interested in any further involvement! The other principal was very concerned about bullying, was working to reduce it and wanted to sign up at the top of the list. The context or climate that the adults create within the classroom and the school directly affect the children's behaviours. From a dynamic systems perspective, as well as from a general systems theory, it is clear that interactions in one frame affect those in another frame. If administrators and teachers turn a blind eye to bullying, it will flourish. If on the other hand, they identify it for the children and are consistent in intervening and following through to deal with bullying, the bully–victim frame will be disrupted and will dissipate.

Effecting change within a school system is extremely difficult, because of the stability that has developed within that system. Reducing bullying in a school requires changes in the cognitions, emotions, and behaviours of the administration and the teachers. Principals and teachers are often unaware of the extent to which their behaviours may promote bullying at school. Their cognitions may support it: kids will be kids, it is not important or serious. Their emotions may sustain bullying in many ways. Occasionally teachers are reluctant to confront a bully, particularly when his behaviour has attracted the attention and allegiance of an entire class. Teachers may not understand the impact on the victim. Identifying the problems and engaging teachers' empathy for the victim is often a critical first step in solving the problems of bullying. Some teachers are bullies themselves, modelling for the children the use of power and aggression. More often, it is the lack of teachers' behaviours that supports bullying. In our playground observations, teachers were observed to intervene in only 4% of the episodes. When they permit bullying by not intervening to stop it, teachers inadvertently promote bullying in their classrooms and schools.

IMPLICATIONS FOR INTERVENTION

Dynamic systems theory, with its accounts of emerging relationships (frames), stability and change, provides clear direction for intervention to reduce bullying. It also provides insight into why it is so difficult, once a frame is established, to change the interactional system. Together with systems theory, we can develop a model of change for interventions within the school. This model needs to take into account the various subsystems within a school and the interrelations among them. Therefore, interventions to reduce bullying must unfold simultaneously at the individual, dyad, peer, classroom, school and family levels.

Dynamic systems theory, together with general systems theory, provide several directions for developing interventions to reduce bullying.

1. In order for patterns to change, systems must lose stability so they may be sensitive to perturbations. To maximize the potential for change, change should be introduced in multiple systems simultaneously. An isolated effort for change at one level will be thwarted by the other systems that remain stable and draw the target system back into line. For example, within interventions to reduce bullying, dynamic systems theory suggests that it is futile to intervene with the bully or victim alone. Not only does each of their behaviours depend on the others, but they are embedded in

the larger frames of the peer group, classroom, and school. There may also be supporting interactional systems at home, suggesting that parents also need to be involved.

2. Because of the interrelatedness of systems, turbulence can be created in one system and have an effect on other systems. If one system is particularly resistant to change (e.g., the bully–victim dyad), it is possible to change it by alterations in other systems (e.g., the peer group). We have worked at giving peers an understanding and a language to support their interventions to stop bullying. Even if peers merely stop providing the audience for bullying, the bully's goal of exhibiting dominance will be thwarted and this may be enough to change the dynamic.

3. Dynamic interactions are supported by cognitions, emotions, and behaviours. Therefore, interventions must target all three of these elements of dynamic systems. Our interventions within schools have aimed to develop an understanding of bullying and an ability to identify it. We have focused specifically on developing empathy and concern for the victim. This has proved to be as important with teachers as it is with children. When teachers really appreciate the distress of victims under their care, they are eager to work for change. The final step of changing behaviour is difficult because even if individuals understand bullying and have concern for the victim, they are drawn into the existing frames by forces that operate on many levels.

We recently experienced a situation exemplifying this pull to homeostasis, or back to former bullying patterns, in a Grade 7 class. We visited the class on the teacher's request. We focused on identifying bullying, its various forms, and discussing the peer processes that support bullying. The students were very engaged in the discussion and we felt all had gone well: the class and teacher were well on their way to reducing bullying. Not two weeks later, we were called back in because the girls had circulated a slam book. This is a book with negative attributes on each page, for which nominations are provided: 'Who is the nerdiest', Who is the stupidest'. This is a form of bullying. What surprised the teacher was that many of the girls (this incident comprised exclusively girls) were very prosocial and cooperative and had not been malicious until that point in the year. We went back into the class and discussed the power of peer pressures. These are the attractors that draw individuals into interactions that their cognitions and emotions would not necessarily support.

SUMMARY AND CONCLUSIONS

The problems of aggression and violence are complex. Dynamic systems theory helps to unravel some of the complexity to increase our understanding of the processes operating at various levels of the problem and points to the multiple intervention targets to ameliorate the problem. The study of bullying and victimization has been hampered by the lack of a theoretical perspective. We believe that the marriage of dynamic systems theory, social learning theory, and systems theory provides the foundation to move beyond our focus on individual bullies and victims to an understanding of the complex processes that underlie and sustain these problems among our school children.

REFERENCES

Bronfenbrenner, U. (1979). *The Ecology of Human Development: Experiments by Nature and Design*. Cambridge, MA: Harvard University Press.

Cairns, R., and Cairns, L. (1991). Social cognition and social networks: A developmental perspective. In D. Pepler and K. Rubin (eds), *The Treatment of Childhood Aggression*, Hillsdale, NJ: Erlbaum.

Craig, W. M., and Pepler, D. J. (1995). Peer processes in bullying and victimization: A naturalistic study. *Exceptionality Education in Canada*, **4**, 81–95.

Craig, W., and Pepler, D. J. (in press). Observations of bullying and victimization on the schoolyard. *Canadian Journal of School Psychology*.

Fogel, A. (1993). *Developing through Relationships: Origins of Communication, Self, and Culture*. Chicago: University of Chicago Press.

Lewis, M. (1995). Cognition–emotion feedback and the self-organization of developmental paths. *Human Development*, **38**, 71–102.

Olweus, D. (1991). Bully/victim problems among school children: Some basic facts and effects of a school-based intervention program. In D. Pepler and K. Rubin (eds), *The Development and Treatment of Childhood Aggression*, Hillsdale, NJ: Erlbaum.

Patterson, G. R. (1982). *Coercive Family Process*. Eugene, Oregon: Castalia.

Pepler, D. J. and Craig, W. M. (1995). A peek behind the fence: naturalistic observations of aggressive children with remote audiovisual recording. *Developmental Psychology*, **31**, 548–53.

Thelen, E., and Smith, L. B. (1994). *A Dynamic System Approach to the Development of Cognition and Action*. Cambridge, MA: MIT Press.

33

The Company They Keep: Friendships and their Developmental Significance*

Willard W. Hartup

**EDITORS'
INTRODUCTION**

On 12 February 1993, 2-year-old James (Jamie) Bulger was lured away from his mother in a busy shopping centre in Liverpool, England, by two 10-year-olds, Robert Thompson and Jon Venables. These children cajoled and pushed the distressed and frightened little boy over two and a half miles, often stopping to 'explain' the situation to concerned passers-by. They then tortured the child, throwing paint at him, striking and kicking him (42 separate injuries resulted from this), and having battered and kicked him to death, finally pushed him onto a railway line, seemingly in an attempt to disguise the murder. Prior to 'capturing' Jamie, the child killers had attempted to entice other children, and it was clear that they had persevered in seeking a victim (Newson, 1994).

On 24 March 1998, in Jonesboro, Arkansas, 11-year-old Andrew (Drew) Golden and 13-year-old Mitchell Johnson donned camouflage gear, stole a van, drove three miles to Drew's grandfather's house, where they broke in and stole four handguns and three powerful hunting rifles. They then went to Westside Middle School, triggered the school fire alarm, and shot dead four young schoolmates (all girls, three aged 12, the fourth 11) and a 32-year-old teacher, firing 22 shots from their armoury of weapons. Their victims were part of an all-girl music class that had been closest to the fire exit and had been first into the line of fire. Mitchell Johnson had vowed to do 'a lot of killing' after being dumped by his girlfriend (she was shot and wounded in the killing spree, but survived), and had told fellow school pupils 'Tomorrow y'all are gonna die', and 'everyone who hates me is going to die'.

* Previously published in *Child Development*, **67** (1996), pp. 1–13.

These two shocking murders took place on opposite sides of the Atlantic, but they had three things in common: the murders were clearly premeditated, the killers were children, and there were two of them. In this important paper Willard (Bill) Hartup begins by citing another murder which shares these three characteristics, and makes a case that would apply to the others mentioned here: 'One conclusion seems relatively certain: this murder was an unlikely event until these two antisocial friends reached consensus about doing it.'

REFERENCE

Newson, E. (1994). Video violence and the protection of children. *The Psychologist*, **7**, (6), 272–4.

Considerable evidence tells us that "being liked" and "being disliked" are **OVERVIEW** related to social competence, but evidence concerning friendships and their developmental significance is relatively weak. The argument is advanced that the developmental implications of these relationships cannot be specified without distinguishing between *having friends, the identity of one's friends*, and *friendship quality*. Most commonly, children are differentiated from one another in diagnosis and research only according to whether or not they have friends. The evidence shows that friends provide one another with cognitive and social scaffolding that differs from what nonfriends provide, and having friends supports good outcomes across normative transitions. But predicting developmental outcome also requires knowing about the behavioral characteristics and attitudes of children's friends as well as qualitative features of these relationships.

On February 16, 1995, in the small Minnesota town of Delano, a 14-year-old boy and his best friend ambushed and killed his mother as she returned home. The circumstances surrounding this event were described in the next edition of the *Minneapolis Star Tribune* (February 18, 1995): The boy had "several learning disabilities – including attention deficit disorder." He had been "difficult" for a long time and, within the last year, had gotten in trouble with a step-brother by wrecking a car and carrying a gun to a movie theater. The mother was described as having a wonderful relationship with her daughter but having "difficulties" with her son. The family dwelling contained guns.

Against these child, family, and ecological conditions is a significant social history: The boy was "...a lonely and unliked kid who was the frequent victim of schoolmates' taunts, jeers, and assaults. He had trouble with school work and trouble with other kids.... He was often teased on the bus and at school because of his appearance and abilities.... He got teased bad. Every day, he got teased. He'd get pushed around. But he couldn't really help himself. He was kind of skinny.... He didn't really have that many friends."

The boy actually had two good friends: one appears to have had things relatively well put together. But with this friend, the subject " ... passed [a] gun safety course for hunting; they took the class together." The second friend (with whom the murder was committed) was a troublesome child. These two boys described themselves as the "best of friends," and spent much time together. The boys have admitted to planning the ambush (one saying they had planned it for weeks, the other for a few hours). They were armed and waiting when the mother arrived home from work. One conclusion seems relatively certain: this murder was an unlikely event until these two antisocial friends reached consensus about doing it.

An important message emerges from this incident: Child characteristics, intersecting with family relationships and social setting, cycle through peer relations in two ways to affect developmental outcome: (a) through acceptance and rejection by other children in the aggregate, and (b) through dyadic relationships, especially with friends. Considerable evidence now tells us that "being liked" by other children (an aggregate condition) supports good developmental outcome; conversely, "being disliked" (another aggregate condition) is a risk factor (Parker and Asher, 1987). But the evidence concerning friendships and their developmental significance is weak – mainly because these relationships have not been studied extensively enough or with sufficient differentiation.

On the too-rare occasions in which friendships are taken into account developmentally – either in diagnosis or in research – children are differentiated merely according to whether or not they have friends. This emphasis on having friends is based on two assumptions: First, making and keeping friends requires good reality-testing and social skills; "having friends" is thus a proxy for "being socially skilled." Second, friendships are believed to be developmental wellsprings in the sense that children must suspend egoism, embrace egalitarian attitudes, and deal with conflict effectively in order to maintain them (Sullivan, 1953). On two counts, then, having friends is thought to bode well for the future.

Striking differences exist, however, among these relationships – both from child to child and from companion to companion. First, enormous variation occurs in who the child's friends are: Some companions are outgoing and rarely get into trouble; others are antisocial; still others are good children but socially clumsy. These choices would seem rather obviously to contribute to socialization – not only by affecting reputations (as the adage admonishes) but through what transpires between the children. Knowing that a teenager has friends tells us one thing, but the identity of his or her friends tells us something else.

Secondly, friendships differ from one another qualitatively, that is, in their *content* or normative foundations (e.g., whether or not the two children engage in antisocial behavior), their *constructiveness* (e.g., whether conflict resolution commonly involves negotiation or whether it involves power assertion), their *closeness* (e.g., whether or not the children spend much time together and engage in many different activities), their *symmetry* (e.g., whether social power is vested more or less equally or more or less unequally in the two children), and their *affective substrates* (e.g., whether the relationship is supportive and secure or whether it is nonsupportive and conflict ridden). Qualitative differences in these relationships may have developmental implications in the same way that qualitative variations in adult–child relationships do (Ainsworth, Blehar, Waters, and Wall, 1978).

This essay begins, then, with the argument that one cannot describe friendships and their developmental significance without distinguishing between *having friends, the identity of the child's friends* (e.g., personality characteristics of the child's friends), and *friendship quality*. In the sections that follow, these relationship dimensions are examined separately and in turn. Three conclusions emerge: First, having friends is a normatively significant condition during childhood and adolescence. Second, friendships carry both developmental advantages and disadvantages so that a romanticized view of these relationships distorts them and what they may contribute to developmental outcome. Third, the identity of the child's friends and friendship quality may be more closely tied to individual differences than merely whether or not the child has friends.

Having Friends

Measurement issues

Children's friends can be identified in four main ways: (*a*) by asking the children, their mothers, or their teachers to name the child's friends and determining whether these choices are reciprocated; (*b*) by asking children to assess their liking for one another; (*c*) by observing the extent to which children seek and maintain proximity with one another; and (*d*) by measuring reciprocities and coordinations in their social interaction. Concordances among various indicators turn out to be substantial, but method variance is also considerable; the "insiders" (the children themselves) do not always agree with the "outsiders" (teachers) or the observational record (Hartup, 1992; Howes, 1989).

Some variation among measures derives from the fact that social attraction is difficult for outsiders to know about. Method variance also derives from special difficulties connected with self-reports: First, children without friends almost always can name "friends" when asked to do so (Furman, in press). Second, friendship frequently seems to investigators to be a dichotomous condition (friend vs. nonfriend), whereas variation is more continuous (best friend/good friend/occasional friend/not friend). Third, whether these categories form a Guttman scale has not been determined, although researchers sometimes assume that they do (see Doyle, Markiewicz, and Hardy, 1994). Fourth, the status of so-called unilateral or unreciprocated friendship choice is unclear. Sometimes, when children's choices are not reciprocated, social interaction differs from when friendship choices are mutual; in other respects, the social exchange does not. Unilateral friends, for example, use tactics during disagreements with one another that are different from the ones used by mutual friends but similar to those used by nonfriends (e.g., standing firm). Simultaneously, conflict *outcomes* among unilateral friends (e.g., whether inter-action continues) are more similar to those characterizing mutual friends than those characterizing nonfriends (Hartup, Laursen, Stewart, and Eastenson, 1988).

Developmental significance

The developmental significance of having friends (apart from the identity of the child's friends or the quality of these relationships) has been examined in three main ways: (*a*) comparing the social interaction that occurs between friends and between nonfriends, (*b*) comparing children who have friends with those who don't, and (*c*) examining the extent to which having friends moderates behavioral outcomes across certain normative transitions.

Behavior with friends and nonfriends Behaviors differentiating friends from nonfriends have been specified in more than 80 studies (Newcomb and Bag-well, 1995); four are cited here. In the first of these (Newcomb and Brady, 1982), school-aged children were asked to explore a "creativity box" with either a friend, or a classmate who was not a friend. More extensive explora-tion was observed among the children with their friends; conversation was more vigorous and mutually oriented; the emotional exchange was more positive. Most important, when tested individually, the children who explored the box with a friend remembered more about it afterward.

Second, Azmitia and Montgomery (1993) examined problem solving among 11-year-olds (mainly their dialogues) working on "isolation of variables" problems either with friends or with acquaintances (the children were required to deduce which pizza ingredients caused certain characters in a series of stories to get sick and die). Friends spontaneously justified their suggestions more frequently than acquaintances, elaborated on their partners' proposals, engaged in a greater percentage of conflicts during their conversations, and more often checked results. Most important, the children working with friends did better than children working with nonfriends – on the most difficult versions of the task only. Clearly, "a friend in need is a friend indeed." The children's conversations were related to their problem solving through engagement in transactive conflicts. That is, task performance was facilitated to a greater extent between friends than between nonfriends by free airing of the children's differences in a cooperative, task-oriented context.

Third, we recently examined conversations between friends and nonfriends (10-year-olds) in an inner-city magnet school while the children wrote stories collaboratively on a computer (Hartup, Daiute, Zajac, and Sholl, 1995). Stories dealt with the rain forest – subject matter that the children had studied during a 6-week science project. Baseline story writing was measured with the chil-dren writing alone; control subjects *always* wrote alone. Results indicate that friends did not talk more during collaboration than nonfriends but, never-theless, (*a*) engaged in more mutually oriented and less individualistic utter-ances; (*b*) agreed with one another more often (but did not disagree more readily); (c) repeated their own and the other's assertions more often; (d) posed alternatives and provided elaborations more frequently; (e) spent twice as much time as nonfriends talking about writing content, the vocabulary being used, and writing mechanics; and (f) spent less time engaged in "off-task" talk. Principal component analyses confirm that the structure of friends' talk was strongly focused on the task (i.e., the text) and was assertively collaborative – reminiscent of the dialogs used by experts and novices as discovered in other social problem-solving studies (Rogoff, 1990). Our stories themselves show that, overall, the ones collaboratively written by friends were better than the ones written by nonfriends, a difference that seems to rest on better use of Standard English rather than the narrative elements included in the text. Results suggest, overall, that the affordances of "being friends" differ from the affordances of "being acquaintances" in social problem solving (Hartup, in press).

Fourth, we examined conflict and competition among school-aged children playing a board game when they had been taught different rules (Hartup, French, Laursen, Johnston, and Ogawa, 1993). Disagreements occurred more frequently between friends than between nonfriends and lasted longer. Conflict resolution, however, differed by friendship and sex: (a) boys used assertions *without rationales* more frequently than girls – but only when friends were observed; (b) girls, on the other hand, used assertions *with rationales* more frequently than boys but, again, only with friends. Sex differences in conflict talk, widely cited in the literature (see Maccoby, 1990), thus seem to be relationship manifestations rather than manifestations of individual children.

Based on these and the other available data sets, a recent meta-analysis identified significant friend versus nonfriend effects across four broad-band categories (Newcomb and Bagwell, 1995): *positive engagement* (i.e., talk, smiling, and laughter); *conflict management* (i.e., disengagement and negotiation vs. power assertion); *task activity* (i.e., being oriented to the task as opposed to being off task); and *relationship properties* (i.e., equality in the exchange as well as mutuality and affirmation). Behaviorally speaking, friendships clearly are "communal relationships" (Clark and Mills, 1979). Reciprocity constitutes their deep structure.

Existing data suggest that four cognitive and motivational conditions afford these distinctive interactions: (a) friends know one another better than nonfriends and are thus able to communicate with one another more efficiently and effectively (Ladd and Emerson, 1984); (b) friends and nonfriends have different expectations of one another, especially concerning assistance and support (Bigelow, 1977); (c) an affective climate more favorable to exploration and problem solving exists between friends than between nonfriends – namely, a "climate of agreement" (Gottman, 1983); and (d) friends more readily than nonfriends seek ways of resolving disagreements that support continued interaction between them (Hartup and Laursen, 1992).

Unfortunately, the developmental significance of these differences is not known. Only fragmentary information tells us about short-term consequences in problem solving and behavioral regulation. Recalled events (Newcomb and Brady, 1982), deductive reasoning (Azmitia and Montgomery, 1993), conflict rates (Hartup et al., 1988), creative writing (Hartup et al., 1995), and social/moral judgements (Nelson and Aboud, 1985) are better supported by transactions with friends than by transactions with nonfriends. But only a small number of investigations exists in each case – sometimes only one. The bottom line: Process-outcome studies are badly needed to tell us whether friends engage in better scaffolding than nonfriends, or whether it only seems like they do. Once process/outcome connections are established, we can then – and only then – conclude that friendships have normative significance (i.e., that children employ their friends adaptively on a daily basis as cognitive and social resources).

Having friends versus not having friends. Does having friends contribute to developmental differentiation (i.e., contribute to individual differences)? For the answer to this question to be affirmative, children who have friends must differ from those who do not.

Cross-sectional comparisons show that, first, children who have friends are more socially competent and less troubled than children who do not; they are more sociable, cooperative, altruistic, self-confident, and less lonely (Hartup, 1993; Newcomb and Bagwell, in press). Secondly, troubled children (e.g., clinic-referred children) are more likely to be friendless than nonreferred control cases (Rutter and Garmezy, 1983). Friendlessness is not always assessed in the same manner in these studies, but the results are consistent: Not one data set suggests that children with friends are worse off than children who do not have them.

Although friended/friendless comparisons are consistent across data sets, the results are difficult to interpret. First, having friends in these studies usually means having good supportive friends; thus having friends is confounded with friendship quality. Secondly, causal direction is impossible to establish: Friendship experience may contribute to self-esteem, for example, but self-confident children may make friends more readily than less confident children.

Longitudinal studies can be more convincing concerning developmental significance. Unfortunately, few exist. Short-term studies suggest that certain benefits accrue across school transitions: First, attitudes toward school are better among kindergartners (5-year-olds) who have friends at the beginning and who maintain them than among those who don't. Making new friends also predicts gains in school performance over the kindergarten year (Ladd, 1990). Secondly, with data collected from 10-year-olds across a 1-year interval, friendship experience enhanced self-esteem (Bukowski, Hoza, and Newcomb, 1991). Thirdly, psychological disturbances have been reported less frequently when school changes occur in the company of good friends than when they don't (Berndt and Hawkins, 1991; Simmons, Burgeson, and Reef, 1988). Having friends thus seems to contribute specifically to affective outcomes across normative school transitions.

One long-term investigation (Bagwell, Newcomb, and Bukowski, 1994) raises questions, however, about "having friends" as a developmental predictor: Eleven-year-old children were identified as either friended or friendless on two separate occasions; subjects were re-evaluated at 23 years of age. Having friends and sociometric status (i.e., social acceptance) *together* predicted school success, aspirations, trouble with the law, and several other outcomes. Unique contributions to adult adjustment, however, were verified only for sociometric status. And even then, when stability in the childhood adjustment measures was taken into account, neither sociometric status nor friendship predicted adult outcomes.

Comment

Overall, the developmental significance of having friends is far from clear. Social interaction between friends differs from social interaction between non-friends, but this does not tell us much more than that these relationships are unique social entities. Correlational studies are difficult to interpret because the effects of having friends are difficult to disentangle from the effects of friendship quality. Short-term longitudinal studies suggest that having friends supports adaptation during normative transitions, but more substantial evidence is needed concerning these effects. Child differences may interact with friendship experience in relation to developmental outcome rather than being main effects. Having friends, for example, may differentiate mainly among children who are vulnerable in some way prior to the transition. Stress associated with developmental transitions is known to accentuate differences among vulnerable children to a greater extent than among nonvulnerable ones (Caspi and Moffitt, 1991). Similarly, developmental interventions often have greater effects on vulnerable than on nonvulnerable individuals (see Crockenberg, 1981).

THE IDENTITY OF THE CHILD'S FRIENDS

We turn now to the identity of the child's friends. Several questions can be asked: With whom does the child become friends? Can the identity of a child's friends be forecast from what we know about the child? What is the developmental significance of the company a child keeps?

Who are children's friends?

Consider, first, that children make friends on the basis of common interests and common activities. Common ground is a sine qua non in friendship relations throughout childhood and adolescence, suggesting that friends ought to be similar to one another in abilities and outlook. Folklore sometimes suggests that "opposites attract," but this notion has not found general support in the empirical literature. The weight of the evidence suggests that, instead, "Beast knows beast; birds of a feather flock together" (Aristotle, *Rhetoric*, Book 11).

Similarities between friends, however, vary from attribute to attribute, in most cases according to *reputational salience* (i.e., according to the importance of an attribute in determining the child's social reputation). Considerable evidence supports this "reputational salience hypothesis": Behavior ratings obtained more than 60 years ago by Robert Challman (1932) showed that social cooperation (an attribute with considerable reputational salience) was more concordant among friends than nonfriends; intelligence (an attribute without reputational salience among young children) was not. Among boys, physical activity (reputationally salient among males) was more similar among friends than nonfriends. Among girls, attractiveness of personality and social network size (both more reputationally salient among females than among males) were more similar among friends than nonfriends.

More recent data also suggest that behavioral concordances among school-aged children and their friends are greater than among children and nonfriends (Haselager, Hartup, Van Lieshout, and Riksen-Walraven, 1995). Peer ratings were obtained in a large number of fifth-grade classrooms centering on three constructs: prosocial behavior, antisocial behavior, and social withdrawal (shyness). First, friends were more similar to one another than nonfriends within each construct cluster (i.e., mean difference scores were significantly smaller). Second, correlations between friends were greater for antisocial behavior (i.e., fighting, disruption, and bullying) than for prosocial behavior (i.e., cooperation, offering help to others) or social withdrawal (i.e., shyness, dependency, and being victimized). These differences may reflect differences among these three attributes in reputational salience: fighting, for example, is more consistently related to reputation than either cooperation or shyness (Coie, Dodge, and Kupersmidt, 1990). Our results also show important sex differences: (a) friends were more similar to one another among girls than among boys in both prosocial and antisocial behavior (see also Cairns and Cairns, 1994), and (b) friends were more similar among boys than among girls in shyness. These gender variations are consistent with the reputational salience hypothesis, too: Being kind to others and being mean to them have greater implications for girls' social reputations than boys', whereas shyness/withdrawal has more to do with boys' reputations than girls' (Stevenson-Hinde and Hinde, 1986).

Concordance data from other studies are consistent with the reputational salience notion: Among adolescents, friends are most similar to one another in two general areas: (a) school-related attitudes, aspirations, and achievement (Epstein, 1983; Kandel, 1978b) and (b) normative activities such as smoking, drinking, drug use, antisocial behavior, and dating (Dishion, Andrews, and Crosby, 1995; Epstein, 1983; Kandel, 1978b; Tolson and Urberg, 1993). Sexual activity among adolescents is also consistent with the reputational salience hypothesis. Among girls (both African-American and white) in the United States, friends have been found to be similar in sexual behavior and attitudes, even when age and antisocial attitudes are taken into account. Among boys, however, sexual activity (especially engaging in sexual intercourse) was not concordant (Billy, Rodgers, and Udry, 1984). The authors argue that sexual activity is more closely related to social reputation among adolescent girls than it is among boys, thus accounting for the gender differences in the results.

Still other investigators, employing the social network as a unit of analysis, have discovered that members of friendship networks are concordant on such salient dimensions as sports, academic activities, and drug use (Brown, 1989). Antisocial behavior also distinguishes social networks from one another beginning in middle childhood (Cairns, Cairns, Neckerman, Gest, and Garieppy, 1988).

Friendship concordances: sources and developmental implications

Similarities between friends are one thing, but where do they come from and where do they lead? Developmental implications cannot be specified without understanding that these similarities derive from three sources: (a) *sociodemographic conditions* that bring children into proximity with one another; (b) *social selection* through which children construct relationships with children who are similar to themselves rather than different; and (c) *mutual socialization* through which children become similar to their friends by interacting with them.

Sociodemographic conditions Demographic conditions determine the neighborhoods in which children live, the schools in which they enroll, and the classes they attend. Concordances among children and their friends in socioeconomic status, ethnicity, and chronological age thus derive in considerable measure from social forces that constrain the "peer pool" and the child's access to it. One should not underestimate, however, the extent to which some of these concordances derive from the children's own choices. Among children attending schools that are mixed-age, mixed-race, and mixed socioeconomically, friends are still more similar to one another in these attributes than nonfriends are (Goldman, 1981; McCandless and Hoyt, 1961).

Selection Some similarities among friends derive from the well-known tendency among human beings (not alone among the various species) for choosing close associates who resemble themselves. Recent studies confirm that the similarity-attraction hypothesis applies to children: Among elementary school children who began an experimental session as strangers, differential attraction was evident in some groups (40%). Within them, more social contact occurred between preferred than between nonpreferred partners, and correlations were higher between preferred than nonpreferred partners in sociability and the cognitive maturity of their play (Rubin, Lynch, Coplan, Rose-Krasnor, and Booth, 1994).

But friendship selection is embedded in assortative processes occurring in larger social networks. Dishion and his colleagues (Dishion, Patterson, and Griesler, 1994) believe that these network concordances emerge through a process called "shopping" in which children and adolescents construct relationships that maximize interpersonal payoffs. Children are not believed to choose friends who are similar to themselves on a rational basis so much as on an experiential one. Accordingly, relationships become established when they "feel right." Similar individuals cleave to one another more readily than dissimilar individuals because they are more likely to find common ground in both their activities and their conversations. Antisocial children are thus most likely to make friends with other antisocial children and, in so doing, their common characteristics merge to create a "dyadic antisocial trait." Similarly, soccer players or musicians make friends, merge themselves dyadically, and set the stage for becoming even more similar to one another.

Selection thus acts simultaneously to determine the identity of the child's friends through two interlocking processes: (a) similarity and attraction occurring within dyads, and (b) assortative network formation occurring within groups. These processes undoubtedly combine differently from child to child in affecting developmental outcome: Cooperative, friendly, nonaggressive children can choose friends resembling themselves from a wide array of choices; antisocial children can also choose their friends on the basis of similarity and attraction – but frequently from a more restricted range of social alternatives.

Mutual socialization   What behavioral outcomes stem from mutual socialization? The weight of the evidence suggests, first, that children and their friends who ascribe to conventional norms move further over time in the direction of normative behavior (Ball, 1981; Epstein, 1983; Kandel and Andrews, 1986). But does antisocial behavior increase over time among children in antisocial networks? Does troublesome behavior escalate among children – especially into criminal activity – through membership in these networks? Answers to these questions have been surprisingly difficult to provide, especially since children perceive their friends as exerting more pressure toward desirable than toward undesirable conduct (Brown, Clasen, and Eicher, 1986). Nevertheless, increases in undesirable behavior through antisocial friends among children who are themselves at risk for antisocial behavior is now relatively well documented (Ball, 1981; Berndt and Keefe, 1992; Dishion, 1990; Dishion et al., 1994). Conversely, "desisting" is forecast as strongly by a turning away from antisocial friends as by any other variable (Mulvey and Aber, 1988).

What occurs on a day-to-day basis between aggressive children and their friends? Jocks and their friends? "Brains" and their friends? One guesses that children model normative behaviors *for* their friends and simultaneously receive reinforcement *from* them. Antisocial children, for example, are known to engage in large amounts of talk with their friends – talk that is deviant even when the children are being videotaped in the laboratory (Dishion et al., 1994, 1995). Ordinary children talk a lot with their friends, too, but the content is not generally as deviant (Newcomb and Bagwell, 1995). Antisocial children use coercion with one another (Dishion et al., 1995); ordinary children, on the other hand, are freewheeling with their criticisms and persuasion but are less likely to be coercive (Berndt and Keefe, 1992; Hartup et al., 1993). Finally, one guesses that friends support one another in seeking environments that support their commonly held worldviews, although not much is known about this.

Other results show that selection *combines* with socialization to effect similarity between friends. Kandel (1978a) studied changes over the course of a year in drug use, educational aspirations, and delinquency in early adolescence, discovering that similarity stemmed from both sources in approximately equal amounts. Relative effects, however, vary according to the norms and the children involved (see Hartup, 1993).

Comment

Children and their friends are similar to one another, especially in attributes with reputational salience. One must acknowledge that effect sizes are modest and that friends are not carbon copies of one another. One must also acknowledge that the reputational salience hypothesis has never been subjected to direct test and it needs to be. Nevertheless, the identity of the child's friends is a significant consideration in predicting developmental outcome. Friends may be generally intimate, caring, and supportive, thus fostering good developmental prognosis. At the same time, the activities in which they support one another (the relationship *content*) may be extremely deviant, suggesting an altogether different prognosis.

FRIENDSHIP QUALITY

Conceptual and measurement issues

Qualitative assessment of child and adolescent friendships currently involves two main strategies: (*a*) *dimensional analysis* through which one determines whether certain elements are present or absent in the social interaction between friends (e.g., companionship, intimacy, conflict, or power asymmetries), and (*b*) *typological* or *categorical analysis*, through which one identifies patterns in social interaction believed to be critical to social development and adaptation (Furman, in press).

Dimensional assessment Most current dimensional assessments are based on "provisions" or "features" that children mention when talking about these relationships (Berndt and Perry, 1986; Bukowski, Hoza, and Boivin, 1994; Furman and Adler, 1982; Furman and Buhrmester, 1985; Parker and Asher, 1993); most instruments tap five or six domains. Domain scores, however, are correlated with one another (Berndt and Perry, 1986; Parker and Asher, 1993), and most factor analyses yield two-factor solutions. Both Berndt (in press) and Furman (in press) argue that "positive" and "negative" dimensions adequately describe most dimensional assessments, although some data sets suggest that more elaborate solutions are warranted (e.g., Ladd, Kochenderfer, and Coleman, in press).

Typological assessment Typological assessment is evolving slowly since the functional significance of friendships remains uncertain. Can one, for example, regard friendships as attachments? Probably not. No one has demonstrated that "the secure base phenomenon," so common among children and their caregivers, constitutes the functional core of children's friendships. Friends have been shown to be secure bases in one or two instances (Ipsa, 1981;

Schwartz, 1972), but one is not overwhelmed with the evidence that children and their friends are bound to one another as attachment objects. Children describe their relationships with friends differently from their relationships with their caregivers – as *more* companionable, intimate, and egalitarian and, simultaneously, as *less* affectionate and reliable (Furman and Buhrmester, 1985). For these reasons, some writers describe friendships as affiliative relationships rather than attachments (Weiss, 1986). The challenge, then, is to describe what good-quality affiliative relationships are.

One new classification system has been devised on the basis of family systems theory (Shulman, 1993). Well-functioning friendships are considered to be balanced between closeness and intimacy, on the one hand, and individuality, on the other. The family systems model suggests three friendship types: *interdependent* ones, with cooperation and autonomy balanced; *disengaged* ones, in which friends are disconnected in spite of their efforts to maintain proximity with one another; and *consensus-sensitive* or *enmeshed* relationships, in which agreement and cohesion are maximized. Empirical data are based largely on children's interactions in a cooperative task adapted from family systems research (Reiss, 1981) and document the existence of interdependent and disengaged relationships – a promising beginning. Once again, however, caution should be exercised: friendship networks may not revolve around the same equilibrative axes as families do.

Developmental Significance

Cross-sectional studies Among the various qualitative dimensions, *support* (positivity) and *contention* (negativity) have been examined most extensively in relation to child outcomes. Support is positively correlated with school involvement and achievement (Berndt and Hawkins, 1991; Cauce, 1986) and negatively correlated with school-based problems (Kurdek and Sinclair, 1988); positively correlated with popularity and good social reputations (Cauce, 1986); positively correlated with self-esteem (Mannarino, 1978; McGuire and Weisz, 1982; Perry, 1987) and psychosocial adjustment (Buhrmester, 1990) as well as negatively correlated with identity problems (Papini, Farmer, Clark, Micke, and Barnett, 1990) and depression – especially among girls (Compas, Slavin, Wagner, and Cannatta, 1986). Results are thus consistent but, once again, impossible to interpret. We cannot tell whether supportive relationships contribute to the competence of the individual child or vice versa.

Longitudinal studies Longitudinal studies dealing with friendship quality (positive vs. negative) emphasize school attitudes, involvement, and achievement. Studying children across the transition from elementary to junior high school, Berndt (1989) measured the size of the friendship network, friendship stability, and self-reported friendship quality (positivity) as well as popularity, attitudes toward school, and achievement. First, network size was negatively related to friendship support as reported by the children, suggesting that children recognize what researchers have been slow to learn, namely, that friendships are not all alike. Secondly, several nonsignificant results are illuminating: Neither number of friends nor friendship stability contributed to changes in school adjustment – either across the school transition or across the first year in the new school. School adjustment was relatively stable across the transition and was related to friendship stability cross-sectionally but not with earlier adjustment factored out. Thirdly, the self-rated supportiveness of the child's friends, assessed shortly after entrance to the new school, predicted increasing popularity and increasingly positive attitudes toward classmates over the next year, suggesting that positive qualities in one's friendship relations support a widening social world in new school environments.

Other investigations focus on friendship qualities as predictors of school adaptation within the school year. Among 5-year-olds enrolled in kindergarten (Ladd et al., in press), for example, those having friendships characterized by "aid" and "validation" improved in school attitudes over the year with initial attitudes toward school factored out. Perceived conflict in friendships, on the other hand, predicted increasing forms of school maladjustment, especially among boys, including school loneliness and avoidance as well as school liking and engagement.

One other investigation (Berndt and Keefe, 1992) focused on both positive and negative friendship qualities and their correlations across time with school adjustment and self-esteem among adolescents (Berndt and Keefe, 1992). Students with supportive, intimate friendships became increasingly involved with school, while those who considered their friendships to be conflict-ridden and rivalrous became increasingly disruptive and troublesome. Friendship quality was not correlated with changes in self-esteem, possibly because self-esteem was relatively stable from the beginning to the end of the year. Additional analyses (Berndt, in press) suggest that developmental prediction is better for the negative dimensions in these relationships than the positive ones.

Other investigators have examined the interactions between stress and social support as related to behavioral outcome. With elementary school children, increases in peer support over several years predict both increasingly better adaptation and better grade point averages (Dubow, Tisak, Causey, Hryshko, and Reid, 1991). Other results, however, suggest that support from school personnel was associated with decreases in distress across a 2-year period but not support from friends (controlling for initial adjustment). Regression models showed that, actually, school grades predicted changes in friends' support rather than the reverse (DuBois, Felner, Brand, Adan, and Evans, 1992). Among adolescents, however, results are more complex: Windle (1992) reported that, among girls, friend support is positively correlated with alcohol use but negatively correlated with depression (with initial adjustment levels factored out). Among boys, friendship support is associated with outcome depending on stress levels: when stress is high, friend support encourages both alcohol use and depression; when stress is low or moderate, both alcohol use and depression are associated with having *nonsupportive* friends.

The dissonances encountered in these results would be reduced considerably were the identity of the children's friends to be known. Children and adolescents with behavior difficulties frequently have friends who themselves are troublesome (Dishion et al., 1995). These friends may provide one another with emotional support, but the interactions that occur between them may not be the same as those occurring between nontroubled children and their friends. Knowing who the child's friends are might account for the empirical anomalies.

Other difficulties in accounting for these results derive from the fact that the referents used in measuring social support in these studies (except in Berndt's work) consisted of friendship networks (the child's "friends") rather than a "best friend." And still other complications arise from the use of one child's assessments of relationship qualities (the subject's) when the evidence suggests that discrepancies between partners may correlate more strongly with adjustment difficulties than the perceptions of either partner alone (East, 1991). Nevertheless, these studies provide tantalizing tidbits suggesting that friendship quality bears a causal relation to developmental outcome.

Comment

What kinds of research are needed to better understand the developmental implications of friendship quality? One can argue that we are not urgently in need of cross-time studies narrowly focused on friendships and their vicissitudes. Rather, we need comprehensive studies in which interaction effects rather than main effects are emphasized and that encompass a wide range of variables as they cycle through time: (a) measures of the child, including temperament and other relevant early characteristics; (b) measures of early relationships, especially their affective and cognitive qualities; (c) measures of early success in encounters with relevant institutions, especially the schools; (d) status and reputation among other children (sociometric status); and, (e) friendship measures that simultaneously include whether a child has friends, who the child's friends are, and what these relationships are like.

Coming close to this model are recent studies conducted by the Oregon Social Learning Center (e.g., Dishion et al., 1994; Patterson, Reid, and Dishion, 1992). Child characteristics and family relations in early childhood have not been examined extensively by these investigators, but their work establishes linkages between coerciveness and monitoring within parent–child and sibling relationships, on the one hand, and troublesomeness and antisocial behavior among school-aged boys, on the other. These studies also establish that poor parental discipline and monitoring predict peer rejection and academic failures, and that these conditions, in turn, predict increasing involvement with antisocial friends. Among children with these early histories, the immediate connection to serious conduct difficulties in adolescence now seems to be friendship with another deviant child. Exactly these conditions existed in the social history of that Minnesota teenager who, together with his best friend, killed his mother early in 1995.

Conclusion

Friendships in childhood and adolescence would seem to be developmentally significant – both normatively and differentially. When children have friends, they use them as cognitive and social resources on an everyday basis. Normative transitions and the stress carried with them seem to be better negotiated when children have friends than when they don't, especially when children are at risk. Differential significance, however, seems to derive mainly from the identity of the child's friends and the quality of the relationships between them. Supportive relationships between socially skilled individuals appear to be developmental advantages, whereas coercive and conflict-ridden relationships are developmental disadvantages, especially among antisocial children.

Nevertheless, friendship and its developmental significance may vary from child to child. New studies show that child characteristics interact with early relationships and environmental conditions, cycling in turn through relations with other children to determine behavioral outcome (Hartup and Van Lieshout, 1995). The work cited in this essay strongly suggests that friendship assessments deserve greater attention in studying these developmental pathways than they are currently given. These assessments, however, need to be comprehensive. Along with knowing whether or not children have friends, we must know who their friends are and the quality of their relationships with them.

Acknowledgments

Presidential address to the biennial meetings of the Society for Research in Child Development, April 1, 1995, Indianapolis, IN. The author is grateful to W. Andrew Collins. Rosemary K. Hartup, Gary W. Ladd, Brett Laursen, and Andrew F. Newcomb for their comments on this manuscript.

References

Ainsworth, M. D. S., Blehar, M. C., Waters, E., and Wall, S. (1978). *Patterns of Attachment: A Psychological Study of the Strange Situation*. Hillsdale, NJ: Erlbaum.

Azmitia, M., and Montgomery, R. (1993). Friendship, transactive dialogues, and the development of scientific reasoning. *Social Development*, **2**, 202–21.

Bagwell, C., Newcomb, A. F., and Bukowski, W. M. (1994). *Early adolescent friendship as a predictor of adult adjustment: A twelve-year follow-up investigation*. Unpublished manuscript, University of Richmond.

Ball, S. J. (1981). *Beachside Comprehensive*. Cambridge: Cambridge University Press.

Berndt, T. J. (1989). Obtaining support from friends during childhood and adolescence. In D. Belle (ed.), *Children's Social Networks and Social Supports* (pp. 308–31), New York: Wiley.

Berndt, T. J. (in press). Exploring the effects of friendship quality on social development. In W. M. Bukowski, A. F. Newcomb, and W. W. Hartup (eds), *The Company They Keep: Friendships in Childhood and Adolescence*, Cambridge: Cambridge University Press.

Berndt, T. J., and Hawkins, J. A. (1991). *Effects of friendship on adolescents' adjustment to junior high school.* Unpublished manuscript, Purdue University.

Berndt, T. J., and Keefe, K. (1992). Friends' influence on adolescents' perceptions of themselves in school. In D. H. Schunk and J. L. Meece (eds), *Students' Perceptions in the Classroom* (pp. 51–73), Hillsdale, NJ: Erlbaum.

Berndt, T. J., and Perry, T. B. (1986). Children's perceptions of friendship as supportive relationships. *Developmental Psychology*, **22**, 640–8.

Bigelow, B. J. (1977). Children's friendship expectations: A cognitive developmental study. *Child Development*, **48**, 246–53.

Billy, J. O. G., Rodgers, J. L., and Udry, J. R. (1984). Adolescent sexual behavior and friendship choice. *Social Forces*, **62**, 653–78.

Brown, B. B. (1989). The role of peer groups in adolescents' adjustment to secondary school. In T. J. Berndt and G. W. Ladd (eds), *Peer Relationships in Child Development* (pp. 188–215), New York: Wiley.

Brown, B. B., Clasen, D. R., and Eicher, S. A. (1986). Perceptions of peer pressure, peer conformity dispositions, and self-reported behavior among adolescents. *Developmental Psychology*, **22**, 521–30.

Buhrmester, D. (1990). Intimacy of friendship, interpersonal competence, and adjustment during preadolescence and adolescence. *Child Development*, **61**, 1101–11.

Bukowski, W. M., Hoza, B., and Boivin, M. (1994). Measuring friendship quality during pre- and early adolescence: The development and psychometric properties of the Friendship Qualities Scale. *Journal of Personal and Social Relationships*, **11**, 471–84.

Bukowski, W. M., Hoza, B., and Newcomb, A. F. (1991). *Friendship, popularity, and the "self" during early adolescence.* Unpublished manuscript, Concordia University (Montreal).

Cairns, R. B., and Cairns, B. D. (1994). *Lifelines and Risks.* Cambridge: Cambridge University Press.

Cairns, R. B., Cairns, B. D., Neckerman, H. J., Gest, S., and Garieppy, J.-L. (1988). Peer networks and aggressive behavior: Peer support or peer rejection? *Developmental Psychology*, **24**, 815–23.

Caspi, A., and Moffitt, T. E. (1991). Individual differences are accentuated during periods of social change: The sample case of girls at puberty. *Journal of Personality and Social Psychology*, **61**, 157–68.

Cauce, A. M. (1986). Social networks and social competence: Exploring the effects of early adolescent friendships. *American Journal of Community Psychology*, **14**, 607–28.

Challman, R. C. (1932). Factors influencing friendships among preschool children. *Child Development*, **3**, 146–58.

Clark, M. S., and Mills, J. (1979). Interpersonal attraction in exchange and communal relationships. *Journal of Personality and Social Psychology*, **37**, 12–24.

Coie, J. D., Dodge, K. A., and Kupersmidt, J. B. (1990). Peer group behavior and social status. In S. R. Asher and J. D. Coie (eds), *Peer Rejection in Childhood* (pp. 17–59), Cambridge: Cambridge University Press.

Compas, B. E., Slavin, L. A., Wagner, B. A., and Cannatta, K. (1986). Relationship of life events and social support with psychological dysfunction among adolescents. *Journal of Youth and Adolescence*, **15**, 205–21.

Crockenberg, S. B. (1981). Infant irritability, mother responsiveness, and social support influences on the security of mother–infant attachment. *Child Development*, **52**, 857–65.

Dishion, T. J. (1990). The peer context of troublesome child and adolescent behavior. In P. Leone (ed.), *Understanding Troubled and Troublesome Youth*, Newbury Park, CA: Sage.

Dishion, T. J., Andrews, D. W., and Crosby, L. (1995). Anti-social boys and their friends in early adolescence: Relationship characteristics, quality, and interactional process. *Child Development*, **66**, 139–51.

Dishion, T. J., Patterson, G. R., and Griesler, P. C. (1994). Peer adaptations in the development of antisocial behavior: A confluence model. In L. R. Huesmann (ed.), *Current Perspectives on Aggressive Behavior* (pp. 61–95), New York: Plenum.

Doyle, A. B., Markiewicz, D., and Hardy, C. (1994). Mothers' and children's friendships: Intergenerational associations. *Journal of Social and Personal Relationships*, **11**, 363–77.

DuBois, D. L., Felner, R. D., Brand, S., Adan, A. M., and Evans, E. G. (1992). A prospective study of life stress, social support, and adaptation in early adolescence. *Child Development*, **63**, 542–57.

Dubow, E. F., Tisak, J., Causey, D., Hryshko, A., and Reid, G. (1991). A two-year longitudinal study of stressful life events, social support, and social problem-solving skills: Contributions to children's behavioral and academic adjustment. *Child Development*, **62**, 583–99.

East, P. L. (1991). The parent–child relationships of withdrawn, aggressive, and sociable children: Child and parent perspectives. *Merrill-Palmer Quarterly*, **37**, 425–44.

Epstein, J. L. (1983). Examining theories of adolescent friendship. In J. L. Epstein and N. L. Karweit (eds), *Friends in School* (pp. 39–61) San Diego: Academic Press.

Furman, W. (in press). The measurement of friendship perceptions: Conceptual and methodological issues. In W. M. Bukowski, A. F. Newcomb, and W. W. Hartup (eds), *The Company They Keep: Friendships in Childhood and Adolescence*, Cambridge: Cambridge University Press.

Furman, W., and Adler, T. (1982). *The Friendship Questionnaire*. Unpublished manuscript, University of Denver.

Furman, W., and Buhrmester, D. (1985). Children's perceptions of the personal relationships in their social networks. *Developmental Psychology*, **21**, 1016–22.

Goldman, J. A. (1981). The social interaction of preschool children in same-age versus mixed-age groupings. *Child Development*, **52**, 644–50.

Gottman, J. M. (1983). How children become friends. *Monographs of the Society for Research in Child Development*, **48** (3, Serial no. 201).

Hartup, W. W. (1992). Friendships and their developmental significance. In H. McGurk (ed.), *Childhood Social Development* (pp. 175–205), Hove, UK: Erlbaum.

Hartup, W. W. (1993). Adolescents and their friends. In B. Laursen (ed.), *Close Friendships in Adolescence* (pp. 3–22), San Francisco: Jossey-Bass.

Hartup, W. W. (in press). Cooperation, close relationships, and cognitive development. In W. M. Bukowski, A. F. Newcomb, and W. W. Hartup (eds), *The Company They Keep: Friendships in Childhood and Adolescence*, Cambridge: Cambridge University Press.

Hartup, W. W., Daiute, C., Zajac, R., and Sholl, W. (1995). *Collaboration in creative writing by friends and nonfriends*. Unpublished manuscript, University of Minnesota.

Hartup, W. W., French, D. C., Laursen, B., Johnston, K. M., and Ogawa, J. (1993). Conflict and friendship relations in middle childhood: Behavior in a closed-field situation. *Child Development*, **64**, 445–54.

Hartup, W. W., and Laursen, B. (1992). Conflict and context in peer relations. In C. H. Hart (ed.), *Children on Playgrounds: Research Perspectives and Applications* (pp. 44–84), Albany: State University of New York Press.

Hartup, W. W., Laursen, B., Stewart, M. I., and Eastenson, A. (1988). Conflict and the friendship relations of young children. *Child Development*, **59**, 1590–1600.

Hartup, W. W., and Van Lieshout, C. F. M. (1995). Personality development in social context. In J. T. Spence (ed.), *Annual Review of Psychology*, **46**, 655–87.

Haselager, G. J. T., Hartup, W. W., Van Lieshout, C. F. M., and Riksen-Walraven, M. (1995). *Friendship similarity in middle childhood as a function of sex and sociometric status.* Unpublished manuscript, University of Nijmegen.

Howes, C. (1989). Peer interaction of young children. *Monographs of the Society for Research in Child Development*, **53** (Serial no. 217).

Ipsa, J. (1981). Peer support among Soviet day care toddlers. *International Journal of Behavioral Development*, **4**, 255–69.

Kandel, D. B. (1978a). Homophily, selection, and socialization in adolescent friendships. *American Journal of Sociology*, **84**, 427–36.

Kandel, D. B. (1978b). Similarity in real-life adolescent pairs. *Journal of Personality and Social Psychology*, **36**, 306–12.

Kandel, D. B., and Andrews, K. (1986). Processes of adolescent socialization by parents and peers. *International Journal of the Addictions*, **22**, 319–42.

Kurdek, L. A., and Sinclair, R. J. (1988). Adjustment of young adolescents in two-parent nuclear, stepfather, and mother-custody families. *Journal of Consulting and Clinical Psychology*, **56**, 91–6.

Ladd, G. W. (1990). Having friends, keeping friends, making friends, and being liked by peers in the classroom: Predictors of children's early school adjustment? *Child Development*, **61**, 1081–1100.

Ladd, G. W., and Emerson, E. S. (1984). Shared knowledge in children's friendships. *Developmental Psychology*, **20**, 932–40.

Ladd, G. W., Kochenderfer, B. J., and Coleman, C. C. (in press). Friendship quality as a predictor of young children's early school adjustment. *Child Development*.

Maccoby, E. E. (1990). Gender and relationships: A developmental account. *American Psychologist*, **45**, 513–20.

Mannarino, A. P. (1978). Friendship patterns and self-concept development in preadolescent males. *Journal of Genetic Psychology*, **133**, 105–10.

McCandless, B. R., and Hoyt, J. M. (1961). Sex, ethnicity and play preferences of preschool children. *Journal of Abnormal and Social Psychology*, **62**, 683–5.

McGuire, K. D., and Weisz, J. R. (1982). Social cognition and behavior correlates of preadolescent chumship. *Child Development*, **53**, 1478–84.

Mulvey, E. P., and Aber, M. S. (1988). Growing out of delinquency: Development and desistance. In R. Jenkins and W. Brown (eds), *The Abandonment of Delinquent Behavior: Promoting the Turn-around*, New York: Praeger.

Nelson, J., and Aboud, F. E. (1985). The resolution of social conflict between friends. *Child Development*, **56**, 1009–17.

Newcomb, A. F., and Bagwell, C. (1995). Children's friendship relations: A meta-analytic review. *Psychological Bulletin*, **117**, 306–47.

Newcomb, A. F., and Bagwell, C. (in press). The developmental significance of children's friendship relations. In W. M. Bukowski, A. F. Newcomb, and W. W. Hartup (eds), *The Company They Keep: Friendship in Childhood and Adolescence*, Cambridge: Cambridge University Press.

Newcomb, A. F., and Brady, J. E. (1982). Mutuality in boys' friendship relations. *Child Development*, **53**, 392–5.

Papini, D. R., Farmer, F. F., Clark, S. M., Micke, J. C., and Barnett, J. K. (1990). Early adolescent age and gender differences in patterns of emotional self-disclosure to parents and friends. *Adolescence*, **25**, 959–76.

Parker, J. G., and Asher, S. R. (1987). Peer relations and later personal adjustment: Are low-accepted children at risk? *Psychological Bulletin*, **102**, 357–89.

Parker, J. G., and Asher, S. R. (1993). Friendship and friendship quality in middle childhood: Links with peer group acceptance and feelings of loneliness and social dissatisfaction. *Developmental Psychology*, **29**, 611–21.

Patterson, G. R., Reid, J. B., and Dishion, T. J. (1992). *Antisocial Boys*. Eugene, OR: Castalia.

Perry, T. B. (1987). *The relation of adolescent self-perceptions to their social relationships*. Unpublished doctoral dissertation, University of Oklahoma.

Reiss, D. (1981). *The Family's Construction of Reality*. Cambridge, MA: Harvard University Press.

Rogoff, B. (1990). *Apprenticeship in Thinking*. New York: Oxford University Press.

Rubin, K. H., Lynch, D., Coplan, R., Rose-Krasnor, L., and Booth, C. L. (1994). "Birds of a feather...": Behavioral concordances and preferential personal attraction in children. *Child Development*, **65**, 1778–85.

Rutter, M., and Garmezy, N. (1983). Developmental psychopathology. In E. M. Hetherington (ed.), P. H. Mussen (series ed.), *Handbook of Child Psychology: Vol. 4. Socialization, Personality, and Social Development* (pp. 775–911), New York: Wiley.

Schwartz, J. C. (1972). Effects of peer familiarity on the behavior of preschoolers in a novel situation. *Journal of Personality and Social Psychology*, **24**, 276–84.

Shulman, S. (1993). Close friendships in early and middle adolescence: Typology and friendship reasoning. In B. Laursen (ed.), *Close Friendships in Adolescence* (pp. 55–72), San Francisco: Jossey-Bass.

Simmons, R. G., Burgeson, R., and Reef, M. J. (1988). Cumulative change at entry to adolescence. In M. Gunnar and W. A. Collins (eds), *Minnesota symposia on child psychology* (Vol. **21**, pp. 123–50), Hillsdale, NJ: Erlbaum.

Stevenson-Hinde, J., and Hinde, R. A. (1986). Changes in associations between characteristics and interaction. In R. Plomin and J. Dunn (eds), *The Study of Temperament: Changes, Continuities and Challenges* (pp. 115–29), Hillsdale, NJ: Erlbaum.

Sullivan, H. S. (1953). *The Interpersonal Theory of Psychiatry*. New York: Norton.

Tolson, J. M., and Urberg, K. A. (1993). Similarity between adolescent best friends. *Journal of Adolescent Research*, **8**, 274–88.

Weiss, R. S. (1986). Continuities and transformations in social relationships from childhood to adulthood. In W. W. Hartup and Z. Rubin (eds), *Relationships and Development* (pp. 95–110), Hillsdale, NJ: Erlbaum.

Windle, M. (1992). A longitudinal study of stress buffering for adolescent problem behaviors. *Developmental Psychology*, **28**, 522–30.

Part VII

CHILDREN AT RISK

34

HELEN KELLER:
AN EXTRAORDINARY LIFE

Alan Slater

Sensory impairments are commonly a cause of developmental problems. Blind children often experience difficulties in understanding the spatial world, and deaf children are often slow in acquiring language. However, such disabilities do not *necessarily* lead to handicap (see article 21, by Petitto and Marentette, for an account of language learning through signing in deaf children). Helen Keller was the first deaf-blind person to achieve international acclaim and to make a huge success of her life. She was a normally hearing and seeing child until a fever deprived her of these senses when she was around 19 months. The first 19 months were almost certainly important to her subsequent development (see article 14 for the relevance of infant memories for later development), but she was later to learn language using the sense of touch. Helen became multilingual, and even learned to speak. One of her biggest successes was in demonstrating, by example, that extreme sensory disability can be overcome. This brief account of her life concentrates on her early education, with an emphasis on language and communication.

Without her teacher, Anne Sullivan, who was with her from childhood until her (Anne's) death in 1936, Helen Keller would almost certainly have remained trapped in an isolated, confused, and frustrating world. Anne Sullivan was extremely gifted, and many books, films, plays, articles and other accounts have been given of her life with Helen. The stage version of the play *The Miracle Worker* was a smash hit. A troubled Anne Bancroft, who played Anne, complained that the reaction of the audience distressed her. In the first act the applause was as great for her as it was for Patty Duke, who played Helen (Patty Duke portrayed Helen both on stage and on screen, and she won an Oscar for this role in 1963), but thereafter applause for Patty Duke remained considerable while for Miss Bancroft it subsided to a polite trickle. This mirrored real life: people were ecstatic about Helen, and often indifferent to Teacher – there are many gifted, intelligent and articulate people in the world, but very few who are also blind and deaf!

The two greatest characters in the 19th century are Napoleon and Helen Keller. Napoleon tried to conquer the world by physical force and failed. Helen tried to conquer the world by power of mind – and succeeded.

(Mark Twain)

Helen Adams Keller was born on 27 June 1880 in Tuscumbia, a little town in northern Alabama. Helen was a perfectly normal child and developed normally, even precociously, through infancy. Then, at 19 months, in February 1882, disaster struck and she was afflicted by a fever that was so intense that it was feared that she might die. No-one seemed quite sure what the fever was – it was given the medical term of 'acute congestion', which could mean anything. However, it abated 'as mysteriously and suddenly as it had begun', but it left Helen both blind and deaf.

Helen's parents, of course, grieved and despaired as to their daughter's development, and a few years later they consulted the famous inventor Alexander Graham Bell, in Washington, who devoted considerable time to the education of the deaf. He advised them to contact the head of the Perkins Institute for the blind in Boston, since this Institute had had considerable success in teaching both the blind and the blind-deaf. Helen's meeting with Dr Bell began a lifetime's friendship between the two, and she later dedicated her autobiography *The Story of My Life* (1902) to him. In late 1886 there came a letter from the Perkins Institute to say that a teacher had been found for Helen, and her teacher arrived in Tuscumbia on 3 March 1887, three months before her seventh birthday, and the remarkable story of her life had begun.

Teacher and Teaching

Helen's teacher was Anne Sullivan (she later married the theatre critic John Macy, and is often referred to as Anne Sullivan Macy). Anne was born at Springfield, Massachusetts. Very early in life she became almost totally blind, and she entered the Perkins Institution for the blind on 7 October 1880, when she was 14 years old. Later her sight was partially restored and she became the private instructor of a blind, deaf and dumb girl, whom she was soon to describe as 'the sweetest and loveliest little girl in the world'. Their devotion to each other was total. Only three times in Anne's life (she died on 20 October 1936) would they be separated for more than a few days, and Anne's job as Teacher was 24 hours a day. The author Samuel Clemens (Mark Twain) wrote: 'It took the two of you to make a complete and perfect whole.' Helen wrote of 'teacher...who has made my darkness beautiful and rent asunder the iron

PLATE 34.1   Portrait of Helen Keller (*sitting*) with Anne Sullivan and Alexander Graham Bell. They are simultaneously using three modes of communication: spoken language between Anne and Dr Bell, manual alphabet between Helen and Dr Bell, and lip reading between Helen and Anne (photograph *c.* 1894, reprinted courtesy of the American Foundation for the Blind, Helen Keller Archives)

gates of silence', and after Teacher's death she wrote in her journal – 'Every hour I long for the thousand bright signals from her vital beautiful hand. That was life!'

THE EARLY YEARS

The period of infancy is vital to children's development. Although we cannot easily remember any of the events of the first two years, they are the essential foundation for subsequent development: 'Those impressions for a time lost their names but the percepts were not lost.' By the time she was 19 months old Helen had already learned to walk, to acquire language, had learned feeding and toilet habits, to distinguish herself from others, to recognize herself, to acquire a sense of self, and to become attached to and love her parents, to develop a sense of security. It has been known for over 100 years that it is easier to develop speech in a child who has had speech in late infancy than to create speech in a deaf-born child.

The effects of the first 19 months on Helen's subsequent development are not easy to quantify, but one example will perhaps indicate their importance. Prior to her illness one of the first words Helen learned was the word for water, which she pronounced as 'wha-wha', and this was the first word she really understood after her recovery. Within days of Teacher's arrival she learned several words. These words were spelled into her hand using the manual alphabet (see below), but, as she says, in *The Story of My Life*, 'I did not know that I was spelling a word or even that words existed; I was simply making my fingers go in monkey-like imitation.' On 5 April 1887, came the breakthrough. Anne took Helen to the pump-house, close to the house, made her hold her mug under the spout, and as the water flowed she spelled W-A-T-E-R into her hand. This was the moment that Helen realized that 'everything had a name': 'that living word awakened my soul, gave it light, hope, joy, set it free! There were barriers still, it is true, but barriers that in time could be swept away.' Anne Sullivan wrote that 'All the way back to the house she was highly excited, and learned the name of everything she touched....' Helen's education had begun with a vengeance. (Many years later, in June 1960, a fountain was dedicated at Radcliffe College [where Helen took her degree] in memory of Anne Sullivan. At the dedication 80-year-old Helen said one word – 'Water'.)

Amongst others, two things are worth noting about Helen's education. The first is her eagerness to learn. Prior to the arrival of her teacher she became aware of her inability to communicate in the way that others did, and without understanding the difference between her and others she became desperately frustrated. 'The desire to express myself grew....I felt as if invisible hands were holding me, and I made frantic efforts to free myself. I struggled....I generally broke down in tears and physical exhaustion.' 'I cannot remember when I first realized that I was different from other people; but I knew it before my teacher came to me. I had noticed that my mother and my friends did not use signs as I did when they wanted anything done, but talked with their mouths.' When she was given the means to communicate she grasped it, literally, with both hands.

The second is her considerable intellect and phenomenal powers of concentration and memory. In the summer of 1887, soon after her 7th birthday, she understood the meaning of abstract thoughts and concepts. Anne Sullivan spelled into her hand 'I love Helen', and Helen then tried to understand the concept of 'love'. A day or two later Helen was trying to understand how to string beads in a sequence of different sizes into symmetrical groups, and having got it wrong Miss Sullivan touched her forehead and spelled 'Think'. Now she understood – 'the word was the name of the process that was going on in my head', and her education proceeded apace. She then understood other abstract concepts such as love....It is notable that an understanding of abstract concepts usually occurs around 11 years of age.

HELEN KELLER'S PERSONALITY AND APPEARANCE

Depite her handicaps Helen Keller had many things in her favour. Perhaps the most important of these was her teacher, Anne Sullivan, without whom she would never have become a 'free spirit'. When she lost her sight and hearing, 'My mind remained clear and active' – and she retained her desire to learn. Her mother, Kate Adams, was a striking beauty – a 'Memphis Belle' – and Helen inherited her mother's looks. Helen had immense energy, and she seemed always to be happy: she was later to write 'Happiness is a condition of the mind, and has very little to do with outward circumstances.' In 1889 the director of the Perkins Institute for the blind produced a report on Helen which attracted massive publicity. It seemed that all the world was fascinated by his account of this amazing child, who was displaying such considerable intellectual development despite being both blind and deaf. Those who met her were unfailingly impressed and captivated: 'Such a happy, rapturous face. No sign of deprivation, darkness or suspicion, but life, light and love' wrote one correspondent of 11-year-old Helen. 'The liveliest and happiest girl in the world' wrote another. 'Chestnut-haired Helen, with her radiant, loving personality, ceaseless mental activity and originality of expression provided proof anew that man was touched by the divine' (Lash, 1980). In her fifties Helen wrote 'All my life I have lived in a dark and silent world, and I seldom think of my limitations, and they never make me sad,' and on her 60th birthday, 'I find life an exciting business.'

LANGUAGE AND COMMUNICATION

Helen was taught by means of the manual alphabet, which was the only way to reach the mind of a child whose primary means of communication was through the sense of touch. This was invented many years previously by a group of Spanish monks who used it to communicate without breaking their vow of silence. It consists of simple movements of one person's hand on the palm of another, each touch spelling a letter. With practice it can be used effortlessly, and the expert can spell around 60 or more words a minute. In *The Story of My Life*, Helen wrote 'I do not feel each letter any more than you see each letter separately when you read. Constant practice makes the fingers very flexible, and some of my friends spell very rapidly – about as fast as an expert writes on a typewriter. The mere spelling is, of course, no more a conscious act than it is in writing.'

Helen, Teacher and others communicated with the manual alphabet throughout their lives. With its use Helen was able to enjoy visits to the theatre: 'I enjoy having a play described to me while it is being acted on the stage far more than reading it, because then it seems as if I were living in the midst of stirring events.' Helen also learned different braille systems, she learned to type, and with immense dedication and concentration she even learned to speak! In a speech to the Association to Promote the Teaching of Speech to the Deaf, at Mt Airy, Philadelphia, Pennsylvania, 8 July 1896, she said 'I use speech constantly, and I cannot begin to tell you how much pleasure it gives me to do so.' She also learned to lip-read, which she did by placing her hand on the speaker's lips. The Italian opera singer Enrico Caruso was the first international singing star. He sang for her the aria of the blinded, chained Samson from *Samson et Delila* as both of them – and all in the room – wept: she 'listened' to him by running her fingertips over his vocal chords and lips.

Helen also became multilingual. She learned Greek, Latin, German and French, and apparently she spoke German and French better than English. Her intellectual development was such that she graduated *cum laude* from Radcliffe College (a branch of Harvard University) in 1904.

LANGUAGE AND TOUCH

We are accustomed to thinking of language as a verbal means of communication, and of thought as subvocal activity. We can understand language being learned (in the deaf) by signing, so that it is represented visually. For Helen Keller, of course, neither of these means of communication was available and for her, language resided in the sense of touch and in her hands. She commented that 'They mean the world I live in – they are eyes, ears, channels of thought and good will. Sooner would I lose my health and even the ability to walk . . . than the use of these two hands.' She often appeared nervous because her hands were rarely still, and many commentators remarked on the 'bird-like' fluttering movements of her hands, since she would talk to herself, and think, by using the manual alphabet: 'When she is walking up or down the hall or along the veranda, her hands go flying along beside her like a confusion of birds' wings.' When she was in her seventies she wrote '. . . even now, in moments of excitement or when I wake from sleep, I occasionally catch myself spelling with my fingers'. When *The Story of My Life* appeared in 1902 it was hailed as a literary masterpiece. Her linguistic abilities are remarkable testimony to the 'language instinct', that language is amodal and can be learned to a high level irrespective of the sensory modality by which it is acquired.

INSIDE HELEN KELLER'S MIND

It would be of great interest to understand Helen's mental processes, to appreciate the actual images in her mind, but it is paradoxically her skilful use of language that makes this a matter of guesswork. She wrote such passages as 'a mist of green', of 'soft clouds tumbling over each other in the sky' and of 'blue pools of dog violets and the cascades of golden primroses' – expressing ideas and images that she could not possibly experience.

When the Empire State Building was completed (in 1931) Helen Keller went to its top:

I will concede that my guides saw a thousand things that escaped me from the top of the Empire State Building, but I am not envious. For imagination creates distances that reach to the end of the world. It is as easy for the imagination to think in stars as in cobble-stones....

There was the Hudson – more like the flash of a swordblade than a noble river. The little island of Manhattan, set like a jewel in its nest of rainbow waters, stared up into my face, and the solar system circled about my head! Why, I thought, the sun and the stars are suburbs of New York, and I never knew it! I had a sort of wild desire to invest in a bit of real estate on one of the planets....

Perhaps what is most important is what the mind brings to the information from the senses, rather than the richness and variety of the sensory information itself. William James, the father of modern psychology, wrote to her:

It is no paradox that you live in a world so indistinguishable from ours...it makes no difference in what shape the content of our verbal material may come. In some it is more optical, in others more motor in nature. In you it is motor and tactile, but its functions are the same as ours, the relations meant by the words symbolizing the relations existing between the things.

An Extraordinary Life

Throughout her life Helen Keller was a tireless campaigner for the deaf, the blind, and the deaf-blind: she worked for the American Foundation for the Blind from 1924 until her death. She went on several world tours, and at each country she visited was met by huge crowds, all eager to catch a glimpse of 'the miracle worker'. A film, *Deliverance*, was made of her life, she wrote several books, and she met and corresponded with the rich and the famous. These included kings, queens, presidents, poets, authors, singers, actors and others – a who's who of the times. When she met Einstein he commented 'I have been a great admirer of you always.' In 1931 H. G. Wells, who met her on a lecture tour of the United States, called her 'the most wonderful being in America'. Alexander Graham Bell said that 'I feel that in this child I have seen more of the Divine than has been manifest in anyone I ever met before.' Helen and her teacher went on lecture tours, and they gave a vaudeville act describing their early days together. Helen's energy allowed her to continue visiting foreign countries until she reached about 80 years old, when strokes made her withdraw into private life. She died in Connecticut on 1 June 1968.

References

Helen Keller (1902). *The Story of My Life*.
Joseph P. Lash (1980). *Helen and Teacher: The Story of Helen Keller and Anne Sullivan Macy*. Barnes and Noble (reprinted 1997).

35

Children of the Garden Island*

Emmy E. Werner

EDITORS'
INTRODUCTION

Emmy Werner describes the developmental outcome of a cohort of 698 children, who were born on Kauai, the Garden Island, in 1955. Her 30-year study concentrates on those children who were 'high risk', experiencing reproductive stress, discordant and impoverished homes, and often alcoholic or mentally disturbed parents. Many of these children went on to experience considerable problems of their own, but others developed healthy personalities, stable careers, and strong interpersonal relationships. There were two main factors that contributed to the latter children's success. One source of such resilience was constitutional: as infants they were described by their parents as 'active', 'affectionate', 'cuddly', 'easygoing' and 'even-tempered'. As school children they tended to ask for help when needed, concentrated on their assignments, and while not especially gifted they used whatever talents they had effectively.

The second factor that led to resilience lay in the environment and its interaction with the children's personalities. The children were highly sociable and had at least one close friend and often several. In particular they seemed to find a great deal of emotional support and nurturance. When this support was not available from their biological parents (perhaps when the father was absent, or the mother was mentally ill), they would often find it from substitute parents within the family, such as grandparents or siblings, or from regular baby-sitters.

The important point is that high-risk factors do not lead inevitably to poor adaptation, delinquency and hopelessness. Werner concludes that 'The life stories of the resilient individuals on the Garden Island have taught us that

* Previously published in *Scientific American*, **260** (1989), pp. 106–11.

competence, confidence and caring can flourish even under adverse circumstances if young people encounter people in their lives who provide them with a secure basis for the development of trust, autonomy and initiative.'

In 1955, 698 infants on the Hawaiian island of Kauai became participants in a 30-year study that has shown how some individuals triumph over physical disadvantages and deprived childhoods.

OVERVIEW

Kauai, the Garden Island, lies at the northwest end of the Hawaiian chain, 100 miles and a half-hour flight from Honolulu (see plate 35.1). Its 555 square miles encompass mountains, cliffs, canyons, rain forests, and sandy beaches washed by pounding surf. The first Polynesians who crossed the Pacific to settle there in the eighth century were charmed by its beauty, as were the generations of sojourners who visited there after Captain James Cook "discovered" the island in 1778.

The 45,000 inhabitants of Kauai are for the most part descendants of immigrants from Southeast Asia and Europe who came to the island to work on the sugar plantations with the hope of finding a better life for their children. Thanks to the islanders' unique spirit of cooperation, my colleagues Jessie M. Bierman and Fern E. French of the University of California at Berkeley, Ruth S. Smith, a clinical psychologist on Kauai, and I have been able to carry out a longitudinal study on Kauai that has lasted for more than three decades. The study has had two principal goals: to assess the long-term consequences of prenatal and perinatal stress and to document the effects of adverse early rearing conditions on children's physical, cognitive, and psychosocial development.

The Kauai Longitudinal Study began at a time when the systematic examination of the development of children exposed to biological and psychosocial

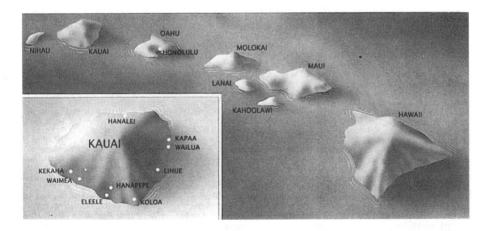

PLATE 35.1   Kauai, the Garden Island, lies at the northwest end of the Hawaiian archipelago. The towns that participated in the Kauai Longitudinal Study are shown in the inset. Lihue is the county seat; it is about 100 miles from Honolulu, the capital of Hawaii

risk factors was still a bit of a rarity. Investigators attempted to reconstruct the events that led to physical or psychological problems by studying the history of individuals in whom such problems had already surfaced. This retrospective approach can create the impression that the outcome is inevitable, since it takes into account only the "casualties," not the "survivors." We hoped to avoid that impression by monitoring the development of all the children born in a given period in an entire community.

We began our study in 1954 with an assessment of the reproductive histories of all the women in the community. Altogether 2,203 pregnancies were reported by the women of Kauai in 1954, 1955, and 1956; there were 240 fetal deaths and 1,963 live births. We chose to study the cohort of 698 infants born on Kauai in 1955, and we followed the development of these individuals at 1, 2, 10, 18, and 31 or 32 years of age. The majority of the individuals in the birth cohort – 422 in all – were born without complications, following uneventful pregnancies, and grew up in supportive environments.

But as our study progressed we began to take a special interest in certain "high-risk" children who, in spite of exposure to reproductive stress, discordant and impoverished home lives, and uneducated, alcoholic or mentally disturbed parents, went on to develop healthy personalities, stable careers, and strong interpersonal relations. We decided to try to identify the protective factors that contributed to the resilience of these children.

Finding a community that is willing or able to cooperate in such an effort is not an easy task. We chose Kauai for a number of reasons, not the least of which was the receptivity of the island population to our endeavors. Coverage by medical, public-health, educational, and social services on the island was comparable to what one would find in communities of similar size on the US mainland at that time. Furthermore, our study would take into account a variety of cultural influences on childbearing and child rearing, since the population of Kauai includes individuals of Japanese, Philipino, Portuguese, Chinese, Korean, and northern European as well as of Hawaiian descent.

We also thought the population's low mobility would make it easier to keep track of the study's participants and their families. The promise of a stable sample proved to be justified. At the time of the two-year follow-up, 96 percent of the living children were still on Kauai and available for study. We were able to find 90 percent of the children who were still alive for the 10-year follow-up, and for the 18-year follow-up we found 88 percent of the cohort.

In order to elicit the cooperation of the island's residents, we needed to get to know them and to introduce our study as well. In doing so we relied on the skills of a number of dedicated professionals from the University of California's Berkeley and Davis campuses, from the University of Hawaii, and from the island of Kauai itself. At the beginning of the study five nurses and one social worker, all residents of Kauai, took a census of all households on the island, listing the occupants of each dwelling and recording demographic information, including a reproductive history of all women 12 years old or older. The interviewers asked the women if they were pregnant; if a woman was not, a card with a postage-free envelope was left with the request that she mail it to the Kauai Department of Health as soon as she thought she was pregnant.

Local physicians were asked to submit a monthly list of the women who were coming to them for prenatal care. Community organizers spoke to women's groups, church gatherings, the county medical society and community leaders. The visits by the census takers were backed up with letters, and milk cartons were delivered with a printed message urging mothers to cooperate. We advertised in newspapers, organized radio talks, gave slide shows, and distributed posters.

Public-health nurses interviewed the pregnant women who joined our study in each trimester of pregnancy, noting any exposure to physical or emotional trauma. Physicians monitored any complications during the prenatal period, labor, delivery, and the neonatal period. Nurses and social workers interviewed the mothers in the postpartum period and when the children were 1 and 10 years old; the interactions between parents and offspring in the home were also observed. Pediatricians and psychologists independently examined the children at 2 and 10 years of age, assessing their physical, intellectual, and social development and noting any handicaps or behavior problems. Teachers evaluated the children's academic progress and their behavior in the classroom.

From the outset of the study we recorded information about the material, intellectual, and emotional aspects of the family environment, including stressful life events that resulted in discord or disruption of the family unit. With the parents' permission we also were given access to the records of public-health, educational, and social-service agencies and to the files of the local police and the family court. My collaborators and I also administered a wide range of aptitude, achievement, and personality tests in the elementary grades and in high school. Last but not least, we gained the perspectives of the young people themselves by interviewing them at the age of 18 and then again when they were in their early 30s.

Of the 698 children in the 1955 cohort, 69 were exposed to moderate prenatal or perinatal stress, that is, complications during pregnancy, labor, or delivery. About 3 percent of the cohort – 23 individuals in all – suffered severe prenatal or perinatal stress; only 14 infants in this group lived to the age of two. Indeed, 9 of the 12 children in our study who died before reaching two years of age had suffered severe perinatal complications.

Some of the surviving children became "casualties" of a kind in the next two decades of life. One out of every six children (116 children in all) had physical or intellectual handicaps of perinatal or neonatal origin that were diagnosed between birth and the age of two and that required long-term specialized medical, educational, or custodial care. About one out of every five children (142 in all) developed serious learning or behavior problems in the first decade of life that required more than six months of remedial work. By the time the children were 10 years old, twice as many children needed some form of mental-health service or remedial education (usually for problems associated with reading) as were in need of medical care.

By the age of 18, 15 percent of the young people had delinquency records and 10 percent had mental-health problems requiring either in- or outpatient care. There was some overlap among these groups. By the time they were 10, all 25 of the children with long-term mental-health problems had learning problems as well. Of the 70 children who had mental-health problems at 18, 15 also had a record of repeated delinquencies.

As we followed these children from birth to the age of 18 we noted two trends: the impact of reproductive stress diminished with time, and the developmental outcome of virtually every biological risk condition was dependent on the quality of the rearing environment. We did find some correlation between moderate to severe degrees of perinatal trauma and major physical handicaps of the central nervous system and of the musculo-skeletal and sensory systems; perinatal trauma was also correlated with mental retardation, serious learning disabilities, and chronic mental-health problems such as schizophrenia that arose in late adolescence and young adulthood.

But overall rearing conditions were more powerful determinants of outcome than perinatal trauma. The better the quality of the home environment was, the more competence the children displayed. This could already be seen when the children were just two years old: toddlers who had experienced severe perinatal stress but lived in middle-class homes or in stable family settings did nearly as well on developmental tests of sensory-motor and verbal skills as toddlers who had experienced no such stress.

Prenatal and perinatal complications were consistently related to impairment of physical and psychological development at the ages of 10 and 18 only when they were combined with chronic poverty, family discord, parental mental illness or other persistently poor rearing conditions. Children who were raised in middle-class homes, in a stable family environment, and by a

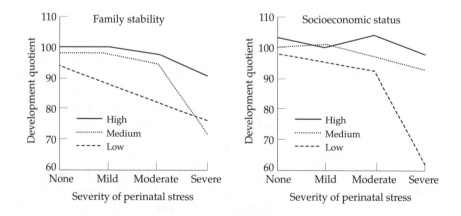

FIGURE 35.1 Influence of environmental factors such as family stability (a) or socioeconomic status (b) in infancy. The "developmental quotients" derived from tests given at 20 months show that the rearing environment can buffer or worsen the stress of perinatal complications. Children who had suffered severe perinatal stress but lived in stable, middle-class families scored as well as or better than children in poor, unstable households who had not experienced such stress

mother who had finished high school showed few if any lasting effects of reproductive stress later in their lives (see figure 35.1).

How many children could count on such a favorable environment? A sizable minority could not. We designated 201 individuals – 30 percent of the surviving children in this study population – as being high-risk children because they had experienced moderate to severe perinatal stress, grew up in chronic poverty, were reared by parents with no more than eight grades of formal education or lived in a family environment troubled by discord, divorce, parental alcoholism or mental illness. We termed the children "vulnerable" if they encountered four or more such risk factors before their second birthday. And indeed, two-thirds of these children (129 in all) did develop serious learning or behavior problems by the age of 10 or had deliquency records, mental-health problems, or pregnancies by the time they were 18.

Yet one out of three of these high-risk children – 72 individuals altogether – grew into competent young adults who loved well, worked well, and played well. None developed serious learning or behavior problems in childhood or adolescence. As far as we could tell from interviews and from their record in the community, they succeeded in school, managed home and social life well, and set realistic educational and vocational goals and expectations for themselves when they finished high school. By the end of their second decade of life they had developed into competent, confident, and caring people who expressed a strong desire to take advantage of whatever opportunity came their way to improve themselves.

They were children such as Michael, a boy for whom the odds on paper did not seem very promising. The son of teen-age parents, Michael was born prematurely, weighing four pounds five ounces. He spent his first three weeks of life in a hospital, separated from his mother. Immediately after his birth his father was sent with the US Army to Southeast Asia, where he remained for two years. By the time Michael was eight years old he had three siblings and his parents were divorced. His mother had deserted the family and had no further contact with her children. His father raised Michael and his siblings with the help of their aging grandparents.

Then there was Mary, born after 20 hours of labor to an overweight mother who had experienced several miscarriages before that pregnancy. Her father was an unskilled farm laborer with four years of formal education. Between Mary's fifth and tenth birthdays her mother was hospitalized several times for repeated bouts of mental illness, after having inflicted both physical and emotional abuse on her daughter.

Surprisingly, by the age of 18 both Michael and Mary were individuals with high self-esteem and sound values who cared about others and were liked by their peers. They were successful in school and looked forward to the future. We looked back at the lives of these two youngsters and the 70 other resilient individuals who had triumphed over their circumstances and compared their behavioral characteristics and the features of their environment with those of the other high-risk youths who developed serious and persistent problems in childhood and adolescence.

We identified a number of protective factors in the families, outside the family circle, and within the resilient children themselves that enabled them to resist stress. Some sources of resilience seem to be constitutional: resilient children such as Mary and Michael tend to have characteristics of temperament that elicit positive responses from family members and strangers alike. We noted these same qualities in adulthood. They include a fairly high activity level, a low degree of excitability and distress, and a high degree of sociability. Even as infants the resilient individuals were described by their parents as "active," "affectionate," "cuddly," "easygoing," and "even-tempered." They had no eating or sleeping habits that were distressing to those who took care of them.

The pediatricians and psychologists who examined the resilient children at 20 months noted their alertness and responsiveness, their vigorous play, and their tendency to seek out novel experiences and to ask for help when they needed it. When they entered elementary school, their classroom teachers observed their ability to concentrate on their assignments and noted their problem-solving and reading skills. Although they were not particularly gifted, these children used whatever talents they had effectively. Usually they had a special hobby they could share with a friend. These interests were not narrowly sex-typed; we found that girls and boys alike excelled at such activities as fishing, swimming, horseback riding, and hula dancing.

We could also identify environmental factors that contributed to these children's ability to withstand stress. The resilient youngsters tended to come from families having four or fewer children, with a space of two years or more between themselves and the next sibling. In spite of poverty, family discord, or parental mental illness, they had the opportunity to establish a close bond with at least one caretaker from whom they received positive attention during the first years of life.

The nurturing might come from substitute parents within the family (such as grandparents, older siblings, aunts or uncles) or from the ranks of regular baby-sitters. As the resilient children grew older they seemed to be particularly adept at recruiting such surrogate parents when a biological parent was unavailable (as in the case of an absent father) or incapacitated (as in the case of a mentally ill mother who was frequently hospitalized).

Maternal employment and the need to take care of younger siblings apparently contributed to the pronounced autonomy and sense of responsibility noted among the resilient girls, particularly in households where the father had died or was permanently absent because of desertion or divorce. Resilient boys, on the other hand, were often firstborn sons who did not have to share their parents' attention with many additional children in the household. They also had some male in the family who could serve as a role model (if not the father, then a grandfather or an uncle). Structure and rules in the household and assigned chores were part of the daily routine for these boys during childhood and adolescence.

Resilient children also seemed to find a great deal of emotional support outside their immediate family. They tended to be well liked by their classmates and had at least one close friend, and usually several. They relied on an informal network of neighbors, peers, and elders for counsel and support in times of crisis and transition. They seem to have made school a home away from home, a refuge from a disordered household. When we interviewed them at 18, many resilient youths mentioned a favorite teacher who had become a role model, friend, and confidant and was particularly supportive at times when their own family was beset by discord or threatened with dissolution.

For others, emotional support came from a church group, a youth leader in the YMCA or YWCA, or a favorite minister. Participation in extracurricular activities – such as 4-H, the school band, or a cheerleading team, which allowed them to be part of a cooperative enterprise – was also an important source of emotional support for those children who succeeded against the odds.

With the help of these support networks, the resilient children developed a sense of meaning in their lives and a belief that they could control their fate. Their experience in effectively coping with and mastering stressful life events built an attitude of hopefulness that contrasted starkly with the feelings of helplessness and futility that were expressed by their troubled peers.

In 1985, 12 years after the 1955 birth cohort had finished high school, we embarked on a search for the members of our study group. We managed to find 545 individuals – 80 percent of the cohort – through parents or other relatives, friends, former classmates, local telephone books, city directories, and circuit-court, voter-registration and motor-vehicle registration records and marriage certificates filed with the State Department of Health in Honolulu. Most of the young men and women still lived on Kauai, but 10 percent had moved to other islands and 10 percent lived on the mainland; 2 percent had gone abroad.

We found 62 of the 72 young people we had characterized as "resilient" at the age of 18. They had finished high school at the height of the energy crisis and joined the work force during the worst US recession since the Great Depression. Yet these 30-year-old men and women seemed to be handling the demands of adulthood well. Three out of four (46 individuals) had received some college education and were satisfied with their performance in school. All but four worked full time, and three out of four said they were satisfied with their jobs.

Indeed, compared with their low-risk peers from the same cohort, a significantly higher proportion of high-risk resilient individuals described themselves as being happy with their current life circumstances (44 percent versus 10 percent). The resilient men and women did, however, report a significantly higher number of health problems than their peers in low-risk comparison groups (46 percent versus 15 percent). The men's problems seemed to be brought on by stress: back problems, dizziness and fainting spells, weight gain, and ulcers. Women's health problems were largely related to pregnancy and childbirth. And although 82 percent of the women were married, only 48 percent of the men were. Those who were married had strong commitments to intimacy and sharing with their partners and children. Personal competence and determination, support from a spouse or mate, and a strong religious faith were the shared qualities that we found characterized resilient children as adults.

We were also pleasantly surprised to find that many high-risk children who had problems in their teens were able to rebound in their twenties and early thirties. We were able to contact 26 (90 percent) of the teen-age mothers, 56 (80 percent) of the individuals with mental-health problems, and 74 (75 percent) of the former delinquents who were still alive at the age of 30.

Almost all the teen-age mothers we interviewed were better off in their early thirties than they had been at 18. About 60 percent (16 individuals) had gone on to additional schooling and about 90 percent (24 individuals) were employed. Of the delinquent youths, three-fourths (56 individuals) managed to avoid arrest on reaching adulthood. Only a minority (12 individuals) of the troubled youths were still in need of mental-health services in their early thirties. Among the critical turning points in the lives of these individuals were entry into military service, marriage, parenthood, and active participation in a church group. In adulthood, as in their youth, most of these individuals relied on informal rather than formal sources of support: kith and kin rather than mental-health professionals and social-service agencies.

Our findings appear to provide a more hopeful perspective than can be had from reading the extensive literature on "problem" children that come to the attention of therapists, special educators and social-service agencies. Risk factors and stressful environments do not inevitably lead to poor adaptation. It seems clear that, at each stage in an individual's development from birth to maturity, there is a shifting balance between stressful events that heighten vulnerability and protective factors that enhance resilience.

As long as the balance between stressful life events and protective factors is favorable, successful adaptation is possible. When stressful events outweigh the protective factors, however, even the most resilient child can have problems. It may be possible to shift the balance from vulnerability to resilience through intervention, either by decreasing exposure to risk factors or stressful events or by increasing the number of protective factors and sources of support that are available.

It seems clear from our identification of risk and protective factors that some of the most critical determinants of outcome are present when a child is very young. And it is obvious that there are large individual differences among high-risk children in their responses to both negative and positive circumstances in their care-giving environment. The very fact of individual variation among children who live in adverse conditions suggests the need for greater assistance to some than to others.

If early intervention cannot be extended to every child at risk, priorities must be established for choosing who should receive help. Early-intervention programs need to focus on infants and young children who appear most vulnerable because they lack – permanently or temporarily – some of the essential social bonds that appear to buffer stress. Such children may be survivors of neonatal intensive care, hospitalized children who are separated from their families for extended periods of time, the young offspring of addicted or mentally ill parents, infants and toddlers whose mothers work full time and do not have access to stable child care, the babies of single or teen-age parents who have no other adult in the household, and migrant and refugee children without permanent roots in a community.

Assessment and diagnosis, the initial steps in any early intervention, need to focus not only on the risk factors in the lives of the children but also on the protective factors. These include competencies and informal sources of support that already exist and that can be utilized to enlarge a young child's communication and problem-solving skills and to enhance his or her self-esteem. Our research on resilient children has shown that other people in a child's life – grandparents, older siblings, day-care providers, or teachers – can play a supportive role if a parent is incapacitated or unavailable. In many situations it might make better sense, and be less costly as well, to strengthen such available informal ties to kin and community than it would to introduce additional layers of bureaucracy into delivery of services.

Finally, in order for any intervention program to be effective, a young child needs enough consistent nurturing to trust in its availability. The resilient children in our study had at least one person in their lives who accepted them unconditionally, regardless of temperamental idiosyncrasies or physical or mental handicaps. All children can be helped to become more resilient if adults in their lives encourage their independence, teach them appropriate communication and self-help skills, and model as well as reward acts of helpfulness and caring.

Thanks to the efforts of many people, several community-action and educational programs for high-risk children have been established on Kauai since our study began. Partly as a result of our findings, the legislature of the State of Hawaii has funded special mental-health teams to provide services for troubled children and youths. In addition the State Health Department established the Kauai Children's Services, a coordinated effort to provide services related to child development, disabilities, mental retardation, and rehabilitation in a single facility.

The evaluation of such intervention programs can in turn illuminate the process by which a chain of protective factors is forged that affords vulnerable children an escape from adversity. The life stories of the resilient individuals on the Garden Island have taught us that competence, confidence, and caring can flourish even under adverse circumstances if young children encounter people in their lives who provide them with a secure basis for the development of trust, autonomy, and initiative.

Further Reading

Kauai's Children Come of Age. Emmy E. Werner and Ruth S. Smith. University of Hawaii Press, 1977.

Vulnerable but Invincible: A Longitudinal Study of Resilient Children and Youth. Emmy E. Werner and Ruth S. Smith. McGraw-Hill Book Company, 1982.

Longitudinal Studies in Child Psychology and Psychiatry: Practical Lessons from Research Experience. Edited by A. R. Nichol. John Wiley & Sons, 1985.

High Risk Children in Young Adulthood: A Longitudinal Study from Birth to 32 Years. Emmy E. Werner in *American Journal of Orthopsychiatry*, Vol. **59**, No. 1, pp. 72–81 (January 1989).

36

Learning and Development in Children with Down's Syndrome

Jennifer G. Wishart

EDITORS' INTRODUCTION

Down's syndrome is one of the commonest, and most easily detectable, genetic disorders. It is invariably associated with severe learning difficulties, and the children experience difficulties in the moderate to severe range when faced with everyday learning skills. Jennifer Wishart looks at how children with Down's syndrome approach the task of learning. She describes their performance in three tasks: *operant learning* (the ability to detect that their activity, a foot-kick, causes the movement of a brightly-coloured mobile); *searching for hidden objects* and scores in *formal assessments* of intelligence.

The children's performance on these tasks leads to the conclusion that cognitive development in children with Down's syndrome cannot be understood simply in terms of a slowed-down version of normal development. Rather, development in these children seems to follow different pathways from those seen in normally-developing children. The key features which are characteristic of early cognitive development in Down's syndrome are 'the growing use of avoidance strategies when faced with cognitive challenges, the less-than-efficient use of existing problem-solving skills, the failure to consolidate existing cognitive skills into the repertoire, and the increasing reluctance to take the initiative in learning'. It is probable that these problems are compounded by the persistent experience for these children of failure in learning tasks, making it likely that, as they get older, motivational problems and underperformance will increasingly depress both the acquisition and development of new skills.

Down's syndrome is the most common known cause of severe learning disability and is a genetic disorder in which three, rather than the usual two, copies of chromosome 21 are present. Chromosome 21 is the smallest of the 23 human chromosomes and although the 1500 or so excess genes resulting from the third copy are in all other respects normal, the resulting imbalance in the genome leads to a highly complex phenotype in which both physical and mental development are significantly disrupted (Epstein et al., 1995; Stratford and Gunn, 1996; Selikowitz, 1997).

World-wide, approximately 100,000 children are born each year with Down's syndrome. The risk of giving birth to a child with Down's syndrome is significantly greater in women over 35 but, contrary to common belief, two-thirds of all children with the syndrome are born to mothers within the normal child-bearing age range. Widespread availability of maternal serum screening in developed countries has made significant inroads into incidence rates in both younger and older maternal age groups but although theoretically capable of 90% efficiency, current programmes are detecting only around 40% of affected pregnancies (Mutton, Alberman and Hook, 1996).

Down's syndrome is invariably associated with some degree of learning disability but cognitive ability levels in individual children vary widely, over 50–60 IQ points (Carr, 1994). The majority of children, however, experience difficulties in the moderate to severe range when faced with learning everyday skills. This article looks at how children with Down's syndrome approach the task of learning. It addresses the question of whether a specific 'style' of learning is associated with the syndrome and if so, whether this changes as the children grow older and their experience of learning increases. In our own research we have looked in particular at whether children with Down's syndrome may be *adding* to their already-existing difficulties by making inefficient use of those skills which they do develop and by using avoidant strategies when presented with opportunities for learning new skills. Our longitudinal data suggest that with increasing age, the children often change from being active and relatively able problem-solvers into progressively more reluctant learners. Deficits in their motivation to learn would appear to be significantly undermining their progress, not only delaying the acquisition and consolidation of new skills but also denying them the full benefits of skills they already have.

Surprisingly little attention is currently being paid to the contribution of motivational deficits to learning difficulties in children with Down's syndrome, or indeed to the role of psychological factors in general in determining developmental outcome. Despite the very large numbers of children affected by the syndrome and the intrinsic interest of Down's syndrome itself, only a very small number of psychologists are investigating how the condition directly affects behavioural development. In comparison with the attention directed at Down's syndrome by the biological sciences, psychological research on the syndrome is very thin on the ground indeed. Children with Down's syndrome are much more likely to be used as control children in studies of normal cognitive development or autism than studied in their own right. As a result, we are still a disappointingly long way from understanding the exact nature of their learning difficulties. Until we can improve on present levels of knowledge, our ability to help them to compensate for their difficulties remains severely limited.

EARLIER WORK ON COGNITIVE DEVELOPMENT IN DOWN'S SYNDROME

It is over a century since Langdon Down first described Down's syndrome and between then and now there have been a great many studies of cognitive ability in children with Down's syndrome (for overviews, see Gibson, 1978; Cicchetti and Beeghly, 1990; Carr, 1994). Some highly insightful research – with findings still useful today – was carried out during this time but unfortunately much of this earlier body of work on Down's syndrome has little current relevance. This is because most of the children in studies carried out prior to the 1960s were being raised in institutions. If there is one psychological fact which is almost universally accepted, it is that institutional life does nothing for the development and maintenance of cognitive skills – in anyone, with or without Down's syndrome.

By the late 60s and early 70s, the majority of children with Down's syndrome were being brought up by their parents in the family home. Here too, though, there are problems with many of the studies carried out, albeit of a quite different kind. Attitudes towards Down's syndrome were much more enlightened by this time and a great deal of research carried out in these years undoubtedly had the very best interests of the children at heart. In their enthusiasm to help, however, many studies regrettably paid insufficient attention to the rudimentary rules of scientific enquiry. As a result, some of their findings are at best often impossible to evaluate, and at worst, potentially highly misleading.

Early intervention studies from this period are perhaps the worst culprits in this respect. Many of the first, ground-breaking programmes claimed very high success rates in raising achievement levels in young children with Down's syndrome. The majority, however, assessed success only by comparing the progress of children in their programme against available developmental norms for children with Down's syndrome. These norms were typically drawn from children almost all of whom would have been institutionalized from birth; little use was made of concurrent control groups of children who were living at home but not receiving early intervention. It would have been very surprising indeed if *any* group of children with Down's syndrome being brought up at home in the 70s and 80s had not exceeded norms from institutionalized children of the 50s and 60s, regardless of whether they were receiving early intervention or not. This, it must be remembered, was a time when interest in early child development was at a peak, when the importance of the mother–child relationship was exalted to its highest-ever level, and which saw the emergence of a completely new industry – 'educational' toys. Early stimulation was seen by many as holding the key to enhancing intelligence levels – in children both with and without learning disabilities – and this increase in learning opportunities was soon reflected in earlier ages of achieving many developmental milestones.

Objectively evaluating the efficacy of these first early intervention programmes was in any case virtually impossible. Many programmes involved only very small numbers of children and were often under constant revision during the period of intervention. Basic features of the intervention – such as age of the child at entry, length of participation in the programme, frequency and content of sessions, level of input expected from parents – were often poorly controlled and varied greatly from programme to programme. Those who designed and implemented the programmes often reported major gains in the young children with Down's syndrome receiving early intervention but independent reviewers were generally far less impressed by the measurable levels of success achieved by most programmes (see, e.g., Haydn and Dmitriev, 1975; Spitz, 1986; Gibson and Harris, 1988; Spiker and Hopmann, 1996). Many gains proved to have very poor 'tenacity' and therefore had little true developmental value. Any advantage was very short-lived and children not being given any specific training soon caught up (see, e.g. Sloper, Glenn and Cunningham, 1986).

The widespread availability of early intervention programmes is often given the credit for the higher levels of competence which today's young children with Down's syndrome show. To a great many researchers, however, it seems just as likely that these advances stem from the better management of the children's health problems, the more positive attitudes of their parents and teachers, and their greatly increased access to education and a more normal lifestyle. There is indeed some concern amongst professionals that an uncritical belief in the direct efficacy of early intervention may lead people to underestimate the degree of learning difficulties likely to show up in post-infancy years and to persist throughout childhood and into adult years.

COGNITIVE ABILITIES IN CHILDREN WITH DOWN'S SYNDROME

Children with Down's syndrome show enormous individual variability in the ages at which specific cognitive milestones are reached and in the levels of cognitive achievement ultimately reached (see, e.g., Cunningham, 1987; Carr, 1994). However, it does them no favours not to recognize the problems that nearly all of them face in learning even very basic childhood skills. Many children with Down's syndrome do not progress much beyond the intellectual capabilities of the average 6–8-year-old and a significant number do not achieve even that; mastering language skills, whether spoken or written, also remains a major problem for a great many (see, e.g., Fowler, 1990; Rondal, 1996).

Cognitive skills – along with language skills – have thus far proved very resistant to attempts at facilitative intervention but lack of success to date does not imply by any means that we should give up on our efforts.

There are considerable grounds for believing that with a better understanding of the very *specific* nature of the learning difficulties experienced by children with Down's syndrome, much more effective methods of intervening may still be found. The emphasis here is very much on the word 'specific'. The specific nature of these difficulties is likely to demand a major change in our approach to teaching children with Down's syndrome, one which recognizes, for example, their short-term memory problems, their deficits in auditory and visual sequential memory, and the relative strength of their visual over their auditory processing ability (Marcell and Armstrong, 1982; Varnhagen, Das and Varnhagen, 1987; Bower and Hayes, 1994). Current models of educational intervention do not typically recognize the specific educational needs of children with Down's syndrome and in all likelihood make some very wrong assumptions about how development proceeds in Down's syndrome. This may well be why we have seen much less progress than we might have hoped for to date, especially in older children (Wishart, 1993b; Buckley et al., 1996).

The Nature of Cognitive Development in Down's Syndrome

It is widely assumed, implicitly if not always explicitly, that cognitive development in children with Down's syndrome can basically be understood in terms of a slowed-down version of normal development: that it is only the rate and endpoint that distinguishes their development from that of other children. This seems unlikely to be an accurate characterization of the nature of development in Down's syndrome. It seems far more likely that there are significant and very important differences in how development unfolds in children with Down's syndrome, some of these stemming as much from crucial differences in the psychological environment in which they learn as from the biological disadvantages they carry from birth.

Maintaining that development in children with Down's syndrome is fundamentally different may not be the favoured viewpoint but it does fit with the large body of data from the neurosciences showing major differences in the structure of the Down's syndrome brain and in how it works (see, e.g., Uecker, Mangan, Obrzut and Nadel, 1993). It is clear that children with Down's syndrome are at a considerable disadvantage when it comes to the basic 'tools' for learning. This inherent biological disadvantage can only be compounded by the adverse psychological effects of always being in the slow lane when it comes to learning. For most children with Down's syndrome, progress in virtually all developmental domains typically takes much longer, failure is more frequent, and the expectations of those around them, whether parents or professionals, are typically low. All of this must make learning a very different experience for the child with Down's syndrome. Provided with a far-from-perfect set of tools for learning and with a very different psychological environment in which to learn, it would surely be remarkable if development in Down's syndrome children did *not* follow different pathways from those seen in normally-developing children from a very early stage.

INCREASING AGE, INCREASING PROBLEMS?

One of the more robust findings about cognitive development in Down's syndrome is that IQ level typically declines with increasing age. Carr (1985) reviewed a large number of IQ studies carried out between 1961 and 1982, looking at data from over 2500 children who had been tested at varying intervals and at various ages between birth and 18 years. She found evidence of a steep drop in IQ between 1 and 3 years, with this decline continuing through to age 13 (the highest age level for which there were sufficient data to plot developmental trends), although lessening in slope. The same pattern also emerged in one of our own more recent cross-sectional studies of development in 35 children with Down's syndrome aged 3 months to 5 years, despite the fact that all of our children had been receiving early intervention in the form of regular visits from an educational home visitor (Duffy, 1990; Wishart, 1996).

One of the main aims of our research programme has therefore been to try to pinpoint some of the factors underlying this failure to maintain developmental rate. The following is a brief overview of some of our findings along with some illustrative data. The children with Down's syndrome in our studies have ranged in age from birth to 14 years. In longitudinal studies data collection has extended from 1 to 5 years, depending on the age of subjects at entry and the nature of the study in question. In all of the studies, control groups of children without Down's syndrome have been included to allow direct evaluation of difference versus delay theories of development. Typically, normally-developing children were matched with the children with Down's syndrome either for chronological age or for stage in development, depending on the focus of the particular study. As will be apparent from some of the findings, however, 'matching' is a somewhat misleading and sometimes meaningless concept when it comes to Down's syndrome. Children with Down's syndrome simply do not respond in test situations in the same way as normally-developing children, even when they achieve similar 'scores'. Children with Down's syndrome do not even provide satisfactory matches for themselves at times: often, their responses on a given test fluctuate greatly over two identical, closely-spaced testing sessions, with successes in the first session no longer demonstrated in the second session and 'failures' turning into successes.

Findings from the three sets of studies to be outlined below – on operant learning, object concept development, and IQ test performance – all demonstrate some of the key features which would appear to define early development in Down's syndrome: the growing use of avoidance strategies when faced with cognitive challenges, the less-than-efficient use of existing problem-solving skills, the failure to consolidate newly-acquired cognitive skills into the repertoire, and the increasing reluctance to take the initiative in learning.

Developmental Trends in Operant Learning

Our studies of operant learning provide the most direct evidence that young children with Down's syndrome very quickly learn to depend on the support of others in learning contexts, even when that support is not needed. Operant learning studies investigate the ability of children to detect that their activity has caused something to happen. Understanding this kind of relationship is basic to learning and is also essential to the formation of any belief in self-efficacy – that you have some control over what happens around you and to you.

Fifty infants with Down's syndrome aged between birth and 2 years old took part in cross-sectional and longitudinal studies (Wishart, 1990, 1991, 1993a). Because of the poor muscle tone often present in the early years, a task requiring minimal motor skills was used. The children were seated securely in a baby chair. If they kicked either foot through 60 degrees this broke a light beam, causing a 1-second rotation of a brightly-coloured mobile. Usually, when this sort of contingency is noticed, kicking rate typically rises and is often accompanied by smiling or excited vocalizations (Watson, 1984; Rovee-Collier, 1987). The criterion adopted for having detected the relationship between kicking and turning was a 50% increase in each infant's personal baseline kicking rate.

These studies were basically about control and the exercise of control. The computer programme allowed two main features of the task to be varied:

- in *contingent* sessions, the mobile would turn if, and only if, the child kicked through the beam; in some sessions, the mobile would turn every time the child kicked, i.e. 100% of the time; in others, kicking would only work 80% of the time (with 1 in 5 kicks being 'cancelled' randomly by computer);
- in mixed *contingent/non-contingent* sessions, the mobile would also occasionally randomly turn by itself, around 10% of the time, although the child had not kicked.

These reinforcement conditions were selected to mimic aspects of real-life learning; real life is not always so generous as to provide a reward for effort on every occasion and sometimes things happen because someone else did something, not you. The objective was to find out which ratio of success to failure in controlling the mobile's movements would encourage the most active exploration of the contingency. We also wanted to investigate whether providing free reinforcement was helpful or unhelpful to the learning process.

As would be expected, the children with Down's syndrome did less well on these tasks than normally-developing children of the same chronological age: they were generally slower to detect the relationship between their kicking and the mobile's turns, were less active in their response to withdrawal of control in extinction periods (when the computer turned off the mobile and kicking was no longer effective), and were less responsive to the introduction of 'free', non-contingent reinforcement, usually an intriguing event to normally-developing infants. The children were eventually able to solve this problem in all its various versions but developmental trends in response to the non-contingent turns of the mobile proved to be of some concern in the longitudinal subjects. Although still aware of their potential to control the mobile and still clearly keen to see it go round, the older children often simply sat and watched the 'free' turns, not bothering to kick for themselves at anything like the rate seen in contingent-only parts of the same testing session. Effectively, they were relinquishing much of their control over what was going on around them, happy simply to watch rather than participate most of the time.

The cross-sectional operant data in table 36.1 illustrate just how differently children with and without Down's syndrome react at different ages and developmental stages when given the opportunity to explore and control aspects of their environment. The table shows data from 16 children with Down's syndrome, four at 6, 12, 18 and 24 months, each matched with two different normally-developing children, one of the same chronological age, the other a younger child of the same mental age. There were two experimental sessions, one with and one without 'free' turns (with order of presentation counterbalanced). Although five of the older children with Down's syndrome were already walking, most were prepared to sit through most of both 18-minute testing sessions with very little complaint, alert and interested and often showing considerable signs of pleasure at each rotation of the mobile, whether produced by themselves or by the computer. In marked contrast, control children with a developmental or chronological age over 6 months retained little interest in either task after the contingency between their actions and the mobile's turns had been fully explored: they refused to sit any longer, fretting or protesting loudly, and usually co-operating for even shorter times in the second session than the first. Protests typically subsided, however, as soon as they were allowed out of the chair and given some other problem to solve, such as an object concept task. The passivity of the children with Down's syndrome in the same situation – reflected not only in the differences in 'co-operation' levels but also in their responses to non-contingent input – clearly has very negative implications for future developmental progress.

TABLE 36.1 Operant learning studies: mean length of co-operation (minutes) at four age levels (cross-sectional data)

Age of Down's syndrome subjects	Session	Down's syndrome subjects	CA matched subjects	MA matched subjects
6 months	1	14.13	11.00	10.00
	2	15.75	11.75	7.25
12 months	1	14.50	3.25	10.25
	2	14.38	1.25	7.13
18 months	1	15.88	1.00	2.63
	2	14.20	0.25	1.13
24 months	1	13.50	0.00	1.13
	2	12.50	0.00	0.88

CA: chronological age; MA: mental age
Source: Wishart, 1991

Object Concept Development

The second set of illustrative data is drawn from studies of object concept development (Wishart, 1988, 1993a, b). It is not necessary to go into any great detail about object concept development itself but it is important to note that the cognitive skills crucial to succeeding on these tasks are considered by many psychologists to be key ones. 'Object concept development' is a wonderfully obscure term for something that is really very simple. We all have to learn at some early point, for example, that objects exist independently of our actions, and that they continue to exist in exactly the same form even when we cannot see them or act upon them. We also have to learn that no object can be in two places at one time and that all objects have unique identities, that two objects seen at different times may look identical but are not necessarily the same object, and so on.

A series of hiding tasks of increasing complexity are used to assess how much infants understand about objects and about the physical laws that govern their movements. The easiest tasks involve hiding a small, attractive toy fully or partially under some sort of occluder, typically a cup or small cloth; in the most difficult tasks, the child must choose from two or more identical occluders, after a hiding sequence in which the position either of the toy or of the occluders has been changed.

Thirty infants with Down's syndrome aged between birth and 2 years 9 months took part in a longitudinal study. We used four levels of task. Although there was already evidence to suggest that children with Down's syndrome are considerably delayed in acquiring each of the stages in object concept development, we decided to try all levels of task with all ages of subject. Testing sessions were fortnightly, with the same person carrying out the testing on all occasions.

The data we shall look at here relate only to the second easiest task, a task commonly known as the AAB task. This task is typically solved by the average child somewhere between 8 and 10 months. A toy is hidden three times, in one of two identical occluders positioned at A and B, in the sequence AAB. There is no sleight of hand and the infant sees the object being hidden each time. Success requires the infant to search at B on the B trial on 4 out of 4 AAB trials; in longitudinal studies, success is required in two consecutive sessions. Prior to 8–10 months, the characteristic error made by normally-developing infants is to continue to search at A on the B trial, i.e. at the place where the toy has previously been found. All children, no matter how intelligent they are, will have produced this error at some point in their development. Early experience with this sort of problem can lead to success at a younger age, but longitudinal studies have shown that the characteristic error still reliably appears in testing sessions prior to this success (Wishart and Bower, 1985).

In our studies, we found that infants with Down's syndrome produced exactly the same AAB error as normally-developing infants but here effectively the similarities ended. Taking the more positive aspects of our data first, mean age of first success on this task was $7\frac{3}{4}$ months for control infants and $10\frac{1}{2}$

TABLE 36.2   Mean age of success (in months) on four levels of object concept task

DOWN'S SYNDROME CHILDREN			

Longitudinal data

	TASK 1	TASK 2	TASK 3	TASK 4
Mean age*	7.75	10.50	19.25	18.0
Range	6.25–10.75	7.25–14.0	14.5–26.75	11.0–25.25

NORMALLY-DEVELOPING CHILDREN			

Longitudinal data

	TASK 1	TASK 2	TASK 3	TASK 4
Mean age*	4.75	7.75	12.25	14.5
Range	4.0–5.75	4.75–8.5	9.25–14.25	10.25–17.0

Cross-sectional data (Wishart and Bower, 1984)

	TASK 1	TASK 2	TASK 3	TASK 4
Age* at which 75% of subjects passed	5.0	10.0	15.0	22.0+

* All ages rounded up to nearest 0.25 months.
Source: Wishart, 1993a

months for infants with Down's syndrome; the range of age of success is also worth noting: 7.25 to 14 months. The infants with Down's syndrome may have taken longer to achieve their first success on this task than the normally-developing infants but the mean age at which they did so was not far off cross-sectional norms for age of acquisition of this stage; a small number of infants in fact succeeded at surprisingly early ages. This was true of performance on higher-level tasks too (see table 36.2).

These early ages of first success were deceptive, however. Figure 36.1 shows the performance profile of one of these early achievers over a period of 12 months, between 6 and 18 months of age. It reflects the instability in development which we found to be typical of many of our young subjects with Down's syndrome. This subject first succeeded on the AAB task at $7\frac{1}{2}$ months and kept this up over five testing sessions, a period of 2 months. This could not just have been lucky guessing. Thereafter, her performance proved to be much less stable however. Her subsequent failures were sometimes the result of a refusal to engage in sufficient trials to be credited with a pass (4/4 correct searches at B) rather than of clearly erroneous search on any trial (M−). Success could sometimes be restored by hiding chocolate or a rusk instead of a toy but this strategy was not always successful (M+). More typically, although watching the hiding carefully and clearly capable of precise search, this little girl would either sweep both cups to the floor or simply pick the same cup on each trial, a very low-level strategy which at best would give a 50% return rate (and, of course would count as a 'fail').

This was not the only problem. The subjects with Down's syndrome also produced counterproductive behaviours in response to tasks which were 'difficult', difficult, that is, in terms of their current developmental level. In this case, engagement was more clearly withdrawn, with difficult tasks often actively avoided after only one or two trials, either with protests or by

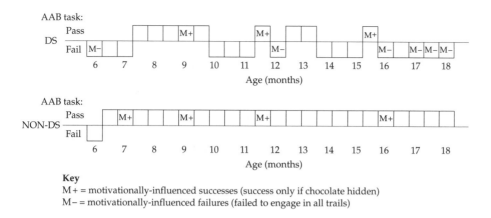

Key
M+ = motivationally-influenced successes (success only if chocolate hidden)
M− = motivationally-influenced failures (failed to engage in all trails)

FIGURE 36.1   Longitudinal profiles of two age-matched subjects on the AAB task

resorting to diversionary strategies such as pretending to be very interested in something else, turning on the charm, or producing some sort of 'party-trick' (such as blowing raspberries) to divert the tester into some other, off-task activity.

These counterproductive behaviours cannot simply be written off as perfectly normal responses to being repeatedly presented with a task which is now 'easy' or being faced with a task that is just too difficult. Normally-developing children typically work hard at *all* levels of these tasks, whether they are above or below their current developmental level in terms of difficulty, with occasional lapses in interest usually easily overcome with coaxing or chocolate (see figure 36.1). Normally-developing children usually enjoy showing off their abilities – why is it that children with Down's syndrome would rather respond in a way that avoids running the risk of error, even when they should have a good chance of succeeding?

BEHAVIOUR IN FORMAL ASSESSMENTS

One last set of data – relating to how children with Down's syndrome behave in formal assessment situations as opposed to psychological experiments – is perhaps worth looking at (Wishart and Duffy, 1990; Wishart, 1993a). The data already given above indicate that the differences in development in children with Down's syndrome and in children without Down's syndrome may be more significant than the similarities in their development. In assessing Down's syndrome children, we nevertheless make great use of psychometric tests, tests that have been standardized on normally-developing children – tests like the Bayley Scales of Infant Development, the Stanford Binet Test, or the Wechsler Scales of Intelligence, for instance. We then describe the child with Down's syndrome in terms of his or her 'mental age' (MA), a term referring to the mental ability that would be expected in the average child of that number of years. The validity of such tests rests on the assumption that test performance will be a reasonably accurate reflection of the skills available to the child and that all children will be equally motivated to demonstrate those skills in a test setting.

Intuition alone would suggest that the child whose learning experience has been characterized by frequent failure might well approach a situation which is clearly designed to test the limits of their abilities in a different way from a child whose experience of success and failure has been more favourable. We have found that the diversionary and delaying tactics, the non-committal responses, the misuse of social skills – the behaviours we see at younger ages – all re-appear in various guises at later ages when children are faced with standardized 'IQ' tests. The tests we have been using are the Mental Scales of the Bayley Scales of Infant Development and the Kaufman Assessment Battery for Children (KABC). In some cases, when we have tested children on two separate but closely-spaced sessions, we have found performance to vary on as many as 30% of the test items presented, with children passing items previously failed and failing items previously passed. This has often meant that two very different IQs resulted from these two testing sessions, neither presumably reflecting accurately the full range of skills available to the child at that point in his or her development.

Table 36.3 shows the number of items on which performance changed between two closely-spaced sessions in a group of 18 Down's syndrome children aged 6 months to 4 years. There were 74 instances in which the children's performance improved on a test item in the second session and 91 instances in which their performance deteriorated in the second session. There is no indication of this instability in mean overall scores at any of the six age levels – these were very similar over sessions. This should sound a warning note about the confidence that can be placed in findings from studies in which subjects were 'matched' on IQ. It is not very feasible that all 74 instances of fail-to-pass changes can be put down to true increases in the children's competencies in the intervening period – there was, after all, only a very short time – a couple of weeks – separating the two testing sessions. The 91 pass-to-fail changes are less ambiguous. Clearly the required behaviour *was* already in the

TABLE 36.3   Test–retest stability on Bayley items at six age levels

| Age (months) | Testing session | | No. test items on which performance varied over two sessions | |
| | I | II | Fail-to-pass | Pass-to-fail |
	Mean raw score (AE)			
6	55.3 (4.5)	53.3 (4.5)	12	19
12	77.3 (7.0)	75.6 (7.0)	10	15
18	100.0 (11.0)	99.7 (11.0)	11	13
24	109.0 (13.0)	108.7 (13.0)	16	16
36	131.3 (19.0)	130.3 (19.0)	12	15
48	142.3 (22.0)	142.3 (22.0)	13	13
		Totals	74	91

AE: age equivalent level (months)
Source: Wishart and Duffy, 1990

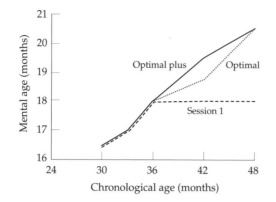

FIGURE 36.2   The effects of instability on IQ profile

child's repertoire at that age but for some reason it was not reproduced in the second testing session.

The effects on development of these fluctuations in performance profiles can be seen in figure 36.2. Few of the Bayley items permit chance success; passes, unlike fails, are likely to be genuine. Figure 36.2 shows the relationship of MA scores to chronological age (CA) for a child tested twice with the Bayley every 3 months between the ages of 30 and 48 months. 'Session 1' points give the score achieved in the first of the two testing sessions presented at each age level. From these, it looks as if this child's development plateaued between 36 and 48 months, and that no developmental progress was made over this year. What could happen, though, if at each age level we were to credit her with all of the items on which she had scored a pass, regardless of whether this was on the first or second of the two closely-spaced sessions? From these 'optimal' scores, it is clear that new skills *were* being gained over the months but that the effects of these on her score were being cancelled out by her failure to reliably reproduce skills gained earlier. The 'optimal-plus' scores credit all items passed up to and including that testing session, irrespective of those items' reliability in sessions beyond that of initial acquisition. What the 'optimal-plus' scores illustrate is the potential for constant progress – *if only* each new skill had been consolidated into the repertoire and used to the full. Our analyses of behaviour during testing showed that two-thirds of the pass-to-fail cases and half of the fail-to-pass cases in this group of children were associated with evidence of inadequate engagement in the task. This fits with the suggestion that psychological as well as biological factors have an important influence on how development progresses.

The degree to which these psychological factors are open to intervention remains to be determined. Although high-achieving individuals with Down's syndrome may not be representative of the average, they none the less demonstrate that the condition does not in itself place a 'fixed' ceiling on cognitive development which is inevitably very low. Given that early intervention, professional input, and full-time schooling are now the norm, the wide differences seen in ability levels are not likely to stem simply from 'brighter' children having had more opportunities to learn than others. There *is* some evidence of a link between favourable developmental outcome and those factors which influence IQ in the rest of the population – factors such as level of parental education and socio-economic status – but this link is far from strong. The evidence is also not strong that variability in IQs in children with Down's syndrome is closely correlated with variability in parental IQ.

Clearly psychological as well as biological factors are at work in determining developmental outcome in Down's syndrome and until we gain a better understanding of how these interact we shall remain unable to explain why it is that some individuals with Down's syndrome succeed in mastering so much more than others do. A closer developmental investigation of the learning process itself (rather than its products) and a more detailed analysis of the contexts in which we expect children with Down's syndrome to learn could well pay rich dividends. It is also important to remember that the potential for further cognitive growth continues well beyond adolescence in those with Down's syndrome (Carr, 1994). It is therefore important that any lesson to be learnt from research into cognitive development in children with Down's syndrome should also be appraised for its potential relevance to older age groups. Many of the psychological obstacles to learning which appear to dog early childhood must also operate in later life. At later ages, it may be even *more* likely that motivational deficits and underperformance will depress both the acquisition and the development of new skills.

ACKNOWLEDGEMENTS

This article is an updated version of a chapter which first appeared in 1996 in *Down's Syndrome: Psychological, Psychobiological and Socioeducational Perspectives*, edited by J. A. Rondal, J. Perera, L. Nadel and A. Comblain (London: Colin Whurr). A more extensive account of the topics can be found in *New Approaches to Down's Syndrome*, edited by B. Stratford and P. Gunn (London: Cassell, 1996). The collaboration – and patience – of the children and families who took part in the studies is gratefully acknowledged, as is the funding support of the Medical Research Council of Great Britain (grant no. 9311518N).

REFERENCES

Bower, A., and Hayes, A. (1994). Short-term memory deficits and Down's syndrome: A comparative study. *Down's Syndrome: Research and Practice*, 2, 47–50.

Buckley, S., Bird, G., and Byrne, A. (1996). The practical and theoretical significance of teaching literacy skills to children with Down's syndrome. In J. A. Rondal, J. Perera, L. Nadel and A. Comblain (eds), *Down's Syndrome: Psychological, Psychobiological and Socioeducational Perspectives* (pp. 119–28), London: Colin Whurr.

Carr, J. (1985). The development of intelligence. In D. Lane and B. Stratford (eds), *Current Approaches to Down's Syndrome* (pp. 167–86), London: Holt, Rinehart & Winston.

Carr, J. (1994). Long term outcome for people with Down's syndrome. *Journal of Child Psychology and Psychiatry*, 35, 425–39.

Cicchetti, D., and Beeghly, M. (eds) (1990). *Children with Down Syndrome: A Developmental Perspective*. New York: Cambridge University Press.

Cunningham, C. (1987). *Down's Syndrome: An Introduction for Parents*. London: Souvenir Press.

Duffy, L. (1990). *The relationship between competence and performance in early development in children with Down's syndrome*. Unpublished Ph.D. dissertation, University of Edinburgh.

Epstein, C., Hassold, T., Lott, I. T., Nadel, L., and Patterson, D. (eds) (1995). *Etiology and Pathogenesis of Down's Syndrome*. New York: Wiley-Liss.

Fowler, A. (1990). Language abilities in children with Down syndrome. In D. Cicchetti and M. Beeghly (eds), *Children with Down Syndrome: A Developmental Perspective* (pp. 302–28), New York: Cambridge University Press.

Gibson, D. (1978). *Down's Syndrome: The Psychology of Mongolism*. Cambridge, England: Cambridge University Press.

Gibson, D., and Harris, A. (1988). Aggregated early intervention effects for Down Syndrome persons: Patterning and longevity of benefits. *Journal of Mental Deficiency Research*, **32**, 1–17.

Haydn, A. H., and Dmitriev, V. (1975). The multidisciplinary preschool programme for Down's Syndrome children at the University of Washington Model preschool center. In B. Z. Friedlander, G. M. Sterritt and G. E. Kirk (eds), *The Exceptional Infant: Vol. 3. Assessment and Intervention*, New York: Brunel/Mazel.

Marcell, M. M., and Armstrong, V. (1982). Auditory and visual sequential memory of Down syndrome and non-retarded children. *American Journal of Mental Deficiency*, **87**, 86–95.

Mutton, D., Alberman, E., and Hook, E. B. (1996). Cytogenetic and epidemiological findings in Down syndrome, England and Wales 1980–1993. *Journal of Medical Genetics*, **33**, 387–94.

Rondal, J. A. (1996). Oral language in Down's syndrome. In J. A. Rondal, J. Perera, L. Nadel and A. Comblain (eds), *Down's Syndrome: Psychological, Psychobiological and Socioeducational Perspectives* (pp. 99–118), London: Colin Whurr.

Rovee-Collier, C. K. (1987). Learning and memory in infancy. In J. D. Osofsky (ed.), *Handbook of Infant Development (2nd edn)* (pp. 98–148), New York: Wiley.

Selikowitz, M. (1997). *Down's Syndrome: The Facts*. Oxford: Oxford University Press.

Sloper, P., Glenn, S. M., and Cunningham, C. C. (1986). The effect of intensity of training on sensori-motor development in infants with Down's syndrome. *Journal of Mental Deficiency Research*, **30**, 149–62.

Spiker, D., and Hopmann, M. R. (1996). The effectiveness of early intervention for children with Down syndrome. In M. J. Guralnick (ed.), *The Effectiveness of Early Intervention: Directions for Second Generation Research* (pp. 271–306), Baltimore: Brookes.

Spitz, H. H. (1986). Preventing and curing mental retardation by behavioral intervention: An evaluation of some claims. *Intelligence*, **10**, 197–207.

Stratford, B., and Gunn, P. (eds) (1996). *New Approaches to Down's Syndrome*. London: Cassell.

Uecker, A., Mangan, P. A., Obrzut, J. E., and Nadel, L. (1993). Down syndrome in neurobiological perspective: An emphasis on spatial cognition. *Journal of Clinical Child Psychology*, **22**, 266–76.

Varnhagen, C. K., Das, J. P., and Varnhagen, S. (1987). Auditory and visual memory span: Cognitive processing by TMR individuals with Down syndrome or other etiologies. *American Journal of Mental Deficiency Research*, **91**, 398–405.

Watson, J. S. (1984). Bases of causal inference in infancy: Time, space and sensory relations. In L. P. Lipsitt and C. K. Rovee-Collier (eds), *Advances in Infancy Research: Vol. 3* (pp. 152–65), Norwood: Ablex.

Wishart, J. G. (1988). Early learning in infants and young children with Down's Syndrome. In L. Nadel (ed.), *The Psychobiology of Down Syndrome* (pp. 7–50), Boston: MIT Press.

Wishart, J. G. (1990). Learning to learn: The difficulties faced by infants and young children with Down's Syndrome. In W. I. Fraser (ed.), *Key Issues in Research in Mental Retardation* (pp. 249–61), London: Routledge.

Wishart, J. G. (1991). Taking the initiative in learning: A developmental investigation of infants with Down's Syndrome. *International Journal of Disability, Development and Education*, **38**, 27–44.

Wishart, J. G. (1993a). The development of learning difficulties in children with Down's syndrome. *Journal of Intellectual Disability Research*, **37**, 389–403.

Wishart, J. G. (1993b). Learning the hard way: avoidance strategies in young children with Down's syndrome. *Down's Syndrome: Research and Practice*, **1**, 47–55.

Wishart, J. G. (1996). Avoidant learning styles and cognitive development in young children with Down's syndrome. In B. Stratford and P. Gunn (eds), *New Approaches to Down's Syndrome*, London: Cassell.

Wishart, J. G., and Bower, T. G. R. (1984). Spatial relations and the object concept: A normative study. In: L. P. Lipsitt and C. K. Rovee-Collier (eds), *Advances in Infancy Research: Vol. 3* (pp. 57–123), Norwood, NJ: Ablex.

Wishart, J. G., and Bower, T. G. R. (1985). A longitudinal study of the development of the object concept. *British Journal of Developmental Psychology*, **3**, 243–58.

Wishart, J. G., and Duffy, L. (1990). Instability of performance on cognitive tests in infants and young children with Down's Syndrome. *British Journal of Educational Psychology*, **59**, 10–22.

37

COGNITIVE DEVELOPMENT AND COGNITIVE DEFICIT*

Uta Frith

Cognitive deficits – in the mind – are caused by biological deficits in the **OVERVIEW** brain. Cognitive deficits both affect and are affected by development. The resulting developmental disorder is manifested in a wide variety of behavioural signs and symptoms which are highly variable and influenced by general factors such as experience, compensation and motivation. Illustrations will be taken from autism and dyslexia. The core symptoms of each of these biologically based disorders can be explained in terms of a unique cognitive deficit.

The study of mental life is the study of thinking, knowing and feeling. This is the subject of cognitive psychology. Where do thoughts, knowledge and feelings come from? This is the question of cognitive development. The question is almost impossibly difficult, but it has one answer that is very simple: the development of the mind comes from the development of the brain.

Reproduction and growth are hazardous processes. Minor problems in brain development can occur so early in life that the very course of mental development is set onto a deviant path. Later intervention with social or other environmental means cannot reset this path though it can certainly smooth it. An example which highlights the three most important aspects of this kind of developmental disorder is congenital cortical blindness. First, there is a deficit which cannot be made good; second, development ensures that there is growth and learning in all unaffected areas; and third, there is adaptation to the deficit,

* Previously published in *The Psychologist, Bulletin of the Bristish Psychological Society*, **5** (January 1992), pp. 13–19.

much of which can be supplied by the environment in the form of special tools and compensatory education.

By studying the effect of abnormality on development we can get a glimpse into the inner workings of this deeply hidden process. By studying the effect of development on abnormality we can find out more about the nature of mental impairment. In normal development everything goes together with everything else; learning to walk goes together with learning to think, to socialise and to communicate; it also goes together with physical growth. Development is under some powerful central control and takes its inexorable course regardless of attempts to help or hinder it along its way. In this pattern of global change the existence of separate components can only be guessed at. There are, however, enough indications that the seemingly impenetrable monolith of the mind contains different elements that merely wait to be discovered.

Could it be that some of these buried elements are so independent as to be subserved by independent brain systems, with their own pathways and their own purpose-made neurotransmitters? Could there be brain damage of a type that only affects a single specialist system? What effect would such damage have on the mind and its development?

The two examples of developmental disorders that I have studied, autism and dyslexia, are each cases of biologically caused syndromes arising from some subtle brain abnormality, occurring probably well before birth. Of course, these disorders are very different from each other, with different causes and effects, autism being by far the more severe. However, in each case a wide range of characteristic behavioural phenomena can be derived from a unique and particular cognitive deficit.

For a long time anatomical evidence for brain abnormalities in autism and dyslexia did not exist and consequently biology tended to be ignored in psychological accounts. Now such evidence does exist, but further technological advances, such as brain imaging processes, will be necessary in order to identify exactly what damage in what brain system at what point in development causes these disorders. We are therefore still in a position to have to make assumptions about their biological basis. Would it be wise to reserve judgement and to allow for the possibility of purely social-environmental causes? Not necessarily, since such "caution" has dangerous consequences, influencing as it must, ideas on prevention and treatment. Simply because we do not yet know the precise brain dysfunction responsible does not mean that we should ignore biology.

The general model shown in figure 37.1 suggests possible links between biological causes and behavioural manifestations of a disorder. Clearly, we cannot jump straight from brain to behaviour in one leap. We need a bridging level. This level is the domain of cognitive processes. They are what lies in between biological and behavioural phenomena. (I should note here that this definition of cognitive processes does away with the old contrast between 'cognitive' and 'affective'. Feelings, i.e. mental states that can be inferred from behaviour and linked to physiological states, are prime examples of cognitive processes.)

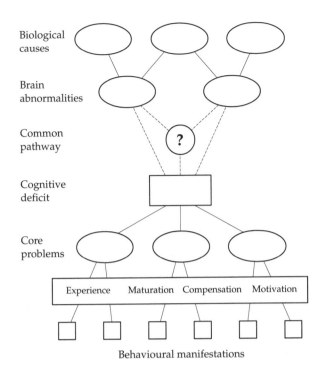

Biological causes

Brain abnormalities

Common pathway

?

Cognitive deficit

Core problems

Experience   Maturation   Compensation   Motivation

Behavioural manifestations

FIGURE 37.1   Developmental disorders: model

In figure 37.1 the disorder in question is defined by the lack of a single component at the cognitive level. At the biological level the origin of the disorder is left open as being due to any one of several causes. The disorder is therefore not identified by a unique etiology. It is possible that each of the causes affects the development of one and the same brain system. In this case, we can speak of a common pathway, in the brain, which would be a good way of defining the disorder. If this could be done, we would have a real link between mind and brain.

In what way can the cognitive level define the disorder? Why not the behavioural level, which at least has the advantage of being in the realm of the directly observable? There is a reason: Behaviour is ever changing and almost infinitely variable. Behavioural symptoms of one and the same underlying problem vary and change with development. In fact this is the basic lesson from the developmental approach to developmental disorders.

Of course, we must use behaviour as our observable basis. However, diagnosis of the disorder is only *guided* by behavioural symptoms, guided towards the hypothesis of a particular underlying problem. This diagnostic hypothesis then has to be tested in the usual way by making specific predictions. The behaviour in question may well appear to shade seamlessly from normal to abnormal, but, if we have a cognitive theory, we can find sharp cuts in this apparent continuum. Superficially similar behaviours may then fall into separate categories. For example, reading words and non-words may well appear to be much the same sort of thing, and so might acts of sabotage and of deception. As we shall see later, in each case, a clean cut can be made between them.

Another consequence of the developmental approach is that one has to take into account the effects of such factors as experience, instruction, social support, maturation and compensation. If all these factors are favourable then development means increasing adaptation, and often dramatic improvement in performance. If they are unfavourable then the expected improvements with age will be disappointing or even absent. In some cases of delayed development catching up is possible, but in others, delay can be very damaging. Likewise, precocious development is not necessarily something to be pleased about. In the end it may well be that the child who walked late will win the race.

Children with severe and obvious mental impairment from birth are studied by few researchers. Yet they hold the key to the problem of how brain abnormality affects the development of the mind. These children are the unfortunate victims of brain damage so pervasive and so early in life that all aspects of their mind and the whole of their development are blighted. The consequences for mental and physical functions are often devastating. Yet here too we find the powerful effects of maturation, experience and, if damage is not too extensive, compensation.

Autistic children are just one subgroup of this large group of severe developmental disorders, except that for autism to result, the damage has to have affected one particular component of the brain – and hence of the mind. Over and above this component it often affects other components as well. The more extensive the damage, the less chance of compensation by drawing on general processing resources.

The cost of pervasive brain damage is a reduction in general processing capacity. It can be measured by standard IQ-tests. How can we measure the cost of specific damage? The success of this enterprise depends on finding the right comparison groups and tasks. Merely to demonstrate that there is poor performance on a particular task is not enough. We must also demonstrate that there is good performance on another task identical in every way – except that it does not involve the targeted cognitive mechanism. This describes an experimental technique of making cuts in otherwise homogeneous behaviour. It is an attempt to 'carve nature at the joints', to use Huxley's famous words. If we have a hypothesis about a specific deficit, then we can predict where the joints are.

What happens where there are behavioural impairments but where these are not due to underlying cognitive deficits? The impairments might be due to unfavourable general factors in such areas as are indicated in the lower part of figure 37.1, factors that modify behaviour on a broad front. Because they act on behaviour fairly directly and indiscriminately we would predict impairments throughout a broad range of tests. In contrast, if there was a cognitive deficit in a particular mechanism then we would expect impairments in only those behaviours that depend on this mechanism.

There are ways then of disentangling specific and general deficits. However, the danger of misdiagnosing someone as having a specific deficit when they do not, is always present, as is the danger of not diagnosing such a deficit when it in fact exists.

For 'carving nature at the joints' you need a theory about the underlying bone structure. When testing for a cognitive deficit you certainly need to adopt a theory. I am delighted to quote here authorities as diverse as Charles Darwin and Agatha Christie, who each advocated that observation must be guided by theory. In *The Sittaford Mystery* the young heroine has just presented her theory to her boyfriend:

> 'It's awfully ingenious' said Charles, 'but I don't believe for a minute it's true.' 'We'll assume that it is true', said Emily firmly. 'I am sure that in the detection of crime you mustn't be afraid to assume things.'

I quote this little scene because I find it very encouraging. The detection of crime and the detection of cognitive deficits (which are, so-to-speak, crimes of nature) are much the same. The encouraging part is that Emily was completely wrong in her assumptions, but if she had not made them, no progress in the investigation would have been made.

I shall now turn to the example of dyslexia, as illustrated in figure 37.2. One hypothesis about the underlying cognitive deficit in dyslexia is that there is a problem with phonological analysis of speech sounds. This hypothesis rests on

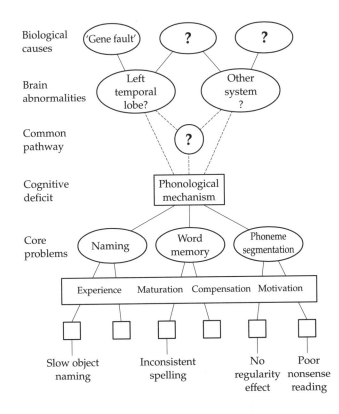

FIGURE 37.2 Dyslexia: model

the convergence of a large body of work carried out in several different centres. The assumption of a phonological deficit leading to classic developmental dyslexia does not rule out that there may be other types of deficit leading to other types of dyslexia, for instance, a deficit in the visual system.

In figure 37.2 we can see that there are various suggestions for affected brain functions in dyslexia. Any of these would lead to the specific cognitive deficit proposed. In turn, this deficit would lead to three putative core problems in naming, short-term memory and phoneme segmentation. It is important to note that these problems are not directly concerned with reading and writing, though learning to read and write in an alphabetic script depends on phoneme segmentation ability.

From the hypothesised cognitive deficit certain predictions can be made. One prediction is that dyslexic readers would be very poor at non-word reading, but not necessarily at word reading. Words, as long as they are familiar and have been memorised as visual patterns, can be recognised by visual means. But non-words which are seen for the first time have to be decoded into speech sounds. The acquisition of decoding skills depends on phoneme segmentation skills, and should therefore be hampered in dyslexics.

The most relevant comparison group for dyslexic children turned out to be younger, normally reading children who had achieved a similar level of expertise with word recognition. Maggie Snowling and I predicted that our young dyslexic readers, despite maturation, experience and motivation (which had allowed them to reach a Reading Age of 8 to 10 years at the chronological age of 10 to 12) would not have acquired the facility in alphabetic skills that is essential for the fast letter-to-sound decoding of novel words.

Our prediction was confirmed (see figure 37.3). A cut could be found. What might have been thought of as a fairly homogeneous group of behaviours, namely reading words that merely vary in terms of their familiarity, revealed a sharp divide. Furthermore, we can see that in the case of normal readers there was a small but noticeable difference in the ease with which they read regular and irregular words, but no such difference was shown by the dyslexics. For them it did not seem to matter whether a word would be called regular or

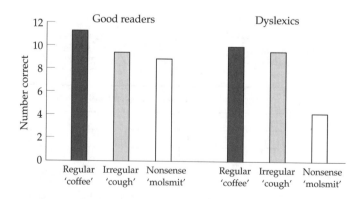

FIGURE 37.3 Reading words and non-words in normal and dyslexic children (based on Frith and Snowling, 1983)

irregular. Of course, it only matters if you are concerned with letter-to-sound translation. If you are not, then the very concept of regular spelling must seem odd. For the dyslexic all spellings are peculiar, including those which can be produced by regular alphabetic principles.

It is not the case, however, that dyslexic children do not acquire *any* skill with alphabetic material. Very often they do – though sometimes by near superhuman effort. More than other developmental disorders dyslexia is marked by high degrees of compensation. Surface behaviour in the older and well motivated dyslexic child can be extremely deceptive. Such a child can be a good reader having acquired a large sight vocabulary and a hard-won measure of alphabetic skills.

We could also make the prediction that dyslexics make many spelling errors that do not follow phonetic principles, but arise instead from less than perfect visual memory images. Dyslexics should show differences in this respect from children who are not very good at spelling for other reasons and who are not suffering from a phonological deficit.

Figure 37.4 presents a comparison of poor spellers and dyslexics, showing that the groups can be differentiated in just this way. They made the same number of errors, but we can see a cut. In non-dyslexic poor spellers (just as in good spellers) errors which result in a form that is phonetically plausible were much more frequent than those that do not. The dyslexics, who were hypothesised to have specific problems with phonological analysis and hence poor alphabetic skills, made fewer phonetically plausible errors. In fact their errors could equally often be put into one as into another category of spelling errors. In this case the category 'phonetically plausible' may be misleading, as near-misses of visually remembered spellings have a high chance of being phonetically close to the target word in any case.

If the general model is correct then the prediction is that dyslexics should have problems with naming and short-term memory as well as with the

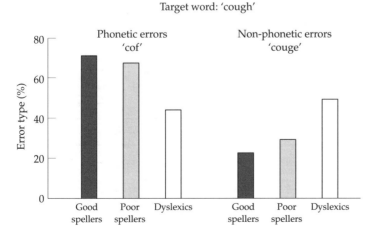

FIGURE 37.4   Types of spelling errors made by 12-year-olds (based on Frith, 1980)

manipulation and segmentation of phonemes. There is no picking and choosing: if they have a specific deficit, then they cannot be impaired on just one or other of the abilities that depend on the underlying cognitive mechanism. Of course, task performance may not always reflect the deficit since there is compensation and, of course, any particular performance impairment can also be shown for reasons other than an underlying cognitive deficit. It might be shown, for instance, as due to inadequate teaching, or a lack of motivation to perform. Here it is important to recall that the definition of dyslexia, as a syndrome, is at the cognitive level and not at the behavioural level. The existence of reading and writing difficulties need not necessarily signal dyslexia. In cases where we do not find the predicted cuts between hypothesised intact and impaired abilities we reject the hypothesis of a specific deficit. We may diagnose a more general problem instead.

It seemed straightforward to identify a specific cognitive deficit for dyslexia, which after all is famous for being a specific disability. In fact, it has proved extremely difficult to pin down the deficit, and it is still far from clear how to conceptualise the phonological mechanism in question. It is also not yet clear what we should regard as the core symptoms of the syndrome.

In the case of autism, the task of identifying a specific cognitive deficit appeared, initially, extraordinarily difficult. Far from the expectation that there would be a single specific deficit to account for the complex pattern of

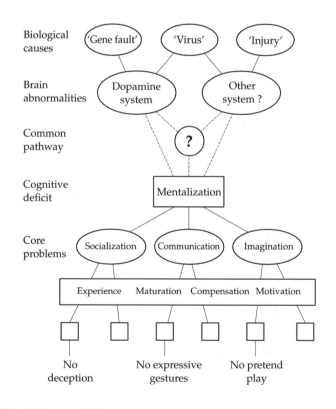

FIGURE 37.5   Autism: model

symptoms, there was the strong possibility that autism was a typical example of multiple deficits. Indeed, the most widely used diagnostic descriptions classify autism as a pervasive developmental disorder rather than as a specific disorder. However, it is in the case of autism that the search for a cognitive deficit has been most successful, as illustrated in figure 37.5.

The core symptoms of autism have been well established by epidemiological and follow-up studies. They form a triad of impairments in socialisation, communication and imagination which persist throughout life. The behavioural manifestation of these impairments is modified by development to such an extent that we find a highly variable picture. Thus there is no definitive set of behaviours that would once and for all serve as markers for autism at any point in time. Likewise, there are as yet no biological markers. However, we can explain the triad of impairments by the hypothesis of a single cognitive deficit. This theory was worked out and tested at the MRC Cognitive Development Unit with the collaboration of Tony Attwood, Simon Baron-Cohen, Francesca Happe, Sue Leekam, Alan Leslie, John Morton, Josef Perner, Amitta Shah, Fran Siddons, Beate Sodian, and Laila Thaiss.

The deficit concerns a mental component that has to do with representing mind itself. This component is responsible for an ability that we termed mentalising. It is also responsible for what has been called an everyday theory of mind, or folk psychology. By this is meant our normal human tendency to attribute systematically and productively thoughts, beliefs and feelings to people. The existence of folk psychology shows how intensely aware we are of having thoughts and of other people having different thoughts. The deficit we postulate implies that autistic individuals lack this awareness.

In order for this explanation to work it is again necessary to show failure and success in tasks that are only distinguished by whether or not they involve the critical cognitive capacity: mentalising. It is also important to make sure that autistic children have all the prerequisites necessary for understanding the tasks, including language competence, ability to remember the relevant events, interest in the task, and motivation to perform well. The research technique is again one of trying to show cuts between components of cognitive processing that otherwise seem to belong to one apparently monolithic entity.

I will here refer to just three examples where the nature of the cognitive deficit is revealed by this technique. Figure 37.6 shows the results of an observational study where we found that autistic subjects, in contrast to Down's syndrome adolescents and young normal four-year-olds, did not use expressive gestures which are designed to manipulate mental states. Nevertheless, they freely used instrumental gestures which are designed to manipulate physical behaviour.

Figure 37.7 shows that autistic children of relatively high ability perform well when asked to place pictures in a sequence so as to make a 'story' when the 'story' in question can be understood as a sequence of actions (figure 37.8), but perform poorly when the story critically involves mentalising, i.e. taking into account the protagonist's mental state, in this case ignorance: 'The boy doesn't know there is a hole in the bag' (figure 37.9). Again the contrast with Down's syndrome children is as great as that with five-year-olds.

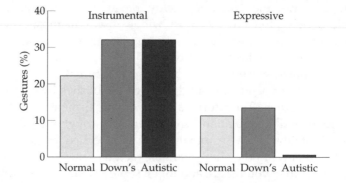

FIGURE 37.6 Gestures in social interactions in autistic subjects and controls (based on Attwood, Frith and Hermelin, 1988)

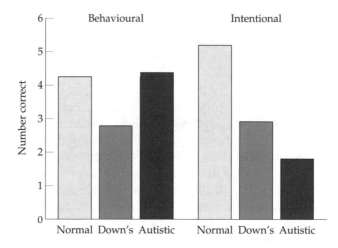

FIGURE 37.7 Sequencing performance in autistic subjects and controls (based on Baron-Cohen, Leslie and Frith, 1986)

FIGURE 37.8 Example of "behavioural" sequence (based on Baron-Cohen, Leslie and Frith, 1986)

FIGURE 37.9   Example of sequence involving "mentalising" (based on Baron-Cohen, Leslie and Frith, 1986)

Figure 37.10 shows that autistic children of a wide range of ability and age were successful when they could use a padlock to physically prevent a baddie from getting a reward (figure 37.11), but failed when, in the absence of a padlock, they had to manipulate the baddie's belief by telling him, falsely, that the box was locked (figure 37.12). As before, this was in marked contrast to controls.

The results never show a total failure in the autistic group (aged between 5 and 20 years), nor a 100 per cent success in the control groups (non-autistic mentally handicapped children of similar age, and normal children aged 3 to 5 years). This is because of the direct influence on test performance of such general modifying factors as experience, motivation and compensation. We must remember that each test is only a remote probe to the cognitive capacity that it is designed to assess. We are measuring performance at the behavioural level, but we cannot measure directly the underlying ability at the cognitive level.

Autistic people who succeed on some mentalising tasks demonstrate how experience and compensation may camouflage a deficit. We do not yet know,

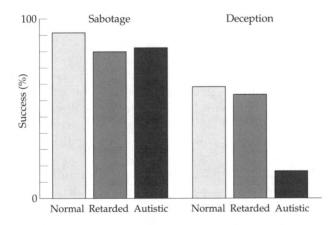

FIGURE 37.10   Sabotage and deception in autistic subjects and controls (based on Sodian and Frith, in press)

FIGURE 37.11 Example of sabotage task (based on Sodian and Frith, in press)

but are currently investigating, whether in these cases the deficit is still there, whether its manifestation is modified by favourable factors, or whether there is a mild form of the deficit.

The general implication of the studies is that the monolith of the mind can indeed be broken up. The study of abnormal development allows us to discover specific components that have long been hidden. Theories about different components of the mind guide us to discover the cuts in the otherwise smooth continuum of behaviour. Without a cognitive theory every behaviour shades into every other. Individual differences in behaviour of a perfectly normal kind merge smoothly with variable behavioural signs that are due to cognitive deficits.

We can find normal children who make as many or more spelling mistakes as children suffering from a specific phonological deficit leading to poor alphabet skills. We can find normal individuals who find it so difficult to engage in reciprocal affectionate relationships that they compare unfavourably with some autistic people who have an earnest desire to make friends. With a cognitive theory the differences can be uncovered and the underlying

FIGURE 37.12   Example of deception task (based on Sodian and Frith, in press)

discontinuities can be revealed. The sources of the discontinuities are at the cognitive level. This is why the definition of the biologically based syndromes of autism and dyslexia is properly placed at the cognitive rather than the behavioural level. For progress in biological investigations we still have to wait. However, for the cognitive explanation it does not matter how many different biological causes will be found.

Of course, besides dyslexia and autism there are other developmental disorders that are due to specific cognitive deficits, for instance language impairments and motor coordination disorders. There are also many disorders of behaviour in childhood that are not biologically caused and that are not due to specific deficits.

We started off with the metaphor of blindness for specific and congenital developmental deficits. Dyslexia can be seen as word-blindness and autism as mind-blindness. The metaphor is helpful as a means of thinking about the education and management of children suffering from a disorder. Clearly, it would be foolish to make a blind person embark on a programme of eye exercises, but it would be wise to remove dangerous objects from their vicinity.

People can be made mindful of the needs of the blind person, and the physical environment can be adapted so as to be safe for someone who cannot see. Exactly the same applies to people with word-blindness or mind-blindness.

Is it unkind to speak of a 'deficit' in the mind? Is it kind to treat a handicapped person as if they were fit and healthy? To me it is a very false idea of kindness not to acknowledge that someone, through no fault but nature's, suffers from a biological disorder. Surely, to recognise that some people have a disorder means to recognise that they have a right to an allowance being made for their handicap. This is at least a first step towards a kinder treatment.

It is not kind to pretend that people are not blind when in fact they are. Nor is it kind to push people if there is little spare capacity. Compensation is a costly process. When mental resources have to be marshalled where they are sparse, then one should think twice about insisting that they are used. There are some remarkably optimistic implications from the concept of cognitive deficits in developmental disorders. Once the deficit has been recognised – it can be left alone. Compensation and diversion into other fields are often possible – but not always necessary. Rather than demanding of handicapped children that they make continuous efforts, we should learn to recognise their often heroic struggle. We can respect the difference.

Acknowledgements

Figures 37.8, 37.9, 37.10, 37.11 and 37.12 are reprinted with kind permission from Axel Scheffler. Figure 37.8 is reprinted from Frith, U., *Autism: Explaining the Enigma*, Oxford: Blackwell, 1989. Figures 37.11 and 37.12 are from Sodian, B., and Frith, U., *Journal of Child Psychology and Psychiatry*, vol. **33** (in press), Pergamon Press.

References

Attwood, A., Frith, U., and Hermelin, B. (1988). The understanding and use of interpersonal gestures by autistic and Down's syndrome children. *Journal of Autism and Developmental Disorders*. **18**, 2, 241–57.

Baron-Cohen, S., Leslie, A. M., and Frith, U. (1986). Mechanical, behavioural and intentional understanding of picture stories in autistic children. *British Journal of Developmental Psychology*, **4**, 113–25.

Frith, U., and Snowling, M. (1983). Reading for meaning and reading for sound in autistic and dyslexic children. *British Journal of Developmental Psychology*, **1**, 329–42.

Frith, U. (1980). Unexpected spelling problems. In U. Frith (ed.), *Cognitive Processing in Spelling*, London: Academic Press.

Sodian, B., and Frith, U. (in press). Deception and sabotage in autistic, retarded and normal children. *Journal of Child Psychology and Psychiatry*.

38

HEAD START: CRITICISMS IN A CONSTRUCTIVE CONTEXT*

Edward Zigler and Sally J. Styfco

EDITORS' INTRODUCTION

Project Head Start began in the 1960s during the Johnson administration's War on Poverty, and it is one of America's favourite social programmes. Its aim is to provide education and self-help opportunities to enable economically disadvantaged preschoolers to improve their lives, and to break what might otherwise be an inevitable cycle of deprivation as disadvantage passes from one generation to the next. Zigler and Styfco consider recent attacks on Head Start, and provide a fair judgement of Head Start's value. In his first Congressional address President Clinton described the programme as a sound social investment deserving of additional support. Zigler and Styfco argue that Head Start is an evolving concept, and 'In the hands of the Clinton Administration, this evolution will continue so that Head Start can again be "the nation's pride".'

OVERVIEW

Recent criticisms of Head Start have arisen as a result of unrealistic expectations; loosely generalized evidence; and misunderstood, incomplete research. But they have forced advocates to focus on administrative problems that make Head Start less effective than it could be. This healthy climate of critical discussion has led to plans to improve program services and to proceed with expansion in a more thoughtful manner. The debate has sparked further ideas to optimize the Head Start approach and make the program more responsive to the needs of children and families in poverty.

Project Head Start has enjoyed unprecedented popularity in recent years. The preschool program has earned rare bipartisan support among the nation's

* Previously published in *American Psychologist*, **49**, 2 (February 1994), pp. 127–32.

lawmakers, who have doubled its budget in the past five years and have promised "full funding" so that all eligible children can attend. The reasons for this political favor are economic: Head Start has come to be regarded as a sound investment, a cost-effective means of reducing school and social failure among children in poverty.

Just when long-held hopes for expansion turned to reality, the nation's love affair with the project began to wane. Head Start does not make children smarter, critics cried, and any benefits it does have fade away soon after children begin school. What had been called America's favorite social program, "the nation's pride" (National Head Start Association, 1990), was now derided as a "scam," a national boondoggle that was wasting precious tax dollars (Hood, 1992).

The brash attacks from those opposed to Head Start on ideological grounds were probably to be expected. What was surprising, however, was that Head Start's friends began to join in the fault finding. Problems with quality – long recognized and already being addressed through legislation – were suddenly highlighted. Head Start teachers were not adequately trained or paid. Parents were not as involved as they should be. Families were not receiving the support services they needed. Perhaps the strongest blows came from the Office of the Inspector General (1993a, 1993b), which reported that health services – widely regarded as Head Start's most successful feature – were not being delivered to all participants and that some grantees could not even spend all their new expansion funds.

Although there is merit to the criticisms, there is also good reason why Head Start has so many supporters. The project has served over 13 million children and their families since 1965, and most of them do not understand the controversy over their warm memories. Counted among Head Start's friends are President Clinton and Donna Shalala, Secretary of Health and Human Services, both of whom have offered assurances that the nation is not about to give up on Project Head Start. Believing the program to be fundamentally sound and worthy of expansion, they have promised to study its problems and support quality improvement efforts as well as better planning for growth. Secretary Shalala has appointed the Advisory Committee on Head Start Quality and Expansion to make recommendations on both counts. The group probably would not have convened without the current wave of public criticism – which has thus already done some good.

The purpose of this article is to analyze the criticisms about Head Start constructively. We will look at the problems associated with unrealistic expectations, inadequate and misunderstood research, deteriorating quality, and rapid growth. Head Start now has the opportunity to address these difficulties and become stronger as it grows.

WHAT CAN HEAD START ACCOMPLISH?

Before a fair judgment of Head Start's value can be made, Americans must decide what they want from their Head Start program. Do we really want to believe that a year or two of early intervention can guarantee a high school diploma or end poverty and crime? If so, our hopes are too high, and the project's actual results will seem disappointing.

Overoptimism about the potential of Head Start began before the first centers opened their doors. The nation had declared a War on Poverty, fully expecting to conquer this enemy by arming its victims with education and self-help opportunities. Although most antipoverty programs developed under the Equal Opportunity Act of 1964 targeted poor adults, Head Start was designed to enhance school readiness among their children. (For a history of the program, see Zigler and Muenchow, 1992, and Zigler and Valentine, 1979.)

The project was developed by a planning committee of 14 professionals in medicine, early education, and mental health. Their recommendations, presented in February 1965, were also extremely optimistic considering that the project was to be a six-or eight-week summer program for children about to enter school. The planning document embraced a "whole child" philosophy that called for comprehensive programming: Head Start's goals would be to improve physical health, enhance "mental processes" (particularly conceptual and verbal skills), and foster social and emotional development, self-confidence, relationships with family and others, social responsibility, and a sense of dignity and self-worth for both the child and family.

School readiness

Despite the broad range of goals the planners wrote for Head Start, early evaluations focused almost exclusively on changes in children's IQ test scores. At the time, a popular view within developmental psychology was that intelligence could be raised dramatically by brief environmental enrichment. On a practical level, tests of intelligence had already been developed and were relatively easy to administer. On the other hand, some concepts such as social competence and parental empowerment that were part of Head Start's agenda had no accepted definitions or assessment tools. (See Zigler and Trickett, 1978, for a discussion of IQ, social competence, and evaluation of early intervention.)

The fixation on intellectual effects was fed by early studies showing that children's IQ scores soared by at least 10 points and their achievement levels rose after just a few weeks of Head Start. Then researchers at Ohio University and the Westinghouse Learning Corporation reported that the achievement gains faded away after children began school (Cicirelli, 1969). Although there were serious methodological problems with the Westinghouse evaluation, subsequent studies of Head Start and other early intervention programs reached the same conclusion: Preschool graduates generally show immediate gains in intelligence and achievement test scores, but these benefits do not appear to be permanent (Consortium for Longitudinal Studies, 1983; Haskins, 1989; McKey et al., 1985; Woodhead, 1988).

Regardless of whether or not Head Start graduates continue to achieve well, the point is that they are achieving better when they leave the program. Head Start prepares children for school. This is a realistic objective and is consistent with the national education goal that all children be ready to learn when they begin elementary school. But readiness to learn carries the expectation that they *will* learn and have successful educational careers. Can the benefits of preschool last forever? This question is at the heart of the debate over Head Start's value.

Can early intervention have lifetime effects?

The 1960s dream of creating the Great Society has long been abandoned. Yet the hope that Head Start could change lives still lingers – partly because of its origins and partly because of the highly publicized results of the Perry Preschool Program – a program with few resemblances to Head Start.

The Perry Preschool Program (Berrueta-Clement, Schweinhart, Barnett, Epstein, and Weikart, 1984), conducted by researchers at the High/Scope Educational Research Foundation, involved 58 children who participated for one or two years during the 1960s. Like most enrichment programs before Head Start, the focus was on preschool education, although there was a home visitation component to enable parents to reinforce the curriculum at home. Also like most other programs, evaluations revealed no drastic, permanent increases in IQ or achievement test scores. Unique in the field, however, were the comprehensive, long-term assessments undertaken by the investigators. The Perry graduates have now been followed through age 27 for their status on indices as wide-ranging as criminality, family structure, and career success (Schweinhart, Barnes, and Weikart, 1993).

Another first in the Perry project was a cost–benefit analysis. The researchers estimated the savings to society resulting from better social competence among Perry graduates, including reduced grade retention, welfare usage, and crime, and increased school completion and employment rates. They reported that for every dollar spent on the preschool program, taxpayers saved $3 to $6 by age 19 (Barnett, 1985) and $7 by age 27 (Schweinhart et al., 1993).

The Perry results have never been replicated because no other program has been subjected to such extensive evaluation. The longitudinal data that do exist are nonetheless encouraging. One rigorous investigation was conducted by the Consortium for Longitudinal Studies (1983), a group of researchers who retested children who had attended 11 preschool programs (2 of them Head Start) during the 1960s and early 1970s. The results showed benefits that persisted until many children had reached 12 or more years of age: They were less likely to be assigned to special education classes and were somewhat less likely to be retained in grade. Similar findings were revealed in the Head Start Synthesis Project, a meta-analysis and review of over 200 studies specific to Head Start. Program graduates were also found to have better health, immunization rates, and nutrition, as well as enhanced socioemotional characteristics (McKey et al., 1985). A study of thousands of sixth through eighth graders who had attended Head Start in 33 programs throughout Philadelphia showed that they had better school adjustment than did peers who had no preschool (Copple, Cline, and Smith, 1987). In another study of three waves of Head Start graduates (over 1,900 children in all) who were at the end of high school, the oldest cohort performed better academically than did control subjects (Hebbeler, 1985).

Although much of this research has technical problems that make the findings tentative, the results are all in the same direction: Head Start enhances school readiness and may have enduring effects on aspects of social competence. Do these benefits justify expansion and the costs that will be involved? The answer hinges on the response to our earlier question about what Americans expect from their Head Start program.

The evidence – disappointing to some – is that early intervention cannot guarantee success in life. As positive as the Perry results were, for example, over 30% of the preschool graduates had been arrested at least once by the time they were young adults, and one-third dropped out of high school. By age 27, 59% had required some type of social services in the past decade. In Hebbeler's (1985) study, the academic performance of one Head Start group was superior to that of control subjects but was far below that of the middle- and upper-class students with whom they attended school. Similarly, students who attended the Chicago Child–Parent Centers, a program with many resemblances to Head Start, had better high school graduation rates than did others in the school system but still did not approach national norms (Fuerst and Fuerst, 1993).

The empirical literature thus delivers good news and bad news. The bad news is that neither Head Start nor any preschool program can inoculate children against the ravages of poverty. Early intervention simply cannot overpower the effects of poor living conditions, inadequate nutrition and health care, negative role models, and substandard schools. But good programs can prepare children for school and possibly help them develop better coping and adaptation skills that will enable better life outcomes, albeit not perfect ones. The current disillusion with Head Start stems from overselling its benefits, but the evidence gives real reason not to undersell them.

GAPS IN EXISTING RESEARCH

Head Start is probably the most extensively evaluated social program in American history, but most of this work was conducted when the concept was new and hopes were high. During the 1980s federal support of program research waned. Research, evaluation, and demonstration efforts consumed 2.5% of Head Start's budget in 1974 but declined to 0.11% by 1989 (National Head Start Association, 1990). The Advisory Panel for the Head Start Evaluation Design Project (1990) lamented the lack of an organized database on Head Start, particularly concerning which program features work best and for whom.

The need for empirical guidance is acute not only to inform program improvements but because the population served by Head Start has changed over time. The environments in which poor children are raised now involve more homelessness, street violence, illegal drugs, and young, single-parent families. The number of dysfunctional families has soared. A program that was state-of-the-art in the 1960s could not be expected to meet the needs of today's economically disadvantaged families.

Another reason for more extensive study is to quiet the critics: The exciting benefits of the Perry Preschool have led many to believe that, because there are no parallel data for Head Start, the project has no benefits. This is certainly not the case; but empirical proof, although positive, is far from overwhelming. If an evaluation parallel to that of High/Scope was conducted for graduates of quality Head Start programs, the national project might be found to be more beneficial than the Perry program because of its more comprehensive services.

Testing this supposition should not be difficult. Yet, despite the voluminous research on Head Start, little work has been done to illuminate the range of its effects. Head Start programs are required to have six components: preschool education, health screening and referral, mental health services, nutrition education and hot meals, social services for the child and family, and parent involvement. Yet evaluators have focused almost exclusively on the preschool education component and its effects on intelligence and achievement. Possible benefits to physical health, nutritional status, social behavior, parents' child-rearing abilities, family functioning, parental empowerment, and community development have been underevaluated and undervalued.

The area in which Head Start has undoubtedly had its strongest impact is in physical health, and this benefit will magnify now that the project is authorized to deliver health services to participants' siblings. Program performance standards require that all enrolled children receive medical screenings, immunizations, dental exams, and corrective treatment if needed. A high percentage of them do. Although the Office of the Inspector General (1993a) reported that only 43.5% of participants were fully immunized according to program guidelines, the number increased to 84% when commonly accepted standards of medical practice were applied. Independent confirmation comes from a review by Zigler, Piotrkowski, and Collins (in press), who found 88% full immunization using the same standards. Head Start is also becoming a major provider of early diagnostic and screening services required for children covered under Medicaid, and it delivers many of the services to handicapped preschoolers and their families mandated under the Individuals with Disabilities Education Act. Additional health benefits derive from the nutritious meals and snacks served at each center and the nutrition counseling provided to many participating parents.

Head Start's effect on families is another outcome that has not received deserved attention. In 1991–92, 94% of families in need of supportive services received them (Brush, Gaidurgis, and Best, 1993). Each year thousands of low-income parents obtain jobs and training through Head Start. Over 35% of the staff are parents of enrolled children or graduates, and many have earned Child Development Associate credentials and have entered careers in early childhood care and education (Collins, 1990). Parents have also reported improved relationships with their children (National Head Start Association, 1990) and greater life satisfaction and psychological well-being resulting from the program's supportive social network (Parker, Piotrkowski, and Peay, 1987).

A few studies have shown that the presence of a Head Start program enhances a community's capacity to meet local needs (see McKey et al.,

1985). In one survey, almost 1,500 institutional changes in the educational and health systems were identified in 48 communities that housed Head Start centers (Kirschner Associates, 1970). A more recent General Accounting Office (1992) report praised Head Start's methods of linking families with local services, judging this approach far more successful than efforts to create new services or delivery mechanisms.

Head Start's contributions to the fields of early childhood education and intervention have also been substantial. Prior to Head Start, preschool programs were child-centered and focused on academic readiness skills. Head Start's two-generation, multidisciplinary approach spurred the development of more sophisticated theories and effective practices. The project has served as a national laboratory for the design and evaluation of new methods of intervention (see Valentine, 1979). It has experimented with services in home-based programs, child care settings, and schools – many of which have benefited children of all socioeconomic groups. Head Start also pioneered the nation's family support movement (Zigler and Freedman, 1987).

There are many other ways Head Start might benefit children and families that remain unexplored. We do not know if there is an influence on future delinquency or welfare rates. One study showed that after at least sixth grade, Head Start graduates had better school attendance records (Copple et al., 1987), which suggests that they might have fewer discipline problems. (See Yoshikawa, 1994, and Zigler, Taussig, and Black, 1992, for discussion of the evidence linking early intervention with reduced delinquency.) Another possible effect is that siblings benefit from their parents' involvement in Head Start and the family support they receive, as has been found in studies of other programs (reviewed by Seitz and Apfel, in press). If so, Head Start's impact is much broader than has been suggested by the research, nearly all of which has been limited to participating children.

FIXING HEAD START

Three decades of experience with early intervention have proved the obvious: Only good programs produce good results. Zigler warned the US Senate (1990) that "Head Start is effective only when quality is high.... Below a certain threshold of quality, the program is useless" (p. 49). When poorly implemented, it is also a false promise to the children and families who enroll.

Head Start program performance standards, implemented in 1975, dictate what services each program must provide, and they are the principal vehicle for monitoring quality. The standards are enforced through annual self-report data required of each grantee and on-site inspections, which are supposed to be conducted every three years. However, staffing for program oversight has declined drastically over the years, although Head Start has become larger. Nationally, only one in five centers was monitored in 1988 (Chafel, 1992). This improved to 35% in 1992 (Horn, 1993), another indication of the positive results criticism can bring. Often these visits cannot be conducted because travel money has all but disappeared from regional office budgets. Funds for training and technical assistance to help programs correct problems and update their methodology have also declined.

Years of inadequate funding have also taken a toll on services delivery. During the 1980s, the average expenditure per child fell in both real and inflation-adjusted dollars (Rovner, 1990), straining the ability of local centers to provide all the program components in the manner intended. For example, many programs have no coordinators for health, parental involvement, or family support, and these positions are often combined with others (National Head Start Association, 1990). In 1991–92, social service staff had caseloads higher than 94 children, nearly triple that recommended (Office of the Inspector General, 1993a). A common response to the complaint that children are not receiving required medical services is that they are receiving care, but overworked administrators do not have time to do the record keeping.

Preschool education, never universally strong in Head Start, was further threatened by an inability to pay teachers competitive wages. Today even the most experienced teachers receive only about $15,000. It is no wonder that fewer than half of Head Start teachers have college degrees. These facts are significant because caregiver training and stability have been identified as essential to quality care and directly responsible for positive developmental outcomes in children (Whitebook, Howes, and Phillips, 1989). Low wages can lead to high turnover, but attrition in Head Start is considerably lower than that in other early care and education programs (Collins, 1990; Kisker, Hofferth, Phillips, and Farquhar, 1991). Only 31% of Head Start centers experience any turnover, but their rate is a shocking 64% (Kisker et al., 1991).

Rapid expansion has created its own set of problems. Between FYs 1992 and 1993 alone, projections were to add 5,000 classrooms and 100,000 children (Administration on Children, Youth and Families, 1993). The Office of the Inspector General's report (1993b) and discussions with program directors have highlighted Head Start's growing pains. Some centers have not had enough time to recruit the additional children they are supposed to enroll. A widespread problem is the inability to find qualified staff because they are not available or will not work for the low pay offered. Space is a major problem, with some centers having to operate with double sessions because new classrooms cannot be located and prepared quickly. Long-awaited expansion is now so sudden that it is proceeding without a plan.

Over the years Head Start's quality problems have not gone unnoticed. Two major advisory committees, convened on the project's 15th and 25th anniversaries, stressed many of the problems just discussed and made recommendations for corrective action (US Department of Health and Human Services, 1980, and National Head Start Association, respectively). Other analyses have likewise concluded that upgrading quality must be a top priority (e.g., Chafel, 1992; Washington and Oyemade, 1987; Zigler, Styfco, and Gilman, 1993).

This advice went largely unheeded until expansion began in earnest with the Human Services Reauthorization Act of 1990. The Act specifies that after inflation, 25% of expansion funds are to be used for quality improvements. Half of the set-aside is reserved for increased salaries and benefits. It is to be hoped that the recommendations of the Advisory Committee on Head Start

Quality and Expansion will not gather dust so long before policymakers enact more detailed plans to strengthen services and to pace growth in the number of grantees and participants.

DIVERSIFYING HEAD START

Expansion and quality improvement are priority areas for Head Start at this time, but we have learned that the highest-quality preschool experience can never be potent enough to last a lifetime. For optimal developmental outcomes, children must have their needs met throughout their growing years. Policymakers must begin to plan for extended services to maximize the gain on their preschool investment.

The rationale for serving younger children is clear: Waiting until a child is three or four years old is waiting too long. Preventive services are more effective than remedial ones. Children who are healthy, who have sound relationships with their primary caregivers, and who have received adequate nurturing and stimulation will have the socioemotional foundations needed for learning in preschool and beyond (Zero to Three: National Center for Clinical Infant Programs, 1992).

Head Start moved in the direction of serving families and children from birth when the first Parent and Child Centers (PCCs) opened in 1967. There are now 106 PCCs providing supportive services and parent education for children up to three years of age. There are no performance standards for Head Start programs serving infants and toddlers, however, so the PCCs remain ill-defined, and their overall effectiveness is unknown.

The Clinton Administration has expressed interest in plans to design a zero-to-three Head Start. With more public schools offering prekindergarten, very young children might become Head Start's target population in the future. To inform this program development, a multidisciplinary committee should be appointed to plan a comprehensive intervention for at-risk families beginning prenatally. To avoid the errors of its predecessor, the new program should be piloted on a small scale, evaluated, and then expanded gradually.

A common complaint about Head Start is that graduates soon lose the academic and cognitive gains they made in preschool. This criticism is more appropriately directed toward the elementary schools they attend, for this is where the preschool advantage fades. To continue the momentum toward success, there must be a smooth transition to the school environment and coordinated programming that builds on prior learning.

Project Follow Through was begun in 1967 to continue Head Start services to graduates through Grade 3, but its mission was never fulfilled (see Doernberger and Zigler, 1993). The concept survives in the Head Start Transition Project (see Kennedy, 1993), now implemented in 32 demonstration sites. Local Head Start and public school personnel work with parents to introduce each child to the new school experience. Comprehensive services, parental involvement, and family support are to be continued from kindergarten through Grade 3.

There is a small but convincing body of evidence (reviewed by Zigler and Styfco, 1993) that supports the premise of the Transition Project: Longer, coordinated intervention produces longer lasting gains. Once the models overcome the trials of implementation, it will be compelling to move the project into the educational mainstream. We have developed a plan to do so using current federal education expenditures (Zigler and Styfco, 1993). A large part of the Department of Education's budget (more than $6 billion annually) is spent on Chapter 1 of the Elementary and Secondary Education Act of 1965. Chapter 1 is a compensatory education program that over the years has shown little effectiveness (see Arroyo and Zigler, 1993). To make a difference in the education of low-income children, school officials must put aside the ineffectual educational model of Chapter 1 and adopt on a large scale the proved model of Head Start. Our proposal is for Chapter 1 to follow Transition Project plans and become the school-age version of Head Start. As Head Start expands to eventually serve all eligible children, Chapter 1 can continue their intervention in grammar school—long enough for them to get a solid footing in the long process of formal education.

Steps to extend the length of the Head Start intervention are proceeding slowly, as they should, while quality improvement is addressed. These changes are possible because Head Start is not only a program but an evolving concept (Zigler, 1976). In the hands of the Clinton Administration, this evolution will continue so that Head Start can again be "the nation's pride."

References

Administration on Children, Youth and Families, (1993, January). *Project Head Start: Statistical fact sheet.* Washington, DC: U.S. Department of Health and Human Services.

Advisory Panel for the Head Start Evaluation Design Project. (1990). *Head Start research and evaluation: A blueprint for the future.* Washington, DC: Administration for Children, Youth and Families.

Arroyo, C. G., and Zigler, E. (1993). America's Title I/Chapter 1 programs: Why the promise has not been met. In E. Zigler and S. J. Styfco (eds), *Head Start and Beyond: A National Plan for Extended Childhood Intervention* (pp. 73–95), New Haven, CT: Yale University Press.

Barnett, W. S. (1985). *The Perry Preschool Program and its long-term effects: A benefit–cost analysis* (High/Scope Early Childhood Policy Papers, No. 2). Ypsilanti, MI: High/Scope Educational Research Foundation.

Berrueta-Clement, J. R., Schweinhart, L., Barnett, W., Epstein, A., and Weikart, D. (1984). *Changed Lives: The effects of the Perry Preschool Program on youths through age 19.* Ypsilanti, MI: High/Scope Educational Research Foundation.

Brush, L., Gaidurgis, A., and Best, C. (1993). *Indices of Head Start Program Quality.* Washington, DC: Pelavin Associates.

Chafel, J. A. (1992). Funding Head Start: What are the issues? *American Journal of Orthopsychiatry,* **62**, 9–21.

Cicirelli, V. G. (1969). *The impact of Head Start: An evaluation of the effects of Head Start on children's cognitive and affective development* (Report presented to the Office of Economic Opportunity, No. PB-184-328). Washington, DC: Westinghouse Learning Corporation.

Collins, R. C. (1990). *Head Start salaries: 1989–90 staff salary survey*. Alexandria, VA: National Head Start Association.

Consortium for Longitudinal Studies (ed.), (1983). *As the Twig is Bent: Lasting Effects of Preschool Programs*. Hillsdale, NJ: Erlbaum.

Copple, C., Cline, M., and Smith, A. (1987). *Paths to the future: Long-term effects of Head Start in the Philadelphia school district*. Washington, DC: U.S. Department of Health and Human Services.

Doernberger, C., and Zigler, E. (1993). Project Follow Through: Intent and reality. In E. Zigler and S. J. Styfco (eds), *Head Start and Beyond: A National Plan for Extended Childhood Intervention* (pp. 43–72), New Haven, CT: Yale University Press.

Fuerst, J. S., and Fuerst, D. (1993). Chicago experience with an early childhood program: The special case of the Child–Parent Center program. *Urban Education*, **28**, 69–96.

General Accounting Office, (1992). *Integrating human services* (Report No. GAO/HRD-92-108). Washington, DC: Author.

Haskins, R. (1989). Beyond metaphor: The efficacy of early childhood education. *American Psychologist*, **44**, 274–82.

Hebbeler, K. (1985). An old and a new question on the effects of early education for children from low income families. *Educational Evaluation and Policy Analysis*, **7**, 207–16.

Hood, J. (1992, December). *Caveat emptor: The Head Start scam* (Policy Analysis No. 187). Washington, DC: Cato Institute.

Horn, W. F. (1993). *Administration on Children, Youth and Families: Accomplishments, FY 1989 to FY 1993*. Washington, DC: Administration on Children, Youth and Families.

Kennedy, E. M. (1993). The Head Start Transition Project: Head Start goes to elementary school. In. E. Zigler and S. J. Styfco (eds), *Head Start and Beyond: A National Plan for Extended Childhood Intervention* (pp. 97–109), New Haven, CT: Yale University Press.

Kirschner Associates. (1970). *A national survey of the impacts of Head Start centers on community institutions*. Albuquerque, NM: Author.

Kisker, E. E., Hofferth, S. L., Phillips, D. A., and Farquhar, E. (1991). *A profile of child care settings: Early care and education* (vol. 1). Washington, DC: U.S. Department of Education.

McKey, R. H., Condelli, L., Ganson, H., Barrett, B., McConkey, C., and Plantz, M. (1985). *The impact of Head Start on children, family, and communities: Final report of the Head Start Evaluation, Synthesis, and Utilization Project* (DHHS Publication No. OHDS 85-31193). Washington, DC: U.S. Government Printing Office.

National Head Start Association. (1990). *Head Start: The nation's pride, a nation's challenge* (Report of the Silver Ribbon Panel). Alexandria, VA: Author.

Office of the Inspector General. (1993a). *Evaluating Head Start expansion through performance indicators* (Report No. OEI-09-91-00762). Washington, DC: U.S. Department of Health and Human Services.

Office of the Inspector General. (1993b). *Head Start expansion: Grantee experiences* (Report No. OEI-09-91-00760). Washington, DC: U.S. Department of Health and Human Services.

Parker, F. L., Piotrkowski, C. S., and Peay, L. (1987). Head Start as a social support for mothers: The psychological benefits of involvement. *American Journal of Orthopsychiatry*, **57**, 220–33.

Rovner, J. (1990). Head Start is one program everyone wants to help. *Congressional Quarterly*, **48** (16), 1191–5.

Schweinhart, L. J., Barnes, H. V., and Weikart, D. P. (1993). *Significant benefits: The High/Scope Perry Preschool Study through age 27* (Monographs of the High/Scope Educational Research Foundation, No. 10). Ypsilanti, MI: High/Scope Press.

Seitz, V., and Apfel, N. H. (in press). Parent-focused intervention: Diffusion effects on siblings. *Child Development*.

U.S. Department of Health and Human Services. (1980). *Head Start in the 1980s: Review and Recommendations*. Washington, DC: Author.

U.S. Senate. (1990, August 3). *Human Services Reauthorization Act of 1990: Report to accompany H. R. 4151* (Report No. 101–421). Washington, DC: Author.

Valentine, J. (1979). Program development in Head Start: A multifaceted approach to meeting the needs of families and children. In E. Zigler and J. Valentine (eds), *Project Head Start: A Legacy of the War on Poverty* (pp. 349–65), New York: Free Press.

Washington, V., and Oyemade, U. (1987). *Project Head Start: Past, Present, and Future Trends in the Context of Family Needs*. New York: Garland.

Whitebook, M., Howes, C., and Phillips, D. (1989). *Who cares? Child care teachers and the quality of care in America* (Final report, National Child Care Staffing Study). Oakland, CA: Child Care Employee Project.

Woodhead, M. (1988). When psychology informs public policy: The case of early childhood intervention. *American Psychologist*, **43**, 443–54.

Yoshikawa, H. (1994). Prevention as cumulative protection: Effects of early family support and education on chronic deliquency and its risks. *Psychological Bulletin*, **115**, 28–54.

Zero to Three: National Center for Clinical Infant Programs. (1992). *Heart Start: The Emotional Foundations of School Readiness*. Arlington, VA: Author.

Zigler, E. (1976). Head Start: Not a program but an evolving concept. In J. D. Andrews (ed.), *Early Childhood Education: It's an Art? It's a Science?* (pp. 1–14), Washington, DC: National Association for the Education of Young Children.

Zigler, E., and Freedman, J. (1987). Head Start: A pioneer of family support. In S. Kagan, D. Powell, B. Weissbourd, and E. Zigler (eds), *America's Family Support Programs* (pp. 57–76), New Haven: Yale University Press.

Zigler, E., and Muenchow, S. (1992). *Head Start: The Inside Story of America's most Successful Educational Experiment*. New York: Basic Books.

Zigler, E., Piotrkowski, C., and Collins, R. (in press). Health services in Head Start. *Annual Review of Public Health*.

Zigler, E., and Styfco, S. J. (1993). Strength in unity: Consolidating federal education programs for young children. In E. Zigler and S. J. Styfco (eds), *Head Start and Beyond: A National Plan for Extended Childhood Intervention* (pp. 111–45), New Haven, CT: Yale University Press.

Zigler, E., Styfco, S. J., and Gilman, E. (1993). The national Head Start program for disadvantaged preschoolers. In E. Zigler and S. J. Styfco (eds), *Head Start and Beyond: A National Plan for Extended Childhood Intervention* (pp. 1–41), New Haven, CT: Yale University Press.

Zigler, E. F., Taussig, C., and Black, K. (1992). Early childhood intervention: A promising preventative for juvenile delinquency. *American Psychologist*, **47**, 997–1006.

Zigler, E., and Trickett, P. (1978). IQ, social competence, and evaluation of early childhood intervention programs. *American Psychologist*, **33**, 789–98.

Zigler, E., and Valentine, J. (eds). (1979). *Project Head Start: A Legacy of the War on Poverty*. New York: Free Press.

39

The Domain of Developmental Psychopathology*

L. Alan Sroufe and Michael Rutter

Sroufe and Rutter offer the proposition that individual functioning is coherent, and understandable, across periods of apparently discontinuous growth, and despite fundamental changes in manifest behaviour. The primary aim of developmental psychopathology is '*the study of the origins and course of individual patterns of behavioral maladaptation*, whatever the age of onset, whatever the causes, whatever the transformations in behavioral manifestation, and however complex the course of the developmental pattern may be' (their italics). They give examples of ways in which patterns of adaptation in childhood may be related to later disordered behaviour, with a view to developing an understanding of the processes that underlie both change and continuity in development and in patterns of adaptation.

EDITORS' INTRODUCTION

It is the "developmental" component of developmental psychopathology that distinguishes this discipline from abnormal psychology, psychiatry, and even clinical child psychology. At the same time, the focus on individual patterns of adaptation and maladaptation distinguishes this field from the larger discipline of developmental psychology. In this essay a developmental perspective is presented, and the implications of this perspective for research in developmental psychopathology are discussed. A primary consideration is the complexity of the adaptational process, with developmental transformation being the rule. Thus, links between earlier adaptation and later pathology generally will not be simple or direct. It will be necessary to understand both individual patterns of adaptation with

OVERVIEW

* Previously published in *Child Development*, **55** (1984), pp. 17–29.

respect to salient issues of a given developmental period *and* the transaction between prior adaptation, maturational change, and subsequent environmental challenges. Some examples are discussed, with special attention to the case of depression.

Understanding the origins, nature, and course of psychological disorders at various ages presents researchers with inordinately challenging problems. For decades researchers and theorists have acknowledged the complexity of predicting adult psychopathology from measures in childhood. Freud (1920/1955, pp. 167–8), in fact, concluded that such prediction was "impossible":

> So long as we trace development from its final outcome backwards, the chain of events appears continuous, and we feel we have gained an insight which is completely satisfactory or even exhaustive. But if we proceed the reverse way, if we start from the premises inferred from the analysis and try to follow these up to the final result, then we no longer get the impression of an inevitable sequence of events which could not have been otherwise determined. We notice at once that there might have been another result, and that we might have been just as well able to understand and explain the latter.... Hence the chain of causation can always be recognized with certainty if we follow the line of analysis (i.e., reconstruction), whereas to predict it...is impossible.

Kohlberg, LaCrosse, and Ricks (1972), who viewed this problem of predictability as "the single most important area of study of clinical theory and practice with children" (p. 1217), were able to conclude 5 decades later that adult disorder was, in fact, predictable from broad indicators of early maladaptation (school failures, poor peer relations, pronounced antisocial behavior). Adult status was predictable from "various forms of competence and ego maturity rather than the *absence* of problems and symptoms as such" (p. 1274). At the time of their review little was known about specific processes by which child adaptation might lead to adult disorder or even how to best conceptualize early patterns of adaptation. In particular, the role of emotional factors was unclear. "In neither case is intrapsychic emotional disturbance a useful or basic aspect of the predictive picture, though emotional disturbance is involved in both schizophrenia and criminality. On emotional-disturbance grounds alone, however, prediction is currently impossible" (p. 1271). This task of predictability, now more broadly defined as understanding the changing manifestations of patterns of adaptation (or maladaptation) over time and the links between patterns of adaptation across time, remains a central task for the field of developmental psychopathology.

Not long ago developmental psychopathology was described as a field that "hardly exists yet" (Achenbach, 1974, p. 3). Even now, it might best be described as an "emergent" discipline. Still, one may discern the dimensions and shape – the domain – of the discipline. Sketching the extensions and boundaries of this special field of inquiry is the purpose of this essay.

The very name of the discipline provides a starting point for defining the scope and particular quality of this field. First, it is concerned with development and is therefore closely wedded to the whole of developmental psychology. The methods, theories, and perspectives of developmental psychology are important tools of inquiry. Second, the focus is on pathology, that is, developmental deviations. Developmental psychopathology may be defined as *the study of the origins and course of individual patterns of behavioral maladaptation*, whatever the age of onset, whatever the causes, whatever the transformations in behavioral manifestation, and however complex the course of the developmental pattern may be.

BOUNDING THE FIELD

Developmental psychopathology is a special discipline within developmental psychology and is distinguished from this larger field in its emphases. It also is distinct from abnormal psychology and psychiatry in that its scope is broader than the description, differentiation, and treatment of disordered behavior, although it is related to these disciplines. And it is fundamentally distinct from clinical child psychology and child psychiatry, though interaction among these disciplines is important.

Developmental psychopathology and clinical child psychology

The discipline is distinct from abnormal child or clinical child psychology and child psychiatry for two basic reasons: (1) Within developmental psychopathology there is equal concern with child pathology, its relation to nondisordered behavior, *and* with the origins of disordered behavior that does not appear in clinical form until adulthood; and (2) differential diagnosis, treatment techniques, and prognosis – the stock and trade of the clinical child psychologist and child psychiatrist – are of secondary interest to the developmental psychopathologist. These endeavors are, of course, closely related. Differential diagnosis is critical for any research on psychopathology, and treatment course and prognosis often are linked to developmental changes. But there is a difference of emphasis. The developmental psychopathologist is concerned with the origins and time course of a given disorder, its varying manifestation with development, its precursors and sequelae, and its relation to nondisordered patterns of behavior.

Thus, developmental psychopathologists may be just as interested in a group of children showing precursors of a disordered behavior pattern, but not developing the disorder proper, as the group that in time manifested the complete pathology. For example, Robins (1966, 1978) points out that 70% of adult antisocial disorders can be linked to antisocial behavior in childhood, an unusually direct connection. Still, half or more of antisocial children do not show antisocial disorders in adulthood, some showing quite different forms of adult pathology and some showing no apparent disorder at all. Moreover, while degree and variety of childhood problems are important predictors, some children with only mild (or no apparent) behavioral or emotional problems become severely disordered adults. Questions that arise concern both those antisocial (and other problem) children who are not disordered as adults and those children relatively free from problems who *are* disordered as adults. Through such comparative study, developmental psychopathologists seek to shed light on factors mediating and/or modifying the development of the disorder.

Descriptive research on the problems of children (e.g., Achenbach's, 1966, patterns of "externalizing" and "internalizing" behaviors) and research on specific childhood disorders such as Tourette syndrome (Cohen, Shaywitz, and Young, 1979; Quinn and Thompson, 1980) and childhood autism (Wing, 1976) are within the domain of developmental psychopathology, but such research is not coextensive with it. First, developmental psychopathologists are interested in childhood behavior problems but also in the ties between behavior problems and normal development and socialization, especially across time (e.g., that boys generally are socialized toward "externalization"). Second, disordered behavior is examined in terms of its deviation from the normal developmental course. Disordered patterns of behavior are illuminated by considering usual patterns of adaptation vis-à-vis the developmental issues of a given period (see below). Third, some pathological conditions (such as autism) are characterized by a distortion of the developmental process. The developmental psychopathologist would be concerned both to investigate the nature of these developmental distortions and to do so in ways that threw light on the developmental interrelationships between different aspects of functioning – in the case of autism among cognition, conation, and affect (Rutter and Garmezy, 1983). Fourth, as stated above, developmental psychopathologists are interested in nonpathological childhood patterns as they may forecast later disorder and even patterns normally predictive of disorder but which, for reasons to be discovered, do not do so with a particular subgroup of subjects.

Abnormal psychology and psychiatry

The broad interest in individual patterns of adaptation also distinguishes the new field from abnormal psychology or psychiatry in general. In seeking to understand the development and manifestation of patterns of maladaptation, developmental psychopathologists must also understand developmental aspects of successful adaptation. Competence and incompetence, vulnerability and "invulnerability," are two sides of the same coin (Garmezy, 1974b). Characteristics or histories that buffer individuals against stress or that provide them with attitudes, orientations, and skills that promote successful coping with stress, and how these change across development and circumstances, are of as much concern as factors that produce vulnerability to stress or coping failures.

Risk research is in many ways paradigmatic developmental psychopathology. Within prospective, longitudinal risk research one examines not only the different developmental course of risk subjects and controls but, especially, the development of those at-risk subjects who do and do not ultimately develop the disorder (Garmezy, 1974a; John, Mednick, and Schulsinger, 1982; Robins, 1978). By thoroughly understanding factors that pull subjects toward or away from increased risk at various age periods, one not only acquires a deeper understanding of development (one goal of this field) but one also gains valuable information for primary prevention. Thus, individuals who never show clinically disordered behavior may offer as much to our inquiry as those who are severely maladapted.

Developmental psychology

Despite this interest in competence as well as incompetence, and individual adaptation of all forms, developmental psychopathology certainly does not encompass all of developmental psychology. Developmental psychology has been concerned with the universal processes of normal development. This includes not only the age range and sequences generally surrounding the emergence of certain capacities, but also the changing manifestation of a capacity with development, the changing impact of context on a given capacity, and its changing organization with other capacities (Collins, 1982). The developmentalist studying attachment, for example, would focus on the changing organization of attachment behaviors in the first year, the timing of their integration into a specific attachment, witnessed by separation distress and integrated greeting reactions, and stability and variation across cultures (e.g., Ainsworth, 1967). As another example, the ability to take the perspective of another (role taking) is studied by examining its precursors, its changing dependence on context, its movement toward a more particularized understanding of the other, its relation to other aspects of cognitive development, and its other correlates (Damon, 1977; Selman, 1980). Or, finally, peer relations are traced from roots in earlier interaction into the preschool and elementary school years, where qualitative changes occur and "friendship" emerges, with deeper understanding of reciprocity and equity (Hartup, 1983). In all cases the concern is with the general trends – the normative developmental process.

Such basic developmental research is of great importance to developmental psychopathologists, but it is not exclusively part of our domain. Rather, knowing that formation of attachment is a salient issue during late infancy, that commonly various capacities (role taking, empathy, self-control) are integrated in serving beginning peer relations in the preschool, and so forth provides the springboard for the developmental psychopathologist's own research. Once salient issues are defined for a given developmental period, individual patterns of adaptation with respect to those issues (and their consequences) may be examined. Once usual processes of behavior coordination and integration (and changing organization with development) are established, failures to achieve such organization or atypical patterns of organization may be defined (Sroufe, 1979). All of this is within the domain of developmental psychopathology.

A DEVELOPMENTAL PERSPECTIVE

Numerous investigations previously have related developmental psychology to psychiatry and to the study of psychopathology. Of particular importance for historical perspective are Hartmann's (1950) "Psychoanalysis and Developmental Psychology," Anthony's (1956) "The Significance of Jean Piaget for Child Psychiatry," and Wolff's (1960) "The Developmental Psychology of Jean Piaget and Psychoanalysis." Each of these authors points to the importance of a developmental perspective for understanding disordered behavior. Only by understanding the nature of the developmental process – with progressive transformation and reorganization of behavior as the developing organism continually transacts with the environment – is it possible to understand the complex links between early adaptation and later disorder.

More recently, Eisenberg (1977) and Rutter (1980) have discussed the concept of development as an integrating theme in psychiatry. Rutter summarized it this way:

> It is not just that some disorders involve a distortion of personality development, or that some have their roots in physical or experiential traumata in childhood or that some involve a genetically determined interference with the normal developmental process, or that some last for so many years that considerations of developmental causes and consequences are unavoidable. Rather it is that the process of development constitutes the crucial link between genetic determinants and environmental variables, between sociology and individual psychology, and between physiogenic and psychogenic causes. Development thus encompasses not only the roots of behavior in prior maturation, in physical influences (both internal and external) and in the residues of earlier experiences, but also the modulations of that behavior by the circumstances of the present. [p. 1]

In this section we will provide a brief outline of what is meant by a developmental perspective. We will point out the implications of a developmental perspective for the problems of continuity and change in behavior (the problem of prediction). And we will illustrate how a developmental perspective is different from merely seeking congruences between early and later disorders or a cataloguing of disorders at different ages.

Guiding propositions underlying a developmental perspective

While there is no single developmental theory, there are a number of agreed-upon guiding propositions that underlie all major developmental positions. These propositions, which in a sense define a developmental perspective, have been summarized by Santostefano (1978):

Holism This is the proposition that the meaning of behavior can only be determined within the total psychological context. Thus, two "manifestly similar" behaviors may have quite different meanings (pathological or otherwise), while quite dissimilar behavior may be equivalent in different contexts (see also Sroufe and Waters, 1977).

Directedness Critical here is the idea that persons do not simply react passively to environmental input. Even at the outset there are built-in biases and thresholds such that some stimulation is more likely to receive a response ("psychological givens"), and in time the person becomes an increasingly active shaper of the environment (Sroufe, 1979). Later experience is not a random influence on individuals because persons selectively perceive, respond to, and create experience based on all that has gone on before. A child that isolates himself is not experiencing the same nursery school class as the child who engages other children.

Also relevant here is the idea that development does not occur as a series of linear additions. Rather, development is characterized by reorganization of both old and new elements. Thus reorganized, even previously existing elements are transformed. The "same" behavior may have totally new meaning with development, just as it may have different meanings in different contexts.

Differentiation of modes and goals   In general, individuals develop toward both increasing flexibility and increasing organization. "The availability of multiple means and alternative ends frees the individual from the demands of the immediate situation, enabling him to express behavior in more delayed, planned, indirect, organized, stage-appropriate terms and to search for detours that acknowledge opportunities and limitations of the environment while permitting successful adaptation" (Santostefano, 1978, p. 23). This concept of increasingly flexible behavioral organization provides a criterion for examining individual differences in adaptation and, in particular, developmental deviations.

Mobility of behavioral functions   With development, earlier forms of behavior become hierarchically integrated within more complex forms of behavior (Werner, 1957). "Although subordinated, earlier forms of behaving remain potentially active" (Santostefano, 1978, p. 24). The individual does not operate only in terms of behaviors that define a single stage. Especially in periods of stress, early modes of functioning may become manifest. It is assumed that more recently integrated patterns of behavior are most susceptible to disruption, giving way to the earlier, less differentiated forms. A clear implication here is that a disordered pattern of adaptation may in many circumstances lie dormant, only to be manifest in periods of increased stress or in very particular circumstances. Suomi and his colleagues (Suomi, in press) have identified a group of at-risk monkeys who show disordered behavior that changes in form with age. However, disordered behavior is shown *only* during periods of marked transition. At other times these monkeys appear indistinguishable from others.

The concept of "mobility of function" puts a new perspective on the psychoanalytic concept of "regression." One need not posit a going back in time. Previous modes of function are currently available and are part of the person's ongoing adaptation, at times promoting improved fit to the environment, though at other times compromising growth. Not the presence or even the employment of less differentiated, early modes connotes pathology, but rather their inflexible use with regard to the ongoing adaptational task.

The problems of continuity and change

Perhaps the central proposition underlying a developmental perspective is that the course of development is lawful. Not only is it posited that there is a common general course of development, followed by normal and retarded individuals alike (Cicchetti and Sroufe, 1978), but that there is a coherence to the course of each individual's development. Such a position is not incompatible with the notions of discontinuity or plasticity (Rutter, in press-a).

Such an expectation of coherence is distinct from an expectation of behavioral stability over time, which rarely obtains. Some time ago Kohlberg et al. (1972) outlined some of the complexities in predicting adult mental health from childhood behavior. Among other things, they pointed to the lack of stability of particular "emotional symptoms," the manifestation of which would be influenced by situation as well as by developmental level. Still they argued, with substantial support, that the child's general pattern of adaptation would better predict later pathology. More useful than specific symptoms would be assessment of the child's "awareness of, and mode of coping with, the developmental task in question" (p. 1246). In criticizing the then widely used GAP diagnostic categories for implying a "trait stability of prognosis," they pointed to more complex developmental models of continuity. "In these more complex models, a childhood conflict is maintained as a theme in later development but its relationship to type of pathology, or indeed its healthy or unhealthy resolution, is determined by developmental events up through adulthood" (p. 1227).

Within the notion of coherence, both change and continuity, in a broad sense, are embraced. Hinde (1982) provides an enlightening example of continuity in the face of dramatic change. The caterpillar is "adapted as a growing machine and also adapted to change dramatically to fulfill the functions of adulthood. But even where the tissues are almost completely broken down and the body is redeveloped in a new form, continuity is not totally absent: larval experience may affect the subsequent behavior of the moth" (p. 91). Equally complex examples may be cited for humans, as when reliable contact seeking in infants predicts self-reliance in preschool children and when girls reared in institutions later marry men with severe psychosocial problems (51% compared with 13% in control subjects) (see Rutter, in press-a, and Sroufe, 1979, for numerous examples in later and early development, respectively). The continuity lies not in isomorphic behaviors over time but in lawful relations to later behavior, however complex the links.

The proposition is that individual functioning is coherent across periods of discontinuous growth and despite fundamental transformations in manifest behavior. Disordered behavior generally does not simply spring forth without connection to previous quality of adaptation, or without changing environmental supports or altered environmental challenges. Even where qualitative change in functioning occurs, as when a well-functioning individual later shows severely disordered behavior (due to environmental and/or physiological factors), it is presumed that the particular form of maladaptation will be related to the adaptational history. Change, as well as continuity, is lawful and therefore reflective of coherent development.

Inflexible employment of modes of functioning and limitations (or distortions) in perceiving opportunities or challenges in the environment compromise later environmental transactions in particular ways. Inflexible, undifferentiated behavior, while perhaps not leading to manifest pathology in a given benign environment, would forecast later pathology in more challenging environments. And the particular pattern of adaptation would forecast specific vulnerabilities in the face of given environmental challenges (Greenspan, 1981; Murphy and Moriarty, 1976; Sroufe, 1983).

The link between early adaptation and later disorder

Rutter (1981, in press-a) previously has listed a number of ways in which early experience (early adaptation) might be connected to later disorder. These include rather direct connections, for example, where (1) experience leads to disorder at the time, which then persists; (2) experience leads to bodily changes that influence later functioning; and (3) there are altered patterns of behavior at the time, which only later take the form of disorder. Others are less direct: (4) early events may change the family circumstances, which in time produce disorder; (5) sensitivities to stress or coping styles are modified, which then later "predispose" the person to disorder (or buffer the person against stress); (6) experiences alter the individual's self-concept or attitudes, which, in turn, influence the response to later situations; and (7) experience influences behavior through effects on the selection of environments or on the opening up or closing down of opportunities.

Here, we would elaborate a complex developmental view of the person–experience transaction and its connection to later disordered behavior. First, a series of developmental issues (table 39.1), based on the collective experience of numerous developmentalists, may be outlined (Erikson, 1963; Kohlberg

TABLE 39.1   Salient developmental issues

Age (Years)	Issues
0–1	Biological regulation; harmonious dyadic interaction; formation of an effective attachment relationship
1–2$\frac{1}{2}$	Exploration, experimentation, and mastery of the object world (caregiver as secure base); individuation and autonomy; responding to external control of impulses
3–5	Flexible self-control; self-reliance; initiative; identification and gender concept; establishing effective peer contacts (empathy)
6–12	Social understanding (equity, fairness); gender constancy; same-sex chumships; sense of "industry" (competence); school adjustment
13+	"Formal operations" (flexible perspective taking; "as if" thinking); loyal friendships (same sex); beginning heterosexual relationships; emancipation; identity

Source: Adapted from Sroufe, 1979.

et al., 1972; Kopp, 1982; Piaget and Inhelder, 1969; Sander, 1962; Sroufe, 1979; Sullivan, 1953). These issues are broadly integrative, cutting across affective, cognitive, and social domains. For example, effective peer relations is more than a set of skills; affective components play a central role in social competence (Sroufe, Schork, Motti, Lawroski, and LaFreniere, in press). Moreover, issues at one developmental period also are seen as laying the groundwork for subsequent issues. Sander (1975), for example, has described the movement from dyadic regulation within the caregiver–infant system toward self-regulation and sees this as the major adaptational task of early development.

Second, individual adaptation may be viewed with respect to these salient developmental issues. As examples, each infant forms an attachment with the caregiver, each relationship having its particular qualities. Each toddler evolves a particular way of dealing with both the fact of its separateness from the caregiver and its continued dependency. Each child develops a particular orientation toward peers and styles of engaging and responding to them. For each child these adaptations (the accomplished "fit" between the child and this aspect of environment) are unique. They are based on the given characteristics of the child and the environment with which the child reciprocally interacts. This adapted organism then faces subsequent developmental issues and subsequent experiences from within that unique adaptation, thus transforming as well as being transformed by later experience.

It is in this way that an adaptation that may be serviceable at one point in development (e.g., avoiding an abusing caregiver, blunting or controlling emotional experiences, etc.) may later compromise the child's ability to maximally draw upon the environment in the service of more flexible adaptation. Thus, a given pattern of early adaptation could lead a child to isolate himself from peers or to alienate them, to avoid emotionally complex and stimulating social commerce, or to respond to such complexity in an impulsive or inflexible manner. Even such patterns may not be viewed as pathological (in the clinical sense) and certainly may be viewed as "adapted," in the sense that the child continues to strive toward a "fit" with the environment. But if the adaptation compromises the normal developmental process whereby children are increasingly able to draw emotional support from age-mates (as well as give it), and to stay engaged in social commerce despite the frequent emotional challenge of doing so, the individual may be sacrificing an important buffer against stress and, ultimately, psychopathology. Inadequate peer relations is a powerful predictor of later psychopathology (John et al., 1982; Kohlberg et al., 1972; Roff and Ricks, 1970). This may be both because it is a sign of early adaptational failure, broadly defined, and because of the role of social relations (social support) as buffers against stress in later life.

Within this view the "unifying" quality of the developmental perspective may be seen. Regardless of whether particular patterns of early adaptation are to a greater or lesser extent influenced by inherent dispositions or by early experience, they are nonetheless the patterns of adaptation. Their consequences are of interest. The developmentalist is interested in the "how" of person–biology–experience interactions more than trying to determine which is more important (Anastasi, 1958). Even given late-arriving genetic influences, contemporary and ongoing adaptation nonetheless remains an important consideration. And even granting the importance of changing environment, the person nonetheless engages that environment in terms of previous adaptation. The tendency of the person to assimilate new environments to former patterns of adaptation, and the particular accommodation (change) the person achieves within a changing environmental context, both require an understanding of the adaptational history.

IMPLICATIONS FOR RESEARCH IN PSYCHOPATHOLOGY

What are the implications of a developmental perspective for research on childhood disorders and the developmental antecedents of adult psychopathology?

First, normal processes of development are viewed with respect to what they may contribute to an understanding of disordered behavior. As just one example, Bobbitt and Keating (in press), drawing upon the work of Dodge (e.g., Dodge and Frame, 1982), have discussed the case of childhood aggression. Aggressive boys, it seems, show a deviation from usual attributional processes, attributing hostile intent in the face of ambiguous provocations directed at them. "Thus the attributional error is a potentially dysfunctional social cognitive skill that mediates aggressive activity in these boys" (Bobbitt and Keating, in press, p. 43). In general, one would examine the malfunctioning child in terms of deviation from normal development in addition to manifest symptomatology.

The concern with normal developmental processes includes consideration of sex differences and, especially, differences in the socialization of males and females. Both symptomatology and behavior patterns predictive of later disorders differ for males and females. For example, in the John et al. (1982) study it was found that teacher reports of undercontrol ("emotional reactions persist"), irritability, disturbing and inappropriate behavior, and disciplinary problems, predicted later schizophrenia in high-risk males, but not females. Being "nervous," not reacting when praised, and being "content with isolation" were predictive for females but not males. Ineffective peer relations (being "lonely and rejected") was predictive for *both* males and females. These findings are consistent with the cultural tendency to socialize males toward "externalizing" and females toward "internalizing" patterns of behavior[1] (and also point to the broad significance of peer effectiveness as an indicator of quality of adaptation).

Second, it is clear that a developmental perspective dictates a new approach to the problems of classification and categorization of children. Current diagnostic classification schemes pay scant attention to development. Apart from (or in addition to) clinical diagnosis, it is important that children be assessed in terms of their patterns of adaptation with respect to issues of the given age. While some gesture in this direction was made in the multiaxial approach of DSM III, much further work is needed in this regard. Considerable effort will be required to define patterns of adaptation, to group them meaningfully, and to validate them against both contemporaneous and cross-age criteria. Ainsworth (Ainsworth, Blehar, Waters, and Wall, 1978) has shown the feasibility of this task with her classification scheme of infant–caregiver attachment, and beginning efforts at classification of patterns of adaptation through the preschool years have been made (Greenspan, 1981; Sroufe, 1983).

Third, and perhaps most fundamental, the nature of the developmental process itself, characterized by progressive adaptation and transformation, provides a unique orientation for conducting research on the origins and course of late-appearing psychopathology. This perspective alerts researchers to broaden the search for antecedents of pathology away from phenotypically similar patterns of behavior in early life and toward particular adaptational failures that are defined in terms of salient issues of the given age period. The adaptational solution at a given developmental period is examined in its own terms. Antisocial behavior and overdependency are not salient issues in infancy; therefore, it is not surprising that such assessments bear little relation to later behavior (Kagan and Moss, 1962). Overdependency in the preschool period does predict later behavior. Moreover, a failure to show the expected progression from emotional dependency to instrumental dependency (using adults and peers as resources) may be most predictive of all. To some extent the adaptational precursors of most disorders are yet to be empirically determined. Therefore, at this time, we would do well to categorize patterns of adaptation (and maladaptation) in terms of the child's management of salient age-period issues, leaving open the question of how direct links to later behavior may be. For example, "Attention Deficit Disorder" may or may not be related to early hyperactivity, distractability, or impulsiveness, or such characteristics may be differentially imbedded in an overall adaptational pattern for children later bearing this diagnosis.

The power of this focus on age-defined adaptational issues already has been demonstrated in general developmental studies. Flexible impulse control, high self-esteem, relative absence of behavior problems, and effective peer relations in the preschool all have been predicted strongly by assessments focused specifically on the salient issues of earlier periods, for example, the quality of infant–caregiver attachment (e.g., Sroufe, 1983). These are the very factors suggested to show strong links to later behavior, including disorder (Kohlberg et al., 1972; Rutter, in press-b). It does not seem likely that measures of infant–infant play would bear much relation to later peer competence. Similarly, the strongest predictors of later pathology are not likely to be early replicas of the behavioral indicators of adult pathology. The strongest predictors are likely to be adaptational failures, defined in age-appropriate terms.

Tracing the course of a particular disorder would necessarily be complex, given the nature of development, and will require theoretically guided, longitudinal research. Early patterns of adaptation influence later adaptation, but not in a simple, linear manner. Both general developmental advances as well as changing circumstances interact with prior adaptation in producing subsequent adaptation. Transformation is the rule. An infancy predictor of aggression in the preschool years is avoidance of the mother following a brief laboratory separation (Main and Weston, 1982; Sroufe, 1983). Thus, a failure of emotional expression (clinging), when such would have been expected, predicted later hostile aggression. Pommeling the caregiver (another form of maladaptation in this context) does not predict later hostile aggression, though it does predict other forms of later maladaptation, including low frustration tolerance and ineptness with peers. Avoidance of the caregiver in infancy also predicts strong dependency on preschool teachers (Sroufe, Fox, and Pancake, 1983). This is paradoxical only if one assumes isomorphism of behavior over time. When one rather looks at patterns of adaptation in terms of how they equip the child to face subsequent developmental issues, such developmental findings (and predictions) become understandable.[2]

Robins (1966) provided an early example of how developmental transformation may emerge in studies of pathology. When children seen at psychiatric clinics were followed into adulthood, there was, indeed, a higher incidence of severe pathology in comparison with a control group. Childhood problems even predicted adult schizophrenia. But it was not the shy, withdrawn child that tended to manifest schizophrenia in adulthood. (Indeed, such childhood symptoms were not associated with adult pathology at all.) Rather, it was children characterized by impulsiveness, aggression, and antisocial behavior who were over-represented in the schizophrenia group. Schizophrenia was predicted by childhood maladaptation, but the developmental link was complex. These results are supported by the findings of John et al. (1982) for males, discussed above. Interestingly, at-risk males who later were borderline schizophrenics (vs. schizophrenia proper) were earlier described as "anhedonic, isolated, and distant."

The general point is that developmental psychopathologists would be open to non-isomorphic antecedents and complex routes to adult disorder. In the sense of a direct tie between adult disorder and the same disordered behavior in childhood, it is clear already that often little connection exists (with exceptions such as antisocial disorders; Robins, 1978). But the likelihood of more complex antecedents, especially in the sense of childhood patterns of adaptation that leave individuals differentially vulnerable to adult disorders, remains very real indeed.

To return to the question of predicting adult disorder from childhood assessments, we may now summarize the existing literature as follows: (1) Broad-based indicators of adaptational failure (inadequate peer relations, antisocial behavior, achievement problems) during the school years do predict adult disorders with some power. This likely is due to their integrative nature, encompassing socioemotional and cognitive aspects, and to their ties to major developmental issues. (2) These broad-band indices, especially peer relations and general conduct disturbances, predict adult disorders broadly, rather than specifically. (3) Specific patterns of emotional development, in the absence of general adaptational failure, do not predict adult disorder at all well.

The implication of this set of findings is that future research should be aimed at the predictive power of specific patterns of behavioral/emotional organization *within* the context of general, developmentally appropriate assessments of adaptational failure.

The case of depression

For a number of reasons depressive disorders provide a useful case for illustrating the nature and utility of a developmental perspective (Rutter, in press–b). First, there are notable, age-related changes that surround the manifestation of depression that call for analysis within the framework of normative developmental psychology. Second, depression seems rather clearly to have both biological and experiential determinants, thus calling upon the integrative role of a developmental perspective. Finally, while depressive disorders apparently exist in childhood, they are far more prevalent in adulthood, making it clear that there can be no simple link between childhood and adult conditions.

Salient age dependencies with regard to depressive phenomena include the following: (1) prior to the second half of the first year, infants show no grief reaction in the face of loss; (2) infantile sequences of protest, despair, and detachment in the face of loss remain in force until about age 4–5 years; (3) disorders with both the cognitive and affective components of depression probably first appear after infancy, being somewhat more common in boys; (4) there is a sharp increment in the frequency of depression with puberty, depression then being notably more common in girls; (5) depression becomes even more common in adulthood. These age changes are of interest in their own right, but they are of even greater interest when viewed within a broader developmental perspective. The proneness toward depression in girls in the face of adolescent challenge becomes more sensible in light of differential socialization patterns. Girls in our culture are socialized toward compliance, inhibition, passivity, and reliance on others.[1] Thus, the depressive pattern of symptom expression is congruent with their socialization history. Viewing events as outside of their own control (Seligman's [1975] learned helplessness) may be a critical feature. The earlier depression in boys, which may or may not be a different phenomenon, is generally nested within a constellation of other conduct-disturbance problems. This again highlights the importance of differential socialization, boys being shaped toward externalizing symptomatology and away from expression of tender feelings. It also calls on the developmental literature on self-concept and self-esteem. Here, one may be tapping feelings of low self-worth, which may be separate from factors of vulnerability and helplessness experienced by adolescent girls (or a different kind of vulnerability).

The age changes cited above also stimulate hypotheses concerning biological factors – hormonal changes with puberty, endorphin functioning in adults, and so forth. A developmental perspective is not in competition with genetic or other biological positions. But the emphasis is on the integration of the biological and psychological. No doubt in part due to hormonal and other developmental changes, the adolescent girl has an increased consciousness of her vulnerability, a vulnerability which now includes sexual exploitation, pregnancy, and its consequences for a young, ill-prepared woman. It is these increased vulnerabilities and their differential meaning that may be the key to understanding why puberty is associated with depression in only some girls. Neither genes nor hormonal changes directly cause depression.

In general, depression may be viewed in terms of the interaction of experience, stress, and age-related biological and psychological factors. It is not likely to be due to stress alone, since similar stressors (at least on the surface) are not as likely to lead to depression in children, nor do all adults develop depression in the face of similar stressors. It cannot be due to biological factors alone, because certain experiences (especially loss of a parent before age 11) predispose women to adult depression (Brown and Harris, 1978). Yet most persons who experience a loss do not show depression later, so particular experiences cannot be considered causal (sufficient) either. While this may, in part, reflect greater biological vulnerability in some individuals, it also seems likely that the meaning of the early loss experience – the pattern of adaptation with respect to the loss by the individual and her family – leaves individuals more or less vulnerable in the face of later stress experiences (Bowlby, 1980). Failure to grieve or pathological patterns of mourning may leave the individual ill-equipped to deal with later loss or other stress.

Finally, we come to perhaps the most important implication of the developmental perspective – its role in the search for developmental antecedents of adult depression. Certain facts are germane: (1) children diagnosed as depressive are not likely to be so diagnosed as adults, and when adult depression has been preceded by a psychiatric disorder, the child generally had not been diagnosed as depressed; and (2) on the other hand, when presence of specific affective symptoms is used as a predictor, setting aside childhood diagnosis, a strong link can be shown between manifest depression in child clinic cases and adult depression in these same subjects (Zeitlin, 1972, 1982).

These apparently paradoxical findings are readily reconciled from within a developmental perspective. In children, depressive features occur within a broader constellation of behaviors, including aggression, school failure, anxiety, antisocial behavior, and poor peer relations. These latter characteristics dominate the diagnostic process. Such adaptational failures are of broad significance, as suggested by the fact that poor peer relations persist even when the child's depression subsides. Adaptational failures in childhood, defined in terms of salient developmental issues (inadequate development of self-control, ineffective peer relations), will predict adult disorder, but they are not sufficiently specific for the prediction of adult depression. Thus, most children with conduct disorders are not depressed as adults. Only when the more specific pattern of adaptation is considered (poor peer relations, conduct disturbances, *and* specific affect disturbances) is adult depression predicted. Note that the children studied by Zeitlin all had been psychiatric cases; it is unlikely that the specific affect aberration, in the absence of the broader adaptational failure, would predict adult depression. Rather, presence of both the general, age-related adaptational failure and the particular pattern of maladaptation are required for predicting the adult disorder.

The developmental psychopathologist would look broadly for the antecedents of later depression, with an appreciation for the complexity of developmental transformations. Beyond childhood depression itself, our interest is in the various outcomes of childhood depression, even if adult depression is not well represented among them, and in the roots of adult depressive reaction, whatever they may be and however they may change with age.

But the search for antecedents is not random or totally empirical. It is guided by considerations of developmental theory and established developmental knowledge. Perhaps most central is consideration of the salient socioemotional issues during various periods of development. Knowing, for example, that the 1-year-old has the capacity for specific loss reaction, one might look to atypicalities in affective reactions to separations at that time. It is noteworthy that some infants react to very brief separations with detachment, a pattern shown normally only following prolonged separation. As another example, knowing that the 4–5 year period is a time of notable reorganization with respect to the control and expression of feelings would suggest that short-term longitudinal observations be undertaken to examine patterns of self-regulation and modification of affect surrounding this transition. The manner of controlling and expressing both anger and sadness change at this time, and there are wide individual differences in patterns of adaptation observed (Block and Block, 1980; Greenspan, 1981). While linkages in patterns of adaptation across the early years have been established in several samples of children (Sroufe, 1979, 1983), the significance of atypical patterns of affect expression and self-regulation for later pathology remains to be explored more fully. It would be expected that early patterns of adaptation, characterized by overcontrol, undercontrol, or poorly modulated affect expression, would be related, albeit complexly, to later affective disorders.

CONCLUSION

When the "developmental" aspect of developmental psychopathology is underscored, distinctions between this discipline and abnormal child psychology and child psychiatry become clear. Basically, in developmental psychopathology the focus is on the ontogenetic process whereby early patterns of individual adaptation evolve to later patterns of adaptation. The aim is to understand the origins and course of disordered behavior, whether disorder emerges in earliest childhood or not until adulthood. At times, studying the course of adaptation in selected nondisordered individuals also is of great interest, since such study may shed light on protective factors and on the development of disorder in others.

Ultimately, there is more to developmental psychopathology than even establishing links between pathology and earlier or later behavior; rather, the focus is on understanding processes underlying both continuity and change in patterns of adaptation. How does the prior adaptation leave the individual vulnerable to, or buffered against, certain kinds of stresses? How do particular patterns of adaptation, at different developmental periods, interact with a changing external environment (or physiology) to produce subsequent adaptation? What mechanisms yield certain patterns of adaptation relatively impervious to change, while others are readily changed, and how do these mechanisms change with development?

These and other such complex developmental questions likely will come to center stage in the next decade of research in developmental psychopathology. Generally, these studies will require costly and taxing longitudinal research (Kohlberg et al., 1972). But in the end, such research can yield valuable information for guiding early intervention and primary prevention. Such goals provide the central justification for the existence of this special discipline.

ACKNOWLEDGMENTS

This paper was supported in part by a program project grant from the National Institute of Child Health and Human Development (5POI-HD-05027).

NOTES

1. Block, J. H. *Personality development in males and females: The influence of differential socialization.* Paper presented in the Master Lecture Series of the American Psychological Association, New York, 1979.
2. A system of early dyadic regulation, which has as one of its principles infant avoidance of the caregiver in times of stress, precludes a smooth transition to self-regulation (Sander, 1975). An infant within this system has little opportunity to evolve flexible modes of psychological contact seeking, expectations of adult availability, or gradually increasing self-reliance. Being required to provide one's own emotional reassurance (or flexible arousal modulation) in times of stress is beyond the 1-year-old's capacity. Only a rigid blocking of the emotional response is possible, a strategy which leaves the child much in need of the physical and emotional closeness central to the infancy period. When emotionally responsive adults later are available, such a child expresses these strong biological needs for contact, which, although deflected, have not been extinguished. While in stressful circumstances these children also avoid their preschool teachers, at other times they show desperate and intense contact. Children with histories of secure attachment do not exhibit high emotional dependence in the nursery school, presumably because they have evolved more age-appropriate (flexible) modes of functioning vis-à-vis teachers (Sroufe, Fox, and Pancake, 1983).

REFERENCES

Achenbach, T. The classification of children's psychiatric symptoms: A factor-analytic study. *Psychological Monographs*, 1966 **80** (whole No. 615).

Achenbach, T. *Developmental Psychopathology* New York: Ronald, 1974.

Ainsworth, M. *Infancy in Uganda: Infant Care and the Growth of Love.* Baltimore: Johns Hopkins Press, 1967.

Ainsworth, M., Blehar, M., Waters, E., and Wall, S. *Patterns of Attachment.* Hillsdale, NJ: Erlbaum, 1978.

Anastasi, A. Heredity, environment, and the question of "how?" *Psychological Review*, 1958, **65**, 197–208.

Anthony, E. J. The significance of Jean Piaget for child psychiatry. *British Journal of Medical Psychology*, 1956, **29**, 20–34.

Block, J. H., and Block, J. The role of ego control and ego resiliency in the organization of development. In W. A. Collins (ed.), *Minnesota Symposia on Child Psychology* (vol. 13), Hillsdale, NJ: Erlbaum, 1980.

Bobbitt, B., and Keating, D. A cognitive-developmental perspective for clinical research and practice. In P. Kendall (ed.), *Advances in Cognitive-behavioral Research and Theory* (vol. 2), New York: Academic Press, in press.

Bowlby, J. *Attachment and Loss* (vol. 3). New York: Basic, 1980.

Brown, G., and Harris, T. *Social Origins of Depression*. London: Tavistock, 1978.

Cicchetti, D., and Sroufe, L. A. An organizational view of affect: Illustration from the study of Down syndrome infants. In M. Lewis and L. Rosenblum (eds), *The Development of Affect*. New York: Plenum, 1978.

Cohen, D., Shaywitz, B., and Young, J. Central biogenic amine metabolism in children with the syndrome of multiple tics of Gilles de la Tourette. *Journal of the American Academy of Child Psychiatry*, 1979, **18**, 320.

Collins, W. A. (ed.). The concept of development. *Minnesota Symposia on Child Psychology* (vol. 15). Hillsdale, NJ: Erlbaum, 1982.

Damon, W. *The Social World of the Child*. San Francisco: Jossey-Bass, 1977.

Dodge, K., and Frame, C. Social cognitive biases and deficits in aggressive boys. *Child Development*, 1982, **53**, 620–35.

Eisenberg, L. Development as a unifying concept in psychiatry. *British Journal of Psychiatry*, 1977, **131**, 225–37.

Erikson, E. *Childhood and Society* (2nd edn) New York: Norton, 1963.

Freud, S. The psychogenesis of a case of homosexuality in a woman. In J. Strachey (ed. and trans.), *The Standard Edition of the Complete Psychological Works of Sigmund Freud* (vol. 18), London: Hogarth, 1955. (Originally published, 1920).

Garmezy, N. Children at risk: The search for the antecedents of schizophrenia, I: Conceptual models and research methods. *Schizophrenia Bulletin*, 1974 (a), No. 8, 14–90.

Garmezy, N. The study of competence in children at risk for severe psychopathology. In E. Anthony and C. Koupernik (eds), *The Child in his Family* (vol. **3**), New York: Wiley, 1974 (b).

Greenspan, S. *Psychopathology and Adaptation in Infancy and Early Childhood*. New York: International Universities Press, 1981.

Hartmann, H. Psychoanalysis and developmental psychology. *The Psychoanalytic Study of the Child*, vol. **5**, 1950.

Hartup, W. Peer relations. In E. M. Hetherington (ed.), *Carmichael's Manual of Child Psychology. Vol. 4: Social and Personality Development*, New York: Wiley, 1983.

Hinde, R. *Ethology*. London: Fontana, 1982.

John, R., Mednick, S., and Schulsinger, F. Teacher reports as a predictor of schizophrenia and borderline schizophrenia: A Bayesian decision analysis. *Journal of Abnormal Psychology*, 1982, **91**, 399–413.

Kagan, J., and Moss, H. *From Birth to Maturity*. New York: Wiley, 1962.

Kohlberg, L., LaCrosse, J., and Ricks, D. The predictability of adult mental health from childhood behavior. In B. Wolman (ed.), *Manual of Child Psychopathology*, New York: McGraw-Hill, 1972.

Kopp, C. Antecedents of self-regulation: A developmental perspective. *Developmental Psychology*, 1982, **18**, 199–214.

Main, M., and Weston, D. Avoidance of the attachment figure in infancy: Descriptions and interpretations. In C. M. Parkes and J. Stevenson-Hinde (eds), *The Role of Attachment in Development*, New York: Basic, 1982.

Murphy, L., and Moriarty, A. *Vulnerability, Coping and Growth*. New Haven, Conn.: Yale University Press, 1976.

Piaget, J., and Inhelder, B. *The Psychology of the Child*. New York: Basic, 1969.

Quinn, A., and Thompson, R. Tourette's syndrome: An expanded view. *Pediatrics*, 1980, **66**, 420–4.

Robins, L. *Deviant Children Grown Up*. Baltimore: Williams & Wilkins, 1966.

Robins, L. Sturdy childhood predictors of adult antisocial behavior: Replications from longitudinal studies. *Psychological Medicine*, 1978, **8**, 611–22.

Roff, M., and Ricks, D. (eds). *Life History Research in Psychopathology* (vol. **1**). Minneapolis: University of Minnesota Press, 1970.

Rutter, M. Introduction. In M. Rutter (ed.), *Scientific Foundations of Developmental Psychiatry*, London: Heinemann, 1980.

Rutter, M. Stress, coping and development: Some issues and some questions. *Journal of Child Psychology and Psychiatry*, 1981, **22**, 323–56.

Rutter, M. Continuities and discontinuities in socio-emotional development: Empirical and conceptual perspectives. In R. Harmon and R. Emde (eds), *Continuities and Discontinuities in Development*, New York: Plenum, 1983 (a) (*in press*).

Rutter, M. The developmental psychopathology of depression: Issues and perspectives. In M. Rutter, C. Izard and P. Read (eds), *Depression in Childhood: Developmental Perspectives*, New York: Guilford, in press (b).

Rutter, M., and Garmezy, N. Developmental psychopathology. In E. M. Hetherington (ed.), *Carmichael's Manual of Child Psychology. Vol. 4: Social and Personality Development*, New York: Wiley, 1983.

Sander, L. Issues in early mother–child interaction. *Journal of the American Academy of Child Psychiatry*, 1962, **1**, 141–66.

Sander, L. Infant and caretaking environment. In E. J. Anthony (ed.), *Explorations in Child Psychiatry*, New York: Plenum, 1975.

Santostefano, S. *A Biodevelopmental Approach to Clinical Child Psychology*. New York: Wiley, 1978.

Seligman, M. *Helplessness: On Depression, Development, and Death*. San Francisco: W. H. Freeman, 1975.

Selman, R. *The Growth of Interpersonal Understanding*. New York: Academic Press, 1980.

Sroufe, L. A. The coherence of individual development. *American Psychologist*, 1979, **34**, 834–41.

Sroufe, L. A. Infant–caregiver attachment and patterns of adaptation in preschool: The roots of maladaptation and competence. In M. Perlmutter (ed.), *Minnesota Symposia in Child Psychology* (vol. **16**), Hillsdale, NJ: Erlbaum, 1983.

Sroufe, L. A., Fox, N., and Pancake, V. Attachment and dependency in developmental perspective. *Child Development*, 1983, **54**, 1615–27.

Sroufe, L. A., Schork, E., Motti, F., Lawroski, N., and LaFreniere, P. The role of affect in emerging social competence. In C. Izard, J. Kagan, and R. Zajonc (eds), *Emotion, Cognition and Behavior*, New York: Plenum, in press.

Sroufe, L. A., and Waters, E. Attachment as an organizational construct. *Child Development*, 1977, **48**, 1184–99.

Sullivan, H. S. *The Interpersonal Theory of Psychiatry*. New York: Norton, 1953.

Suomi, S. Social development in Rhesus monkeys: Consideration of individual differences. In A. Oliverio and M. Zappella (eds), *The Behavior of Human Infants*, New York: Plenum, in press.

Werner, H. The concept of development from a comparative and organismic point of view. In D. Harris (ed.), *The Concept of Development: An Issue in the Study of Human Behavior*, Minneapolis: University of Minnesota Press, 1957.

Wing, L. *Early Childhood Autism*. Oxford: Pergamon, 1976.

Wolff, P. The developmental psychology of Jean Piaget and psychoanalysis. *Psychological Issues*, 1960, **2** (1, Monograph No. 5).

Zeitlin, H. *A study of patients who attend the children's department and later the adults' department of the same psychiatric hospital*. Unpublished M.Phil. dissertation, University of London, 1972.

Zeitlin, H. *The natural history of psychiatric disorder in children*. Unpublished M.D. thesis, University of London, 1982.

INDEX